ONE WEEK LOAN

Andrzej Walicki

Marxism and the Leap to the Kingdom of Freedom

The Rise and Fall of the Communist Utopia

STANFORD UNIVERSITY PRESS

STANFORD, CALIFORNIA   1995

Stanford University Press
Stanford, California
© 1995 by the Board of Trustees of the
Leland Stanford Junior University
Printed in the United States of America

CIP data appear at the end of the book

Stanford University Press publications are
distributed exclusively by Stanford University
Press within the United States, Canada, Mexico,
and Central America; they are distributed
exclusively by Cambridge University Press
throughout the rest of the world.

Original printing 1995
Last figure below indicates year of this printing:
05 04 03 02 01 00 99 98 97 96

To Marzena

Acknowledgments

This book, which was finished in September 1992, is mostly a result of several years of my research and teaching at the University of Notre Dame. Several chapters are directly related to my graduate courses on "The Marxist Conception of Freedom," "Soviet Marxism," and "The Marxist Theory of Communism."

Work on this book was also supported by the following institutions: the Social Philosophy and Policy Center at the University of Bowling Green (Ohio), where I spent the spring semester of 1989; the J. S. Guggenheim Memorial Foundation, whose fellowship in 1990–91 enabled me to enjoy several months of productive work and lively scholarly contacts in Russia; and finally, the Humanities Research Centre of the Australian National University (Canberra), which offered me three months' visiting fellowship from May through August 1992. To all these institutions, grateful acknowledgment is made.

Among friends and colleagues to whom I feel indebted for helping me to persist in coping with the vast and often thankless subject of this book, I should mention the following:

Dr. Zbigniew Pelczynski, from Pembroke College, Oxford, who in 1980 became interested in my views on Marxism and asked me to write an essay on "The Marxian Conception of Freedom" for the book *Conceptions of Liberty in Political Philosophy* (ed. Z. Pelczynski and J. Gray, London, 1984); Professor Leszek Kolakowski, an old friend who read this essay in 1981 and, despite his declining interest in the subject, encouraged me to continue my work in this field; Sir Isaiah Berlin, who read my article "Marx and Freedom," commented on it in a long letter to me, and recommended it for publication in the *New York Review of Books*; and finally, Professor T. H. Rigby, from the Australian National University, who read the last two chapters, commented on them, and above all, supported my hope that a book by an intellectual historian might prove interesting and relevant to political scientists.

I am grateful also to Mrs. Elisabeth Short, the research assistant in the History of Ideas Unit in the Australian National University, for reading chapters 4, 5, and 6 and greatly improving my style. Of course, she is not responsible for the final linguistic shape of this work.

Contents

A Note to the Reader

Russian names are transliterated in accordance with the Library of Congress system, even if the quoted source used a different transliteration. Exceptions to this rule are those names well known in a different form, such as Dostoevsky or Trotsky, to English-speaking readers.

The name Dzierżyński (Dzherzhinskii) is written in accordance with its Polish spelling, because Polish names (exactly like English, German, or French names) should not be mechanically transliterated from the Russian.

The word *communist* appears with an initial capital letter when referring to specific Communist parties or party members but is lowercased when referring to a current of thought justifying the abolition of private property and market economy. This is an important terminological distinction, since one could be a Communist party member without believing in communism, and vice versa. It is obvious that the two meanings of the term overlap and that in many cases it is impossible to decide which connotation prevails. Hence, in deciding about proper handling, a certain degree of arbitrariness could not be avoided.

To keep the notes to manageable proportions and to assist the reader, page references to the many quotations from the works of Marx, Engels, Marx and Engels, and Lenin appear in parentheses in the text. Works by Marx, Engels, or Lenin alone appear with an identifying "M," "E," or "L," respectively; those by Marx and Engels, with "M&E." For example, Marx's *Selected Writings* are cited thus (M, SW, 279), while Marx and

Engels's *Selected Works* appear in this form (M&E, *SW*, 143), and so on. Following are listed the abbreviations of this type the reader will encounter in the text.

Work by Engels

AD   *Anti-Dühring: Herr Eugen Dühring's Revolution in Science.* Moscow, 1978 [1947].

Works by Lenin

A   *The Lenin Anthology.* Ed. Robert Tucker. New York, 1975.
CW   *Collected Works.* 45 vols. Moscow, 1960–70.
PSS   *Polnoe sobranie sochinenii.* 5th ed. 55 vols. Moscow, 1958–65.
SW   *Selected Works.* 3 vols. Moscow, 1977 [1963].
SR   *The State and Revolution.*

Works by Marx

C   *Capital.* 3 vols. New York, 1967.
G   *Grundrisse: Foundations of the Critique of Political Economy.* Harmondsworth, Eng., 1973.
PCEF   *Pre-Capitalist Economic Formations.* Int. Eric Hobsbawm. New York, 1964.
SW   *Selected Writings.* Ed. David McLellan. New York, 1985.
TOM   *Texts on Method.* Trans. and ed. Terrell Carver. Oxford, 1975.
TSV   *Theories of Surplus Value.* Moscow, 1969.

Works by Marx and Engels

BW   *Basic Writings on Politics and Philosophy.* Int. L.S. Feuer. London, 1984 [1959].
C   *Correspondence, 1846–1895.* Sel., ed., trans. D. Torr. London, 1936.
CW   *Collected Works.* New York, 1975–.
RME   *The Russian Menace to Europe.* Glencoe, Ill., 1952.
SC   *Selected Correspondence.* Moscow, 1956.
SW   *Selected Works.* 3 vols. Moscow, 1969.
W   *Werke.* Berlin, 1956–.

Marxism and the Leap to
the Kingdom of Freedom

Introduction

The aim of this book is to carefully reconstruct Marx and Engels's theory of freedom, to highlight its centrality for their vision of the communist society of the future, to trace its development in the history of Marxist thought, including Marxism-Leninism, and to explain how it was possible for it to be transformed at the height of its influence into a legitimization of totalitarian practices.

To understand the problem of freedom in Marxism, we must realize that for Marx, as for Hegel, freedom was the organizing principle of his entire philosophy of history—a philosophy designed to demonstrate the necessity of communism, conceived as the "kingdom of freedom." An analysis of the Marxist theory of freedom, therefore, requires a detailed reconstruction of Marxist views on the different stages and preconditions of freedom, on the alleged necessity of developing toward communism, and finally, on communism as the ultimate liberation of the human species. The scope of such an investigation has to be very broad, covering in fact the entire history of Marxism *as communism*—that is, of Marxism as a historical justification of communism, as a vision of the communist future, and as an ideological and pseudoscientific legitimization of revolutionary attempts to realize the communist ideal.[1] The range of this broad topic is well defined by Engels's famous words on "the leap from the kingdom of necessity to the kingdom of freedom." The "kingdom of necessity" refers to the Marxist conception of historical necessity as paving the way for freedom; the "leap to the kingdom of freedom" refers to the doctrine of "scientific socialism" and to the conception of the dictatorship of the proletariat; the "kingdom of freedom" refers to the Marxist conception of communism and its attempted realization in the Soviet Union.

This problematic does not cover all aspects and ramifications of Marxist theory. It can be said that Marxism as a theory of communism is old-fashioned Marxism, dogmatic and utopian at the same time, sharply contrasting with the "living Marxism"—the scientific and critical part of Marx's legacy—that is, still a method of radically criticizing different aspects of the capitalist system. Yet whether we like it or not, the dogmatic and utopian side of Marxism is of utmost importance for understanding communist totalitarianism and therefore should not be passed over in silence or conveniently forgotten. It is certainly possible to be a Marxist without being a dogmatic communist, or even a communist at all (as is usually the case with academic Marxists in the West), but adherence to noncommunist Marxism does not justify ignoring the Marxist roots of twentieth-century communism or treating the latter as a merely Russian or "Eastern" development. Unfortunately, such a practice has been, and still is, common among "Western Marxists" and the broad range of Marxist sympathizers in the post-Stalin period. Most of them, especially in Anglo-Saxon countries, either had little interest in the communist utopia or tried very hard to make communism respectable, democratic, and commonsensical; hence they did their best to extricate their Marxism from such strange ideas as the abolition of the market (and, ultimately, money) or simply tried to ignore this side of Marx's legacy.[2] In fact, this attitude was strongly supported by events in the countries of "really existing socialism": after several decades of talking about "market socialism" and "reform communism," even highly placed members of official Communist parties, East and West, could conveniently forget that in Marx's view socialism was to be a *totally marketless* society. In this way Marxism has become diluted, domesticated, as it were, and deprived of its widely utopian revolutionary aspect. But precisely because of this it is now necessary to "defamiliarize" Marxism by paying proper attention to its utopian, millenarian features. Otherwise we cannot grasp the close connection between the two aspects of the Bolshevik revolution: its Marxist ideology and its totalitarian outcome.

The Marxist genesis of the Bolshevik totalitarian project does not explain, of course, all features of communist totalitarianism; it explains only the ideological legitimation and utopian goals of Bolshevik rule—that is, its specifically "ideocratic" aspect. I do not wish to diminish, let alone ignore, the role of nonideological, historical and social, factors in the formation of the Soviet system. Nevertheless, I intend to show that the part played by ideological factors was relatively independent and for a long time of decisive importance. Interpreting Russia's communist experiment as the consequence of Russia's unique political culture amounts in fact to explaining the crucial problem away. It is no doubt the easiest way of exculpating Marxism and putting all blame on factors external to it and absent in the West. One would be more honest to admit, as Etienne Balibar did, that "communism as idea or ideology is at the heart of European political thought" and that its collapse in the Soviet Union is a historic event of universal significance.[3] Without the communist ideology provided by Marxism, the historical development of the former tsarist empire (and, later, of East-Central Europe) would have been fundamentally different from what it was. The postrevolutionary polity might have been undemocratic, but it would not have been totalitarian. Without the tremendous authority of Marxism, claiming a virtual monopoly of truth and the last word on both social science and universal progress, Russia, together with the other countries in its sphere of influence, would have been spared the uniquely cruel experiment of "constructing communism," of being compelled to follow a preconceived utopian blueprint. This experiment was also unique in its duration and its institutionalization of consistently totalitarian power structures. Utopian strivings are present in all great revolutions, but the communist revolution in Russia was first one in which these impulses prove strong enough to become firmly institutionalized and to determine for several decades the entire development of this large country, with its complex, if relatively backward, economy and sophisticated culture. It can safely be said that this historical anomaly, contradicting all assumptions of historical materialism as a theory of precommunist history, would not have been possible without a firm belief in the scientific character of Marxist communism and an equally firm conviction of its inevitability on a global scale.

Because of this, a comprehensive historical study of the Marxist conception of freedom—that is, of Marxism as an axiological justification of communism—must deal with its relationship to Soviet-style totalitarianism as its most important practical result. One might assume the legitimacy of such a task to be beyond question, yet great efforts have been made to portray Marxism and communist totalitarianism as two distinct, virtually unrelated phenomena. In the writings of many Western Sovietologists, the relationship between the Soviet system and Marxist ideology has been either marginalized or denied outright; hence, to present this system as a flawed but nonetheless genuine attempt to realize Marxist communism involves the risk of being accused of right-wing bias or intellectual poverty. Similarly, many Marxologists have consciously avoided the analysis of Marx's ideas for their potential dangers, as manifested in Marxist-inspired totalitarian systems. Analyses of this sort have often been contemptuously dismissed as expressions of a cold war mentality, as intellectually obsolete, unfair, and disreputable. It is not surprising, therefore, that many Western radicals today write of the end of communism as if this epochal event bore no relation whatever to Marxism.[4]

I do not attribute this situation to the intellectual and political sympathies of individual scholars. In my opinion, there are two main reasons for it, and they are interconnected: first, that Marxism in the West, increasingly self-conscious and choosing to call itself "Western Marxism,"[5] was no longer seen as inseparable from communist ideals; and second, that the East European communist regimes defined themselves as "really existing socialism," stressing thereby their commitment to the maintenance of the status quo rather than to the "building of communism," and so were no longer viewed as militantly ideological. Most Western radicals learned to appreciate Marxism as a critical theory of history, with special emphasis on the capitalist system, yet they remained strangely blind to the centrality and paramount historical importance of Marxist "scientific socialism," with communism as its ultimate goal. Very few realized that the communist idea of freedom presupposed the total abolition of civil society and the market economy by subjecting social forces to conscious rational control in a totally planned economic system. The whole notion of communism came to be associated not so much with a body of ideas as with existing communist regimes, irrespective of their factual commitment, or lack of it, to communist ideology. This thoroughly misleading shift of emphasis in the understanding of both communism and Marxism was paralleled and supported by the evolution of "really existing socialism" in the Soviet Union and, still more, in East-Central Europe, where Communist parties tried to extricate themselves from their ideological heritage and sought ways of combining one-party rule with some form of marketization. As a result, the meaning of the word *communism*, as applied to the countries of "really existing socialism," was dissociated, as it were, from specifically communist ideological connotations and came to mean simply the monopoly of power by a single party calling itself communist, without regard for its actual relationship to the communist ideal.

This drastic change of the original meaning of communism greatly facilitated, of course, the left-wing tendency to save Marxism from any responsibility for the Soviet-style regimes. At the same time, it strengthened the right-wing habit of ignoring the importance of changes in these regimes: no change seemed to matter as long as a Communist party retained a monopoly on political power.

In my opinion, this way of thinking is now one of the chief obstacles to a better understanding of both "communism" (as a recently collapsed system) and Marxism. Our views of communism should not be based on our knowledge of the countries of "really existing socialism" in their recent stage of advanced de-ideologization and their open or disguised abandonment of their communist commitments. Nor should our views of Marxism be determined by Western academic Marxism, especially its American variety. As the ideology of the militantly communist movement, Marxism was not a method of historical criticism designed to unmask all ideological rationalizations and illusions, but rather a comprehensive "New Faith" that combined powerful beliefs with quasi-scientific certitude—a faith that imbued its followers with an exceptionally strong feeling of self-righteousness as well as an unshakable confidence in ultimate victory. As such, Marxism was the most influential form of secularized millenarianism and the most utopian (although pretending to be anti-utopian) modern ideology. Its utopian aspect consisted not just in its vision of a communist future but included "scientific socialism," which, ironically, had been seen as the overcoming of all utopian forms of socialist thinking. Its ultimate aim, presented as both the conscious purpose and the necessary outcome of an objective, law-governed, historical process, was described as "the kingdom of freedom." This was, of course, a peculiar interpretation of freedom, being fundamentally different from the liberal definition of freedom as opposition to arbitrary coercion by other people. But it was important both that the aim of communism should be the realization of freedom and that true human freedom should be seen as possible *only under communism*. In other words, Marx and Engels's communism and their conception of freedom were essentially identical—hence the importance of my topic.

The relevance of the Marxist conception of freedom for an understanding of communist totalitarianism derives from the historical fact that the latter came into being as the result of a conscious, strenuous striving to realize the former. The Russian Revolution suppressed "bourgeois freedom" to pave the way for the "true freedom" of communism. Totalitarianism was a by-product of this immense effort. Shigalev, a character in Dostoevsky's novel *The Possessed*, says: "I started out with the idea of unrestricted freedom, and I have arrived at unrestricted despotism."[6] One is tempted to conclude that this is a fairly accurate description of what actually happened in Russia.

The most obvious and visible link between the Marxist conception of freedom and the Bolshevik revolution is the intransigent hostility displayed toward the market. Lenin was more hostile to the capitalist mode of distribution (market exchange) than to capitalism as a mode of production because the latter could assume the form of rationally controlled state capitalism, while the former was in his view the epitome of anarchy, uncontrollability, and dependence on blind, quasi-natural spontaneity. But the same is true of the founders of Marxism. To put it briefly, Marx conceived of freedom as conscious, rational control over economic and social forces. The main enemies of such freedom were the "blind forces" of the market; freedom would only be realized by rational planning, by liberating people from objective dependence on things and alienated social forces. Hence he was inevitably *more hostile to the market than to capitalism as a system of large-scale factory production*: the capitalist factory was for him a great step forward to rational planning and organization, while the market was synonymous with anarchy and blind necessity. For Engels, the antimarket utopia took the form of a belief that the monetary exchange economy would disappear *within* capitalism as a result of its further centralization. He visualized communist society as a well-organized factory in which social and economic forces would be totally controlled and thus transformed from "master demons" into "willing servants." In this way he envisaged a "mono-organizational" society[7]—an ideal the Bolsheviks consciously tried to realize in the Soviet Union.

Although antimarket utopianism, incompatible with the complexity of modern societies, sheds much light on the fate of socialism in the Soviet Union, it should not be seen as the sole ideological reason for Soviet totalitarianism. The total suppression of freedom in the Bolshevik state found justification in many other elements of Marxist theory, all significantly related to the Marxist conception of freedom. This book examines all these elements and attempts to show that Marxism-Leninism was a legitimate outgrowth of the original theory. Of course, it does not deny that Marxism, like other complex ideologies, had many faces and was subject to different interpretations, depending not only on different readings of the original doctrine but also on different historical conditions. We know that before World War I, Marxist ideology was most influential in two countries, Germany and Russia, but only in Russia did a Marxist-inspired pretotalitarian party emerge and only there was the collapse of the monarchy followed by the establishment of a totalitarian state. As mentioned earlier, many researchers see this as proof of a special affinity between totalitarianism and Russian national culture, but such a conclusion does not do justice to the complexity and richness of Russia's cultural heritage.[8] It is conceivable, without adducing such cultural factors, that Russian economic backwardness, especially in conjunction with the catastrophe of the war, created a better chance for the growth of Marxist communism than did the more advanced conditions obtaining in Germany. But it is not accurate to say that the German Social Democrats were more faithful to original Marxism than were the Russian Bolsheviks. As far as Marxist communism was concerned, the opposite was true. The democratic practice of the German party was not a development toward communism; rather, it was a case of a workers' party dissociating itself from communist dogma, although for a time paying lip service to it. Bernstein was right in pointing out the glaring contradiction between the party's practical activity and its declared commitment to Marxist revolutionary communism. After World War I, German Social Democracy underwent a process of consistent decommunization that culminated in a conscious break with Marxism. In contrast, Russian Bolsheviks showed a remarkably stubborn and long-lasting commitment to Marxist communism. Hence they should be regarded as the only Marxist party that dared to embark on the practical realization of Marxist communist ideals.

Communist totalitarianism is seen in this book as the result of a "politically forced development," to use Löwenthal's expression,[9] aimed at the realization of a Marxist communist utopia. It is clear, therefore, that I am dealing with a specifically communist phenomenon, and not with a sociopolitical system allegedly shared by the Stalinist Soviet Union and Nazi Germany.[10] The term *totalitarianism*, in this context, means a dictatorship that not only deprives people of political and civil freedom but also aspires to control their minds and consciences, demanding not only passive conformity but active participation as well, keeping people under ruthless ideological pressure, in a state of continuous mobilization. The closest approximation to this ideal type was, of course, Soviet Stalinism. Paradoxically, it used the Marxist conception of freedom (freedom as conscious, rational control) to justify its suppression of freedom. This was because reliance on conscious regulation and centralized planning presupposed a vertical structure of command, "iron discipline," and "single will." The emphasis on ideological control was justified, in turn, by the Engelsian view that communist liberation required learning "scientific socialism" and accepting its guidance. This belief in the magic omnipotence of "the only correct theory" fostered the view that universal indoctrination was the surest way to collective freedom. In this way Engels's claim that a "truly scientific world-view" is a necessary condition of liberation paved the way for an ideocratic tyranny. The free market of ideas had to be liquidated as mercilessly as the free market of commodities.

Seen from this perspective, communist totalitarianism appears as a thoroughly ideological system, not only because of its aspiration to ideocratic rule, but also for its dependence on ideological legitimation. It was unable to develop self-regulating economic mechanisms; neither could it legitimate itself in nonideological terms. Hence, it could not survive the inevitable process of deideologization.

The last section of the book gives a concise analysis of the dismantling of Stalinism, involving not only the gradual detotalitarization but also the partial decommunization of "really existing socialism." In this connection I present and critically analyze Western discussions between the totalitarian school and its opponents, known as revisionists. Many representatives of the former used and abused for political reasons the term *totalitarianism*, trying to prove that all changes in the Soviet Union were negligible, since its "totalitarian essence" allegedly remained unchanged. As a result, the notion of totalitarianism became broad and vague, losing its original content and its theoretical usefulness. Some revisionists, in turn, tried to prove that the totalitarian model had always been useless and irrelevant. My own position is that the theory of totalitarianism in general, and of Marxist totalitarianism in particular, must be preserved in a modified version, stressing the inevitability of its decomposition in a long process of detotalitarization. It is useful to recall in this connection that such a view was not alien to the original theorists of the totalitarian phenomenon.[11]

Let me end these introductory remarks with a personal statement on two points. The first offers an additional explanation of the attention I have devoted to developments in the People's Poland. I am convinced that a parallel study of the fate of totalitarianism and "really existing socialism" in the Soviet Union and Poland is justified by the fact that Poland was the weakest link in international communism and "the freest country in the Soviet bloc."[12] For that reason, Poland became the scene of the earliest and most advanced, although difficult and discontinuous, detotalitarization. Hence, a comparison of the changes in the Soviet Union with the much more rapid developments in Poland is, I think, a good way of showing the range of possible differences between the countries of the Soviet bloc and so avoiding the widespread error of generalizing about Soviet-style socialism on the basis of the Soviet Union example alone. I readily admit that reasons of an autobiographical nature are also involved. It is no exaggeration to say that the problems dealt with in this book were also personal problems that throughout my adult life I have been anxious to clarify for myself. My immediate experience of socialism was in Poland, but I constantly tried to compare it with the situation in Russia. As a rule, this greatly helped me broaden my perspective and avoid popular anti-Russian stereotypes. In later years I was able to view these problems through Western eyes, which also proved very helpful. All my judgments, however, derive not so much from following the guidelines of this or that school of Western Sovietology or Marxology, but rather from my individual experience of the problems in question. I think, therefore, that the presence of this biographical, experiential element deserves to be made explicit here.[13]

The second point concerns the political message of this book. My first writings on Marxism and freedom appeared at a time when communist regimes were still strong and when the idea of an imminent collapse of communism seemed completely unrealistic.[14] Now, however, the situation is different. Soviet and East European communism (or rather "really existing socialism," since none of the so-called communist regimes has ever claimed to have achieved communism) lies in ruins, Communist parties have been dissolved, and, especially in Poland, demands for a settling of accounts with former party functionaries grow ever louder. In this new context I feel it proper to stress that my critique of communist theory and practice is far from reducing the history of communism to a series of crimes. Without denying its criminal aspects, I see communism rather as a historical tragedy. My exposition of the dangerous, sinister aspects of communist ideology is not intended to provide arguments for decommunization in the sense of wholesale reprisals and discrimination against former party members. I treat Marxist communism as an ideology that has compromised itself but that nevertheless deserves to be seen as the most important, however exaggerated and, ultimately, tragically mistaken, reaction to the multiple shortcomings of capitalist societies and the liberal tradition. Otherwise I would not have written this book.

1

Marx as Philosopher
of Freedom

1.1 Preliminary Remarks

The term *freedom* appears in Marx in a variety of contexts, both positive and negative, and the problematic of freedom, as conceived by him, has different dimensions or components that should be distinguished, although not separated, from one another. It can safely be said that most errors in presenting the problem of freedom in Marx's thought stem from concentrating exclusively on one of its dimensions while neglecting, or simply ignoring, its other, equally important aspects.

One of the main reasons for the frequency of such errors is the peculiar status of the conception of freedom in Marx's thought. It is simultaneously a central question and a marginal question: central on the philosophical plane and marginal on the legal-political plane. Contrary to common opinion, the whole Marxian philosophy of history and man, as well as his vision of the communist society of the future, revolve around the problem of freedom, and not merely the issue of distributive justice.[1] If it is possible for a Marxist to speak of the "meaning of history"—in the sense of history having an inner direction and a preordained end in which the final destiny of humankind would find its fulfillment—then for Marx (who in this respect is faithful to Hegel), this meaning lies in the realization of freedom. But the Marxian philosophy of freedom is not directly translatable into the language of law and politics. Legal and political conceptions and safeguards of freedom are essentially a secondary matter for Marx, since freedom, in his view, depends on the extent of humankind's domination over nature and the degree of rational, conscious control over social relations, and not on this or that legal-political system.

Broadly speaking, four groups of problems are peculiarly relevant to Marx's theory of communist freedom.

First, Marx is well known as a severe critic of the classical liberal conception of freedom—of the concept of the "free contract" between capitalist and worker, of the "formal" and "negative" character of bourgeois liberty, and especially of the liberal notion of human rights. He pretended to have "unmasked" the class content of liberal freedom and accordingly rejected its claims for universal significance (although in his more sober moments he reluctantly acknowledged its relative value).

Second, Marx is equally well known as the founder of historical materialism—a deterministic (or quasi-deterministic) (see chapter 2, section 1) theory of social development which stresses that all human ideals are class bound and dependent on economic interests and that socioeconomic systems cannot be freely chosen, since both their sequence in time (their diachronic aspect) and their inner logic (their synchronic aspect) is always subject to objective necessity independent of human will.

Third, Marx powerfully influenced the course of history as a prophet of communism, a utopian visionary for whom communism meant "truly human freedom." Such freedom, according to Marx's vision, concerned humans as species beings and would restore the unity of humankind, reconciling human individual existence with human species essence. This highly speculative conception of ultimate God-like liberation depended on the "positive overcoming" of private property and the exchange economy. In this utopian vision the abolition of the market was more important than the socialization of property. After all, property could be de-alienated; in fact, the expression "individual property" had a positive connotation in Marx's thought, as the opposite of the estranged and dehumanized "private property."[2] But a de-alienated and humanized market was for him a contradiction in terms. The "blind forces of the market" were, in his view, synonymous with human beings' enslavement by their own products, with the state of humiliating dependence on things, and therefore the opposite of "truly human freedom." His ideal of communism presupposed the restoration of an unmediated social unity through consciously planned and "directly socialized" production, which left no room for the alienating mechanisms of the market.

Finally, Marx created an all-embracing philosophy of history, combining his scientific method of explaining historical processes (historical materialism) with his quasi-millenarian vision of collective earthly salvation in the communist society of the future. This philosophy made use of the notion of causal necessity but at the same time interpreted history as a teleologi-cal, meaningful process leading inevitably to universal human liberation, i.e., to the full, unfettered development of humans' species powers. As will be shown, freedom was conceived of by Marx as the only standard for transcultural appraisal, the only common yardstick for measuring histori-cal progress by comparing and appraising different modes of production and different socioeconomic systems.[3] As such, this conception provided the broadest common framework for a coherent interpretation of all the different dimensions and components of Marx's views on freedom.

It is easy to note the inner connection between Marx's critique of lib-eralism and his historical materialism, as well as between his vision of communism and his historiosophy of freedom. As a critic of the bourgeois worldview and as a "materialistic" interpreter of history, Marx was rather cynical about freedom, seeing its hitherto known forms as illusions of con-sciousness, if not conscious deception, and mercilessly unmasking their "class content." But in his communist utopia, as well as in his general phi-losophy of history, Marx attached central importance to freedom. This was not a contradiction, since he defined freedom in a rather unconventional manner, being consciously opposed not only to the liberal conception but also to the usage of the term in ordinary speech. To put it briefly, freedom was conceived by him not as an absence of external coercion or constraint, but *as the ability to live in accordance with man's essential nature*, that is, as *the opposite of dehumanization*. He did not concentrate on the problem of governmental intervention in private life because, in his view, the very existence of a private sphere, in which individuals were allowed to pursue their particularist egoistic aims, was a symptom of dehumanization, i.e., of unfreedom. He could not express his conception of freedom in the language of law and politics because he refused to regard civil and political liberty as central to human liberation. He concentrated instead on *humankind's capacity to control the conditions of its own self-objectification*, and from this point of view the most libertarian period of legislation, that of classi-cal liberalism, appeared to be a period of the uncontrolled domination of "blind economic forces" and hence of the least freedom. Finally, and most importantly, he was concerned not with individual freedom here and now but with species freedom—that is, the liberation of humans' "communal nature" and the maximization of their collective power at the final, commu-nist phase of human history. True, he also endorsed a concept of individual freedom, but only as a part of communist freedom—as individual partici-pation in "communal freedom" and as full unfettered development of the capacities of the species in each individual human being. It never occurred to him that actual human beings might not want to be "liberated" from their egoism, particularism, and other features incompatible with what he saw as humans' species essence. Hence it is not enough to say that his

ideal of the emancipation of humankind was different from the liberal
ideal of individual freedom: these two ideals are not merely "different" but
incompatible, mutually exclusive.

This aspect of Marx's conception of freedom was perfectly understood
by Lukács, a thinker who penetrated most deeply the Promethean and
romantic spirit of the Marxian utopia. He wrote:

> Above all one thing must be made clear: freedom here does *not* mean the freedom
> of the individual. This is not to say that the fully developed communist society will
> have no knowledge of the freedom of the individual. On the contrary, it will be
> the first society in the history of mankind that really takes this freedom seriously
> and actually makes it a reality. However, even this freedom will not be the same
> as the freedom that bourgeois ideologists have in mind today. In order to achieve
> the social preconditions necessary for real freedom, battles must be fought in the
> course of which present-day society will disappear, together with the race of men
> it has produced.

"The present generation," says Marx, "resembles the Jews whom Moses led
through the wilderness. It must not only conquer a new world, it must also perish
in order to make room for the people who will be equal to a new world." For the
"freedom" of the men who are alive now is the freedom of the individual isolated
by the fact of property which both reifies and is itself reified. It is a freedom *vis-
à-vis* the other (no less isolated) individuals. A freedom of the egoist, of the man
who cuts himself off from others. . . . The *conscious* desire for the realm of freedom can only mean consciously taking the steps that will really lead to it. And
in the awareness that in contemporary bourgeois society individual freedom can
only be corrupt and corrupting because it is a case of unilateral privilege based
on the unfreedom of others, this desire must entail the renunciation of individual
freedom. It implies the conscious subordination of the self to that collective will
that is destined to bring real freedom into being. . . . This conscious collective will
is the Communist Party.[4]

The last sentence refers to Leninist innovation—the conception of the
vanguard party. But the rest of the quoted passage is an excellent summary
of Marx's view. It is to Lukács's credit that he shows so clearly the close
logical connection between Marx's philosophy of freedom and the Leninist
solution to the "organizational problem."

However, let us not anticipate the final conclusions of the present study,
but formulate instead a few more preliminary remarks about the four main
components of the theme of freedom in Marx's thought.

By "bourgeois freedom" Marx meant primarily freedom of private individuals in the sphere of civil society. Following Hegel, he defined civil
society as a sphere of conflicting egoistic interests competing or struggling
with each other within the framework of a legal order reflecting the rules
of commercial exchange. Marx wrote: "At first there is *commerce*, and
then a *legal order* develops out of it. . . . In a developed trade the exchang-

ers recognize each other tacitly as equal persons and owners of the goods to be exchanged respectively by them. . . . This practical relation, arising through and in exchange itself, only later attains a *legal form* in contracts, etc." ("Notes on Adolph Wagner," M, *TOM*, 210). Hence, "bourgeois freedom" boils down, in fact, to the freedom of selling and buying; its more lofty aspects, such as the liberal conception of civil rights and personal liberty, serve merely as a convenient mask for the "liberty of capital freely to oppress the workers." Marx attacked liberals with fury, treating them as shameless apologists for bourgeois exploitation. He refused to agree that economic compulsion, unlike direct coercion, was compatible with freedom and repeatedly asked how a contract between a proletarian and a capitalist could be called "free" if the former acted under threat of death by starvation. In his "Speech on the Question of Free Trade," delivered at the beginning of 1848, he warned the workers: "Gentlemen! Do not be deluded by the abstract word Freedom!—whose freedom? Not the freedom of our individual in relation to another, but freedom of capital to crush the worker. Why should you desire further to sanction unlimited competition with this idea of freedom, when the idea of freedom itself is only the product of a social condition based upon Free Competition?" (M&E, CW, 6:463–64).

Free trade, Marx continued, would not contribute to the freedom and prosperity of workers. On the contrary, it would increase competition among them and thereby increase the intensity of their exploitation. But in spite of this, Marx wanted the workers to support the free trade system as a system paving the way for the liberation of their class *in the future*. "The Protective system in these days," he wrote, "is conservative, while the Free Trade system works destructively. It breaks up old nationalities and carries antagonism of proletariat and bourgeoisie to the uttermost point. In a word, the Free Trade system hastens the Social Revolution. In this revolutionary sense alone, gentlemen, I am in favor of Free Trade" (ibid., 465).

The timing of the Social Revolution and the final liberation of the proletariat was not very important in this reasoning. It is legitimate, therefore, to ask "whose freedom" was close to Marx's heart. To answer this question, we have to pass from Marx's critique of "bourgeois freedom" to his historical materialism, his vision of the communist society of the future, and his all-embracing philosophy of history.

It is obvious that Marx was largely indifferent to the fate of workers as empirically existing individuals. He was perfectly ready to sacrifice the present generation of workers for the sake of their future liberation as a class, a supra-individual whole—a class, it might be added, that was charged with the mission of bringing about a universal emancipation of humankind. The liberation of the working class was identical, in his view, to the liberation of Humanity. Hence he was committed to the cause of universalism but not to that of ethical individualism. He never accepted the principle that "society's obligation runs first of all to its living citizens";[5] neither did he accept Kant's view that each individual must be treated as an end in himself, and never as a means. On the contrary, Marx was used to treating individuals, as well as entire classes and nations, as mere instruments of history and to justifying this instrumental attitude by the greatness of the final result of historical development: the universal collective liberation of humankind, tantamount, as he saw it, to the liberation of superior capacities inherent in the species nature of humans. In other words, new, superior human beings of the communist future, no matter how remote, were incomparably closer to his heart than were now-existing human beings. Using the Nietzschean distinction, one may say that Marx passionately loved what was far off (*Fernstenliebe*) and exhibited a conspicuous lack of love for his own neighbor (*Nächstenliebe*). This programmatic historiosophical "instrumentalism" had much in common with the Hegelian philosophy of history, sharing with it the same contempt for "sentimental" concerns about the price of progress, the same unshakable conviction that the fate of "particular individuals," or particular groups, does not really matter.[6]

The habit of conceiving human liberation as a long, cruel historical process in which entire generations and classes have to be ruthlessly sacrificed for the sake of the unfettered development of human beings in the future is perhaps one of the most characteristic, although sometimes conveniently forgotten, features of Marx's thought. The workers' unease about such justification of their past and present sufferings could be amply compensated, in Marx's view, by the claim that their class was fulfilling a unique historical mission. But what about slaves? They, as a class, had no such reward for their sufferings in Marx's view of history, and yet Marx did not hesitate to justify slavery. His vision of future universal human liberation demanded full development of humankind's productive forces, and slavery was, in his view, a necessary precondition of economic growth. He wrote:

Direct slavery is as much the pivot of our industrialism today as machinery, credit, etc. Without slavery no cotton; without cotton no modern industry. Slavery has given value to the colonies; the colonies have created world trade; world trade is the necessary condition of large-scale machine industry. Thus, before the traffic in Negroes began, the colonies supplied the Old World with only very few products and made no visible change in the face of the earth. Slavery is therefore an economic category of the highest importance. Without slavery North America, the most progressive country, would be transformed into a patriarchal land. You have only to wipe North America off the map of the nations and you get anarchy, the total decay of trade and of modern civilization. But to let slavery disappear is to wipe North America off the map of the nations. And therefore, because it is an economic category, we find slavery in every nation since the world began. (letter to P. V. Annenkov, Dec. 28, 1846, M&E, SW, 1:523–24)

Let us turn now to Marx's conception of communist freedom.

Marx attacked the "bourgeois liberal" idea of freedom as being merely "negative" and "formal." This accusation, however, does not contain anything *specifically* Marxist. Many non-Marxist thinkers share the view that true freedom should be conceived "positively"—as the maximization of our capacities and a way of increasing our ability to attain desired goals. Underlying this view is a powerful philosophical tradition, and it is no exaggeration to say that in our century this view has become widespread even among convinced supporters of liberal democracy. Many people who call themselves liberals easily accept John Dewey's view that freedom is "the effective power to do specific things."[7] I shall try to show that this conception involves an important misunderstanding and terminological confusion and results, especially in the case of liberals, from too hastily making concessions to Marx and other socialist critics of the liberal tradition. Nevertheless, it is obvious that endorsing such a view does not make one a Marxist. The same is true of those innumerable critics of liberalism who think, like Marx, that the liberal conception of freedom, at least in its classical version, is too individualistic, too divisive, and therefore incompatible with the communal spirit. It is necessary to remember that Marx's conception of "positive" and "communal" freedom should not be separated from his equation of "true freedom" with communism, on the one hand, and from his general view of history, on the other. To do so would reduce this conception to ahistorical platitudes and deprive it of its specifically Marxist content and context.

To understand Marx's conception of communist freedom, we must realize that it referred to *a mode of existence in which humans are integrated and self-determining*—that is, in which their actions correspond to their true self, their innermost identity.[8] This "existential" (as opposed to "legal" or "political") notion of freedom can be traced back to Hellenistic tradition, which defines salvation or liberation as "a coming to the true self and the gaining of self-control."[9] Marx's own original variant of this old and venerable conception can be seen as resulting from his peculiar interpretation of its two components: the "true self" and "self-control."

By "true self," i.e., by the area of proper identification, Marx meant nothing less—and nothing more—than man's species essence. He assumed, therefore, that all other more narrow and concrete areas of identification— such as group consciousness, corporate ties, religious affiliation, historical tradition, nationality, and so forth—were ultimately different forms of alienation from man's essential nature. In this sense Marx seemed to share the eighteenth-century view that "when man is freed from everything that is not wholly himself, what remains as the actual substance of his being is man in general, mankind, which lives in him and in everyone else." But this similarity was only partial and should not mislead us. The classical Enlightenment conception of freedom took it for granted that the subjects of freedom were actually existing human individuals and that each of them (as Kant put it) should be treated as an end, not merely as a means. In addition, freedom from "the 'intermediate' circles and middle levels that separated men from mankind" was interpreted as freedom from estate barriers and other *feudal* restrictions, hence as a justification of free competition and the policy of "laissez faire, laissez aller." [10] In contrast to this, Marx developed a communist conception of freedom, fiercely anticapitalist and leveled against all forms of "bourgeois egoism." Hence it was quite natural for him to treat humanity as a whole, and not empirically existing individuals, as the real subject and bearer of freedom. [11] His communism, conceived as "the real reappropriation of the human essence by and for man" (see below, section 3), was to fulfill human destiny through an act of *collective* liberation of human beings from all forms of imprisonment in particularist and (therefore) not truly human spheres of existence. This was to take place on the ruins of capitalism, in the communist society of the future. In other words, Marx's freedom was conceived of not as individual freedom here and now, but rather as a collective salvation in history. Its introduction was to be the historical mission of the proletariat—a class totally uprooted, free from all attachment to institutions and traditions of the past, stripped from everything except its bare humanity, and therefore having nothing to lose and everything to gain. The proletariat, wrote young Marx, is "a class with radical chains, a class in civil society that is not a class of civil society, a social group that is the dissolution of all social groups, a sphere that has a universal character because of its universal sufferings and lays claim to no particular right, because it is the object of no particular injustice but of injustice in general. This class can no longer lay claim to a historical status, but only to a human status. . . . It is, finally, a sphere that cannot emancipate itself without emancipating itself from all other spheres of society and thereby emancipating these other spheres themselves. In a word, it is the complete loss of humanity and thus can only recover itself by a complete redemption of humanity" ("Towards a Critique of Hegel's *Philosophy of Right: Introduction*," M, *SW*, 72–73).

This definition of the proletariat's liberating mission was logically bound up with the assumption that communism, owing to its universal character, could not prevail in isolation. The necessary precondition of communism, Marx reasoned, was the "universal intercourse," the universal objective interdependence, created by the capitalist world market. The task of the proletariat as the universal class was to replace this alienating, enslaving interdependence with a conscious, rationally organized form of all-human unity. Hence, communism, in Marx's view, was "only possible as the act of the dominant people 'all at once' and simultaneously. . . . The proletariat can thus only exist world-historically, just as communism, its activity, can only have 'a world-historical' existence" (*The German Ideology*, M&E, *CW*, 5:49).

The other component of the ancient Greek conception of freedom— "self-control"—was reinterpreted by Marx in accordance with his general view on the importance of material production for the development of the inherent creative capacities of the human species. He understood self-control as primarily "the determination and control of one's objectification."[12] He meant by this, above all, the establishment of rational, conscious control over economic forces, conscious mastery over human collective fate, the replacement of "blind, natural" necessities by free, teleological activity consonant with human essence.[13] Thus, human freedom was conceived by him as the opposite of the spontaneous, quasi-natural order of the market, as the liberation of human beings, as rational creatures capable of conscious self-determination, from the rule of the "invisible hand." Of course, he regarded this task as achievable only through the communist regulation of production and exchange on a world scale. Hence he described communist freedom as involving "the abolition of the alien attitude [*Fremdheit*] of men to their own products" and "dissolving into nothing the power of the relation of supply and demand" (ibid., 48). In other words, it was to be a universal reintegration of humanity through the abolition, or, rather, the positive overcoming of the divisive, alienating institutions of class society: private ownership of the means of production and the market.

Another specific feature of Marx's conception of freedom is his invariably historical approach to the problem. He was very consistent in presenting communism as the final outcome of human history and in stressing the necessity of all stages of this painful historical development. But he was not always consistent in his interpretation of the notion of "historical necessity." His historical materialism has usually been interpreted as a rigidly deterministic account of human historical praxis or even as a variant of technological determinism.[14] His theory of communism, however, assumed the possibility of consciously steering historical processes and therefore of liberating humankind from dependence on "objective laws" of historical or economic development. This gave rise to two opposite and seemingly incompatible interpretations of his philosophy of history: "scientific Marxism," on the one hand, and humanistic neo-Marxism, on the other.[15] The "scientific Marxists" see Marx primarily as the discoverer of the objective and inevitable laws of history; in contrast, humanistic neo-Marxists are deeply embarrassed by the "necessitarian" aspect of Marxism and sometimes try to explain it away by showing that the "scientific determinism" of so-called classical Marxism was really an invention of Engels and a deep distortion of the authentic philosophy of Marx.[16] In fact, both sides have serious arguments supporting their respective views. The publication of Marx's early works should not be considered as invalidating the earlier "classical" interpretation, thereby reducing it to a sort of grotesque philosophical misunderstanding. It is not as simple as that. It can now safely be said that Marx should not "be called a historical determinist if this means that human actions are univocally determined by historical laws and social circumstances."[17] But we must explain at least why the author of *Capital* employed not only the modes of expression peculiar to Hegel (M, C, 1:29) but also the language of deterministic naturalism. Why did he propound such notions as "the natural laws of capitalist production" or "tendencies working with iron necessity toward inevitable results"? (ibid., 19).

Of course, such an explanation, involving, as it would, the entire dialectic of freedom and necessity in Marx's thought, cannot be given in a few sentences. What can and needs to be explained in these preliminary remarks is rather the legitimacy of bringing together the "deterministic" and "voluntaristic" aspects of Marxism as the two sides of his historiosophy of freedom. Marx invoked the authority of science; Engels and the theorists of "classical Marxism" even tried to present Marxism as the most perfect form of scientism in social theory. Nonetheless, it is useful to remember that for most of these theorists, the notion of "historical necessity" was strongly associated with the meaningful pattern of history, not with a purely mechanical naturalistic determinism. Their belief in the immanent meaning of history was often much stronger than that of voluntaristic neo-Marxists, and the publication of Marx's early writings only strengthened this crucial element of the classical Marxists' worldview. Whether consciously or not, they used the term *necessity* as a value-laden concept, presupposing the existence of a rational inner structure of history. The French philosopher Maurice Merleau-Ponty was perfectly right in proclaiming that "in its essence Marxism is the idea that history has a meaning—in other words, that it is intelligible and has a direction." To remain a Marxist in the classical sense to him meant to believe in the rationality of history, to uphold this intense belief even at the time of universal skepticism and despair: "In this sense Marxism is not a philosophy of history; it is *the* philosophy of history and to renounce it is to dig the grave of Reason in history."[18] A similar view was expressed by Leszek Kolakowski, who stressed in one of his early works that the deeply experienced and fully assimilated communist faith endows the individual with *the most intense* feeling of meaningfulness in life.[19] The number of such testimonies is truly infinite; if I have chosen to employ these two, it is because they were made by sophisticated philosophers whose knowledge, as well as their deeply personal experience, of Marxism cannot be doubted. And it should be noted that both these testimonies refer primarily to the deterministic, or "scientific," Marxism.

It is legitimate, therefore, to claim that the search for meaning in history constitutes an essential feature of Marxism, both in its "deterministic" and in its "voluntaristic" interpretation—for the former even more so than for the latter. And it cannot be doubted that Marx defined freedom not in terms of free will—that is, as the lack of any determination—but in terms of unfettered, all-round development—that is, as autonomous self-determination. Owing to this, he saw a threat to freedom not only in externally imposed necessity, but also, and no less, in the meaningless contingency of human existence. From this perspective the contrast between "classical," or "scientific," Marxists, who sought support for their vision of universal human emancipation in the working of inexorably "objective" laws of history, and "humanistic" neo-Marxists, who treated "objective laws" as merely illusions of the reified consciousness, turns out to be less sharp than might have been expected and is definitely nonreducible to the simple dualism of determinism versus voluntarism.

1.2   Civil and Political Liberty: A Confrontation with Liberalism

Let us pass now to the exposition of the critical part of Marx's views of freedom.

In Marx's view the liquidation of different forms of personal dependence, such as direct slavery or feudal bondage, should not be treated as the equivalent of achieving freedom. Historically, the abolition of personal dependence was followed by the enormous strengthening of depersonalized and reified forms of dependence, and this process could by no means be described as an increase in human freedom. If capitalism had liberated the workers, it was only in the sense that it replaced extraeconomic compulsion with an even more merciless economic compulsion. If it liberated humankind from dependence on extrahuman nature, this was achieved at the cost of subjecting people to the merciless rule of economic laws that functioned independently of their will and confronted them like an objective and hostile force of nature. Thus, freedom in the positive sense, as the actual possibility of controlling one's fate, had not increased either for the workers or for humanity as a whole. On the contrary, in many respects the rise of capitalism brought about a marked increase in unfreedom.

It was this aspect of Marx's view of freedom that most deeply impressed his contemporaries and that was central to his entire theory of capitalist development: to his conception of primitive accumulation as necessarily entailing the wholesale expropriation of small producers; to his view of the nature of bourgeois exploitation and of the proletarian condition ironically described as "freedom from the means of production"; and, finally, to his analysis of the historical role and alienating function of the social division of labor. Let me illustrate this point with two characteristic quotations.

In the *Manifesto of the Communist Party* we read:

Modern industry has converted the little workshop of the patriarchal master into the great factory of the industrial capitalist. Masses of laborers, crowded into the factory, are organized like soldiers. As privates of the industrial army they are placed under the command of a perfect hierarchy of officers and sergeants. Not only are they slaves of the bourgeois class, and of the bourgeois state; they are daily and hourly enslaved by the machine, by the overlooker, and, above all by the individual bourgeois manufacturer himself. . . . In bourgeois society capital is independent and has individuality, while the living person is dependent and has no individuality.

And the abolition of this state of things is called by the bourgeois abolition of individuality and freedom! And rightly so. The abolition of bourgeois individuality, bourgeois independence, and bourgeois freedom is undoubtedly aimed at. (M&E, CW, 6:491, 499)

And in *Capital* we find: "For the conversion of his money into capital, therefore, the owner of money must meet in the market with the free laborer, free in the double sense, that as free man he can dispose of his labor-power as his own commodity, and that on the other hand he has no other commodity for sale, is short of everything necessary for the realization of his labor-power" (M, C, 2:166).

In other words, the conditions necessary for capitalist development comprise not only the abolition of serfdom but also the "liberation" of small producers from their means of production. Such liberation, however, brought into being a new form of social exploitation that, in Marx's view, was the most merciless of all forms of exploitation—one completely unscreened, deprived of any personal bond between exploiter and exploited, unsoftened by any religious or moral considerations. Its nakedness was otherwise a progressive factor, greatly simplifying social relations, unveiling the very essence of class oppression, and thus, for the first time in history, enabling the oppressed to attain a true understanding of the reasons for their miserable position and of the means of changing it.

This assessment of capitalism as socioeconomic formation was extended to the entire capitalist superstructure, institutional and ideological. In the modern representative state, Marx maintained, the bourgeoisie "conquered for itself exclusive political sway. The executive of the modern state is but a committee for managing the common affairs of the whole bourgeoisie." The same is true of all "bourgeois notions of freedom, culture, law, etc." Addressing the bourgeoisie, Marx and Engels wrote: "Your very ideas are but the outgrowth of the conditions of your bourgeois production and bourgeois property, just as your jurisprudence is but the will of your class made into a law for all, a will whose essential character and direction are determined by the economical conditions of existence of your class" (M&E, CW, 6:486, 501, 501).

In this way Marx came to undermine the basic assumption of liberalism: the belief in the autonomous value of political and legal safeguards of liberty. It was easy to conclude from his general view of capitalism, as well as from his general theory of the relationship between "the base" and "the super-structure," that political and civil freedom was merely an illusion serving the selfish interests of the bourgeoisie. Interestingly, the authors of the *Manifesto of the Communist Party* clearly perceived the danger of using this view to idealize precapitalist conditions, including patriarchal feudal absolutism, and explicitly warned against doing so. They stressed that in the backward conditions of Germany, the workers should support the liberal bourgeoisie in its struggle against feudal aristocracy and feudal monarchy; thus, Marx and Engels sharply distanced themselves from the so-called true socialists who, driven by a utopian and sentimental anticapitalism, chose instead to hurl "the traditional anathemas against liberalism, against representative government, against bourgeois competition, bourgeois freedom of the press, bourgeois legislation, bourgeois liberty and equality; and to preach to the masses 'that they had nothing to gain, and everything to lose, by this bourgeois movement'" (ibid., 511). But in no sense did this amount to recognition of the intrinsic value of the bourgeois liberal conception of political and civil liberty. Marx and Engels supported a tactical alliance with bourgeois liberalism as a historical force, without making any concessions to liberalism as a worldview or political theory. In other words, they supported bourgeois liberalism in the same way in which they supported the system of free trade—that is in "the revolutionary sense alone," as a movement destroying patriarchal feudal illusions, laying bare the antagonism of proletariat and bourgeoisie and thereby hastening the victory of the social revolution.

As already mentioned, Marx's own views on freedom were developed as a philosophical, or, rather, a historiosophical, conception in which problems of political and civil liberty, central to liberalism as political doctrine, were deprived of autonomous significance and thus marginalized, as it were. In contrast to liberals, Marx was interested chiefly in the freedom of the human species realized in history through increasing rational control of humankind over nature and social forces. This radical difference in focus led him to conclude that classical liberalism brought about the greatest alienation and reification of social forces, the culmination of humankind's enslavement by blind economic forces. His historical materialism drew on an analysis of "bourgeois liberty" as merely an illusion of consciousness, a hypocritical self-embellishment or even a conscious deception. No wonder, therefore, that Marx was often cynical about civil rights and democratic forms of government. Unlike many of his later followers (especially in Russia), he refrained from arguing that all forms of bourgeois government were "essentially the same" and that from the communist point of view there was no difference between, say, military dictatorship and bourgeois democracy. But even the most ardent defenders of his libertarian credentials have to concede that he was extremely reluctant in expressing his "underlying respect" for civil and political freedom. Richard N. Hunt attributed this reluctance to Marx's peculiar "moral constipation."[20] It seems, however, that it would be more proper to point out that Marx's residual respect for Western liberal values was merely a vestige of his bourgeois upbringing and not a part of his communist vision of human liberation.

Historians of ideas can safely say that Marx's paradigm of freedom and the liberal paradigm are incommensurable, in T. S. Kuhn's sense.[21] This is a useful point for all who are not sufficiently aware of the essential incompatibility of the Marxist and the liberal traditions.[22] On the other hand, comparing the two paradigms of freedom and highlighting the differences between them might yield instructive results, important especially for a better understanding of Marx's conception.

In the classical liberal conception, only man-made obstacles to individual effort can be described as limitations to freedom.[23] The opposite of freedom is not one's dependence on some necessity governing the world of things (e.g., the anonymous market mechanism), but one's dependence on the arbitrary will of another human.[24] We can be free from external compulsion, coercion, or constraint, but we cannot be free from natural necessity. Freedom is the opposite of prohibition, compulsion, and constraint, but not the opposite of internalized determination, let alone objective laws of nature. Hence, the liberal conception of freedom does not depend on the acceptance of "the freedom of the will"; it pertains not to the will but to the agent. Most liberals readily agree with Locke that "the question is not proper, whether the will be free, but whether a Man be free."[25] The question of "the freedom of the will" should not be confused with the question of "the freedom of the subject of will." The subjects of will (individuals) are free when nobody forbids them to do what they want (or coerces them to do what they do not want), and usually they are quite indifferent as to whether what they want (i.e., the content of their will) is determined by society and history. They feel free when they act in accordance with *their own* will, their true self, and are not concerned with the speculative problem of whether the content of their will, their identity, was freely chosen or shaped by a number of biological, social, and historical factors. After deeper reflection one could even grant that "freedom of the will," in the sense of the absence of the determination of will, diminishes the seriousness and value of human freedom, since it makes will into something accidental, a caprice. The famous words of Luther—"here I stand, I *cannot* do otherwise"—expressed both a conscious, free choice and an internal necessity of just such a choice.

Another feature of the liberal conception of freedom is (or should be) a clear conceptual distinction between freedom and power, or freedom and capacity. Individuals are free when *nobody forbids* them to act in accordance with their own will, and it is irrelevant whether those actions *can* bring about the results expected by them. *Lack of freedom* should not be confused with *lack of ability*. One's freedom is always limited by one's ability; if I am permitted to pursue my own goals but incapable of reaching them, I should complain about my own limitation, not about lack of freedom. I am *not* a slave if my physical strength does not enable me to do certain things, but I am a slave if my physical strength is not at my own disposal. If I want to run but cannot because I have a broken leg, this is an accident of fate, a misfortune but not servitude; lack of freedom, servitude, would be at issue if I was able to run but *was not allowed* to do so. Similarly, I am not unfree when I cannot think creatively, but I am unfree if my creative thinking has been suppressed by forcible indoctrination. Freedom thus conceived is therefore not *positive liberty* or ability to attain desired ends. It is *negative liberty*—freedom from commands and prohibitions imposed on an individual by others.[26] One may add that legal norms do not contradict freedom, since their character is universal and impersonal. Rule of law excludes arbitrariness and therefore secures freedom under law; admittedly it sets definite limits to freedom, but within those limits it guarantees the individual a sphere of privacy free from the interference of other people and any authority. It is just this sphere of independence, in which one is free from all interference and at the same time left alone and at one's own risk, that is the proper sphere of freedom.

One can see at once that the Marxian conception of freedom had nothing in common with "negative liberty." Rather, it was a perfect example of conceiving freedom as "positive liberty" or, using Isaiah Berlin's words, "the freedom which consists in being one's own master."[27] That Marx considered not human arbitrariness but dependence on the world of things (or reified social relations) to be the greatest threat to the "mastery over one's fate" had deep roots in the tradition of classical German philosophy. The axiological premise of this philosophy was the feeling that a human being's dependence on things (subject on object, consciousness on elemental and uncontrolled processes) is something deeply humiliating and unworthy of a rational creature. Antiliberal implications of such an axiology can be seen most clearly not in the mature Hegel, who accepted the existence of "civil society" as an autonomous sphere of particular, private interests, but in the young Hegel and especially in Fichte. Fichte's enthusiasm for freedom was a blatant denial of the respect for liberal "negative liberty." Freedom for him meant not "the inalienable rights of the individual" but the rule of ego over nonego, the victory of the subjectivity of the human world over the objectivity of nature. At this point Fichte's similarity to Marx ends, but it is worth recalling that freedom thus conceived was perfectly compatible with the Fichtean ideal of "the closed state," which regulated all spheres of the life of individuals. In Fichte's utopia (considered to be a socialist utopia by the Marxists of the Second International), the rational totalitarian state was treated as an instrument of freedom, an instrument of the collective ego that controls and determines itself, subjects itself to laws, and in this way liberates itself from the humiliating power of the blind necessity that governs the world of things.[28]

This example of Fichte highlights another point that needs elucidation, namely, the problem of the subject of freedom. It is important to ask *what* is to be set free: transcendental ego or empirical ego, the human species or really existing particular individuals. Classical liberals tried to secure individual freedom, stressing mostly its negative aspect and taking it for granted that the term *individual* refers to empirically existing human beings, imperfect as they are, pursuing their different particular interests and often colliding with one another (hence the necessity of law and the state). For Marx, as for Fichte, it was entirely different. Marx was concerned with the positive freedom of the human species—that is, with the unfettered and optimal development of man's species essence. He was outspokenly cynical about individuals as members of bourgeois civil society; their freedom was, in his view, nothing more than unfettered egoism, "freedom to collide with one another and to engage in exchange within this freedom" (M, G, 163–64). When he used the term *individual* with a positive connotation, he meant something completely different—namely, the de-alienation of man through an incarnation of human species powers in the universally developed individual human beings of his communist utopia. He took it for granted that such individuals would be perfect embodiments of universal human essence and therefore would not collide with one another.

It is sometimes stressed that Marx, in contrast to the "true socialists," was genuinely sympathetic to democratic radicalism. This is partially true. Before becoming a communist he was a radical democrat, and even as a communist he did not cease to support the cause of democratic radicalism in Germany; after all, he was editor-in-chief of the radical newspaper *Neue Rheinische Zeitung* after publishing the *Manifesto of the Communist Party* (although, on the other hand, he quite unscrupulously used this newspaper for propagating communist ideas). But quite irrespective of how deep and genuine was Marx's sympathy for democracy, it should be clear that it was not a sympathy for *liberal* democracy. We have become accustomed to identifying democracy with its liberal variety, but in fact democracy and liberalism were, at Marx's time, two different ideologies, drawing from different sources and answering different questions. They are distinguishable not only historically but analytically as well. Democracy is concerned with the problem of the *source* of political power ("Who governs me?"), while liberalism tries to cope with the problem of the legitimate scope of public power ("How far does government interfere with me?");[29] the first revolves around the conception of the sovereignty of the people, derived in modern times from Rousseau, while the second is bound up with the conception of inalienable human rights—a conception setting definite limits to governmental power, including the power of a democratically elected government, and thus undermining the very notion of sovereignty, in the sense of unlimited authority.[30] True, in the struggle against absolute monarchies the idea of popular sovereignty was, as a rule, inseparable from the idea of human rights; thus, the French Revolution proclaimed both conceptions at once in the "Declaration of the Rights of Man and Citizen." However, it soon turned out that these were different ideas, often admittedly supporting each other but also able to produce wholly different consequences. This was very clearly shown by Benjamin Constant in his famous lecture on modern freedom as compared with the "freedom of the ancients" (1819).[31] He defined ancient (democratic) liberty as participating in political power, taking an active part in collective sovereignty—in other words, as political democracy extending its rule over all spheres of human life. In contrast to this, he argued, the essence of modern (liberal) freedom is precisely the existence of a private sphere with which no state, even the most democratic, has the right to interfere. Thus, ancient freedom—*unlimited* popular sovereignty—is fundamentally incompatible with modern freedom—the freedom of the private individual—as the Jacobin phase of the French Revolution all too clearly showed. Therefore, political freedom can be accepted by liberals only if the rights of man are recognized as prepolitical and unalienable, as *limiting* the scope of political power irrespective of its source. If the autonomy of the private sphere is sufficiently protected, political democracy may function as a guarantee of modern liberty; if not, an undemocratic but limited government is greatly preferable to the omnipotence of a democratic state.

Marx also sharply distinguished between modern liberalism and ancient democracy, but in value judgments he diametrically differed from Constant. In his early writings Marx often complained about the loss of ancient freedom, defining it as communal freedom founded on commonly shared purposes and values.[32] On the eve of his conversion to communism, in a programmatic letter to *Deutsch-Französische Jahrbücher* (May 1843), he wrote about it thus: "The self-confidence of the human being, freedom, has first of all to be aroused again in the hearts of these people. Only this feeling, which vanished from the world with the Greeks, and under Christianity disappeared into the blue mist of the heavens, can again transform society [*Gesellschaft*] into a community [*Gemeinschaft*] of human beings united for their highest aims, into a democratic state" (M&E, *CW*, 3:137).

Contrasting *Gemeinschaft* with *Gesellschaft*—a theme developed later in a classical sociological study by Ferdinand Tönnies[33]—was typical of all German critics of capitalist economies and of the liberal ideologies of the more advanced Western countries. German conservative romantics and German socialists shared common ground in criticizing *Gesellschaft* as an alienated form of social intercourse, as based on mechanical interplay of commercial interests and wholly lacking spiritual dimension. These conservatives, however, saw a remedy for this—and the foundation of a true *Gemeinschaft*—in revealed religion and unreflectively accepted tradition, while the socialists dreamed about a rational community striving for common, consciously chosen aims and consonant with universally human values. The emphasis on rationality (as opposed to spontaneous adjustment to "blind forces") and on the need of consciously chosen common *ends* (as opposed to plurality of individual ends realized within the framework of commonly accepted *rules* of conduct) made the socialists deeply hostile toward "*bürgerliche Gesellschaft.*" A radicalization of this attitude might likely lead to a wholesale condemnation of the monetary exchange economy, which would be the next step in Marx's ideological evolution. After his conversion to communism, he conceived of modern "civil society" (*bürgerliche Gesellschaft*) as involving a profound discrepancy between humans' existence and their species essence. Conversely, the true community (*Gemeinschaft*) came to be seen by him as presupposing the replacement of the market economy by a conscious regulation of production and consumption.

Extremely important from this point of view is Marx's article "On the Jewish Question" (1844). This was a fierce attack on the principles of "civil society" in the name of the democratic principle of the sovereignty of the people, an attack on "private freedom" (Constant's "modern freedom") in the name of "public freedom" (Constant's "ancient freedom"). In this article, Marx made a sharp distinction between the rights of man and the rights of citizens. The first are the rights of private individuals seeking a legal guarantee of their negative freedom; the second are the rights of political participation—that is, giving people their share in political decision making in the public sphere of human existence. Marx condemned the first category outright. "The right of man to liberty," he argued, "is not based on the union of man with man, but on the separation of man from man." Human rights guarantee the freedom of an individual as an isolated, self-sufficient monad; the practical application of such freedom is the right to private property, and the essence of such freedom is the law of egoism, which "leads man to see in other men not the realization but the limitation of his own freedom" (M, *SW*, 53).

This severe condemnation of the very concept of the rights of man, the cornerstone of the liberal worldview, resulted because Marx, as Buchanan aptly put it, "thought of rights exclusively as boundary markers which separate competing egoists," or, to put it differently, because the concept of a person as essentially a bearer of rights was, in Marx's eyes, "a radically defective concept that could only arise in a radically defective form of human society."[34] Man as the subject of rights and the egoistic economic subject of capitalist civil society were, for him, two sides of the same coin.[35]

Marx's attitude toward the rights of the citizen—the rights of political participation—was much more complex. Like many German thinkers he was under the spell of the ancient polis democracy. He deplored the privatization of life in modern times and sharply contrasted the public freedom of the ancient Greek citizen with the private, egoistic freedom of the modern bourgeois. In his early "Critique of Hegel's Philosophy of Law" (1843) he even expressed a hope that universal suffrage (a universalization of the rights of political participation) would abolish the dualism of state and civil society by liquidating the autonomy of the private sector and making civil existence inessential in contrast to political existence (ibid., 27–30, 32–35). This, he thought, would amount to a restoration of the ancient heroic virtues, as contrasted with bourgeois egoism.

In a true democracy, Marx wrote, constitutional laws do not have autonomous existence: they are only "the self-determination of the people; subject to change in accordance with the people's sovereign will. Republican government should not be mistaken for democracy. The republic is a mere state *form*, as is the monarchy. This is clearly shown by the fact that property relationships, that is the *content* of the state, are almost the same in the North American republic and in the Prussian monarchy" (ibid., 29). In Marx's view this proved that the content of the state might contradict its form. In order to eliminate the contradiction between democratic political form and undemocratic content, it was necessary to extend the democratic principle of popular sovereignty to the economic sphere through subjecting economic relations to collective control. In other words, no sphere of life should remain exempt from public regulation, and, consequently, all legal safeguards of private freedom, freedom from intervention, should be abolished.

We can see from this how inimical Marx was to liberal values even in the precommunist stage of his ideological development. He saw no positive value in privacy; his ideal was the total subordination of the private sphere to the public sphere, the extension of the scope of political decisions to all spheres of life and thus the abolition of the autonomous existence of the economy. He accepted political freedom only on condition that it was *not* combined with the rights of man, conceived of as the right of individuals to limit the scope of collective control over them and thus to restrain popular sovereignty. If we define totalitarianism as unlimited power, we have to agree with Friedrich Hayek that liberalism is the opposite of totalitarianism, while democracy wielding totalitarian power is perfectly conceivable.[36] True, it is difficult to imagine the realization of such a possibility in a modern industrial society in which the people's will is truly respected, that is, not artificially molded by more or less subtle indoctrination from above. But the ideal of totalitarian democracy, which was the ideal of the young Marx, does not contain any logical contradiction.

Commenting on the French "Declaration of the Rights of Man and Citizen," Marx wrote:

It is already paradoxical that a people that is just beginning to free itself, to tear down all barriers between different sections of the people and form a political community, should solemnly proclaim (Declaration of 1791) the justification of egoistic man separated from his fellow men and the community. Indeed, this proclamation is repeated at a moment when only the most heroic devotion can save the nation, and is therefore peremptorily demanded, at a moment when the sacrifice of all the interests of civil society is raised to the order of the day and egoism must be punished as a crime (Declaration of the Rights of Man . . . 1793). This fact appears to be even more paradoxical when we see that citizenship, the political community, is degraded by the political emancipators to a mere means for the preservation of these so-called rights of man, that the citizen is declared to be the servant of egoistic man, the sphere in which man behaves as a communal being is degraded below the sphere in which man behaves as a partial being. Finally that it is not man as citizen but man as bourgeois who is called the real and true man. (ibid., 54)

The young Hegel expressed very similar thoughts. He too deplored the privatization of life in modern times, sharply contrasted the world of freedom of the ancient "citizen" with the freedom of the modern "bourgeois," saw in the French Revolution an attempt to recreate the heroic "ancient liberty," and was disappointed by the fiasco of those efforts.[37] But the mature Hegel abandoned these conceptions in favor of a more complex one recognizing the autonomy of modern civil society, and thus he moved closer to the liberal doctrine. It is important to realize, therefore, that the young Marx criticized Hegel's *Philosophy of Law* not only for its bureaucratic authoritarianism, combined with a tolerance for various semifeudal institutions, but also, and perhaps above all, for its acceptance of important elements of classical liberalism.

Marx's essay "On the Jewish Question" throws much light on the consistently illiberal character of his own conception. For instance, he deplores the state's lack of resolve in crushing the autonomy of civil society in the following words:

Of course, in times when the political state is born violently as such out of civil society, when man's self-liberation tries to complete itself in the form of political self-liberation [an allusion to the French Revolution], the state must go as far as abolishing, destroying religion, but only in the same way as it goes as far as abolishing private property, at the most, by declaring a maximum, by confiscation or a progressive tax, or in the same way as it abolished life, by the guillotine. In moments of particular self-consciousness political life tries to suppress its presupposition, civil society and its elements, and to constitute itself as the real, harmonious life of man. However, this is only possible through violent opposition to its own conditions, by declaring the revolution to be permanent. The political drama therefore ends necessarily with the restoration of religion, private property, and all the elements of civil society, just as war ends with peace. (ibid., 47)

In this manner the total suppression of civil society by an omnipotent state was presented as the victory of harmonious species life, and the bourgeois state was condemned for its inherent inability to achieve this ideal.

In developing this thought Marx concluded that every political emancipation—that is, the unfettering of the political spirit without abolishing the autonomous network of egoistic interests constituting civil society—was a far cry from genuine human emancipation. Instead of freeing individuals from religion and property, it gave them religious freedom and freedom to own property; instead of freeing them from the egoism of business, it gave them freedom to engage in business (ibid., 56). Characteristically, this list of important "freedoms from" did not include the basic one, the cornerstone of the entire edifice of freedom: namely, freedom from political coercion.

How to translate Marx's critique of "political emancipation" into a working practical program may be open to debate. It is certainly arguable that Marx himself did not advocate immediate, wholesale expropriations or compulsory atheization. But it is clear, nevertheless, that his vision of building harmonious human existence on the ruins of civil society was a totalitarian utopia and that taking this seriously fully justified violent means.

Having become a full-fledged communist, Marx ceased to be puzzled by the fate of the rights of citizens in capitalist societies. His historical materialism made it clear to him and to his followers that under capitalism politics *must* serve the egoistic interests of man as "bourgeois" and that to think otherwise amounted to cherishing petty bourgeois democratic illusions. As long as capitalism existed, civil society was stronger than the state, and the political sphere was merely a superstructure whose autonomy in relation to the economic sphere could only be relative.

With this conclusion, Marx's attitude toward political democracy underwent a considerable change. Political freedom ceased to be for him an end in itself and became instead a means of struggle, a means whose value was relative, depending on many different factors. He no longer thought of political freedom as being able to resurrect the ancient public virtues and curb bourgeois egoism; on the contrary, it followed from his analysis of the capitalist system that such freedom was always more formal than real, serving the interests of the propertied classes and therefore deserving to be unmasked rather than glorified. The young Engels formulated this conclusion even earlier and more strongly, writing in "Progress of Social Reform on the Continent": "Democracy is, as I take all forms of government to be, a contradiction in itself, an untruth, nothing but hypocrisy (theology, as we Germans call it), at the bottom. Political liberty is sham-liberty, the worst possible slavery; the appearance of liberty, and therefore the reality of servitude" (M&E, CW, 3:393).

The Russian populists, who belonged to the most eager readers of *Capital*, concluded from it that parliamentarianism was a deception, an instrument of bourgeoisie class rule, and hence not worth fighting for. Such sentiments were not isolated; the German "true socialists" preceding Marx held similar views and later so did the anarcho-syndicalist ideologists of the workers' movement who invoked Marx. Marx himself, despite appearances, was in fact far from drawing such conclusions. In *The Eighteenth Brumaire of Louis Bonaparte*, he developed the idea that parliamentary governments created by the bourgeoisie could become instruments of the socialists and that the bourgeoisie, in order to preserve its class rule, would have to resort to dictatorship. The bourgeoisie needed peace, while parliamentary governments "live in struggle and thanks to struggle." Marx continued:

Parliamentary governments live on discussion so how can they forbid discussion? Every interest, every social institution is transformed here into universal thoughts; as a thought it is the subject of debate; how can any interest or institution rise above thinking and impose itself as a dogma of faith? The struggle of speakers on the rostrum provokes the struggle of the hooligans of the press, a discussion club in parliament is necessarily supplemented by discussion clubs in drawing rooms and public bars, the representatives by appealing ceaselessly to popular opinion justify popular opinion in expressing its true opinion in petitions. Parliamentary governments leave all to majority decisions, hence the considerable majorities outside parliament also want to decide. If fiddles play at the summit of the state, is it to be wondered that people dance at the bottom? (ibid., 11:142)

This is very far indeed from condemning parliamentarism and treating it exclusively as an instrument of bourgeois oppression.

There is even more unambiguous support for political freedom in a remark by Engels condemning the first Polish Marxists (the Equality, or *Równość*, group) for renouncing the struggle for Polish independence. In a letter to Kautsky (Feb. 7, 1882), Engels wrote: "It appears that the editors of *Równość* have been impressed by the radically sounding phrases of the Geneva Russians" (i.e., the Russian anarchists and populists who dismissed political questions as allegedly irrelevant to social revolution). In the same letter he gave a theoretical explanation of his and Marx's position: "Every Polish peasant or worker who wakes up from the general gloom and participates in the common interest encounters first the fact of national subjugation. This fact is in his way everywhere as the first barrier. To remove it is the basic condition of every healthy and free development. Polish socialists who do not place the liberation of their country at the head of their program appear to me as would German socialists who do not demand first and foremost repeal of the anti-socialist law, freedom of the press, association and assembly. In order to be able to fight one needs first a soil to stand on, air, light and space. Otherwise all is idle chatter" (M&E, *RME*, 117).

There is no doubt that this remark by Engels adequately expressed the position of both friends. Since he condemned equally the so-called political indifferentism of Russian populists, it is worth noting that Chernyshevskii, one of the "fathers of Russian populists," finally came to a similar conclusion and expressed it in a similar way. His comrades in exile, sharing the current populist opinions, were amazed when he profferred the following assessment of political freedom: "You, gentlemen, say that political freedom cannot feed a hungry man. Quite true. But can, for example, air feed a hungry man? Of course not. Nevertheless, without food man can survive a few days, while without air he will not survive even ten minutes. Just as air is indispensable to the life of individual man, so political freedom is indispensable to the proper functioning of human society." [38]

And yet, in spite of similarities, these wise words expressed a position that on closer examination turns out to be essentially different from that of Marx and Engels. True, they could not be accused of a nihilist attitude toward political freedom. They deeply hated "patriarchal feudal absolutism" and, in contrast to the Russian populists, repeatedly emphasized that capitalism with political democracy is, as a rule, much better, much more progressive than capitalism with another kind of political superstructure. But, in contrast to Chernyshevskii, they never came to the conclusion that political freedom should be supported for its own sake, as a principle. Under capitalism, they thought, political freedom can further capitalist progress; sometimes it can even serve as a *means* of proletarian class struggle, but as a part of the capitalist superstructure, it can never be a form of true freedom. This was for them axiomatic: they were convinced that in class societies true freedom could not exist, while in the classless society of the future there would be no more conflicts, people would live in accordance with their species essence, and the entire sphere of politics would become superfluous.

Thus, the Russian populists were not mistaken when they saw in Marx an uncompromising unmasker of "bourgeois freedom." They were mistaken only in drawing from Marxism such *practical* conclusions as the view that political freedom was completely irrelevant to the solution of the social question, that it could only worsen the situation of the common

people, and that socialists should combat it as strengthening only the possessing classes and thereby blocking the chances for socialism in Russia.[39]
These views, quite irrespective of their value for fostering an understanding
of some specific problems of backward agrarian countries entering a phase
of rapid modernization, could not be legitimately deduced from Marx's
stance on political freedom.

Before the reprinting of Marx's essay "On the Jewish Question" in 1902,
most readers of his works did not realize that "bourgeois freedom" on
the legal and political plane meant for him two interrelated but different
conceptions: political freedom realized in the functioning of representative organs of state power, and freedom as the nonintervention of the state
into a broadly conceived sphere of "private life," which comprised the
whole sphere of civil society. It is this *second* form of "bourgeois freedom,"
praised by classical liberal writers, that Marx attacked with true fury as
a particularly shameless form of hypocrisy that served the interests of the
stronger. In his view, "formal" and "negative" freedom—i.e., freedom as
merely the absence of compulsion (more precisely, extraeconomic compulsion)—was entirely worthless to one who had no means to realize his aims
and thus could not become "master of his fate."

This view, shared with Marx by both socialist and conservative critics of capitalism, was quickly and generally accepted by the radical left.
Chernyshevskii (in his populist phase) compared freedom in this sense to
the right to eat from gold plates: What advantage is it if nobody forbids
me to do so if I know that I shall never acquire the means to purchase a
gold dinner service?[40] However, this comparison proves more than it tries
to demonstrate: it shows not only the weakness but also the strength of the
classical liberal conception of freedom. In the converse situation in which
one who can afford to purchase a gold dinner service is forbidden to do so
because the ownership of such things is the monopoly of the ruling caste,
the arbitrariness of such a prohibition would so violate one's sense of freedom and dignity as to be far more painful than the situation described by
Chernyshevskii.

The examples Marx gives are more convincing, but the strong aspect of
Marx's conception of freedom simultaneously constitutes its weakness. In
the nineteenth century, when workers made contracts without coercion but
under the threat of starvation, it was necessary to point out all the limitations of the liberal idea of "negative freedom," which Marx did with great
force. He was also largely right when he argued that freedom conceived
purely negatively is not an ideal adequate to man's Promethean greatness.
It would be wrong to judge Marx guilty of not stressing the contradiction
between compulsion, in all its forms, and human subjectivity, which was so
dear to him. One must rather assume that he considered the contradiction
to be something self-evident, perhaps worth dealing with in works on Asi-

atic despotism but not in an analysis of economically developed European society.

Such a diagnosis certainly enjoyed profound historical justification. The optics of history change, however, and so it is not strange that our century has seen the problem of freedom through a new lens. In developed capitalist countries today, workers are not helpless and are not threatened with death from starvation. However, the cruel and tragic history of twentieth-century communist movements has demonstrated that it was premature to treat "Asiatic despotism" as something that in no way could threaten Europe. It has become evident that economic progress and even social emancipation of oppressed classes can go hand in hand with an increased role of social and political compulsion and that various forms of "positive freedom" in the form of so-called economic and social rights can be secured to workers by totalitarian states, but that such situations surely cannot be considered triumphs of freedom. Given this, Berlin's assertion that there indeed are more important things than freedom, that he is willing to accept the limitations of freedom for the sake of solving burning social problems but that he opposes the identification of freedom with the improvement of economic conditions and with progress toward social equality is especially convincing.[41]

The ideas of the contemporary Western radical left, which as a rule draws its inspiration from Marx, also provide a serious argument in favor of the thesis of nineteenth-century liberals that freedom consists, above all, in the absence of dependence on alien arbitrary will. What is the point of the left's ceaseless attacks on manipulation, advertising, and deliberate creation of "artificial" wants? The goal is to convince the inhabitants of well-to-do countries with market economies that the market mechanisms on which they depend are not at all "objective" but rather are steered by the deftly hidden conscious will of a small handful of producers and monopolists, and hence that a dependence on such mechanisms is, in essence, a dependence on alien will—that is, a lack of freedom. If freedom were understood as the opposite of dependence on the anonymous "course of events" and not as the absence of dependence on alien decisions, such conceptions, assuming the existence of a kind of capitalist "conspiracy" against society, would be wholly unnecessary.

Marx distanced himself from such conceptions in a wholly unambiguous way. In the preface to the first edition of *Capital*, he wrote: "I paint the capitalist and the landlord in no sense *couleur de rose*. But here individuals are dealt with only insofar as they are the personifications of economic categories, embodiments of particular class-relations and class-interests. My standpoint, from which the evolution of the economic formation of society is viewed as a process of natural history, can less than any other make the individual responsible for relations whose creature he socially remains, however much he may subjectively raise himself above them" (M, C, 1:20–21).

It seems proper to also say a few words about Marx's relationship to the evolution of liberalism—that is, its transition from the classical liberalism of the nineteenth century to the welfare state liberalism of our times.

Marx criticized liberalism from a position wholly outside the liberal tradition, but his criticism served, and still serves, as a mighty catalyst, making liberal theorists more and more alive to the social dimensions of freedom. How has this been possible?

The main reason for this was, undoubtedly, the vast extension of the government's responsibilities—that is, of the scope of conscious decision making—into the economic sphere. What had usually been regarded as a sphere of natural necessity came to be treated as a sphere of conscious regulation. This made liberals more and more susceptible to learning from Marx's criticism of "bourgeois freedom." The situation in which poor people cannot afford to buy a great many things (although nobody forbids them to buy anything) could no longer be treated as resulting simply and solely from a lack of capacity rather than a limitation of freedom. If social relations and the distribution of national income came to be seen as subject to conscious decisions, then the very fact that poor people are poor could be explained (rightly or wrongly) as the outcome of a man-made social system and, thus, as a limitation of poor people's freedom. True, it would be straining matters somewhat to apply this interpretation to early capitalist societies in which social engineering was unknown and uncontrolled economic forces functioned, as Marx so often stressed, like natural forces. But this interpretation became less strained as conscious regulation of the economy increased and the resultant social consequences became more predictable. This explains, I think, the increasing complication of the liberal conception of freedom and the readiness of some left-wing liberals to embrace Marxism.[42] Of course, no genuine liberal or neoliberal could accommodate Marx's view that the real subject of freedom was humanity as a whole and that individual freedom, conceived as unfettered self-realization, would appear only under communism. Nevertheless, Marx's critique of "bourgeois freedom" helped liberals become acutely aware that freedom of personality, broadly conceived, implies not only freedom from arbitrarily imposed constraints but also the possibility of the free development of inherent human capacities. It cannot be denied that in this particular sense, the ideal of freedom demands not only independence from the arbitrary will of another, but also the removal of those social and economic conditions that hamper the fullest possible development of the individual. The ideal of freedom, therefore, demands not only a minimalization of external constraints, but also the creation of optimal conditions for everyone's fullest personal development.

The evolution in this direction was greatly facilitated by the fact that the Aristotelian notion that things have essences that need self-actualization and full expression, a notion underpinning Marx's conception of humans' species essence,[43] was not alien to the mainstream liberal tradition. T. H. Green, the main theorist of British neoliberalism, preserved the classical liberal view of "negative liberty" as the core meaning of freedom but proposed extending the notion of freedom beyond this core meaning to a "metaphorical" sense that involved "a positive power or capacity of doing or enjoying something worth doing or enjoying, and that, too, something that we do or enjoy in common with others."[44] Another neoliberal theorist, B. Bosanquet, defended "negative liberty" as a necessary condition of freedom but insisted at the same time that freedom broadly conceived concerns much more than absence of coercion, or threats of coercion, by others. Liberty positively defined is "being oneself," freely realizing one's nature, and "the fullest condition of liberty is that in which we are ourselves most completely."[45] This seems to be close to Marx's conception of freedom as unfettered self-realization. Also, it seems obvious that negative liberty is not sufficient to secure full self-realization.

Nevertheless, the similarity between Marx's freedom and the neoliberal conception of positive individual freedom is very superficial, while the difference remains profound. Unfortunately, an awareness of this point is not in itself sufficient. I shall therefore try to sum up in three points of fundamental importance.

First, in the liberal interpretation, the "new" positive freedom remains aim independent and, in this sense, can be seen as an extension of the "old" negative freedom.[46] This interpretation imposes on the government the obligation to commit itself to creating conditions in which every individual can develop more fully and with greater ease, but it does not say anything about the desired *direction* of personal development; neither does it limit individual freedom of choice by endowing the public authority with the paternalistic right to decide what is good for people and the power to impose this decision on the population. Also, this interpretation does not identify freedom with any positive idea of what humans should be like; it does not say, for instance, that individuals should become "communal beings," asserting their individuality in harmony with somebody else's vision of the universal human essence. It does respect individuals' "negative" freedom by not depriving them of the right to determine for themselves their needs and wishes and, in fact, enhances this freedom by increasing the number of possible individual choices. It also endorses a pluralistic society by recognizing the multiplicity of human needs and interests, thus excluding the Marxian vision of conscious collective control over all spheres of social life, eliminating pluralism in the name of universality and rationality.

Second, in the liberal tradition freedom inescapably focuses on individuals such as they exist under given conditions, while in Marxian tradition freedom applies primarily to the entire human species. Marx conceived of freedom as consisting of the full self-realization of human beings' species essence, while the neoliberals, following J. S. Mill, assumed that human beings had their own *individual* essence or nature, their own peculiar and inborn endowment that might or might not be realized during their lifetime.[47] Hence, the neoliberals were concerned with the fullest possible self-realization of actually existing individuals, while Marx concentrated on the "liberation" of superior capacities inherent, he believed, in humankind as a species. This explains the ease with which he was ready to sacrifice living people for the cause of the future liberation of humanity. He did not conceive of the possibility that even after the abolition of capitalism, people might remain as egoistic and philistine as before, unwilling to raise themselves to the level of "species beings." However, the logic of his position made it clear that such recalcitrant individuals should be seen as prisoners of bourgeois individualism, and as such subject to collective "reeducation" or simply "forced to be free."

Finally, the neoliberals did not see the market as the worst enemy of human freedom. On the contrary, they believed that the spontaneous order of the market was the only form of large-scale social cooperation that (to use Mill's words) provided individuals with the liberty to frame "the plan of their life to suit their own character . . . to pursue their own good in their own way." The neoliberals also remained firmly convinced that a market economy was preferable from the point of view of collective welfare. This was so because, as Mill put it, "mankind are greater gainers by suffering each other to live as seems good to themselves, than by compelling each to live as seems good to the rest."[48] Such views were, of course, incompatible with Marx's ideal of "communal freedom," which was to be achieved through all-embracing collective planning.

We must conclude, therefore, that the left-wing liberals who try to see in Marx an ally in their fight against right-wing libertarians or liberal conservatives are, in fact, deeply mistaken. Marx's ideal of the emancipation of humankind was essentially different from the liberal ideal of individual freedom, both in its "old liberal" and in its "new liberal" versions.

1.3   The Story of Self-Enriching Alienation: A General Outline

We can now turn to a closer examination of the Marxian "historiosophy of freedom"—that is, Marx's philosophy of history as the development of freedom and his philosophy of freedom as the immanent meaning of history.

It seems to me that one can speak of "the meaning *of* history" in the strict sense only if one admits some metaphysical, absolute point of reference for history as a whole. In Christianity, for example, the meaning of history is determined by the eschatological perspective of collective resurrection and the Last Judgment. According to Hegel the meaning of history is realized in the process of "self-enriching alienation." The Absolute Spirit alienates (externalizes) itself in time so that it may, after achieving the climax of alienation, absorb into itself its alienated contents and by so doing raise itself to the level of self-consciousness. Hence history emerges from the absolute and returns to it; its end is predetermined already at its beginning. We can find numerous antecedents of this Hegelian schema (as Kolakowski has extensively shown) [49] in the Neoplatonic tradition of that current of Christian thought which developed the theme of God enhancing himself through the Fall. The crossing of this tradition with Hegelianism resulted in the philosophico-historical conception of the Romantics, frequently linked with chiliastic ideas. An inquiry into the meaning of history is fully justified and has a clear answer for all these conceptions—from Neoplatonic mysticism to the maximally rationalized and relatively secularized (although, in fact, no less mythical) Hegelian schema.

The matter is quite different for Marxism, which took on its distinct shape, after the Feuerbachian discovery that the secret of Hegelian philosophy is theology, as a consequence of accepting and *radicalizing* the "antitheological" postulates of Feuerbachism. This resulted in the exclusion of the metaphysical perspective and thereby the question of the metaphysical meaning of history. Hence Marx did not consider questions such as why history exists at all, what was before it, and what will be after it. If he perceived in history some positive "inner direction," what he sought to answer was not a metaphysical question about the "meaning of history," but a much more modest question about *meaning in history*, the question whether historical events constitute some meaningful structure *inside history*.

With this qualification we can safely claim that Marx elaborated a general philosophy of history—a philosophy that, like Hegelianism, saw history as a dialectical process of developing freedom, a *meaningful* process having an inner direction and a final goal. Freedom was defined in this philosophy as the fullest, freest self-actualization of human species being (*Gattungswesen*), as the truest possibility for the unfolding of human nature, revealing all its inherent capacities and its potential richness. Development, in turn, was conceived as the dialectical movement of self-enriching alienation. This concept, central to the entire Marxian philosophy, assumed, to put it briefly, that in order to develop oneself, one must exteriorize one's forces and subject oneself to alienation, because only in this way can what is potential and latent become actual and self-conscious.

The term *alienation*—originally a theological term taken up and developed by Hegel, Feuerbach, and other German thinkers—means, first, going out of itself, becoming something different from and alien to its essence, and, second, giving something away, relinquishing something of one's own being, undergoing an amputation as it were. In this sense the Incarnation was the alienation of God, who had to relinquish his divine attributes to assume a nondivine corporeal form; in a similar sense Hegel wrote about the alienation of the Spirit (*Geist*), which had to exteriorize itself to constitute the material world.[50] Self-enriching alienation is the concept of a dialectical movement through alienation to self-enrichment. Thus, the entire period of man's separation from God after the Fall could be interpreted as a journey from Paradise lost to Paradise not only regained but also enriched by the knowledge of what is good and what is bad, by freedom and consciousness. Similarly, in Hegelian philosophy the Absolute Spirit alienates itself in time so that it can, after achieving the climax of alienation, absorb into itself its alienated contents and thereby enrich itself, raise itself to the level of self-consciousness.

Marx is known to have been deeply impressed by Feuerbach's reversal of the Hegelian (and Christian) view of alienation: by his claim that it was not the Absolute Spirit that had alienated itself in the world and in man but, on the contrary, that it was man who had alienated his generic essence by externalizing it in the image of God. According to a widespread view, Feuerbach, in contrast to Hegel, "regarded alienation as an altogether negative phenomenon," as something purely evil, bringing about no positive values.[51] This view, however, seems to be erroneous. Undoubtedly, Feuerbach stressed the negative aspect of alienation, but nevertheless he too saw it as a self-enriching process. By creating God, he reasoned, humankind had impoverished itself, as it were, and, moreover, had become dominated by its own creation; however, overcoming this alienation would entail the absorption of divine attributes by human beings, thus making them truly divine beings.

Marx followed Feuerbach in relating his theory of alienation to humans' being, but his own theme was socioeconomic alienation through the social division of labor under conditions of private ownership of the means of production, a process that entered its culminating phase with the development of modern capitalism. He saw the capitalist market as a force created by humans but alien from them, having its own quasi-natural laws of development that opposed and dominated individuals, thwarting their aims, instead of being subjected to their conscious control. Thus, humans became enslaved by their own products, by things; even interhuman relations became reified, taking on the appearance of the objective relations between commodities in the process of exchange, completely independent of human will. This "commodity fetishism," or reification, was, in Marx's view, the worst, and a peculiarly capitalist, form of alienation.

By contrast, Marx described communism as "the positive abolition of private property and thus of self-alienation and therefore the real reappropriation of the human essence by and for man"; as "the complete and conscious return of man conserving all the riches of previous development for man himself as a social, i.e. human being"; as "the genuine solution of the antagonism between man and nature and between man and man," "the true solution of the struggle between existence and essence, between objectification and self-affirmation, between freedom and necessity, between individual and species"; and, finally, as "the solution to the riddle of history" knowing itself to be this solution (M, SW, 89).

This quotation from the young Marx is remarkably revealing. It perfectly fits the pattern of self-enriching alienation, since humankind's return to itself is seen as self-enrichment, as a return on a higher level. It shows communism as the preordained goal of history, thus exposing the teleological structure of the Marxian philosophy of history. Finally, it describes communism as necessary for the sake not of equality but of the full self-actualization of the human essence—that is, for the sake of freedom, as Marx understood it. And, as we shall see, despite many qualifications, despite the appearance of a naturalist scientism, this same mythical pattern of thought is to be found in the works of the mature Marx, the author of *Capital*.

What, however, was to be the realization of freedom in the entire historical process? What did Marx understand by freedom realizing itself through all consecutive stages of history?

The self-actualization of the human essence in history—that is, the realization of freedom—was, in Marx's view, a process of liberating humankind from the domination of things, both in the form of physical necessity and in the form of reified social relations. In order to liberate themselves, to develop all capacities inherent in their species nature, human beings must be able to exercise conscious rational control over their natural environment and over their own social forces. Hence, freedom in this conception has two aspects. In the relation "man versus nature," it consists in the maximization of the power of the human species achieved through the development of productive forces. In the relation "man versus society," freedom means for Marx conscious shaping by humans of the social conditions of their existence, thereby eliminating the impersonal power of alienated, reified social forces. In the first case the subject of freedom was abstract collectivity; what was at stake was the development of humankind, freeing itself from the dependence on nature at the expense of the ever-increasing alienation and ever-increasing enslavement of the individual. In the second

case freedom was to become experienced by concrete, individual representatives of the species reabsorbing into themselves their alienated and
"socialized" (i.e., reified) powers by subjecting their social relations, as
well as their intercourse with nature, to conscious rational control. In both
cases, however, freedom is conceived as the ability to control one's fate,
i.e., as positive freedom; also in both cases it is opposed not to arbitrary
coercion but to the uncontrolled objectivity of impersonal forces—both
natural forces and the forces of historically produced "second nature," that
is, the quasi-natural functioning of alienated social forces.

Despite this common denominator, these two aspects of freedom were
clearly distinguished by Marx, both conceptually and historically. In history their relation was inversely proportional: "In the same measure in
which mankind achieves power over nature, man seems to fall under the
power of his own baseness" (M&E, CW, 14:655). From the viewpoint
of power of man over nature, capitalism appeared as a triumph of freedom, the culminating point of progress so far. But from the viewpoint of
the power of humankind over its own social relations, capitalism was the
greatest denial of freedom, the most complete subordination of individuals
to alienated and reified social forces. What the bourgeoisie calls personal
freedom (we read in *The German Ideology*) amounts, in the end, to leaving
the fate of particular individuals to the play of chance, which is the reverse of blind necessity, which governs the totality of social life. In the
literal version: "This right to the undisturbed enjoyment, within certain
conditions, of fortuity and chance has up till now been called personal
freedom." Under conditions of feudalism, all individuals were, above all,
members of a definite estate and as such were protected against the elemental character of impersonal social forces; their estate membership was
"a feature inseparable from individuality" and thus a defense of individuality against reification. In capitalism, however, the mighty power of reified
forces, brought into play by the development of the social division of
labor and worldwide market exchange, had destroyed personal bonds and
interconnections. "Thus in imagination, individuals seem freer under the
dominance of the bourgeoisie than before, because their conditions of life
seem accidental; in reality, of course, they are less free, because they are to
a greater extent governed by material forces" (ibid., 5:80–81, 78–79).

As we can see, freedom in Marx's conception was inseparable from
rationality, or rational predictability, and opposed to the irrationality of
chance.[52] Capitalism was condemned for not being rational enough, and
the final victory of freedom was seen as the replacement of market mechanisms with "production by freely associated men, consciously regulated by
them in accordance with a settled plan" (M, C, 1:84).

To understand Marx's assessment of capitalism, and its huge significance
for the conception of history as the realization of freedom, it is worth

recalling Marx's dependence on Hegelianism, a dependence evident just as much in the tendency to identify freedom with rationality, or rational control, as in the general schema of self-enriching alienation. According to Lukács, in Hegel's *Phenomenology of Mind* the capitalist epoch was considered to be "the most alienated and thus most progressive,"[53] since in the past progress had to be paid for by alienation. Only after reaching the highest stage of alienation (externalization)—after developing, at the price of alienation, all its potential—could the Absolute Spirit begin its "return journey" leading to the overcoming of alienation without losing the results of development. The young Marx translated this Hegelian thought into the language of the dialectic of socioeconomic relations. This helped him interpret the two aspects of freedom as two successive stages in the history of self-enriching alienation: the maximization of the productive powers of the species at the cost of alienation (capitalism) and the de-alienation of these powers through rational collective planning (communism).

Such is the general pattern, the triadic scheme, of Marx's historiosophy of freedom that underlies all his works, though, of course, it is most pronounced and explicit in his early philosophical writings. Marx quickly realized that a teleological conception of the meaning of history was too closely related to speculative idealism and therefore difficult to reconcile with the program of historical materialism. Hence, already in *The Holy Family* and *The German Ideology* we find a number of statements decisively rejecting all teleology on a macrohistorical scale. History itself, repeats Marx, does nothing; man is at once the actor and the author— the only author—of the historical drama. From this viewpoint a change of the definition of communism is very significant: "Communism is not for us a *state of affairs* which is to be established, an *ideal* to which reality [will] have to adjust itself. We call communism the *real* movement which abolishes the present state of things" (M&E, CW, 5:49).

Despite these caveats it would be difficult to maintain that Marx's remarks about the *totality* of the historical process do not implicitly contain the conviction that it forms a certain meaningful structure. Equally difficult would be an attempt to reduce the Marxian notion of "necessity" to a mere illusion of consciousness of the capitalist epoch. Rejecting an a priori postulated, metaphysical "meaning of history," Marx was at the same time inclined to search in history (of course, only on the scale of humanity) for an internal, dialectical meaning. This in turn strengthened his conviction that history is governed by necessity and that this necessity is a "meaningful" one, which led him to conclude that human destiny is more than the outcome of a certain conjunction of accidents guaranteeing a favorable solution to the historical drama. In other words, Marx saw in history the working of a rational necessity, not just the "natural necessity" he writes about in the preface to the first edition of *Capital*. Despite his often forceful denials (especially in *The Holy Family* and *The German Ideology*), it was a necessity resembling secularized Providence or Hegelian "Reason in history," making use, in a "cunning" way, of man to achieve various ends of its own, ends that only in the final stage of history were to become identical with man's conscious goals.

In all this there could exist no 100 percent consistency. Rather, there was a constant tension between the search for philosophical meaning and the desire to avoid falling into a speculative philosophico-historical construction. In some of Marx's statements from the period of his intellectual "maturity," antiteleological lines of thought were reinforced by the recognition of the multivariant nature of the historical process; this occurred first in *Grundrisse* in connection with the so-called Asiatic mode of production and later (in the 1877 letter to the editors of the journal *Otechestvennye zapiski* and in the February–March 1881 drafts of a letter to Vera Zasulich) in connection with the recognition of a possibly noncapitalist path for the development of backward countries (M, *SW*, 573–80).[54] But this does not change the fact that *on a global scale*, history was seen by Marx as a huge process of alienation and reintegration—a process that admitted, in certain phases, different paths of development, provided that these paths in the final result led to one goal. The plurality of the variants of development did not contradict the idea of a fundamental unilateral directionality of development. One ought therefore agree with Berlin, who states that according to Marx, "the gradual freeing of mankind has pursued a definite irreversible direction. . . . History does not move backwards or in cyclical movements: all its conquests are final and irreversible."[55]

However, Marx's essential faithfulness to the conception of self-enriching alienation manifested itself differently at different stages of his intellectual evolution: from the explicit embrace of this conception in *Economic and Philosophic Manuscripts* (1844) to deliberate attempts to conceal it behind, or rather underneath, the seemingly "naturalistic scientific" structure of *Capital*. Hence, it is useful to present different aspects of this conception in chronological order and, for the sake of clarity and conciseness, to limit our presentation to those works of Marx that are especially important in this respect.

1.4   The Paris *Manuscripts*: Human Essence Lost and Regained

We should start, of course, with Marx's early writings, among which his *Economic and Philosophic Manuscripts* (the Paris *Manuscripts* of 1844) occupy the central place.

The easiest way to grasp the originality of Marx's conception of self-enriching alienation is to compare it, following his own guidelines, with the relevant views of Hegel and Feuerbach.

The process of alienation, Marx argued, must have an agent, a subject. In Hegelianism, however, the story of self-enriching alienation is about the absolute idea alienating itself in nature (static alienation) and then raising itself to the level of self-consciousness, thus enriching itself by self-knowledge, through human history. In this way "real man and real nature become mere predicates or symbols of this hidden, unreal man and un-real nature. The relationship of subject and predicate to each other is thus completely inverted: a mystical subject-object or subjectivity reaching be-yond the object, absolute subject as a process." Such a subject, of course, cannot engage in productive activity, which presupposes physical effort; its only activity is thinking, the only labor known to it is abstract, mental labor. Alienation is identified with objectification, and the entire objec-tive world is treated as objectification of self-consciousness. The human essence is homogeneous with the divine essence because it is the same as self-consciousness; "all alienation of man's essence is therefore nothing but the alienation of self-consciousness." Consequently, "what needs to be transcended is not that man's being objectifies itself in an inhuman man-ner in opposition to itself, but that it objectifies itself in distinction from, and in opposition to, abstract thought" (ibid., 109, 102, 100). Liberation, therefore, is nothing else than de-alienation of self-consciousness, to be achieved through thought and in the sphere of thought.

Following Feuerbach, Marx conceived the subject of alienation not as Hegelian Absolute Spirit but as a "real man of flesh and blood, stand-ing on the solid, round earth and breathing in and out all the powers of nature." Such a subject is not a "pure" subject, idealistically conceived. It is an objective being, endowed with certain physical, biological qualities; "it only creates and posits objects because it is posited by objects, because it is by origin natural. Thus in the act of positing it does not degenerate from its 'pure activity' into creating an object; its objective product only confirms its objective activity, its activity as an activity of an objective, natural being" (ibid., 103, 103–4).

However, Marx continued, "man is not only a natural being, he is a human natural being. This means that he is being that exists for himself, thus a species-being that must confirm and exercise himself as such in his being and knowledge." He is a being who strives for independence and "a being only counts itself as independent when it stands on its own feet and it stands on its own feet as long as it owes its existence to itself" (ibid., 105, 94). Independence therefore presupposes autocreation, and this is precisely what distinguishes man from other natural beings. The humanization of the human species is a product of a long historical process of *autocreation through collective labor* (ibid., 95). Thus, for humans, nature is not something ready-made or given; rather it appears to them as nature "formed in human history," "fashioned by industry." Through labor people shape both external nature and themselves, their senses, their faculties. Industry should be conceived as "the open revelation of human faculties" or as "the real historical relationship of nature to man." Similarly, natural science should be conceived as a powerful instrument of human historical praxis and thereby "lose its one-sidedly materialist, or rather idealistic, orientation" (ibid., 94, 93, 93). In other words, natural scientists should become aware that science deals only with the "nature for man," that "nature in itself" is a materialistic metaphysics, while science divorced from practice, aiming at purely theoretical, disinterested truth, is an idealistic illusion.

In this manner Marx wanted to distinguish his standpoint from both idealism, seeing man as disembodied subject, and metaphysical, contemplative materialism, conceiving humans as passive natural objects. "We see," he wrote, "how consistent naturalism or humanism is distinguished from both idealism and materialism and constitutes at the same time their unifying truth" (ibid., 104). This unifying truth consisted, according to him, of the view of man as a truly unique part of nature: a natural being capable of autocreation, growingly independent of nature, endowed with the possibility of achieving a conscious, rational self-determination. The realization of this possibility—freedom—was in Marx's view (as in Hegelianism) the inner content and the ultimate goal of history.

However, the tragic law of development through alienation demands sacrifices. The human species can develop only by exteriorizing its inner faculties, objectifying its activity, and losing control over it, thus creating an external, autonomous world that confronts people as an alien force of nature and grows at the expense of individual human beings. This alienated world of human products, the objects of political economy, is a form of human self-creation that lays the foundation for man's liberation from the yoke of external nature while being at the same time a form of human self-enslavement. Human labor assumes the form of *alienated* labor—that is, an activity alienating (1) nature from man, (2) man from himself, and also (3) man from his species (ibid., 81–82). The activity of alienated labor increases man's freedom in relation to external nature but, at the same time, brings about the degradation of man as a rational, self-conscious being. This state of affairs affects all humans but above all the workers, who deny themselves in their work while feeling freely active only in their animal functions of eating, drinking, and procreating (ibid., 80). The relation between the worker and the products of his work becomes inversely proportional: "The more powerful becomes the alien, objective world that he creates opposite himself, the poorer he becomes in his inner life and the less he can call his own." Thus, the general scheme here is the same as in

. Feuerbach, which Marx fully recognized. "It is the same in religion," he commented. "The more man puts into God, the less he retains in himself." But economic alienation was, in his view, the primary phenomenon, explaining religious alienation, not vice versa: "Religious alienation as such occurs only in man's interior consciousness, but economic alienation is that of real life, and its abolition therefore covers both aspects" (ibid., 78–79, 79, 89).

The only bonds keeping together a world of people alienated from one another, from nature, from their products, and from their species essence are the same forces in which the self-alienation of humankind achieved its most extreme expression—namely, the division of labor and monetary exchange. Both create mutual external dependencies while destroying all inner ties stemming from human beings' communal nature. Both increase human power over external nature at the cost of dehumanization. Marx was especially fascinated by the miraculous power of money to exchange everything for everything and thus to achieve the colossal extension of interhuman relation at the cost of utter alienation. He called money "the true agent both of separation and of union," "the externalized and self-externalizing species-being of man" (ibid., 110).

Economic alienation results not only from putting people under the rule of objects created by them, but also, and particularly, from putting the workers under the yoke of the owners of private property (ibid., 84). In Marx's view all slave relationships were just modifications and consequences of this basic relationship of the workers to their products. Hence, the abolition of private property was tantamount to general human emancipation. But this abolition should have nothing in common with "crude communism"—that is, "a regression to the unnatural simplicity of the poor man without any needs" (ibid., 88). On the contrary, it was to be the *positive* transcendence of private property—that is, the abolition of private property under conditions of highly developed needs and universal needs. *Private* property was to be abolished, but property, in the sense of the genuine *appropriation* of the products of labor by laborers, should be restored in its true meaning and firmly established. In other words, the abolition of private property would provide a positive solution to the struggle "between objectification and self-affirmation," enabling working people to reappropriate the objects created by them by liquidating the autonomous power of these objects and reducing them to the obedient organs of the extended body of humankind.

Conceived in this way, communism, in Marx's view, signified the final end of the drama of self-enriching alienation, "the abolition of human self-alienation and therefore the real reappropriation of the human essence by and for man." This contention seems to contradict Marx's words that "communism is the necessary form and dynamic principle of the immediate future, but communism is not as such the goal of human development" (ibid., 89, 96). This apparent contradiction, however, boils down to different usages of the term *communism*. In his *Manuscripts* Marx distinguished three forms of communism, and it is clear that his words about communism, which "is not as such the goal of human development," referred to the second form of communism—that is, to the existing communist movements—which was much superior to "crude communism" (the first form). But these movements still inadequately grasped the *positive* essence of private property, defining their goal as the simple negation of private property, and were therefore still imprisoned and contaminated by it (ibid., 88–89). There was, however, the third and highest form of communism: the final reconciliation between existence and essence, the "solution to the riddle of history." This third form of communism was, of course, the goal of human history, but it could no longer be defined as the *negation* of private property, since with the disappearance of private property, communism conceived as its negation would also be doomed to disappear. Similarly, atheism would have no meaning at the stage when religious alienation was positively transcended; people who have regained their divine attributes no longer need a denial of God (ibid., 95).

As the *positive* abolition of private property—that is, as the final return of humans to their essential nature after a long, painful development through alienation—communism would bring about a truly unheard of, unimaginable feast of universal liberation. It would usher in the complete emancipation of all human senses and qualities: the eyes and ears of the de-alienated people of the future would be completely different from the crude inhuman eyes and ears of the dehumanized people of the present (ibid., 92). True, individuals would remain mortal, but for Marx this was not a serious problem. "The individual," he reasoned, "is the social being. . . . The individual and the species-life of man are not different, although, necessarily, the mode of existence of individual life is a more particular or more general mode of species-life." Hence, what is mortal is merely the particular, the inessential. On this ground Marx based his hope that the superior human beings of the de-alienated future would feel their essential identity with the species so strongly that personal mortality would cease to be perceived as a tragedy. In this sense the third form of communism was for him the universal reintegration and the "true solution of the struggle between individual and species" (ibid., 91, 89).

It is no exaggeration to say that communism, so conceived, was a secularized, immanentized version of the millenarian vision of collective earthly salvation. It would establish not only perfect unity of social and personal life, but also perfect harmony between human essence and existence, thus transcending the normal human condition and giving man God-like status. Seen in this light, the deepest content of Marx's *Manuscripts* amounts to nothing less than a soteriological myth, a new secular gnosis, an initiation to the mystery of human self-deification. The Russian religious philosopher Sergei Bulgakov was right in claiming that the early works of Marx should be seen as a philosophical enrichment of the Feuerbachian idea of man as divine being.[56] Marx agreed with Feuerbach that "the divine being is nothing else than the human being" and that "all the attributes of the divine nature are, therefore, attributes of the human nature."[57] At the time of composing his *Economic and Philosophical Manuscripts*, Marx was enthusiastic about Feuerbach and even wrote to him saying that his works provided "a philosophical basis to socialism" (ibid., 113). His enrichment of Feuerbach's conception consisted in explaining the historico-economic reasons of human alienation, as well as in interpreting de-alienation as not a merely intellectual self-liberation but as the outcome of collective human emancipation carried out by the proletariat and inaugurating the communist millennium. As can easily be seen, this historico-economic (and, in this sense, "materialistic") reinterpretation of Feuerbachian ideas resulted in combining the Promethean "religion of Man" with a messianic-millenarian scheme in which the proletariat played the role of a collective messiah leading humankind to the millennial kingdom.

A sort of "positive counterpart" to Marx's story of alienation of labor can be found in his "Excerpts from James Mill" (1844). Here young Marx once more indulged in a vehement condemnation of the money economy, describing money as "the complete domination of the alienated thing over man" and claiming that monetary exchange and production for market necessarily lead to mutual enslavement. In contrast to this, he continued, production "in a human manner" would be a free expression of life, affirming both the producer and his fellow humans. The description of this idea, summed up in four points, shows how close Marx was by then to the German "true socialists," whom he so severely criticized in his later works for their verbal pomposity and incorrigible sentimentality. Thus, for instance, Marx's "truly human" producer describes his imaginary feelings toward the recipient of his product in the following convoluted way: "I would have been for you the mediator between you and the species and thus been acknowledged and felt by you as a completion of your own essence and a necessary part of yourself and have thus realized that I am confirmed both in your thought and in your love. In my expression of my life, I would have fashioned your expression of your life, and thus in my own activity have realized my own essence, my human, my communal essence" (ibid., 114, 118, 122).

Nevertheless, the theoretical importance of this text should not be disregarded. "Excerpts from James Mill" is invaluable in showing the axiological premises of Marx's intransigent hostility toward the market economy and production for sale (commodity production) in general. In the exchange economy, he argued, "what links our productions together is not the human essence. . . . Each of us sees in his own product only his own selfish need objectified, and thus in the product of another he only sees the objectification of another selfish need independent and alien to him." Owing to this, work ceases to be self-realization, becoming instead merely a means to live; private property in the sense of nonalienated individual property (i.e., the legitimate extension of one's self) becomes "externalized private property" of the means of production, giving birth to wage labor— that is, to "the alienation and disconnection between labor and the man who labors" (ibid., 120, 118). Mutually enriching communal cooperation becomes degraded into an objective, functional interdependence in which producers try to maneuver others into a position of dependence on their products (ibid., 120). What was domination of person over person is now the general domination of the thing over the person, of the product over the producer. This "complete domination of the alienated thing over man" is "fully manifested in money" (ibid., 118).

Economic alienation, in close relation with religious alienation, is also the major theme of Marx's essay "On the Jewish Question," discussed above in another context. It seems useful to read this text, as well as other texts of the early Marx, against the background of ideas developed in the works of Moses Hess, the greatest theorist of "true socialism."

In his *Economic and Philosophic Manuscripts*, Marx mentioned Hess, along with Engels, as the only German socialist whose writings were comparable in originality and value to the works of the French and English socialists (ibid., 76). He pointed specifically to two articles published by Hess in 1843: "Philosophie der Tat" ("Philosophy of Action") and "Die Eine und Ganze Freiheit" ("One and Total Freedom").

The first of these articles developed the main idea of August Cieszkowski's *Prolegomena zur Historiosophie*—namely, the "philosophy of action." [58] To be more precise, the article was an attempt to reinterpret this idea in the spirit of Feuerbach's anthropological materialism, on the one hand, and French utopian socialism, on the other. The possibility of such reinterpretation arose from a number of common points discernible in all these thinkers. Cieszkowski and Feuerbach, both following the example of the Fourierists and the Saint-Simonians, favored the rehabilitation of matter, nature, and sensuality. Feuerbach's anthropology and Cieszkowski's "philosophy of action" were both conceived of as a reconciliation of nature with logic, feeling with thought, the real with the ideal. According to both, ancient times were the epoch when humans were not yet divorced from nature; both stressed, each in his own fashion, the connection of Hegel's idealism with Christianity and wanted to resolve the painful dualism characterizing, in their opinion, the life and thought of the Christian epoch. Hess repeated these views, adding to them economic themes: the theme of labor and the theme of property. Philosophy of Spirit, he argued, must become Philosophy of Action, thus raising itself to overcome the dualism between thought and matter. At this stage, labor as toil would be replaced by labor as pleasure, as free activity. Following the transformation of an external God into the internal, immanent divinity, material property would be transformed into "spiritual property, conceived as an activity, not an object, as a verb, not a noun. Material property is an objectification, alienation of spirit." Its abolition is therefore necessary for freedom, because freedom is nothing else than "self-consciousness of active spirit, the overcoming of natural determination through self-determination." "The true history of spirit begins where natural determination ends, where spirit is fully developed, endowed with mature self-consciousness and knowledge of its action. With this knowledge begins the realm of freedom at whose gate we are standing and rattling." [59]

In the second article Hess developed Cieszkowski's view that philosophy should become practical and popular and express itself in social action. In contrast to Cieszkowski, however, Hess combined this view with a radical stance on religious and political matters. Many of his statements closely resemble well-known pronouncements of Marx. Being radical, he claimed, means eradicating the roots of one's slavery. Religion is spiritual slavery, an opiate of the people, intoxicating them and subjugating their consciousness and will to be free. The distinction between religious and political slavery is purely formal: both annihilate moral force and freedom, reducing human existence to that of a working slave, on the one hand, and an animal seeking pleasure, on the other. To achieve freedom one must, therefore, combat both religion and politics, both church and state.

The next step in the development of Hess's philosophy was his important work *On the Essence of Money*. In this work, he defined money as the "product of mutually alienated men, or the alienated Man." [60] Selling oneself, Hess contended, means becoming reified (*verdingt*).[61] Being a slave is a morally neutral, natural human condition in the world of universal robbery, while hiring oneself is immoral because it amounts to selling oneself voluntarily. Hence, the ancient world was superior to the Christian world. Christianity is self-alienation raised to the status of a principle, the bad conscience of corrupted humanity. Christianity sanctifies an immoral dualism: free immaterial soul, on the one hand, and enslaved body, on the other; or slavery on earth and freedom in heaven. "Money, the essence of the contemporary huckstering world, is the *realized* essence of Christianity." [62] God is but idealized capital, heaven is the *theoretical* world of hagglers. The direct slavery of antiquity is replaced by an indirect slavery that is much worse, destroying all social bonds, sanctifying egoism, bringing about the complete self-alienation of humankind. Community is reduced to a mere means to private ends, the public sphere is separated from the private sphere, social ties are destroyed and replaced by a cash nexus. Slavery thereby becomes mutual and universal.[63]

The Middle Ages, Hess maintained, were much better, because medieval estates and corporations, although pursuing egoistic aims and limited in their particularisms, nevertheless had a social character and were permeated, although only to a limited extent, by a communal spirit.[64] In contrast to this, in the modern epoch serfdom has become universal, and social conduct is completely deprived of any noble motivation. Predatory instincts reign supreme, people affirm themselves in money, in the "alienated social blood." [65] Christianity is, in fact, the fulfillment of the predatory mission of the Jews. In ancient Israel bloody sacrifice was only a prototype; in medieval Christianity, a religion of predatory animals, this sacrifice took the mystical form of consuming the blood of God-man; in the contemporary world, this mystical theophagy is replaced by an open and quite prosaic anthropophagy. In this way all people have become predatory animals, bloodsuckers, "Jews," capitalistic sharks.[66]

However, money also performs a positive, necessary function in this utterly dehumanized world. It is a substitute for human ties, the inhuman means of interhuman communication, the only form of contact between isolated beings, a reified social force. Without money people would be deprived of all mutual contacts.[67] But in order to achieve true social unity, an inner organic unity, it is necessary to get rid of this dead external form of interhuman contact, to replace abstract, indirect, external means of contact objectified by money with direct, inner, truly human ties that unite human beings from within, without mediation of things, by means of values grounded in human nature. In this manner all alienation—religious, political, and economic—would be abolished, resulting in a truly human organic community, a veritable kingdom of freedom.

In Marx's essay "On the Jewish Question," the same vocabulary and very similar thoughts are evident, for example:

What is the secular basis of Judaism? Practical need, selfishness. What is the secular cult of the Jew? Haggling. What is his secular god? Money. . . .

Christianity had its origin in Judaism. It has dissolved itself back into Judaism. . . .

Christianity is the sublime thought of Judaism; Judaism is the vulgar practical application of Christianity. But this practical application could only become universal after Christianity as the perfect religion had completed, in a theoretical manner, the self-alienation of man from himself and from nature.

Only then could Judaism attain general domination and make externalized man and externalized nature into alienable, saleable objects, a prey to the slavery of egoistic need and the market.

Selling is the practice of externalization. As long as man is imprisoned within religion, he knows only how to objectify his essence by making it into an alien, imaginary being. Similarly, under the domination of egoistic need he can only become practical, only create practical objects by putting his products and his activity under the domination of an alien entity and lending them the significance of an alien entity—money. (ibid., 58, 61–62)

The similarities between Hess and Marx are striking: their views parallel on religious alienation and socioeconomic alienation, on God and money. They share the same image of the predatory, huckstering nature of Judaism; the same general conception of the relationship among Judaism, Christianity, and capitalism; the same curious blend of romantic anticapitalism, sentimental socialist utopia, Feuerbachian antireligious philosophy, and left-Hegelian political radicalism. Both Hess and Marx display the characteristic result of the encounter between socialism and the Teutonic spirit: romanticism and obscure philosophical speculation. Both employ a strong admixture of the anti-Semitic stereotypes current in German popular culture, but this does not necessarily imply a personal anti-Semitism. If these popular stereotypes could have been so strong in Hess, who became one of the founders of Zionism, then their presence in Marx's thought should not be seen as a feature peculiar to him as an individual and expressing his alleged Jewish self-hatred.[68]

Hess published his philosophy of money in 1845, a year after Marx's essay "On the Jewish Question." Nevertheless, the influence of Hess's ideas on Marx's essay is very probable, although Marx's influence on Hess is also possible. In his multivolume biography of Marx and Engels, Cornu stressed that during his stay in Paris (October 1843 through February 1845), Marx was in very close contact with Hess and that the obvious similarities in their views on economic alienation and on money can be attributed to a mutual exchange of thoughts.[69]

By showing these similarities I am not motivated by a desire to vindicate the significance of Hess as a direct precursor of Marx. I want rather to dispel the illusion of the almost absolute originality and exceptional philosophical value of Marx's early works. In fact the young Marx, like Hess, was an organic product of German "true socialism," the current of thought mercilessly criticized and maliciously ridiculed by Marx in his later works. He succeeded in distancing himself from this speculative variety of socialism only in 1845, when he elaborated the main tenets of his so-called historical materialism.

1.5 *The German Ideology*: The Division of Labor and the Myth of Human Identity

The next step in the development of Marx's views on freedom is *The German Ideology*, a long manuscript written by him with Engels in 1845–46.

Only in 1932 did it appear in print, after having been rejected by the publisher and abandoned by the authors to "the gnawing criticism of the mice" (preface to *A Critique of Political Economy*, ibid., 390).

In many respects *The German Ideology* was a critical response to Stirner's manifesto of radical philosophical egoism, published in 1844 under the title *Der Einzige und sein Eigentum* (*The Ego and His Own*).[70] This well-written, provocative book contains a sharp critique of Feuerbachianism. Feuerbach, Stirner argued, was right in asserting that the secret of speculative philosophy was theology and that God was nothing more than alienated human essence. But he was totally wrong in believing that his replacement of the religion of God by a religion of Man would promote the cause of genuine human liberation. In reality the religion of Man, the deification of man's species essence, was only a new way of combating egoism and thereby enslaving really existing individuals. This was so because all variants of universalism and essentialism were effective means of ideological repression. Individuals do not have "essences" and therefore do not have to repress their natural egoism in the name of such fiction as "the Human Species." They should fight against all forms of the "tyranny of the universal," be it religion of God or religion of Man, Christian morality or state law, the Hegelian Absolute Spirit or the Feuerbachian "anthropoteism." Individuals should behave as unscrupulous egoists and thus assert their sovereign dignity, their absolute freedom.

As a communist, Marx could not sympathize with this unabashed glorification of egoism. Nonetheless, he learned from Stirner that the Feuerbachian philosophy of man was indeed too reminiscent of Christianity and that its essentialist language might be an easy target for attack.[71] Hence, becoming more critical of Feuerbach, Marx ceased to see himself as Feuerbach's disciple. Marx realized, as Engels put it in *Ludwig Feuerbach and the End of Classical German Philosophy*, that "the cult of abstract man, which formed the kernel of Feuerbach's new religion, had to be replaced by the science of real men and their historical development" (M&E, SW, 3:360). True, Marx was moving in this direction already in his Paris *Manuscripts*. But only in 1845–46, in his "Theses on Feuerbach" and *The German Ideology*, did he elaborate the concept of a self-conscious historical materialism.

"It is not consciousness that determines life, but life that determines consciousness" (M&E, CW, 5:37). With this aphorism Marx hoped to provide new ground for post-Hegelian discussions on human liberation. The young Hegelians, and even Feuerbach, saw human beings as enslaved by different ideological alienations, illusions of consciousness that had assumed an independent existence; hence, they concentrated on revolting against these imaginary beings and on replacing them with "thoughts corresponding to the essence of man." This, according to Marx, was an expression of an idealistic illusion, of a naive belief that purely intellectual critique can bring about a genuine intellectual liberation and that the latter might be equivalent to general human emancipation. In fact, however, the road to liberation is much longer and more difficult: illusions of consciousness are rooted in the forms of human cooperation, alienated ideas reflect alienated forms of social life, and intellectual liberation on a mass scale is not conceivable without the *social* emancipation of the masses. Moreover, the degree of social emancipation depends not only on class struggle and the revolutionary energy of the masses, it also depends, above all, on the degree of economic achievement and, particularly, technological development. "Preconditions of the real liberation of man" were described by Marx as follows:

The "liberation" of "man" is not advanced by a single step by reducing philosophy, theology, substance and all the rubbish to "self-consciousness" and by liberating "man" from the domination of these phrases . . . "it is possible to achieve real liberation only in the real world and by real means" . . . "slavery cannot be abolished without steam-engine and the mule jenny, serfdom cannot be abolished without improved agriculture, and, in general, people cannot be liberated as long as they are unable to obtain food and drink, housing and clothing in adequate quality and quantity." "Liberation" is a historical and not a mental act, and it is brought about by historical conditions, the [level] of industry, com[merce], [agri]culture, [intercourse]. (ibid., 38)

In developing these thoughts further, Marx pointed out that by the term *social* he meant "the co-operation of several individuals" and that a given mode of cooperation, or a *social* stage, was always combined with a definite mode of production, or *industrial* stage. It followed from this that the level of social and industrial development of a given nation "is shown most manifestly by the degree to which the division of labor has been carried" (ibid., 43, 32). At the same time, however, the degree of the development of the division of labor is the measure of human self-alienation.

In explaining this view, Marx made use of the classical analyses of the negative aspects of the social division of labor in the works of Adam Ferguson and Adam Smith but interpreted these analyses in the light of the idea of the alienating character of commodity production as such.[72] In Marx's conception human cooperation in primitive, small-scale natural economies was nonalienated but limited in scope and therefore incapable of developing the productive capacities of the species. Hence the tragic necessity of developing through alienation: the increase of human control over external nature could only be achieved at the cost of losing control of economic forces.

In tribal society, Marx argued, the division of labor was confined to a further extension of the natural division of labor existing in the family;

thus "social structure was limited to an extension of the family," preserving patriarchal despotism but, at the same time, exercising conscious control over its production, resources, and distribution. Under feudalism the division into estates became strongly marked, but social division of labor remained merely budding: in agriculture natural economy still prevailed, while "in industry there was no division of labor in the individual trades and very little between them."[73] Full development of the social division of labor came into being only at the capitalist stage, when production became narrowly specialized and destined for a broader, more anonymous market, a power subject to its own laws, created by men but uncontrollable by them, thwarting their plans and cruelly playing with their lives. In this manner spontaneous division of labor, stemming from the need for commodity exchange, brought about a situation in which people became enslaved by their own products. Marx defined this process in terms of his theory of alienation:

This consolidation of what we ourselves produce into a material power above us, growing out of our control, thwarting our expectations, bringing to naught our calculations, is one of the chief factors in historical development up till now. . . . In history up to the present it is certainly likewise an empirical fact that separate individuals have, with the broadening of their activity into world-historical activity, become more and more enslaved under a power alien to them (a pressure which they have conceived of as a dirty trick on the part of the so-called world spirit, etc.), a power which has become more and more enormous and, in the last instance, turns out to be the *world market*.[74]

At this point, however, Marx could apply his dialectical historiosophy of freedom: the worst alienation turned out to be self-enriching, and universal mutual enslavement proved to be a necessary condition for universal mutual liberation. The world market, Marx reasoned, would liberate individuals from various national and local barriers, bring them into practical connection with the material and intellectual production of the whole world, and thus put them in a position to acquire the capacity to enjoy this all-sided production of the whole earth.[75] In this way universal human intercourse would create not only an all-round dependence, but also the possibility of an all-round development of each individual. All-round dependence, the *natural* form of world historical cooperation of individuals, would be transformed by the communist revolution into a *voluntary* world historical cooperation and would thereby put an end to human alienation. Freely associated individuals would gain control and conscious mastery over their social power. Communist regulation of production and exchange would thus create a truly human world in which people, as rational and conscious beings, would feel free and at home, exercising full conscious control over their products instead of allowing products to enslave them in an alien world. Personal freedom would no longer be confused with "the right to the undisturbed enjoyment, within certain conditions, of fortuity and chance."[76] Personal freedom would be realized in accordance with its true meaning—that is, as rational, conscious self-determination presupposing individuals' control and direction of their self-objectification and harmonious, communal relation to others.[77]

Certain observations need to be made at this juncture. As we can see, the word *free* was, in Marx's usage, a synonym for "consciously regulated" and the opposite of "natural" (meaning "alien," existing independently of humans). Freedom was also associated with rationality and hence opposed to chance. The word *spontaneous* meant "not subordinated to a general plan of freely combined individuals" and therefore evoked associations with blind natural necessity, not freedom (M&E, CW, 5:83). In other words, Marx is here much closer to Hegel than to Feuerbach: like the former, he excludes the "natural" from his notion of freedom, defining human freedom in terms of rational and conscious activity—that is, an overcoming of "merely natural" determinations.

Another Hegelian feature of this conception is the identification of freedom with the self-aggrandizement of the creative subject, which conquers and absorbs everything outside itself in order to become, in the full sense, itself.[78] Unlike Hegel, Marx did not deal with the relationship between the Absolute Spirit and the world; he dealt only with the relationship between humankind, as the creative subject of history, and the human products, which had become independent of men by taking the form of a quasi-objective "second nature." In this interpretation, freedom meant the establishment of full control over people's alienated forces and, finally, their full reabsorption by the superior, universally developed human beings of the communist future. Communism, in Marx's view, was to be the triumph of humankind's free self-creation, the final overcoming of economic and social alienation: "Communism for the first time consciously treats all naturally evolved premises as the creations of hitherto existing men, strips them of their natural character and subjugates them to the power of the united individuals. . . . The reality which communism creates is precisely the true basis for rendering it impossible that anything should exist independently of individuals, insofar as reality is nevertheless only a product of the preceding intercourse of individuals" (ibid., 81).

Thus, the liberation of individuals from dependence on the "blind" and "irrational" forces of the market was seen by Marx as the ultimate triumph of individual freedom. However, to avoid a semantic trap, we must realize that by "individuals" Marx meant individual specimens of the species, not *individualized* human beings. His concept of an integral, all-round development of each individual presupposed an equal participation in the species—that is, the opposite of individuation within the species. This is a fundamental difference and amounts to the difference between species collectivism (communism) and liberal individualism. This difference can clearly be seen if we compare Marx's conception of the social division of labor with the relevant views of James Madison, one of the Founding Fathers of American democracy. For Madison, social division of labor stemmed from "different and unequal faculties for acquiring property," i.e., from the primordial and irreducible individual diversity of human beings.[79] For Marx, this diversity was not the cause but the result of the division of labor—a result of man's alienation from his species nature, something that had to be overcome at the stage of man's communal reintegration.

The victory of communism presupposed the abolition of social division of labor (ibid., 78). This view, the main conclusion of *The German Ideology*, makes it clear that free individuals in a communist society were conceived of by Marx as individual specimens of humankind, and not as specific, qualitatively different individualities, products of the differentiating function of the division of labor. They were to be "communal beings" because "only within the community has each individual the means of cultivating his gifts in all directions." They were not to be free to develop their specific, particular individualities that distinguished them from other individuals; on the contrary, they were to be free to develop their *common* human nature—that is, not in an individual, specific direction but as all-round human beings capable of satisfying all their own needs without becoming dependent on others and without being imprisoned in a particular exclusive sphere of activity. In communist society, Marx wrote, it will be possible for each individual "to do one thing today and another tomorrow, to hunt in the morning, fish in the afternoon, rear cattle in the evening, criticize after dinner, without ever becoming hunter, fisherman, shepherd or critic" (ibid., 78, 47).

In spite of the somewhat jocular tone, Marx really meant what he wrote. He did not want, of course, a return to the primitive natural economy preceding the development of the division of labor; such retrospective utopias were explicitly prohibited by his general theory of history. His utopianism was more imaginative and definitely futuristic. But, nonetheless, an idealized image of the natural economy was an important constitutive element of his thinking. He visualized the communist society of the future as a dialectical return to a natural economy on a higher level and in a macroscale. In this sense he would have agreed with his Russian critic, the populist theorist Nikolai Mikhailovskii, that the archaic natural economy and socialism represent two different *levels* of the same *type* of socioeconomic organization.[80] His favorite esoteric idea of self-enriching alienation convinced him that the stage of exteriorization and alienation of one's inner content must be followed by the *reappropriation* of this content, thereby achieving a return to oneself on the highest level. In practice, this meant that industrial development achieved through the social division of labor—that is, through the alienation of humans' species powers—should give way to communist freedom, which would de-alienate these powers by replacing the power of capitalist industry and the all-round dependence on the world market with the power of freely united and universally developed individuals. Thus, the realization of communism would bring about the appearance of a new and vastly superior race of human beings. Marx boldly believed that the appropriation of the existing totality of productive forces through the expropriation of their private owners would result in "the development of individual capacities corresponding to the material instruments of production. The appropriation of a totality of instruments of production is, for this very reason, the development of a totality of capacities in individuals themselves" (ibid., 87).

What could be added to this fantastic utopia outlined by authors who otherwise described themselves as resolute anti-utopians? Only a few details more, such as the abolition of the state, the disappearance of professionalism in art (since every member of society would be able to become an artist without professional teachers), and even the abolition of the state of affairs in which "individuality is subservient to chance" (ibid., 438)—in a word, "The true solution of the struggle between existence and essence," as promised in the *Economic and Philosophic Manuscripts*.

This utopian edifice was to secure the realization of the Marxian idea of freedom. It is surprising that many scholars, otherwise very critical of Marxism and keenly aware of the dangers of unbridled utopianism, find this idea very attractive and worthy of passionate defense. Kolakowski, for instance, wrote about it as follows:

The restoration of man's full humanity, removing the tension between individual aspirations and the collective interest, does not imply a denial on Marx's part of the life and freedom of the individual. It has been a common misinterpretation by both Marxists and anti-Marxists to suppose that he regarded human beings merely as specimens of social classes, and that the "restoration of their species-essence" meant the annihilation of individuality or its reduction to a common social nature. On this view, individuality has no place in Marxist doctrine except as an obstacle in the way of society attaining to homogeneous unity. No such doctrine, however, can be derived from *The German Ideology*.

Marx, Kolakowski continued, criticized the situation in which "people confronted one another as representatives of the impersonal forces that ruled the world—goods, money, or civil authority—while the individual's 'freedom' meant a lack of control over the conditions of his own life, a state of impotence *vis-à-vis* the external world. To reverse this reification and restore man's power over things is likewise to restore his individual life, the possibility of all-round development of his personal aptitudes and talents."[81]

Let us examine, as briefly as possible, this strange reasoning. Freedom conceived as full, conscious control of people's collective fate presupposes, of course, the *ability* to control—that is, a public body able to exercise effective control over all spheres of social life. This would immediately liquidate the sphere of the "uncontrollable," i.e., "negative" individual freedom. Moreover, the replacement of self-regulating impersonal mechanisms by conscious decisions would severely restrict the scope of individual freedom in the positive sense as well. "For," said Marx, "it is the association of individuals (assuming the advanced stage of modern productive forces, of course) which puts the conditions of free development and movement of individuals under their control" (ibid., 80). This can only mean that dependence on things will be replaced by a situation in which the development and movement of individuals will be controlled by an association, or, to put it differently, in which impersonal dependence will be exchanged for total personal dependence on a collective body. It would seem that no genuine liberal could see this as an increase of personal freedom.

But what about freedom from the dependence on things, freedom as individuals' conscious mastery over their products? It does not seem that such freedom could ever be attained. Products produced on a mass scale, including the products of knowledge, naturally tend to become autonomous, to have a life of their own, so to speak, bringing about unintended— sometimes disastrous, sometimes beneficial—results, and differing among different groups of the population. Would it really be an increase of freedom if everything were made fully predictable and firmly controlled? In such a fully controlled social universe there would be no element of chance, no room for adventure, no individual choice of one's own way in the pursuit of happiness. In this sense Hayek was probably right when he wrote, "Freedom means that in some measure we entrust our fate to forces which we do not control."[82]

Finally, Marx's ideal of collective freedom is obviously incompatible with pluralism and social differentiation. It presupposes the abolition of the division of labor, which also means the "abolition" of specialized, "individualized" individuals who have different skills and interests. True, in contrast to such egalitarian communists as Babeuf or Tkachev, Marx explicitly rejected the idea of leveling downward as well as all conceptions of the forceful regimentation of society. He also made it clear that humans' mastery over their fate was to be realized not through a dictatorship of an enlightened elite but rather through participatory democracy: "Modern universal intercourse cannot be controlled by individuals, unless it is controlled by all" (ibid., 88).

However, universal participatory democracy is completely unsuitable for modern, complex, pluralistic societies. Kolakowski stressed elsewhere that for both historical and technical reasons participatory democracy "is obviously impracticable in any community larger than a medieval Swiss village."[83] How could Marx imagine that a communist society based on "modern universal intercourse," and therefore extended to global dimensions, might allow all its members an equal share in decision making? How was it possible to believe that all these different individuals could harmoniously cooperate with one another, pursue the same aims, fully agree with one another as to the common good, accept the same criteria of rationality, and, above all, espouse the same hierarchy of values?

The only possible explanation is that Marx saw free individuals of the future not as *individualized* human beings, but as "species beings," or "communal beings." He agreed that freedom meant self-determination, to act in accordance with one's true self, but he sharply differed from individualistic liberalism in his definition of "true self." He would not have agreed that "individual freedom is the freedom that is limited by individuality"[84] or that it means the unfettered development of the uniqueness and specificity of individuals and thus demands more and more room for social differentiation. True self, he thought, cannot be something different from fundamental human essence. Once people are freed from everything that is not wholly themselves, they will be left with their essential identity as human beings, as specimens of the same species. In that case, and *only* in that case, could they be expected to merge together in rational unanimity, to share the same values and to strive for the same collective aim, to cooperate with one another without conflict, without mediation of things (such as money), and, of course, without separate political bodies serving as instruments of mediation or moderation.

The dangers inherent in this wildly utopian vision were clearly perceived by a Russian liberal, Pavel Novgorodtsev, who wrote about it at the beginning of our century, before the publication of *The German Ideology*. Marx's theory of man as a species being was known to him from Marx's essay "On the Jewish Question," which he rightly interpreted as a manifesto of collectivism demanding a complete socialization of man. The separate existence of the political sphere, Novgorodtsev argued, is a necessary precondition of individuality and freedom. Individuals as species beings—that is, as directly and totally socialized—are no longer individualized and independent. They may be better morally, if they have overcome their egoism, and more powerful, if they have succeeded in embodying in themselves the capacities of their species, but they are no longer anything more than a specimen of the species.[85]

In his essay on "The Myth of Human Self-Identity," Kolakowski expressed very similar views. He pointed out that "the dream of a perfectly unified human community," deeply rooted in European culture and embraced by so many socialist thinkers, is the deepest source of totalitarian utopias the practical consequences of which are always destructive of freedom. He wrote: "There is no reason to expect that this dream can ever become true except in the cruel form of despotism; and despotism is a desperate simulation of paradise."[86]

As should be evident, I fully share this view. I want only to add that it could be legitimately applied to *The German Ideology*, despite Kolakowski's defense of this text. It seems that there are only two possible ways of interpreting this curious utopia: either as a program for abolishing all self-regulating mechanisms of society by subjecting all spheres of human life to conscious regulation by "associated producers," or, more radically, as a vision of the perfect unification of humankind. The first case would involve a kind of democratic totalitarianism that could function only under the unlikely conditions of universal unanimity or, at least, universal readiness to conform to collective pressures. The second interpretation evokes associations with mystico-metaphysical dreams of overcoming sinful individualization and returning to the original Oneness. In both these interpretations, however, individual freedom—that is, freedom of *individualized* human beings, freedom as diversity and pluralism, as individual autonomy and the possibility of "being different"—is resolutely excluded. Herein lies the essential root of Marx's hostility toward the division of labor—the source of differentiation and individuation—and of his dream of restoring (on "a higher level," to be sure) the undifferentiated wholeness of the human species.

1.6 *Grundrisse*: The World Market as Alienated Universalism

Marx's *Grundrisse*—a series of seven notebooks drafted by Marx during the winter of 1857–58 but published in the German original only in 1953—is a text more difficult and probably more mature than *The German Ideology*. It has rightly been noticed that "among the many of Marx's works which first appeared in print in the twentieth century the *Grundrisse* represents unquestionably the most significant new development, comparable in importance only to the *Theories of Surplus Value* and the *Economic and Philosophic Manuscripts* of 1844" (foreword, M, G, 7). For our purposes, the value of this badly written and unfinished book is truly exceptional: it provides a bridge between Marx the philosopher and Marx the economist, thus showing the close connection between his philosophy of freedom and his theory of capitalism as a socioeconomic formation.

The introduction to *Grundrisse* contains an important and often quoted generalization:

The more deeply we go back into history, the more does the individual, and hence also the producing individual, appear as dependent, as belonging to a greater whole:

in a still natural way in the family and in the family expanded into a clan; then later in the various forms of communal society arising out of the antitheses and fusions of the clans. Only in the eighteenth century, in "civil society," do the various forms of social connectedness confront the individual as a mere means towards his private purposes, as external necessity. But the epoch which produces this standpoint, that of the isolated individual, is precisely that of the hitherto most developed social (from this standpoint, general) relations. The human being is in the most literal sense a *zoon politicon*, not merely a gregarious animal, but an animal which can individuate itself only in the midst of society. (ibid., 84)

So far, so good. Marx seems to be endorsing the classical liberal view according to which capitalism brings about the individuation of people and their liberation from blood ties and communal bonds. He clearly distanced himself from conservative romantic and feudal socialist thinkers who accused capitalism of disintegrating and "atomizing" society. In developing his views he pointed out that, in fact, "bourgeois society is the most developed and the most complex historic organization of production" (ibid., 105). Hence it is a very cohesive society, held together by a highly developed division of labor and a system of differentiated needs—that is, by an unbreakable reciprocal dependence on production and consumption. Members of such a society are not akin to atoms, since atoms have no needs and do not have to engage in exchange with one another.

However, in bourgeois society, "various forms of social connectedness confront the individual as a mere means towards his private purposes, as external necessity." This observation might have been readily endorsed by the conservative romantic critics of capitalism and by all other thinkers who set against modern industrial civilization an idealized vision of a truly human organic community. Marx's description of "civil society" is as unflattering as is Ferdinand Tönnies's view of *Gesellschaft*.[87] But such similarities might be misleading, since the specificity of Marx's thought can be grasped only in his dialectic of self-enriching alienation. Bourgeois society is seen by him as a tremendous progress and a tremendous regression at the same time. It is progress because it has developed, although in an alienated form, "the universality of individual needs, capacities, pleasures, productive forces, etc., created through universal exchange." The "old view, in which the human being appears as the aim of production . . . seems to be very lofty when contrasted to the modern world, where production appears as the aim of mankind and wealth as the aim of production." In fact, however, "when the limited bourgeois form is stripped away," wealth (*Reichtum*) turns out to be nothing else than the chief value in Marx's axiology, namely "the absolute working out of [man's] creative potentialities."[88] But the price to be paid for realizing this value is horrendous. This is so, because "in bourgeois economics—and in the epoch of production to which it corresponds—this complete working-out of the human content appears as a total emptying-out, this universal objectification as total alienation, and the tearing down of all limited, one-sided aims as sacrifice of the human end-in-itself to an entirely external end. This is why the childish world of antiquity appears on one side as loftier" (ibid., 488, 488, 488, 488).

In this way the human species develops through alienation and within alienation. The esoteric side of Marx's thought is revealed here once more as a variant of the old gnostic story about breaking the primordial unity and embarking on the long way toward universal reintegration, a way that passes necessarily through fragmentation, alienation, and other forms of painful imperfection. In Marx's version this was a tragic story of humankind that realized its immanent purpose at the cost of its individual members. Agnes Heller summarized this as follows:

In the course of its process of development, humanity can only realize the possibilities that accord with its given nature as a species. . . . It is on the social plane as a whole that men develop their given qualities in accordance with the species (at least up to a certain point); but human beings as individuals do not participate in the wealth of the social whole. Whilst the individual, subordinated to the division of labor, remains poor (in the broadest sense of the word), there is a parallel enrichment of the species. The highest level of enrichment reached so far, i.e., capitalism, is also the peak of individual impoverishment.[89]

But precisely because this is so, the possibilities of developing within alienation are exhausted, and since that moment the idea of freedom as de-alienation ceases to be a retrospective utopia, becoming instead a legitimate and necessary aim of further progress. Thus, only at this stage does the final goal of human liberation become compatible with the direction of the dialectical movement of history.

From the point of view of the present book, the main difference between *Grundrisse* and *The German Ideology* is the shift of focus: while in the latter work the greatest threat to freedom is seen in man's subjugation to the social division of labor, in *Grundrisse* freedom is analyzed in the context of a developed money economy, i.e., in the context of conditions presupposing maximum freedom of competition and exchange. Marx's picture of capitalism is thereby made even darker and its criticism even more radical. After all, the thesis that narrow specialization caused by the social division of labor limits individuals' freedom of choice and prevents the free development of all their capacities is *as such* less paradoxical and less radical than considering economic freedom to be the greatest enemy of individual freedom. But this is precisely the main thesis of the conception of freedom contained in *Grundrisse*.

It is not the individuals who are set free by free competition; it is rather capital which is set free. As long as production resting on capital is the necessary, hence the fittest, form for the development of the force of social production, the movement of individuals within the pure conditions of capital appears as their freedom; which is then also again dogmatically propounded as such through constant reflection back on the barriers torn by free competition. Free competition is the real development of capital. . . . This kind of individual freedom is therefore at the same time the most complete suspension of all individual freedom, and the most complete subjugation of individuality under social conditions which assume the form of objective powers, even of overpowering objects—of things independent of the relations among individuals themselves. (ibid., 650, 652)

Further, on the subject of money:

The dissolution of all products and activities into exchange values presupposes the dissolution of all fixed personal (historic) relations of dependence in production, as well as the all-sided dependence of the producers on one another. . . . The reciprocal and all-sided dependence of individuals who are indifferent to one another forms their social connection. This social bond is expressed in *exchange value*, by means of which alone each individual's own activity or his product becomes an activity and a product for him; he must produce a general product—*exchange value*, or, the latter isolated for itself and individualized, *money*. On the other side, the power which each individual exercises over the activity of others or over social wealth exists in him as the owner of *exchange values*, of *money*. The individual carries his social power, as well as his bond with society, in his pocket. Activity, regardless of its individual manifestation, and the product of activity, regardless of its particular make-up, are always *exchange value*, and exchange value is a generality, in which all individuality and peculiarity are negated and extinguished. This indeed is a condition very different from that in which the individual or the individual member of a family or clan (later, community) directly and naturally reproduces himself, or in which his productive activity and his share in production are bound to a specific form of labor and of product, which determine his relation to others in just that specific way.

The social character of activity, as well as the social form of the product, and the share of individuals in production here appear as something alien and objective, confronting the individuals, not as their relations to one another, but as their subordination to relations which subsist independently of them and which arise out of collisions between mutually indifferent individuals. The general exchange of activities and products, which has become a vital condition for each individual—their mutual interconnection—here appears as something alien to them, autonomous, as a thing. (ibid., 156–57)

Thus, in Marx's view, economic freedom results in the subjugation of people to the rule of things, as symbolized by money. Interestingly, Marx was fully aware of the inverse relationship between reified impersonal dependence and personal dependence on other people: "The less social power the medium of exchange possesses . . . the greater must be the power of the community which binds the individuals together, the patriarchal relation, the community of antiquity, feudalism and the guild system. . . . Rob the thing of this social power and you must give it to persons to exercise over persons" (ibid., 157–58).

Radoslav Selucký drew attention to this passage, and made very appropriate comments, when he wrote:

What follows from Marx's logic is this: on the one hand, the market [objective dependence] destroys personal dependence; on the other hand, personal independence is based on objective dependence. Free individuality, according to Marx, could be based only on the universal development of individuals, which presupposes the abolition of objective dependence (the market). Marx is not concerned with the fact that by overcoming the *objective dependence* of man through the abolition of the market he at the same time destroys the very foundation of man's *personal independence*. . . .

If there is only the alternative between personal dependence and objective dependence, then everyone must make a choice. The incapability of a social scientist to identify with either of these two possibilities had led and must lead to utopia. Marx himself decided in favor of utopia. His synthesis rests on the following assumption: *at the moment when the division of labor and scarcity die out*, the commodity production with market relations would die out as well, while the independent (autonomous) position of producers as the foundation of their personal independence, equality and freedom could be preserved.[90]

What should be added to this analysis is only an explanation of Marx's amazingly neglectful, offhand treatment of the problem of personal freedom. He consciously minimized its importance because the preoccupation with personal freedom was, in his view, a typical feature of bourgeois liberalism, that is, of the view of freedom that was directly opposite his own. In sharp contrast to the liberals, he rejected the view that in comparison with personal dependence, which characterizes patriarchal, tribal, and feudal relations, impersonal reified dependence, or interdependence, involved an increase of freedom. On the contrary, he continued to maintain, as he put it in *The German Ideology*, that members of bourgeois society are in fact "less free, because they are to a greater extent governed by material forces" (M&E, CW, 5:78–79). He conceded that their freedom *seems* to be greater than under feudal bondage but stressed that "on closer examination" this turns out to be a mere illusion (M, G, 164). Objective dependency relations, he explained, allow greater freedom only to particular individuals who "may by chance get on top of these relations" but do not change the basic relation between the exploiting and the exploited class; hence, they involve "certain definite relations of personal dependency," but stripped of all illusions and, in addition, greatly strengthened by the appearance of "objectivity," that is naturalness and permanence. As a matter of fact, an objective dependency relation "is nothing more than social relations which have become independent," or "the reciprocal relations of production separated from and autonomous of individuals"; their "objectivity," therefore, is merely an illusion of consciousness, an illusion helping the oppressed reconcile themselves to their fate through belief in its naturalness and objective inevitability. Owing to this, Marx commented, this belief "is of course consolidated, nourished and inculcated by the ruling classes by all means available" (ibid., 164–65, 165).

Let us dwell for a while on this reasoning. It does not explain why "objective dependency" should be worse, from the point of view of freedom, than personal dependency. Rather, it shows Marx's reluctant acknowledgment of the fact that most people feel personal dependency to be worse, as well as his awareness that belief in the objective character of existing dependency relations makes the task of the revolutionary overthrow of the system especially difficult, if not impossible. Hence his attempt to prove that "objectivity" is merely an illusion of consciousness—an attempt that resembles the views of the Left-Hegelians (who specialized in combating different "illusions of consciousness") and contradicts his own view of alienation as a necessary phase of development, and not merely a phenomenon of consciousness. On the other hand, however, it is obvious that his view of capitalism as the epoch of the greatest suppression of individual freedom was a dogmatic assumption that derived from his general theory, which claims that the mastery of the human species over nonhuman nature (the task of capitalist industrialization) could be achieved only at the expense of human beings as individuals. For this reason capitalism could not be seen by him as a progression of freedom in the relation "man versus society." But he was ready, of course, to see it as a self-enriching sort of alienation—that is, an unfreedom that was laying the foundation for universal liberation in the future.

The triadic scheme underlying this conception contained many brilliant sociological insights, as follows:

Relations of personal dependence (entirely spontaneous at the outset) are the first social forms, in which human productive capacity develops only to a slight extent and at isolated points. Personal independence founded on objective [*sachlicher*] dependence is the second great form, in which a system of general social metabolism, of universal relations, of all-round needs and universal capacities is formed for the first time. Free individuality, based on the universal development of individuals and on their subordination of their communal, social productivity as their social wealth, is the third stage. The second stage creates the conditions for the third. (ibid., 158)

At this second stage, characterized by a highly developed division of labor and exchange mediated by money, production is no longer *directly* social. Individuals are subsumed under social production, but not vice versa, since they are unable to manage it as their "common wealth." The idea that a money economy might be subject to rational control in the interest of the community seemed to Marx "erroneous and absurd" (ibid., 158–59). This was another of his many essentialist and aprioristic assumptions, which he put forth elsewhere as follows: "The essence of bourgeois society consists precisely in this, that *a priori* there is no conscious social regulation of production" (M, *SW*, 525). Conceived in this way, capitalist society was opposed to two different forms of social production and distribution: to precapitalist societies (patriarchal, ancient, or feudal) in which distribution is based "on a natural or political super- and subordination of individuals to one another," on the one hand, and to the future society of free individuals associated on the basis of common appropriation and control of the means of production (M, *G*, 159). This future society would stand in antithesis to the market economy, since exchange of the products of labor would no longer be private and mediated by money.

Bourgeois freedom, Marx argued, consists in reciprocal interdependence and indifference of isolated private individuals. But the other side of this private independence, the inevitable product of private exchange, is "complete dependence on the so-called world market." In describing this dependence Marx used not only the term *alienation* but also the term *reification* (*Versachlichung*); he wrote, for instance, that "the existence of money presupposes the objectification [*Versachlichung*] of the social bond." He appreciated the role of the market in providing economic knowledge but, characteristically, reduced this problem to conscious, articulated knowledge while completely disregarding the possibility that the "tacit knowledge" (Hayek's expression) inherent in the operation of the market might be incomparably greater than the amount of information accessible to outward observers of these operations.[91] By definition, as it were, the practical application of knowledge meant for him conscious regulation, while self-regulation was synonymous with alienation. Hence, the market as such was a sphere of alienation, while institutions "whereby each individual can acquire information about the activity of all others" (e.g., lists of current prices, rates of exchange, different statistical data, and so on) were treated as efforts to overcome alienation (ibid., 159, 160, 161). Of course, these efforts could never succeed: under the conditions of a money economy, alienation is unavoidable.

Marx's feelings toward the world market were by no means one-sidedly negative. The world market represented for him universal alienation, but it was also a form of universal interconnection, universal intercourse. It is instructive to analyze, sentence by sentence, what he said about it in *Grundrisse*.

"It has been said and may be said that this is precisely the beauty and the greatness of it: this spontaneous interconnection, this material and mental metabolism which is independent of the knowing and willing of individuals, and which presupposes their reciprocal independence and indifference" (ibid., 161). Obviously, Marx was not referring here to his own views: for him spontaneity meant lack of conscious, rational freedom, and being independent of the knowing and willing of individuals was synonymous to a humiliating alienation. The positive view of the market presented by him belongs to the classics of liberal political economy. The contrast between this view and his own values shows the inadequacy of the widespread opinion that attributes to classical liberals a one-sidedly rationalistic view of society. Marx was, in fact, a more consistent supporter of the rationalization of social life; from his point of view, capitalism was not rationalistic enough.

"And, certainly, this objective connection is preferable to the lack of any connection, or to a merely local connection resting on blood ties, or on primeval, natural or master-servant relations" (ibid., 161). Of course: all-round dependence created by the world market is a victory of universalism, albeit in an alienated form. All-round, objective dependence of the victims of capitalist alienation is the necessary condition for all-round development of the de-alienated human beings of the future.

Equally certain is it that individuals cannot gain mastery over their own social interconnections before they have created them. But it is an insipid notion to conceive of this merely *objective bond* as a spontaneous, natural attribute inherent in individuals and inseparable from their nature (in antithesis to their conscious knowing and willing). This bond is their product. It is a historic product. It belongs to a specific phase of their development. The alien and independent character in which it presently exists *vis-à-vis* individuals proves only that the latter are still engaged in the creation of the conditions of their social life, and that they have not yet begun, on the basis of these conditions, to live it. It is the bond natural to individuals within specific and limited relations of production. (ibid., 161–62)

This passage is more difficult and certainly open to divergent interpretations. It seems, however, that its essential meaning coincides with the famous sentence from Marx's preface to his *Contribution to the Critique of Political Economy*: "No social order ever perishes before all the productive forces for which there is room in it have developed" (M, SW, 390). Universal social interconnection still appears to people as objective and alien because they are still engaged in the capitalist phase of self-creation, because capitalist productive forces, i.e., exteriorized and alienated powers of humankind (*Vermögen*), still have room for further development. Before the stage of self-consciousness and freedom begins, the stage of development through alienation must be completed. But this is a law of human self-creation in history, not an entirely objective and immutable law of nature.

The rest of the quoted paragraph confirms this interpretation, while at the same time raising it, as it were, to a higher level of historiosophical abstraction.

Universally developed individuals, whose social relations, as their own communal [*gemeinschaftlich*] relations, are hence also subordinated to their own communal control, are no product of nature, but of history. The degree and the universality of the development of wealth where *this* individuality becomes possible *supposes production on the basis of exchange values as a prior condition*, whose universality produces not only the alienation of the individual from himself and from others, but also the universality and comprehensiveness of his relations and capacities. In earlier stages of development the single individual seems to be developed more fully, because he has not yet worked out his relationships in their fullness, or erected them as independent social powers and relations opposite himself. It is as ridiculous to yearn for a return to that original fullness as it is to believe that with this complete emptiness history has come to a standstill. (M, *G*, 162; italics added)

Thus, production on the basis of exchange values, and hence the total alienation, the "complete emptiness" bound up with it, is an unavoidable condition for achieving the highest stage of human development: that of "universally developed individuals." The unfolding of human essence in history is a dialectical movement involving three phases: the phase of primitive, undifferentiated fullness, presupposing economic self-sufficiency, that is, natural economy; the phase of total alienation, of the total destruction of human beings' primitive fullness through the development of the division of labor, universal exchange, and universal mutual dependence; and, finally, the phase of de-alienation in which human beings regain their "fullness" without losing the universality and comprehensiveness of their relations. In this third stage social relations will be subordinated to communal control. In other words, production will no longer be based on exchange values. The forces that brought about the alienated development of human relations and capacities—that is, the money economy and the world market—will be abolished and replaced by a conscious regulation of economic and social processes.

The term *communal control* testifies that Marx tried to preserve his youthful commitment to participatory democracy. He was obviously not aware, or not willing to acknowledge, that "a human planning agency must be hierarchically organized or it will display the very lack of control that constituted its raison d'être."[92] But he *was* fully aware that, to quote him once more, "the less social power the medium of exchange possesses . . . the greater must be the power of the community which binds the individuals together" (ibid., 157). Hence he must have been aware that, in spite of his constant use of the term *free individuals*, his vision of human liberation involved a tremendous strengthening of social cohesiveness and of communal power over the individual. His "free individuals" were to be free as specimens of the human species, not as individualized beings pursuing their own aims, which were not necessarily identical with communal aims; they were to be liberated from reification and alienation, but their dependence on the power of the community was to be increased, not loosened. Marx could sincerely believe that this would be "true freedom" because he was concerned with the freedom of humans as "communal beings." If freedom meant "living according to one's own nature," then the definition of freedom was naturally dependent on the definition of what constituted true human nature, our true selves. There is no doubt that, for Marx, the true self was identical with "communal essence." True, unlike the majority of collectivists, he wrote about "free individuals" in a positive sense, thus creating the impression that he subscribed to individualist values. But this is deeply misleading. "Free individuals" in Marx's sense are not individualists seeking maximum independence from their community, immune to its pressures and interpreting self-determination as being determined by their own unique individuality and not by their general human essence. Marx's use of this term reverts to the vocabulary of the Feuerbach-inspired Paris *Manuscripts*—that is, it expresses the standpoint of humanistic naturalism, as opposed to the abstractions of speculative idealism and all other forms of alienated consciousness. In other words, his usage of the term *free individual* had no anticollectivistic connotations; it meant "individuals free from alienation," not "individuals free from dependence on others." Hence, his vision of the universal liberation of humankind does not include safeguards for individual liberty. It concentrates on overcoming human dependence on "vast, impersonal forces,"[93] such as the reified social power of capital, while completely neglecting the classical problems of preventing direct coercion, personal tyranny, and other nonreified threats to human freedom. It did not occur to him that the aspiration for freedom as collective self-mastery, as conscious control over the fate of humankind, might create such a concentration of power in which safeguards for individual freedom would be more needed than under the conditions of unfreedom caused by the processes of reification and alienation.

1.7   Self-Enriching Alienation in *Capital* and the Abandonment of Youthful Optimism

In comparison with *Grundrisse* or *The German Ideology*, let alone the Paris *Manuscripts*, the philosophical content of *Capital* is not very impressive. Small wonder that most Marxists of the Second International did not see it as a philosophical work. Nevertheless, reading *Capital* against the background of Marx's earlier works, which were mostly unknown in the "Golden Age of Marxism," enables us to see it as another chapter in Marx's story about self-enriching alienation.

Above all it shows the price that has been paid for capitalist progress. It stresses that the passage from natural economy to commodity production had to involve the expropriation of immediate producers, a process that in its classical form had been accomplished "with merciless vandalism, and under the stimulus of passions the most infamous, the most sordid, the pettiest, the most meanly odious." But even irrespective of these evil passions, capitalist progress had to be cruel and merciless. The atrocities of primitive accumulation could not be avoided; small producers *had* to be expropriated to set free social productive powers and thus avoid "universal mediocrity." Petty industry had to be annihilated to enable "the transformation of the individualized and scattered means of production into socially concentrated ones." All this "expropriation of the great mass of the people from the soil, from the means of subsistence, and from the means of labor" was "the prelude to the history of capital" (M, C, 1:714, 713–14, 713, 713). Its further history, consisting of the development of a money economy and the division of labor, led, on the one hand, to the maximum development of productive forces, but, on the other, to the maximum alienation of labor, an extreme reification of social relations ("commodity fetishism") and the disintegration of the human personality. As the splitting up of labor into partial activities progressed, "collective laborers" developed at the expense of individual laborers, who were condemned to ever more monotonous and one-sided work, being transformed in the end into automatons carrying out one activity during their whole lives. The products of "socialized" labor, i.e., divided and alienated labor, were the products of everyone and, at the same time, of no one. These products were wholly impersonal, took on an independent life in an anonymous market, and subjugated their producers. The poorer and more inhuman the life of individual workers became, the greater and more concentrated became the social, although alienated, power of capital. But the "immanent laws of capitalistic production" also created objective conditions for, and the necessity of, capitalism's undoing.

Hand in hand with this centralization, or this expropriation of many capitalists by few, develop, on an ever-extending scale, the co-operative forms of the labor-process, the conscious technical application of science, the methodical cultivation of the soil, the transformation of the instruments of labor into instruments of labor only usable in common, the economizing of all means of production by their use as the means of production of combined, socialized labor, the entanglement of all peoples in the net of the world-market, and with this, the international character of the capitalistic régime. Along with the constantly diminishing number of the magnates of capital, who usurp and monopolize all advantages of this process of transformation, grows the mass of misery, oppression, slavery, degradation, exploitation; but with this too grows the revolt of the working-class, a class always increasing in numbers, and disciplined, united, organized by the very mechanism of the process of capitalist production itself. The monopoly of capital becomes a fetter upon the mode of production, which has sprung up and flourished along with, and under it. Centralization of the means of production and socialization of labor at last reach a point where they become incompatible with their capitalist integument. Thus integument is burst asunder. The knell of capitalist private property sounds. The expropriators are expropriated. (ibid., 714–15)

This summary of the ideological message of *Capital* was the most influential text in Marx's entire legacy, inspiring generations of revolutionaries and providing them with "scientifically proved certainty" of the imminent worldwide collapse of capitalism (the famous "Zusammenbruchstheorie") and of the worldwide victory of the workers' movement. It was their vision of the Apocalypse and the Last Judgment, to be followed by a communist millennium.

As can easily be noticed, this Marxist myth contained two prophecies: the authoritative statement about the (allegedly) imminent and unavoidable immizerization of the workers (so-called *Verelendungstheorie*), and the promise of ultimate deliverance at the end time. This reflected the inner logic of millenarism, according to which terrestrial salvation must be preceded by a period of tribulation and utter misery. It was also consistent with the triadic scheme of self-enriching alienation. Marx himself presented his conception of the appearance and disappearance of capitalist property in terms of the Hegelian version of this scheme, writing about it as follows:

The capitalist mode of appropriation, the result of the capitalist mode of production, produces capitalist private property. This is the first negation of individual private property, as founded on the labor of the proprietor. But capitalist production begets, with the inexorability of a law of Nature, its own negation. It is the negation of negation. This does not re-establish private property for the producer, but gives him individual property based upon the acquisitions of the capitalist era: i.e., on cooperation and the possession in common of the land and of the means of production. (ibid., 715)

Marx's *Capital* paints with dark colors not only the initial stage of the capitalist phase of world history, the period of "primitive accumulation," but also the capitalist "socialization of labor," i.e., the process of creating positive conditions for socialism. In Marx's interpretation, this was a process of progressive development but, at the same time, a process of dehumanization. He formulated the general law of this double process in these words:

The one-sidedness and the deficiencies of the detail laborer become perfections when he is a part of the collective laborer. The habit of doing only one thing converts him into a never failing instrument, while his connexion with the whole mechanism compels him to work with the regularity of the parts of a machine. . . .

In manufacture, in order to make the collective laborer, and through him capital, rich in social productive power, each laborer must be made poor in individual productive powers. . . .

Some crippling of body and mind is inseparable even from division of labor in society as a whole. Since, however, manufacture carries this social separation of branches of labor much further, and also, by its peculiar division, attacks the individual at the very roots of his life, it is the first to afford the materials for, and to give a start to, industrial pathology. (ibid., 330, 341, 342–43)

These phenomena had been already described before Marx, although in another language, by the romantic conservative critics of capitalist civilization and also by the representatives of the so-called economic romanticism, such as Sismondi. After Marx these subjects were taken up by the Russian populists, who derived their knowledge of the dehumanizing results of capitalist development mainly from *Capital*. They drew from it the conclusion that one should oppose capitalist development, put a brake on its dynamism, for the sake of preserving or restoring the integral character of individuals and personal, immediate, and nonreified social bonds. The populists and the representatives of "economic romanticism" (as opposed to romantic conservatives) added to this egalitarian arguments, setting against capitalism a vision of an egalitarian community of direct producers.

Marx drew a wholly different conclusion. He proclaimed that alienation and reification would be overcome at the time when "the life-process of society, which is based on the process of material production" throws off the fetishistic veil and becomes transformed into "production by freely associated men, and is consciously regulated by them in accordance with a settled plan" (ibid., 84). At the same time he rejected the thought of reaching this end at the price of stopping or weakening the development of productive forces. Conscious, planned control of production on a macrosocial scale was, in his judgment, possible only after the completion of the spontaneous process of socializing labor, hence, after such a perfection of self-regulating market mechanisms of cooperation as would make the economy of a given society a finely regulated and excellently functioning productive system. In the conflict between preindustrial harmony and disharmonious, alienating industrialism, Marx chose industrialism; in the conflict between egalitarianism and productivism, he chose productivism. He did not even hesitate to praise Ricardo for voicing the principle of "production for production's sake," since that principle meant for him "the development of the richness of human nature as an end in itself" (M, *TSV*, pt. 2, 118). The Russian Marxist Anatol Lunacharskii was therefore right when he stated that in the dispute between "God," or "the principle of justice," and "Satan," or "the will for power," the will for intensive development, the author of *Capital* stood on the side of "Satan."[94]

The maximal development of alienated productive forces of humanity was to be followed, of course, by the positive overcoming of alienation—that is, the level of historical development on which humans as individuals would be able to reappropriate the wealth created in previous epochs and bring it under their sovereign dominion. In the remark about Ricardo quoted above, Marx severely criticized Sismondi, attributing to him the desire to arrest the development of the species in order to safeguard the welfare of the individual. He added, however, that at the final stage, the interests of the individual and those of the species would coincide.

Apart from the barrenness of such edifying reflections [as represented by Sismondi], they reveal a failure to understand the fact that, although at first the development of the capacities of the *human* species takes place at the cost of the majority of human individuals and even classes, in the end it breaks through this contradiction and coincides with the development of individuality; the higher development of individuality is thus only achieved by a historical process during which individuals are sacrificed, for the interests of the species in the human kingdom, as in the animal and plant kingdoms, always assert themselves at the cost of the interests of individuals, because these interests of the species coincide only with the *interests of certain individuals*, and it is this coincidence which constitutes the strength of these privileged individuals. (M, *TSV*, pt. 2, 118)

It is difficult to exaggerate the importance of this statement, although as an answer to Sismondi it is obviously weak, entirely missing the point. Sismondi was concerned with the fate of real, living individuals and therefore could hardly be consoled by the idea that sacrificing them for the development of the species would cease to be necessary in the remote future. Neither would he accept the alleged necessity of sacrificing ordinary individuals for the interests of *certain* individuals, or even for the sake of the higher development of the individuality of the human beings of the future. All these reasonings sharply contrasted with the principle of ethical individualism, since they asserted, with quite amazing brutality, the indisputable priority of the interests of the species. Marx's belief that human sufferings of the past and present would be compensated for when the individuals of the future de-alienated the wealth of collective human beings by absorbing it into themselves had nothing in common with treating each individual as an end, never as a means. True, Marx insisted that the future flourishing of the human species must be manifested in the appearance of superior individuals, incarnating the fullest development of humans' species capacities and infinitely surpassing the undeveloped and degraded human beings of the presocialist epochs of history. So he was not a "collectivist" in the sense of extolling the gray anonymous masses, the herd animals, the gregarious beings; he dreamt rather of a kind of "superman"—not in the sense of a new species, but a superman by virtue of the full realization of man's species capacities. But if "collectivism" is meant as the priority of "the general," the readiness to sacrifice individuals for the sake of their group, class, or the entire species, if its essential features are the contemptuous neglect of privacy and the insistence that individuals can exercise their "true freedom" only in community as "communal beings," then Marx's worldview should, of course, be classified as a quite extreme variant of collectivism. The quasi-Nietzschean features of this worldview, combined with the view of history as human self-creation through self-enriching alienation, make this view peculiarly destructive of humanitarian values. This conception involves not only an easy justification of all the cruelties of history, but also the active encouragement "to make history" without regard to the human price of progress. Added to this, the stress on autocreation justifies, in turn, all kinds of voluntaristic experiments on human beings. The inner logic of the ideal of conscious self-creation can provide arguments (although Marx himself was only marginally interested in this problem) for attempts to improve the biological quality of the species by eugenics, publicly controlled family planning, and so forth. After all, these are important ways of exercising conscious mastery over the fate of the human species.

But let us return to *Capital*. The main theme of this book is not freedom but necessity—a "meaningful necessity," to be sure, paving the way for freedom. Hence, our discussion of the problem of freedom in *Capital* must concentrate on the relations between necessity and freedom in history, especially in the capitalist epoch.

Marx's prefaces to the first and second German edition of *Capital* greatly contributed to legitimizing the view of him as a rigid, scientific determinist who believed in the "iron laws" of history and proclaimed their complete independence of "human will, consciousness, and intelligence" (M, C, 1:19, 27). Literally interpreted, such views would amount, of course, to a denial of the very idea of autocreation, to a complete reversal of Marx's earlier thesis (as expressed in *The German Ideology*) that social reality is nevertheless "only a product of the preceding intercourse of individuals themselves" and therefore that the task of communism is to "render it impossible that anything should exist independently of individuals" (M, SW, 179). We know now that this was not the case. The works of young Lukács and other "neo-Marxists," as well as the development of "Marxology" after the publication of Marx's early works, made it clear that the author of *Capital* had not radically departed from his earlier philosophy of history. It remains a fact, nonetheless, that he chose to use the language of naturalistic determinism, and this had a considerable impact on the understanding of his theory.

In principle, the conviction that there is determinism in history should not be dangerous to freedom. "Determinism versus indeterminism" is the problem of the freedom of the will, while the question of human freedom is not dependent on our solution of the theoretical problem of "liberum arbitrium." We are concerned with freedom to act in accordance with *our* will, and not with the problem of "freedom to will what we will." There is no logical connection between these two problems: libertarian institutions can be supported from both indeterminist and determinist standpoints, and the same is true of all sorts of tyranny. Nevertheless, *on a psychological level* historical determinism is often felt to be incompatible with our sense of freedom. Everything depends on how we perceive the alleged "laws of history." It makes a great difference if we perceive them as truly "natural" or not, if we identify ourselves with them or feel them as an alien force. In the case of identification, the feeling of being determined by history, that is, of representing a historical force, adds seriousness and value to our self-determination. Awareness that there is an element of necessity in our freedom does not reduce us to the role of mere puppets; rather, it endows us with a sense of mission, makes our freedom meaningfully related to our innermost essence and not something contingent, a matter of mere caprice. But this is so only when the final outcome of different activities is unknown and unpredictable, when the results, all of them causally determined, are felt to be dependent on their relative strengths, on the energy of our respective wills (determined, but nevertheless *ours*), and not known in advance, preordained by factors entirely alien to us. In other words, if somebody succeeds in persuading us that some of our actions are doomed to failure whereas other actions have a scientific guarantee of success, our feeling of freedom—that is, our freedom of action, of having a historical alternative—is distressingly diminished. On the other hand, those of us who *want* to act in the prescribed direction will benefit from the certainty that we *have* to win, since history itself is on our side.

It has rightly been noticed that the notion of the "iron necessity" of historical development "applies in Marx primarily to socio-economic formations, not to individuals."[95] Marx seemed to assume that educated individuals could make their own, right or wrong, historical choices. Hence, he often used the notion of "historical necessity" as a means of warning his ideological enemies that their cause was doomed, thus undermining their morale and self-confidence. Needless to say, he used the same rhetoric to embolden his supporters. He was skillful in manipulating the idea of "historical inevitability," having learned this morally doubtful art not from positivistic scientists but from Hegel. Already in 1846 he wrote to Annenkov: "Are men free to choose this or that form of society for themselves? By no means" (ibid., 192).

In the prefaces to *Capital*, Marx merely repeated this statement. His German readers, he stressed, should not imagine that they could choose a noncapitalist way of development. The story of the development of capitalism in England applies also to them, because "the country that is more developed industrially only shows, to the less developed, the image of its own future" (M, C, 1:19). One nation can and should learn from others, but the latecomers to the arena of history should rid themselves of illusions that successive phases of normal economic development can be bypassed or removed by legal enactments. In other words, capitalism cannot be avoided; one can only shorten and lessen its birth pangs (ibid., 20).

A good response to this reasoning was provided by Mikhailovskii, who argued that to Western socialists, Marxist theory would provide arguments for the necessity and desirability of socialism, but that socialists from a backward country like Russia would draw from the theory less comfortable conclusions: they would be forced to agree that the preconditions of socialism were as yet nonexistent in their country and that the image of the immediate future was to be found in Marx's descriptions of the atrocities of primitive accumulation. Moreover, Marxist historical determinism would force them to accept all the consequences of capitalist progress in spite of the full knowledge of how much harm and pain these would bring to the people.

All this "maiming of women and children" we have still before us and, from the point of view of Marx's historical theory, we should not protest against them because it would mean acting to our detriment; on the contrary, we should welcome them as the steep but necessary steps to the temple of happiness. It would be, indeed, very difficult to bear this inner contradiction, this conflict between theory and values which in many concrete situations would inevitably tear the soul of a Russian disciple of Marx. . . . His ideal, if he is really a disciple of Marx, consists, among other things, in making property inseparable from labor, so that the land, tools and all the means of production belong to the workers. On the other hand, if he really shares Marx's historico-philosophical views, he should be pleased to see the producers being divorced from the means of production, he should treat this divorce as the first phase of the inevitable and, in the final result, beneficial process. He must, in a word, accept the overthrow of the principles inherent in his ideal. This collision between moral feeling and historical inevitability should be resolved, of course, in favor of the latter.[96]

In his (unpublished) answer to Mikhailovskii's article, Marx declared that he had never intended to present his "historical sketch of the genesis of capitalism in Western Europe" as "an historic-philosophic theory of the *marche générale* imposed by fate upon every people." He stressed that the laws of capitalist accumulation, as analyzed in *Capital*, applied exclusively to Western Europe and emphatically disclaimed any ambition on his part to create "a general historico-philosophical theory" (M&E, C, 354).[97] Finally, he resolutely rejected Mikhailovskii's suggestion that *Capital* implied a negative attitude toward the efforts of Russian revolutionary populists who tried to find for their country a path of development different from, and better than, that of the West.

It is difficult to believe that this declaration could have been written entirely in good faith. True, Marx certainly did not want to persuade Russian revolutionaries to give up their socialist hopes, since he knew only too well that this would undercut their revolutionary energy and thereby greatly weaken the entire revolutionary movement in Europe. But, characteristically, he completely ignored Mikhailovskii's concern about sparing people's sufferings. He insisted instead on arguing that *Capital* did not contain any universal prescription for progress and that under special circumstances even the capitalist phase could sometimes be avoided. All these explanations and qualifications are more or less acceptable, but Marx's main contention—the alleged lack of any "general historico-philosophical theory"—was either a tactical retreat (to put it mildly) or simply a lie. Marx's theory of self-enriching alienation, which underlay all his theoretical construction, is undoubtedly a "general historico-philosophical theory," a theory justifying evil as bringing about beneficial results in the future. This was precisely the kind of theory that was bound to create the moral dilemmas described by Mikhailovskii. It was not necessarily a theory about the inevitability of capitalism, although it was seen as such by the first generation of Marxists. But it *was* a theory of development through the sufferings of alienation, a historiosophical theodicy, an apologia for the necessary cruelties of progress. Its true meaning for backward countries was clearly revealed in Marx's article on "The Future Results of the British Rule in India," which summarizes the point: "When a great social revolution shall have mastered the results of the bourgeois epoch, the market of the world and the modern powers of production, and subjected them to the common control of the most advanced peoples, then only will human progress cease to resemble that hideous pagan idol, who would not drink the nectar but from the skulls of the slain" (M, SW, 336).

Division of labor and commodity production were in Marx's historiodicy a necessary evil through which humankind must pass in order to achieve the full and harmonious realization of its species essence. Division of labor was the main target of his attacks in *The German Ideology*. But it is important to note that with the passage of time, his attitude toward division of labor became more ambivalent, more complex.[98] At the same time, commodity production, production for money and the "atomic" freedom bound up with it, came to be seen by him as *the worst* evil, the most complete form of human alienation. He began to reconcile himself to the division of labor as a necessary form of rationalization of productive processes and to insist that it was perfectly conceivable *without* monetary exchange and production for sale. In *Capital* he stressed that the "division of labor is a necessary condition for the production of commodities, but it does not follow, conversely, that the production of commodities is a necessary condition for the division of labor. In the primitive Indian community there is social division of labor, without production of commodities. Or, to take an example nearer to home, in every factory the labor is divided according to a system, but this division is not brought about by the operatives mutually exchanging their individual products. Such products can only become commodities with regard to each other, as result of different kinds of labor, each kind being carried on independently and for the account of private individuals" (M, C, 1:49).

Chapter 14 of the first volume of *Capital* contains a section entitled "Division of Labour in Manufacture, and Division of Labour in Society." Although both of these two forms of division of labor are accused of entailing "some crippling of body and mind" of workers as individuals, the first is praised by Marx for introducing principles of efficient organization and rational planning, while the second is conceived of as surrendering control over production and exchange, thus bringing about the rule of things over man. The importance of this distinction justifies, I think, this extensive quotation from Marx:

> The division of labour in the workshop implies concentration of the means of production in the hands of one capitalist, the division of labour in society implies their dispersion among many independent producers of commodities. While within the workshop, the iron law of proportionality subjects definite numbers of workmen to definite functions, in the society outside the workshop chance and caprice have full play in distributing the producers and their means of production among the various branches of industry. . . . The *a priori* system on which the division of labour, within the workshop, is regularly carried out, becomes in the division of labour within the society, an *a posteriori*, nature-imposed necessity, controlling the lawless caprice of the producers, and perceptible in the barometrical fluctuations of the market-prices. Division of labour within the workshop implies the undisputed authority of the capitalist over men, that are but pawns of a mechanism that belongs to him. The division of labour within the society brings into contact independent commodity-producers, who acknowledge no other authority but that of competition, of the coercion exerted by the pressure of their mutual interests, just as in the animal kingdom, the *bellum omnium contra omnes* more or less preserves the conditions of existence of every species. The same bourgeois mind which praises division of labour in the workshop, life-long annexation of the labourer to a partial operation, and his complete subjection to capital, as being an organization of labour that increases its productiveness—that same bourgeois mind denounces with equal vigour every conscious attempt to socially control and regulate the process of production, as an inroad upon such sacred things as the right of property, freedom and unrestricted play for the bent of the individual capitalist. It is very characteristic that the enthusiastic apologists of the factory system have nothing more damning to urge against a general organization of the labour of society, than that it would turn all society into one immense factory. (ibid., 336–37)

In historical hindsight, the falseness of the view that the concentration of the means of production implies that these be fully controlled by *one* capitalist, or that the division of labor within the workplace implies the undisputed authority of *one* individual, is obvious and does not require comment. What is somewhat concealed in the above quotations and should be made clear for a better understanding of Marx's conception of freedom is the fact that, in spite of his gloomy picture of both forms of the capitalist division of labor, he saw the worst evil not in the "despotism in the workshop" but in the "anarchy of the market" and did not deny that the socialist society of the future would bear some resemblance to "one immense factory" (ibid., 337). In fact he had already said something similar in his *Poverty of Philosophy* (1847), writing: "Society as a whole has this in common with the interior of a workshop, that it too had its division of labor. If one took as a model the division of labor in a modern workshop, in order to apply it to a whole society, the society best organized for the production of wealth would undoubtedly be that which had a simple chief employer, distributing tasks to the different members of the community according to a previously fixed rule" (M&E, CW, 6:184).

This surprisingly naive idealization of what we today call "the command economy" is to be found also in Marx's views on the inner organization of capitalist factories, and this fact should not be obscured by his concentration on the dark side of industrialization. What was not explicitly said in *Capital* was stated in Engels's works, especially in his *Socialism: Utopian and Scientific*. There we find a clear distinction between the "old" (spontaneous) and the "new" (consciously planned) division of labor, i.e., the "division of labor upon a *definite plan*, as organized in the factory." Engels emphasized that the latter had become stronger than the former. The growth of trusts was, in his eyes, a phenomenon that paved the way for socialism: "In the trusts freedom of competition changes into its very opposite—into monopoly; and the production without any definite plan of capitalistic society capitulates to the production upon a definite plan of the invading socialistic society" (M&E, SW, 3:136, 144).

Marx was more cautious in expressing positive views about capitalist factories or corporations, but his conception of freedom nonetheless *required* the recognition of the superiority of "factory despotism" over the "freedom of the market." This was so because freedom, understood as conscious mastery over human collective fate, presupposed, in his view, the full control of the economy—that is, the abolition of independently acting private subjects of economic activity, the replacement of self-regulating mechanisms of the market by "directly social" production, in other words, by "production upon a definite plan." Hence he had to condemn "atomic" freedom and to see it as the main source of reification, i.e., the worst form of human alienation. Commodity production and the free market meant for him a society in which "the behavior of men in the social process of production is purely atomic. Hence, their relations to each other in production assume a material character independent of their control and

conscious individual action" (M, C, 1:96). In this sense individual freedom in the economic sphere, i.e., freedom of private economic activity,
seemed incompatible with individual freedom conceived as conscious self-
determination. All these considerations led him to conceive of socialism,
or "the co-operative society," as a society characterized by the absence of
commodity production and monetary exchange. In his "Marginal Notes to
the Program of the German Workers' Party," written in 1875 and published
posthumously by Engels under the title *Critique of the Gotha Program*,
he wrote about this society in uncompromising terms: "Within the co-
operative society based on common ownership of the means of production,
the producers do not exchange their products; just as little does the labor
employed on the products appear here *as the value* of these products, as
a material quality possessed by them, since now, in contrast to capitalist
society, individual labor no longer exists in an indirect fashion but directly
as a component part of the total labor" (M&E, SW, 3:17).

This entailed not only the end of unplanned production but also the
end of unplanned consumption, or, to put it differently, the abolition of
individual freedom in the sphere of consumption, as guaranteed by money.
Some of Marx's contemporaries saw very clearly the dangers of such an
aim. Franz Mehring, for instance, accused Marx of wanting to establish the
realm of freedom on the ruins of "individual freedom in defining our needs"
and concluded from this that Marx's teaching might provide justification
for the worst possible tyranny.[99]

The unfreedom caused by alienation and reification stemming from developed commodity production and monetary exchange had no parallel
in precapitalist social formation, no matter how restrictive or despotic in
all other respects. The lack of individual independence characteristic of
primitive societies, such as that of the ancient Indian community or the
Peruvian Inca state, was idealized in *Capital* as a lack of mutual estrangement (*Fremdheit*) and thus as a form of communal freedom, as a state of
affairs in which human products were not alienated by their producers and
therefore not allowed to get out of control (M, C, 1:91).[100] In the Middle
Ages everyone was dependent, but precisely because of this there was "no
necessity for labor and its products to assume a fantastic form different
from reality. . . . No matter, then, what we may think of the parts played
by the different classes of people themselves in this society, the social relations between individuals in the performance of their labor appear at all
events as their own mutual personal relations, and are not disguised under
the shape of social relations between the products of labor" (ibid., 81–82).

Thus, "commodity fetishism," owing to which social relations between
people assume in their eyes "the fantastic form of a relation between things"
(ibid., 77), did not exist in the Middle Ages, that is, at the early stage of
commodity production. This meant for Marx that the phenomenon of reifi-

cation was also absent. Personal dependence in a hierarchically constructed authoritarian system had not yet been replaced by objective (*sachlicher*), reified dependence, and this, in Marx's view, meant less alienation and therefore more freedom. In contrast to the liberals, Marx obviously felt that reified forms of social relations—that is, such relations of dependence as are seen as something "objective" and "natural"—are more destructive of human freedom than is clearly perceived personal dependence. In his *German Ideology* he expressed his view explicitly, stressing that it was merely an illusion to see individuals as freer under the dominance of the bourgeoisie than before; in reality, he maintained, the opposite was true (M&E, CW, 5:78–79). In *Capital* he developed the theory of commodity production and "commodity fetishism," which provided additional arguments for the same conception of the historical fate of freedom.

Marx's idealization of the natural economy in primitive communism went much further. In a letter to Engels of March 25, 1868, he legitimized this idealization by stressing that what is oldest often contains the germ of what is newest; consequently, he found it normal that "looking beyond the Middle Ages into the primitive age of each nation" was becoming more and more widespread among socialists (M, *PCEF*, 140). In later years he was delighted to find powerful support for such tendencies in Morgan's *Ancient Society* (1877). He agreed with Morgan that the socialist order of the future would restore on a higher level the equality, freedom, and brotherhood of ancient kinship society. At the end of life, in the drafts of his famous letter to Vera Zasulich, he quoted Morgan's words in support of the view that communism would be "a revival in a superior form" of an archaic type of society (M&E, *SW*:3, 153–54).[101]

According to Ernest Gellner, Morgan "saved Marxism" by helping Marx "replace the linear philosophy of history, characteristic of Hegelianism, which leads from slavery to freedom, by a new, so to speak, 'detour' soteriology that is distinctively Marxist: from freedom to freedom via alienation."[102] In fact, however, this "detour soteriology" had always been present in the idea of self-enriching alienation, which was the foundation stone of Marx's historiosophy of freedom. Hence, Morgan's role has to be defined more modestly, as providing Marx with new arguments for defending his philosophy of history against contamination by positivistic conceptions of linear progress.

The difference between the Russian populists and Marx in their respective idealizations of "archaic society" can be defined axiologically. For the populists, archaic social structures were mostly a paragon of equality, while Marx saw them as embodying an important aspect of freedom: freedom as human control over human products. Engels, in his *Origin of the Family, Private Property and the State*, did not hesitate to conclude that in this respect "barbarity" was definitely superior to civilization. In ancient societies, he argued, "production was carried on within the most restricted limits, but—the producers exercised control over their own product. This was the immense advantage of barbarian production that was lost with the advent of civilization; and to win it back on the basis of the enormous control man now exercises over the forces of nature, and of free association that is now possible, will be the task of the next generations" (ibid., 278).

The "immense advantage" indicated in this quotation was the advantage of the self-sufficient natural economy over all forms of exchange: "When the producers no longer directly consumed their product, but let it go out of their hands in the course of exchange, they lost control over it. They no longer knew what became of it, and the possibility arose that the product might some day be turned against the producers, used as a means of exploiting and oppressing them" (ibid., 279). These words also belong to Engels, but the extreme prejudice against exchange expressed in them was not his own invention. In Marx's *Capital* this prejudice was expressed with such force that many socialist theorists, including such first-rate scholars as Neurath and Bauer, came to follow Marx in seeing socialist economy as a natural economy in macroscale.[103] To be sure, Marx and Engels—once more in accordance with the idea of self-enriching alienation—combined their hostility toward exchange with a clear awareness that what they saw as its negative aspect was a necessary price for developing human capacities through "universal intercourse." Nevertheless, "free" unplanned exchange was, in their eyes, not an expression of freedom but a denial of it. True freedom in the economic sphere was conceived by them as antithetical to the liberals' "economic freedom"; it was defined by them not as "freedom of selling and buying" but as conscious control over production and distribution. And from this point of view, the primitive natural economy could indeed be seen as superior to commodity production and monetary exchange, as deserving to be restored on a higher level, and, in a sense, as providing a ready-made model for the socialist future.

An extreme, almost caricatured expression of this view is to be found in the parallel Marx drew between the socialist economy of the future and the economic activities of Robinson Crusoe (M, C, 1:81). In both cases there is a single subject of economic activity, although in one case it is simply an individual, while in the other it is the collective, which is endowed with a single will and working in accordance with a settled plan (ibid., 84). In neither case do different kinds of labor involve the existence of different, independent subjects of economic activity exchanging their products "privately" and "freely," that is, without concern about the common good and without any rational planning. Owing to this, Marx maintained that under socialism "all the characteristics of Robinson's labor are repeated" (ibid., 83).

But how to ensure that "freely associated individuals" will really act like a single individual? The very idea of such a possibility presupposed two rather risky assumptions. First, that all individuals could be raised (or, rather, reduced) to their common species essence; second, that the human essence could be fully expressed in each individual. The first of these assumptions was, for Marx, an axiom. He never ceased to believe that all humans, as members of the same species, have basically the same interests and that only their division into different classes prevents them from acting in accordance with a rational consensus. But he was becoming more and more skeptical about the second assumption, which involved his early vision of human liberation as developed in the period of the *Economic and Philosophic Manuscripts* and *The German Ideology*. As discussed, in this early period he believed in the total de-alienation of humankind through the process of overcoming the division of labor; he even postulated the "transformation of labor into self-activity" since the very word *labor* meant for him, by then, the alienated activity, the realm of unfreedom (M&E, CW, 5:88).[104] Under socialism labor was to be de-alienated, that is, changed into diversified, comprehensive activity; "forced activity," imposed on individuals "through an exterior, arbitrary need" was to give way to work that would be a "free expression" of human life and therefore a "free enjoyment of life" ("On James Mill," M, SW, 122). The price to be paid for this final outcome was to be very high, because it had to be prepared for by capitalist industrialization—that is, by the *alienated* development of human capacities, leading to "complete dehumanization" (M, SW, 93). But the species capacities of humankind, developed at the cost of human beings as individuals, were to be de-alienated through "the development of a totality of capacities in the individuals themselves" (M&E, CW, 5:87). Thus, division of labor could be overcome without losing its achievements in mastering nature; this, of course, presupposed the reappropriation of the species capacities of humankind by individual human beings; in other words, human beings as individuals would be raised to the level achieved by humankind as a species. A more optimistic utopia could hardly be imagined. Humankind would continue its Promethean mission of subjugating nature and, at the same time, do this without employing the Puritan work ethic, without subjugating itself to rigorous discipline; productivity would continue to increase while at the same time becoming transformed into free creativity, free enjoyment of life.

In Marx's later works this ultraoptimistic vision gave way to a more realistic conception, one more in agreement with the harsh laws of material production as described in *Capital*. Marx apparently came to the conclusion that freedom as "mastery over collective fate"—that is, as conscious, rational control, which allowed humans to avoid humiliating dependence on both blind necessities and chance—was not compatible with replacing labor with free self-expression and self-enjoyment; that rational planning could not go together with the abolition of the division of labor, i.e., with allowing individuals to do whatever they wanted and to develop themselves in all possible directions. Hence, it was necessary for him to reconcile himself to the division of labor, and he did so precisely by distinguishing between the division of labor in society, which presupposed the uncontrolled decentralized economic activity of different independent producers, and the division of labor in the factory, which was based on a settled plan and strict control of everybody's work. He continued to condemn the former while positing the latter as a model for the socialist society of the future.

Unlike Engels (section 2.6), Marx was aware that conscious, rational control over the economy, even if it really enabled humans to steer their history and to avoid all the unintended consequences of their actions, could not be equated with freedom in the fullest sense of the term. He continued to dream about freedom as unrestrained self-realization, although he ceased to believe that it could be achieved in the economic sphere. Hence, he sharply divided human life into two spheres—productive and nonproductive—and stressed that freedom could not be realized in both of them. This new conception assumed that, "in fact the realm of freedom actually begins only where labor which is determined by necessity and mundane considerations ceases; thus in the very nature of things it lies beyond the sphere of actual material production." In the sphere of production, freedom "can only consist in the socialized man, the associated producers, rationally regulating their interchange with Nature, bringing it under their common control, instead of being ruled by it as the blind forces of Nature; and achieving this with the least expenditure of energy and under conditions most favorable to, and worthy of, their human nature. But it nonetheless still remains a realm of necessity. Beyond it begins that development of human capacities which is an end in itself, the true realm of freedom, which, however, can blossom forth only with this realm of necessity as its basis. The shortening of the working day is its basic prerequisite" (M, C, 3:820).

In other words, the maximal development of productive forces and their subjection to conscious planned control is merely a *condition* of authentic freedom. It is an indispensable condition, as only it will enable human beings to acquire the material means and the free time needed to satisfy comprehensive, "abundant," truly human needs. But it should not be treated as the realization of true freedom. Even under socialism, productive work would not become a sphere of individuals' free self-realization and self-activity, but would remain a sphere of purely instrumental activity, a means to live and not a free expression of life, not an end in itself.

This amounted to the abandonment of the most ambitious and most optimistic idea of Marx's communist utopianism—namely, the idea of the "abolition of labor" through its transformation into an end in itself: nonalienated self-realization, free self-activity, which would enable individuals to joyfully participate in the life of the species. The realization of true freedom—the unfettered development of all human capacities—was dependent on the shortening of the work day. Marx assumed, of course, that people would devote their free time to creative activities; in this matter he continued to manifest an exaggerated optimism that he did not attempt to justify. He was convinced that in the affluent society of the future (naturally a *socialist* society, since he excluded the possibility of mass affluence under capitalism), artificial needs, or those degrading to humans, would not appear. The Promethean vision of humans as creative beings, ever present in his works, inclined him to believe that the achievement of the opportunity for free, comprehensive, creative development of personality would be fully utilized by individuals and that the victory of socialism would be followed, in the language of his earlier works, by an increasingly perfect fulfillment of human essence in existence, by an increasingly rapid diminution of the difference between "true man" and "man really existing."

But this is only one side, one face, of Marx's utopia, namely, its humanistic face, overoptimistic, of course, but not harmful. If Marx's conception of freedom could be reduced to the idea of shortening the work day in order to release individuals' free creativity, it would be very easy to absolve him from all responsibility for subsequent totalitarian interpretations of his legacy. Unfortunately, we must remember that the other side of Marx's conception is his firm conviction, a conviction central to his entire philosophy of human history, that the necessary condition for "truly human freedom" is "freedom in the realm of necessity"—that is, total control over the economy, full suppression of the freedom to produce, exchange, and consume. Marx changed his views on the division of labor, but money, free exchange, and production for sale by autonomous economic agents (in other words, self-regulating mechanisms of the market) remained for him an anathema. He modeled his vision of the division of labor under socialism on what he himself called the "despotism of the workshop" or "the organization of the labor of society in accordance with an approved and authoritative plan" (M, C, 1:337). What this amounted to, in fact, was nothing less than abandoning the hope that under socialism individuals would become "universally developed," and thus restored on a higher level to their original "wholeness," while simultaneously increasing the emphasis on the necessity of authoritarian control. Engels (as usual) made this even more explicit, stressing the importance of the principle of authority in all social organizations, especially in industry, where there is virtually no place for individual autonomy (Engels, "On Authority," M&E, SW, 2:377). The victory of socialism would not change this at all. Quite irrespective of how and by whom decisions would be made—by "a delegate placed at the head of each branch of labor" or by a majority vote—"the will of the single individual will always have to subordinate itself, which means that questions are settled in an authoritarian way. . . . Wanting to abolish authority in large-scale industry is tantamount to wanting to abolish industry itself" (ibid., 377).

This says much, but still not enough, about socialism as an "association of free producers." Neither Marx nor Engels proved capable of imagining the terrible consequences of attempts to realize their utopian vision of a totally controlled economy. If such an economy were to develop in accordance with a rational, authoritative plan, it would be necessary to suppress not only individual freedom but also group freedom, and hence all forms of direct democracy, which is ironic, since the ideal of direct democracy, as embodied, for instance, in the Greek polis and other forms of "ancient society," was so close to their hearts. If unintended results were to be avoided, then control from above would have to be truly all-embracing and ruthless. If market forces, including money, were to be totally eliminated, then freedom to define individual needs through buying or not buying would have to give way to authoritarian decisions and plans on what people really needed, in what quantities, in what order, and so forth. And since such decisions always depend on the common scale of values, implementing them would not be possible without strenuous efforts to create, or impose, an intellectual and moral unanimity. The end result is only too well known.

All these consequences necessarily follow from the conception of freedom, or the precondition of freedom, as "conscious control over history," and it is precisely this conception that shaped communism as a mass movement. The ideal of the full, all-round development of human beings is rooted in the entire tradition of European humanism, but the conception of an all-embracing conscious control over man's economic activities is distinctively Marxian. The humanist ideal as such has little to do with communism, while the Marxian conception of control is embodied in the entire communist program. As a rule, rank-and-file communists did not even know that Marx, in his unfinished draft of the third volume of *Capital*, defined "the true freedom" as freedom to develop humans' higher, creative capacities; in other words, as freedom from the mundane necessities of productive labor, freedom whose realm lies "beyond the sphere of actual material production." But as long as communism was taken seriously, all communists were convinced that the basic prerequisite of communist liberation was total control over the economy—that is, the replacement of the spontaneous order of the market by conscious planning. And this was to be only the first step toward gaining total control over human beings' collective fate and thus realizing the ideal of freedom as rational collective self-mastery.

However, striving for such control always entails the striving for control over society by a minority that arrogates to itself the right to steer others. If such a minority wants to realize the utopia of "total freedom," in the sense of total control over the direction of history, it must obviously secure for itself total control over *all* spheres of social life—not only over the sphere of production, but also over nonproductive spheres as well.

S. Rainko, a Polish Marxist, formulated this logic as follows:

Socialist society is a social experiment on a macro-historical scale. This is its first and fundamental peculiarity. For the first time in the evolution of the human species, man dared to direct his global history—not only certain events in history but the entire historical process. This immediately implies two conclusions. Every experiment must be steered and organized. And every experiment must be preceded by a theory. The organizer of the socialist experiment is the party of the working class, and the theory, which guides it in this task, is Marxism-Leninism.[105]

This is precisely the point: monopolistic rule of a single party, guided by a single theory. As we shall see, Marx would not have agreed with this conclusion, but, nevertheless, this Leninist innovation harmonized perfectly with Marx's idea of rational self-determination of the human species through conscious control over man's self-objectification. Paradoxically, he saw this conception of conscious control as defining the necessary foundation of human freedom.

1.8   The Vision of the Future: The Transition Period and the Final Ideal

For many decades Marx's socialism was understood as the opposite of utopian blueprints for the future. In other words, it was believed that Marx and Engels, in contrast to utopian socialists, had no "ideal of the future"; their theory provided scientific knowledge of the inexorable laws of history, not a utopian fantasy. It was repeated endlessly that "scientific socialists" do not indulge in ahistorical thinking, do not share the eighteenth-century belief in the omnipotence of rational legislation, and do not claim to possess a ready-made vision of the future.[106] This view was, of course, powerfully endorsed by Engels in his *Socialism: Utopian and Scientific*. In comparison with this classical treatise, Marx's critique of utopian socialism was less systematic and, perhaps, less consistent as well. Nevertheless, it cannot be denied that he too strongly disliked to be seen as a "utopian," that is, as somebody committed to an a priori, ready-made ideal of the future. In his view "utopian" tendencies were deeply foreign to the mature working class. In "The Civil War in France," his analysis of the Paris Commune, he wrote: "The working class did not expect miracles from the Commune. They have no ready-made Utopias to introduce *par décret du peuple* [by decree of the people]. They know that in order to work out their own emancipation, and along with it that higher form to which present society is irresistibly tending by its own economical agencies, they will have to pass through long struggles, through a series of historic processes, transforming circumstances and men. They have no ideals to realize, but to set free the elements of the new society with which old collapsing bourgeois society itself is pregnant" (M, SW, 545).

In fact, Marx's thinking was strongly permeated by utopianism. In spite of his denials, he was committed to a definite ideal of the future. True, this ideal was not described in detail; nonetheless, it was clear enough and easily recognizable: Marx's socialism involved the abolition of commodity production and monetary exchange.[107] In other words, it was a vision of a totally marketless economy. Today this most essential truth about Marxism is not widely known, even among people who call themselves Marxists. In the West this is due either to widespread ignorance of the genuine Marxist tradition or to a fear of discrediting socialism as a workable alternative to the capitalist system.[108] In "postcommunist" countries, as well as those countries (like China or Vietnam) where Communists are still in power, enlightened and open-minded Marxists continue to do everything possible to forget the dreadful dogma of classical Marxism; even hardliners, despite their fear of the self-regulating market, have proved to be no longer interested in keeping alive the spirit of Marx's economic utopianism. But historical facts cannot be changed. We must agree with Ernest Mandel's summary of Marx's view on the nature of socialist economy:

Marx and the Marxist tradition are unambiguous on the subject: socialism, as "the first phase of communism," is characterized by the absence of commodity production. . . . For Marx and Marxists, there are only two basically different ways in which needs and resources can be balanced in any given society: either *a priori* in a conscious way (regardless of whether this is done democratically or despotically, based upon prejudice, magic rites, religion, habit, tradition, or based upon the application of science, whether it is "irrational" or "rational"); or *a posteriori* through the operation of the law of value, i.e., objective laws operating behind the backs of "economic agents." Schematically, and in the last analysis, *a priori* adaptation of social resources to social needs implies social property of the means of production and labor which is directly recognized as social labor. *A posteriori* adaptation of social resources to social needs implies private property, implies labor which is spent in the form of private labor and which is not immediately and directly recognized as social labor.[109]

This quotation enables us to gain a firm grasp of two additional aspects of the Marxian ideal of socialism: first, of its backward-looking aspect, evident in its admiration for primitive societies in which "conscious regulation" balances needs against resources in accordance with tradition, religion, or even magic rites and prejudices, and, second, its theoretical compatibility with both democracy and despotism.

Democracy in this context means, of course, not liberal democracy but a variety of collectivism strong enough to subordinate the life plans and life goals of all individuals to one collective plan and one set of collective goals. This is, in other words, the democracy described by Marx in his early essay "On the Jewish Question": a government by the people unrestricted by individual rights, offering freedom as participation but not freedom as individual autonomy. In later years in a letter to J. Weydemeyer of March 5, 1852, Marx described this form of democracy as suitable for the "dictatorship of the proletariat" (M&E, SW, 1:528). He was fairly vague in defining the latter, but Engels was right in asserting that his lifelong friend saw the first historical embodiment of this dictatorship in the Paris Commune.[110] Hence, Marx's writings on the Commune are a key to understanding his views of the transition period.

Marx criticized the Commune for insufficient revolutionary resolve but at the same time highly praised it as a form of direct participatory democracy that combined legislative and executive functions, got rid of bourgeois parliamentarianism and "the sham independence" of the judicial functionaries, and suppressed the standing army, substituting for it the armed people (M, SW, 542). He did not fail to stress that this direct form of people's rule differed profoundly from representative democracy, stressing especially its radical "deprofessionalization" of all state functions, i.e., its ability to dispense with parasitic bureaucracy. He was fond even of such archaic detail as "formal instruction" for the delegates, thus writing, for instance: "The rural communes of every district were to administer their common affairs by an assembly of delegates in the central town, and these district assemblies were again to send deputies to the National Delegation in Paris, each delegate to be at any time revocable and bound by the *mandat impératif* [formal instructions] of his constituents" (ibid., 542).

Understandably, Marx was especially enthusiastic about the Commune's efforts to abolish capitalist private property and thus transform the means of production "into mere instruments of free and associated labor." He saw these efforts as leading toward communism, because only communism could give a sound basis for a principle of cooperative production: "If cooperative production is not to remain a sham and a snare; if it is to supersede the Capitalist system; if united cooperative societies are to regulate national production upon a common plan, thus taking it under their own control, and putting an end to the constant anarchy and periodical convulsions which are the fatality of Capitalist production—what else, gentlemen, would it be but Communism, 'possible' Communism?" (ibid., 545).

But how was it possible to combine direct participatory democracy, i.e., the most decentralized and, indeed, anarchic form of decision making, with comprehensive rational planning and efficient control over production and distribution? There is no doubt that Marx's ideal was *democratic* planning, that is, planning as rational decision making based on consensus. However, it is equally indubitable that the inner logic of his idea of planned economy led him toward accepting authoritarian principles in the sphere of material production, to visualizing the society of the future as "one immense factory," and thus to the idea that the "realm of freedom" begins where labor determined by necessity ceases. In this way, in contrast to some "Western Marxists" of our century, he tended to abandon the overoptimistic view that at a certain level of general affluence, labor could be transformed into free self-activity. He stressed that human wants constantly increase and therefore exert a constant pressure on human productive activity, irrespective of the level of development of productive forces. "Just as the savage must wrestle with Nature to satisfy his wants, to maintain and reproduce life, so must civilized man, and he must do so in all social formations and under all possible modes of production. With his development this realm of physical necessity expands as a result of his wants; but, at the same time, the forces of production which satisfy these wants also increase." Thus, people will never free themselves from the severe discipline of productive labor. On the contrary, in this sphere freedom can consist only in instrumental rationality, enabling people to maximize the efficiency of their productive efforts and to bring them under conscious control. As we know, Marx readily acknowledged that this means only "freedom within the realm of necessity" and not "the true realm of freedom," i.e., "that development of human energy which is an end in itself" (M, C, 3 : 820, 820). But it is obvious that freedom as conscious control over the economy was for him *not only* a necessary means of shortening the work day and thus making room for the "true realm of freedom." He saw it also as liberating people from the rule of "blind forces" and thus as a value in itself and a foundation of the entire edifice of freedom.

If this is so, we can clearly see that Marx's view of the nature of socialist economy was not easily compatible with his ideal of communal democracy. Productivity, efficiency, and rational control can hardly be achieved through direct universal participation. Even if we assume, as Marx did, that in a classless society the interests of all people are basically the same, it does not follow that their capacity for rationally understanding these interests is also the same. Hence arises the inevitable tension between freedom as "rational, conscious control" and freedom as universal participation in decision making. On the one hand, Marx wanted the radicalization of democracy through the extension of the principle of popular sovereignty to the economic sphere; by the "dictatorship of the proletariat" he meant the hegemonic power of the working class as a whole, taking for granted its division into different parties as well as the rights of free expression, assembly, and association for the entire population.[111] On the other hand, however, there cannot be any doubt that the inner logic of the Marxian conception of freedom demanded that in the case of conflict control over the economy, as the very essence of socialism, could not be sacrificed for the sake of popular demands, since the latter, after all, might be chaotic, self-contradictory, and incompatible with economic rationality.

Another important source for the clarification of Marx's vision of the future is his *Critique of the Gotha Program*. As the most elaborate pro-grammatic document in Marx's legacy it exercised great influence on the Marxist parties of the Second International (especially on the German Social Democrats) as well as on the theory and practice of Russian com-munism. Hence, we must present and analyze its relevant fragments.

In discussing the problem of distribution in the program of the workers' party, Marx distinguished between two phases of communist society: the lower, transitional phase in which communism is "still stamped with the birth marks of the old society from whose womb it emerges," and the higher phase, embodying the communist final ideal (M&E, *SW*, 3:17). Lenin (and after him all Soviet Marxists) called the first of these phases *socialism*, reserving the name *communism* for the second (L, *SR*). For the sake of convenience we will accept this terminology.

The first phase of the new society is described by Marx as preserving inequalities that stem from the application of the bourgeois conception of "equal right" but abolishing monetary exchange, thus equating price with labor cost. In other words, it was to be a society radically curtailing the role of exchange by substituting labor certificates for money, thus elimi-nating the exploitation of workers: "The social working day consists of the sum of the individual hours of work; the individual labor time of the individual producer is the part of the social working day contributed by him, his share in it. He receives a certificate from society that he has fur-nished such and such an amount of labor (after deducting his labor for the common funds), and with this certificate he draws from the social stock of means of consumption as much as costs the same amount of labor. The same amount of labor which he has given to society in one form he receives back in another" (M&E, *SW*, 3:17–18).

The inequality arising from this arrangement is no longer class inequality but merely a reflection of the differences among individuals, or among the circumstances of their life. Nevertheless, the principle of "equal right," i.e., of applying to everyone an *equal standard*, makes these inequalities quite conspicuous. One man is superior to another physically or mentally and so supplies more labor for the same amount of time or can labor for a longer time; further, one worker is married, another not; one has more children than another; and so on and so forth. But the principle of "equal right" is blind to all these differences. Therefore, Marx reasoned, *equal* right is an unequal right for unequal labor. It recognizes no class differences, because everyone is only a worker like everyone else; but it tacitly recognizes unequal individual endowment and thus productive capacity as natural privileges. *It is, therefore, a right of inequality, in its content, like every right.* Right by its very nature can consist only in the application of an equal standard; and unequal individuals (and they would not be different individuals if they were not unequal) are measurable only by an equal standard in so far as they are brought under an equal point of view, are taken from one *definite* side only, for instance, in the present case, are regarded *only as workers* and nothing more is seen in them, everything else being ignored. (ibid., 18–19)

The same applies to different life circumstances or family situations; a single worker and a worker maintaining a big family are entitled to the same share in the social consumption fund if their labor performance is equal.

Thus, in Marx's view, communist society in its lower (socialist) phase was to remain a strictly nomocratic system, i.e., a system operating through general, abstract and formal, rules.[112] Using Hayek's terminology, we may say that it was to be a rule-bound society, and not yet an end-connected community.[113] As discussed above, for Marx, who had already in 1843 defined his ideal as "a community of human beings united for their highest aims," this was a serious defect. He thought, however, that such defects were inevitable at the early stage of communism. Right, he argued, "can never be higher than the economic structure of society and its cultural development conditioned thereby" (ibid., 19).

This sentence implies that the concept of right obtaining at the lower stage of communism, a concept "stigmatized by a bourgeois limitation" (ibid., 18) would be replaced at the higher phase of communism by a communist right that would no longer be a right of inequality. But this would clearly contradict Marx's earlier statement that *every* right is a right of inequality, since "right by its very nature can consist only in the application of an equal standard." If the defect of *every* right (and law) consists in the application of the same general rules to all people, irrespective of the differences in their individual endowments and social situations, then a right free from this defect would be a contradiction in terms.

In one of the best books on Marx's vision of communism, Stanley Moore explains this contradiction by pointing out that in Marx's *Critique of the Gotha Program*, the term *right* (*Recht*) is used in two different senses: in the sense of the general, formal rules of the civil law, and in the Hegelian sense of a "higher right," including not only general rules but also patterns of solidarity and characterizing such communities as family, on the one hand, and political state, on the other.[114] This might be partially true, but it does not contradict the traditional interpretation according to which the development of communism would entail the withering away of law. Marx was deeply influenced by the classical "*Gesellschaft* paradigm of law,"[115] which claimed that the goddess Justice must be blindfolded, that is, deliberately blind to all circumstances that cause her to deviate from treating all people as equal before the law. On the other hand, he was steeped in the socialist tradition that questioned the fairness of legal justice, saw law as such as serving the interests of the stronger, and demanded the replacement of law-based civil society with a fraternal community. Hence there can be no doubt that "higher right" of the developed communist society was, in his view, not a legal concept but a communal principle presupposing the abolition of law.

Fully developed communism was to be qualitatively different from its lower transitional phase, as Marx described it: "In a higher phase of communist society, after the enslaving subordination of the individual to the division of labor, and therewith also the antithesis between mental and physical labor, has vanished; after labor has become not only a means of life but life's prime want; after the productive forces have also increased with the all-round development of the individual, and the springs of co-operative wealth flow more abundantly—only then can the narrow horizon of bourgeois right be crossed in its entirety and society inscribe on its banners: From each according to his ability, to each according to his needs!" (ibid., 19).

Thus, to put it briefly, the common feature of both phases of communism was to be the public ownership of the means of production and the abolition of the market. This would have amounted to achieving the basic prerequisite of freedom: total control over economy, and the liberation of individuals from enslavement by their own products. But full freedom, freedom as de-alienation and equal participation by each individual in developing all the riches of humankind's communal essence, was to be achieved only in the second phase: the phase of pure communism, i.e., communism free from the birthmarks of the old society and developing "on its own foundations" (ibid., 17).

There are several points to be made about this conception. First, even the lower "socialist" phase of communist society was conceived by Marx as a marketless social system. Some elements of exchange economy were to be preserved in it, but money was to be abolished and labor certificates could not replace capital: they could not be invested, bring interest, and allow the existence of middlemen. Thus Lenin was right when he interpreted Marx as saying that the abolition of the market was to be the *first step* toward construction of communism, not its crowning achievement.

This interpretation, although fully consistent with Marx's inflexible hostility toward commerce, has been questioned by those Marxist theorists, or Marxologists, who wanted to prove that Marxist socialism did not really involve the elimination of the market. Stanley Moore supported this thesis by pointing out that in the *Manifesto of the Communist Party* Marx and Engels envisioned a different type of socialism, a socialism with a mixed economy that allowed the coexistence of different forms of property and combined planning with the market.[116] In fact, however, these more realistic ideas referred not to socialism but to the short period between the victory of the proletarian revolution and the emergence of the early phase of the new society. In his *Critique of the Gotha Program* Marx clearly distinguished this period from the first ("socialist") phase of communist society: "Between capitalist and communist society lies the period of the revolutionary transformation of the one into the other. Corresponding to this is also a political transition period in which the state can be nothing but the revolutionary dictatorship of the proletariat" (ibid., 26).

Hence, the realization of the final ideal of communism was to be preceded, in Marx's view, by *two* transition periods: a short revolutionary period of the dictatorship of the proletariat and a longer period of the first phase of communist development (i.e., the period of socialism). Marx clearly assumed, on the one hand, that the dictatorship of the proletariat could not coincide with socialism and, on the other, that socialism (unlike the dictatorship of the proletariat) would not tolerate any form of money economy and private property.

Second, there is a striking contrast between Marx's gloomy pessimism about the possibility of reforms within capitalist society and his somewhat unexpected return to an ultraoptimistic view of fully developed communism. He wanted German workers to expect no peaceful reforms and did not even sympathize with the intentions of the reformers. Thus, for instance, he resolutely opposed the idea of the prohibition of child labor: "A general prohibition of child labor," he argued, "is incompatible with the existence of large-scale industry and hence an empty, pious wish. Its realization—if it were possible—would be reactionary, since, with a strict regulation of the working time according to the different age groups and other safety measures for the protection of children, an early combination of productive labor with education, is one of the most potent means for the transformation of present-day society" (ibid., 29). However, he assumed that under fully developed communism, the existence of large-scale industry (which was to be preserved as a means of man's control over nature) would be somehow compatible not only with putting an end to the "enslaving subordination of the individual to the division of labor," but also with the full de-alienation of labor (transforming it from "only a means of life" into "life's prime want") and the complete elimination of scarcity. Such a vision contradicted his more sober conception that even under communism productive labor would remain "a realm of necessity" and that the "true realm of freedom" would be realized beyond the sphere of material production. It was much closer to Marx's youthful dreams about communism as "the solution of the riddle of history," the overcoming of all forms of alienation and the perfect realization of human species freedom.

How can this lack of consistency be explained? In attempting to answer this question, we must consider that in *Capital* (including its unfinished volumes), Marx was above all a scholar applying his critical method of historical materialism to explain the capitalist system, past and present. In his notes on the program of the German workers' party, he had to deal with the final aims of the workers' movement, and this preoccupation with the future revealed once more the utopian dimension of his thought, his deep attachment to his early communist ideal. This provides a partial explanation of his attempt to revise the ideal of communist freedom in the third volume of *Capital*, on the one hand, and his yielding to the temptation of communist utopianism in his *Critique of the Gotha Program*, on the other. But this was not merely a difference in emphasis. Despite his own conviction that his historical materialism provided a scientific basis for communism, Marx's final ideal could not be derived from historical materialism as a method and a theory of history. Moore has correctly pointed out the existence of "an unresolved tension between the principles of philosophical communism and historical materialism." He formulates this thesis more strongly by stating that "the conflict between communism and historical materialism" is "a key to the dialectic of Marxism." [117]

According to Moore, however, historical materialism did provide a scientific justification for a broadly conceived socialism: socialism as a "classless economy" in which central planning would somehow be combined with the market. In other words, Moore thinks that Marx's analysis of capitalist development substantiated his conclusion about the inevitable replacement of competitive capitalism by a system based on "co-operation and the possession in common of the land and of the means of production" (M, C, 1:715). At the same time, Moore is aware of the horrible consequences of the practical implementation of the idea of the abolition of markets and subscribes to the Eurocommunist view of the need for "a reasoned rejection of communism as a final ideal." [118] Hence he distances himself from Marx's view on the first phase of the new society expressed in *Critique of the Gotha Program*, calling attention instead to an alternative Marxist conception of socialism: a conception combining markets with planning, outlined (as he wrongly believes) in the *Manifesto of the Communist Party*. Moore also indicates that in the third volume of *Capital* (in the passage concerning the "realm of necessity" and the "realm of freedom" quoted above), Marx conceded that the trends he predicted in the development of the forces of production were insufficient in themselves to produce the transition from socialism to communism.[119] In this way the tension between Marx's communism and Marx's historical materialism was eliminated by abandoning the first in the name of the latter.

My endorsement of Moore's main thesis does not entail sharing his other views. My analyses in this book allow me to contend that historical materialism, whatever can be said about its value as a theory of history or a heuristic device, does not substantiate Marx's vision of the future *as a whole*—that is, not only his ultimate communist soteriology (end of all alienations, "true realm of freedom"), but also his belief in gaining total conscious control over the economy (i.e., the basic prerequisite of freedom, or "freedom within the realm of necessity"). Accepting Marx's "socialism" while rejecting his final ideal would not lead us very far, because the idea of total rational control over the spontaneity of life, involving in the first place the abolition, or at least the severe restriction, of all exchange, was fundamental for his entire vision of the future, both in its "lower" and "higher" phases. But, happily, this idea cannot be logically derived from historical materialism, for very simple reasons. Historical materialism deals with historical processes as made, but not designed, by humans. In other words, it is a theory of the unintended results of human actions—that is, of creating history within the structure of alienation,[120] without the possibility of controlling its course, predicting its outcome, or, least of all, directing it toward a consciously chosen collective aim. In contrast with this, Marx's theory of communism (including "socialism" as its "lower phase") presupposes the conscious steering of historical processes—that is, the creation of history on the basis of rational knowledge and in accordance with freely chosen aims, as an expression of the innermost essence of our common human nature. This theory assumes, therefore, that consciousness would no longer be determined by life, that human beings would be not only actors in but also authors of their history. Hence, Marx's theory of communism was in fact radically separated from his historical materialism and could be interpreted as a promise that the so-called objective laws of economic development dealt with by the latter would cease to exist in the future. This is what Lukács had in mind when he described historical materialism in its classical form as *"the self-knowledge of capitalist society"*—that is, as the theoretical explanation of man's enslavement by things and not a theory of communist liberation.[121]

If so, how to explain Marx's stubborn lifelong commitment to the communist ideal? Moore thinks that it had nothing to do with Marx's views on history and can be explained only "in terms of the superiority of communism as an ideal of distributive justice."[122] We know, however, how contemptuous Marx was toward the moralizing, ahistorical notions of "fair distribution," "equal right," and other "obsolete verbal rubbish" (M&E, SW, 3:19). We cannot doubt that he was a "historicist" in the sense of interpreting everything in the light of his general conception of history. But his general all-embracing interpretation should not be identified with the theory of historical development provided by historical materialism. That is why, in preliminary remarks, I have carefully distinguished between Marx's historical materialism and his all-embracing historiosophy founded on the ancient myth of self-enriching alienation and culminating in the vision of communism as human beings' earthly salvation. Historical materialism deals only with the second act of humans' historical drama, with the story of their development *in* alienation and *through* alienation. In contrast with this, Marx's conception, or vision, of communism concerns the third and final act of this drama: the story of humanity's de-alienation and reintegration. These two stories were structurally interrelated as parts of the great underlying myth, but they were not parts of a single scientific theory.

Of course, Marx was not aware of this fact, which explains many of his incorrect prophecies, as well as his inconsistencies and hesitations. The same applies to most of his followers. From the vantage point of the present time, the paradoxical duality of Marx's intellectual legacy can clearly be seen. On the one hand, it was the main source of communist mythology, including its worst manifestations; on the other hand, however, it proved able to inspire many great minds in the social sciences and to provide students of social theory with an instrument of critical analysis, destroying all illusions of consciousness, including communism. For a long time historical materialism was used as a scientific legitimization of communists' claims to monopolistic leadership and ideological infallibility; at the same time, nonetheless, it provided an intrasystemic "revisionist" opposition to communist rule, providing ready-made intellectual tools for a critical analysis and disowning of the system. The collapse of communism, or rather, of "actually existing socialism," can easily be explained in Marxist terms. No such explanation, however, would be honest without showing the fundamental flaws of Marx's theory of communism or without defining Marx's share of responsibility for the consequences of the well-known attempts at the practical implementation of the theory.

1.9   Capitalism and Freedom in the Post-Marxian Sociological Tradition: The Case of Marx Versus Simmel

The proposed distinction between Marxism as historical materialism and Marxism as historiosophical soteriology has a typological nature and thus can rarely be drawn with precision and clarity. Most of Marx's works belong to both types of Marxism, and no clear line divides one from another. This is particularly true of Marx's conception of the relationship between capitalism and freedom, which was one of the central themes both in Marxian "materialist" analysis of capitalist development and in his mythological scheme of development through alienation. Hence this theme contains both social science and gnostic mythology. As a theorist of communism, Marx interpreted the first in the light of the second, but it is perfectly possible to refrain from following his example and instead present and evaluate his views on capitalism and freedom without linking them to his mythological vision of the future. In doing this we should try to disentangle Marx's contributions to sociological knowledge from his value judgments.

The experience of our times has made it clear that there is no reason to believe that any form of comprehensive planning would prove superior to developed market economies in increasing the productivity of labor and thereby enabling people to shorten their work day. It is equally evident that comprehensive planning as such is intrinsically incompatible with both individual freedom and the complexity of culture. The more perfect the model of such planning, the less room it leaves for individual life plans and pursuit of happiness. And, of course, it is quite obvious that people living under "actually existing socialism" did not perceive planning as an embodiment of rationality and a remedy against alienation. On the contrary, they perceived the constraints created by planning and other forms of "conscious control" over the economy as deriving from arbitrary decisions and therefore as more irritating and humiliating than objective dependence on the anonymous forces of the market.

Marx, however, saw the problem of "men's dependence on other men" versus "men's dependence on things" in a completely different way. In his view, the worst form of dehumanization, hence of unfreedom, was dependence on things, not dependence on the will of other people; hence, he did not hesitate to state that the reified human relationships characteristic of capitalism were more destructive of freedom than were different forms of personal dependence in precapitalist social formations (see the discussion above in section 6). Taking into account all the cruel restrictions on human freedom that obtained under feudalism or in "the ancient society," this was indeed a very bold and provocative claim. Such a claim could have been made only by a man for whom it was utterly important to belie the liberal conception of freedom as embellishing capitalism and thereby serving the interests of bourgeois exploiters, a man who wanted at all costs, even at the expense of simple common sense, to define freedom differently, not only as in opposition to coercive commands or prohibitions, but also, above all, as in opposition to the blind force of things and reified (*sachlicher*) human relationships, as embodied in the quasi-natural mechanism of the capitalist market. This was precisely the case with Marx, his scale of values, and his political aims. No wonder, then, that subordination to the conscious and rational decisions of the planning authorities, acting in the name of all humans as "species beings," was for him a form of promoting the cause of human freedom, while subordination to self-regulating market forces, symbolized by money, represented nothing less than the utter degradation of human beings as free, conscious agents. From this point of view capitalism, the most developed form of the monetary exchange economy, appeared especially destructive of human freedom. This was so because the world of universal objective dependence created by capitalism reduced human beings, including members of the ruling class, to mere puppets who were ruled by their own products and who accepted this humiliating state of affairs as their fate (M, G, 158).

There is a certain logic and truth to this view, but there is also a certain blindness and a complete inability to see the other side of the coin. To render justice to this other side, it is useful to compare Marx's view of the relationship between capitalism and freedom with the relevant views of some post-Marxian classics of sociology. Such a comparison, or confrontation, is only natural. After all, classical sociology focused on the same problems as did Marx. According to Jürgen Habermas, "Sociology arose as the theory of bourgeois society: to it fell the task of explaining the course of the capitalist modernization of traditional societies and its anomic side effects." [123] These words help us see Marx's role in originating the classical sociological tradition. It was he who produced the first and most influential theory of bourgeois society and bourgeois progress. The constant return to the problems that were raised and defined by him showed remarkable evidence of continuity in the classical sociological tradition. But precisely because of this, his theory of capitalism should not be analyzed merely on its own terms, in isolation from later theories that deal with the same problems and arrive at different conclusions.

Of course, a detailed comparative study of the problem of capitalism and freedom in Marx and in post-Marxian sociological tradition is a theme for a separate, full-length book. In the present context I can only provide a brief illustration of the thesis that some central "Marxian problems" can be seen in a very different perspective and that their analysis can lead to very different results.

Marx believed that the main causes of the extreme human alienation in developed capitalist societies inhered in the division of labor, which destroyed the "wholeness" of human beings, and in commodity production, which imposed on humans the tyranny of an alien entity—money. The first of these causes has been dealt with by Emile Durkheim in his classic work *The Division of Labor in Society*; the second has been analyzed in depth by Simmel in *The Philosophy of Money*. Both of these thinkers differed from Marx by being much more sensitive to the problem of individual freedom. This difference in their scale of values led them to conclusions that radically undermined Marx's gloomy view of the fate of human freedom in the capitalist system.

Marx's distinction between "relations of personal dependence" and "personal independence founded on *objective* dependence" (ibid.), which were characteristic, respectively, of precapitalist and capitalist societies, is paralleled by Durkheim's distinction between "mechanical" and "organic" (functional) social solidarity. Mechanical solidarity characterizes societies in which the division of labor is not developed, whose members are therefore undifferentiated, and whose cohesion is secured by a mandatory set of beliefs and severe punishments for all deviations from accepted standards. The absence, or underdevelopment, of the social division of labor forces the members of such societies to be multifunctional, to develop their capacities in all directions, which makes them "all-round" (though they do not excel in any specialized activity) and hence similar to each other; owing to this, their solidarity is based on likeness, on identical ways of life and ideological unanimity. Under such conditions individual freedom is neither possible nor required. It is impossible because of strict collective supervision over individual conduct; it is nonrequired because, as a rule, the scope of individual consciousness is identical with that of collective consciousness, so that ideological conformity is felt as natural and individual deviations are too rare and too weak to create a need for institutionalized pluralism. In contrast to this, "organic solidarity," based on functional interdependence created by the division of labor, minimizes the need for social supervision and uniform collective consciousness. Social cohesion stemming from homogeneity and conformity is replaced by the natural complementarity of specialized functions, which creates room for pluralism, for individual autonomy, for individualization and rationalization of consciousness, both intellectual and moral. In other words, capitalist modernization is not destructive of individual freedom (as Marx thought) but creates conditions for its emergence.

Durkheim was fully aware of the problems raised by Marx. He readily conceded that the modern "organic" form of solidarity makes human relations mediated by things and deprives these relations of moral content and common purpose. He was also aware that freedom as individualization, i.e., freedom to be different, to develop in a chosen direction, is in conflict with developing in all directions and thereby becoming a "complete human being, one quite sufficient unto himself."[124] His criticism of solidarity based on the division of labor was often reminiscent of Marx's diatribes against egoistic individuals under the rule of things. Thus, for instance, he wrote:

We see what this real solidarity consists of; it directly links things to persons, but not persons among themselves. . . . Consequently, since it is only through the medium of persons that things are integrated in society, the solidarity resulting from this integration is wholly negative. It does not lead wills to move towards common ends, but merely makes things gravitate around wills in orderly fashion.

Because real rights are thus limited, they do not cause conflicts; hostility is precluded but there is no active coming together, no consensus. Suppose an agreement of this kind were as perfect as possible; the society in which it exists—if it exists alone—will resemble an immense constellation where each star moves in its orbit without concern for the movement of neighboring stars. Such solidarity does not make the elements that it relates at all capable of acting together; it contributes nothing to the unity of the social body.[125]

In spite of many such strictures, Durkheim, in contrast to Marx, did not try to deny that transition from tradition-based societies to capitalism brings about an immense increase in individual freedom. He was concerned that liberation from all restraints might be destructive of society, but he nevertheless treated individual freedom as a separate autonomous value and did not contribute to terminological confusion by identifying freedom with other values, such as moral consensus, social integration, and so forth. Unlike Marx, he did not confuse the problem of freedom with that of alienation and therefore did not equate the increase of alienation with the reduction of freedom. Therefore he had no doubts that individuals are freer when (to use Marx's words) "the social connection between persons is transformed into a social relation between things" (ibid., 157). Durkheim stressed that functional interdependence, originating in the highly developed division of labor, minimizes the rule of coercion in social life and liberates individuals from subordination to the collective conscience and consciousness. The problem of alienation was not thereby ignored; in fact, Durkheim devoted much attention to it and was greatly concerned with its negative consequences for social life. At the same time, however, a certain degree of alienation was, in his eyes, a necessary price for individual freedom.

A comparison of the philosophies of money put forth by Marx and Simmel is even more instructive. Simmel's views are symmetrically opposite to those of Marx: his analysis is parallel to Marx's presentation of the transition from personal dependence to objective dependence, but his value judgments, and consequently his conclusions concerning freedom, are completely different. Peter L. Berger commented on this as follows: "In an ingenuous reversal of the Marxian view of money as an instrument of 'reifying' oppression, Simmel argued that the very abstraction of money (which becomes generalized in a money economy) frees the individual from the bondage of concrete social allegiances. . . . This meant liberation, socially, and economically, and, eventually, politically as well."[126]

It is illustrative to compare the relevant views of the two thinkers in some detail. While Marx saw money as the loathsome symbol of universal alienation and enslavement by things, Simmel concentrated on showing the immense role of monetary exchange in winning and securing individual freedom. Subordination to individual personalities, he reasoned, is always much worse than subordination to a strictly objective organization.[127] The growth of individual freedom in history can be measured by the increasing depersonalization of human obligations. Direct slavery is the most personal and most complete form of dependence. The bondsman, who owes the master specific services limited in time, is freer than the slave but less free than the manorial serf, who owes the landlord payment in kind; the latter is less free than the peasant, who can replace payment in kind with money payment. This is so because payment in kind is still a form of personal bondage, while money payment is "the form most congruent with personal freedom." "The lord of the manor who can demand a quantity of beer or poultry or honey from a serf thereby determines the activity of the latter in a certain direction. But the moment he imposes merely a money levy the peasant is free, insofar as he can decide whether to keep bees or cattle or anything else."[128] The replacement of natural services by monetary payments is an increase of freedom for both sides, since a person receiving capital has a much greater freedom of choice than a person entitled to specific personal services.[129] Thus, it is precisely the abstract, impersonal quality of money, as well as its "magic" capacity to change everything into everything, that makes the money economy a powerful factor for personal liberation.

Like exchange in general, Simmel continues, monetary exchange does not necessarily mean taking something away; there are cases similar to intellectual exchange in which "each is mutually and equally enriched by the others." This greatly reduces the human tragedy of competition. In contrast to simple taking away or giving, exchange presupposes "an objective appraisal, consideration, mutual acknowledgement."[130] Exchange is a wonderful means for combining justice with changes in ownership and its aims are best served by money, a means of exchange characterized by divisibility and unlimited convertibility.[131] Owing to this, a "money economy is able to increase individual liberty to its fullest extent, that is, to release it from that primary form of social values in which one person has to be deprived of what the other receives."[132]

Simmel was, of course, fully aware that the developed money economy develops our needs and therefore greatly and constantly increases our mutual dependence. "Compared with modern man," he wrote, "the member of a traditional or primitive economy is dependent only upon a minimum of other persons."[133] He stressed, however, that dependence on many makes room for independence. In the market economy human dependence, or rather interdependence, is greater in scope but looser and, above all, depersonalized:

While at an earlier stage man paid for the smaller number of his dependencies with the narrowness of personal relations, often with their personal irreplaceability, we are compensated for the great quantity of our dependencies by the indifference towards the respective persons and by our liberty to change them at will. And even though we are much more dependent on the whole of society through the complexity of our needs on the one hand, and the specialization of our abilities on the other, than are primitive people who could make their way through life with their very narrow isolated group, we are remarkably independent of every *specific* member of this society. . . . This is the most favorable situation for bringing about inner independence, the feeling of individual self-sufficiency.[134]

This independence should not be confused with indifference and isolation; it involves distance but not complete alienation from each other: "If every human relationship consists of elements of closeness and distance, then independence signifies that distance has reached a maximum, but the elements of attraction can just as little disappear altogether as can the concept of 'left' exist without that of 'right.'"[135]

As we can see, in all of these points Simmel's standpoint is diametrically and symmetrically opposite to that of Marx. While Simmel shared the classical liberal view that the worst form of unfreedom is the personal dependence characteristic of precapitalist formations, Marx thought that the worst enslavement of the human species, as collective subject, occurs with the objectification and reification of human relationships brought about by capitalism. Thus, for Simmel depersonalization meant freedom, while for Marx it meant suppression of freedom. Consequently, Simmel welcomed the money economy as promoting personal liberation, as increasing the freedom of both the obliger and the obligee, while for Marx money symbolized mutual alienation and enslavement, the destruction of communal ties and the replacement of these by universal mutual dependence. Simmel readily agreed that the money economy increases the scope of mutual dependence but stressed that this dependence is looser and objectified, thus making more room for individual freedom. Marx did not really appreciate the increase of individual mobility and choice resulting from the marketization of the economy; rather, he saw these as making individuals more dependent on mere chance and stressed that the capitalist world market develops at the cost of the fragmentation and subjugation of individuals. True, he treated this as a necessary and ultimately beneficial process, but dialectical reasoning, which supported this conclusion, did not affect his adamant hostility toward the free exchange of commodities: in his view, "universal intercourse" in the world market would create the material conditions for universal liberation, but this final positive result would be achieved *only* after the abolition of the monetary exchange economy and its replacement by "directly social production." For Simmel, money transactions involved mutual acknowledgment as independent subjects; for Marx, they symbolized subjugation to blind quasi-natural forces. What Simmel appreciated as interpersonal distance, which diminished collective pressure and thereby created space for individual freedom, Marx saw as mutual estrangement, which transformed human beings into isolated egoists and thus alienated them from their human nature. And if, in Simmel's estimation, "freedom means living according to one's own nature"[136] (a definition Marx would have been able to accept), then alienation from human nature amounts, of course, to the loss of freedom.

The main difference between Marx and Simmel, as far as the problem of freedom is concerned, boils down to their different assessments of the role and meaning of reification and of human dependence on things in general. Like Marx, Simmel paid much attention to the processes of objectification and reification but, in contrast to Marx, he treated them as furthering the cause of freedom. He wrote about this as follows:

Thus we can observe the distinctive parallel movement during the last three hundred years, namely on the one hand the laws of nature, the material order of things, the objective necessity of events emerge more clearly and distinctly, while on the other we see the emphasis upon the independent individuality, upon personal freedom, upon independence [Fürsichsein] in relation to all external and natural forces becoming more and more acute and increasingly stronger. . . . Individual freedom grows to the extent that nature becomes more objective and more real for us and displays the peculiarities of its own order so that this freedom increases with the objectification and depersonalization of the economic universe.[137]

Equally important is the difference between how Marx and Simmel conceived of the role of money in changing the relationship between people and their property. Marx distinguished between capitalist private property and the property of immediate producers, which is based on personal labor and therefore constitutes, as it were, an extension of human beings. From this point of view it was natural to see the development of the money economy as bringing about the dehumanization of property, the expropriation of direct producers, and the alienation of laborers from their products. Simmel saw money in a different light: he thought that money should be credited with making owners *independent of their property*, thereby freeing them from exclusive preoccupation with it. Possessing a garden or a farm makes owners dependent on their property, while possessing money makes them free to do whatever they want. Similarly, "humanized" and "personalized" possession of specific objects determines the consciousness of owners to a much greater extent than does possession of something abstract, impersonal, and easily convertible. In this context Simmel directly referred to "Marx's question of whether the consciousness of men determines their being or their being determines their consciousness." His answer to this question was: "The more fundamentally and intensively the possession is really owned, that is made useful and enjoyed, then the more distinct and determining will be the effects upon the internal and external nature of the subjects. Thus there is a chain from being to having and from having back to being." Money dissolves this dependency on things. In other words, the possession of money creates the possibility of "the independence of being from possessing and of possessing from being," thus increasing human freedom in relation to the world of things.[138]

Simmel's philosophy of money also develops the idea of a causal relationship between the development of the money economy and the rise of modern rationalism. Money, he argued, "is concerned only with what is common to all, i.e., with the exchange value which reduces all quality and individuality to a purely quantitative level." The same is true of rationalism, and because of this the "money economy and the domination of the intellect stand in the closest relationship to one another."[139] As a representative of *Lebensphilosophie*, which was deeply concerned with the fate of the irrational qualitative elements of human life, Simmel deplored this development; as an intellectual, however, he welcomed it and described it as an increase of freedom. As is known, similar problems are dealt with in Weber's theory of the development of Western rationalism, a theory that stresses not only monetary exchange but also progressive bureaucratization, seeing the future in terms of an "iron cage" with little place for individual freedom. This pessimism concerning the fate of freedom in "rationalized" industrial societies deeply influenced the "Western Marxists" who, following Georg Lukács, tried to identify Weber's "rationalization" with Marx's "reification."[140] But Marx's theory of reification was leveled, first of all, against commodity production—that is, against the market economy—and by no means against the idea of rational regulation of all spheres of life (i.e., not against rationalization in Weber's sense). Unlike the thinkers of the Frankfurt school, Marx protested against reification while remaining faithful to the tradition of Western rationalism. He accused capitalism of *insufficiently* rationalizing social life and allotted to socialism the mission of bringing the process of rationalization to its logical end through the elimination of the money economy and the transformation of society into one economic subject, one immense factory. The idea of conscious rational control was, in his eyes, a remedy *against* reification. He failed, however, to explain how such control could be exercised by "freely associated producers" and how it was possible to save "rational control" from degenerating into "bureaucratic control." And, of course, he failed to understand that a deliberate wholesale rationalization of socioeconomic life would ultimately prove fatal for human reason itself. Like other rationalists, he stubbornly insisted that "the use of reason aims at control and predictability" without realizing that "the process of the advance of reason rests on freedom and the unpredictability of human action." His commitment to communism made him unable to see that "for advance to take place, the social process from which the growth of reason emerges must remain free from its control."[141]

The preceding quoted words belong to Hayek, but they aptly summarize what seems to be the common ground of Simmel's liberalism and his *Lebensphilosophie*. Both as a liberal and as a "philosopher of life," Simmel defended the spontaneity of life against rational bureaucratic regulations. His spirited defense of the money economy, and of free exchange in general, was an important part of this strategy.

It should be stressed that Simmel did not ignore the Marxian problematic of people's changing relationship to their products, and he never tried to deny the importance of alienation and reification. On the contrary, Marx's analysis of the capitalist factory as developing the productive capacities of humankind at the cost of individual laborers was seen by Simmel as a peculiar case of a more general phenomenon he called "the tragedy of culture." He described this tragedy as a situation in which subjective culture (i.e., cultural development of individual persons) cannot reach the level of objective culture—that is, the objectified cultural world created by humans but no longer controlled by them,[142] a world in which human products have become alienated from individual human beings and too complex to be absorbed by them, in which these products take on a life of their own and are capable of developing in separation from, or even at the expense of, subjective culture. But Simmel did not follow Marx's dreams about the reabsorption, or reappropriation, of humankind's alienated riches. Alienation was for Simmel a part of the human condition, a necessary price to be paid for the complexity of civilization and culture as well as for individual freedom. From his point of view, Marx's vision of a "directly socialized production"—that is, of a marketless economy in which human relationships would become simple and transparent—was a backward-looking utopia, an impossible dream about returning (on a "higher level," to be sure) to the simplicity of a natural economy. And, of course, Simmel had to regard such a vision as deeply inimical to individual freedom.

The contrast between the views of Marx and Simmel, which is sharpest in their respective theories of the relationship between freedom and monetary exchange, stems ultimately from their different value judgments about what constitutes the greatest violation of freedom: personal dependence or objective dependence, imposition of alien arbitrary will or domination by things, which prevents people from controlling their collective fate. Historical experience, as well as empirical studies of social psychology, provide many arguments in favor of Simmel's judgment. It is not necessary to involve, in this connection, the totalitarian temptation inherent in the Marxian conception of freedom or the testimony of those who have experienced totalitarian tyranny. Hatred of personal dependence, of being directed by others, the greater readiness to accept objective, or quasi-objective, necessity than to be obedient to arbitrary prohibitions and commands is, at a certain level of development, a universal human phenomenon. In the patriarchal conditions of a premodern society, personal dependence may be acceptable or even sought after, but movement toward individualization and rationalization of consciousness makes such dependence irrevocably and increasingly incompatible with the experience of freedom. To deny this universal truth would have amounted to a deliberate challenge to common sense—not the trivial common sense so much despised by the disciples of Hegel, but common sense as the accumulated experience of humankind.

Does it follow that Marx's conception of freedom should be dismissed as entirely false and irrelevant? I do not think so. There is some truth in Lukes's view that this conception "cannot be ignored by those who profess to take liberty seriously."[143] As a historical account of different sources of unfreedom, it identifies a number of problems of crucial importance for the understanding of modernity. The linkage of this conception to the image of communist utopia often resulted in a very biased, one-sided interpretation of these problems, but even so (as Simmel's case clearly shows) it is usually possible to make use of its findings in a different theoretical and axiological framework. Anyhow, it can safely be said that it is only superficial knowledge of Marx's theory of freedom that makes it really dangerous for liberal democratic values. A deeper and more comprehensive analysis of this theory's content, especially in the light of its historical fate, should rather bring about a better understanding of the merits, as well as a more profound self-awareness, of its main historical opponent—the liberal tradition.

Even the most resolute rejection of Marx's conception of freedom as a feasible alternative to liberalism does not justify a nihilistic attitude toward Marx's intellectual legacy. It would be difficult to deny that Marx's historical materialism contains many profound, critical insights into the nature of modern industrial societies that enjoy the benefits of political freedom and a developed market economy. In such societies ignorance of Marxism, including Marx's theory of freedom, would amount to a dangerous complacency, although uncritical acceptance of Marxist ideas would certainly lead to even more dangerous results. Hence, it is understandable that many nonconformist Western intellectuals see in Marxism above all a humanist ideal of man as a real "master of his fate" and a powerful source of inspiration for the critique of reified social conditions. But even more understandable is the fact that under the repressive regimes of "actually existing socialism," the nonconformist intellectuals of East-Central Europe were inclined to see Marxism mainly as an instrument of ideological oppression, as legitimizing power exercised without popular will, and as providing an argument for the suppression of political and economic freedom.

It has often been said that liberalism is a "Eurocentric" doctrine, abso-lutizing some Western ideas and totally irrelevant for the rest of the world. There may be some truth in this, if liberalism is understood as an ideology justifying a certain strategy of economic development—a strategy that has proved successful in the West but has failed, as yet, to produce similar re-sults elsewhere. But even so, it does not follow that the liberal conception of freedom is suitable only for the West. On the contrary, it is especially needed in those countries that have begun to modernize their economies under the auspices of authoritarian or totalitarian governments. It would be truly arrogant to claim that liberalism is good only for wealthy West-erners. Arguably, the reverse is true: as a conception of freedom, liberalism is of universal significance, while the relevance of the Marxist conception is limited to the democratic and affluent countries of the West.[144] In other words, Marx's critique of the limitations of liberal democracy may serve as a freedom-increasing force mostly, if not exclusively, in affluent liberal democratic countries—that is, countries in which the liberal conception of freedom is firmly entrenched and that for this reason can *afford* to criticize its shortcomings. These shortcomings are sometimes very real, and there-fore the legitimacy of "Western Marxism" as a current of thought is beyond question. But "Western Marxists" should be aware that *uncritical* use of Marx's ideas, under the comfortable shelter of liberal democracy, as a rule amounts to a selfish, short-sighted indulgence in political and intellectual irresponsibility.

2

Engels and "Scientific Socialism"

2.1 The Problem of "Engelsian Marxism"

My reconstruction of Marx's philosophy of freedom has been based mostly on his early essay "On the Jewish Question," his *Economic and Philosophic Manuscripts*, *The German Ideology*, *Grundrisse*, and, of course, *Capital*. The first of these texts, published in 1844, was little known in the period of the Second International, while the other three were, at that point, completely unknown: their publication took place only in the years 1927–32, and their influence came to be felt only after World War II. Thus, they did not belong to the classical canon of Marxist texts that was established in the "Golden Age" of Marxism.[1] The greatest Marxist thinkers of that time—the generation of "classical Marxists"—knew Marx mostly as the author of *Capital*, but the philosophical content of this work could not be discovered, let along properly understood, without Marx's philosophy of human alienation as presented in his earlier works. The "classical Marxists" did not know such terms as *alienation* or *reification* and did not suspect that Marxism contained in itself the old mythical story of self-enriching alienation—that is, the story of paradise lost and paradise regained.

Many "classical Marxists" were not greatly interested in philosophy; neither were they aware of Marx's deep roots in classical German idealism. For them, Marx was not a philosopher but a great economist, a theorist of capitalist development and a master of class analysis who provided the workers' movement with a solid scientific foundation, who predicted and guaranteed the movement's future victory. This gave them a deep feeling of participation in a great and meaningful historical process, as well as an illusionary certainty of possessing a faultless guide for action. As a rule, nothing more was required. The fateful tendency to transform Marxism into an all-embracing philosophical worldview was by then only beginning. Its chief representative was Marx's lifelong friend and collaborator Friedrich Engels,[2] who after Marx's death became universally recognized as the greatest theorist within the Marxist movement. It was he who established the central tradition in interpreting Marxism, giving it the names "historical materialism" and "scientific socialism." He was less successful in his attempts to provide Marxism with an ontological foundation in terms of Hegelianized, dialectically interpreted materialism. This was not surprising, since in the last decades of the nineteenth century, everything associated with Hegelianism was felt, at least in Germany and in East-Central Europe, to be philosophically obsolete and difficult to combine with the dominant spirit of naturalistic scientism. Nonetheless, even this aspect of Engelsian Marxism was embraced, codified, and further developed by Plekhanov, the "father of Russian Marxism," who made the adherence to "dialectical materialism" a necessary condition of being a "true Marxist." This view of Marxist "orthodoxy" was taken up by Lenin and Stalin and became a distinctive feature of Soviet Marxism-Leninism.

But let us return to Marxism's Golden Age. It is no exaggeration to say that Engels was by then a more important and influential Marxist theorist than Marx himself. It was Engels who wrote "the most influential works in the Marxist tradition"[3]—*Anti-Dühring, Socialism: Utopian and Scientific*, and *Ludwig Feuerbach and the End of Classical German Philosophy*. A *Dictionary of Marxist Thought* reminds us that these works, including also *The Origin of the Family, Private Property and the State*, "consolidated his [Engels's] position as a philosopher of even greater importance than Marx during the epoch of the Second International."[4] In the most comprehensive history of Marxism, we read that "along with *Capital*, these works are the basic source from which three or four generations of readers have imbibed their knowledge of scientific socialism and its philosophical background."[5] In another classical work on Marxism, the historical role of Engels's main works is assessed as even greater than the role of *Capital*: "It was from them, rather than from *Capital* (not to mention Marx's early writings, which were still largely unknown), that most Socialists drew their mental picture of the world."[6]

If so, it is arguable that, regardless of their inherent *philosophical* value, the *historical* importance of Engels's works was greater than that of Marx's. It is also legitimate to ask why contemporary historians of Marxism, including Kolakowski, have tended to neglect Engels and instead stress the importance of Marx's early works. Such neglect might be justified philosophically, but not historically. From the historical point of view, the opposite standpoint (i.e., that emphasizing the importance of Engel's ideas) is certainly more justified. After all, Engels's works, his interpretation of Marxism, inspired powerful revolutionary movements, while the reception of the ideas of young Marx cannot lay claim to a comparable world historical significance.

A deliberate de-emphasizing, or even an ostentatious ignoring, of Engels's contribution to Marxism has become a distinctive feature of so-called Western Marxism. Perry Anderson has rightly observed that "Western Marxism, in fact, was to start with a decisive double rejection of Engels's philosophical heritage—by Korsch and Lukács, in *Marxism and Philosophy* and *History and Class Consciousness* respectively. Thereafter, aversion to the later texts of Engels was to be common to virtually all currents within it, from Sartre to Colletti, and Althusser to Marcuse." [7] In most cases, the reasons for this were quite evident. It was necessary to rescue Marxist philosophy from becoming monopolized by Soviet philosophers who, relying heavily on Engels, transformed it into a hopelessly schematic and philosophically obsolete "dialectical materialism." The awareness of the growing irrelevance of "classical" Marxism, coupled with the increasing evidence of the philosophical poverty and totalitarian character of Marxism-Leninism, worked against Engels, since he was made responsible for both forms of Marxist orthodoxy: the old orthodoxy of prewar German Social Democracy and the new orthodoxy of Soviet Marxism. Paradoxically, Marx himself was in a much better position. He was not a popularizer, and to all those who defined themselves as Marxists, he was known for his critical distance. Above all, however, the publication of his previously unknown early writings threw a new light on his oeuvre, showing him to be a sophisticated philosopher whose ideas had not been fully assimilated (and thereby compromised) by the hitherto existing forms of the communist movement. This made it possible to claim that he had been misunderstood and thus not responsible for the practical consequences of his teaching—that his ideas, properly interpreted, could still serve the cause of individual freedom. In fact, this was not the case, since Marx's theories contained only a more sophisticated philosophical justification of communist utopianism. Nevertheless, in 1956 (the year of Khrushchev's "secret speech" on the crimes of Stalin) this unjustified hope was alive in both parts of artificially divided Europe. The young Marx was then the source of inspiration for Eastern European revisionist Marxists (among them Kolakowski) and Western intellectuals who wanted to remain faithful to Marxism. In their view, Marx had presented an unsurpassed philosophical critique of capitalist civilization. It was thus significant and symbolic that the intellectual excitement of the Polish "thaw" of 1955–56 reached Paris, causing Sartre to publish the first version of his essay "Existentialism and Marxism" in the 1957 issue of the Polish monthly *Twórczość*.[8]

In later years, this situation changed. In Eastern Europe, the Marxist revisionists of 1956 had, as a rule, ceased to regard themselves as Marxists.[9] As Marxism itself came to be seen as discredited and irrelevant, the newer forms of revisionism became of marginal importance. Even the ruling parties no longer treated Marxism very seriously, paying lip service to it but, in fact, abandoning more and more of its dogma. Meanwhile, in the West, Marxism won recognition as a respectable, internally differentiated current in academic philosophy and historiography (although characteristically it became greatly weakened in what was formerly its central field: economic theory).[10] Its Western representatives developed Marxism in all possible directions, which was greatly facilitated by, among other things, the unfinished and somewhat ambiguous character of Marx's thought. The Engelsian account of Marxism, irrespective of its obvious dependence on the Victorian spirit or its importance for repressive Soviet orthodoxy, was too clear-cut, authoritative, and all-embracing and left too little room for interpretive ingenuity. Hence, it is understandable that it was not attractive to Western Marxists. But this is, of course, no reason for neglecting it in historical studies, in attempts to understand the appeal, the mobilizing force, and the different functions and consequences—both intended and unintended—of Marxism as a "New Faith,"[11] in the disguise of "scientific socialism."

By saying this, I do not intend to propose a return to the naive view that Marx and Engels were completely single-minded, that they were the proverbial "one spirit in two bodies." On the contrary, I share the view that Engels's works should be published and studied separately from Marx's and that the differences between their respective ideas (even if they themselves were not aware of them) are crucially important for understanding the further development of Marxism. It was probably not accidental that Engels's doctrines were better suited for shaping certain aspects of Soviet Marxism, while Marx's ideas, as expressed in his total oeuvre, proved capable of exercising influence on Western intellectuals of the late twentieth century, even in the Anglo-Saxon countries, which have not produced Marxist-inspired workers' movements.

Although a detailed analysis of the intellectual relationship between Marx and Engels does not fall within the scope of this book, a brief introduction to this complicated issue seems necessary for a proper reconstruction of Marx and Engels's conception, or conceptions, of freedom.

The naive view of the virtual identity of these two thinkers was something an overwhelming majority of Marxists held for an amazingly long time. It has been suggested that Engels himself was instrumental in bringing about this assumption. His ostentatious modesty in defining his own contribution to what he called "scientific socialism" served to conceal views that could not be found in Marx; he thus used Marx's authority to endorse some of his own favorite ideas.[12] If this is the case, Engels's practice of actively shaping the content of Marxism in the name of Marx was extremely clever and extraordinarily successful. How complete this success was can be seen from the following statement by Trotsky: "Marx and Engels were bound together by forty years of titanic mental labor. The most informed and penetrating students of Marxism, like Ryazanov, have been unable—for it is unthinkable in general—to conclusively establish the line of demarcation between their creative work."[13]

The discovery of some essential differences between Marx and Engels is usually attributed to Lukács, the great Hungarian Marxist, whose "heretical" book of 1923, History and Class Consciousness (Geschichte und Klassenbewusstsein), has been described as the main source of the "Western Marxism Paradigm," the "fons et origo" of Western Marxist thought.[14] In fact, direct references to Engels are rather rare in this book, and thus Lukács's critique of Engels remains hidden rather than explicit. According to Lukács, Engels, the author of Anti-Dühring, failed to properly understand Marxian dialectics and the Marxian conception of praxis. He contrasted dialectical interaction with rigid causality, but did not even mention "the most vital interaction, namely the dialectical relation between subject and object in historical process." For Lukács such an oversight implied "a failure to recognize that in all metaphysics the object remains untouched and unaltered so that thought remains contemplative and fails to become practical." In another chapter, Lukács accused Engels of misinterpreting both Hegel and Marx by ignoring the active role of the subject, instead seeing the process of acquiring knowledge as a passive contemplation by an external onlooker. This amounted, in Lukács's view, to a complete misunderstanding of the epistemological implications of the Marxian conception of historical praxis, which Engels replaced by a positivistic conception of "scientific experiment."[15] In fact, according to Lukács: "Scientific experiment is contemplation at its purest. The experimenter creates an artificial, abstract milieu in order to be able to observe undisturbed the untrammelled workings of the laws under examination, eliminating all irrational factors both of the subject and the object."[16] In contrast to this, praxis presupposes an interaction between subject and object—that is, an active relationship, an active involvement—and thus excludes the position of a contemplative observer of purely objective processes.

To clarify the real significance of these accusations, it is necessary to place them in a wider context, to see them as a part of Lukács's struggle for cleansing Marxism from naturalistic scientism and thus restoring the true meaning of Marxist thought. This attempt was leveled not against

Lenin (although his *Materialism and Empiriocriticism* could have easily been made its target) but against the conception of objective laws of history, independent of human will and similar to the laws of nature—the conception in the name of which Kautsky, Plekhanov, and other leading theorists of the Second International criticized the Bolshevik revolution as a voluntaristic experiment that violated the "laws of development" and was therefore bound to fail. At the same time, it was an attempt by Lukács to rediscover and emphasize (in a different way than did Engels) the Hegelian roots of Marxism, to sharply distinguish between Marxian dialectics and positivistic evolutionism, and to offer a consciously antipositivistic account of Marxist theory that was capable of absorbing some of the results of the so-called revolt against positivism in modern philosophy. To achieve these aims, Lukács had to get rid of Engelsian "dialectical materialism," which treated dialectical laws as objective laws of nature and stressed the continuity between natural evolution and human history. In Lukács's view, the "dialectics of nature" could not exist, because the proper sphere of dialectics was the interaction between subject and object in the historical world of broadly conceived human praxis. From this perspective, the objectivity of the economic laws governing capitalist development was merely a "fetishistic illusion," the result of the reification of human relationships characteristic of the capitalist market—in other words, a form of consciousness produced by a historically transient form of human collective activity. Studying these laws "scientistically," that is, from the position of a "detached spectator" (as was true in the case of Engels), amounted to supporting this illusion and giving legitimacy to the reified view of society—to treating society as a kind of "second nature" alien to human beings and subject to an inexorable necessity.[17] In contrast to this, dialectical method aimed at bringing about the dereification and de-alienation of consciousness by destroying the reified character of social phenomena.[18] In other words, the notion of objective "laws of development" reflects only "man's plight in bourgeois society" and even "turns out to be an ideological weapon of the bourgeoisie." Attempts to employ this notion to support the fatalistic optimism of the "objectivistic" account of Marxism were, in Lukács's view, theoretically unfounded and practically harmful, requiring a wait-and-see attitude instead of making people aware that "the historical process will come to function in *our deeds and through our deeds.*"[19]

In fact, Lukács was not the first to question the validity of the "objectivistic" and "necessitarian" interpretation of Marxism characteristic of Engels and (because of him) of the Marxist orthodoxy of the Second International. Some awareness of the differences between Marx and Engels existed earlier (before World War I in Italy) among Marxists and thinkers interested in Marxism, such as Rodolfo Mondolfo, Arturo Labriola, Giovanni Gentile, and Benedetto Croce.[20] Kolakowski has pointed out that "the first to attack Engels's philosophy as radically different from Marx was probably Stanislaw Brzozowski."[21] This Polish thinker saw Marxism as an antinaturalistic "philosophy of action" rooted in the mainstream tradition of German classical philosophy, although unfortunately deeply contaminated in later years by positivistic scientism.[22] In 1905, such ideas were ahead of their time. Like Lukács, Brzozowski interpreted the notion of the so-called objective laws of history as an illusion of consciousness that reflected individuals' loss of control over their own products. Again like Lukács, Brzozowski rediscovered the problems of reification and alienation and understood Marx's philosophy of history not as a theory of "necessary stages of economic development," but in terms of externalization and reappropriation of humans' creative powers. "This theory," he wrote, "ran as follows: man casts behind him the results of his own creativity—religion, art, law, etc.—and treats them as independent beings which he serves; actually, however, he always serves himself, because these independent beings are his own creations. The awareness of this means becoming conscious of one's own riches; it is the reappropriation by man of what he had externalized from himself, and thereby his liberation."[23]

Two years later, in 1907, Brzozowski came to the conclusion that the responsibility for the scientistic distortion of Marxism fell on Engels and wrote an article presenting the contrast between "true Marxism" and "Engelsism." Marx, Brzozowski argued, developed the dialectic of history, while Engels interpreted this dialectic as a part of a "dialectic of the cosmos" and consequently dissolved it in the evolution of nature. Marx went beyond Hegel by "solving the Hegelian problem of *Sein-Denken*," while Engels "returned to a pre-Kantian standpoint." Marx saw history as human active autocreation, whereas Engels reduced history to a "natural," "objective" process. This was so, because Engels took nature as something given and treated humankind as a part of it, while Marx, conscious of the Kantian upheaval in philosophy, adopted an anthropocentric standpoint and knew well that nature or, more precisely, nature within the range of human experience (since we are unable to say anything about nature in itself), is, in a sense, our own creation—that the very term *nature*, if used critically, denotes "the power achieved by human technical ability over the outside world."[24]

Although Brzozowski used the phrase "dialectic of the cosmos," this was no more than a purely verbal concession. In fact, he anticipated Lukács (and later Sartre) in his categorical denial of the legitimacy of the Engelsian "dialectic of nature." After all, he had already defined nature in 1904 as a "product of history," a "historically determined content," in the sense that everything that shapes the content of our concept of nature is the result of the historical development of human praxis. He wrote: "The entire content of human life, both theoretical and practical, belongs to history. History does not lose its autonomy in relation to nature because, as a matter of fact, history encompasses nature. The extra-human world is itself a product of history. . . . History, the world of man's responsibility and action, is a reality logically prior to nature."[25]

In this manner, the Engelsian "dissolving of the dialectic of history in the dialectic of nature" was replaced by a philosophical conception that dissolved nature, as well as the very notion of an objective being, in the dialectical movement of human history.[26] The convergence with Lukács, whose philosophy evolved later in a quite different direction, was in this point truly striking. "Nature is a social category," wrote Lukács, and this meant precisely that the content of our knowledge of nature is "a product of history."[27] He explained: "For the Marxist as an historical dialectician both *nature* and all forms in which it is mastered in theory and practice are *social categories*; and to believe that one can detect anything supra-historical or supra-social in this context is to disqualify oneself as a Marxist."[28]

Brzozowski's critique of Engels was further developed in his long essay "Anti-Engels" (1910). This was not conceived as a program for Marxists, because at that time Brzozowski also wanted to distance himself from Marx. Nevertheless, this essay contains many pre-Lukácsian ideas, especially the critique of scientism and intellectualism as contemplative attitudes characteristic of socially alienated, detached observers and incompatible with the Marxian thesis that the goal is to change the world, not just to interpret it. In Brzozowski's view, Engels was a particularly repulsive representative of this mind-set, looking on history from Olympian heights and deliberately seeing in it "a process which is as indifferent and alien to us as natural processes."[29] Thus Engels's view of life as subject to inevitable laws exemplified the stance of the passive onlooker and also involved the error of pre-Marxian "intellectualism": a receptive conception of cognition and a conviction that social praxis must be preceded and guided by "correct theory." In conclusion, Brzozowski defined Engelsism as a dangerous distortion of Marxism that would demoralize the workers by killing their militant spirit and their feeling of responsibility for their own fate and for the fate of humankind.

As we can see, the dialectical historicism of Brzozowski and Lukács was not a theory of history but rather a theory of the inescapable historicity of human knowledge, as well as a theory of its inescapable species subjectivism. In later years, similar views were put forward by Gramsci, for whom Marxism, as a philosophy of praxis, was a historicist reinterpretation of the "subjectivist conception of reality" characteristic of modern European philosophy. "Objective," Gramsci stressed, "always means 'humanly objective' which can be held to correspond exactly to 'historically subjective':

in other works, objective would mean 'universal subjective.' " He endorsed Lukács's view that "human history should be conceived also as the history of nature" and carried it to its logical conclusion: if nature, as we know it, is a product and part of human history, then why should the concept of dialectic not be applied to it?[30] But this was not meant as a concession to "dialectical materialism." On the contrary, Gramsci agreed that dialectic should not be extended to *extrahuman* nature and went so far as to claim that the very notion of extrahuman nature should be eliminated from Marxism as being a relic of theological thinking (referring in this context to Engels's *Anti-Dühring*).[31] He was equally resolute in cleansing historical materialism (which he preferred to call "philosophy of praxis") from naturalistic accretions. Thus, he insisted that there was nothing ontologically inevitable in the so-called laws of historical development. They were merely "laws of tendency," that is, "not laws in the naturalistic sense or that of speculative determinism, but in a 'historicist' sense," as a historically determined, changing pattern of human interaction.[32] This explained his negative attitude toward sociology, which he considered an offshoot of "evolutionist positivism," "an attempt to produce a so-called exact (i.e. positivist) science of social facts."[33] Interestingly, the same view was expressed much earlier by Brzozowski, for whom the term *sociology* was utterly compromised, being inextricably associated with naturalistic scientism and its search for the "objective laws" of social life.[34]

Gramsci was, of course, aware that the conceptions of the objective laws of history and of development through stages could also be found in Marx. In one of his early articles, Gramsci defined the Bolshevik revolution as "the revolution against Karl Marx's *Capital*." He went on to argue:

In Russia, Marx's *Capital* was more the book of the bourgeoisie than of the proletariat. It stood as the critical demonstration of how events should follow a predetermined course: how in Russia a bourgeoisie had to develop, and a capitalist era had to open, with the setting-up of a Western-type civilization, before the proletariat could even think of its own revolt, its own class demands, its own revolution. Events have exploded the critical schema determining how the history of Russia would unfold according to the canons of historical materialism. The Bolsheviks reject Karl Marx, and their explicit actions and conquests bear witness that the canons of historical materialism are not so rigid as might have been and has been thought.[35]

Thus (and certainly to his credit), Gramsci's reinterpretation of historical materialism by transforming it into a historicist and culturalist philosophy of praxis was leveled *not only* against Engels, but also, unlike Lukács's, against Marx himself. On the other hand, Gramsci tried to explain the deterministic rigidity of classical Marxism by arguing that "the fatalistic conception of the philosophy of praxis" had been useful for a certain period of history and deserved to be buried "with all due honors." "Its role," he claimed, "could really be compared with that of the theory of predestination and grace for the beginnings of the modern world, a theory which found its culmination in classical German philosophy and its conception of freedom as the consciousness of necessity. It has been a replacement for the cry of ''tis God's will,' although even on this primitive, elementary plane it was the beginning of a more modern and fertile conception."[36]

In other words, the belief in the final victory of communism as guaranteed by the inexorable laws of history, though false, nonetheless had performed a useful role by strengthening the energy and self-confidence of the workers' movement. However, the time had come to bury it as a theoretically untenable idea that had been undermined by the unexpected victory of a proletarian revolution in a backward country and was now too primitive to serve as a guide to increasingly complex political praxis.

In spite of Gramsci's acknowledgment that the "fatalistic" interpretation of historical materialism found powerful support in the usual reading of Marx's *Capital* (a reading endorsed by Marx himself in his preface to the first German edition of his magnum opus), it is quite obvious that Engels's contributions to the codification of "classical Marxism" were for him peculiarly uncongenial, for at least two important reasons. First, it was Engels who, with his dialectical materialism, grounded the laws of dialectic in extrahuman nature, thus providing an ontological foundation for a rigidly deterministic account of Marxism and excluding the possibility of seeing Marxism as a philosophy of human praxis, that is, of interpreting it in an antinaturalistic, humanistic, historicist (in the Gramscian sense), and activist manner. Second, it was Engels who defined freedom as "the consciousness of necessity," thus promoting the "fatalistic" (or, rather, necessitarian) interpretation of Marxism, an interpretation that Gramsci wanted to bury with due honors. Therefore, there was no possible doubt that the Gramscian philosophy of praxis was equally anti-Engelsian as the neo-Marxism of Lukács (although, certainly, less extreme in its anti-Engelsism than was Brzozowski's "philosophy of labor").[37]

After World War II, Gramsci, along with Lukács, was recognized as one of the main pillars of Western Marxism. The growing interest in this retrospectively reconstructed intellectual tradition continued to develop, as did a fascination with Marx's early works, in which the insights of Lukács and Gramsci found impressive confirmation. Small wonder that this brought about a situation diametrically opposite to one that obtained earlier, when (to repeat Trotsky's words) even the best specialists on Marxism felt unable to establish a line of demarcation between Marx and Engels. Now even those sympathizers of Western Marxism whose knowledge of Marxism is grossly inadequate know from hearsay that Marx should not be identified with Engels and conclude from this that Engels's works can be simply ignored. The number of books on Marx has increased enormously without a comparable increase in the literature on Engels. There are many academic Marxist philosophers in the West whose knowledge of Engels is almost nonexistent, who analyze Marx as if he were their contemporary, without paying the slightest attention to what was known as "classical Marxism." Most of them simply ignore the fact that "if it is a mistake to treat Engels as an authentic interpreter of Marx, the first person who made that mistake was Marx himself."[38] Marx's works are now being published separately from Engels's (which is good), but English translations of Engels's *Anti-Dühring*—historically, the most important work in the classical Marxist tradition—are available only in Soviet and Chinese editions. On the other hand, however, the theme of "Marx versus Engels" has focused the attention of several serious students of Marxism, which has contributed to a better understanding of both these thinkers.

A survey of the relevant literature on the subject would not be justified here, but it seems useful to refer to two philosophers who have reconstructed and systematized the differences between Marx and Engels clearly and elaborately. One is Leszek Kolakowski, and the other is Norman Levine, author of *The Tragic Deception: Marx contra Engels*.[39]

Kolakowski presented his views on the intellectual relationship between Marx and Engels in his important article "Le marxisme de Marx, le marxisme d'Engels" and in the concluding chapter of the first volume of his *Main Currents of Marxism*. There he summed up his findings by indicating four contrasts: "firstly, between naturalistic evolutionism and anthropocentrism; secondly between the technical interpretation of knowledge and the epistemology of praxis; thirdly, between the idea of the 'twilight of philosophy' and that of its merging into life as a whole; and fourthly, between infinite progression and eschatology."[40]

The elaboration of these points exhibits the strong influence of Brzozowski, Lukács, and Gramsci. Like them, Kolakowski stressed "the latent transcendentalism of Engels's dialectic of nature" and contrasted it with Marx's view that "nature as we know it is an extension of man, an organ of practical activity."[41] He clearly endorsed Brzozowski's view of Marx's philosophy as "historical subjectivism" and used the same term for defining Lukács's and Gramsci's views, sharply contrasting them with "Engels's materialism." Following Lukács, he pointed out the revolutionary and eschatological character of the Hegelian dialectic, discovering the same features in Marx ("the idea of history culminating in the complete unity of man, the identification of existence with essence and the abolition of contingency in human life") and emphasizing their absence in Engels, for whom dialectic meant "ceaseless development and negation, so that no form of Being or society can be final, and the Absolute is always out of reach."[42] Kolakowski, in his earlier work, interpreted this observation politically by stating that Engels's evolutionism was more compatible with reformism than with Marx's eschatology.[43] The same comment was made by Levine, for whom Engels was simply "the first revisionist,"[44] and earlier by Georg Lichtheim, who found it deplorable that Engels, and "following him Kautsky and the orthodox school in general," had transformed Marxism "from the vision of a unique historical breakthrough into the doctrine of a causally determined process analogous to the scheme of Darwinian evolution."[45] One could expect that Kolakowski, having become fully aware of the grave dangers of revolutionary eschatology, would assess this change differently. However, the summary of the Marx-versus-Engels theme in *Main Currents* contains no mention of the political implications of Engels's abandonment of this eschatology, and even at this point the author's sympathies lie with Marx, probably because Kolakowski disliked Engels's naturalistic scientism.

Levine defined Marx's philosophy as "naturalistic humanism," but he did so without any intention to distance himself from antinaturalistic interpretations of Marxism. The term *naturalism* is used in his book in the sense it had for the young Marx—that is, in a sense that had nothing in common with positivistic scientism or Darwinian evolutionism. According to Levine, positivism, unlinear evolutionism,[46] technological determinism, uncritical scientism (coupled with the naive copy theory of knowledge), materialism (in the sense of reducing everything to matter and its motion), misinterpretation of historical praxis, and lack of understanding of human subjectivity characterize Engels's views as distinct from Marx's. All these observations (and this is only a part of a much longer list) fit well the standard model of anti-Engelsian Marxism. Levine fully endorsed this model when he wrote that "Marx's universe was anthropocentric," while "Engels's universe was cosmocentric" and that for Marx "the dialectic was not in nature itself, but in the interaction between man and nature." No wonder he concluded from this that Marx, unlike Engels, could be described as a "dialectical materialist"; he went even further by claiming that the term *historical materialism* was equally unfitting as a definition of Marx's views. He proposed instead to call Marx's position "dialectical *naturalism*" and distinguished it sharply from Engels's materialism.[47]

This insistence on naturalism, completely absent in Lukács, Gramsci, and Brzozowski, for whom this term was firmly associated with the positivistic naturalism of the "exact sciences," constitutes the originality of Levine's approach and adds an important dimension to Kolakowski's analysis of the Marx-versus-Engels problem. The use of the term *naturalism* is, nevertheless, somewhat confusing and requires further explanation. It is not enough to say that naturalism in Levine's usage was different from the scientific naturalism of Darwinian evolutionism; it is necessary to stress that the two naturalisms were mutually exclusive. Neither is it enough to explain this difference by referring to the texts of Feuerbach and the young

Marx; after all, both these thinkers used the term *naturalism* to oppose Hegelian idealism, to vindicate the view of humans as corporeal beings, as part of the really existing material world of nature. It is evident that *in this sense* Engels was a "naturalist" and a Feuerbachian no less than was Marx. Moreover, if this Feuerbachian naturalism amounted to materialism (as was later claimed by Feuerbach himself), then the term *materialism* applied also to Marx, both when he was young and also when he was mature.

To properly understand what Levine really wanted to say, it is better to use the term *essentialism*. Naturalism, in this sense, is a standpoint that asserts that things have "natures," or "essences." From this point of view, we can distinguish between essentialist materialism (Feuerbach's and Marx's) and reductive materialism (a form of atomism characteristic of the mechanistic materialism of the natural sciences).[48] We can also (perhaps more legitimately) interpret materialism in a way that excludes both essentialism and dialectic and, on this basis, question both the materialistic character of Marx's dialectic and the dialectical character of Engels's materialism. But, nevertheless, this perspective enables us to recognize the "profoundly Aristotelian" character of Marx's conception of humans' species essence.[49] Seen from this perspective, Marx appears as a great essentialist thinker, a legitimate successor of both Aristotle and Hegel.[50]

Given these explanations, Levine's view of the main contrast between Marx and Engels becomes perfectly clear. Levine maintained that Engels completely overlooked "the Feuerbachian notion of species being" and hence could not develop a philosophical anthropology. While Marx "combined process with naturalistic [that is, essentialistic] ontology, Engels, conversely, completely overlooked the naturalistic [essentialistic] core, and fell to the other extreme of viewing human nature itself as totally historical. Essence, for Engels, was completely absorbed in flux." This was so because he saw human nature as an evolutionary product. "This evolutionary process was still continuing. It was Engels who wed socialism to Darwinism."[51]

Having no concept of man's species essence, Engels, of course, could not develop a theory of alienation and reification of this essence.[52] It is no wonder, therefore, that he did not use Marx's most important concepts, such as objectification, alienation, reappropriation, and self-affirmation.[53] And it is also no wonder (and at this point the analyses of Levine and Kolakowski converge) that he could not conceive of human history as a process that would come to an end at the time when the human species would overcome its self-alienation, reappropriate its reified forces, and thereby at a higher level reconcile its existence with its essence.

A sharp criticism of Levine's thesis, and of the entire tradition of setting Marx against Engels, is given by Alvin W. Gouldner in his impressive book *The Two Marxisms*. He wrote: "Efforts to resolve differences between Marx and Engels by thus splitting them rest on a most un-Marxist assumption: that Marxism simply cannot be internally contradictory, that there are no real contradictions *within it*, but only differences *between two persons*." Therefore, instead of drawing contrasts between the two thinkers, one should instead distinguish between the two models of Marxism to be found in the writings of both Marx and Engels. Gouldner proposed that these models be called "scientific Marxism" and "critical Marxism," or "structuralist" and "voluntarist." He treated them as heuristic devices that explain the pattern of tensions in Marxist thought, especially the tension between modernism and antimodernism. "Scientific Marxism," he argued, "conceives of men as *other*-grounded, i.e., as produced objects, as products of society, or of society's structured contradictions and of the blind laws expressing these. Critical Marxism, however, stresses that men are doers and producers. In accenting the *self*-groundedness of men, it fuses with recurrent social movements toward a cultural revitalization, that is a 'romanticized' opposition to the 'mechanization' of the modern world, resonating inhibited 'spiritual' sentiments."[54]

There are some merits to this interpretation. It is true that it would be impossible to neatly separate Marx's views from Engels's, that many pages from Marx could be written by Engels, and vice versa.[55] This is especially true of Marx, since Engels was somewhat consistent in his scientism, if only because his philosophy was less complex and did not elaborate on some important themes of Marx's. Thus, Gouldner's typology can be useful in explaining different currents of Western Marxism.

Nevertheless, the point here depends on treating Marx and Engels separately and clearly distinguishing between their views. The difference between Marx and Engels is especially noteworthy in their respective philosophies of freedom. As discussed above, Marx's philosophy of freedom is part and parcel of his historiosophical conception of self-enriching alienation of humans' species essence. Marxologists may legitimately differ in their attitudes toward the Marx-versus-Engels thesis, but those who have most carefully studied this subject agree that such a conception was foreign to Engels's thought. Hence, although Marx and Engels might have used the same words in their condemnations of bourgeois freedom, their respective visions of true liberation were necessarily different. Similarly, although they might have used the same deterministic vocabulary, they nonetheless differed in their understanding of the inner meaning of the "necessary laws of history" and of necessity as such.

2.2 From Pantheism to Communism

To understand the peculiarly exalted role of necessity in Engels's *Weltanschauung* (and, therefore, also some peculiarities in his understanding of freedom), it seems justified to analyze this concept in connection with the deep Calvinist religiosity of his family background.

As is well known, Marx's background was entirely different than Engels's. Marx's father, an educated and prosperous lawyer, was a typical Enlightenment rationalist; his conversion from Judaism to Protestantism, although somewhat facilitated by his admiration for Kant's philosophy of religion, was mostly a pragmatic decision and marked his final assimilation into German society. In contrast, Engels's father represented Calvinism in its fundamentalistic, pietistic, and traditionally puritan form. Thus, it is no wonder that the evolution of Engels's ideas proceeded initially within the confines of a religiously based worldview, as was typical of German intellectuals of the time, including those professionally interested in philosophy.[56] Speculative idealism, especially Hegelianism, came to be felt as too abstract, too remote from existential issues, which created a widespread desire to connect philosophy with broadly conceived practice, to make it relevant in defining one's position in vitally important religious and political questions. Hence, as Engels rightly noticed in *Ludwig Feuerbach*, German post-Hegelian philosophy revolved mostly around religion and politics (M&E, SW, 3:342). Young Marx, for whom religious questions never seriously mattered, was in this respect a less typical post-Hegelian thinker than young Engels.

I will briefly outline those aspects of young Engels's intellectual evolution that seem to be philosophically most important for his understanding of necessity and freedom.

Not surprisingly, the intellectual awakening of young Engels started with his rebellion against his father's Calvinistic pietism. His first journalistic work, "Letters from Wuppertal" (March–April 1839), was a warning against the religious obscurantism growing around Wuppertal, "an area so full of pietist activities" (M&E, CW, 2:17). In a letter of April 8, 1839, to his schoolmate, the future pastor Friedrich Graeber, Engels confessed that he had been a mystic for some time but never a pietist and described his actual position as that of a comparatively very liberal "supernaturalist" with some inclinations toward rationalism. By this he meant primarily the views of the Young Hegelian David Strauss, who in his *Life of Jesus* (1835) interpreted Christianity as one of the manifestations of the Absolute that incessantly incarnates in humankind and constantly develops through higher and higher stages. Later, in a letter of June 15, 1839, he movingly described his tensions between rationalism, as represented by Spinoza, Kant, and Strauss, as well as the representatives of the Young German movement (Ludwig Börne and Karl Gutzkow), and "positive" (i.e., institutionalized) Christianity. He could not believe that the rationalists, who passionately strove for a union with God and a reconciliation between Christianity and modern culture, would after their death "suffer God's wrath physically and mentally without end in the most fearful torments." He could not even agree to condemn those rationalists who had doubted, because they also had been striving for truth. Yet he declared his readiness to defend positive Christianity against all those who arrogantly dismissed it, writing: "I defend this teaching, which derives from the deepest needs of human nature, the longing for salvation from sin through God's grace: but when it is a matter of defending the freedom of reason, then I protest against all compulsion.—I hope to live to see a radical transformation in the religious consciousness of the world—if only I was clear about it in myself!" (ibid., 423, 455, 456).

This painful contradiction resolved when he suddenly adopted a belief in the radical separation of philosophical reason and religion, as a matter of irrational, irreducible feeling. This change occurred through the influence of Schleiermacher, who defined religion as an irrational feeling of absolute dependence born as "an immediate existence-relationship" and inevitably historical in character.[57] In the letter to Graeber of July 12–27, 1839, Engels reported enthusiastically that he was "moved to the core," with tears in his eyes, and that all contradictions had disappeared from his worldview, since he now knew that "religious conviction is a matter of the heart and is only conceived with dogma insofar as dogma is or is not contradicted by feeling." He now understood that "everything God does is mercy, but everything He does is likewise necessity. The unity of these contradictions constitutes an essential part of the essence of God." It is not enough to say that religion, as "an affair of the heart," cannot be undermined by reason; in fact, religion does not need any support from reason and "those whose devoutness is rooted either in their understanding or in their reason have none at all." "The tree of religion," Engels continues, "sprouts from the heart, overshadows the whole man and seeks its nourishment from the air of reason. But its fruits, which contain the most precious heart-blood, are the dogmas, and what goes beyond them is of the Evil one. This is what Schleiermacher teaches and I stand by it" (ibid., 461, 459, 462, 463).

The importance of this testimony is obvious. Engels had finally arrived at a well-defined philosophic-religious standpoint: romantic pantheism, which conceived of freedom as liberation from contingency through rediscovery of the universal presence of divine necessity. Significantly, Schleiermacher's version of this worldview was particularly insistent on necessity, extolling universal determinism as universal dependence on, and participation in, Absolute Being. Engels might not have been aware of it, but the Hegelian definition of freedom, which Engels later embraced in a modified form, was also to be found in Schleiermacher's writings. Like Hegel, Schleiermacher belonged to those thinkers for whom the expression "free necessity" was not a contradiction in terms. Freedom, in his view, was not the absence of necessity; on the contrary, he saw freedom as "necessity incorporated, necessity understood." [58]

In his classic essay "Historical Inevitability," Isaiah Berlin stressed the dangers of deterministic worldviews, but also indicated the reasons for their powerful attractiveness. Being dependent on supraindividual forces that speak "in us" and "through us" relieves us from "the tension, the fear of failure and frustration," provides us with "a sense of membership in an ordered system, each with a unique position to oneself alone." [59] This observation defines the common worldview orientation, or axiological option, underlying romantic pantheism, and Hegelian historicism, as well as the scientistic version of historical determinism, and thus provides a common denominator for the different phases of Engels's intellectual evolution.

The peculiar charm of romantic pantheism consists in its divinization of nature and "oceanic feeling" (Nietzsche's expression) bound up with it. This was precisely the feeling young Engels expressed in an article published in July 1840:

All remembrance of the enemies of light and their treacherous attacks disappear, and you stand upright, proudly conscious of the free, infinite mind! I have had only one impression that could compare with this; when for the first time the divine idea of the last of the philosophers, this most colossal creation of the thought of the nineteenth century, dawned upon me, I experienced the same blissful thrill, it was like a breath of fresh sea air blowing down upon me from the purest sky: the depths of speculation lay before me like the unfathomable sea from which one cannot turn one's eyes straining to see the ground below; in God we live, move and have our beings! We become conscious of that when we are on the sea; we feel that God breathes through all around us and through us ourselves; we feel such kinship with the whole of nature, the waves beckon to us so intimately, the sky stretches so lovingly over the earth, and the sun shines with such indescribable radiance that one feels one could grasp it with the hand. (ibid., 99) [60]

"The last of the philosophers" in this quotation refers to Hegel. The beginning of Engels's conversion to Hegelianism was reported in his letter to Graeber of January 20, 1840: "Through Strauss I have now entered on the straight road to Hegelianism. . . . The Hegelian idea of God has already become mine, and thus I am joining the ranks of the 'modern pantheists' " (ibid., 489).

The parallel expressed here between Engels's feeling for nature and the powerful impact on him of Hegel's idea of the Absolute reveals that Engels's Hegelianism was still of a heterodox variety. A more consistent Hegelianism would have excluded romantic divinization of nature, because in Hegelian absolute idealism, nature was downgraded to the alienated "otherness" of the spirit, not celebrated as "spirit which has become visible" (as was done by Schelling and his romantic followers). Young Engels's view of the relationship between God and the world was inadequately Hegelian as well, since it did not assume a radical immanentization of the Absolute. His quoting of St. Paul's famous words ("*In Deo vivimus, et movemur, et sumus*") strongly suggests that his pantheism was in fact closer to *panentheism*: that is, a standpoint typical of romantic philosophers who tried to reconcile pantheism with the idea of a transcendent God by claiming that all finite things exist in God but refusing to reduce God to pure immanence.[61] Thus, in 1840, Engels's Hegelianism was very superficial and strongly contaminated by a vaguely romantic religiosity.

Engels's further intellectual evolution was so rapid that he had no chance to become a consistent Hegelian. The intellectual situation in Germany at that time was characterized by an acute awareness of the crisis of Hegelian absolute idealism, which was attacked from many quarters for its "pan-logism" and essentialism, for undermining the ontological independence of nature through reducing everything to the dialectic of pure reason, and for examining only the rational world of essences while ignoring the realm of positive existence. Schelling had already, in his Munich lectures of 1827, called Hegelianism a "negative" philosophy preoccupied only with pure concepts and had set against it a program for a "positive" philosophy that would deal with positively existing facts, thus rehabilitating the sphere of experience, including religious experience and actually existing "positive Christianity." Similar ideas were developed by the representatives of the so-called late idealism—Immanuel Hermann Fichte ("the younger Fichte"), Christian Hermann Weisse, and Friedrich Julius Stahl—who used the mystical doctrine of Jacob Boehme to prove that matter was not reducible to spirit and that both the material and the spiritual belong to the essence of the Absolute Being. The young Hegelians (with whom Engels became closely associated when he came to Berlin in 1841) treated a commitment to antireligious rationalism as the main criterion of intellectual progress and therefore saw these ideas as an extreme expression of right-wing German philosophy. However, a similar critique of Hegelian absolute idealism and a similar tendency to "rehabilitate matter" (and nature) appeared also on the extreme left of the German "philosophical parliament." I mean, of course, the early works of Ludwig Feuerbach, whose anthropological materialism was leveled against both Hegelian idealism (as establishing "the tyranny of Reason") and the traditional idea of God (as an alienation of man's species essence, which repressed and degraded really existing human beings). Despite the obvious differences, both forms of attack on absolute idealism had something important in common: the recognition that the real world cannot be reduced to dialectical reason, and that existence (contrary to Anselm's ontological proof of the existence of God) does not logically follow from essence.[62]

The year 1841 was marked by two important philosophical events: the appearance of Feuerbach's primary work, *The Essence of Christianity*, and Schelling's nomination to the chair of philosophy in Berlin, where he started to lecture on the "philosophy of the revelation." The impact of Feuerbach's book on the Left-Hegelian milieu was enormous. According to Engels's retrospective account in *Ludwig Feuerbach*, "the enthusiasm was general; we all became at once Feuerbachians" (M&E, SW, 3:344). *The Essence of Christianity* was generally seen as a frontal attack not only on positive Christianity but on religion as such. Young Engels was delighted by the panic the attack caused among conservatives and, in a satirical poem, parodied their reaction as follows:

> But who comes from the South as lonely as a cloud,
> Disdaining sympathy, himself a one-man crowd,
> A one-man host of Atheists fanatical,
> A one-man treasure store of craft Satanical,
> A one-man fount of wicked blasphemy and shame?
> Help us, Saint John, it's *Feuerbach* of dreadful name!
> (M&E, CW, 2:337)[63]

The expectations raised by Schelling's reappearance on the philosophical scene were also enormous. It was known that he had been called to Berlin by the Prussian authorities to serve as an antidote to Left-Hegelianism, that for many years he had been working on a refutation of Hegelianism, and that he saw himself (to quote once more from Engels) as "the philosophical Messiah" destined to bring about "the fall of Hegelianism, the death of all atheists and non-Christians" (ibid., 192). Curiosity was great, and the old philosopher had an extremely large audience that included some notable Poles and Russians. Many listeners brought with them the awareness that the Hegelian Absolute Spirit was no longer in good shape and did not exclude the possibility that it would fall to Schelling either to overcome the crisis of German idealism or to lay the foundation for a new beginning in philosophy.

Engels, however, did not belong to this group. A year or two earlier, Schelling's religious philosophy might have appealed to his romantic pantheism (or panentheism), but at the current stage of his intellectual development, he was too much involved in Left-Hegelianism and too conscious of the political implications of Schelling's declared intention of assuming "the fact of a revelation." Engels expected that this would mean turning "to the positive philosophy, to the empirical side," in the sense of accepting "facts as they are," thus supporting the conservative view of historical change as held by the "historical school" in jurisprudence.[64] He did not want to hear about "positive theology," because this would strengthen the prestige of all sorts of strait-laced Christian orthodoxies. Hence, at the outset of Schelling's lecture series, Engels declared himself as Schelling's enemy and promised to confidently fight against his ideas.[65] He kept his promise by publishing in 1842 an interesting pamphlet entitled *Schelling and the Revelation: Critique of the Latest Attempt of Reaction Against the Free Philosophy.*

The point of this pamphlet amounted to a defense of Hegel by someone who saw Hegelianism as developed and positively transcended by Feuerbach. Engels concluded this piece by stressing that Hegel was "being attacked from two sides, by his predecessor Schelling and by his younger follower Feuerbach," and by making it clear that "Feuerbach's critique of Christianity is a necessary complement to the speculative teaching on religion founded by Hegel." By treating Feuerbach as a follower of Hegel, Engels obviously underestimated Feuerbach's break with Hegelianism, stressing instead the elements of continuity. Nonetheless, he was fully aware of Feuerbach's rejection of Hegelian idealism in the name of vindicating the independent ontological status of material nature and wholeheartedly endorsed it as the legitimate last word of philosophy. Engels did not fail to mention that in this respect Schelling, at least in his early philosophy of nature, had something in common with Feuerbach and his concept of "naturalism," writing: "The conclusion of modern philosophy, which was at least among the premises of Schelling's earlier philosophy, and of which Feuerbach first made us conscious in all its sharpness, is that reason cannot possibly exist except as mind, and that mind can only exist in and with nature, and does not lead, so to say, a life apart, in separateness from it, God knows where" (ibid., 237, 209).

We can now see the roots of the philosophical differences between Marx and Engels. Unlike Marx, young Engels never fully dealt with Hegel's absolute idealism. Engels's early intellectual evolution revolved around religious, rather than purely philosophical, issues. Hegelianism was for him merely a transition from romantic pantheism to Feuerbachian atheism. In fact, his Hegelianism so quickly fused with Feuerbachianism that he felt no need to independently correct its idealism; Feuerbach did this for him. In addition, his reading of Feuerbach had to be different than Marx's: while young Marx was impressed mostly by Feuerbach's theory of alienation of man's species essence, young Engels embraced Feuerbach's philosophy as a form of materialistic atheism that finally liberated him from the remnants of religiosity.

What remained of Hegelianism in Engels's worldview was, above all, the unshakable belief in rational historical necessity. In this respect, he was different from other Left-Hegelians who, following Bruno Bauer, stressed the activism of critical self-consciousness, which was expressed in the constant negation of all historically given forms of reality.[66] Especially interesting from this point of view is Engels's article "Centralization and Freedom," published in September 1842 in the liberal newspaper *Rheinische Zeitung*, which directly reflects his views on necessity and freedom.

According to a recent work on Marx and Engels, "as a dedicated liberal, Engels mourned the betrayal of the July revolution through the illiberal policies of François Guizot."[67] However, this comment provides a very one-sided idea of Engels's article. Indeed, the article begins by deploring the fact that "the principles of popular sovereignty, of a free press, of an independent jury, of parliamentary government, have practically been destroyed in France." It deplores, in particular, the tendency toward excessive centralization, arguing that the French state was "overstepping its bounds, going beyond its essential nature." But this condemnation of the illiberal French government has been supported not by the liberal argumentation about the "rights of man," but by the Hegelian view of history. Governments, Engels reasoned in an article entitled "Frederick William IV. King of Prussia," should keep pace with the course of history without usurping to themselves the right to change its direction (as this reactionary monarch had attempted to do) or deciding the rhythm of its development (ibid., 355, 356, 360–67). Thus, Engels wrote:

By assuming a right which belongs only to history, the state destroys the freedom of the individual. History has eternally had and will always retain the right to dispose of the life, the happiness, the freedom of the individual, for it is the activity of mankind as a whole, it is the life of the species, and as such it is sovereign; no one can revolt against it, for it is absolute right. No one can complain against history, for whatever it allots one, one lives and shares in the development of mankind, which is more than any enjoyment. How ludicrous it would be if the subjects of a Nero or a Domitian were to complain that they had not been born in an age like ours, when beheading or roasting alive does not happen so easily, or if the victims of medieval religious fanaticism were to reproach history because they did not live after the Reformation and under tolerant governments! As if without the suffering of some, the others could have made progress! Thus, the English workers, who at present have to suffer bitter hunger, have indeed the right to protest against Sir Robert Peel and the British Constitution, but not against history, which is making them the standard-bearers of a new principle of right. The same thing does not hold good for the state. It is always a particular state and can never claim the right, which mankind as a whole naturally possesses in its activity and the development of history, to sacrifice the individual for the general. (ibid., 356–57)

Thus, young Engels fully shared the Hegelian view of world history as a sort of theodicy that justified and sanctioned human suffering as the necessary price for progress. He stressed, however, that no particular government should see itself as an incarnation of historical reason. But despite this important qualification, the idea that history is always right and that complaints against it are always futile was, of course, very dangerous. It did not occur to young Engels that a particular government could claim a monopoly on the scientific knowledge of the laws of history and at the same time see itself as representing the interests of the entire human species. In other words, he did not predict the dangers of ruling in the name of the "correct, scientific understanding of history" or the dangers of the arrogant claim to represent the "true interests" of humankind.

In developing his views Engels explained that he was by no means against centralization. On the contrary, he wanted "to allow it the historical and national right that is its due." Centralization, he maintained, "is the essence, the vital nerve, of the state. Every state must necessarily strive for centralization; every state is centralized, from the absolute monarchy to the republic; America just as much as Russia. . . . Under this centralization, communal administration, everything that affects individual citizens or corporations, can quite well be left free, since *because* centralization is concentrated in a single center, because everything here forms a single unity, its activity must necessarily be general, its competence and powers embracing everything that is of *general* validity, but leaving free everything that concerns only this or that particular individual" (ibid., 358, 358–59).

The idea that a centralized state should leave room for individual freedom and that centralized power should be clearly distinguished from personal power ("the main thing is not the person in the center, but the center itself") was in accordance with the political thought of Hegel (ibid., 359). But Engels's article ended with remarks about the need to transcend the Hegelian ideal of the modern state. Centralization, he argued, "necessarily compels the state to reach out beyond itself, to make itself—the particular—into something universal, ultimate and supreme, and to claim the authority and position that belongs only to history. . . . True *subjective* freedom, which has equal rights with absolute freedom, calls for a different form of realization than the state" (ibid.).

These somewhat enigmatic remarks were the result of Engels's conversion to the utopian communism of Hess, who tried "to marry the spirit of Spinoza to that of Saint-Simon."[68] The idea of a higher form of centralization, providing more space for individual freedom, probably referred to the Saint-Simonian view that economic centralization would create the possibility of replacing the rule over people (i.e., the state as the highest form of political domination) by the administration of things. The idea of transforming the state into "something universal, ultimate and supreme" that could claim "the authority and position that belongs only to history" evokes the millenarian spirit of Hess's communism, which was conceived as the ultimate earthly salvation of humanity.[69] Communism was by definition something universal, representing the entire human species and in this respect comparable to world history. But Engels too hastily agreed to endow the future communist society with the same authority and position that he, as a Hegelian, attributed to universal history; namely (as quoted above), the right—the *absolute* right—"to dispose of life, the happiness, the freedom of the individual." This is revealing not about Engels's intentions, which were certainly benign, but about the objective danger inherent in certain combinations of ideas.

Hess developed his communist ideas in his book *The European Triarchy* (1841). Unlike mainstream Left-Hegelians, he was a religiously inspired thinker; this enabled him to appreciate and assimilate the messianic historiosophy of the Polish Hegelian August Cieszkowski, who predicted that the fusion of German philosophy with French socialism would usher in a universal religious regeneration of humanity.[70] Hess himself also speculated on the "missions" of different nations; according to him, England (as the country with the most developed industry) was to give birth to a social revolution that would bring about a synthesis of German "freedom of thought" (the product of the Reformation) with French "freedom of action" (inaugurated by the French Revolution). Engels, although indifferent to the religious aspect of Hess's views, was greatly interested in these speculations. He had the opportunity to observe England firsthand when he went to work in his father's firm in Manchester in 1842.

Having arrived in England, Engels initially experienced a series of disappointments. Representatives of the nation destined, as he thought, to provide a revolutionary synthesis of German thought with French action proved to be totally uninterested in German philosophy, clinging obstinately to "crude empiricism," combined, as a rule, with old-fashioned religious beliefs, and seeing in social life clashes of interests rather than clashes of principles.[71] However, his initial feeling of astonishment did not prevent him from realizing how much he could learn from closely observing a developed industrial society. He established contacts with British Owenites and Chartists, seeing himself as a sort of bridge between socially radical movements in England and Germany.

In performing this role, Engels developed many themes directly relevant to our topic. Thus, in the Owenite journal *New Moral World* (November 1843) he offered British readers an interesting survey of "Progress of the Social Reform on the Continent." At the beginning of this article, there is a programmatic statement about the transition to communism being the necessary outcome of the development of "the three great and civilized countries of Europe—England, France, and Germany" and the need for the mutual understanding of these nations. Such understanding would involve a clear awareness of the different ways in which the three countries came to the same conclusion: "the French came to it *politically*, the Germans *philosophically*, and the English *practically*, by the rapid increase of misery, demoralization, and pauperism in their country" (ibid., 3 : 392–93).

Engels's analysis of the situation in France reveals that he was no longer a political democrat in any recognizable sense of the term, as this quote clearly shows:

Democracy is, as I take all forms of government to be, a contradiction in itself, an untruth, nothing but hypocrisy (theology, as we Germans call it), at the bottom. Political liberty is sham-liberty, the worst possible slavery; the appearance of liberty, and therefore the reality of servitude. Political equality is the same; therefore democracy, as well as every other form of government, must ultimately break to pieces: hypocrisy cannot subsist, the contradiction hidden in it must come out; we must have either a regular slavery—that is, an undisguised despotism, or real liberty, and real equality—that is Communism. Both these consequences were brought out in the French Revolution: Napoleon established the first, and Babeuf the second. (ibid., 393)

Engels's hostility toward political democracy was shared by the so-called true socialists in Germany. A few years later, in the *Manifesto of the Communist Party*, Marx and Engels condemned this attitude as inappropriate in a backward country: by "hurling the traditional anathemas against liberalism, against representative government, against bourgeois competition, bourgeois freedom of the press, bourgeois legislation, bourgeois liberty and equality" the "true socialists" in fact helped the German governments in fighting the liberal bourgeoisie and, at the same time, expressed and supported the anticapitalist illusions of independent small producers (ibid., 6:510–12). The further development of their views led the authors of the *Manifesto* to a more positive evaluation of political democracy, which sharply distinguished their position from other currents in broadly conceived socialism, such as international anarchism or Russian populism. Nevertheless, a stage of hostile criticism of "merely political" liberation seems to have been necessary for them to separate themselves from all forms of noncommunist social radicalism.

In his presentation of French socialist and communist thinkers, Engels made two critical remarks. First, he expressed his disgust for their use of religious ideas (such as "new Christianity," "new Revelation," and so on), seeing this as a proof of their philosophical immaturity, and he went on to praise the English socialists, who, although without sufficient training in philosophy, had succeeded in liberating themselves from the religious prejudices of the English bourgeoisie. Second, he pointed out that the French communists, as heirs of the distinctively political tradition of French radicalism, combined communism with a commitment to republicanism and intended to overthrow by force the present government of their country, as was shown by "their continual policy of secret associations." Engels objected to this practice, stating that "secret associations are always contrary to common prudence, inasmuch as they make the parties liable to unnecessary legal prosecutions" (ibid., 3 : 397, 397). Thus, from the very beginning of his communism, Engels distanced himself from conspiratorial forms of revolutionary activity, which later were labeled "Blanquism."

In an essay on the situation in Germany, Engels set forth the thesis that in Germany communism had to be philosophical because of the national character of the Germans.

The Germans are a philosophical nation, and will not, cannot abandon Communism, as soon as it is founded upon sound philosophical principles: chiefly if it is derived as an unavoidable conclusion from their *own* philosophy. And this is the part we have to perform now. Our party has to prove that either all the philosophical efforts of the German nation, from Kant to Hegel, have been useless— worse than useless; or, that they must end in Communism; that the Germans must either reject their great philosophers, whose names they hold up as the glory of their nation, or that they must adopt Communism. And this *will* be proved; this dilemma the Germans *will* be forced into, and there can scarcely be any doubt as to which side of the question the people will adopt. There is greater chance in Germany for the establishment of a Communist party among the educated classes of society, than anywhere else. The Germans are a very disinterested nation; if in Germany principles comes into collision with interest, principle will almost always silence the claims of interest. The same love of abstract principle, the same disregard of reality and self-interest, which have brought the Germans to a state of political nonentity, these same qualities guarantee the success of philosophical communism in that country. (ibid., 406–7)

What Engels really says in this extremely interesting quotation boils down to the hope that his compatriots would embrace communism for nationalistic reasons and not because of national interest, but because of considerations of national glory. Not surprisingly, he had to diminish the contribution of French thinkers by stressing that they rejected philosophy, perpetuated religion, and thus could assist the Germans only in the first stages of their development toward communism. English socialists, on the other hand, could safely be praised, as they were unable to compete with the Germans in the sphere of ideas. In his final conclusion, Engels defined their importance for the Germans as follows: "Although our fundamental principles give us a broader base, inasmuch as we received them from a system of a philosophy embracing every part of human knowledge; yet in everything bearing upon practice, upon the *facts* of the present state of society, we find that the English socialists are a long way before us, and have left very little to be done" (ibid., 407, 407).

Equally interesting are three articles on "The Condition of England" written by Engels (in 1844) for German readers.[72] The first of these deals with Thomas Carlyle's *Past and Present*, beginning with an explanation of why the English conservatives, the Tories, were intellectually more interesting than the Whigs and why "a Whig would never have been able to write a book that was half so humane as *Past and Present.*" Of course, this was so because Carlyle's aristocratic critique of the "Mammonism" of industrial society converged in many points with the communist critique of capitalism. In addition, Carlyle endeared himself to Engels because of his interest in German literature and his affinity with German romantic pantheism. Engels was fond of stressing that such pantheism, derived from German literature and similar in spirit to Schelling's philosophy (although not his "positive" philosophy of revelation), had to be seen as a progressive phenomenon in England. "Pantheism itself," Engels argued, "is but the last preliminary step toward a free and human point of view." The German philosophical communists, in his view, had already attained the highest wisdom: they know that "God is man," they "lay claim to the meaning of history" but "see in history not the revelation of 'God' but of man and only of man." But, precisely because of this, they understood the true meaning of Carlyle's attacks on the atheism of bourgeois society. They sympathized with his complaints about the "emptiness," "hollowness," and "soulless-ness" of the age; if this is "atheism," they were also against atheism (so conceived), but they saw the roots of this atheism in religion itself. Religion is the main culprit in depriving humans of their substance and human history of its meaning. This was especially true of Christians, who "by putting forward a separate 'History of the Kingdom of God' deny that real history has any inner substantiality." "By assenting that the culmination of the human species is their Christ, they make history attain an imaginary goal, interrupt it in mid-course and are now obliged, if only for the sake of consistency, to declare the following eighteen hundred years to be totally nonsensical and utterly meaningless" (ibid., 447, 461, 465, 464, 461–63, 464). People like Carlyle were therefore right in pointing out the growing emptiness and meaninglessness of human life, although they were totally mistaken in their romantic idealization of medievalism.

Before proceeding further, it is worthwhile making a brief historico-philosophical comment. Young Engels's ideas are a perfect illustration of the view of communism as, first, a substitute for religion through deifi-cation of man and, second, a secularized version of the millenarian quest for this-worldly collective salvation.[73] The first element of this definition refers to the Feuerbachian theme in Engels's thought. Feuerbach's trans-formative critique of Christianity, summarized in his thesis "God is man, man is God,"[74] was accepted by Engels as the final result of German phi-losophy. The second element, the idea of collective salvation in history, was taken from French sources. The French utopian socialists, especially the Saint-Simonians and Pierre Leroux, who was considered by Engels as one of "the eminent minds" of France (ibid., 399), consciously vin-dicated the millenarian hopes of the early Christians, claiming that the salvation of individual souls in heaven would be followed by the "second salvation," this time a collective salvation on earth, announced and revealed in their own doctrines. The Saint-Simonians developed a theory of religious progress according to which the revelation of Christ, which was confined to the sphere of *private* life, was to be completed by the new, ultimate revelation of Saint-Simon, the "new messiah," whose disciples would bring about the Christianization of *social* and *political* life, thus realizing the Kingdom of God on earth.[75] Even though it did not question the existence of God or the immortality of human souls, this philosophy was a radical departure from traditional Christianity. God was seen by the Saint-Simonians as containing matter in his essence (which was to justify concern about this-worldly life), and immortality was conceived, as a rule, as progressive reincarnation (which was to enable now-living individuals to physically participate, in their new incarnations, in the future Kingdom of God on earth).[76] These ideas, which were consciously opposed to the bourgeois rationalism of the Enlightenment, did not please German radicals and, in fact, made impossible the realization of the Left-Hegelian idea of a "Franco-German intellectual alliance."[77] Nevertheless, the idea of socialism (or communism) as a sui generis terrestrialization of eschatology came to Germany from France. Hess made French ideas a part of his own religious messianism,[78] but at a later stage (having become a Feuerbachian) he transformed them into a secularized, anthropotheistic millenarianism. Young Engels followed his lead.

In his next article on "The Condition of England," Engels developed Hess's view on the monetary exchange economy as the final outcome of human alienation caused by Christianity. The modern Christian state, Engels reasoned, promoted the Christian principle of subjectivity, which amounted in practice to elevating subjective and egoistical individual interests (ibid., 475). This was bound to bring about "universal fragmentation, the concentration of each individual upon himself, the transformation of mankind into a collection of mutually repelling atoms." The abolition of feudal servitude made it even worse, because cash payment became (to quote Carlyle) "the sole relation of human beings." In this matter, Christian spiritualism gave birth to a world devoid of spirit: "Property, a natural, spiritless principle, as opposed to the human and spiritual principle, is thus enthroned, and ultimately, to complete this alienation, money—the alienated, empty abstraction of property—is made master of the world. Man has ceased to be a slave of men and has become the slave of *things*: the perversion of the human condition is complete; the servitude of the modern commercial world, this highly developed, total, universal venality, is more inhuman, and more all-embracing than the serfdom of the feudal era" (ibid., 475–76, 476, 476).

As we can see, young Engels, like young Marx, followed Hess in putting together Feuerbach's conception of religious alienation (God) with Hess's own conception of economic alienation (money), thereby arriving at a wholesale condemnation of modernity. This happened because (this time, *unlike* Marx) Engels was not able to see the process of alienation as self-enriching. He saw it only as an increase in evil, and thus based his hopes not on its positive results (universal interdependence through the world market), but only on the diagnosis that disintegration had achieved its climax and could not go any further: "The disintegration of mankind into a mass of isolated, mutually repelling atoms means the destruction of all corporate, national and indeed of any particular interests and is the last necessary step towards the free and spontaneous association of men. The supremacy of money as the culmination of the process of alienation is an inevitable stage which has to be passed through, if man is to return to himself, as he is now on the verge of doing" (ibid., 476).

The abolition of alienation was to be achieved through the social revolution in England. Somewhat inconsistently with his view of modern nations as totally disintegrated and atomized, Engels drew this conclusion from his favorite conception of the differing characters and historical callings of the foremost nations of Europe: "The Germans, the nation of Christian spiritualism, experienced a philosophical revolution; the French, the nation of classical materialism and hence of politics, went through a political revolution; the English, a nation that is a mixture of German and French elements, who therefore embody both sides of the antithesis and are for that reason more universal than either of the two factors taken separately, were for that reason drawn into a more universal, a social revolution" (ibid., 471).

However, Engels's last article on "The Condition of England" ended on a more sobering note: "The immediate future of England will be a democracy." In developing this view, Engels stressed that this would no longer be the political democracy of the French Revolution "whose antithesis was monarchy and feudalism," but a *social* democracy "whose antithesis is the middle class and property." But he qualified this distinction by emphasizing once more his basic skepticism about *all* forms of democracy. By itself, he argued, democracy "is not capable of curing social ills. Democratic equality is a chimera, the fight of the poor against the rich cannot be fought out on the basis of democracy or indeed of politics as a whole. This stage too is thus only a transition, the last purely political remedy which has still to be tried and from which a new element is bound to develop at once, a principle transcending everything of a political nature.

This principle is the principle of socialism" (ibid., 513, 513).

2.3   Political Economy and Communist Utopia

Engels's new experience as a businessman in Britain made him aware of
the need of translating these ideas into the language of political economy.
He did this in his "Outlines of a Critique of Political Economy," written
at the end of 1843 and published in the next year in *Deutsch-Französische
Jahrbücher*. This work made a profound impression on German radicals,
including Marx, who called it "brilliant" and fully assimilated its main
ideas. True, it was Hess who had showed young Marx the philosophical
relevance of economy, but it was Engels who passed from a purely speculative analysis of "economic alienation" to more concrete economic problems. Anyhow, it is arguable that in 1844 Engels's influence on Marx was
especially important—more important than, at that time, Marx's influence
on Engels.[79]

The critical part of "Outlines" was yet another exercise in condemning
"bourgeois freedom." Engels suggested that even liberal economists no
longer believed in this concept, thus transforming themselves from honest
scholars into shameless apologists for the existing system: "The nearer the
economists come to the present time, the further they depart from honesty. With every advance of time, sophistry necessarily increases, so as to
prevent economics from lagging behind the times. This is why *Ricardo*,
for instance, is more guilty than *Adam Smith*, and *McCulloch* and *Mill*
more guilty than Ricardo." Engels saw the apologetic function of the liberal economy even in the fact that it called itself a "political economy"
and defined its subject as "national wealth." As long as private property
existed, he reasoned, the term *national wealth* had no meaning; similarly,
the science of economy whose "public connections exist only for the sake
of private property" should, if it were honest, call itself *private* economy
(ibid., 420, 421–22).

The immediate consequence of private property—trade—was described
by Engels as immoral in its very nature. He ridiculed the view that trade was
a more humane way of acquiring goods than the highway robbery of the
Middle Ages. In fact, trade allows and fosters the universal use of immoral
means for attaining immoral ends and thus undermines the morality of all.
Its much praised peacefulness destroys social peace by constantly reproducing antagonistic confrontations among people. Its "humane methods"
boil down to a friendly way of cheating—"the more friendly, the more
advantageous." Its indisputable contribution to the intensification of international relations has brought about not the fraternization of peoples, but
"the fraternity of thieves." As a result, "the liberal economic system had
done its best to universalize enmity, to transform mankind into a horde of
ravenous beasts (for what else are competitors?) who devour one another

just *because* each has identical interests with all the others" (ibid., 423, 423, 423).

After this introduction, Engels proceeded to analyze the central categories of a liberal economy, such as value, commodity, capital, competition, monopoly, and so forth. All these analyses confirmed his initial statement that the system described and defended by liberal economists was nothing less than "modern slavery." Special attention was given to Malthusian theory, which "has shown us how in the last instance private property has turned man into a commodity whose production and destruction also depend solely on demand." He even questioned freedom of competition on the grounds that competition necessarily produces monopoly. Otherwise, the word *monopoly* in this context meant something better than unrestricted competition: "Monopoly at least intended to protect the consumer against fraud, even if it could not in fact do so" (ibid., 420, 439–40, 441).

In predicting the future of the system, Engels formulated the following view, which was later repeated in Marx's *Capital* and accepted as an article of faith by all classical Marxists: "In general large property increases much more rapidly than small property, since a much smaller portion is deducted from its proceeds as property expenses. This law of centralization of private property is as immanent in private property as all the others. The middle class must increasingly disappear until the world is divided into millionaires and paupers, into large landowners and poor farm laborers. All the laws, all the dividing of landed property, all the possible splitting-up of capital, are of no avail: this result must and will come, unless it is anticipated by a total transformation of social conditions, a fusion of opposed interests, an abolition of private property" (ibid., 441).

The critical part of Engels's article leads directly to the positive formulation of his conception of truly human freedom in economic activity. He anticipated the development of Marx's views in this respect, and his main conclusion was to be repeated in Marx's *Capital*. This conclusion concerned, of course, conscious comprehensive planning as a means of getting control over the blind forces of the market and thereby attaining a state of rational self-mastery. The law of competition, Engels argued, produces periodical crises because it is "purely a law of nature and not a law of the mind." Hence, it is a law "based on the unconsciousness of the participants. If the producers as such knew how much the consumers required, if they were to organize production, if they were to share it out amongst themselves, then the fluctuations of competition and its tendency to crisis would be impossible. Carry on production consciously as human beings—not as dispersed atoms without consciousness of your species—and you have overcome all these artificial and untenable antitheses" (ibid., 433, 434).

It is noteworthy that young Engels formulated the feasibility of such a solution in a quite modern way, a way reminiscent of the great "calculation debate" of the twentieth century, as a problem of economic calculation that could replace the spontaneous (unconscious) order of the market. He wrote: "The truth of the relation of competition is the relation of consumption to productivity. In a world worthy of mankind there will be no other competition than this. The community will have to calculate what it can produce with the means at its disposal: and in accordance with the relationship of this productive power to the mass of consumers it will determine how far it has to raise or lower production, how far it has to give way to, or curtail, luxury" (ibid., 435).

Needless to say, Engels was totally unaware of the difficulties involved. His reference in this connection to unnamed "English Socialists" and to Fourier clearly shows that he lacked his own ideas on the matter. But from the point of view of the topic of freedom, his carelessness in using the word *community* is even more disturbing. It should have been obvious to him that community as a whole cannot calculate what it can produce. Macroeconomic calculation (regardless of what we think of it) can be made only by an individual, or a group of individuals, and society as a whole cannot be expected to unanimously accept the recommendations of a small group. After all, decisions about what, how much, and what not to produce are important matters that concern everyone, and human preferences and interests, at least in a modern, complex society, are by no means uniform. To achieve such uniformity, planners would have to legally enforce these decisions, which would amount to a "dictatorship over needs." [80] Unrestricted competition had led to crises, but at the same time, it had enormously increased (compared to the natural economy) consumers' freedom to choose. Engels did not take this into account. Above all, however, he wrongly assumed that dependence on another's decisions is more desirable than dependence on things. This conclusion is wrong because dependence on persons is *more* humiliating and *more* destructive of freedom than dependence on depersonalized relations or (quasi) natural laws. As shown earlier, Marx based his entire theory of freedom on this faulty assumption (see Chapter 1, section 6).

It has been observed that, after 1844, "Engels seems to have surrendered political economy wholly to Marx." [81] Because of this, it is appropriate to ask what Marx was to add to Engels's conception of the relationship between human freedom and capitalist development.

Both thinkers agreed that capitalism was a necessary "link in the chain of mankind's universal progress," a link especially important as, in fact, a turning point from the greatest alienation to "the reconciliation of mankind with nature and with itself." [82] Young Engels, however, described only the destructive effects of capitalism, seeing universal destruction, universal atomization, as a necessary premise for universal regeneration. Thus, in his view, nationalities had to be dissolved to give way to universal human fraternity; even the family, "the last vestige of common interests," had to be undermined by the cruel "factory system," because only universal "separation of interests" could enable individuals to join efforts as simple human beings, free and conscious members of the same species (ibid., 424, 424, 423–24).[83] The means of bringing about this destructive, although unintentionally progressive, work was trade. It was extremely characteristic that young Engels, following such haters of trade as Hess and Fourier,[84] concentrated exclusively on commercialization while completely neglecting the spectacular development of capitalist productive forces.

Marx assimilated these ideas in a critical way and developed them in accordance with his own conception of self-enriching alienation. For him, capitalist development involved not only inevitable universal destruction, but also, above all, the creation of *positive* preconditions for communism, such as technological mastery over nature, universal interdependence through the world market, and a level of productivity ensuring universal abundance. Thus, for him capitalism meant an enrichment of humanity, although achieved at the cost of maximum alienation.[85] He stressed that capitalist alienation was a form of development of the human essence: in order to develop its faculties, humans *had* to externalize these faculties, to objectify their activities in an inhuman way and thus lose control over their products.

Already in *The German Ideology* (whose theoretical foundations were worked out mostly by Marx), young Engels had corrected his thesis about capitalist atomization and the alleged "separation of interests" by showing that the division of labor would create new forms of social unity— alienated, to be sure—that would subject individuals to an all-round dependence, leaving little room for "atomic" freedom. In his later works, especially *Grundrisse*, Marx treated the vision of universal atomization as a romantic distortion of the real nature of capitalism. Atoms, he stressed, have no needs; capitalism destroys the relations of personal dependence but replaces them with a strong structure of large-scale objective dependency relations.

However, this more positive view of capitalist achievements did not automatically entail a more positive assessment of freedom under capitalism, but only made it more dialectical. In the relation of man to nature, capitalism greatly increased human freedom (Engels, as we shall see, readily accepted this conclusion), while in the relation of man to society, it brought human alienation to its outer limits, thus maximizing unfreedom. Hence, the more sophisticated treatment of capitalism did not change any part of the adamantly negative attitude toward the liberal conception of freedom. On the contrary, Marx's views on the means of overcoming capitalist

alienation were even more illiberal: he thought that the idea of a conscious regulation of production must be accompanied by the abolition of
money—that is, by making individual consumers totally dependent on the
decisions of "community."

The close friendship between Marx and Engels began at the end of
August 1844, when Engels, returning from England to Germany, stopped
for ten days in Paris. The first fruits of their lifelong collaboration were
The Holy Family and *The German Ideology*. In 1845, Engels published his
first book, *The Condition of the Working Class in England*, which made
his name widely known in Germany.[86] Marx, who by that time had just
achieved his "theoretical self-clarification," saw Engels's book as proof
that his friend had arrived independently at the same theoretical position.
The road from theory to practice was very short: in 1845, both friends were
active in the renascent communist movement in Germany.

In sketching the vision of the communist society of the future, Marx contributed less than Engels, who presented the first and most comprehensive
outline of this vision in his "Speeches in Elberfeld," which he delivered to
a middle-class audience in February 1845. His comments deserve our attention, since there is a lack of similarly detailed description of this vision
in the later writings of both Marx and Engels.

After drawing an appalling picture of the results of free competition,
Engels promised his audience that all these evils would disappear under
communist organization. He was particularly fond of telling how *easily*
and *simply* everything could be arranged, as, for instance, the rational
regulation of production: "Since we know how much, on the average, a
person needs, it is easy to calculate how much is needed by a given number
of individuals, and since production is no longer in the hands of private
producers but in those of the community and its administrative bodies, it is
a trifling matter *to regulate production according to needs*" (ibid., 4:246).

The elimination of unnecessary middlemen, the swindlers, speculators,
agents, exporters, wholesalers, and retailers, will be equally easy: "Just as
one can *easily* know how much cotton or manufactured cotton goods an
individual colony needs, it will be *equally easy* for the central authority to
determine how much all the villages and townships in the country need. . . .
Average annual consumption will only change in proportion to the increasing population; *it is therefore easy* at the appropriate time to determine in
advance what amount of each particular article the people will need—the
entire great amount will be ordered directly from the source of supply"
(ibid., 247; italics added).

This is the first Marxist formulation of the idea of so-called directly
socialized production—that is, production that would eliminate exchange
on the market, thus replacing commodity production by "production for
use." In a strikingly un-Marxist manner, Engels assumed that, just as in

a primitive "natural economy," human needs would not increase. Nevertheless, the term *Marxist* is justified in this case, since Marxologists tend to agree that, from the beginning of 1845 onward, everything written by Marx or Engels represented Marxism—not perfect Marxism perhaps, but still Marxism. Significantly, the quoted passages have been included without qualification in a Soviet anthology of classical Marxist-Leninist texts on communist society.[87]

In publicly delivered speeches destined for publication, Engels preferred to avoid the risk of dealing directly with the sensitive problem of the abolition of the state. He managed, however, to touch on this question by advocating the liquidation of the unnecessarily extensive and complicated system of administrative and judicial bodies. "In communist society," he argued, "this would likewise be vastly simplified, and precisely because—strange though it may sound—precisely because the administrative body in this society would have to manage not merely individual aspects of social life, but the whole of social life, in all its various activities, in all its aspects" (ibid., 248).

This indeed sounds strange—totally administered society as a positive ideal! But the logic behind this conclusion was consistent with the requirement to end the division of social life into two distinct spheres, private and public. Liquidation of this dualism was understood as the abolition of the state (and politics as such) by overcoming political alienation. But Engels, who had never been an anarchist, made it perfectly clear that administration (which he now called "the administrative bodies of the community") would continue to exist, being directed by a "central authority." This was not illogical: liquidation of dualism was conceivable either as dissolving administration in the spontaneous order of civil society, or as swallowing civil society by administration. Having learned from Hegel that civil society was a sphere of conflicting, particular interests, Engels naturally preferred the second solution. Seeing this as the abolition of the state (rather than the abolition of society) was simply a matter of definition: the state was, by his definition, something external and alienated, presupposing the existence of a conflict-ridden society and of the private/public dichotomy. The elimination of conflicts between individuals and social groups would (according to this logic) transform administration into something completely different from what had been called the state.

The same logic applied to law. Civil law would disappear because there would be no private property to defend; conflicts between individuals would become extremely rare and would be "*easily* settled by arbitrators." A standing army would also become useless because "it will be *easy* to train every fit member of society" to defend the country in case of aggression (ibid., 249, 249 [italics added]). (This shows, by the way, that Engels at that time did not exclude the possibility of communism in one country.)

Among other savings of social energy that were to follow, Engels mentioned "the fusing of individual powers into a social collective power" through a thorough reorganization of family life. He fully subscribed to the proposals of Robert Owen as "the most practical and most fully worked out" (ibid., 252). He summarized them as follows:

Instead of the present towns and villages with their separate individual houses standing in each other's way, we should construct large palaces which, built in the form of a square some 1,650 feet in length and breadth, would enclose a large garden and comfortably accommodate from two to three thousand people. . . . What amount of labor and material is squandered under the present system of separate housing—in heating for example! . . . And the preparation of meals—what a waste of space, ingredients, labor, is involved in the present, separate households, where every family cooks its little bit of food on its own, has its own supply of crockery, employs its own cook, must fetch its own supplies separately from the market, from the garden, from the butcher and the baker! . . . And finally, the household itself! Will not such a building be infinitely easier to keep clean and in good condition when, as is possible, this kind of work also is organized and regularly shared out, than the two or three hundred separate houses which would be the equivalent under the present housing system? (ibid., 252–53)

Interestingly, Engels did not envisage the immediate expropriation of manufacturers. Rather, he saw his ideas for the desirable future as a program of peaceful reform that would receive support for the entrepreneurs in the form of "a general progressive tax on capital, at a rate increasing with the size of the capital." He assured his audience that "it is not intended to introduce common ownership overnight and against the will of the nation." And, somewhat curiously, he tried to assuage possible fears by arguing that communism was an organic product of existing society whose embryonic forms had already become generally accepted. "The principle of taxation," he reasoned, "is, after all, a purely communist one. . . . For either private property is sacrosanct, in which case there is no such case as national property and the state has no right to levy taxes, or the state has this right, in which case private property is not sacrosanct, national property stands above private property, and the state is the true owner. This latter principle is the one generally accepted—well then, gentlemen; for the present we demand only that this principle be taken seriously, that the state proclaim itself the common owner and, as such, administer public property for the public good" (ibid., 254, 255, 254).

The reason industrialists should support gradual introduction of communism was, Engels explained, because it was in the national interest of Germany. The system of free trade would ruin German industry because Germany would not be able to successfully compete with England. The system of protectionism, even if fully successful in stimulating industrial development (which Engels thought to be "very improbable"), could only bring Germany to the same point England had reached: "namely the eve of the social revolution." Therefore, there is only one way to avoid "the bloody solution of the social problem": namely, "the peaceful introduction or at least preparation of communism" (ibid., 260, 261, 263).

In 1847, when Marx and Engels joined the newly organized Communist League, Engels elaborated the communist program differently, for he only had to deal with convinced revolutionaries, former members of the League of the Just. The heated discussions that preceded the emergence of the Communist League are relevant for our topic, because both sides— Marx and Engels, on the one, and revolutionary artisans from the League of the Just, on the other—seemed to be genuinely concerned with the problem of freedom.[88] Marx and Engels saw the danger to freedom in the authoritarian tendencies inherent in the Blanquist-type revolutionary conspiracy, as well as in the premature revolution that would have to be carried out against the will of the majority of the population. Their opponents, in turn, suspected the two learned friends of a desire to "establish some kind of aristocracy of intellectuals [Gelehrten-Aristokratie]" and to rule over the people from its "new godly thrones." These accusations were by no means without substance. The revolutionary tailor and chiliastically minded utopianist Wilhelm Weitling was indeed deeply convinced that the communist movement needed an all-powerful dictator, while Marx was certainly not immune from intellectual arrogance, at one point banging the table with his fist and shouting, "Ignorance never did anyone any good!"[89] Historical hindsight enables us to see this confrontation as anticipating a long series of similar clashes in later revolutionary movements.[90]

Engels's new task—providing a draft program for the Communist League—was completed in his catechismal "Principles of Communism." He repeated once more his and Marx's main idea about "the whole of society" running industrial production "according to a fixed plan and according to the needs of all." Such a system presupposed "people of all-round development" who knew all branches of industry and were capable of moving from one to another according to the needs of society and their own inclinations. He outlined a vision of communism as based on universal abundance that would thereby enable every member of society "to develop and exercise all his powers and abilities in perfect freedom," and he boldly claimed that after concentrating all exchange "in the hands of the nation," production would increase enormously and "money will become superfluous." Finally, he did not fail to mention characteristic details such as "the erection of large palaces on national estates as common dwellings for communities of citizens engaged in industry as well as agriculture, and combining the advantages of both urban and rural life without the one-sidedness and disadvantages of either." New aspects of this vision included the provision that children would be "communally educated," thus freeing them from dependence on their parents.[91] New elements also included a higher appraisal of capitalist development and the view that the communist revolution could not succeed in one country alone. Both these elements moderated revolutionary impatience and thus directly supported the main innovation of the program: its strongly anti-Blanquist, antivoluntaristic tendency. Engels emphasized his (and Marx's) rejection of Weitling's view that "mankind is necessarily always ripe for communism or never will be."[92] "Every revolution in property relations," Engels asserted, "has been the necessary result of the creation of new productive forces which would no longer conform to the old property relations." Hence, a communist revolution was not possible before capitalism created necessary premises for it. Furthermore, the phenomenon of social exploitation and oppression had been inevitable in the past, because "so long as it is not possible to produce so much that not only is there enough for all, but also a surplus for the increase of social capital and for the further development of productive forces, so long must there always be a ruling class disposing of these productive forces of society, and a poor, oppressed class" (ibid., 6:347, 353, 347, 351, 351, 354, 348, 349).

Engels's views on the revolution and his practical recommendations for the German communists were also consistently anti-Blanquist. "The Communists," he proclaimed, "know only too well that all conspiracies are not only futile but even harmful. They know only too well that revolutions are not made deliberately and arbitrarily, but that everywhere and at all times they have been the necessary outcome of circumstances entirely independent of the will and leadership of particular parties and entire classes." The transition to communism was, in the long run, a historical necessity, but it could, in principle, be achieved by peaceful methods. Germany was still a relatively backward country, and therefore the immediate task of the German workers would not be an immediate introduction of communism: "In Germany, the decisive struggle between the bourgeoisie and the absolute monarchy is still to come. Since, however, the Communists cannot count on the decisive struggle between themselves and the bourgeoisie until the bourgeoisie rules, it is in the interests of the Communists to help bring the bourgeoisie to power as soon as possible in order to overthrow them again" (ibid., 349, 349, 356).[93]

The *Manifesto of the Communist Party* (for whose final draft "Marx alone was responsible")[94] leaves no doubt that this was also Marx's position. "The Communists," it stated, "do not form a separate party opposed to other working-class parties. They have no interests separate and apart from those of the proletariat as a whole" (ibid., 497). It is difficult to imagine a more anti-Blanquist, or (*avant la lettre*) anti-Leninist statement. The necessity of a temporary alliance with the modern liberal bourgeoisie—as different from and, indeed, opposed to the petty bourgeoisie—was also unambiguously endorsed (ibid., 519). And the ultimate goals of the movement were not even mentioned.

However, there also exists another document in which Marx and Engels defined their position differently—and in a way much closer to the views of their opponents within the Communist League—namely, their "Address of the Central Authority of the League," known commonly as their "March Circular" of 1850. Some Marxologists have described this piece as revealing the true nature of Marx and Engels's views, proving that Lenin was basically right in his claim to have correctly interpreted their political thought.[95] Serious arguments against this view have been put forward by Hunt, who has tried to show that the March Circular was a product of a number of circumstances that distorted Marx and Engels's theory, concluding from this that "it would be best to disregard the document altogether as a source for the political doctrines of Classical Marxism."[96]

It is in any case necessary to briefly examine this matter, which seems appropriate in a chapter on Engels, since he was more consistent than Marx in elaborating the necessitarian (and therefore, anti-Blanquist) aspect of classical Marxism.

The March Circular begins with the postulate of changing temporary allies. In 1848 the liberal bourgeoisie proved to be counterrevolutionary; it became obvious that revolutionary elements could be found, apart from the Communists, only among the democratic petty bourgeoisie—that is, among a social stratum that was far more dangerous for the workers than the treacherous liberal bourgeoisie (ibid., 10:279). Any alliance with a petty bourgeois democracy therefore would require special precautions.

Why so? In Marx and Engels's eyes, the petty bourgeoisie represented an obsolete mode of production whose very existence was doomed; hence, it was treated by them as an objectively reactionary class, often as simply a relic of medievalism. On this ground, the *Manifesto of the Communist Party* expected the revolution to conform to the logic of modernization: modern social classes (i.e., the bourgeoisie and the proletariat) were to fight against the forces of the old regime, including the petty bourgeoisie (ibid., 6:519). Reality, however, diverged from this doctrinaire logic while at the same time making it clearer than ever that revolutionary communists could not fight against absolute monarchy without allies. This situation explains Marx and Engels's reluctant alignment with the petty bourgeois democracy, as well as their warnings against these unwelcome allies. In other words, they reconciled themselves to the necessity of the initial support of the petty bourgeoisie but remained deeply convinced that progress meant centralization; hence, they were adamantly hostile to petty bourgeois aims and values. The petty bourgeoisie, they warned, "will give the feudal lands to the peasants," but the workers "must demand that the confiscated feudal property remain state property and be converted into workers' colonies cultivated by the associated rural proletariat with all the advantages of large-scale agriculture" (ibid., 10:284–85). Communal property, as well as communal civil law, should also be abolished as lagging behind modern civil law and modern private property (ibid., 285). As in France in 1793, the task of a really revolutionary party in Germany was "to carry through the strictest centralization." The petty bourgeois democrats would resist this tendency; they "will work either directly for a federative republic or, if they cannot avoid a single and indivisible republic, they will at least attempt to cripple the central government by the utmost possible autonomy and independence for the communities and provinces. The workers, in opposition to this plan, must not only strive for a single and indivisible German republic, but also within this republic for the most determined centralization of power in the hands of the state authority. They must not allow themselves to be misguided by the democratic talk of freedom for the communities, of self-government, etc" (ibid., 285, 285).

Thus, an alliance with petty bourgeois democracy was indeed far more dangerous for the workers than an alliance with bourgeois liberals. The scope of common aims was much narrower (because of different attitudes toward centralization), and preserving the separate identity of the workers' movement was much more difficult; after all, petty bourgeois elements were active even within the Communist League, and it was easily imaginable that the class conscious proletarian movement might be dissolved in the broader, amorphous movement of the popular masses. This explains why the authors of the March Circular thought it necessary "to establish an independent secret and public organization of the workers' party alongside with official democrats" and why they chose for this organization the slogan: "The Revolution in Permanence." The same aim—preserving the independence of the workers' movement—was to be served by keeping alive the spirit of "direct revolutionary excitement" through encouraging "so called excesses, instances of popular revenge against hated individuals or public buildings" (ibid., 282/287, 282). The authors hoped that such excesses would, from the very beginning, create conflicts between the petty bourgeois democrats and the Communists, thus preventing their close collaboration.

Admittedly, the March Circular must disappoint all who wish to see in Marx and Engels noble-minded, faithful allegiance to democratic values. But having said this, I should also stress that its obvious Jacobinist centralizing tendency was not bound up with Blanquism: the secret organization of the workers' movement was not conceived as a conspiracy aiming at the seizure of political power, but only as a means whereby the attitudes and interests of the proletariat could be discussed independently of outside influences (ibid., 282). Commitment to Jacobinism was in itself yet another proof that despite the "treachery" of the German bourgeoisie, Marx and

Engels remained faithful to the view that historical development must proceed through stages and that a stage equivalent to that of the French Revolution could not be passed over. There were genuine Blanquists among the German Communists, but Marx and Engels did not belong to them. The centralizing tendency was common to Jacobins and Blanquists, but the distinctive feature of Blanquism, as Hunt correctly emphasized, was the rejection of the entire concept of revolution through progressive stages.[97]

It seems worthwhile to make two points here. First, there was an important difference between Marx and Engels's views and the Leninist standpoint on the question of possible allies for the revolutionary workers. Unlike his theoretical masters, Lenin from the very beginning saw his temporary allies as being the peasantry (that is, the rural petty bourgeoisie, according to Marxist criteria) but rejected on principle any form of alliance with bourgeois liberals, whom he defined as the most dangerous enemies of his party. Second, after the dissolution of the Communist League (which took place on Marx's motion at the end of 1852), Marx and Engels consciously chose the role of independent critics, not of leaders of a tightly organized, let alone illegal, vanguard party.[98] In this respect, they differed from Lenin as much as possible.

In his *Peasant War in Germany* (1850), Engels generalized the experience of the radical forces in the revolutions of 1848–50 in Europe by drawing parallels, as well as contrasts, between their defeat and the fates of the Great Peasant War of 1525 in Germany. He concentrated on the tragedy of the radical leader who, like Thomas Münzer, the early prophet of the communist millennium, faced the situation in which their party and their class could not objectively win. Such a leader, Engels maintained, "necessarily finds himself in an unsolvable dilemma. What he *can* do contradicts all his previous actions and principles and the immediate interests of his party, and what he *ought* to do cannot be done. In a word, he is compelled to represent not his party or his class, but the class for whose domination the moment is then ripe. In the interests of the movement he is compelled to advance the interest of an alien class, and to feed his own class with talk and promises, and with the asseveration that the interests of that alien class are their own interests. He who is put into this awkward situation is irrevocably lost" (ibid., 470).

Despite appearances, this analysis was not meant as a warning against betraying one's own movement. Rather, it showed that morality and ideological principle should be sacrificed to the long-term interests of historical progress, which, in such situations, demand support for those progressive forces "for whose domination the movement is then ripe." Münzer was not flexible enough to follow this dialectical logic, and this entailed not only his own decapitation and the crushing defeat of his followers, but also fatal consequences for Germany: the victors were the princes alone and this meant "the deepening and consolidation of German disunity." The results of the revolutions of 1848–50 were, in fact, very different. The proletarian leaders in Germany and France did not imitate Münzer's heroic intransigence, which undoubtedly placed them in an awkward and personally discrediting position, but owing to this the victory did not fall into the hands of reactionary forces. In Germany, the defeat of premature radicalism this time did not profit the minor princes, as in 1525, but rather the big princes: Austria and Prussia. This was a completely different outcome, because "behind Austria and Prussia, there stand the modern big bourgeois, rapidly getting them under their yoke by means of the national debt. And behind the big bourgeois stand the proletarians" (ibid., 480, 482).

In other words, the obvious defeat of the German Communists furthered the cause of capitalist development in Germany and thereby furthered the long-term interests of the German workers. Was Engels not aware that this dialectical reasoning amounted to what he himself described in the above quote as feeding one's own class "with talk and promises, and with the asseveration that the interests of that alien class are their own interests"?

Nevertheless, he certainly did not see himself as being put in an "awkward situation" and "irrevocably lost." This shows clearly that he treated himself, quite correctly, as a theorist of German communism, and not as its practical leader. As such, he was deeply attached to the Hegelian notion of rational historical necessity, which clears its way without paying any attention to the illusions and tragedies of its tools—namely, human beings. He was always proud of the peculiar philosophical capacity of the Germans and saw the German workers as the rightful heirs to this tradition. Therefore, a quarter of a century later, in his preface to the third edition of his *Peasant War*, he gratefully mentioned Hegel and fondly concluded: "Without German philosophy, particularly that of Hegel, German scientific socialism—the only scientific socialism that has ever existed—would never come into being" (M&E, SW, 2:169).[99]

In contrast to utopian socialism, "scientific socialism" (as Engels himself so many times explained) was to refuse to provide any specific details about the future. In fact, however, this was not so. Marx was possibly the most extreme utopian, because his conception of communism presupposed not only common ownership and comprehensive planning, but also complete abolition of market exchange—a conclusion he derived from philosophical speculation, though he failed to support this by any scientific arguments whatsoever.[100] In Engels's case, the discrepancy between programmatic scientism and utopianism is even more visible because, after all, in the early period of his collaboration with Marx, he had indulged in drawing quite detailed visions of communism and had never renounced them in later years. No wonder, therefore, that these early ideas were not allowed to be quietly forgotten. Thus, for instance, Engels's favorite idea of "the abolition of the antithesis between town and country"—an idea taken by him directly from classical utopian socialism[101]—was alive in the Soviet Union as late as the time of Khrushchev, who tried to realize it by his experiments with so-called agrotowns. Similarly, Engels's fantasies about "large communal palaces," which would accommodate thousands of people and enable them to dispense with the burdens of conducting separate family households, were developed with much enthusiasm by Stanislaw Strumilin, one of the foremost Soviet economists of that time.[102] Needless to say, Strumilin's palace communes "were to create conditions for a truly-human, i.e., fully communal life"; families, reduced to "primary units" composed of husband and wife, would be "freed from the burdensome care of dependents and time wasting domestic chores" and thus could participate in "the workers' clubs, libraries, sport organizations and creative, artistic collectives."[103] This only shows that Engels's "scientific socialism" did not really mean breaking with utopianism in the name of science; in actuality, it only gave new, pseudoscientific credibility to very old utopian ideas.

As exercises of imagination and regulative ideas for an overall betterment of society, utopias are undoubtedly a much needed element of human society. But Engels's "scientific socialism" was something different—precisely because it pretended to be scientific. It disclaimed all affinities with utopianism, espousing instead the Hegelian belief in the inexorable laws of history and claiming to possess the key to their "truly scientific" understanding.[104] "Scientific socialism" thus became arrogantly self-confident, and hence, dangerously authoritarian, being convinced of its essential infallibility and completely immune to criticism from the point of view of different value judgments. Its peculiar identification of "the necessary" with "the desirable" and "the justifiable" made it programmatically antisentimental, with an Olympian indifference to the human sufferings that could be interpreted as a necessary price and condition of historical progress. This was also one of its Hegelian features. This view was forcefully manifested in Engels's approach to different "national questions" in the revolutionary times of 1848–50.

2.4   "Historical Necessity" in the World of Nations

On the eve of the Springtime of the Peoples, the *Manifesto of the Communist Party* proclaimed that "the history of all hitherto existing society is the history of class struggles" and that "the working men have no country" (M&E, CW, 6:482, 502). However, the revolutionary events of 1848–49 in the Habsburg Empire and Prussia generated a powerful outburst of nationalist emotions that took the form of a struggle between nationalities rather than classes. Strange as it may seem, the authors of the *Manifesto* were not shocked or even surprised by this.[105] They did not try to weaken national antagonisms by turning revolutionary energy against the ruling, or privileged, classes of each nation. On the contrary, they firmly supported some nationalities against others, thereby claiming to further the cause of all-European revolution. They explicitly denied the equality of nations, ridiculed the romantic ideal of their universal brotherhood, and rejected on principle the universal application of the right of national self-determination. Instead, they divided nations into two groups: "the historical nations," having the right to independence, and "history-less peoples," whose national aspirations were reactionary and absurd. In addition, they themselves were vulnerable to German nationalist feelings, and their revolutionary zeal too easily transformed itself into a crusade against Slavs (except for the Poles) as alleged enemies of European progress and faithful allies of the reactionary Russian Empire. In any case, their newspaper, *Neue Rheinische Zeitung*, did not preach turning wars between nations into war between classes; rather, it proposed achieving a progressive solution to "the German question": a democratic republic unified through an alliance of German revolutionary forces with the "revolutionary nations" of East-Central Europe and a common crusade against Russia.

The policy of the *Neue Rheinische Zeitung* was determined by Marx, who in principle had to endorse everything published in it.[106] Nevertheless, the main expert on national questions was Engels, and what he wrote on this subject deserves careful attention in a study of the different aspects of the Marxist conception of freedom. Let us start with a few quotations from two of Engels's articles of early 1849: "The Magyar Struggle" and "Democratic Pan-Slavism."

In the first of these, Engels divided nations into two categories: "historical nations," i.e., nations taking an active part in history as "standard-bearers of progress," and nations that never played, or failed to play, such a role. In the Habsburg Empire, the first category was represented by the Germans, Magyars, and Poles; the second consisted mostly of the small Slavic nations. Engels, referring to Hegel, called the latter "*residual fragments of peoples*," relics of nations that had been "mercilessly trampled under foot in the course of history." To the same category belonged the Gaels in Scotland, the Bretons in France, and the Basques in Spain. Since history was always right, all these historical losers deserved their lot and could not change it; thus, they were doomed to be "fanatical standard-bearers of counter-revolution and remain so until their complete extirpation or loss of their national character, just as their whole existence is itself a protest against a great historical revolution" (ibid., 8:230, 234, 234).

This sweeping generalization made it clear that the Hungarian Slavs could not have history on their side in protesting against Magyar oppression, especially in a situation in which the Magyars, supported by Polish volunteers and applauded by German revolutionaries, rose against their

Habsburg rulers. Nevertheless, the Slavs dared to use this occasion to settle their accounts with Magyars and to win concessions for themselves from the monarchy. Engels's indignation was boundless. His article ended with the following threat: "At the first victorious uprising of the French proletariat, which Louis Napoleon is striving with all his might to conjure up, the Austrian Germans and Magyars will be set free and wreak a bloody revenge on the Slav barbarians. The general war which will then break out will smash this Slav Sonderbund and wipe out all these petty hidebound nations, down to their very names. The next world war will result in the disappearance from the face of the earth not only of reactionary classes and dynasties, but also of entire reactionary peoples. And that, too, is a step forward" (ibid., 238).

It is difficult to deny that this was an outright call for genocide.[107] But let us pass to Engels's second article, a polemic against Bakunin.

It begins with a critique of "ardent fantasies about the universal fraternal union of peoples" (ibid., 362). In reality, Engels argued, such an idyll is historically impossible: peoples are divided into revolutionary and reactionary groups, and history moves forward through a bloody struggle between the forces of revolution and the forces of reaction (ibid., 363). The choice of side depends on the advancement of civilization. Bakunin, and other romantic believers in "universal liberation," did not pay due attention to "the very diverse degrees of civilization and the consequent equally diverse political needs of the individual peoples." They invoked "justice," "humanity," "freedom," and "fraternity," but these abstract ethical categories *prove absolutely nothing* in historical and political questions" (ibid., 364, 365). To illustrate this point, Engels asked a series of rhetorical questions concerning the war between the United States and Mexico:

Will Bakunin accuse the Americans of a "war of conquest," which, although it deals a severe blow to this theory based on "justice and humanity," was nevertheless waged wholly and solely in the interests of civilization? Or is it perhaps unfortunate that splendid California has been taken away from the lazy Mexicans, who could not do anything with it? That the energetic Yankees by rapid exploitation of the California gold mines will increase the means of circulation, in a few years will concentrate a dense population and extensive trade at the most suitable places on the coast of the Pacific Ocean, create large cities, open up communications by steamship, construct a railway from New York to San Francisco, for the first time really open the Pacific Ocean to civilization, and for the third time in history give world trade a new direction? The "independence" of a few Spanish Californians and Texans may suffer because of it, in some places "justice" and other moral principles may be violated; but what does that matter compared to such fact of world-historic significance? (ibid., 365–66)

Roman Rosdolsky, the best expert on Engels's views on the national question, commented on this quotation, reminding readers that the main reason for the American-Mexican conflict was the revolt of American settlers in Texas, who were slave owners and who protested the abolition of slavery in Mexico.[108] Thus, in a sense, it was a war in defense of slavery. But this reminder would have confused neither Engels nor Marx, since at that time their views on slavery in America were quite unambiguous, as is reflected by what Marx wrote on this subject in a letter to P. V. Annenkov, December 28, 1846: "Without slavery North America, the most progressive country, would be transformed into a patriarchal land. You have only to wipe North America off the map of the nations and you get anarchy, the total decay of trade and of modern civilization. But to let slavery disappear is to wipe North America off the map of nations" (M&E, SW, 1:524).

The theory of international relations contained in Engels's article amounts to a wholehearted endorsement of the Victorian conception of what might be called "the historic right of superior civilization." In a conflict between superior and inferior civilizations or superior and inferior cultures, the superior one is bound to win and rule, and there should be no moral scruples about it. The superior culture must win at all costs because its victory is in the interest of historical progress, of universal human civilization. In history, being "right" means only "being on the side of progress," "being a vehicle of civilization." And civilization, in full accordance with the Victorian stereotype, was identified, of course, with Western civilization, whose main pillars were the "advanced countries" of Europe and the United States.[109] Hence Pan-Slavism, in whatever form, had to be perceived as a mortal threat to the continuity of historical progress.

The specifically Engelsian contribution to this theory derived from Engels's vulgar Hegelianism[110] and his Jacobin-Marxist belief in centralization, both of which were bound up with the Marxist conviction that applying "abstract" moral standards to history was nothing more than an indulgence in sheer sentimentalism and ahistoricism. Three quotations amply illustrate this.

First, on the Hegelian theme of "nonhistorical" peoples: "Peoples which have never had a history of their own, which from the time when they achieved the first, most elementary stage of civilization already came under foreign sway, or which were *forced* to attain the first stage of civilization only by means of a foreign yoke, are not viable and will never be able to achieve any kind of independence" (M&E, CW, 8:367).

Second, on "historical necessity": "What a crime it is, what a 'damnable policy' that at a time when, in Europe in general, big monarchies had become a 'historical necessity,' the Germans and Magyars united all these small, stunted and impotent little nations into a single big state and thereby enabled them to take part in a historical development from which, left to themselves, they would have remained completely aloof! Of course, matters of this kind cannot be accomplished without many a tender national blossom being forcibly broken. But in history nothing is achieved without violence and implacable ruthlessness" (ibid., 370).

Finally, on centralization: "*Now*, however, as a result of the powerful progress of industry, trade and communications, political centralization has become a much more urgent need than it was then, in the fifteenth and sixteenth centuries. What still has to be centralized is being centralized. And *now* the Pan-Slavists come forward and demand that we should abolish a centralization which is being forced on these Slavs by all their material interests!" (ibid., 371).

One might wonder why Hungarian and Polish independence should be seen as compatible with the steady movement toward political and economic centralization. This was so, in Marx and Engels's view, for more than one reason. First, both these nations had their own nationally conscious and politically active "historical class" (i.e., their own nobility) and a long, vivid tradition of their own statehood; hence, they belonged to the category of "historical nations." Second, if considered in their historical boundaries, they represented big (although multiethnic and multilingual) national units, and the necessary centralization might be conceived as centralization *within* independent Hungary and Poland, which would involve, of course, magyarization and polonization of respective minorities (which would have been fully consistent with the Jacobin ideal of a centralized and linguistically homogeneous nation).[111] Finally, and perhaps decisively, Hungarians and Poles were precious allies of the revolutionary forces in Germany, especially in view of the likelihood (and desirability) of a revolutionary war with tsarist Russia. The case of Poland was additionally strengthened by the fact that the three absolute monarchies (Austria, Prussia, and Russia) that had partitioned Poland were the pillars of the reactionary Holy Alliance, whose avowed aim was to prevent revolutions in Europe. Due to this, Western revolutionaries and Polish patriots had common enemies and saw themselves as struggling for the same aim: the overthrow of the "old order" in Europe. Engels was full of admiration for the Poles who, as he put it, "shared the fighting in all the revolutions and revolutionary wars" and thus made the words *Pole* and *revolutionary* synonymous (ibid., 375).[112] He did not hesitate to draw from this a far-reaching conclusion: "For Poles the sympathy of all Europe and the restoration of their nation [i.e., state] are as certain as are for the Czechs, Croats and Russians the hatred of all Europeans and the most bloody revolutionary war of the entire West against them" (ibid., 375).

Of course, the restoration of historical Poland would have entailed territorial losses for the Germans, including the territories with a numerous German minority. But in 1848 Engels was fully prepared to pay this price. He wrote: "Poland must have at least the dimensions of 1772, she must comprise not only the territories but also the estuaries of her big rivers and at least a large seaboard on the Baltic" (ibid., 7:352).

When the revolutionary events were over, Engels's zeal cooled, and he made a critical appraisal of what had really happened. In his *Peasant War*, he expressed satisfaction with the strengthening of the centralizing tendency in Austria, obviously having reconciled himself to the defeat of Hungary (see above, section 3). In his *Revolution and Counterrevolution in Germany* (1852), Engels made some revealing comments about the Polish question. He endorsed the German *"Drang nach Osten"* by stating that "ever since the time of Charlemagne the Germans have directed their most constant and persevering efforts to the conquest, colonization, or at least, civilization of the East of Europe." His positive appraisal of these civilizing efforts included the Teutonic Knights, who had laid "the ground for a far more extensive and effective system of Germanization by the trading and manufacturing middle classes." The capitalist development of the last seventy years had quickened this process, and as a result, the line of demarcation between German and Polish nationalities had entirely changed. This, Engels continued, created a difficult situation for the German revolutionaries who (like himself) enthusiastically proclaimed the necessity of the restoration of Poland. They realized that the Germans, as a first proof of the reality of their sympathy with the Poles, had to begin giving up *"their* share of the plunder." But, Engels confessed, the revolutionaries were also cognizant of the other side of the problem: "Should whole tracts of land, inhabited chiefly by Germans, should large towns, entirely German, be given up to a people that as yet had never given any proofs of its capacity of progressing beyond a state of feudalism based upon agricultural serfdom?" (ibid., 11:43, 44, 45, 45).

In a letter to Marx of May 23, 1851, Engels revealed that he had come to the conclusion that the Germans should never abandon even an inch of the territories east of the line between Memel (Klaipeda) and Cracow (ibid., 38:364).[113] But in the revolutionary year 1848, there existed, he thought, a possibility of a solution that would have been acceptable to both sides: a successful war with Russia. He explained: "The question of delimitation between the different revolutionized nations would have been made a secondary one to that of first establishing a safe frontier against the common enemy; the Poles, by receiving extended territories in the east, would have become more tractable and reasonable in the west; and Riga and Mitau would have been deemed, after all, quite as important as Danzig and Elbing" (ibid., 11:45).[114]

To complete the picture, it should be added that not only the Slavs were seen by Engels as representing an inferior civilization in comparison with Germany. For instance, he was quite disdainful about the Danes, regarding them as being "completely dependent on Germany" and unable to develop economically and culturally without constant German assistance. He wrote about this in justifying the annexation of Schleswig-Holstein: "By the same right under which France took Flanders, Lorraine and Alsace, and will sooner or later take Belgium—by that same right Germany takes over Schleswig; it is the right of civilization as against barbarism, of progress as against stability. . . . This right carries more weight than all the agreements, for it is the right of historical evolution" (ibid., 7:422, 423).

Small wonder that scholars who have pondered over this part of Engels's legacy were often strongly tempted to question its Marxist character. Thus, for instance, Rosdolsky treated Engels's argumentation about "nonhistorical peoples" as "a relic of the idealistic interpretation of history" that "has no place in Marxism." He stressed, correctly, that in the controversy over the future of the Austrian Slavs, "the political romantic Bakunin proved victorious over the political realist Engels" and added that, humanly speaking, it was difficult to understand how a man like Engels could so strongly commit himself to the defense of "historical, geographical, commercial, strategic necessities" and other results of "a thousand years of history." [115] Other scholars, of whom Miklós Molnár is probably the best example, did not treat Engels separately from Marx, proving instead that both thinkers left us a dubious embryonic theory of international politics—a theory deeply embarrassing for later Marxists, who either explicitly distanced themselves from it or simply ignored its existence.[116] Following this line of reasoning we necessarily encounter the problem of whether or not a theory of nations and nationalism can be discovered in Marx's and Engels's writings.

Despite appearances, all these questions—or, to be more precise, some aspects of them—are relevant for a better understanding of Marx and Engels's conception of freedom. Therefore, for the sake of convenience and brevity, I shall limit my comments to three main points: (1) the "Eurocentric" and strongly "Occidentalist" character of Marx and Engels's theory of history, (2) the degree of consistency between their theoretical principles and their political stance in 1848–49, and finally (3) the problem of historical versus nonhistorical nations and Engels's approach to the national question.

First, quite irrespective of the problem of unilinear or multilinear development in the past, Marx and Engels were convinced that capitalist development in the West was the beginning of the great and necessary process of the "unification of the world." The *Manifesto of the Communist Party* stated this in unambiguous terms:

The bourgeoisie, by the rapid improvement of all instruments of production, by the immensely facilitated means of communication, draws all, even the most barbarian, nations into civilization. The cheap prices of its commodities are the heavy artillery with which it batters down all Chinese walls, with which it forces the barbarians' immensely obstinate hatred of foreigners to capitulate. It compels all nations, on pain of extinction, to adopt the bourgeois mode of production; it compels them to introduce what it calls civilization into their midst, i.e., to become bourgeois themselves. In one word, it creates a world after its own image.

The bourgeoisie has subjected the country to the rule of the towns. It has created enormous cities, has greatly increased the urban population as compared with the rural, and has thus rescued a considerable part of the population from the idiocy of rural life. Just as it has made the country dependent on the towns, so it has made barbarian and semi-barbarian countries dependent on the civilized ones, nations of peasants on nations of bourgeois, the East on the West. (ibid., 6:488)

Molnár rightly stressed the paramount importance of these words.[117] After all, they justify the Westernization of the entire world and also explain why their authors, in sharp contrast with latter-day Marxists (both Leninists and Marxisant Westerners), saw dialectical progress even in colonialism.[118] True, Marx and Engels were referring to peaceful conquests by means of progressive commodities. But who would claim that either ever denied the role of force in historical progress (see Engels, "The Role of Force in History," M&E, SW, 3:377–428)? According to Marx's classical formula, in the process of begetting a new social order, force usually performed the role of midwife and, to that extent, was also an economic power (M, C, 1:703). If the world was to become unified on the Western model, if this was a necessary and dialectically progressive process, then this formula also applied to international relations. Indeed, in Marx and Engels's eyes, an absolute moral condemnation of direct conquests was sentimental stupidity.[119] Consider Marx's famous articles on India. The role of England in India was, in his view, fully analogous to the role of the bourgeoisie in world history: in both cases, base interests and brutal methods produced great revolutionary change (M&E, CW, 12:131–32). The price of progress thus achieved was great, but it had to be paid. Marx saw this not as an exception, but as a general rule. Human progress, he wrote, always resembles "that hideous, pagan idol, who would drink the nectar but from the skulls of the slain"; it will cease to be so only "when a great social revolution shall have mastered the results of the bourgeois epoch, the market of the world and the modern powers of production, and subjected them to the common control of the most advanced peoples" (ibid., 222).

Even after the victory of the socialist revolution in the entire world, control over the world economy was to belong, for some time at least, to "the most advanced peoples," that is, to the West. Hence, there is no possible doubt that not only Engels but also Marx firmly believed in "the historic right of superior civilization." In international conflicts both authors did not allow themselves to be guided by abstract moral judgments but instead asked Whose victory is in the interests of universal human progress? And it was consistent with their theory of history that they tended to support "civilized" against "barbarian" or "semibarbarian" countries, "nations of bourgeois" against "nations of peasants," the West against the East.

This statement, however, must be qualified. It was not accidental (to use a favorite Marxist expression) that the shockingly brutal articles against the Austrian Slavs were written by Engels. Marx's views were basically the same, but he was less doctrinaire, usually more sophisticated in expressing his ideas, and certainly less infected by German nationalism. His greater theoretical flexibility was to be shown later in, among other things, his approach to the question of socialism in Russia. His sympathy with the Russian revolutionary populists, who wanted to "skip" the capitalist phase of development, caused him to revise his view and to allow the possibility that a successful revolution would enable Russia to pass directly from "archaic collectivism," as represented by the peasant communes, to modern socialism (see Marx's letter to Vera Zasulich, Mar. 8, 1881, M&E, C, 576–80).[120] Engels did not protest, but after Marx's death returned to the doctrinaire standpoint according to which "it is a historical impossibility for a social standing at a lower stage of economic development to have to resolve the tasks and conflicts which have arisen, and could only have arisen, in a society at a much higher stage of development" (afterword to "On Social Relations in Russia," M&E, SW, 2:403). And it was very characteristic of both his dogmatism and his "Olympian" attitude to human plights that Engels refused to help his populist correspondent in discovering a milder form of capitalist development, insisting instead that capitalism was inevitably bound up with "fearful sufferings and convulsions" which had to be accepted as an ineluctable destiny (letter to N. Danielson, Oct. 17, 1893, M&E, SC, 547). "History," he wrote, "is about the most cruel of all goddesses, and she leads her triumphal car over heaps of corpses, not only in war, but also in 'peaceful' economic development" (letter to N. Danielson, Feb. 24, 1893, M&E, C, 510).

Second, the unqualified support given by the *Neue Rheinische Zeitung* to the Magyars and Poles might seem strange in view of the fact that the political elites of both these nations consisted of the members of the gentry—that is, a class with deep roots in the feudal system.[121] In addition, the backwardness of Poland and Hungary was undisputable, while the Czechs, against whom Engels fulminated in his articles, represented a relatively developed part of the Habsburg Empire. Marx and Engels maintained that East-Central Europe needed an "agrarian revolution" that would overthrow its "patriarchal feudal barbarism" supported by the Holy Alliance of the absolute monarchs of Russia, Austria, and Prussia. If so, why did they choose to strongly support national aspirations of the Hungarian and Polish gentry while at the same time treating the "peasant nations" under Hungarian or Polish rule as hopelessly reactionary, uncivilized, and doomed to extinction? Did they think that the tasks of an essentially anti-feudal revolution would be performed by the nationalist gentry and resisted by the peasants?

Despite its ironic aspects, Marx and Engels's standpoint was explicable, both politically and theoretically. They thought in terms of the European situation *as a whole* and thus concentrated attention on forces that could change the fate of large regions, such as Germany (which was to become a united democratic republic) or historical Poland (whose progress they thought had been artificially arrested by the three partitioning powers). Revolutionary forces in Germany and Poland had, from this perspective, the same enemies: tsarist Russia, which had committed itself to maintaining the reactionary status quo in Germany, and the Prussian monarchy, which served as an outpost of Russian influence in Germany and in Europe. Hence, the restoration of Poland seemed to be the only way of liberating Germany from the restrictions on her progressive development: the domination of Prussia and the tutelage of Russia. Therefore, as Engels noted in "Marx and the *Neue Rheinische Zeitung*," the political program of the *Neue Rheinische Zeitung* came down to two points: "A single, indivisible, democratic republic, and war with Russia, which included the restoration of Poland" (M&E, *SW*, 3:167).

Given such a program, it was perfectly natural to seek an alliance between the revolutionary forces of Germany and the Polish liberation movement, which was led, of course, by the patriotic gentry. The successive Polish uprisings, as well as the development of Polish political thought, left no doubt that the link between national liberation and the revolutionary solution of the agrarian question was well understood by the Polish gentry-radicals. On the other hand, the tragic fate of the last and most democratic Polish uprising—the Cracow uprising of 1846, which had been quenched, with the blessing of Austrian officials, in a bloody peasant *jacquerie* (the so-called Galician massacre) [122]—showed that the peasants lacked elementary political consciousness and could easily go astray, antagonizing progressive forces within the gentry or even directly helping the reactionary monarchy. Besides, Marx and Engels's theory demanded support for the forces of "civilization" and Westernization, and who was representing "civilization" on the vast territories of the former Polish-Lithuanian Commonwealth if not the progressive and educated part of the Polish gentry? The illiterate and backward peasant masses could not be seen, within this theoretical framework, as a progressive force. A Leninist might feel surprised that Jakub Szela, the leader of the peasants who had perpetrated the Galician massacre, was treated by the *Neue Rheinishe Zeitung* as a simple "bandit." [123] In fact, however, such classification was quite consistent with Marx and Engels's theory. The same theoretical and political reasons explain (but do not justify) their contemptuous attitude toward the budding national aspirations of the Galician Ruthenians (Ukrainians) [124]—after all, they were neither representatives of civilization nor political allies of the German revolution.

The same logic applied to the Hungarian question. The *Neue Rheinische Zeitung*, it must be remembered, struggled for the *grossdeutsche* solution of the German question—that is, for the incorporation of Austria into a unified German republic.[125] The Magyar insurgents were reliable allies of the Viennese revolutionaries, while the Croats actively supported the Habsburgs and the Slav Congress in Prague opposed the unification of Germany, offering instead the so-called Austro-Slavic solution.[126] Marx and Engels rejected Austro-Slavism not only as German politicians but also as theorists: it would give too much autonomy to small national units and thus contradict the centralizing tendency of universal progress. If the Habsburg Empire could not be incorporated into Germany in its entirety, then it would have to be divided between the two historical nations: the Germans and Magyars. In that case, Engels wrote in *Revolution and Counterrevolution in Germany*, Bohemia—"surrounded by thoroughly German countries on three sides" and solidly Germanized even in its capital, Prague— was to remain "a portion of Germany," while the other Habsburg Slavs were to become a part of an increasingly unified Hungarian nation (M&E, CW, 11:46).

This was perfectly consistent with historical law, as put forth in the *Manifesto of the Communist Party*, according to which "independent, or but loosely connected provinces with separate interests, laws, governments and systems to taxation, became lumped together into one nation, with one government, one code of laws, one national class interest, one frontier and one custom-tariff" (ibid., 6:488–89). Objections on the grounds of class criteria could not be justified, because, for the authors of *The Communist Manifesto*, revolutionary gentry was certainly preferable not only to the backward peasantry (like the Ruthenians or Slovaks) but also to the lower middle class (which was the social base of the Czech national movement). The *Manifesto* gave this attitude a historical and theoretical foundation, declaring: "The lower middle class, the small manufacturer, the shopkeeper, the artisan, the peasant, all these fight against the bourgeoisie, to save from extinction their existence as fractions of the middle class. They are therefore not revolutionary, but conservative. Nay more, they are reactionary, for they try to roll back the wheel of history" (ibid., 494).

Third, Engels's theory of historical and nonhistorical nations was, of course, deeply involved with all of these theoretical and political analyses. The terminology belongs to Hegel, and admittedly it is curious that Engels did not try to change it. As a historical materialist, he might have been expected to emphasize that historicity is a general human condition and not a privilege of those who acted as independent agents in *political* history. But, after all, many theories, historical "materialism" included, have been couched in terms that are misleading.

According to Rosdolsky, "the theory of 'historic' and 'nonhistoric' peoples is by now long dead, and no one (least of all a Marxist) would want to revive it." [127] This is not quite true; other Ukrainian scholars have provided convincing arguments for this theory's defense. Thus, Ivan L. Rudnytsky pointed out that "the differentiation of nations into historical and non-historical, though first theorized by Hegel, took on independent importance in the legal and administrative practice óf the Habsburg Empire." There were good reasons for this: it was useful and practically necessary to see the difference between plebeian peoples, distinguishable only in terms of ethnicity and not represented by upper classes of their own, and those peoples who had once had their own states, preserved their upper classes together with their ongoing political and cultural traditions, and thus never ceased to be politically and culturally active or to have a full awareness of their distinctive national identity. It is arguable that the case of the Czechs or the Croats was somewhat mixed, but the nineteenth-century Ukrainians or Slovaks, on the one hand, and the Poles and Magyars, on the other, neatly fitted this typology. Rudnytsky summarized this as follows: "The decisive factor in the existence of the so-called historical nations was the preservation, despite the loss of independence, of a representative upper class as the carrier of political consciousness and 'high' culture. Usually, as in the case of Poland and Hungary, this upper class consisted of the landed nobility. . . . Conversely, the so-called non-historical nations had lost (or had never possessed) a representative class, and were reduced to an inarticulate popular mass, with little if any national consciousness and with a culture of predominantly folk character. This differentiation is not an arbitrary theoretical construct, for it is grounded in empirical historical reality." [128]

This, I hope, makes it clear that Engels's theory (or rather, the theory he employed in his articles) was not without foundation and that its usefulness in analyzing the events of 1848–49 was rather obvious. The abusive language in which he couched the theory and the conclusions he drew from it (especially those concerning the future) are another matter.

Another, more general, explanation of Engels's views on the national question, especially as developed by him later, can be found in the history of the term *nation* in Europe. For a very long time, this term had been used in a predominantly political, not an ethno-linguistic, sense; a nation was defined by active citizens of a state, living under the same laws, united in a common political loyalty, and conscious of a common political history.[129] Neither ethnicity nor language was relevant to this definition: thus the French nation (before the homogenizing effects of the Revolution) consisted of people who spoke not only French, but also German, Basque, Italian, Provençal, and so forth. Similarly, the Polish nation was conceived as consisting of all active citizens (members of the gentry), irrespective of their ethnic background; thus it was possible to define oneself as "gente Ruthenus, natione Polonus"—ethnically a Ukrainian, but nationally a Pole. In Hungary, the term *Hungarian nation* was defined politically: as including also the non-Magyar population of historical Hungary. The downfall of the Polish state brought the notion of a stateless nation into common usage, but this did not automatically entail giving up the political conception of nation; on the contrary, Poles saw themselves, and were seen by others, as a legitimate political nation—a nation formed by a common political history and only temporarily deprived of its statehood. In an analogous way, the Germans could see themselves as members of one nation temporarily divided into several states. Defining a nation in terms of language and ethnicity became a common practice only in the second half of the nineteenth century, mostly in Eastern Europe, owing to the "national awakening" of "nonhistorical nations." Of course, such an important shift in the meaning of this important term would not go unnoticed or unresisted.

The greatest resistance to this change was among the political elites of "historical nations." In Poland, stubborn political legitimism characterized (somewhat less obviously) the radical left wing of the insurgents of 1863–64, for whom the abandonment of Poland's historical frontiers amounted to a cowardly betrayal.[130] The radicals assumed that the Ukrainian, Belorussian, and Lithuanian peasants needed only social emancipation (and the introduction of general education in Polish) to define themselves as Poles. Engels made this position a general theoretical principle.

He elaborated this principle in a dispute with the Proudhonists, who opposed the pro-Polish stand of the First International. They claimed that the "principle of nationalities" was a "Bonapartist invention" that was used for reactionary aims and had nothing in common with the class interests of the workers. To refute this reasoning, Engels wrote an interesting article, "What Have the Working Classes to Do with Poland?" (1866). In the piece, in addition to explaining the political importance of the Polish question, he made a sharp distinction between the terms *nationality* and *nation*. A nationality, he argued, was an ethnic group whose natural boundaries were those of language; a nation was a product of political history whose boundaries depended on its "inner vitality" and its ability to be a vehicle of civilization. Every European nation had been composed of many ethnic nationalities, and a great majority of nations were still inhabited by people of different ethnic and linguistic backgrounds. The disintegration of great political nations through separatist movements of ethnic nationalities would be reactionary and absurd and would destroy the results of historical progress. Hence, the "principle of nationalities" had nothing in common with "the old democratic and working-class tenet as to the right of the great European *nations* to separate and independent existence." The right of "the great national subdivisions of Europe to political independence" was indeed "one of the fundamental conditions of the internal liberty of all." But this could not apply to "those numerous small relics of peoples which, after having figured for a longer or shorter period on the stage of history, were finally absorbed as integral portions of those more powerful nations" (ibid., 20:157, 155, 157).

The application of this theory to the Polish question was obvious. Poland was not a mere nationality but one of the historical nations of Europe. Like many other nations in the present or past, she was a multiethnic nation, and if her ethnic minorities had not become fully assimilated, this was mostly due to the Russian intrigues. Engels did not hesitate to assert that the principle of nationalities as such was, in fact, "*a Russian invention concocted to destroy Poland.*" "Therefore," he concluded, "if people say that to demand the restoration of Poland is to appeal to the principle of nationalities, they merely prove that they do not know what they are talking about, for the restoration of Poland means the re-establishment of a State composed of at least four different nationalities" (ibid., 157, 159).

To render justice to Engels, it should be stressed that his rejection of ethno-linguistic criteria as a basis for political vindication was consistent and might also be used against the Germans. Thus, for instance, in his pamphlet *Po and Rhine* (1859), Engels turned this argument against the German minority in northern Italy, arguing that "remnants of peoples" were to be found everywhere and that they should remain incorporated into larger nations, either merging with them or conserving themselves as "merely ethnographic relics with no political significance" (ibid., 16:254).[131]

Rosdolsky made an excellent comment on Engels's article on Poland:

Given the context of the time, one can all too readily understand Engels's struggle against the "principle of nationalities" and the use made of it by Russia and Bonapartism; one can also, for example, very well imagine that neither the Ukrainians nor the Belorussians and Lithuanians were mature enough to form their own states in 1866. From this, however, it does not at all follow that one had good reason at that time to consider these peoples *destined to perish*. But Engels's talk of "relics" and "remnants of peoples long gone by," as well as his comparison of the Serbs, Croats, Ruthenians, Slovaks, Czechs, etc., with the Manxmen and Welsh leave no doubt about his views on this matter. . . . In essence, his views were like a sign inscribed: "*Nonhistoric peoples not admitted!*" He condemned these movements always as movements that "would tend to undo what a thousand years of history have created," that could not be realized "without sweeping from the map Hungary, Turkey and large parts of Germany." Engels did not recognize that sweeping these powers from the map was objectively necessary and also historically progressive.[132]

We can now move on to some general conclusions about what Engels's approach to the national question has to do with the problem of freedom. It follows from the discussion above that Engels's views on the national question in the revolutionary years of the Springtime of the Peoples can be explained both politically and in terms of his (and Marx's) general theory. In addition, Engels's approach to the national question involves antilibertarian aspects of Marxist theory that have implications for possible political purposes.

Unfortunately, many intellectuals, even political moderates, are extraordinarily tolerant of revolutionary rhetoric. As a rule, predictions of inevitable doom and even threats of physical extermination do not arouse great indignation if addressed to "reactionary" social classes. However, analogous predictions and threats definitely become unacceptable if applied to entire nations. Even the practice of classifying certain nations as defending outlived social formations and as therefore being reactionary, from the point of view of general human progress, had become deeply suspicious. In view of this, it is important to be aware that Marx and Engels's theory provided no basis for treating nations differently than classes. On the contrary, Engels followed the logic and spirit of Marxism when he treated entire nations as hindering the development of civilization and therefore doomed to inevitable extinction and also when he divided peoples into those that did not possess the right to self-determination and those that, in addition to having this right, were entitled and indeed, destined, to swallow up and assimilate others. The end result of this approach—the favoring of the bigger and stronger at the expense of the smaller and weaker—is yet another unpleasant aspect of the theory of dialectical historical necessity.

Of course, humanitarianism and freedom are values that do not necessarily coexist, as the possibility of an antihumanitarian libertarianism clearly shows. In the case of Marxism, antihumanitarianism coincided with a shocking disrespect for freedom. The attempt to find historical necessity in past events (whatever we may think about the philosophical and methodological legitimacy of such an endeavor) is not dangerous to freedom, but the situation changes completely if one claims to see historical necessity as predetermining the future. In this case freedom is directly and dangerously threatened. This is so because alleged historical necessity gives those who act in its name an absolute mandate to realize "progress," irrespective of the will of the majority, by any and all possible means; in other words, the belief in the historical necessity of a given course of action removes all "abstractly moral" scruples, thereby justifying all possible violations of freedom. Indeed: "What mercy should be shown to men who stood in the way of History and opposed her will, who rejected the tenets of science and refused to abide by them?" [133]

Nobody knows what Engels would have done if he had had political power. Let us assume that he would have been much more humane and cautious than are his words. But even as it was, his authoritarian style of thought posed a threat to political and intellectual freedom because, in political matters, invoking the notion of scientifically established necessity amounts to an arrogant attempt to solve problems in an authoritarian way—through an abuse of the authority of knowledge. The claim to know the irrevocable verdicts of History liquidates genuinely political argument, replacing it by a technique that both strengthens the self-confidence of one's followers and paralyzes the will of one's opponents. Marx and Engels were probably unaware of these dangers, but unfortunately the history of Marxism made them all too evident.

2.5 Freedom as "Necessity Understood"

The Hegelian synthesis was certainly the climax of German classical philosophy. The Hegelian Left and Feuerbach, on the one hand, and Schelling, with his "philosophy of the Revelation," on the other, were the products of the crisis of Hegelian "absolute idealism." The early writings of Marx and Engels belong essentially, although not entirely, in the same category. They were a part of an ideological situation and a universe of discourse created by Hegelian dialectical idealism, its inner crisis, and Feuerbach's open challenge to it. In other words, they belonged to a period in which German intellectual life was still dominated by philosophers, although, paradoxically, the main topic of philosophical discussion during that time was the insufficiency of "abstract thought" and the need to overcome sterile philosophical speculations.

The revolution of 1848 marked the abrupt and definite end of this transitional period, which Engels noted in *Ludwig Feuerbach*: "The Revolution of 1848 thrust the whole of philosophy aside as unceremoniously as Feuerbach had thrust aside Hegel. And in the process Feuerbach himself was also pushed into the background" (M&E, SW, 3:345).

In Engels's eyes, "the end of philosophy" (that is, German-style speculative philosophy) was irreversible,[134] but the new, "postphilosophical" situation was by no means intellectually advantageous. On the contrary, in 1859 in his review of Marx's *Contribution to the Critique of Political Economy*,[135] Engels presented this situation as a retrogression rather than genuine progress. "The immense bourgeois development after 1848" was accompanied by the parallel development of the natural sciences, but the theorists of this unprecedented scientific progress—Büchner, Vogt, and Moleschott—represented a hopelessly obsolete, vulgar form of the mechanical materialism of the eighteenth century (M&E, CW, 16:473). In fact, they reproduced the most banal form of "the narrow-minded philistine mode of thinking of the pre-Kantian period," that is, "the ordinary, essentially Wolffian, metaphysical method." To Engels, this meant thinking in historical "fixed categories," in contrast to the historicity and protean flexibility of the dialectical method. He saw this as a terrible regress but, at the same time, as a sort of sad inevitability, in view of the fact that the dialectical method was bound up with speculative idealism while the natural sciences had to firmly cling to materialism. From this perspective, it was evident that the dialectic, the precious legacy of Hegelianism, needed a materialist reinterpretation. According to Engels, this had been done by "the German proletarian party" in its "materialist conception of history" (ibid., 473, 469).

The natural sciences, however, remained methodologically obsolete, hampered in their further development by a "metaphysical" (read: non-dialectical, mechanical, antihistorical) form of materialism. Hence, what was needed was *dialectical* materialism. In Engels's review of 1859, this term is absent, but the idea of making natural sciences dialectical, without abandoning their materialist foundations, is clearly present.

In later years, Engels came to the conclusion that the natural sciences did not fail to fulfill this program (although the natural scientists themselves were somewhat slow in becoming aware of this). The main steps in this direction were, as he put forth in *Ludwig Feuerbach*, the discovery of the cell, the transformation of energy, and, above all, the Darwinian theory of evolution (M&E, SW, 3:351). Neither Hegel nor Feuerbach could develop a "historical" conception of nature: Hegel, because nature was for him merely an alienation, a degradation, of the absolute idea (ibid., 343–44), and Feuerbach, because he proved unable to go beyond the materialism of the eighteenth century. But with the appearance of Darwin, the "historical" (read: dialectical) conception of nature had finally become possible (ibid., 351). Darwin had shown that "nature works dialectically and not metaphysically," that "she does not move in the eternal oneness of a perpetually recurring circle, but goes through a real historical evolution" (E, AD, 33). Small wonder that the achievements of Marx (the materialist "historicization" of social sciences) and the discoveries of Darwin (the "historicization" of nature) came to be seen by Engels as comparable and complementary. In his speech at the graveside of Marx, he said: "Just as Darwin discovered the law of development of organic nature, so Marx discovered the law of development of human history" (M&E, SW, 3:162).

In this way, the conception of dialectical materialism came into being. As we can see, it was a product of a peculiarly German philosophical development. It is difficult to imagine a non-German thinker preoccupied with "divesting" Hegelian dialectic "of its idealist wrappings" in order to combine it with the materialism of the natural sciences (M&E, CW, 16:475). Hence, it is inappropriate to attribute to Engels an allegiance to *positivistic* scientism; it is safer to say that he knew little about positivism and used the term *science* in a broader sense, which also included a Hegelian connotation. It is certainly true that Engels was much more interested in, and influenced by, natural sciences than Marx, but it does not follow that he was less interested in stressing the continuing relevance of the German philosophical tradition. His search for a dialectical form of materialism was intended to defend the Hegelian legacy against the so-called vulgar materialism of Vogt, Büchner, and Moleschott, who were also a typically German phenomenon, explicable as an exaggerated reaction against all forms of idealism. And it seems wrong to make too much of Darwin's influence on Engels. True, Engels *was* influenced by Darwin, but even more important is the fact that he interpreted Darwin's importance in a preconceived way: as a corroboration of his own view of a possibility of a dialectical (read: historical) conception of nature.

According to Terrell Carver, "Preoccupation with method" was something peculiar to Engels and "foreign to Marx," whose actual method was eclectic and who, in fact, never employed the dialectical method "either explicitly or implicitly in his works." [136] According to other authors, the opposite was true: it was Engels who profoundly misunderstood dialectic and, in fact, replaced it by an eclectic methodology strongly influenced by the empiricism of the natural sciences. Before proceeding further, it is necessary to comment, however briefly, on these mutually exclusive interpretations.

To begin with, both ignore the fact that, on the *conscious* level, Marx tended to agree with Engels. In his afterword to the second German edition of *Capital*, Marx explicitly accepted the notion of a materialist dialectic and defined its essential features in the same way as Engels: as a historical and critical method that includes "comprehension and affirmative recognition of the existing state of things" but at the same time recognizes the transient nature of that state and the inevitability of its revolutionary negation. Like Engels, Marx strongly protested against the fashion of treating Hegel as a "dead dog" but nonetheless criticized Hegel more thoroughly than did Engels, stressing that even dialectic suffered mystification in Hegel's hands. "My dialectical method," Marx explained, "is not only different from the Hegelian, but is its direct opposite. To Hegel, the life-process of the human brain, i.e. the process of thinking, which, under the name of 'the Ideal,' he even transforms into an independent subject, is the demiurgos of the real world, and the real world is only the external, phenomenal form of 'the Idea.' With me, on the contrary, the ideal is nothing else than the material world reflected by the human mind, and translated into forms of thought. . . . With him [Hegel] it is standing on its head. It must be turned right side up again, if you would discover the rational kernel within the mystical shell" (M&E, *SW*, 2:98).

Thus, the claim that dialectical method was "invented" by Engels and foreign to Marx is here explicitly denied by Marx himself. But, as we can see, the opposite view, attributing to Marx a clear understanding that dialectic cannot be made materialist and applied to nature, is also based on a shaky foundation. It is a fact that Marx wrote the quoted words. It is a fact that Marx was also greatly impressed by Darwin and even contemplated dedicating the first volume of *Capital* to him. And, finally, it is a fact that he did not disapprove of Engels's *Anti-Dühring*. All these facts cannot be explained away.

However, these remarks are intended only as a warning, not as a wholesale dismissal of the problem of Engelsian Marxism. The differences between the philosophical possibilities of Marx's anthropocentric philosophy of praxis and Engelsian Marxism (i.e., "dialectical materialism") were very real and important but, whether we like it or not, the Engelsian account of Marxism became a part of Marx's own views (although, admittedly, it did not completely eliminate elements of the philosophical vision of human development through alienation that dominates Marx's writings from the *Paris Manuscripts* to *Grundrisse*). This was so because, after 1859 (the year of Engels's review of Marx's *Contribution to the Critique of Philosophical Economy* and also of the appearance of Darwin's *Origin of Species*), the philosophical initiative was taken over and effectively monopolized by Engels. In his "Anti-Engels," Brzozowski observed that Marx, as the ideological leader of the First International, was a different man than the Marx of the 1840s. He had greatly regressed as a philosopher; his constant contact with philosophical simpletons and exposure to the influence of Engels rendered him unaware of the genuine foundations of his own thought and indifferent to the philosophical subtleties of his own development.[137] Brzozowski's diagnosis seems to be correct; we can only add to it that Marx's philosophical regress mirrored the general condition of German thought after the German Revolution of 1848–49, which (as Engels put it) had "thrust the whole of philosophy aside."

To grasp the differences between Marx's original philosophical vision and the Engelsian interpretation of Marxism, it is enough to recall Marx's grandiose conception of the development of the human species through self-enriching alienation. A detailed reconstruction of this conception has been provided in chapter 1, showing, among other things, that, despite appearances, even *Capital* was consistent with and can be meaningfully interpreted within the framework of Marx's self-enriching alienation. The point is that this conception *could not have been reconstructed* on the basis of Engelsian Marxism. True, some elements of it can be found in Engels's early writings, but these elements have been eliminated from Engels's mature works, which he (and his contemporaries) considered the codification of Marxism and the theoretical foundation of "scientific socialism."

The main reason for eliminating such elements was Engels's desire to make Marxism as "scientific" as possible. After Darwin, the Aristotelian notion of a species essence, or species nature, seemed obsolete, and Engels did not want to uphold it; he explicitly abandoned these ideas in his article on "The Part Played by Labor in the Transition from Ape to Man." This inevitably led Engels to abandon the idea of the final goal of human history, otherwise so dear to his communist heart. Finally, his conviction that scientificity must coincide with the standpoint of natural science led him to search for a dialectic of nature. Thus, Hegelian dialectic became the opposite of itself. Hegel conceived an *epistemological* dialectic that dealt with the relationships between the active subject and the object of knowledge, or rather between the subject and its different objectifications. Marx transformed this concept into a dialectic of human *historical praxis*; he abandoned the notion of a transcendental subject but substituted for it another conception of subject: the human species as a collective subject that developed its essence through different forms of historical practice. For Engels, the desire to see human beings as part of nature proved so strong that dialectic became subjectless, as it were, dealing instead with objectively existing laws of nature. Dialectics, he wrote, "is nothing more than the science of the general laws of motion and development of nature, human society and thought" (E, *AD*, 172). "Thereby," he commented in his essay on Feuerbach, "the dialectic of concepts itself became merely the conscious reflex of the dialectical motion of the real world and thus the dialectic of Hegel was placed upon its head; or rather, turned off its head, on which it was standing, and placed upon its feet" (M&E, *SW*, 3:362).

Turning something into its opposite is, of course, quintessentially dialectical. Ironically, this happened to dialectic itself, because dialectic without an active subject, dialectic conceived as objective "laws of motion," is, in fact, a contradiction in terms. Such dialectic is no longer a method but rather a preconceived all-embracing conception of the universe. Thus, in spite of his view of the irreversible end of philosophy, Engels returned to the German tradition of elaborating all-comprising systems—a tradition he wittily ridiculed when professed by Dühring.[138]

As we can see, Engels so deeply changed (or distorted) the original meaning of dialectic that it makes little sense to describe this dialectic as a tribute to Hegelianism. But this is not to deny that many of Engels's views had a Hegelian genealogy. To understand Engels's conception of freedom, it is necessary to realize that Hegelianism deeply influenced his views of the laws of history. In *Anti-Dühring*, Engels praised Hegel for presenting history as "no longer a wild whirl of senseless deeds of violence" but as "the process of evolution of man himself." He deeply approved of the Hegelian view that it was "the task of the intellect to follow the gradual march of this process through all its devious ways, and to trace out the inner law running through all its apparently accidental phenomena" (E, *AD*, 34). It is evident, therefore, that Engels had not abandoned his claim to attribute meaning to historical events. True, he no longer thought in terms of the global *meaning of history* (since this would involve an eschatological perspective), but he persisted, nonetheless, in looking for a *meaning in history*—that is, for an inner law that would cause history to be seen as an inherently rational process. Needless to say, the natural sciences could not help him in this endeavor. But classical political economy proved to be much more helpful, because its idea of an "invisible hand" could be easily interpreted as similar to the Hegelian "cunning of Reason." Characteristically, Engels identified the role of economic motives in human conduct with the role of moral evil in history. In *Ludwig Feuerbach*, he praised Hegel for understanding that "evil is the form in which the motive force of history presents itself" and explained this thought as follows: "This contains the twofold meaning that, on the one hand, each new advance necessarily appears as a sacrilege against things hallowed, as a rebellion against conditions, though old and moribund, yet sanctified by custom; and that, on the other hand, it is precisely the wicked passions of man—greed and lust for power—which since the emergence of class antagonisms, serve as levers of historical development—a fact of which the history of feudalism and of the bourgeoisie, for example, constitutes a single continual proof" (M&E, SW, 3:357).

Now we can move on to Engels's conception of freedom. In order to analyze his conception in detail, it is necessary to quote the relevant passage from *Anti-Dühring*:

Hegel was the first to state correctly the relation between freedom and necessity. To him, freedom is the appreciation of necessity. 'Necessity is *blind* only *in so far as it is not understood.*' Freedom does not consist in any dreamt-of independence from natural laws, but in the knowledge of these laws, and in the possibility this gives of systematically making them work toward definite ends. This holds good in relation both to the laws of external nature and to those which govern the bodily and mental existence of men themselves—two classes of laws which we can separate from each other at most only in thought but not in reality. Freedom of the will therefore means nothing but the capacity to make decisions with knowledge of the subject. Therefore the *freer* a man's judgment is in relation to a definite question, the greater is the *necessity* with which the content of this judgment will be determined; while the uncertainty, founded on ignorance, which seems to make an arbitrary choice among many different and conflicting possible decisions, shows precisely by this that it is not free, that it is controlled by the very object it should itself control. Freedom therefore consists in the control of ourselves and over external nature, a control founded on knowledge of natural necessity; it is therefore necessarily a product of historical development. (E, AD, 140–41)[139]

The immediate context of this passage is Engels's polemic against Dühring's views on law—Roman law, Prussian *Landrecht*, and so forth. Nevertheless, Engels completely ignored the entire problematic of freedom under law—that is, of the legal and institutional guarantees of civil and political liberty. This was, no doubt, very characteristic, significant, and consequential; as such, it demands an explanation.

The simplest possible explanation can be derived from the Marxist critique of "bourgeois freedom" as merely formal and fraudulent. This line of reasoning is legitimate, but involves the risk of oversimplification. It is necessary to remember that Marx and Engels were indeed disdainful of negative freedom (freedom as noninterference), which they saw as amounting to the egoism of private property owners, but at the same time, they appreciated positive political freedom (freedom as collective self-determination and active participation in political affairs). This feature sharply distinguished them from Proudhonists, Bakuninists, Russian populists, and other programmatically "antipolitical" socialist movements of their time. Hence, their critique of "bourgeois freedom" does not fully explain Engels's refusal to theorize on political liberty.

A more comprehensive and satisfying explanation is provided by Engels's conception of the "juridical world-view," which was conceived by him as the "secularization of theology" and the "classical world-view of the bourgeoisie." [140] He combined in this conception two different categories of the eighteenth-century belief in rational law: a belief in the omnipotence of rational legislation, bound up with the ideology of state absolutism, and a belief in universally valid and legally claimable human rights, which formed the foundation of the liberal version of the natural rights doctrine. Both were, in his eyes, deeply idealist, ahistorical, and utopian, although otherwise historically progressive as an ideological weapon in the struggle against feudal privilege and irrational traditionalism. Because of this, the juridical worldview was embraced for some time by the early representatives of the proletarian party, who tried to use it against the bourgeoisie— in much the same way as the bourgeoisie had for some time refused to let go of the theological worldview, attempting to use it against the feudal nobility. Hence, for representatives of a mature proletarian party acting in mature capitalist conditions, making use of the juridical worldview would have been totally inappropriate. The postrevolutionary reality in France made it obvious that the "kingdom of reason was nothing more than the idealized kingdom of the bourgeoisie" (ibid., 26). It was natural, therefore, that "the best minds among the early socialists"—Saint-Simon, Fourier, Owen—reacted to this by abandoning "the legal-political arena" altogether, "declaring all political struggle to be worthless." Marx corrected this conclusion, emphasizing the need for political forms of class struggle, but at the same time, he consistently refused to appeal to legalistic or humanitarian emotions and to observe matters through "legally tinted spectacles." His theory marked the final overcoming of the abstract rationalism of the juridical worldview. After Marx, Engels reasoned, it would be

ridiculous to question bourgeois domination from a moral or legal standpoint, to formulate a socialist program in the language of legal demands,
or to postulate a charter of socialist "human rights." Anton Menger, a
"professorial socialist" who wanted to elaborate a juridical foundation of
socialism, "does not seem to know that in the course of their development
the ruling classes have quite definite social functions to fulfill and become
rulers for that very reason," that "the socialists recognize the temporary
historical justification of these classes." Especially Marx "understands the
historical inevitability, or justification, of ancient slaveholders, of feudal
lords in the Middle Ages, and so forth, as the necessary conditions of
human development for a limited historical period; he also recognizes the
historical and textual justification for exploitation, the usurpation of the
work proceeds of others"; his "scientific socialism" is based on "the discovery of an economic principle," and not on abstract, legalistic theories of
justice. This is why "legal rights, which always reflect the economic conditions of a specific society, are treated only in a very secondary manner in
Marx's theoretical studies."[141]

For the same reason, Engels refused to discuss freedom as a politico-
juridical problem. For him, freedom was the question not of right but of
might, of the effective *ability* to realize human purposes. This ability, in
turn, was seen by him as dependent on historically developing economic
conditions and subject to the laws of necessity. Hence, it was logical and
unavoidable that for him freedom was a problem of appreciating, understanding, and mastering necessity. This view of freedom did not logically
entail the elimination of all concern for the minimization of the role of
political coercion in social life, but it did justify treating this concern "in a
very secondary manner."

The idea of freedom as "the control of ourselves" based on knowledge,
i.e., on reason, has a very respectable philosophical genealogy. Its followers
can be found among the greatest philosophers of the world, from Plato and
the Stoic writers to Spinoza, Kant, and Hegel. The number of philosophers
who combined this idea with another component of the Engelsian definition of freedom—*the understanding of necessity*—is, of course, much
smaller. The best-known and most important among them are those who
actually influenced Engels: Spinoza and Hegel.

According to Spinoza, freedom means self-determination: "that thing
will be called free which exists simply by the necessity of its own nature,
and is determined to act by itself alone."[142] In this absolute sense, only God
is free, because God alone is *causa sui*, the cause of his own being. Human
beings, like all finite beings, have to live in the world of necessity; their freedom cannot consist in being independent from causality. It can manifest
itself only as a certain situation, a certain relation to themselves and the
external world. The possibility of human freedom is rooted in rationality;

humans cannot achieve freedom of action, but as rational creatures they can attain freedom in a stoical way, in the purely spiritual sphere, through the understanding that their true self is identical with the rational essence of the world and through conscious acceptance of necessity. Thus, human freedom is not independence from causality, since this would amount to the impossible and disastrous state of being "independent" from God. On the contrary, human freedom consists in eliminating everything that separates us from God, in fully integrating ourselves into the divine universe.

Some German romantics interpreted Spinozism as a vision of liberation through a mystical union with the divine; a union presupposing the annihilation of the rational self. This was wrong because Spinoza's pantheism was a rationalist worldview. For him, liberation did not involve the surrender of rationality in order to become one with the irrational wholeness of the universe. He conceived the universe (God) as rational in its essence and therefore made freedom dependent on the conscious reassertion and strengthening of our own essential rationality. Freedom, in his view, demanded harmony between our existence and our essence; hence, it depended on our endeavor (*conatus*) to persist in being truly rational. This, in turn, involved the notion of freedom as rational control over blind passions and affections; in other words, the rule of the "higher" (rational) self over the "lower" self, the ability to be guided by knowledge and to resist the impulses of blind spontaneity. The more our ideas are adequate, the more freedom we have.[143]

Hegel, for whom the true manifestation of the Absolute was human history (through which the Absolute was raising itself to the level of self-consciousness), concentrated attention on the need to understand the laws of history and to thereby achieve a "reconciliation with reality" (*die Versöhnung mit der Wirklichkeit*). Assuming the immanence of the Absolute (i.e., the immanent presence of the divine element in human beings), he defined human essence as rational and therefore capable of freedom. He even assumed the possibility of human free will, by which he meant truly rational will, free from "natural determinations": in its rationality, such will was identical with the rationality of the Absolute which, of course, *presupposed* freedom. But rationality and freedom were not something given, but something to be achieved through a long and painful historical process. Thus, human history appeared to Hegel as a process of the development of rationality and freedom, a process that had already attained its climax in the modern rational state. Hegelian history therefore had a clear inner meaning, even an absolute meaning, since it was conceived as, in a sense, a development of the Absolute itself. It was governed by necessary laws, but laws that were rational in essence and therefore quite different from the mechanical laws of physical nature. People could not only know them but also *understand* them, identify with them, recognize in them their own rational essence, and thereby experience them as fully compatible with their true freedom.

In accordance with this conception of historical development, individual freedom was conceived by Hegel as conscious and rational self-determination in the sphere of "objective ethics" (*Sittlichkeit*)—that is, the sphere of laws and sociocultural institutions corresponding to the achieved stage of development of Historical Reason.[144] As we can see, the reconciliation with reality, the inner harmony stemming from the understanding of the essential rationality of history, was an important part of this conception. Owing to this, Hegelian philosophy was able to perform a therapeutic role, helping individuals to see their surrounding reality in a completely new light and to invest their lives with a new and deeper meaning. Access to Hegelianism involved, therefore, something more than a purely intellectual commitment: "To enter the school, to become an authentic Hegelian, a person had to undergo an existential transformation, a philosophical 'rebirth.' " [145]

Let us now return to the quoted passage from Engels, on which Kolakowski commented as follows:

> Engels follows the conception of freedom that arose among the Stoics and reached Hegel through Spinoza: freedom is the understanding of necessity. However, "freedom as the understanding of necessity" has a different meaning for Engels than for the Stoics, Spinoza, and Hegel. The free man is not he who understands that what happens must happen, and reconciles himself to it. A man is free to the extent that he understands the laws of the world he is living in and can therefore bring about the changes he desires. Freedom is the degree of power that an individual or a community are able to exercise over the conditions of their own life. . . .
>
> Engels thus puts the question of free will in a different way from his predecessors. He does not ask whether a conscious act of choice is always determined by circumstances independent of consciousness, but rather in what conditions human choices are most effective in relation to the end proposed, whether practical or cognitive. Freedom is the degree of effectiveness of conscious acts—not the degree of independence with regard to the laws which govern all phenomena, whether men are conscious of their operation or not; for, according to Engels, such independence does not exist.[146]

I think that this is, in fact, a very favorable comment—too favorable, perhaps, because it fails to stress the dangerous aspects of Engels's conception.

We can agree with Kolakowski that Engels succeeded in combining the notion of freedom as "necessity understood" with an *activist* attitude, as well as in interpreting knowledge as a means of increasing our power, in accordance with the old saying: *Tantum possumus, quantum scimus.* His linking of this view with an emphasis on rational "control of ourselves" may also be seen as defensible. All conceptions of rational self-government might be dismissed as "puritanical" and contrasted to Marx's ideal of a free creativity,[147] but this is not a reason to see in them a danger to liberty; on the contrary, it is arguable that political liberty is possible only among self-disciplined people, whose conduct is rational and predictable.[148] (This was, by the way, Spinoza's view.) Finally, the larger context of Engels's definition of freedom makes it clear that he was also concerned (although Kolakowski does not mention it) with the "therapeutic" aspect of the "understanding of necessity," but, unlike Hegel, avoided using it as an argument for the status quo. In his interpretation, an understanding of the *rational character* of necessity helped individuals accept the necessity of existing relations while, at the same time, identifying themselves with historical progress. Given such an attitude, Engels, for instance, could easily liberate himself from moralistic scruples and perform the role of a leading communist theorist without ceasing to be a British capitalist. We may like it or not, but as long as this conception was applied *to individuals only*— that is to say, as long as it was *not* combined with the idea of *collective* self-determination—it could not be treated as incompatible with liberalism. After all, the classical liberal idea of the "invisible hand" was also a sort of secularized theodicy, reassuring individuals about the order and meaning inherent in social processes.

Thus, Engels's conception of *individual* freedom—as a conception of freedom versus necessity—might be regarded as reasonable, perhaps even attractive. Its main shortcoming, and (what is much worse) its main trap, was the otherwise obvious fact that it was not linked to any theory of civil and political liberty. But it does not follow that this has anything to do with the very idea of the understanding of necessity. Spinoza and Hegel, Engels's great predecessors in thinking about freedom as necessity understood, were also great theorists of political community. An understanding of necessity and of political liberty are not mutually exclusive. Spinoza was one of the first theorists of a liberal state. Hegel emphasized the rationality of the modern state and drew from this many illiberal conclusions but, nonetheless, respected and philosophically justified the autonomy of civil society, the spontaneous order of the market, and some moderate forms of political freedom.[149] He saw history as a process of increasing rationalization but, at the same time, emphatically rejected the view that *all* spheres of social life had to be subjected to a rational *collective* control.

Engels's conception of freedom was far from being innocent. It was, in fact, very dangerous and pregnant with disastrous consequences. To point out its dangers (which strangely go unnoticed in Kolakowski's comments), it is necessary to place the above quoted passage on freedom in the context of Engels's views on "scientific socialism" as a means of transforming the "kingdom of necessity" into a "kingdom of freedom." When we do this, it becomes evident that Engels, without any argumentation and probably without being fully aware of what was involved, changed the meaning of his conception by illegitimately and illogically substituting a *collective* subject of freedom for an individual subject, thus passing (illegitimately and illogically) from the problem of rational self-determination of individual human beings to that of rational *collective* self-determination.[150] This change was illegitimate and illogical, because, without additional argumentation, the idea of *individual* freedom as rational self-control does not entail the view that all social forces should be rationally controlled and that collective freedom should be defined in opposition to spontaneity. But this was precisely what Marx and Engels did. They reduced Hegelian rationalism to absurdity by claiming that civil society, seen by Hegel as the legitimate preserve of spontaneous social forces, should be abolished, and that collective liberation should consist in an all-embracing rational control of social life. In this context, Engels's view of freedom as the "understanding of necessity" changed the original meaning of freedom so thoroughly that it was to become the most effective justification of communist totalitarianism.

It is striking how deeply ingrained Marx and Engels's disgust and enmity were for spontaneously operating social forces. As Engels wrote:

Active social forces work exactly like natural forces: blindly, forcibly, destructively, so long as we do not understand, and reckon with, them. But when once we understand them, when once we grasp their action, their direction, their effects, it depends only upon ourselves to subject them more and more to our own will, and by means of them to reach our own needs. And this holds quite especially of the mighty productive forces of today. . . . Once their nature is understood, they can, in the hands of the producers working together, be transformed from master demons into willing servants. The difference is as that between the destructive force of electricity in the lightning of the storm and electricity under command in the telegraph and the voltaic arc; the difference between a conflagration, and fire working in the service of man. With this recognition, at last, of the real nature of the productive forces of today, the social anarchy of production gives place to a social regulation of production upon a definite plan. (E, *AD*, 339)

Of course, this transformation must be preceded by a social revolution: "The proletariat seizes political power and turns the means of production in the first instance into state property." Then the state, as an apparatus of oppression, "dies out," because nothing remains to be repressed (ibid., 340, 341). Finally, we have the miracle of the total liberation and regeneration of humanity:

With the seizing of the means of production by society, production of commodities is done away with, and simultaneously, the mastery of the product over the producer. Anarchy in a social organization is replaced by systematic, definite organization. The struggle for individual existence disappears. Then for the first time, man, in a certain sense, is finally marked off from the rest of the animal kingdom, and emerges from the mere animal conditions of existence into really human ones. The whole sphere of the conditions of life which envision man, and which have hitherto ruled man, now comes under the dominion and control of man, who for the first time becomes the real, conscious lord of nature, because he has now become master of his own social organization. The laws of his own social action, hitherto standing face to face with man as laws of nature foreign to, and dominating him, will then be used with full understanding, and so mastered by him. Man's own social organization, hitherto confronting him as a necessity imposed by nature and history, now becomes the result of his own free action. The extraneous objective forces that have hitherto governed history pass under the control of man himself. Only from that time will man himself, with full consciousness, make his own history—only from that time will the social causes set in movement by him have, in the main and in a constantly growing measure, the results intended by him. It is humanity's leap from the kingdom of necessity to the kingdom of freedom. (ibid., 343–44)

Here we have the myth that nourished the messianic hopes of several generations of Marxists. It was Engels, not Marx, who expressed it with the greatest force. All those who, following fashionable trends, tend "to dismiss Engels as a shallow popularizer"[151] should realize that, historically speaking, this was one of most influential and, thereby, most classical Marxist texts. But despite its apparent clarity, it is in fact an obscure text, full of contradictions and open to different interpretations. Why should "active social forces" be treated as destructive and demonic? Who was to understand and master these forces? What could it mean that productive forces "have outgrown all control except that of *a society as a whole?*" (ibid., 338; italics added). Why should a "systematic, definite organization" in which everything is firmly under control (whose control?) be regarded as the triumph of human freedom? Why is the spontaneous order of the market seen as anarchy and a shameful defeat of freedom? Why is only the state oppressive? Why will economic administration liberate?[152] What is the real nature of "historical necessity" if it can suddenly disappear, as it were, and make room for humankind's "free action"? Sometimes Engels suggests that the laws of necessity will be entirely abolished, while at other times he speaks about mastering these laws by means of knowledge, which presupposes that something remains to be understood and mastered. I will consider some of these questions in the next section.

2.6   From Freedom Lost to Freedom . . . Regained?

Like Marx and Hegel, Engels saw freedom as developing in a historical process. The *Manifesto of the Communist Party* describes "the history of all hitherto existing society" as "the history of class struggles" (M&E, CW, 6:482). But this famous phrase was to be subject to correction. Engels added to the English edition of the *Manifesto* (1888) a footnote saying that this was true only of "all *written* history." He further explained:

In 1847, the prehistory of society, the social organization existing previous to recorded history, was all but unknown. Since then, Haxthausen discovered common ownership of land in Russia, Maurer proved it to be the social foundation from which all Teutonic races started in history, and by and by village communities were found to be, or to have been, the primitive form of society everywhere from India to Ireland. The inner organization of this primitive Communistic society was laid bare, in its typical form, by Morgan's crowning discovery of the true nature of the *gens* and its relation to the *tribe*. With the dissolution of these primeval communities society begins to be differentiated into separate and finally antagonistic classes. (ibid., 482n)

What is strange about this explanation is that Engels is silent on the important fact that Marx did have his own theory of a classless society, a theory *presupposed* by his concept of man's communal essence and elaborated (long before Morgan) in detail in *Grundrisse*.[153] Hence, the phrase "the history of class struggles" can be interpreted only as referring to the history of civilization as opposed to "prehistory," not as a result of Marx's alleged ignorance of the very existence of a prehistorical "ancient society."

What Haxthausen and Maurer revealed to Marx was rather the vitality of ancient communal structures and their (at least partial) survival in the historical world. Marx's growing interest in these problems was bound up, among other things, with the need to provide an answer to the question raised by the Russian populists about the relevance of the Russian peasant commune to the "skipping of the capitalist phase" in Russia.[154] Marx's letters to Engels of March 25 and March 14, 1868, make it clear that Maurer's book on the rural commune in Germany was "exceptionally significant" for Marx in connection with the Russian question: as depriving the Russians of "the last trace of ORIGINALITY, even in THIS LINE" (ibid., 42:557, 547). This meant, of course, the rejection of the hope that the existence of communal ownership of land endowed Russia with a unique opportunity to make a direct transition to socialism. But several years later, the heroic struggle of Russian revolutionary socialists caused Marx to change his mind, and Morgan's *Ancient Society* (1877) was used by Marx to support this important theoretical concession.

According to Engels in his preface to *The Origin of the Family*, Morgan "rediscovered in America, in his own way, the materialist conception of history." The materialist conception, Engels explained, is one that defines the determining factor in history as "the production and reproduction of immediate life." By this he meant two kinds of production: the production of the means of subsistence, on the one hand, and the production of human beings themselves, on the other. Thus, the social institutions that govern human existence are conditioned not only by productive forces and the division of labor, but also by the forms of "the propagation of the species." The relative importance of the two kinds of production is inversely proportional: "The less the development of labour, and the more limited its volume of production and, therefore, the wealth of society, the more preponderatingly does the social order appear to be dominated by ties of sex" (M&E, SW, 3:191, 191, 191–92). It followed from this reasoning that what Marx had done for the study of civilization—that is, for the study of territorial groups dominated by the property system and torn by class antagonisms—Morgan did for the study of the earlier precivilizational stage in which human society was based on the ties of kinship.

Engels mentioned in this context the first part of *The German Ideology*, in which "making other men, propagating their kind" was included under three aspects of social activity that "from the very outset, enter into historical development" (M&E, CW, 5:42–43). But otherwise the analogy between material production and production of human beings is, of course, somewhat strained. We can safely say that the source of Morgan's powerful appeal for Marx and for Engels was rather the integration of his findings into a global vision of history. This vision, presented in the final conclusion of Morgan's book, was quoted by Engels at the end of his *Origin of the Family, Private Property and the State*:

Since the advent of civilization, the outgrowth of property has been so immense, its forms so diversified, its uses so expanding and its management so intelligent in the interests of its owners that it *has become*, on the part of the people, *an unmanageable power. The human mind stands bewildered in the presence of its own creation.* The time will come, nevertheless, when human intelligence will rise to mastery over property, and define the relations of the state to the property it protects, as well as the obligations and the limits of the rights of its owners. The interests of society are paramount to individual interests, and the two must be brought into just and harmonious relation. A mere property career is not the final destiny of mankind, if progress is to be the law of the future as it has been of the past. The time which has passed away since civilisation began is but a fragment of the past duration of man's existence; and but a fragment of the ages yet to come. The dissolution of society bids fair to become the termination of a career of which property is the end and aim, because such a career contains the elements of self-destruction. Democracy in government, brotherhood in society, equality in rights and privileges, and universal education, foreshadow the next higher plane of society to which experience, intelligence and knowledge are steadily tending. *It will be a revival, in a higher form, of the liberty, equality and fraternity of the ancient gentes.*[155]

It is understandable why this vision was so enormously attractive to Marx and Engels. Marx found in it his favorite scheme of the self-enriching alienation of the human species. Engels, who also wanted to combine scientificity with the Hegelian search for the rationality of history (something he could not derive from Darwinism), saw in Morgan's vision a version of scientific evolutionism capable of revealing not only the mechanisms of change but also the *meaning* of development. Both enthusiastically welcomed Morgan's explanation of the domination of human beings by their own products and their future liberation from this yoke. Referring to this point, it is justified to say that Morgan "rediscovered in his own way" the central proposition of Marx and Engels's philosophy of history.

Engels's *Origin of the Family* is a popularization of Morgan's book and, at the same time, an attempt at a wholesale integration of its content into the Marxist theory of history. The result of this effort is the extreme idealization of ancient tribalism and an almost Marcusean emphasis on the sexual repressiveness of civilization. Thus, for instance, summarizing Morgan's discoveries about the Iroquois gens, Engels wrote: "And this gentile constitution is wonderful in all its childlike simplicity! Everything runs smoothly without soldiers, gendarmes or police; without nobles, kings, governors, prefects or judges; without prisons; without trials. All quarrels and disputes are settled by the whole body of those concerned—the gens or the tribe or the individual gentes among themselves. . . . There can be no poor and needy—the communistic household and the gens know their obligations toward the aged, the sick and those disabled in war. All are free and equal—including women" (M&E, *SW*, 3:266).

True, this idyll was possible only within the boundary of a tribe; "the confederacy of the tribes already signified the commencement of its downfall." Nonetheless, the inevitable breakdown of this small but harmonious universe appears to us as "a degradation, a fall from the simple moral grandeur" (ibid., 267).

The same "moral grandeur" was found by Engels among the other representatives of "barbarism" (the higher stage of prehistoric culture, following that of "savagery"): the Greek of the Heroic Age, the early Romans, and the Teutonic warriors. The "old freedom" consisted in every case of direct democracy, lack of any oppression, "relative freedom of sexual intercourse," and equality of women. Everywhere the first form of class oppression was "that of the female sex by the male," culminating in indissoluble monogamic marriage dominated by man, being, in fact, "monogamy *only for the women*." And, above all, freedom, equality, and harmony could be preserved only as long as production was carried on "within the most restricted limits" so that "the producers exercised control over their own product" (ibid., 240, 240, 238, 278). The appearance of private property, money, and commodity production amounted to a revolution that marked the transition from "barbarism" to "civilization."

Civilization, Engels argued, "is that stage of development of society at which division of labor, the resulting exchange between individuals, and commodity production, which combines the two, reach their complete unfoldment." He described it as progressive, "revolutionizing the whole hitherto existing society," but painted its emergence in dark colors, illustrating, as it were, the Hegelian thesis of the role of moral evil in history. Thus, for instance, the emergence of the "open society" in Athens was presented by him not as the "Grecian miracle" but as a gloomy process of social disintegration in which the main role had been played by greedy foreign merchants (ibid., 330, 330, 279–80). A similar story repeated itself everywhere, and everywhere the role of commerce was peculiarly destructive, though it functioned to pave the way for cruel, tragic progress, as Engels noted:

As soon as money, and with it the merchant, steps in as a middleman between the producers, the process of exchange becomes still more complicated, the ultimate fate of the product still more uncertain. The merchants are numerous and none of them knows what the other is doing. Commodities now pass not only from hand to hand, but also from market to market. The producers have lost control of the aggregate production of the conditions of their own life, and merchants have not acquired it. Products and production become the playthings of chance.

But chance is only one pole of interrelation, the other pole of which is necessity. In nature, where chance also seems to reign, we have long ago demonstrated in each particular field the inherent necessity and regularity that assert itself in this chance. What is true of nature holds good also for society. The more a social activity, a series of social processes, becomes too powerful for conscious human control, grows beyond human reach, the more it seems to have been left to pure chance, the more do its peculiar and innate laws assert themselves in this chance, as if by natural necessity. . . . These economic laws of commodity production are modified at the different stages of development of this form of production; on the whole, however, the entire period of civilization has been dominated by these laws. (ibid., 331)

By the "entire period," Engels meant "three great epochs of civilization": slavery, feudalism, and capitalism. Each of these epochs caused oppression to be more disguised and hypocritically embellished (ibid., 332, 333).[156] In reality, however, each marked an increase in unfreedom: of mastering people by their own products, of subjugating their conscious will to the blind law of necessity.

To reconstruct Engels's views on the fate of freedom, one must read his *Origin of the Family* together with *Anti-Dühring* (or, to be precise, those parts of this work published separately under the title *Socialism: Utopian and Scientific*). The *Origin of the Family* brings us to the threshold of civilization—that is, to the point when humans lost their ancient freedom; *Anti-Dühring* deals with the development of civilization and culminates in the vision of human ascent from the kingdom of necessity to the kingdom of freedom. As can easily be seen, this tripartite scheme illustrates the dialectical law of the negation of negation—that is, of the restoration on a higher level (the third phase) of what had been negated in the second phase of the process.

At this juncture, however, two remarks should be made. One concerns Engels's interpretation of Morgan's evolutionism; the other, the difference between Engels's view and the view set forth in Marx's *Capital* on the law of the negation of negation in history.

Engels's account of Morgan's alleged rediscovery of a materialist interpretation of history amounts, in fact, to a somewhat trivial observation that people in order to live must both produce themselves and their means of subsistence. We can add to this the general assumption of evolutionism that history develops through stages that are essentially the same for the entire human race (whether this assumption legitimately applies to Marx's view is another question).[157] But apart from this, Engels's work makes it clear that Marx's discovery of the "laws of motion of the human society applied only to the history of civilization, and not to prehistorical cultures"; hence Engels's sharp contrast between civilization and the earlier stages of human evolution brought about the unintended effect of *contrasting* Marx's and Morgan's fields of study. Marx's "laws of motion" were economic laws, or, more precisely, laws of commodity production, while Morgan proved that such laws did not apply to ancient society; if so, it would have been more correct to say that Morgan demonstrated the *limited applicability* of Marx's historical materialism. Engels did not show the evolutionary continuity between prehistory and history, although obviously this was his intention; rather, what he showed was the discontinuity between tribal society, which was still tied to nature by a metaphorical umbilical cord, and civilized society, which was ruled by economic laws (i.e., not *truly natural* laws but laws of *human praxis*), although "asserting themselves *as if* by natural necessity" (ibid., 331). By using the words "as if," Engels implied, in fact, an ontological difference between laws of nature and laws of "second nature" (i.e., the world of human products that had acquired a naturelike independence of conscious human will). Finally, Engels did not bother to explain why the nonexistence of economic laws of commodity production was seen as the most important condition of freedom. After all, societies described by Morgan had established cultural patterns full of constraints, obligatory rituals, and fixed roles that left no room for individual deviation. Why, indeed, should tribal existence be seen as more conducive to freedom than, say, Athenian democracy? Engels's remarks on the destructive role of money (which divided people into creditors and debtors) and commerce (which attracted too many strangers to Athens) did not provide an adequate answer (ibid., 279–80).

What caused Engels to express such doubtful judgments was his decision to define the passage to civilization as the first negation—that is, the greatest watershed in the evolution of hitherto existing society. Marx, at least in *Capital* and *Grundrisse*, considered this watershed as not the passage to civilization, but rather the passage to capitalism. Hence, for him, there was no need to stress the contrast between the old constitution of the Grecian gens and the Athenian state. He could remain faithful to the humanist tradition of idealizing the Greek city-state, because he did not consider antiquity, or even the Middle Ages, to be dominated by the blind laws of commodity production.

The tripartite dialectical scheme employed in Marx's *Capital* described human history not as a process in which the negation of negation was conceived as negation of primitive communal ownership by civilization, which, in turn, was to be negated through the restoration of collective ownership on a higher level, but instead as the negation of individual property through the capitalist expropriation of direct producers, to be followed by the "expropriation of the expropriators," which would restore *individual* property on a higher level (M, C, 1, ch. 32). In *Anti-Dühring*, Engels tried to interpret this third stage as "the reestablishment of individual property, but *on the basis* of the social ownership of the land and of the means of production produced by labor itself"—in other words, as individual ownership of the products (that is, the articles of consumption) but collective ownership of the means of production (E, *AD*, 160–61). But the point is that, for Marx, collective ownership under communism was precisely the restoration of the *individual* ownership of the means of production, understood as the restoration of the direct, nonalienated relationship between producers and their means of production. Thus, for him individual property was the opposite *not* of collective property, but of "dehumanized or estranged property."[158] In this sense, Marx wrote in *The Civil War in France* that the Paris Commune "wanted to make individual property a truth by transforming the means of production, land and capital, now chiefly the means of enslaving and exploiting labor, into mere instruments of free and associated labor" (M&E, *SW*, 2:223).

We can therefore conclude that the difference under discussion has two aspects. First, Marx's triad was a division within civilization, while that of Engels applied to the whole span of human evolution; in other words, Marx continued to exclude prehistory from the history of civilization (seeing the transition to the latter as long and gradual), while Engels (following Morgan) treated civilization as a distinctive phase in the general evolution of the species (which led him to define communism as a dialectical negation of civilization). Second, Marx's conception of freedom emphasized need of de-alienation, while Engels concentrated almost exclusively on control of the fate of human products (conceivable only under fully controllable conditions—i.e., either in a small tribal community or in a fully centralized and therefore totally controlled industrial society). Because of this the replacement of the market by rational planning was seen by Engels as "the leap to the kingdom of freedom," while for Marx it was only the necessary *basis* for freedom.

Let us now return to Engels's view of human history. The first epoch of civilization, that of slavery, was presented by him as an epoch of inevitable historical progress that should not be assessed from a narrow moralistic viewpoint. Slavery was both the result of progress (since, in times of low productivity, prisoners were simply killed) and the cause of further progress. In *Anti-Dühring*, Engels noted: "It was slavery that first made possible the division of labor between agriculture and industry on a larger scale, and thereby also Hellenism, the flowering of the ancient world. Without slavery, no Greek state, no Greek art and science; without slavery, no Roman Empire. But without the basis laid by Grecian culture, and the Roman Empire, also no modern Europe. We should never forget that our whole economic, political and intellectual development presupposes a state of things in which slavery was as necessary as it was universally recognized. In this sense we are entitled to say: Without the slavery of antiquity, no modern socialism" (E, *AD*, 221).

True, in *The Origin of the Family*, we encounter a strikingly different judgment: "It was not democracy that caused the downfall of Athens, as the European schoolmasters who cringe before royalty would have us believe, but slavery, which brought the labor of the free citizen into contempt" (M&E, *SW*, 3:284). But although *The Origin of the Family* was written after *Anti-Dühring*, it did not mark a real change in Engels's views; its Morgan-inspired love of freedom was genuine, but Engels's Hegelian belief in the rationality of history proved much stronger. His view that ancient communities *had* to be dissolved to enable progress—a view expressed in *Anti-Dühring* as an argument for slavery (E, *AD*, 222) [159]—was not abandoned in *The Origin of the Family* but only differently phrased, with more emphasis placed on the tragic cost of progress. In his afterword to "On Social Relations in Russia," Engels repeated this view: he drew a parallel between the disintegration of the Russian peasant commune and the dissolution of the Athenian gens, his aim being to stress the inexorable inevitability of both processes (M&E, *SW*, 2:405).

An important aspect of Engels's view of the transition to civilization was his conception of the emergence and functions of the state.

In the *Manifesto of the Communist Party*, political power was defined as "merely the organized power of one class for oppressing another"; the modern state was called, accordingly, "a committee for managing the common affairs of the whole bourgeoisie" (M&E, *CW*, 6:505, 486). [160] In *Anti-Dühring*, and especially in *The Origin of the Family*, Engels developed this crude conception in a way that made it somewhat more plausible. He upheld the view of the state as a phenomenon bound up with the division of society into classes and serving, as a rule, the interests of the economically dominating class, but he abandoned the extremist version of this view, which stressed direct connection between "political power" and "economic power," reducing the former to a mere tool of the latter. Thus, he argued against Dühring that class oppression does not have to rely on "direct political force" and that the socially dominant class should not be identified with the holders of political power (for instance, economic power might belong to the bourgeoisie and political power to the nobility) (E, AD, 198–203). In *The Origin of the Family*, he pointed out that the state developed organically from the old gentile order by organizing tribal life, for defensive reasons, on a territorial basis, thus replacing the ties of blood by territorial divisions. This entailed the establishment of a *public power*, which no longer directly coincided "with the population organizing itself as an armed force" and consisted "not merely of armed men but also of material adjuncts, prisons, and institutions of coercion of all kinds." The internal functions of this public power, such as levying taxes and "holding class antagonisms in check" necessarily made it an organ that stood *above* society and thus not one that was merely an obedient tool in the hands of one class. As a rule, the state's main function—that of preserving internal order—coincided in practice with supporting the most powerful class and suppressing the oppressed one. In this *indirect* sense, the state of antiquity was the state of slave owners, and the modern representative state was an instrument of exploitation of wage labor by capital. However, Engels added, sometimes "periods occur in which the warring classes balance each other so nearly that the state power, as ostensible mediator, acquires, for the moment, a certain degree of independence of both." Following Marx's analyses (especially in *The Eighteenth Brumaire of Louis Bonaparte*), he mentioned three examples of such a situation: "the absolute monarchy of the seventeenth and eighteenth century, which held the balance between the nobility and the class of burghers," and "the Bonapartism of the First, and still more of the Second French Empire, which played off the proletariat against the bourgeoisie and the bourgeoisie against the proletariat" (M&E, SW, 3:327, 328, 328, 328).

Thus, the state was seen by Engels as a force standing above society (although dependent, as a rule, on the most powerful social force) and using its repressive power for pacifying the destructive manifestations of social conflicts (as a rule, in the interests of the stronger). What was lacking in this conception was not the allowance of the possibility of a certain autonomy of the state, but rather the insight that state officials might have some particular interests of their own.

Despite the quoted declaration about the necessity and progressiveness of slavery, Engels's argumentation for the inevitability of socialism starts with his analysis of the system of petty industry in the Middle Ages. Following Marx, Engels described it as a system in which the instruments of labor, including land, were "small, dwarfish, circumscribed" and therefore belonged to the direct producers—artisans or peasants, freemen and serfs (E, *AD*, 325).[161] (The phenomenon of big estates cultivated by serfs but belonging to the nobility remained unexplained in this description.) The role of capitalism and of its upholder, the bourgeoisie, was to concentrate these scattered and limited means of production. This was done by transforming them "from means of production of the individual into *social* means of production only workable by *a collectivity of men.* . . . In like manner, production itself changed from a series of individual into a series of social acts, and the products from individual to social products" (ibid.; cf. M&E, *BW*, 135).

Since this logic is somewhat strange, we must make sure we have grasped it. For Engels, a capitalist factory was a *social* means of production irrespective of its ownership, for the simple reason that its existence implied "the co-operation of hundreds and thousands of workers." Its social character *as a means of production* had to be distinguished from the fact that it belonged to a private capitalist, who, owing to property rights, appropriated its product. Marx and Engels called this the contradiction between "socialized production" and "capitalistic appropriation" (ibid., 325, 328; cf. M&E, *BW*, 135).

The socialization of production presupposed a relatively high development of the division of labor. In the Middle Ages, the division of labor grew up "spontaneously and upon *no definite plan,*" following the exchange of commodities on the market. In contrast to this "old division of labor," capitalist factories represented a "new division of labor" based on "*a definite plan.*" These factories were islands of socialized production in a sea of individual production. This coexistence of two principles was by no means peaceful and harmonious; their relationship was competitive, and "organization upon a definite plan" proved stronger and more efficient than the spontaneous division of labor. Socialized production was bound to become more and more centralized, while individual producers were doomed to gradual extinction. But even though modern "socialized" industry was bound to win in this "Darwinian struggle for existence," there remained the glaring contradiction between the planned character of production and the unregulated spontaneous character of exchange, or as Engels put it, *"between the organization of production in the individual workshop, and the anarchy of production in society generally"* (ibid., 326, 332, 332; cf. M&E, *BW*, 133, 138, 138).

The general line of Engels's reasoning follows, of course, that of Marx's in *Capital*: Engels's dichotomy of old versus new division of labor corresponds to Marx's distinction between the division of labor in society and the division of labor in the factory. The view of the historical necessity of centralization and of the reactionary character of the petty bourgeoisie is also purely Marxian. But there are also striking differences that continue to go unnoticed or are neglected by most researchers, although the fashion of opposing Engels to Marx should have brought these differences into relief.[162]

In Engels's view, commodity production was a common feature of the entire period of civilization. He conceded that in the Middle Ages, commodity production "was only in its infancy," but at the same time he saw medieval history as dominated by the "spontaneous division of labor." Describing the emergence of capitalism, he wrote: "Into this society of individual producers, of commodity producers, the new mode of production thrust itself. In the midst of the old division of labor, grown up spontaneously and upon *no definite plan*, which had governed the whole of society, now arose division of labor upon *a definite plan*, as organized in the factory; side by side with individual production appeared *social production*" (E, *AD*, 330, 326; cf. M&E, *BW*, 137, 133). According to this description, the whole of medieval society was governed by the laws of spontaneous division of labor, "individual producer" was a synonym for "commodity producer," while "social production"—the novelty introduced by capitalism—meant the division of labor on a definite plan, as organized in the factory. From this perspective, the progressiveness of capitalism consisted essentially in *limiting* the scope of uncontrolled spontaneity ("blind forces") by introducing the principle of socially organized, planned production; a principle inherently hostile to the spontaneous division of labor and inevitably leading to monopoly. In contrast to this, Marx (who was, after all, a much better economist) did not associate the socialization of production exclusively with the division of labor within the factory: for him, it was above all the result of the liberation of commodity production from the fetters of the natural, or seminatural, medieval economy. In this interpretation, socialized production was made possible through the rapid extension of markets—that is, through creating large networks of exchange that were at the same time networks of productive cooperation. Accordingly, social product—i.e., a product about which no individual could say: "this is *my* product" (E, *AD*, 326)—was not necessarily a product of one factory. On the contrary, it was, as a rule, a product of people working in different factories, people who did not know one another and who often even lived in different countries. In other words, Marx did not see market relations as an element of continuity between feudalism and capitalism. Rather, he emphasized the qualitative difference between the restricted local markets of the Middle Ages and the national and international markets of the capitalist era. Unlike Engels, he saw the victory of the modern centralizing tendency not only in the planned organization of capitalist factories, but also in the apparent anarchy of the capitalist market. We must not forget that he saw the world market as the greatest achievement of capitalism, as the economic unification of humankind.

Another difference can be detected in Marx and Engels's views on the relation between capitalist development and the "blind laws of necessity." For Engels, the lack of conscious control over social relations was a common feature of all societies based on the production of commodities. Seen from this perspective, capitalist factories represented the first step toward the victory of conscious organization over blind spontaneity. Marx, however, saw this quite differently: for him, medieval producers exercised some control over their products and did not allow social relations to assume "the fantastic form of a relation between things" (M, C, 1:77; see chapter 1, section 7). They were subject to different forms of personal dependence, but precisely because of this, their social relations were transparent and "commodity fetishism" did not exist. This fetishism appeared only at the mature (i.e., capitalist) stage of commodity production. It followed from this that capitalism was different in this respect from all precapitalist social formations. Engels (who, characteristically, did not use the term *commodity fetishism*) completely overlooked, or ignored, this aspect of Marx's *Capital*.

Finally, it is striking that Engels says almost nothing about the human tragedy of the direct producers. He seems to have forgotten what he himself had written about this in his *Condition of the Working Class in England* (M&E, CW, 4).[163] The expropriation of small producers, the separation of individuals from their means of production—that is, the social process described by Marx as the greatest turning point in the history of hitherto existing society—is barely mentioned in Engels's account of capitalist development.[164] No wonder that he presents the result of this process—the early capitalist factory—only in its positive aspect.

All these differences were linked to Marx and Engels's different conceptions of the law of "negation of negation" in history. Marx contrasted capitalism with all precapitalist forms of human development; the capitalist revolution was, for him, the greatest watershed in history. Engels put more emphasis on continuity in his treatment of capitalism: for him, capitalism was a new mode of production *within* civilization and a new phase in the development *of* civilization. Underlying Marx's account of capitalist development was the dramatic visionary story of self-enriching alienation, but this was not the case with Engels's account. Whether the two thinkers were aware of this difference is another matter.

Engels's tendency to look for continuity was also manifested in his conception of the emergence of the technological and organizational premises of socialism. In his view, the productive superiority of big factories, and of the principles of conscious planning they represented, led inevitably to the replacement of competition by monopolies (E, *AD*, 336; cf. M&E, *BW*, 143). "The producers on a large scale in a particular branch of industry in a particular country unite in a 'Trust,' a union for the purpose of regulating production. They determine the total amount to be produced, parcel it out among themselves, and thus enforce the selling price fixed beforehand." Engels saw this as the result of *rebellion of* the mode of production (large-scale factories) rebelling against the mode of exchange (the "anarchic" market). He was so euphoric about this idea that he even called it the factual capitulation of capitalist production "to the production upon a definite plan of the invading socialistic society" (ibid.).

The next step would be the undertaking of the direction of production by the official representative of the capitalist society—the state (ibid., 337; cf. M&E, *BW*, 143). In Engel's diagnosis, this must be so because the existence of private capitalists, deprived of any historical justification, had become superfluous (ibid., 341; cf. M&E, *BW*, 147–48). The capitalists themselves, he argued, were becoming increasingly aware of the social character of production and partially *recognized* this fact by reducing their role in managing the industry (ibid., 345; cf. M&E, *BW*, 151). First came joint stock companies, and then trusts. This paved the way for state capitalism under which all social functions of the bourgeoisie would be performed by salaried employees.

A rather peculiar aspect of Engels's analysis was his view that the further development of monopolistic capitalism would be hindered by, of all things, money. He thought that this would usher in an economic catastrophe, which he described as follows: "The contradiction between socialised production and capitalist appropriation ends in a violent explosion. The circulation of commodities is, for the time being, stopped. Money, the means of circulation, becomes a hindrance to circulation. All the laws of production and circulation of commodities are turned upside down. The economic collision has reached its apogee. *The mode of production is in rebellion against the mode of exchange*" (M&E, *BW*, 141).[165]

This prediction, though seemingly absurd, was quite logical to someone for whom rational planning (represented by the monopolies) was irreconcilable with the "anarchy of the market." From this point of view, money, as a guarantee of the "anarchic" freedom of consumption, was indeed a hindrance to a rationally planned circulation. Consistent planning demanded the abolition of the monetary exchange economy.

Engels's text does not make it clear whether state capitalism was, in his view, a stage preceding the socialist revolution or, rather, a brief alternative to the revolutionary solution. In any case, his analysis was that the bourgeoisie had become politically and intellectually bankrupt and incapable of leadership and that they hindered further economic progress. Therefore the time had come for the proletarian revolution and for the final triumph of freedom: "The proletariat seizes the public power, and by means of this transforms the socialized means of production, slipping from the hands of the bourgeoisie, into public property. By this act, the proletariat frees the means of production from the character of capital they have thus far borne, and gives their socialized character complete freedom to work itself out. . . . In proportion as anarchy in social production vanishes, the political authority of the state dies out. Man, at last the master of his own form of social organization, becomes at the same time the lord over nature, his own master—free" (E, *AD*, 345–46; cf. M&E, *BW*, 151–52).

But, Engels reminded us, this "humanity's leap from the kingdom of necessity to the kingdom of freedom"[166] will not be possible without scientific understanding of necessity. Happily, this understanding has been provided, and imparted to the now oppressed proletarian class, by scientific socialism—"the theoretical expression of the proletarian movement" (ibid., 346; cf. M&E, *BW*, 152).

What does it really mean, this collective self-mastery based on scientific knowledge? The phrase "the leap from necessity to freedom" suggests the abolition of all necessary laws, but Engels's general definition of freedom envisions only understanding and making use of necessity. On the other hand, Engels describes the "blind laws" of commodity production not as "natural" but only "naturelike," thus suggesting their ontological difference from the "natural laws of motion" inherent in the dynamic structure of the universe. Similarly, in his essay on Feuerbach, Engels described social laws as resulting from the conflicts of innumerable individual wills operating at cross-purposes and thus escaping any individual's control, thereby bringing about entirely unintended results. In this sense, laws governing the domain of history are independent of anyone's will and *analogous* to the laws governing "the realm of unconscious nature" (M&E, *SW*, 3:365–66).[167] "Analogy" does not mean "identity"; "naturelike" (*naturwüchsig*) does not mean "nature"; "second-nature" (the world created by man, although subject to its own "naturelike" laws) is therefore fundamentally different from "first nature" (i.e., the world of nonorganic and organic matter). If "the autonomy and uncontrollability" of the second nature is in fact the result of the uncontrollable character of commodity production, then the transition to socialism can be interpreted as the abolition of social laws. In this new situation, the technological mastery over the first nature will strengthen human collective power without producing unintended results. Reasoning along these lines, it is possible to interpret Engels's vision of emancipation as profoundly voluntaristic, quite close, in fact, to the voluntaristic Marxism of young Lukács.

There is a doctoral dissertation (unfortunately unpublished) in which all these problems are analyzed in depth, showing an unexpected complexity and at the same time a fundamental ambiguity in Engels's thought. Its author, Steven M. Vogel, claims that Engels's conception of second nature treats its laws as laws of alienated human praxis—that is, as something that should be not merely understood but also abolished, overthrown in a victorious proletarian revolution. In this manner, the notion of alienation has been reintroduced in Engels's writings at the expense of his material- istic determinism.[168] Vogel is fully aware that "this thesis if fully developed stands in contradiction both to the fundamental metaphysical thesis of the ontological unity of society and nature and to the specific Engelsian notion that nature is dialectical." [169] Indeed, if the laws of dialectic are general laws of motion, and not laws of interaction between subject and object, then the notion of alienation loses its basis; and if social laws can be abolished, then the thesis of the ontological unity of society and nature is no longer tenable.

The existence of contradictions in Engels's thought cannot be denied. Most of them, however, form a distinctive pattern that confirms the other- wise well-known truth that the unity and coherence of a worldview (as distinct from theoretical coherence) may consist in the particular logic of its contradictions or in the structured character of its inner tensions. The speci- ficity of Engels's worldview consisted in a syndrome of tensions between Hegelian rationalism and natural science materialism; his necessitarianism, therefore, was divided between scientistic determinism (excluding such notions as "rational necessity" or "meaning of history") and the Hegelian conception of necessity, which was deeply involved with the search for rationality and meaning in historical processes. On the whole, Engels was not a positivist but rather a post-Hegelian thinker, who wanted to bury Hegelian idealism but at the same time save the Hegelian view of history as a meaningful process that led inevitably to the victory of rationality and freedom. But this means also that freedom in his view presupposed rationality, and rationality, in turn, presupposed necessity—although, of course, not the blind, irrational necessity of a spontaneous process. And this, I think, provides the key to the proper understanding of his vision of liberation: His "leap from the kingdom of necessity to the kingdom of freedom" meant, in fact, the transition from the kingdom of irrational spontaneity, where necessary laws operate behind the backs of its agents, to the kingdom of reason, which exercises maximum control within the limits of objective necessities.

Let us briefly develop this thought. Engels's historical materialism as- sumes that historical processes are determined by the development of pro- ductive forces and that the latter are subject to the inexorable law of cen- tralization. Thus, the decentralized individual production of the Middle Ages gave way to production in capitalist factories; under capitalism, the law of centralization brought about the concentration of capital and the replacement of free competition by monopolies; this created objective conditions for the final act of centralization—that is, for socialism, which would transform the entire country into "one great factory." Engels certainly did not think that the necessity of steadily increasing centralization was merely a law of alienated human praxis, that is, a law that would be abolished together with capitalism. Certainly not! He saw this law as inherent in the very nature of modern technology, in the very nature of economic rationality, and, thereby, in the very nature of socialist freedom. He did not dream about liberating workers from the physical, technological, and organizational necessities of a maximally rationalized and efficient productivity; he knew that such liberation presupposed strong self-discipline. But such self-discipline, which he called "control over ourselves," was a part of his definition of freedom. Therefore, he contemptuously dismissed the anarchist critique that accused him and Marx of being authoritarians and centralizers. His answer to these accusations made it absolutely clear that he never thought of freeing people from the rule of what he saw as truly objective and rational necessities. In his 1874 essay "On Authority," he used as an example a cotton-spinning mill, concluding:

Keeping the machines going requires an engineer to look after the steam engine, mechanics to make the current repairs, and many other laborers, whose business it is to transfer the products from one room to another, and so forth. All these workers, men, women and children, are obliged to begin and finish their work at the hours fixed by the authority of the steam, which cares nothing for individual autonomy. The workers must, therefore, first come to an understanding on the hours of work; and these hours, once they are fixed, must be observed by all, without exception. Thereafter particular questions arise in each room and at every moment concerning the mode of production, distribution of materials, etc., which must be settled at once on pain of seeing all production immediately stopped; whether they are settled by decision of a delegate placed at the head of each branch of labor or, if possible, by a majority vote, the will of the single individual will always have to subordinate itself, which means that questions are settled in an authoritarian way. The automatic machinery of a big factory is much more despotic than the small capitalists who employ workers ever have been. At least with regard to the hours of work one may write upon the portals of these factories: *Lasciate ogni autonomia, voi che entrate!* [Leave, you that enter in, all autonomy behind!] If man, by dint of his knowledge and inventive genius, has subdued the forces of nature, the latter avenge themselves upon him by subjecting him, in so far as he employs them, to a veritable despotism, independent of all social organization. Wanting to abolish authority in a large-scale industry is tantamount to wanting to abolish industry itself, to destroy the power loom in order to return to the spinning wheel. (M&E, BW, 520–21)[170]

Indeed, this point could not have been made clearer: the price for the subjugation of the forces of nature, through the development of man's productive forces, is the despotism of the productive regime, a despotism that is independent of all social organization and therefore cannot be abolished along with capitalism. If this is so, however, then what did Engels mean when he wrote his solemnly enthusiastic words about the leap to the kingdom of freedom?

To put it most simply, he meant the abolition of the spontaneous order of the market and its replacement by conscious, rational control over human products. It is evident, therefore, that laws of *exchange*—that is, the blind laws of the market—did not have, in his view, the same ontological status as the general laws of motion governing *production* as human intercourse with nature. Hence, it is justified to say that the laws of the market, in contrast to the laws of material production, were, in his view, naturelike, but not natural, pertaining to the second nature and only analogous to the laws of unconscious nature.[171] Engels's explanation of the origin of the laws of the market did not involve the Marxian notion of the alienation of human essence, but nonetheless he employed the concept of alienation in a less speculative sense—that is, as a "human being's estrangement from, and lack of control over, his own products."[172] This estrangement and lack of control were derived by Engels from the nature of commodity production. Engels believed that this lack of control was reflected in religious consciousness in the Calvinist doctrine of predestination. As he noted, predestination implied that "in the commercial world of competition success or failure does not depend upon a man's activity or cleverness, but upon circumstances uncontrollable by him" (M&E, *BW*, 96). This diagnosis brings us very close to Gramsci's view that an uncritical belief in the objectivity of the laws of the market is little more than a secularized version of Calvinism.

Anyhow, the main task of socialism was to abolish commodity production (i.e., production for market) and thereby liberate conscious agents from the tyranny of blind laws. Freedom in this sense was to be collective rational self-mastery, the conscious steering of history on the basis of scientific knowledge. The benefits for the individual boiled down to predictability—the avoidance of unintended results. But predictability was to be achieved at the cost of living in a totally controlled society, which is hardly compatible with the notion of individual freedom.

Thus, we can reasonably doubt whether Engels's kingdom of freedom really deserves its name; whether his account of the fate of freedom in history really does resemble the ancient story of freedom regained. Economic forces were to lose their demonic nature and become instead "willing servants," but the pressure of efficiency and the severe regime of factory work were to remain. The state as political power (i.e., as the organ of class rule) was to wither away, but entire social life was to be regulated by one public authority—an authority that could not tolerate spontaneity or pluralism, since this would lead immediately to the loosening of control, and hence to a weakening of the rational collective freedom, by unleashing of "chance" and blind forces. Individuals' dependence on unpredictable impersonal forces would thereby be minimized, Engels claimed in "On Authority," but their dependence on authorities, "no matter how delegated," would proportionately increase (ibid., 522). Such an ideal might be appealing to those who value order over freedom and for whom "spontaneous order" is not order at all. Perhaps it is not accidental (as the Marxists like to say) that Engels was a self-made military expert and liked to be called "General."

It is important to recall that Marx did not endorse Engels's view of the kingdom of freedom. He came to see this ideal as freedom in the kingdom of necessity. Socialization and rationalization of production, Marx argued, would liberate people from the rule of blind forces and thus create "conditions most favorable to, and worthy of, their human nature"; but this achievement "still remains a realm of necessity." The true realm of freedom "begins only where labor which is determined by necessity and mundane considerations ceases." To exercise our freedom, we need free time in which we can pursue "that development of human capacities which is an end in itself." But this should not be confused with a lack of civilized needs and withdrawal from collective work. Marx was emphatic that the full development of human capacities, which he identified with freedom, presupposes maximum development of the production sphere. The true realm of freedom, he stressed, "can blossom forth only with this realm of necessity as its basis" (M, C, 3:820).

This is, to be sure, a more acceptable conception. But it cannot be isolated from the entire context of Marx's work, since this would sever the connection between socialism and freedom, which was certainly not Marx's intention. He did not intend to say that freedom equals free time in *any* highly developed industrial society; he intended to define freedom as the socialist organization of productive forces (i.e., truly human development in the realm of necessity) *plus* free time for the development of those human capacities that cannot unfold in the productive sphere. We can safely assume that Engels was not against this correction. Nonetheless, the difference in emphasis remains and has given rise to very different interpretations of Marxism.

2.7 The Dual Legacy

Engels's role in the history of Marxism and Marxist-inspired workers' movements was strikingly varied. As an ideologist and practical advisor of the German and international workers' movements, he left us a very different legacy than as a philosopher, a codifier of Marxism, and an unrepentant communist utopian. With a certain (but not too great) oversimplification, we can say that in his first role he exercised decisive influence on German Social Democracy, while in the second, he found his most ardent and dogmatic followers in Russia. It was an ironic dualism. On the one hand, as an indefatigable systematizer and popularizer of Marx's ideas, he did more than anybody else to spread the doctrine called Marxism and to create the image of its infallibility. On the other hand, he shared Marx's concern about the legitimacy of the term *Marxism* and did not want to have uncritical followers, especially, perhaps, in Russia.[173] A. M. Voden, a Russian social democratic writer who visited Engels in 1893, reported: "Engels would prefer the Russians—and everybody else too—to stop fishing around for quotations from Marx and Engels and begin thinking instead in the way that Marx would have thought in their position. If the word Marxist has any right to exist, it is only in that meaning."[174]

After the dissolution of the Communist League in 1852, Marx and Engels took a consistently anti-Blanquist stand. In 1879, in their "Circular Letter" to the German Social Democratic party, they strongly protested against the tendency to claim that "the working class of itself is incapable of its own emancipation," further declaring: "We cannot co-operate with people who openly state that the workers are too uneducated to emancipate themselves and must first be freed from above by philanthropic big bourgeois and petty bourgeois. If the new Party organ adopts a line corresponding to the views of these gentlemen, a line that is bourgeois and not proletarian, then nothing remains for us, much though we should regret it, but publicly to declare our opposition to it, and to dissolve the solidarity with which we have hitherto represented the German Party abroad" (M&E, SW, 3:89, 94).

Although the circumstances were different and "philanthropic bourgeois" should, of course, be distinguished from "professional revolutionaries," nevertheless the "Circular" can be legitimately interpreted as containing a strong condemnation, *avant la lettre*, of the Leninist disbelief in the independent self-development of the workers' movement. How it could be reconciled with "scientific socialism," which, as the anarchists were quick to notice, emphasized the need for theoretical guidance (and thereby for theorists as leaders), is another question. In the present context, it is sufficient to note that the conception of a party inseparable from the broad legally operating movement of the masses was remote from revolutionary voluntarism. The anarchist critique of this conception was a critique from the left. And the anarchists had good reason to maintain that the Paris Commune, which was generally seen and extolled as the first truly proletarian revolution, was closer in spirit to anarchism than to the orderly movement led by the German Social Democrats.

Despite their initial understandable and unavoidable enthusiasm for the Commune, the leaders of the German party were becoming more and more inclined to share this view. Marx himself, although only in a private letter, qualified the high appraisal of the Commune in his *Civil War in France* by stating that "it was simply the uprising of one town in exceptional circumstances" and that "the majority in the Commune was not socialist and could not be so."[175] After Marx's death, the organizational successes of the Second International and of the German Social Democracy (especially after the annulment of Bismarck's antisocialist law in 1890) created the almost universally held conviction that the center of the European revolutionary movement had shifted from France to Germany. From this perspective, the Paris Commune did not look like a new beginning so much as the closing of the romantic period of revolutionary struggle on the barricades.[176]

In this context, the aging Engels wrote the text that is usually seen as his testament: the introduction to the 1895 edition of Marx's *Class Struggles in France*. In this introduction Engels advocated the legal parliamentary method of struggle. The revolutionary hopes of 1848, Engels argued, had proved to be an illusion. The Europe of that time was not yet ripe for the elimination of capitalism, and rebellion in the old style (i.e., street fighting with barricades) had become an anachronism (M&E, *SW*, 1:187–204). But it also happened that "the bourgeoisie and the government came to be much more afraid of the legal than of illegal action of the workers' party, of the results of elections than those of rebellion." Thus, Engels concluded, "the irony of history turns everything upside down. We, the 'revolutionists,' the 'overthrowers'—we are thriving far better on legal methods than on illegal methods and overthrow. The parties of Order, as they call themselves, are perishing under the legal conditions created by themselves. They cry despairingly with Odilon Barrot: *la legalité nous tue*, legality is the death of us; whereas we, under this legality, get firm muscles and rosy cheeks and look like life eternal. And if we are not so crazy as to be driven to street fighting in order to please them, then in the end there is nothing left for them to do but themselves break through this fatal legality" (ibid., 196, 202).

Admittedly, "Engels denied being a legalist at all cost."[177] He did not abandon the aim of overthrowing bourgeois rule; on the contrary, he thought that the bourgeoisie would defend itself by breaking its own laws, thus triggering revolutionary action. But, nonetheless, he provided an authoritative endorsement of the legal parliamentary method of struggle. This did not involve a sacrifice on his part: after all, he abhorred the Reign of Terror[178] and already had (in his *Origin of the Family*) treated the democratic republic as "an inevitable necessity," "the form of state in which alone the last decisive struggle between proletariat and bourgeoisie can be fought out" (ibid., 3:329). His "testament" was a logical outcome of his intellectual evolution, of his patriotic pride in the electoral successes of

German Social Democracy, and finally of his deterministic view of history. His necessitarian position did not allow him to argue with history: if historical facts proved a certain theory, and the hope based on it, to be merely an illusion, then history must be right and theory wrong. Otherwise, history would be merely a plaything of chance, not an orderly, law-abiding, essentially rational process.

Another reason for Engels's preference for legality was his growing concern about Germany's national security. He predicted an all-European war in which Germany would be attacked from both east and west, by Russia and France. He reacted to the Franco-Russian alliance by writing an article to *Almanac*, the organ of the French workers' party led by Jules Guesde and Paul Lafargue, in which he solemnly warned his French readers: "If the French Republic were to enter the service of his Majesty the Czar, Autocrat of all the Russians, the German socialists would fight them—regretfully, of course, but they would fight them." [179] Unlike Lenin, Engels wanted to avoid the war, not to turn it against class enemies within his country; for him, the necessary condition of the proletarian seizure of power in Germany was peace, because war, as he saw it, would bring the bourgeoisie and the workers together in the common effort of defending the fatherland.[180] He thought that in a war against Russia, Germany would represent the interest of the entire proletariat of Europe, and he saw this view as identical with the standpoint of *Neue Rheinische Zeitung* of 1848.[181] In his excellent article "The Foreign Policy of Russian Czarism" (1890), Engels reminded readers that it had been the contribution of Marx, "first in 1848 and repeatedly since, to have emphasized that . . . the Western European labor parties must of necessity wage an implacable war against Russian Czarism" (M&E, *RME*, 25). And he was not alone in this thinking; during his lifetime this was the predominant view of the German Social Democrats. August Bebel declared on many occasions that, in the case of a war with Russia, his old age would not prevent his aim "to shoulder a rifle." At the Erfurt Congress of the party, he told the delegates in the presence of Engels: "If Russia, the refuge of cruelty and barbarism, the enemy of all human culture, attacks Germany in order to partition and destroy her . . . then we are as much interested, and more so, than those who stand today at the head of Germany, and we will fight against the attack." [182]

Engels did not object. On the contrary, he thought about the threatening war in practical terms and advised Bebel, who was the party's leading spokesman in the Reichstag, that in the case of attack, socialist deputies should vote for war credits. In a letter to Bebel of October 13, 1891, Engels defined his position as follows: "If we are convinced that the thing will start next spring, we could hardly be opposed to the credits on principle, and then we should be in a pretty desperate position. The lick-spittle parties would boast that they had been right, and that we had to eat our own words. Also, such an unexpected change of front would cause appalling friction within the party—and internationally as well."[183]

To avoid these consequences, the party should vote credits only for such measures "which will bring the present army nearer to a people's militia, which will simply strengthen our defences, which will train and arm all men who have not yet enlisted, from seventeen to sixty, and which will dispose them in fixed cadres, without increasing all that 'control.' "[184] But the regular army need not feel endangered by this levy in mass:

> We cannot demand that the existing military organization should be completely altered while the danger of war persists. But if there is an attempt to take the great mass of men who are fit for service but have not been trained and train them as well as possible and dispose them in cadres—for real fighting, not for parading and all that nonsense—then that is an approach to our idea of the people's militia, which we can accept. If the danger of war increases, we can tell the government that we should be ready, if they made it possible for us by decent treatment, to give our support against the foreign enemy—on the presupposition that they will fight relentlessly and use every means, even revolutionary means. If Germany is attacked from east and west, all means of self-defence are good. The existence of the nation is then at stake, and we, too, have a position to maintain and a future which we have won by hard fighting.[185]

Lenin, for whom the German Socialists' voting for war credits in 1914 was a shameful scandal, was aware of Engels's position in 1891. In a letter to Inessa Armand of November 30, 1916, he tried to defend this position on the grounds that for the Germans a war with Russia and France would have been *by then* "a peculiar variety of *national* war" (L, CW, 35:251). The awkwardness of this explanation is obvious, especially in view of the fact that a few years later an official Leninist account of the so-called crisis of international socialism in 1914 included a categorical assertion that the war of 1870–71 was the last national war in Europe.[186] The best comment on this is the fact that Engels's letter to Bebel, quoted above, has been excluded from Soviet editions of Engels's correspondence, and its very existence has been passed over in silence.[187] The same is true for Engels's article "The Foreign Policy of Russian Czarism": its intended publication in the journal of *Bolshevik* in 1934 was personally forbidden by Stalin.[188]

However, from the point of view of the German Social Democrats, it was perfectly natural to legitimize their conduct in 1914 by referring to Marx and Engels's view of the need to defend Germany against tsarist Russia.[189] After all, people like Lenin, Martov, and Rosa Luxemburg (on whose motion the Stuttgart Congress in 1907 defined "the internationalist duties" of the socialist parties in the case of war[190]) represented a world that had very little in common with mainstream social democratic thinking in Germany. Neither Lenin's "defeatism" (manifested already in his attitude toward the Russo-Japanese War of 1904–5) nor Luxemburg's fanatical and sectarian condemnation of all sorts of "social patriotism" could be treated as typical of European socialism of their time. German Social Democracy saw the proletariat as the best representative of Germany's national interest—that is, as the "national class" (although the *Manifesto of the Communist Party* saw workers in this role only after they had acquired "political supremacy") (M&E, CW, 6:502–3). Accordingly, its practical policy interpreted the class interest of the proletariat more and more broadly, sought for allies among the progressively minded middle class, and embarked willy-nilly on the path of reformism. This practical reformism—as long as it did not try to revise the theoretical foundations of Marxism—had Engels's support and could legitimately invoke his authority.

Thus, in a broad sense, Engels's "Testament" was not only his introduction to *Class Struggles in France* but also his other writings of the last five years of his life, including the letters in which he warned against dogmatism and narrow-mindedness in interpreting historical materialism (M&E, BW, 434–51). It is justified to say that this part of his legacy was in harmony with mainstream social democratic thinking in Germany. Our topic, however, is not Engels as a politician but Engels as a theorist. Therefore, we must focus on another part of his legacy: his disastrous mythology of "scientific socialism" and his philosophical conception of freedom.

After the "collapse" of the Second International in 1914, Lenin felt an acute need to cut himself off from the very term *social democracy*. In April 1917, he formally proposed to abandon the old name of his party (the Russian Social Democratic Labor party) and instead to call it the Communist party (retaining the word *Bolshevik* in brackets). To justify this motion, he referred to a passage from Engels, stressing that Engels had written it in the last period of his life (see *The State and Revolution*, L, SW, 2:296). This passage is quoted in full as follows:

It will be noticed that in all these articles. . . . I call myself not a Social Democrat but a Communist. Those who called themselves Social Democrats in different countries at that time were far from advocating takeover by society of all the means of production. In France a Social Democrat was a democratic republican with more or less genuine, though invariably vague, sympathies for the working class—such people as Ledru-Rollin in 1848 and the Proudhonist "Radical Socialists" of 1874. In Germany the Lassalleans called themselves Social Democrats; but though large numbers of them had come to see the necessity for socialization of the means of production, Lassalle's demand for producers' cooperatives with state aid remained their sole officially recognized program. For Marx and me it was therefore quite impossible to choose such an elastic term for our specific point of view. Today the situation is quite different and the name can pass—however unsuitable it remains for a party whose economic program is not merely socialist in general but specifically communist, and whose ultimate political aim is to overcome the entire state and consequently democracy as well.[191]

The immediate cause of Lenin's decision was his bitter political disappointment in the German "comrades," but it is important to realize that this decision was also theoretically justified and that Lenin had good reasons to support it by involving the authority of Engels. In spite of his commonsensical practical moderation, Engels remained deeply attached to the communist utopia of his youth, while mainstream social democratic thinkers of the end of the century were increasingly, cautiously, but consistently, distancing themselves from this utopian vision. This was done under the convenient pretext that the immediate task of the party was to take political power through the gradual transition to socialism. This being the case, it was argued, preoccupation with the tasks of a more remote future would be contrary to the scientific approach to social change. Engels readily agreed, seeing this attitude as consistent with scientific socialism; he even idealized this approach as a manifestation of the praiseworthy self-discipline of the German workers. After his death, however, it soon became clear that the reluctance to theorize about the "final ideal" also reflected something else. The rise of the revisionist movement, initiated by Engels's closest collaborator, Eduard Bernstein, showed that communism had become uncongenial to the social democratic mentality and that many clearly saw its ineradicable utopian nature. Bernstein proposed to distinguish between the two sides of Marxism—scientific and utopian—with the aim of eliminating the latter. In his view, the German Social Democratic party had become a party of reforms and should abandon the practice of couching its real aims in the old revolutionary phraseology. This stance also involved an attack on the very notion of the final goal as a relic of revolutionary millenarism. As Bernstein declared: "What is generally called the ultimate goal of socialism is nothing to me; the movement is everything." [192]

Karl Kautsky, "the pope" of the German orthodox Marxists, disagreed with Bernstein; this enabled Lenin, who badly needed recognition among the leaders of the Second International,[193] to continue seeing Kautsky as a theoretical authority. But the most adamant and principled resistance to revisionism came from the east. Rosa Luxemburg attacked Bernstein furiously, stating that for her the final goal was everything and the movement was only a means for its attainment. Plekhanov could not understand why Bernstein was criticized by the party leaders so mildly and, above all, why he was allowed to remain a party member. If Lenin was more restrained in expressing similar feelings, it was only because of the fact that he was then little known outside Russia and could not afford intervention in the affairs of the German party.

But in 1917 everything was different. Lenin felt that his party—under his leadership, to be sure—was the only legitimate and worthy successor of the entire legacy of genuine Marxism. In his April theses, he abandoned, without discussion, all traditional tenets of Russian Marxism, all views about Russia's immediate future, which hitherto distinguished Russian Marxists from Russian populist socialists. He no longer spoke about passing through the phase of capitalist development and political freedom. He explicitly rejected the social democratic (and Engelsian) acceptance of the democratic republic as the most progressive form of the state—the form (to quote Engels) "in which the decisive struggle between the proletariat and bourgeoisie can be fought out" (M&E, SW, 3:329; cf. L, SW, 2:39). He decided that the time had come for the Bolshevik seizure of power and for Russia's direct transition to socialism. And in arguing for calling his party "Communist," he reaffirmed his unyielding devotion to the final ideal. Socialism, he reaffirmed, is not enough: "Our Party looks farther ahead: socialism must inevitably evolve gradually into communism, upon the banner of which is inscribed the motto, 'From each according to his ability, to each according to his needs'" (L, SW, 2:60).

In this manner, Lenin rejected the social democratic part of Engels's legacy, reaffirming instead a boundless commitment to what Lenin saw, not without reason, as the very heart of Marx and Engels's teaching— their vision of the communist future. And communism was nothing else than Marx and Engels's ideal of freedom. Lenin avoided formulating it in this way, since, in his view, the word *freedom* was too compromised. But he, of course, firmly remembered Engels's formula for humanity's "leap from the kingdom of necessity to the kingdom of freedom" and wanted his party to be the chosen instrument of this great, world-transforming work of universal liberation.

Of course, these brief formulas cannot substitute for a closer analysis of Lenin's position (which will be explored in chapter 4). At this point we need only avoid misinterpretation. Thus, it is necessary to emphasize that Lenin's decision to embark on a socialist revolution in a backward country did not amount, in his view, to the rejection of "scientific socialism." Lenin subjected the tenets of "scientific socialism" to reinterpretation, but it did not occur to him to renounce the claim of acting in accordance with a "scientific understanding of history." On the contrary, he made full use of the legitimizing device inherent in the conception of scientific socialism, claiming that all his actions derived from a correct understanding of the laws of history. It was Engels who provided Lenin with the most authoritative assurance about the proletarian revolution as humanity's leap from the kingdom of necessity to the kingdom of freedom. In Lenin's view, Engels "scientifically proved" that the proletarian seizure of public power would and should result in gaining full mastery over humankind's social organization through the immediate abolition of the blind forces of the market. Engels's vision of the tasks of the socialist revolution "scientifically justified" Lenin's voluntaristic policy of a direct transition to socialism. This policy, called War Communism, was by no means a pragmatic response to the exigencies of civil war in Russia (see chapter 4, section 8). Rather, it was a grandiose social experiment, an exercise in revolutionary utopianism, directly inspired by Engels's unshakable belief in the miraculous power of the centralized decision making that was to replace the "anarchy of the market" and thus make humanity its own conscious master.

German Social Democrats, who clung to the view that revolutions could not be "made" because they are the result of deep historical processes and not of a deliberate action of a party, understood "scientific socialism" in a different way. For them, Engels's analysis of the steadily increasing scope of centralized planning *within* capitalist society, combined with his frank acknowledgment of the failure of attempts to accelerate the course of history by means of armed uprisings, provided decisive arguments against revolutionary voluntarism. And this was in tune with their necessitarian interpretation of "scientific socialism." For a consistent scientific determinist (as was the case with Kautsky and other influential theorists of German Social Democracy), Engels's formula of freedom as the "understanding of necessity" could only mean that facts must be accepted and that the "subjective factor" play only a limited, modest role in historical processes.

Thus, as we can see, Engels's legacy, and especially his conception of freedom, had two widely different aspects and could be subject to diametrically opposite interpretations. Engels himself, proud of the achievements of the German workers, endorsed in his last year the social democratic interpretation of Marxism. But the irony of history, which he found in historical events, proved very bitter in his case. The inner logic of the "scientific" and antivoluntaristic interpretation of Marxism proved to be more and more difficult to combine with Engels's favorite beliefs: his belief in Marxism as a comprehensive scientific theory, and his utopian belief in the communist ideal. The outbreak of revisionism after his death and the practical embracement of a semirevisionism by the orthodox leaders of the German Social Democrats were only the first steps toward the formal abandonment of the commitment to communism, to be followed, after several years, by the inescapable renunciation of the Marxist character of the party.[194]

The fates of Marx and Engels's ideas in Lenin and Stalin's party were quite different. In chapter 1, I discussed how Marx's philosophy of freedom—his violent critique of liberalism and the market, his conception of freedom as conscious, rational control over spontaneous forces (stemming from the identification of spontaneity with blind necessity), and his exclusive concern with *species* freedom (i.e., unfettered development of human beings' species capacities), combined with a contemptuous attitude toward *individual* freedom (especially freedom in the "egoistic" pursuit of one's interests)—could be used to pave the way for totalitarianism. The same views were advocated by Engels, but on the whole his unintended contribution to the philosophical underpinning of totalitarianism was even greater, for two reasons: his invention of "dialectical materialism," which transformed Marxism into an all-embracing philosophical system containing ready-made answers to all possible questions, and his conception of freedom as the understanding of necessity. The latter provided totalitarian leaders with a dangerously flexible formula by means of which it was possible to justify both extreme voluntarism (that is, belief in the omnipotence of those who "correctly understood" the laws of history) and extreme fatalism (a necessary component in breaking the will to resist through invoking the authority of the inexorable and entirely objective "historical necessity").

The evolution of German Social Democracy is yet another proof that belief in determinism is, in itself, not inimical to freedom. The most dangerous aspect of the Engelsian conception of freedom is, therefore, not its necessitarianism but what it says about correct understanding of necessity: to make it conscious and then to act in accordance with this consciousness. According to Engels, uncontrolled social forces "work exactly like natural forces: blindly, forcibly, destructively," so long as we do not understand them. "But when once we understand them, when once we grasp their action, their direction, their effects, it depends only upon ourselves to subject them more and more to our own will," to transform them "from master demons into willing servants" (E, *AD*, 339; cf. M&E, *BW*, 145).

Although by "social forces" Engels meant economic forces, his quoted words and his entire conception of freedom provided a perfect rationale for attempts to transform an entire society into a "willing servant" of those who "know better and see further," who have "correctly understood" history and can therefore speak in its name, whom history itself has given the mandate to rule. And who can doubt that Lenin saw his party as the chosen instrument of History? If freedom was "necessity made conscious," his party was surely the embodiment of this consciousness. The will to control everything, to eliminate irrational pluralism and blind spontaneity, could be presented as the will to freedom.

Marx and Engels, despite their often arrogant self-confidence, did not see themselves as infallible. But, nonetheless, the very concept of scientific socialism entailed a claim to possess scientific knowledge, not only of the past but also of the general direction of future history. Karl Popper was right in regarding such a claim as undermining the democratic principle of power legitimization and justifying instead a particularly self-confident, hence particularly repressive, authoritarian leadership. Indeed, possessors of the only correct knowledge of the meaning and laws of history have a right, even a duty, to ignore the opinions of the ignorant majority; if they are in power, they have the right, the duty, to realize historical necessity, even against all, with the help of police, bayonets, and tanks. They may, of course, admit a mistake in this or that specific matter, but they derive from "scientific socialism" the certainty that the course of history is irreversible, that History itself has given their party a mandate to exercise power, and hence under no circumstances can they give up this power.

A second dangerous consequence of this manner of thinking is a pseudo-rationalistic constructivism: the conviction that an understanding of the "laws of development" supplies unambiguous directives as to the only correct action. In practice, this means that individuals who allegedly have understood the laws of historical development ought to shape reality in accordance with their *theory* of what is necessary, even if it is contrary to accumulated experience and common sense. Such an attitude has little in common with determinism: the consequence of historical determinism shows a respect for facts, for the realities of life, and not the rejection of these realities in the name of theoretical dogma. "Scientific socialists" may, however, ignore the resistance that life offers theory, since they are convinced that they have "understood" the deeper "laws" of history and so ought to be guided by this understanding and not by an opportunistic respect for superficial empirical reality. In this way Engels's formula about necessity understood could easily be used to transform Marxism into the opposite of historical determinism—into a convenient tool of voluntaristic arbitrariness. It was sufficient justification of such arbitrariness to proclaim that the laws of history had become understood and that those in power understood them best.

Finally, the conception of freedom as the understanding of necessity justified attempts at the total indoctrination of society. In this respect, Engels's unintended contribution to Stalinist totalitarianism was especially important. It was he who had done the most to legitimize the transformation of Marxism into an all-embracing view of the world, claiming to represent the highest level of "scientificity." And since "true knowledge" was made all-embracing and everything was dependent on it, then indoctrination had to be all-embracing too. The enslavement of minds could present itself as an attempt at bringing people to "true understanding," or "adequate consciousness," thus creating conditions for their liberation.

These attempts at indoctrination were, in their way, wholly logical, although they confirmed once more that those who made them were not, as a matter of fact, authentic believers in historical determinism. If these leaders had been, they would have trusted in the functioning of objective laws, which do not need any attempts at social engineering. In reality, however, these leaders made the victory of their ideal dependent on the "correct understanding" of the laws of history, and this understanding was not all that it might be; the fear that people persistently would not understand the supposedly necessary direction of history was perfectly well founded. If freedom consists in the correct understanding of history, then mass indoctrination was naturally a preparation for freedom, a *condition* of freedom. According to a well-known formula, one had to "force people to be free."

Of course, the transformation of Marx and Engels's ideas into the legitimation of totalitarianism and the instrument of its rule over the minds and consciences of the people was the result of a process that did not occur in a historical and social vacuum. It is arguable, however, that without a utopian goal (conceived, paradoxically, as the kingdom of freedom) and a firm conviction of having History and Science on its side, communist totalitarianism could not have emerged, survived, and become what it was. If it had relied on force alone, it would not have been able to mobilize active popular support, to create the grotesque cult of the omniscient and omnipotent leader, and to mesmerize the progressive intellectuals of the West. If it had not aimed at the realization of a utopian vision, it would not have needed to combine cruelty with absurdity.

Perhaps it is rather doubtful praise, but human beings as a rule do not dare to commit great crimes on a mass scale without being inspired by a powerful faith. It so happened that a portion of Marx and Engels's views, irrespective of their intentions, provided the basis of the most powerful and dangerous secular faith of our century. Almost everywhere, this faith is now dead, but its consequences are still with us.

Marx and Engels's legacy should not be reduced to their most compromised conceptions, such as "scientific socialism" or the idea of the abolition of the market. Nevertheless, these conceptions are basic to their misconceived view of human liberation. Hence, they should be carefully studied not only by historians of social philosophy and political thought, but also by all who want a better understanding of the tragic historical fates of those countries that have passed through the ordeal of "utopia in power."

3

Variants of "Necessitarian" Marxism

3.1 Karl Kautsky: From the "Historical Necessity" of Communism to the "Historical Necessity" of Democracy

The preceding chapters have illustrated the effects of Engels's codification of Marx's ideas on the multidimensional Marxian philosophy of freedom. Broadly speaking, these effects resulted in so-called "classical Marxism," or "Marxism of the Second International," the central notion of which was that of "necessity." Kolakowski has rightly observed that "belief in historical necessity, and in particular the 'objective' necessity of socialist society, was to Kautsky the cornerstone of Marxism and the essential difference between scientific and utopian socialism."[1] The same can be said of other "orthodox Marxists" of this epoch. This could hardly be otherwise, since the meaning of "orthodox Marxism" was defined on the pages of Kautsky's *Die Neue Zeit*, the first programmatically Marxist theoretical journal, published since 1883 with the aim of destroying "eclectic socialism" and achieving victory for "consistent Marxism." It was Kautsky who was, in fact, "the father of the terms 'Marxist' and 'Marxism' in the meaning they have assumed in our vocabulary."[2] His authority as the chief theorist of the Second International was universally acknowledged, and his influence was truly enormous. He was even more important than Marx and Engels in the intellectual development of the younger generation of

Marxists from Russia and East-Central or southern Europe.[3] According to Nikolaevskii, Kautsky enjoyed more popularity in Russia than any other Western political thinker in his time.[4] A similar testimony to Kautsky's unmatched popularity in Russia can be found in Lenin's writings.[5] Small wonder, therefore, that Kautsky's account of Marxism, which was dependent on the Engelsian account, has been seen as orthodox and classical.

However, a closer examination reveals that the views of the other leading theorists of the Second International were not always identical with Kautskian orthodoxy. Despite their common emphasis on historical necessity, these theorists sometimes differed quite substantially, although they were not always aware of it. Some of these differences were relevant, both theoretically and practically, to the Marxist understanding of freedom. To show this, I shall briefly examine the problem of necessity and freedom in the views of three prominent representatives of "necessitarian Marxism": Kautsky, Plekhanov, and Luxemburg.

Anderson has noted that after Marx and Engels, "the whole geographical axis of Marxist culture" shifted "towards Eastern and Central Europe."[6] Indeed, Kautsky, Plekhanov, and Luxemburg were representatives of this shift. Karl Kautsky (1854–1938) was born in Prague and typified (as he himself liked to point out) the ethnic mixture of the Habsburg Empire: his father was Czech, with Polish family connections; his mother was German, with Hungarian or Croat connections.[7] Only the first years of his political activity were bound up with the Austrian Socialist party. At the beginning of 1880 he moved to Zurich and joined the circle of German socialists who had congregated there to avoid the antisocialist law in Germany. He experienced this as a broadening of his horizons and decided to work for the outlawed German Social Democratic party (SPD).

Kautsky's conversion to Marxism began in Austria as a result of his reading Engels's *Anti-Dühring*, to which (as he later confessed) he owed his understanding of Marx's *Capital*.[8] His education in Marxism continued in Zurich, where he systematically studied Marx and Engels's writings under the guidance of his older friend, Eduard Bernstein (the future theorist of revisionism). In 1881, he first met Marx and Engels, and although he did not succeed in making a very good impression on them, the contact was established.[9] When Kautsky, as the editor of *Die Neue Zeit*, moved to England (because the antisocialist law made it too difficult to continue publishing the journal in Germany), Marx was no longer alive, but Engels was there and soon became a sort of personal mentor and frequently consulted advisor. Kautsky's first major books—*Thomas More und Seine Utopie* (1888) and *Die Klassengegensätze von 1789* (1889)—were "written under Engels's tutelage."[10] However, Kautsky did not become Engels's disciple in philosophical matters, which cannot be attributed to Kautsky's "complete lack of understanding of philosophical problems."[11] There certainly have been many "dialectical materialists" whose understanding of philosophy was no better. Among the reasons for Kautsky's indifference to Engels's philosophical undertakings was Kautsky's different intellectual background: he was greatly influenced by Darwinian evolutionism but completely untouched by Hegelianism. But the most important reason simply was his view that Marxism applies only to the social sciences and should not aspire to become an all-embracing philosophy. This view was widely shared by other Social Democrats in Germany. Among the major theorists of the Second International, only Plekhanov wanted to transform Marxism into a comprehensive philosophy based on Engelsian dialectical materialism.[12] As we shall see, this exerted a truly fatal influence on the course of Marxism in his native Russia.

Of course, lack of philosophical ambition did not protect Kautsky from being influenced by the prevailing intellectual trends of his time. His desire to adhere to a strictly scientific standpoint made him especially susceptible to the influence of naturalistic evolutionism and positivistic scientism. As a result, he laid the foundations for the so-called positivistic interpretation of Marxism that was characteristic of the Second International and was often confused with Engelsian Marxism, although it differed from the latter by lacking both "the Hegelian component" and the tendency to philosophize about nature.[13] The basic premises of this interpretation are best revealed in Kautsky's work *Ethics and the Materialist Interpretation of History* (1906). For this reason, it seems justified to take this work as a starting point for a discussion of Kautsky's views, even though doing so departs from chronological order.

Kautsky well knew that Marx and Engels did not like to derive socialism from the demands of morality. Such a moralistic approach to socialism was seen by them as ideological (in the pejorative sense) or utopian, a position stubbornly defended by those socialists (mostly French) who had failed to raise themselves to the level of a nonsentimental scientific theory.[14] The "necessitarian" account of Marxist theory strengthened this tendency, exposing Marxism to the accusation of being nothing but a variety of historical fatalism. On the other hand, some sympathizers of Marxism—most notably the neo-Kantians and the Austro-Marxists (who were also influenced by Kant)—came to the conclusion that the causal justification of socialism provided by Marxism could be (and indeed should be) supplemented by ethical justification.[15] Kautsky's *Ethics* contains a direct polemic against this standpoint, a rejection of the neo-Kantian "ethical socialism" in the name of "scientificity." His main thesis, fully consonant with Engels's view of freedom, is that the choice of goals should not depend on a free moral option but solely on the scientific knowledge of necessity: "It was the materialist conception of history which, for the first time, fully deprived the moral ideal of its status as a directing force in the development of society, and taught us to derive our social goals exclusively from knowledge of the given material foundations."[16]

But what about the social roots of knowledge, the Marxist view of consciousness as determined by social existence—that is to say, as necessarily class bound and value dependent? Kautsky's position on this question was that of an uncritical believer in "pure science," "objectivity," and value neutrality. He conceded that even "in a man like Marx . . . the presence of a moral ideal occasionally breaks through into his scientific investigation," but he assured his readers that such a man "is continually aiming, and rightly, to banish it whenever possible." Science, he explained, "is never concerned with anything but the recognition of the necessary. It may reach the stage of issuing imperatives but this should only be as a consequence of insight into necessity. It must avoid putting forward an imperative which cannot be shown to be grounded as a necessity in the 'world of phenomena.' Ethics must always remain an object of science; the purpose of science is to investigate and conceptualize moral instincts and moral ideals; but it must not derive from them any directives as to the kind of results to be arrived at. Science stands above ethics; its results are no more moral or immoral than necessity can be moral or immoral."[17]

Thus, "ethics as an object of science" cannot be a normative discipline. Its proper task is the explanation of the genesis, function, and transitional character of moral norms. The specificity of Kautsky's contribution to such explanations was his claim that moral norms should not be exclusively historical, separating human history from the wider realm of natural history. Human society, he reasoned, is a part of nature, and morality is not something distinctively human; most forms of human behavior are products of natural evolution through progressive adaptation to the environment and can be traced back to the animal kingdom. Even the most altruistic feelings are not peculiar to human nature but, as Darwin showed, can be found among animals. In fact, moral norms evolved at the prehuman stage of evolution are much more stable and strong than those produced by human history as expressions and instruments of different class interests: "The specifically human aspect of morality is subject to continual change." In this sphere, not only morality but even immorality are only relative concepts: "The only form of absolute immorality would be the absence of those animal instincts and virtues which man has inherited from social animals."[18]

Of course, the neo-Kantian socialists saw this position as amounting to a surrender to ethical skepticism.[19] Indeed, this stance did not provide a compelling *ethical* reason for choosing socialism over capitalism. Kautsky, however, did not intend to indicate such a reason; for him, socialism was justified by historical necessity, scientifically understood. This, in his view, was the strongest argument against skepticism. In his reply to Otto Bauer, a leading Austro-Marxist, Kautsky asked: "How can scepticism arise out of the recognition of necessity?"[20]

The Kautskian notion of necessity is different from both the mechanical necessity of physical sciences and the rational necessity of Hegelianism. Kautsky distinguished between necessity and inevitability, explaining this distinction as follows: "If we speak of the necessity of the victory of the proletariat and of socialism that follows therefrom, we do not mean that victory is inevitable, or perhaps, as many of our critics perceive it, [that victory] must come of itself with fatalistic certainty, even if the revolutionary class does nothing. Here necessity is understood in the sense of the only possibility of further development."[21]

In other words, socialism would not come about as an inevitable, though unintended, result of human history. Unlike all other social arrangements, it must be intended and struggled for. The necessity of socialism derived from its role as a prerequisite to further development, since the alternative would be the demise of civilization. This was not an improvised response of Kautsky to answer reformist opponents; the same conception of necessity is to be found in his commentary on the Erfurt Program: "As things stay today capitalist civilization cannot continue; we must either move forward into socialism or fall back into barbarism."[22] Thus, it is not correct to attribute to Kautsky "confidence in historic inevitability" and to sum up his policy in the words: "socialism is guaranteed by the law of history in any case."[23] What was inevitable, in Kautsky's view, was the development and imminent collapse of capitalism, but it did not follow from this that the victory of socialism would automatically follow. On the contrary, socialism was dependent on will and consciousness guided by objective scientific knowledge.

It should be noted that this view of the necessity of socialism did not remain uncontested. Eduard Bernstein, for instance, thought that a genuine necessity did not require conscious acceptance. Capitalism was a necessary phase of economic development because it arrived as an outcome of spontaneous processes, not as a result of conscious collective efforts. If socialism demanded conscious struggle for its introduction and depended for its functioning on conscious will rather than spontaneous self-regulation, then, Bernstein concluded, it was not grounded in causal determinism and could be justified only as an ethical ideal.[24] In this manner, this theorist of empirically minded pragmatic revisionism found a common language with the neo-Kantians.

A direct consequence of Kautsky's conception of the necessity of socialism was the view that the goals of the workers' party must be formulated on the basis of objective scientific knowledge, and that the class consciousness of the workers should be shaped from without—by those who possess such knowledge. In an article Lenin was quick to quote in his *What Is to Be Done?*, Kautsky expressed this view in a wholly unambiguous way:

Modern socialist consciousness can arise only on the basis of profound scientific knowledge. Indeed, modern economic science is as much a condition for socialist production as, say, modern technology, and the proletariat can create neither the one nor the other, no matter how much it may desire to do so; both arise out of the modern social process. The vehicle of science is not the proletariat, but the *bourgeois intelligentsia*: it was in the minds of individual members of this stratum that modern socialism originated, and it was they who communicated it to the more intellectually developed proletarians who, in their turn, introduce it into the proletarian class struggle where conditions allow that to be done. Thus, socialist consciousness is something introduced into the proletarian class struggle from without [*von Aussen Hineingetragenes*] and not something that arose within it spontaneously [*urwüchsig*].[25]

Lenin's use of this quotation should not mislead us. It is not true that Lenin's *What Is to Be Done?* was fully consistent with the Marxist orthodoxy of his time.[26] Even less true is Kolakowski's claim that "Lenin's theory of the party as vanguard was based on the doctrine formulated by Kautsky."[27] There is a marked, obvious difference between professional revolutionaries, who aim above all at the seizure of political power, and socialist scholars, who try to attain a fully objective understanding of necessity—in other words, between the revolutionary vanguard, which is threatened by the spread of a trade union mentality among the workers, and the socialist elite, whose main aim is to avoid the danger of revolutionary voluntarism by coordinating the activities of the party with the scientific understanding of objective conditions. The only common element in the two positions is that both reject a reliance on "spontaneity," and this stance is indeed closely related to the very essence of Marxism. Although Marx and Engels might sincerely believe that the workers would liberate themselves and that communists need not even organize themselves into a separate party, their vision of liberation nevertheless assumed rational control over spontaneity (*Manifesto of the Communist Party*, M&E, CW, 6:497). In their view, spontaneity was something to be overcome; it was blind, irrational, and thus incompatible with true freedom.

At this juncture, however, it is necessary to point out a very important difference between Kautskian Marxism and the Marxism of Marx and Engels, which Kolakowski highlighted as follows:

In Kautsky's evolutionist doctrine there is of course no room for eschatology or any belief in the general "meaning" of history. . . . There is no such thing in reality as the paradigm of human nature returning into itself after an age-long state of fission and restoring the unity between the object and subject of history. We are the spectators of a necessary process of changes which have no "meaning" in themselves and cannot reveal any to scientific investigation, for science has nothing to do with values and is only concerned with necessity of the "laws" of nature.[28]

This excellently drawn contrast between Marx and Kautsky does not fully apply to Engels. In a sense Engels was a bridge between the two. On the one hand, he abandoned Marx's essentialism and therefore could not see the meaning of history as reflected in the development of man's inherent capacities through self-enriching alienation that led finally to the full reconciliation of human existence with human essence. On the other hand, he did not abandon the Hegelian belief (whether it was philosophically consistent or not) in the meaning of history, and he saw this meaning in history's inherent and increasing rationality. Hence the term "historical necessity," if applied to long-term historical processes, meant for him "rational necessity," not merely the value-neutral "natural necessity."

Thus, Kautsky's determinism deprived history of its meaning. This is probably the main reason for the utter contempt with which his "positivistic" account of Marxism is treated among those Marxists or "Marxisant" intellectuals who see Marx through the prism of his early writings. But this is also the main reason why Kautsky proved able to preserve his common sense and his human decency at the time of the great catastrophes of our century.

Let us now return to Kautsky's career in the ranks of German Social Democracy.

In 1890, shortly before the expiration of the antisocialist law, Kautsky returned to Germany and took an active part in the preparation of the national congress of his party. During his work on the party program, which came to be known as the Erfurt Program, he was recognized as the leading theorist of the party. The entire theoretical part of the program was, in fact, written by him and remained for many years the most influential document of the international workers' movement. Its importance derived from its Marxist character (being the first deliberately Marxist party program) and from its endorsement by Engels, who found no theoretical errors in it.[29] After the program's acceptance by the party in 1891, Kautsky wrote in 1892 an extensive commentary on its theoretical part entitled *Das Erfurter Programm in seinem grundsätzlichen Teil erläutert* (1892; translated into English as *The Class Struggle*). This book-length commentary, officially commissioned by the party, became his "most famous and most translated work."[30]

Of course, a comprehensive analysis of the *Erfurt Program* does not fall within the scope of this book. In what follows I shall concentrate on three interrelated topics: (1) Kautsky's view of the necessary laws of capitalist production, (2) his view of the society of the future, and, finally, (3) his view of the changing conceptions of freedom.

The first chapter of the *Erfurt Program* bears the title "The Passing of Small Production." In accordance with Engels, Kautsky described capitalist development as a process of centralization and concentration that leads inevitably to the overthrow of decentralized small production as a relic of the Middle Ages. He left no doubt that "the days of handicraft, of independent production, are numbered."[31] Hence, the industrial workers should not seek allies among the small producers. They should realize that their class is the only progressive class of capitalist society, that "the proletariat is the only one among the working classes that has grown steadily in energy, in intelligence, and in clear consciousness of its purpose." Its only possible allies in the struggle for socialism are "the idealists among the upper classes"; of course, only those of them who have "not only the requisite theoretical insight" but also "the courage and strength to break with their class."[32]

Kautsky readily admitted, and even stressed, that the necessary "dissolving of the middle classes" and the unavoidable proletarianization of small producers was an extremely painful process. He painted the situation of the industrial workers in dark colors, showing them as enslaved by the machines that had, in the hands of the capitalists, "made the burden of labor unbearable."[33] He described the condition of the wage earner as "worse than that of the medieval apprentice": unlike the latter, the proletarian did not live in the same house as his master nor eat at the same table, which thus doomed him to permanent starvation.[34] Nevertheless, the socialists should not commit themselves to helping the small producers in their struggle for survival: "To assist them *as producers* by fortifying them in the retention of their outlived method of production is impossible, for it is opposed to the course of economic development." The only means of assisting them (after all, Kautsky was a humanitarian) was to defend their interests *as consumers* (how this could be done remained unexplained) and to promote their intellectual development. With their needs developed and intellectual horizons broadened, the most intelligent among the small producers would become aware of the misery and hopelessness of their status in capitalist society, and this would cause them to rebel, to "pass directly into the ranks of the militant, purposeful proletarians."[35]

In his analyses of new tendencies in the development of capitalism, Kautsky made use of Marx's *Capital* (especially in writing about the alleged "falling off in the rate of profit") but, as a rule, closely followed Engels's account. Like Engels, he saw the growth of large-scale production and the emergence of trusts and syndicates as a necessary and progressive process leading to "the concentration of more and more capitalist undertakings into a single hand, be that the hand of a single capitalist, or of a combination of capitalists who legally constitute one person." The progressiveness of this process consisted, in his view, not only in an increase in productivity but also in the general rationalization of the economy. He learned from Engels (and from Marx as well) that large-scale production represented the principle of rational planning and thus limited the scope of the "anarchy of the market." Therefore, Kautsky was confident that the increasing amalgamation of capitalist companies in the hands of a few firms would pave the way for socialism, which would complete this process by uniting all factories "into one large concern" capable of satisfying all the needs of the population. He stressed that such a "single economic mechanism" must organize production and distribution on the scale of the entire state, since only the state had the necessary dimensions to serve as a framework for it. And he made it clear that socialist society, organized in this way, would be economically like "one great factory." Socialist society, he wrote, "is nothing more than a single gigantic industrial concern" in which both production and distribution were "carefully regulated." [36]

This dreadful vision of an entire society transformed into one economic subject was fully consistent with Marx and Engels's conception of replacing the old spontaneous division of labor with a new technical division of labor based on a "definite plan," thus fully eliminating the "anarchy of the market." This society would represent Marx's idea of a collective Robinson Crusoe—that is, a single subject of economic activity, endowed with a single will, satisfying all his needs himself, and therefore having full control over the products of his work (see chapter 1, section 7). But what about the workers' freedom to change their work at will, to develop in all directions as well-rounded human beings, "to do one thing today and another tomorrow?" (M&E, CW, 5:47).

We must remember that *The German Ideology* (where this idea of freedom was best formulated), as well as other early writings of Marx, remained unpublished at that time, and interpretations of Marxism at that time were based on *Capital* and *Anti-Dühring*. At the same time, the anarchists' attacks on Marx's followers were well remembered, and therefore the matter of freedom was treated rather defensively by Marxists. Kautsky devoted an entire section of his *Erfurt Program* to this problem, and his treatment of it left no room for utopian illusions.

Socialist society, he argued, would offer its members security and comfort, but not the kind of freedom possible only under conditions of small-scale market production. Whether we like it or not, "it is true that socialist production is irreconcilable with the full freedom of labor, that is, with the freedom of the laborer to work when, where and how he wills. But this freedom of the laborer is irreconcilable with any systematic, co-operative form of labor, whether the form be capitalist or socialist. Freedom of labor is possible only in small production, and even there only up to a certain point." The socialization of production through the division of labor had developed at the expense of the workers' freedom: "Freedom of labor has come to an end, not only in the factory, but wherever the individual worker is only a link in a long chain of workers. It does not exist either for the manual worker or for the brain worker employed in any industry." True, the workers enjoyed one type of freedom under capitalism: they could change employers. But even under capitalism "the natural tendency of the economic development of modern society" increasingly limited this freedom. The advent of socialism would eliminate this freedom altogether as incompatible with rational planning. Kautsky did not see this as an important change for the worse, but neither did he try to present it as an increase in freedom. He set this idea forth frankly and honestly: "In a socialist community, where all the means of production are in a single hand, there is but one employer; to change him is impossible. . . . In this respect the wage-earner today has a certain freedom in comparison with the worker in a socialist society." [37]

So in what sense, if any, can socialism be seen as an increase of freedom? In answering this question, Kautsky closely followed the famous comment on freedom in the third volume of *Capital* (see chapter 1, section 7). First, he pointed out that in the socialist economy, the lack of freedom would "lose its oppressive character" because the entire organization of social life would be rational and comprehensible and would serve the interests of all. In this respect, the strict rules of the economy of the future would be similar to the rules of contemporary trade union organizations; although "laid down minutely and enforced strictly," these rules would not be seen as unbearably restricting personal liberty. Also, the working day would be substantially reduced, and this would give the workers "freedom from the necessity of toil." Leisure would cease to be a privilege based on exploitation; all would have time for harmonious development of their faculties, for "disinterested search for truth," or for "striving after the ideal." Hence, socialism deserved the overwhelming support of the "cultured classes," which under capitalism were completely dependent on the market and could not afford to produce or even to learn "anything which cannot be turned into money." The workers would also enjoy the possibility of disinterested learning; their thirst for knowledge had already been wakened, but only socialism could satisfy it. [38]

In conclusion, Kautsky defined socialist freedom as follows:

It is not the freedom of labor, but the *freedom from labor*, which in a socialist society the use of machinery makes increasingly possible, that will bring to mankind freedom of life, freedom for artistic and intellectual activity, freedom for the noblest enjoyment.

That blessed, harmonious culture, which has only once appeared in the history of mankind and was then the privilege of a small body of select aristocrats, will become the common property of all civilized nations. What slaves were to the ancient Athenians, machinery will be to modern man. [39]

This typical humanistic intellectual conception was, for Kautsky, a favorite view of freedom, and he returned to it several times in his later works. In *Social Revolution*, he defined the socialist mode of production as communism in the sphere of material production and anarchism in the sphere of spiritual creativity.[40] In his *Ethics*, he juxtaposed the following three conceptions of freedom: (1) the primitive Christian conception according to which freedom was simply "freedom from all work after the manner in which the lilies of the field neither spin nor weave yet are provided for," (2) the bourgeois conception of "freedom to make use of one's property in economic life to achieve maximum profit according to one's discretion," and (3) the social democratic conception that sees freedom as the increase of free time "in which to enjoy scientific and artistic pursuits, the fruits of free life."[41] He also stipulated that social and personal freedom should be distinguished from political liberty.

It is interesting to note that in our times the ideal of freedom as liberating culture from the rule of the economy (and thus offering to all what had once been an aristocratic privilege and what under capitalism had been threatened by complete extinction[42]) has been associated with the names of the programmatically antipositivist and antiscientistic Western Marxists such as Georg Lukács and Herbert Marcuse. It is important, therefore, to recall that something very similar was preached by the positivistically minded chief theorist of the Second International.

But let us return to Kautsky's *Erfurt Program*, an important feature of which was the full endorsement of the central idea of Marx and Engels's communism; the abolition of commodity production. The chapter on the "State of the Future" begins with a motto from the party program saying that socialism means "the conversion of private ownership of the means of production into social ownership *and* the conversion of commodity production into socialist production."[43] The conjunction *and* indicates that these are two different tasks and that the accomplishment of the first one is not enough,[44] a point that is reiterated in the section on "Socialism and Freedom." Kautsky began his argument with a brief polemic against the view that "socialism destroys economic freedom, the freedom of labor" and introduces instead "a despotism in comparison with which the most unrestricted absolutism would be freedom." He conceded that this "fear of slavery" had even caused some socialists to look for a way to combine socialist ownership with the market economy. He resolutely rejected such ideas as self-contradictory and leading in practice to a surrender to capitalism. Proponents of such views, he argued, "want to have communism and production for sale together. Theoretically, this is absurd; in practice it could amount to nothing more than the establishment of voluntary cooperative societies for mutual aid."[45]

László Szamuely, a Hungarian scholar and supporter of the idea of a "socialist market economy," turned his attention to the semiforgotten fact that the Erfurt Program and Kautsky's commentary on it committed socialists to the struggle for total abolition of the monetary exchange economy and, by the same token, to a fantastic utopia that introduced on a macroscale the old principles of natural economy, such as allocation in kind, barter instead of commerce, and so on.[46] He pointed out the connection between this fact and the Bolsheviks' efforts to achieve a direct transition to a "centralized natural economy."[47] He stressed the backward-looking aspect of such strivings, an aspect of which Kautsky himself was not totally unaware, as is evident from his comment that "the system of socialist production . . . will and must have certain features in common with the older systems of communal production, in so far, namely, as both are systems of cooperative production for use."[48] Szamuely also made some fascinating observations about the evidently retrograde character of some parts of Kautsky's program, such as the idea that the first step toward socialism would entail changing from taxation to payments or services in kind (similar to feudalism)[49] or the view that a drastic shrinkage in the exportation and importation of products would be necessary for the self-sufficiency of the socialist economy.[50]

In conclusion, Szamuely summarized the conceptions of the German Social Democrats at the end of the nineteenth century as follows: "(1) They considered it as an axiom that commodity production was incompatible with socialism and regarded its liquidation as one of the tasks of the proletarian revolution; (2) they interpreted socialist economy as a centrally controlled, self-sufficient industrial plant; (3) they held that the 'naturalization' of economic relations was indispensable in the period of transition to socialism."[51]

What is lacking in this otherwise convincing and penetrating analysis is the derivation of all these views from Marx and Engels. After Engels's *Origin of the Family*, the backward-looking "tribalist" aspect of the Marxist ideal should have been evident (although admittedly only Popper and Hayek have analyzed it in sufficient detail). A certain idealization of the natural economy (and, to a certain extent, of all precapitalist formations) is also visibly present in Marx's *Capital*. Szamuely was, of course, right when he indicated that Kautsky's idea of deliberately minimizing all international exchange of products contradicted Marx's view of the necessity and progressiveness of the "unification of mankind" through the world market. But it is also true that Marx's vision of the moneyless economy of the future, especially his view of it as a single economic subject, a collective Robinson Crusoe, strongly suggests the autarchy and closedness inherent in the notion of a natural economy. We know Marx's answer to this: he thought that the dialectical return to a natural economy would be achieved on the world scale and thus would not involve any shrinkage of the scope of economic interdependence. The German Social Democrats, however, apparently did not exclude the possibility of "socialism in one country"— for some time, at least. If the socialist economy within the framework of one state was to abolish commodity production, it was logical for social- ists to want it to be as self-sufficient as possible.[52] The more international exchange, the more difficult it would be to exercise effective control over it. Hence, it is understandable that Kautsky wanted only such international exchange of products (not commodities!) as would not endanger "the eco- nomic independence and safety of the several nations." And, in his view, this danger could be avoided because "a co-operative commonwealth co- extensive with the nation could produce all that it requires for its own preservation."[53]

We must remember that this reasoning is strictly conditional: in a coun- try that has abolished commodity production, a return to a sort of natural economy, the striving for maximum autarchy, would have been justified and unavoidable. But the point is that the very ideal of abolishing the monetary exchange economy was, in Kautsky's case, not a product of his own thinking as a theorist of a great workers' party, but something he inherited, as it were, from his ideological masters. Kautsky never followed Bernstein in openly challenging Marx and Engels's authority, but never- theless after Engels's death he did begin, somewhat slowly and hesitantly, to think on his own and reduce thereby his dependence on them. The first thing he did was to disentangle the main task of socialism (i.e., the socialization of the means of production) from the communist moneyless utopia. Thus, in his *Social Revolution* (1902) he abandoned the view that the abolition of monetary exchange was an immediate task of a socialist revolution. This was an important change, which amounted to a revision of the Erfurt Program, but its theoretical justification did not go beyond a commonsensical argument about money, as follows:

Money is the hitherto best known simplest means of permitting the turnover of products and their allocation to the individual members of society to take place in as complicated a machinery as is—with its infinitely developed division of labor— the modern mode of production; money is the means of enabling everybody to satisfy his needs according to his individual inclination (of course, within the limits of his economic power). Money as a means of turnover will be indispensable as long as no better one is found. Of course, it will lose several of its functions, at least in domestic turnover, above all its role as a *measure of value*.[54]

Szamuely viewed Kautsky's new standpoint as revealing a much greater sense of reality but as theoretically meager: "Why does money remain? Be- cause nothing better has been found. Products have prices, but no value, or they also have a value but this must be found somewhere in the historical past. In a word, if I so wish it, the product is a commodity; if not, it is not [although the notion of commodity and commodity production does not even appear in this work of Kautsky]. If Kautsky's earlier views showed many common features . . . with the ideology of War Communism, his later arguments remind us, as regards both their level and their content, mostly of the pragmatic-eclectic 'theories' of the forties and fifties." [55]

From an economic point of view, little can be added to this comment, but it should be remembered that eclecticism is hard to avoid for one making the first hesitant attempts to loosen the grip of rigid dogmatism. And in the context of the problematic of freedom, it should be stressed that Kautsky's motivation did not amount to narrowly practical, pragmatic considerations. In fact, he quite explicitly stated that he was concerned with individual freedom and saw money as an irreplaceable guarantee for a free choice of consumer goods.

However, Kautsky's final liberation from the grip of the communist utopia occurred only after the Bolshevik revolution and the nightmare experiments of War Communism in Soviet Russia.[56] In his book *Die proletarische Revolution und ihr Programm* (1922), which was a synthesis of the experiences of the European workers' movement during the years of war and revolutionary upheavals,[57] he dismissed communism as probably no more than "a pious wish, similar to the Millennial Kingdom." In the name of freedom, he rejected the abolition of money and the entire "one nation, one factory" model, arguing as follows:

Without money only two kinds of economy are possible: First of all the primitive economy already mentioned. Adapted to modern dimensions, this would mean that the whole of the productive activity in the State would form a single factory, under one central control, which would assign its tasks to each single business, collect all the products of the entire population, and assign to each business its means of production and to each consumer his means of consumption in kind.

The ideal of such a condition is the prison or the barracks.[58]

This time, Kautsky (as befitted a "renegade") did not try to conceal that his new position involved a partial parting of the ways with Marx. Kautsky quoted Marx's arguments against money and corrected him, pointing out that he'd presented only one side, that the abolition of money would entail a historical retrogression. Money, Kautsky wrote,

first facilitated the greatest development of the division of labor, and consequently of the productive forces, which eventually reached such a level that general equality of conditions of life is no longer, as was once the case, only possible with general intellectual barbarism, but is compatible with a high degree of general civilization.

Socialism is called upon to remove the degrading effects of money. They arise from private property in the source of life and in the socially created wealth, which has hitherto been closely bound up with money. The abolition of this private property will make an end of the curse which has hitherto attached to money.

But we must avoid going so far as to abolish the great things which money has created, the extension of the division of labor, variety of production, and freedom of personality.

Socialism must connote an advance upon, and not a retreat from, capitalism. A relapse would not be tolerated by individuals of the present who have passed through the school of capitalist production, with its great variety of products and its great independence of personality.[59]

As we can see, this position perfectly coincided with Simmel's views on the connection between a money economy and individual freedom (see chapter 1, section 9). Kautsky was probably not aware of this and did not need to be. The important thing is that he proved able and bold enough to see the source of Marx's communist vision in the backward-looking utopias of the past, which he had been studying all his life. For instance, the settlements of the Anabaptists were "based upon a communism not only of production but also of consumption, involving the complete abolition of freedom of personality, as the 'elders' assigned to each individual not only his work and his food rations, but also his pleasures, even his wife."[60] The communistic organization of the Jesuits of Paraguay was based on similar principles. But what was possible in small, or relatively small, organizations (the state of the Jesuits in the days of its greatest expansion numbered about 150,000 inhabitants),[61] based entirely on natural economy could not be a model for a modern socialist state. "Soviet Russia," Kautsky concluded, "was the first and will doubtless be the last attempt of this kind."[62]

The importance of this analysis can hardly be exaggerated. For the first time in the history of Marxism, the ideal of the abolition of the monetary exchange economy—the very essence of Marxian communism—had been treated by an influential Marxist theorist as amounting in practice to the abolition of consumers' freedom and as being derived from the archaic ideal of the "communism of consumption."[63] It is clear that Kautsky's distinction between "communism of production" and "communism of consumption" coincided with Marx's distinction between two phases of communism, known in common parlance as the distinction between socialism (the "lower phase") and communism (the "higher phase"). Thus, Kautsky's rejection of the communism of consumption (inherent, as he had shown, in the idea of the abolition of money) was nothing less than an outright rejection of what had been seen for so long as the final goal of the workers' movement. In other words, Kautsky's stance amounted to the claim that socialism did not involve a commitment to communism, as Marx and Engels saw it. Even more, his position implied a critique of communism as being reactionary in its deepest essence, a warning against the menace of communism to freedom, and an expression of confidence (overoptimistic, to be sure) that after the Soviet experiment, communism would not be able to raise its head again.

The brutal and primitive methods of War Communism acted as a powerful catalyst in developing and clarifying Kautsky's ideas, but equally important in this respect was the dispersal of the freely elected Constituent Assembly and the period of anarchy and terror that followed. Kautsky's reaction to this period was his book *Die Diktatur des Proletariats* (1918), which made it clear that Marx's unfortunate expression "the dictatorship of the proletariat" did not mean "a dictatorship in the literal sense." [64]

It was not true, Kautsky argued, that socialism was the goal and democracy merely a means. Both were means toward the same end—namely, the emancipation of the proletariat—and both were equally necessary. [65] Democracy, however, was possible without socialism, while socialism without democracy was unthinkable. All known cases of socialized production without democracy, such as the Jesuit state in Paraguay or the Dutch colonial system in Java, were examples of patriarchal despotism incompatible with modernity and therefore had nothing in common with socialism. [66] Furthermore, "non-democratic socialism" was a contradiction in terms, because socialism presupposed "the will to socialism" in the majority of the population. This will could not appear without the "maturity of the objective conditions," being "first implanted in the masses when large-scale industry is already highly developed and its predominance over small industry unquestionable; when the dissolution of large-scale industry would be a retrograde, indeed an impossible, step; when the workers in the large-scale industry can aspire to ownership of the means of production only in collective form; and when the small industries which exist are deteriorating so fast that their owners can no longer derive a good living from them." [67]

Whatever we think about this argument, it is certainly not true that Kautsky could not "say precisely what constitutes 'ripeness' for socialism." And it is only partially true that "it is meaningless to criticize a revolutionary movement for taking no account whether the situation is ripe, since its ripeness is demonstrated by the movement's very success." [68] Kautsky answered this objection, comparing an impatient revolutionary movement to a pregnant woman who performs "the most foolish exercises in order to shorten the period of gestation" and thereby causes a premature birth: "the result of such proceedings is, as a rule, a child incapable of life." Another possible answer was, of course, the classical argument about the imminent relapse into a retrograde form of despotism. Kautsky saw this possibility as a danger inherent in all elitist and conspiratorial forms of socialist movements. "Masses," he argued, "cannot be organized secretly and, above all, a secret organization cannot be a democratic one." If the masses were immature and socialists saw themselves as messianic saviors who could afford to be contemptuous of democracy (as was the case for such pre-Marxian socialists as Blanqui or Weitling),[69] then the most likely outcome was something similar to the Jesuit state in Paraguay.[70]

What is, therefore, the meaning of Marx's thesis that between capitalism and socialism lies the period of the dictatorship of the proletariat? Kautsky conceded that although this was a rather unfortunate expression, it could not have meant a dictatorial form of government. A class, he soberly recalled, can rule but cannot govern.[71] Marx and Engels saw the Paris Commune as a dictatorship of the proletariat; hence, proletarian dictatorship was compatible, in their view, with full political freedom for all the democratic forces of society. What Marx was talking about, then, was not "a form of government" but "a state of affairs" in which the workers, because of their sheer numbers as well as their revolutionary spirit, exercised a predominant influence.[72] This was to be a transitional period, not to be confused with any sort of governmental arrangement, least of all with the dictatorship of a single party. "Party and class," Kautsky explained, "do not necessarily coincide. A class can split up into different parties and a party can have members from different classes."[73]

This simple statement, reflecting the parliamentary experience of the Social Democratic party (SPD), contradicted everything in Lenin's interpretation of Marxism. Equally anti-Leninist was Kautsky's definition of the dictatorship of the proletariat: "the rule of the proletariat on the basis of democracy."[74] To make things even worse, Kautsky thought it necessary to emphasize that democracy signified not only the rule of the majority but also, and no less, the protection of the minority.[75] Instead of scorning simple, commonsensical freedom, he defined the essence of socialism as "freedom and bread for all." Freedom, he wrote, "is not less important than bread. Even well-to-do and rich classes have fought for their freedom, and not seldom have made the biggest sacrifices for their convictions in blood and treasure. The need for freedom, for self-determination, is as natural as the need for bread."[76]

An interesting aspect of Kautsky's discussion of freedom is his full awareness that democratic freedom in everyday life might seem less attractive than revolutionary heroism and could even lead to undesirable results. He admitted that mass organizations under democracy were too much concerned with petty practical details, which served to contract workers' minds into narrow circles and reduced interest in, or caused outright contempt for, theory. This was why German workers had once been more theoretically minded than American or English workers and why the Russian workers were currently more interested in theoretical questions than were the German workers.[77] As we can see, this was an important concession to Lenin's view of the negative consequences of what he called "the trade-union mentality." Kautsky hoped, however, that "the degenerating influence of democracy on the proletariat" would disappear with the shortening of the working day. This hope allowed him to declare: "It were indeed extraordinary if the possession of freedom necessarily made men more narrow and trivial than its absence. The more democracy tends to shorten the working day, the greater the sum of leisure at the disposal of the proletariat, the more it is enabled to combine devotion to large problems with attention to necessary detail. And the impulse thereto is not lacking."[78]

In *The Dictatorship of the Proletariat* Kautsky does not accuse the Bolsheviks of evil intentions or of aiming for political power for themselves; on the contrary, he criticizes them for yielding to the anarchic impulses of the masses and for the genuine inability to create a strong but democratic governmental power.[79] The book's conclusion sounds a conciliatory note of historical understanding and a cautious expression of hope: "Dictatorship as a form of government in Russia is as understandable as the former anarchism of Bakunin. But to understand it does not mean that we would recognize it; we must reject the former as decisively as the latter. . . . The essential achievements of the Revolution will be saved, if dictatorship is opportunely replaced by democracy."[80]

Of course, this was not advice Lenin wanted to follow. In a long and indignant reply in *The Proletarian Revolution and the Renegade Kautsky*, Lenin called Kautsky a renegade and described his pamphlet as "a most lucid example of that utter and ignominious bankruptcy of the Second International about which all honest socialists in all countries have been talking for a long time" (L, *SW*, 3:17).

Kautsky, in his turn, was quickly losing his last illusions. He made it clear that a social revolution, in contrast to a merely political one, was a gradual process that could not be artificially accelerated by political coercion.[81] His new book on revolutionary Russia, entitled *Terrorismus und Kommunismus* (1919), proclaimed the complete bankruptcy of Bolshevik methods as leading only to "that form of socialism which has been called Asiatic; but unjustly, for Asia has given birth to a Confucius and a Buddha. It would be more exact to call it *Tartar* socialism." Accordingly, he maintained that "the task of European socialism, as against communism," was to dissociate itself from Bolshevism and thereby avoid a situation in which the moral catastrophe resulting from the latter would lead to "the catastrophe of socialism in general."[82]

Apart from moral condemnation, *Terrorism and Communism* contains many interesting observations and attempts at theoretical explanation. Thus, for instance, Kautsky was the first to formulate the hypothesis about "a new kind of class society." He criticized the workers' councils as a form of arbitrary rule of one class (and thus by no means a "school of democracy"), showing at the same time how the inevitable anarchization of industry forced the Communists to subject the councils to the absolute and arbitrary authority of "a new class of governors" and how "this new class gradually appropriated to itself all actual and virtual control." In this way the substitution of democracy for the arbitrary rule of workers' councils, which was to serve for the "expropriation of the expropriators," gave place "to the arbitrary rule of a new form of bureaucracy. Thus it has been made possible for this latter to render democracy for the workmen a complete dead letter; since the working-class community has, at the same time, been driven into greater economic dependence than it ever had to endure before." [83]

It is worthwhile noting that the fate of the workers in Lenin's "workers' state" was by no means Kautsky's only concern. As a democrat, Kautsky took to heart the fates of the other classes as well, pointing out that the situation of the nonproletarian strata (the former bourgeois, the small middle class, and intellectuals), "in so far as they show any opposition," was much worse: "Deprived of all political rights, and robbed of all means of subsistence, they are from time to time forced to do compulsory labor of the most objectionable kind, for which in return they receive rations of food, which barely represent the most wretched form of hunger rations, or, more truly said, starvation rations. The infernal state of such slavery can only be compared with the most horrible excesses that capitalism has ever shown. The creation of this state of affairs is the original and most characteristic act of the Bolsheviks. It represents their first step towards the emancipation of the human race." [84]

As a Marxist, Kautsky tried, of course, to provide a sociological explanation of the Bolsheviks' victory. He agreed with the Russian Mensheviks that it was the war that had decimated or dispersed the conscious elements among the proletariat, mobilizing instead the backward masses.[85] He wrote: "Those among the labouring classes in Russia who had been trained on Marxist lines were dead or swept away by the backward masses, who had suddenly awakened to life. It was the pre-Marxist ways of thought that gained the upper hand, ways such as were represented by Blanqui, Weitling or Bakunin. . . . In the case of the Bolsheviks, Marxism had no power on the situation. The mass psychology overruled them, and they allowed themselves to be carried away by it. Doubtless in consequence of this they have become the rulers of Russia. It is quite another question what will and must be the end of it all." [86]

Finally, Kautsky's book also contains some embryonic theories that bear no relation to Marxism. One of these provides an epistemological justification of democracy. Dictatorship, Kautsky reasoned, could be justified if those who exercised it possessed absolute truth; this, however, was impossible. There was no such thing as absolute truth; there was only "a process of knowledge," of acquiring and exchanging information and opinion, in which all citizens should democratically participate. Without democracy, decision making in a modern complex society was necessarily flawed, being based on inadequate knowledge.[87] Did Kautsky realize that this argument undermined the very essence of "scientific socialism"—the arrogant claim to having achieved a scientific understanding of necessity and therefore, being able to offer the communists a mandate to rule in the name of history? Unfortunately, we cannot know this. Nonetheless, it is evident that Kautsky's vindication of democracy did not undermine his determinism, but undermined only the belief that the knowledge of the laws of history could be attained and monopolized by a single party or leader.

Another embryonic theory reveals the role of articulated speech, and of communication in general, as means of understanding others and thereby of making people more peace loving and amicable.[88] In this context Kautsky stressed the positive role of intellectuals as sui generis specialists in communication and, of course, of the process of democratization that destroyed the barriers dividing estates and increased the importance of a common national language.[89] The result of this democratization was the modern nation within which even class struggles were waged in a civilized and enlightened manner that avoided brutalities and upheld the common good. Kautsky pointed out that he had already outlined this conception of the humanizing effect of democracy in his *Social Revolution* (1902).[90] He could also have mentioned his study *Die moderne Nationalität* (1887), in which he defined modern nationhood as a linguistic community embracing all classes of the population.[91] From the point of view of contemporary social science, it is interesting to note the presence of certain convergences between Kautsky's conception of the increasingly important and humanizing role of communication and Habermas's theory of "communicative action." Kautsky, of course, could not match Habermas as a philosopher, but nonetheless it seems significant that in both cases a deeper reflection on "communicative action" resulted in an emphasis on the role of democratic consensus in society.

Kautsky's last book on Soviet Russia bears the title *Von der Demokratie zur Staatssklaverei* (1921). From the point of view of the problematic of necessity and freedom, this book's main contribution consists in its development of the theory of democracy as a historical necessity for modern industrial society, both capitalist and socialist. Kautsky saw this necessity as stemming from the increased tasks of the state under increasingly complex economic and technical conditions. It followed from this view that the Bolshevik dictatorship in Russia was a historical anomaly, explicable as a product of specifically Russian conditions but nonetheless bound for an inevitable downfall. The best alternative to Bolshevism would be a social democratic republic similar to that established in independent Georgia (and quickly overthrown by Russian intervention).[92] In the meantime, the socialists should energetically resist Bolshevik activities in the international arena as amounting to a plot against the working classes of Europe.

The rejection of the communist ideal and the wholehearted commitment to the cause of democracy in Russia did not lead Kautsky to abandon Marxism as a method and a general theory of history. On the contrary, in 1927 he published a large volume entitled *Die materialistische Geschichtsauffassung*. He saw this book as his magnum opus, but it remained little known, which, as Kolakowski observed, was so for good reasons: by then Marxist doctrine had been almost monopolized by the Russian Communists, while the German Social Democrats, having broken with the Communists, had lost interest in the theoretical foundations of socialism and weakened their links with Marxist tradition.[93]

3.2 Georgii Plekhanov: "Historical Necessity" as Utopian Ideal

Although the belief in "historical necessity" was the cornerstone of the entire edifice of the "orthodox" Marxism of the Second International, as developed mostly by the theorists of German Social Democracy, its intensity was variable and the very meaning of necessity was subject to different interpretations. It so happened that the most inflexible necessitarian was not Kautsky, or any other German, but the Russian theorist Georgii Valentinovich Plekhanov (1856–1918), who was known as the "father of Russian Marxism."

The reasons explaining this fact can be found in the ideological situation that preceded the birth of Plekhanov's Marxism and that shaped his intellectual development. The peculiarities of this situation had a larger significance. In every country that was economically backward but intellectually developed, and thus exposed to the influence of Marxism, the intelligentsia faced the same difficult choice between the necessity of modernization and the requirements of social justice. For nineteenth-century socialists, who tended to equate modernization with bourgeois development on the Western model (as seemed to be suggested by Marx himself), this was a particularly difficult and painful dilemma. As we shall see, Plekhanov's Marxism was an attempt to eliminate this dilemma by persuading himself and his followers that a problem of choice did not exist, because human decisions could not change the inexorable laws of history.

The problem of the role of subjective and objective factors in history already had appeared in Russia in the 1830s as a result of the widespread influence of Hegelianism. The Russian Hegelians of the so-called Stankevich Circle, especially the literary critic Vissarion Belinskii and the future theorist of anarchism Mikhail Bakunin, interpreted Hegelianism as a philosophy of objective rational necessity the understanding of which should lead to a philosophical "reconciliation with reality."[94] Both Belinskii and Bakunin passed through a period of such reconciliation, experiencing its therapeutic psychological effects but soon finding it incompatible with their rebellious nonconformist "subjectivity." In later years, as an ideologist of anarchism, Bakunin recalled this episode of his life with disgust, condemning "historical objectivism" as a convenient excuse for cowardly passivity.[95] This was in tune with the voluntarist ethos of Russian populist socialism, as expressed in Petr Lavrov's and Mikhailovskii's "subjective sociology."[96] This theory claimed that the so-called objective laws of history were merely spontaneous tendencies of development that could be effectively opposed by the subjective factor (i.e., human will and consciousness), as expressed in the activity of a revolutionary party or in the deliberate intervention by the state. The emergence and popularity of this view was understandable given the fact that sociological "objectivism," manifesting itself as Spencerian evolutionism, or belief in the "iron laws of political economy," was then the main ideological weapon for all who wanted to compromise socialism, especially socialism in a backward country, as merely a utopian dream based only in wishful thinking.

However, there also existed the tendency to provide objectivist arguments for populist socialism: to present it as a theory adequately reflecting some peculiarities of the Russian condition, having an objectively existing social basis in communal ownership of the land, and offering an objectively defensible program of noncapitalist modernization of the country. The young Plekhanov—as one of the leaders of the populist party Land and Freedom and later the head of the separate populist organization Black Repartition[97]—was a peculiarly consistent representative of this objectivist trend. This was so for at least three reasons: first, his conviction that political movements must have a viable social basis; second, his sharply critical attitude toward the People's Will, a terrorist party whose heroic voluntarism was seen by him as irresponsible adventurism; and, finally, his growing fascination with Marxism, which he interpreted as a fully scientific and therefore entirely objective justification of socialism in the advanced countries of the West. His commitment to the populist idea of a direct transition to socialism depended on the viability of the Russian peasant commune. Therefore, when a book by V. I. Orlov on *Communal Property in the Moscow District* convinced him that the disintegration of the peasant commune was a natural and irresistible process, he had no other option than to accept the view that Russia had to pass through a "capitalist phase."[98] Happily, Marxism enabled him to do so without abandoning his allegiance to socialism. Thus, he proclaimed himself a Marxist and in 1883 transformed his Black Repartition organization into the Emancipation of Labor group, which was the first programmatically Marxist Russian organization. Characteristically, this group came into being in Geneva and never tried to establish itself in Russia; the remoteness of socialism in Russian justified concentration on those activities (mostly theoretical) that could be conducted in emigration.

In political terms, Plekhanov's organization defined itself as social democratic. These words were to be a part of its name, but the idea was dropped for tactical reasons: two members of the group, Lev Deutsch and the ex-terrorist Vera Zasulich, thought that in the minds of Russian revolutionaries "social democracy" was too firmly associated with parliamentary activities (for which there was no place in Russia) and resolute avoidance of revolutionary methods of struggle.[99] Nevertheless, Plekhanov's sympathy for the SPD was outspoken, and the terms *social democratic* and *Marxist* were, in his writings, almost synonymous. This meant that Marxism was for him not only a theory of socioeconomic development (which undermined the populist theory of Russia's "exceptionalism"), but also a definite political option. Being a Marxist, Plekhanov reasoned, involved acceptance of a certain conception of the proper relationship between socialism and "political struggle," a conception radically different from the extreme views that had dominated the pre-Marxist revolutionary movement in Russia. First of all, Marxists knew that the highest form of class struggle was political struggle and would therefore resolutely reject the nihilistic attitude toward politics preached by the anarchists. Second, Marxists living under absolute monarchy in a country not yet ripe for socialism must fight for political liberty, in alliance with bourgeois liberals, and must resolutely reject the classical populist standpoint that dismissed the struggle for political freedom as bourgeois in its content and even suggested that a liberal constitution in Russia would only strengthen the possessing classes and thereby ruin the chances for socialism.[100] Third, Marxists knew that revolutions were social processes that could not be "made" by a group of devoted militants; hence they must eschew Blanquism—that is, the attempt to seize political power and impose socialism from above. In Russia the most extreme advocate of a seizure of political power by the revolutionary vanguard (which was to be followed by a period of socialist dictatorship) was Petr Tkachev, whose ideas exerted some influence on the People's Will. Both as a populist and as a Marxist, Plekhanov opposed Tkachev and the People's Will. We can therefore say that social democracy for him meant an emphatic commitment to political struggle combined with a continued, and even strengthened, opposition to Blanquism. In an article criticizing Blanquist tendencies among the People's Will, Plekhanov drew a sharp distinction between the Marxist idea of a dictatorship of the proletariat and the Blanquist concept of the dictatorship of a revolutionary elite, writing: "No executive, administrative, or any other committee is entitled to represent the working class in history." [101]

Another aspect of Plekhanov's political program, as set forth in *Social-ism and the Political Struggle* (1883), *Our Differences* (1885), and his other works of the 1880s, was its adamant Westernism. The great mission of the Russian workers was, from this point of view, to complete the Western-ization of Russia begun by Peter the Great. A seizure of power by revolu-tionary socialists would only hinder this process and would be a disaster that in the end could only result in a long step backward. Authentic social-ism could only be established when economic development and proletarian class consciousness had attained a level of maturity. Political authorities trying to organize from above socialist production in an underdeveloped country would be forced "to seek salvation in the ideals of 'patriarchal and authoritarian communism,' only modifying those ideals so that national production is managed not by the Peruvian 'sons of the sun' and their offi-cials but by a socialist caste. But even now the Russian people is too far developed for anybody to flatter himself with the hope that such experi-ments on it could be successful. Moreover, there is no doubt that under such a guardianship the people, far from being educated for socialism, would even lose all capacity for further progress or would retain that ca-pacity only thanks to the appearance of the very economic inequality which it would be the revolutionary government's immediate aim to abolish." [102]

The conclusion of this argument was that Russia must first finish the phase of capitalism she had already entered.[103] Russia's transition to social-ism cannot be direct; neither should it be made through a process of a permanent revolution: "To bind together in one two so fundamentally different matters as the overthrow of absolutism and the socialist revolu-tion, to wage revolutionary struggle in the belief that these elements of social development will *coincide* in the history of our country *means to put off the advent of both.*" [104] A sufficiently long time must elapse be-tween the political revolution (i.e., the overthrow of tsarism) and the future socialist revolution to enable capitalist forces of production to become fully established and the Russian proletariat to receive political training in a law-abiding parliamentary state. The interval might well be shorter than in the West, because in Russia (owing to Western influence) the socialist movement was organized very early, while capitalism was still in its in-fancy. Thanks to their early adoption of Marxism, Russian socialists could accelerate the development of proletarian class consciousness among the Russian workers. On the other hand, the capitalist stage should not be too brief; it was possible to shorten this "natural" process, but every attempt to shorten it too much or to replace it by an "artificial" process entailed the danger of an undesirable "chemical change." [105]

The views outlined above provided a firm foundation for Plekhanov's interpretation of Marxism, which his further intellectual development did not lead him to abandon. Thus, he was hardly exaggerating when he wrote a quarter of a century later that in the controversies between the Bolsheviks and the Mensheviks he remained committed to the ideas worked out by the Emancipation of Labor group.[106]

For the revolutionary populists, Plekhanov's program of passing through a capitalist phase amounted in practice to a betrayal of socialism. Lev Tikhomirov, the leading theorist of the People's Will, dismissed this idea as psychologically unacceptable: a true socialist, he argued, would never agree to support the development of capitalism, especially if he had learned from Marx's *Capital* how much suffering it involved for the masses. He compared Plekhanov to a Christian missionary trying to persuade the savages that slavery was necessary for civilization and that for that reason they had to become slaves.[107]

Plekhanov anticipated such reactions and did not try to win the battle on moral grounds. Instead, he insisted on representing scientific objectivism, which is concerned only with what really is, not with what should be according to some subjective ideal. And, of course, he invoked in this connection the scientific authority of Marx. But the trouble was that Marx himself did not share Plekhanov's views on Russia. Plekhanov knew of this from Marx's letter to Vera Zasulich of March 8, 1881, in which Marx explicitly endorsed the populist view that Russia could achieve "social regeneration" (i.e., a successful transition to socialism) on the basis of the peasant commune.[108] However, this important letter, kept in the archives of the Emancipation of Labor group, was published only in 1924. Why was it not shown to anybody outside the group? In 1881 Plekhanov and Zasulich were still populists; they did not publish Marx's letter because they thought that he intended to elaborate his views on the chances of populist socialism in Russia in a pamphlet specially devoted to this subject. But why did they refrain from publishing it after Marx's death? Unfortunately, deliberate concealment is the most probable hypothesis. In fact, this hypothesis has been confirmed by a Russian Menshevik, E. Yur'evskii, in an article published in the emigré *Sotsyalisticheskii vestnik* in which he asserted that Marx's diagnosis

contradicted all ideas which Plekhanov, in the process of overcoming populism, worked out on the basis of *Capital*. Marx's letter to Zasulich mercilessly refuted all his conclusions, all his theoretical constructions. The thesis that the advanced countries show the backward ones the image of their own future was deprived by this letter of its universal applicability. Russia was put by it, as it were, outside the scope of the process of Westernization. It removed the foundation of the certainty with which Plekhanov answered the question: where are we going? Therefore, when Zasulich received this letter, Plekhanov instructed her not to talk about it. In 1885, after the publication of his sharp attacks on the populism, he went even further: he convinced Zasulich (who always followed him) that it would be better to forget Marx's letter altogether, because it supported the populist illusions and made struggle against them more difficult. I learned this from Plekhanov's wife, Rosaliia Markovna.[109]

Of course, Plekhanov could have sincerely believed that as far as Russia was concerned his own interpretation of Marxism was more consistent and scientific than Marx's casual thoughts. Nonetheless, Plekhanov was fully aware that for a socialist the acceptance of the capitalist development of his country was a tragic decision, justifiable only in the name of objective necessity. This was, after all, his own dilemma and the main reason for the peculiarly necessitarian quality of his Marxism. "Scientific understanding of necessity," in accordance with Engels's famous formula, was Plekhanov's main argument against populist "subjectivism" and the main reason for his growing self-confidence, bordering on intellectual arrogance, that resulted from his becoming infected (through Engels) with the Hegelian bacillus. It is no exaggeration to say that Plekhanov came to see himself as the living embodiment of the correct scientific understanding of historical necessity. This was the final outcome of his intellectual evolution in which the very notion of necessity changed its meaning.

At the beginning, Plekhanov's notion of necessity was strongly influenced by positivistic evolutionism. The "inner necessity" of development meant for him normal, natural development, as opposed to the different "anomalies" that could result from external interference. In this sense, capitalist development was for Russia a necessity but not an absolute inevitability; it was a necessity if Russia was to develop, but this did not exclude other possibilities, as, for instance, a retrogression into authoritarian communism. At other times, however, Plekhanov flatly rejected any possibility of choice, claiming that his political program was based on an understanding of the "objective laws of development," that the validity of its prognosis could be demonstrated with "mathematical exactness," and that its goals would be realized as surely as tomorrow's sunrise.[110] In his early Marxist works (*Socialism and the Political Struggle* and *Our Differences*), the first argument was more in evidence, whereas later, the second rationale prevailed. Scientific socialists, he insisted, strive for socialism not because it is desirable, but because it is the next stage in the "magnificent and irresistible forward-march of History." "Social Democracy swims with the tide of History," and the causes of historical development "have nothing to do with human will or consciousness." [111]

This shift of emphasis was caused by the special function that necessity was to perform in Plekhanov's worldview. He shared the populist conviction, formed under the influence of Marx's *Capital*, that capitalist development of Russia would necessarily entail expropriation of the peasantry and thus bring about enormous suffering for the masses.[112] This required him to explain his readiness to endorse such a high price for progress; his best explanation was, of course, to interpret capitalist development as an *absolute* and *rational* historical necessity. A merely empirical, statistical necessity would not sufficiently justify such acceptance of human suffering. In other words, he needed a theodicy, and he found it in the idea of a necessary, *rational, meaningful* unfolding of history. Hence, he could not be fully satisfied by the positivistic determinism of Kautsky, a determinism in which there was no place for the "meaning of history." He sought for inspiration in the great metaphysicians: in Spinoza, whom he saw as a great predecessor of Marxism,[113] and above all in Hegel. The necessity to which he appealed could not be a simple necessity of facts, to endorse such sacrifice merely for facts would be nothing more than simple opportunism. Therefore, it had to be conceived as an ontological necessity, a necessity inherent in the rational structure of the universe. It was, in a word, the rational necessity of Spinoza, made dynamic and historical by Hegel and reinterpreted scientifically by Marx. To become reconciled with such a necessity was, indeed, something inspiring and lofty; it gave a powerful feeling of historical mission and a certainty of final victory.

Nevertheless, Plekhanov did not simply identify the recognition of necessity with freedom. He understood that necessity might appear to individuals as an external power that threatens to crush them unless they surrender. And he knew well that invoking historical necessity was very effective in ideological struggle, that necessitarian arguments were excellent for intimidating people, disarming them intellectually and morally, and forcing them to submission. This awareness is well expressed in one of his notes on Hegel: "*Hegelian objectivism.* The difference between individual reason and the reason of the world. There is no harmony between *individual ideas* and the universal reason. Hegel's answer to this was: your ideas are senseless. Our subjective reason cannot serve as a criterion for social development. The entire philosophy of Hegel aimed at suppressing the individual."[114]

Undoubtedly, Plekhanov pursued the same aim in his merciless polemics against different "subjectivists." But he himself experienced the idea of rational necessity as giving meaning to his life and immensely increasing his freedom. He explained this in his philosophical works, above all *The Development of the Monistic View of History* (1894), the pamphlet *On the Question of the Individual's Role in History* (1898), and a series of important articles on the Russian Hegelian Vissarion Belinskii. Our subject in this book justifies paying close attention to Plekhanov's arguments. Let us start with his most general explanation, which is set forth in the second of the aforementioned works.

Rudolph Stammler, a famous neo-Kantian philosopher of law, remarked that if socialism was as necessary as a lunar eclipse, then there was no need for a socialist party.[115] Plekhanov reacted to this comment by pointing out that in history the activity of each individual was a necessary link in the chain of causation and could sometimes greatly influence events, although this activity could not change the general direction of development. But the historical role of great individuals does not depend on their free will; on the contrary, only those individuals can perform an important historical role whose will is fully determined, who are propelled by an inner necessity, and who can apply to themselves Luther's words: "Here I stand, I cannot do otherwise." Plekhanov's other examples were the Calvinists, who believed in divine predestination; Moses and the other prophets of Israel; and Cromwell, who "also regarded himself as a Divine instrument." Plekhanov contrasted these individuals with those whose will was not sufficiently determined, or rather was determined by different conflicting forces, which gave them the illusion of free choice. In reality, he argued, such people suffered from a Hamlet-like inability to choose: their will was weakened, their energy was paralyzed, and as a result they were capable "only of complaint and reflection."[116]

Thus, Plekhanov continued, true freedom consisted in the internalization of necessity, the conscious identification with it, and thereby in making necessity free and freedom . . . necessary. He wrote: "When the consciousness of the non-freedom of my will presents itself to me only in the form of the complete subjective and objective impossibility of behaving otherwise than I am doing, and when, at the same time, my given actions are at the same time those that I find the most desirable of all possible actions, then necessity becomes identified in my mind with freedom, and freedom with necessity; then, I am non-free only in the sense that *I cannot upset this identity of freedom and necessity; I cannot contrapose them to each other; I cannot feel the restraint of necessity. But such an absence of freedom* is at the same time *its fullest manifestation.*"[117]

The populists rejected historical necessity on moral grounds: first, the necessity of capitalist progress contradicted their socialist moral ideal, and second, above all, the price for this progress was too high and involved too much human suffering. Plekhanov's answer to this was that ethicism (or subjectivism) always leads to "the morass of dualism" and makes it impossible to achieve freedom. Those who are paralyzed by moral scruples will never be able to identify with necessity and to transform it into freedom. The Russian disciples of Marxism had liberated themselves from such scruples, while the populists had not, and thus, he concluded, "it is a question of that moral restraint which curbs the energy of those who have not parted company with dualism; the restraint that causes suffering to those who are unable to bridge the gulf separating ideals and reality. Until the individual has won *such* freedom through a courageous exertion of philosophical thought, he does not fully belong to himself, his own moral torment being his shameful payment to the external necessity confronting him. But then, as soon as that same individual casts off the yoke of that painful and shameful restriction, he is born for a new, full and hitherto unfamiliar life; and his *free* activities will be the *conscious* and *free* expression of *necessity*."[118]

Plekhanov's articles on Belinskii show that his own identification with necessity was not an easy process, even if we assume that he easily renounced moral scruples (which is highly unlikely). This process was difficult because he had to recognize two historical necessities at the same time: the necessity of a "capitalist phase" (i.e., of the class rule of the bourgeoisie after the overthrow of autocracy) for the immediate future, and the necessity of socialism for the remote future. For someone who identified himself with historical forces struggling for socialism, the acceptance of a capitalist phase involved, of course, a calculated "reconciliation with reality" that would put multiple restraints on his freedom of action.

The relevance of Belinskii's philosophical development to the controversy between the populists and the Marxists was discovered and set forth by Mikhailovskii in 1894. Polemizing with the "legal Marxist," Petr Struve, whom he accused of an "aggressive contempt for the human individual," Mikhailovskii compared Struve's Marxism to Belinskii's Hegelianism of the 1830s.[119] Toward the end of 1837 Belinskii, under the influence of Hegel's famous thesis "What is real is rational, what is rational is real," came to the conclusion that it was necessary to become "reconciled" to reality, to humble oneself before the "Reason of History" and to renounce forever all "moralism," "subjectivism," and "abstract heroism." Quoting some relevant utterances of Belinskii, Mikhailovskii suggested that there existed an analogy between Belinskii's "reconciliation" and Russian Marxism: in both cases the conflict between personality and historical reality was resolved in favor of the latter, and the resolution consisted of the subordination of the individual to an allegedly rational and beneficial necessity. Belinskii, however, at last came to himself, cursed his "base reconciliation with base reality," and revolted against historiosophical theodicy, refusing to accept its claim that human suffering might be justified.[120]

Plekhanov's article "Belinskii and 'Rational Reality'" was in a sense an answer to Mikhailovskii. In contrast to the populist publicist, Plekhanov was deeply fascinated not by Belinskii's revolt against reality but by his reconciliation with it. In Plekhanov's interpretation the period of reconciliation was a time of Belinskii's most remarkable efforts to overcome idealistic subjectivism, recalling Schiller and the "abstract rationalism" of the Enlightenment—a time when the Russian intelligentsia, in the person of Belinskii, discovered that ideals, in order to exert a positive influence, should be anchored in social reality, should reflect its inherent tendencies, not just noble but abstract daydreams and idealistic wishful thinking. Belinskii, according to Plekhanov, was in this period "a sociological genius" who "in the Hegelian doctrine of the rationality of everything real felt instinctively the only possible foundation of social science." Belinskii's error consisted not in his general attitude toward reality but in his too static understanding of it, in the identification of the dynamic reason of reality (i.e., the progressive tendencies inherent in it) with the existing empirical reality of Russia. His revolt against Hegel did not correct this error; on the contrary, this revolt was in essence a return to utopianism, the "theoretical original sin" that could not be justified theoretically, although it was fully justified as an outburst of suppressed passions.[121] Plekhanov, however, was fond of adding that Belinskii himself had been aware that a subjective revolt did not amount to a theoretical solution: after all, Belinskii had expressed the view that his idea of reconciliation was sound and needed only to be coupled with the dialectical idea of negation.

Intelligent readers of Plekhanov's article were inevitably drawn to the conclusion that there was a close analogy between Belinskii's rejection of abstract heroicism and Plekhanov's own rejection of the abstract populist idea of a direct transition to socialism. The Marxism adopted by Plekhanov and his comrades could also be called a specific variant of reconciliation with reality (the reality of Russian capitalism) in the name of historical necessity, a reconciliation that had, of course, been purged of Belinskii's error and represented the acceptance of dynamic reality as a process of becoming coupled with the idea of negation. It is interesting to note that in his unfinished *History of Russian Social Thought* Plekhanov had intended to draw this parallel between Belinskii's reconciliation with reality and Russian Marxism.[122]

In this manner, Plekhanov presented Belinskii as virtually a precursor of Russian Marxism (or, more accurately, of his particular version of Marxism). Plekhanov did not think, however, that there was any contradiction between this portrayal and the "subjective" sociologists' claim to Belinskii as their ideological predecessor. Belinskii, Plekhanov admitted, had not entirely succeeded in overcoming his utopianism; in his negation of Russian reality he had frequently abandoned the dialectical view in favor of the subjectivist attitudes of Enlightenment rationalism (*prosvetitel'stvo*). The Russian Marxists aligned themselves on Belinskii's strong side, whereas subjective sociology harked back to his weak side, to the "theoretical original sin" shown in his moral revolt against Hegelianism. In later years Plekhanov tried to demonstrate that the Bolsheviks' subjectivist tactics also sprang from this "original sin." It is significant that to the end of his life, Plekhanov continued to draw attention to Belinskii's struggle against utopianism, feeling impelled to warn the victorious Bolshevik party against the dangers of an "abstract ideal."[123] Equally characteristic was Plekhanov's wish to be buried in St. Petersburg next to the grave of Belinskii.

We can now turn to Plekhanov's main philosophical work, his *Development of a Monistic View of History*, published in Russia under the pseudonym N. Beltov. This work was an attempt to conceptualize the intellectual history of modern Europe in such a way as to show Marxism to be its crowning achievement. Plekhanov divides this history into the same three phases he discovered in Belinskii's intellectual development. The first phase—that of the abstract ideal—was embodied in Enlightenment rationalism, which used the subjective yardstick of individual human reason to evaluate social realities. The second phase—that of the discovery of historical necessity, applied, as a rule, in its conservative interpretation—was German idealistic philosophical tradition culminating in Hegelianism. The third and final phase—that of the reconciliation of the ideal with objective necessity—was inaugurated by Marx. The two additional chapters of the book deal with French historians of the Restoration and the utopian socialists. Plekhanov presented both groups as precursors of Marxism: the first because they formulated the socialist ideal; the second, because they offered a sociological interpretation of necessity and emphasized the importance of class struggle.

The most important (especially from the point of view of the problematic of freedom) are the last two chapters: on German idealism and on Marxism. Having paid due homage to Spinoza, Plekhanov credited German idealists with the discovery that "*freedom presupposes necessity, necessity passes entirely into freedom.*" They understood that for rational beings, dependence on chance was more humiliating than dependence on necessary laws, without which everything would be unpredictable and therefore incompatible with rational freedom. Moreover, the idealists also understood that history is not a plaything of chance, but unfolds in an innerly rational way, exhibiting a meaningful pattern of development. Hegel, the greatest of the German idealists, defined history as "*progress in the consciousness of freedom, progress which we must understand in its necessity.*" [124]

In his account of Marxism Plekhanov depended entirely on Engels. The development of productive forces emancipated humans from nature's yoke but gave rise to a new dependence, a new variety of slavery: economic necessity. This happened because the growing complexity of the social process of production made it uncontrollable, and producers thus became enslaved by their own creation. However, the very logic of the development of production made it possible to understand the cause of human enslavement by economic necessity. This understanding (provided by Marxism) offered "the opportunity for a new and final triumph of *consciousness* over *necessity*, of *reason* over blind *law.*"

In this manner, exactly as with Engels, the strictly necessitarian interpretation of history ended in the understanding of necessity and the voluntaristic "grand finale," as described here:

Thus dialectical materialism not only does not strive, as its opponents attribute to it, to convince man that it is absurd to revolt against economic necessity, but it is the first to point out *how to overcome* the latter. Thus is eliminated the *inevitably fatalist* charater inherent in *metaphysical materialism*. And in exactly the same way is eliminated every foundation for that pessimism to which, as we saw, consistent *idealist* thinking leads of necessity. The individual personality is only foam on the crest of the wave, men are subjected to an iron law which can only be discovered, but which cannot be subjected to the human will, said Georg Büchner. No, replies Marx: once we have *discovered* that iron law, it depends on us to overthrow its yoke, it depends on us to make *necessity* the obedient slave of *reason*.

I am a worm, says the idealist. I am a worm while I am ignorant, retorts the dialectical materialist: but I am a god when I *know. Tantum possumus, quantum scimus . . .*

Dialectical materialism says that human reason could not be the demiurge of history, because it is itself the *product* of history. But once that product has appeared, it *must* not—and in its nature it *cannot*—be obedient to the reality handed down as a heritage by previous history; of necessity it strives to transform that reality after its own likeness and image, *to make it reasonable.*

Dialectical materialism says, like Goethe's Faust: *Im Anfang war die That!* [In the Beginning was the Deed!]

Action (the activity of men in conformity to law in the social process of production) explains to the dialectical materialist the historical development of the reason of social man. It is to action also that is reduced all his *practical philosophy. Dialectical materialism is the philosophy of action.*[125]

According to Kolakowski, Plekhanov's position amounted to "the denial of any basic distinction between the study of nature and that of society." Like Kautsky, Plekhanov was "also convinced that social processes can be studied in the same completely objective way as natural phenomena . . . in the same way as geological formations." [126] In fact this is a somewhat oversimplified statement. True, Plekhanov stressed that "the spirit of research" was "absolutely the same" in Darwin and Marx; at the same time, however, he pointed out that "the investigation of Marx begins precisely where the investigation of Darwin ends." This was so because animal species, as studied by Darwin, develop under the influence of their *physical* environment, while the historical development of humans is explicable (according to Marx) "by the characteristics of those social *relations* between men which arise when social man is acting on *external nature.*" [127] Thus, the *subject* of social sciences was seen by Plekhanov as qualitatively different from the subject of, say, geology. One can say that Plekhanov considered the laws of history to be naturelike rather than simply natural, to apply Engel's distinction (see chapter 2, section 6). It is also evident that Plekhanov followed Engels (and differed from Kautsky) in attributing a rational meaning to history. Finally, despite his explicitly expressed disgust with excessive interest in Marx's early writings,[128] as well as his definite rejection of the notion of human essence, his philosophy of history retained some semblance of the Marxian scheme of self-enriching alienation. As the quoted passages clearly show, Plekhanov saw history as a process in which an individual loses control over his products, allowing them to develop autonomously, and thus becomes "*the slave of his own creation.*"[129] But at the end of the long ordeal, individuals do attain scientific understanding of their plight and, armed with correct knowledge, pass from the rule of self-imposed necessity to the kingdom of freedom.

As we can see, all these ideas derived from Engels, not from Kautsky. The ideas of Engels enabled Plekhanov to draw directly from Hegel and to develop his concept of necessity as dialectical, teleological, and rational, that is, in conscious opposition to the mechanistic determinism of the natural sciences. In his article "For the Sixtieth Anniversary of Hegel's Death," Plekhanov called on Marxists to be "faithful to the spirit of Hegel's philosophy," defining it as "the irresistible striving to the great historical goal, a striving which nothing can stop."[130] It should be obvious that the necessity of the great march of history conceived in this manner was something very different from natural necessity, which is observable in the growth of geological formations.

By being "faithful to the spirit of Hegel's philosophy," Plekhanov also meant something else. He drew a parallel between Marx's conception of the mission of the proletariat and Hegel's view on the missions of world historical individuals and world historical nations, agreeing with Hegel that all bearers of the new historical principle should have the absolute right to override everything that hindered them in their realization of their mission. He quoted with satisfaction Hegel's words that nobody can have any rights against those who are "the vehicle of the present stage of development of the universal spirit."[131]

It should be equally obvious why this Hegelianized Marxism posed an incomparably greater danger to individual freedom than did the positivistic account of Marxism typical of the Second International. The slightest acquaintance with Hegelianism reveals that true knowledge must be the knowledge of dialectical totality—hence, Plekhanov's striving to transform Marxism into an all-embracing philosophical system of dialectical and historical materialism. And if human liberation was made dependent on knowledge, on correct scientific understanding of necessity, then it was perfectly logical to claim that anarchy in the intellectual sphere could not be tolerated. Deviation from the only correct knowledge could be tolerated neither at present, because there was only one correct understanding of historical necessity, nor in the future kingdom of freedom, because correct knowledge was to be the very foundation of freedom. If freedom consisted in rational, conscious control over humans' collective fate, a control made

possible because of "correct scientific knowledge," then it logically followed that freedom of action could not be understood as lack of omnipresent "scientific" guidance of human conduct. Although for tactical reasons
Plekhanov did not elaborate on this point, he did not hesitate to be explicit in private conversations, as Alexei M. Voden recounted: "I had to
admit that Plekhanov had frequently said to me that, when 'we' were in
power, 'we' would naturally allow freedom to none but 'ourselves.' . . .
In answer to my question as to who should logically be recognized as the
monopolists of liberty, Plekhanov replied: the working classes, under the
leadership of comrades who had properly understood Marx's teaching and
had drawn from it the correct conclusions. When I asked whether there
was an objective criterion for the proper understanding of Marx's teaching
and for the correct conclusions to be drawn from it, Plekhanov confined
himself to the comment that all this was 'sufficiently clearly' set out in his
[Plekhanov's] works." [132]

It was not possible to legitimize one's political position by referring to
a mandate derived from the faultless understanding of history in combination with allowing the workers' movement to develop spontaneously and
to escape the tutelage of its Marxist leaders. Neither could this position be
combined with an unconditional commitment to the rule of law or popular sovereignty, which explains Plekhanov's agreement with Lenin at the
Second Congress of the Russian Democracy (1903).[133] He supported Lenin
on two points of crucial importance: in his claim that consciousness must
be introduced to the workers' movement from without, and in his general attitude toward "formal democracy." In what is known as Plekhanov's
"Jacobin Speech" at the Congress, he said:

If it were necessary for the success of the revolution to restrict the effect of one or
another democratic principle, it would be criminal to stop at such a restriction. As
my own personal opinion I would say that even the principle of universal suffrage
should be regarded from the point of view of this basic principle of democracy I
have just mentioned. Hypothetically it is conceivable that we, Social Democrats,
may have occasion to come out against universal suffrage. . . . The revolutionary
proletariat could restrict the political rights of the upper classes the way these
classes once restricted the political rights of the proletariat. The fitness of such a
measure could only be judged by the rule: *salus revolutionis suprema lex.* The same
point of view should be adopted by us on the question of the duration of parliaments. If, on an impulse of revolutionary enthusiasm, the people were to elect a
very good parliament, a sort of Chambre Introuvable, we should try and make it
a long parliament; and if the elections turned out to be unfavorable, *we should try
and dismiss it not in two years' time, but if possible in two weeks.*" [134]

It is no wonder that Lenin thought it convenient to recall these words
in January 1918, in connection with Plekhanov's objections against the

Bolshevik terror. On the eve of the dispersal of the freely elected Constituent Assembly, he reprinted the quoted passage in full, commenting that it "might have been written specially for the present day" (L, CW, 42:47).

However, Plekhanov's alliance with Lenin did not last long. Soon after the Second Congress he rejoined his old friends, now the Mensheviks, and became an unrelenting critic of Lenin. He became aware that the main motivation behind Lenin's critique of the theory of the workers' "spontaneity" was not the defense of the role of scientific (i.e., objective) theory (which under Russian conditions demanded patience and moderation), but rather his conception of the vanguard party (which, in contrast to the emphasis on theory, led to a dangerous exaggeration of the role of the "subjective factor" in history). Having realized this, Plekhanov condemned Leninism as a new and particularly perilous version of the theoretical original sin of the Russian revolutionary intelligentsia.

Most of the differences that divided Plekhanov from Lenin were directly relevant to the cause of freedom in Russia. All of them concerned the problem of the capitalist phase in Russia's development and, consequently, of the character of the Russian Revolution.

Before 1917 Lenin agreed with Plekhanov that Russia had to pass through a capitalist phase and that the Russian revolution would have a "bourgeois-democratic content." This was the main tenet of the Marxist orthodoxy in Russia. For Plekhanov, however, this meant capitalism not only in an economic base, but also in a political superstructure. Thus, for instance, he saw parliamentary government as an *essential* feature of the capitalist phase and stressed from the very beginning in his polemics against the populists that without bourgeois parliamentarism, Russia's capitalist development would not be completed.[135] Characteristically, he supported this view not by showing the autonomous value of parliamentary institutions, but rather by pointing out their specifically bourgeois character. All forms of government, he reasoned, were essentially forms of class rule; all of them enabled the ruling class "to use the organized force of society in defense of its interests and for the suppression of all social movements which directly or indirectly endanger these interests"; hence, all of them were forms of dictatorship.[136] But precisely because of this the bourgeois revolution in Russia would have been impossible without first establishing the political dictatorship of the bourgeoisie; in other words, if the Russian Revolution was to be bourgeois in its content, it should pave the way for the class rule of the capitalists and the political rule of the bourgeois liberals. Lenin's 1905 conception of a bourgeois revolution led by the proletariat in alliance with the revolutionary peasantry and aimed politically against the liberals was, from Plekhanov's point of view, either sheer nonsense or a disguised expression of a desire to skip over a necessary phase of development.

By taking this position, otherwise fully consistent with his theoretical views, Plekhanov placed himself at the extreme right wing of Russian Marxism. Even the most moderate Mensheviks distanced themselves from his tactics, regarding them as self-defeating.[137] His publicly expressed view that the armed insurrection of the Moscow workers in 1905 was a political error contributed to a further increase in his isolation within his own party. He won instead the praise of P. N. Miliukov, the leader of the Kadet party, who said: "If all the comrades of G. V. Plekhanov understood what the most outstanding of their leaders understands, and if they were as little discomfited as he by the praises of the 'liberal bourgeoisie'! My God, how that would simplify the explanation of our present political problems and how strongly it would advance their solution."[138]

Another important feature of Plekhanov's political tactics was his resolute opposition to the idea of a revolutionary alliance between workers and peasants. This standpoint found support not only in his "orthodox Marxism" (his view that small producers represented the most obsolete form of production),[139] but also, increasingly, in his conception of the cultural peculiarities of Russian history.

All people who knew Plekhanov were impressed by his impeccably Western manners but noticed at the same time something Mongolian about his features, which Plekhanov was fond of attributing to his Tartar ancestry.[140] There was a certain similarity between his attitude toward Russian history, on the one hand, and his own family history, on the other: he wanted Russia to become impeccably Western but not to conceal the oriental features of its heritage.

According to Plekhanov, medieval Russia had wavered between the West and the East. The moving of its political center from Kiev to Moscow, the Tartar yoke, and the emergence of the Muscovite autocracy marked the victory of the Asiatic influence. Muscovite Russia was a typical case of "oriental despotism." "Its social life, its administration, the psychology of its inhabitants—everything in it was alien to Europe and very closely related to China, Persia, and Ancient Egypt."[141]

The social basis of Russian despotism was the state ownership of the land, which created a total dependence of all classes on undivided and unlimited political power. The "enserfment" of the population was thereby made universal; even the landed aristocracy lost its independence and became transformed into "servitors of the state." In this way Russian autocracy developed into something completely different from Western absolutism. In the West absolute monarchy came into being together with modern private property and private law, guaranteeing the personal freedom of property owners. Despite his favorite saying "*L'état c'est moi!*" Louis XIV was not, and could not be, an oriental despot, because—unlike Russian autocrats—he could not claim that all land in France belonged to him.[142]

The reforms of Peter the Great turned Russia toward the West but did not touch the Russian peasantry; hence, it remained the mainstay of Russian "Asiaticism." Another great achievement of Westernization—the reforms of Alexander II—did not produce a radical change in this respect, because the main cell of the old Asiatic order of rural Russia—the peasant commune—was allowed to survive. As members of village communities, Russian peasants preserved intact the old Asiatic mentality, being deeply servile and hostile to modern values.[143] Therefore, in Plekhanov's view, they were in fact a reactionary force, and their alleged revolutionism, as exhibited in the 1905 revolution, amounted to primitive anarchic impulses.

This view of the Russian peasantry explains Plekhanov's resolute rejection of Lenin's ideas on the nationalization of land. Plekhanov proposed instead the municipalization of land or, if this proved impracticable, the division of land among individual peasants. Under Russian conditions, he argued, the nationalization of land would strengthen both the Asiatic mentality of the masses, who would see themselves as slaves of the state, and the despotic psychology of the rulers, who would see themselves as owners of the country. In an article entitled "On the Agrarian Problem in Russia" (1906), he summed up this position as follows: "A division of land among the peasants unquestionably would have many inconveniences from our point of view. But as compared with nationalization it would have the enormous superiority of striking the definite blow at the old order lying at the base of all the great Oriental despotisms. But nationalization of land would be an attempt to restore in our country that order which first received some serious blows in the eighteenth century and has been quite powerfully shaken by the course of economic development in the second half of the nineteenth century."[144]

This was indeed a complete reversal of the views Plekhanov had held as a populist; for populists, the survival of the peasant commune was a question of life and death. Now he was more radical and consistent in his antipopulist Westernism than the liberals from Miliukov's party; he could afford to be outspokenly antipeasant because as a Marxist he felt himself free from bourgeois scruples and as a political exile he did not need to take into account electoral considerations. For the same reasons he was able to appreciate the progressiveness of Prime Minister Stolypin's agrarian reform, which aimed at dismantling the commune, while the mainstream Russian liberals, as members of the Kadet party, treated Stolypin as merely a counterrevolutionary henchman and thought that political expediency demanded the wholesale condemnation of everything he did.[145]

During the war Plekhanov took a consistently social patriotic position (arguing, of course, that German victory would be a catastrophe for the proletarian revolution). In March 1917, after the overthrow of the tsarist regime, he returned to Russia. He was welcomed by crowds under red banners, but his hope of influencing events did not materialize. He was too isolated from the Left, and Marxist pride did not allow him to join the bourgeois liberals, so, he was active only in the tiny group of his followers, which published its own newspaper *Edinstvo*. He saw the tragedy of the revolution in the inability of Russian socialists to ally themselves firmly with the liberals. He criticized the Mensheviks, whom he treated as "half Leninists," for the inconsistency of their views on the revolution and their role in it: in accordance with their theoretical credo, they stressed its bourgeois character while rejecting alliance with the liberals as well as liberal leadership, as if a bourgeois revolution could be carried on without bourgeois parties, as if capitalism were possible without capitalists.[146] He accused Kerenskii's government of lack of energy in combating the "waves of anarchy"; even the Kadet party was, in his eyes, too soft on the radical Left, being permeated with "Zimmerwald-Kienthal spirit" and not resolute enough in defense of the fatherland. Lenin's "April Theses" summoning the Bolsheviks to embark on a socialist revolution were, according to Plekhanov, the ravings of a madman.[147] (Lenin repaid him in kind, calling him an "ex-Marxist" and, later, "the ill-famed renegade from Marxism" [L, SW, 2:33, 263].) His position was so adamant and well known that shortly after Lenin's seizure of power, Plekhanov was invited to occupy a ministerial post in a counterrevolutionary coalition. He rejected the offer, but this gesture reflected only his personal tragedy: "I have given forty years to the proletariat, and I will not shoot it down when it is going along the wrong way."[148] In the depth of his heart he was convinced that the Bolshevik revolution was a historical catastrophe and was tormented by his own responsibility for it, asking himself: "Did we not begin the propaganda of Marxism too early in backward, semi-Asiatic Russia?"[149] He died with the painful consciousness that his lifelong activity had helped produce results other than those he had anticipated; in other words, he felt he had been deceived by his idol, History.

Plekhanov's tragedy was that of a Russian Westernizer who wished for his country a "normal," "European" development that would follow a rational sequence of phases and would always be perfectly in tune with "inner," economic and cultural, growth. On the one hand, his Marxism assumed that it was necessary to develop the class antagonism between proletariat and bourgeoisie; on the other hand, it proclaimed the need to educate Russian workers in the spirit of "scientific socialism," to prepare them to accept, for a generation or two, the rule of their class enemy. The psychological impossibility of an equal commitment to each of these two aims should have been obvious. For Plekhanov, however, mass psychology was merely a subjective factor that, in the final instance, must subordinate itself to objective and rational necessity. In this manner the concept of rational necessity, which was to save him once and for all from the trap of utopianism, turned out to be his own utopia.

We should not forget that the father of Russian Marxism—despite his intellectual intolerance and cynical attitude toward moral values—sincerely desired more freedom for his country. But, unfortunately, this side of his activity proved fruitless, while his codification of Marxist philosophy—aimed at transforming it into a "*complete* world-view" (i.e., a worldview in which "*each* of its aspects is connected in the closest way *with all the others*") [150]—was a direct and lasting contribution to Leninism and Stalinism. In 1921 Lenin instructed young party members: "You *cannot* hope to become a *real*, intelligent Communist without making a study— and I mean *study*—of all of Plekhanov's philosophical writings, because nothing better has been written on Marxism anywhere in the world" (L, CW, 32:94). In accordance with this instruction, Plekhanov's works on "diamat" and "histmat" (dialectical and historical materialism) became under Stalin an obligatory component of official indoctrination. Their content was, of course, interpreted in such a way as to conceal the conflict between Plekhanov's objectivism and Leninist voluntarism. What was really important was their wonderfully authoritarian spirit—the spirit of absolute self-confidence stemming from the possession of "the correct, scientific understanding of necessity." This spirit served well the cause of those who presented themselves as "historical necessity embodied" and for whom the freedom of others was not a value but merely an obstacle in "the irresistible striving to the great historical goal." [151]

All this was, to be sure, a travesty, but it was a travesty Plekhanov somehow deserved. After all, he never acknowledged that he valued freedom for its own sake. On the contrary, even in his last article, in which he protested against the Bolshevik terror and the dispersal of the Constituent Assembly, he invoked only historical necessity. He recalled Engels's "brilliant thought" that "without ancient slavery modern socialism would have been impossible," using it as an argument for the need of Russia's "passing through the capitalist phase." [152] Thus, instead of defending liberty, he once more sternly warned of the danger of going against necessity. Unfortunately, historical necessity could justify not only the need for Russia to pass through capitalism but also, in the hands of Plekhanov's successors, through modern slavery.

3.3 Rosa Luxemburg, or Revolutionary *Amor Fati*

Rosa Luxemburg (1871–1919) is known mostly as the main figure in the radical left wing of the workers' movement in Germany: first in the SPD and later, after the collapse of the Second International, in the revolutionary Spartacus League, which formed the nucleus of the Communist party of Germany. Nonetheless, it would be utterly misleading to classify her as a German. As her biographer rightly notices: "Throughout her life in Germany she remained a self-conscious Easterner" who saw her true fatherland in the international revolutionary working class.[153] She joined the SPD because she saw it as the main party of the Second International and as "the purest incarnation of Marxian Socialism."[154] The proletarian revolution in Germany seemed to her to be imminent and of crucial importance for the fate of international socialism. She shared this conviction with all Marxists of her generation in eastern and East-Central Europe, Lenin included.

Luxemburg was born in Zamość, a small Polish-Jewish city in the Lublin province of the Congress Kingdom of Poland, the daughter of an affluent and assimilated (i.e., polonized) Jewish family. Her parents spoke Polish, and "her father especially took an interest in Polish affairs."[155] After high school in Warsaw, she studied at Zurich University, where she wrote a doctoral thesis on Polish industrial development. In the meantime the Congress Kingdom witnessed a spectacular upsurge of the workers' movement, which culminated in the so-called Łódź rebellion of 1892, a nine-day-long spontaneous mass strike that broke out on the May holiday and was bloodily suppressed by the police. These events mobilized Polish socialist intellectuals to organize the Polish Socialist party (PPS) in 1892, which combined socialism with a commitment to national liberation. Luxemburg was close to the group of Polish socialists in Zürich (including L. Jogiches, J. Marchlewski, A. Warski) who saw the PPS as a danger to the class character of the worker's movement in Poland and decided to counteract it.[156] They published the paper *Workers' Cause* and in 1894 formally constituted themselves as the Social Democracy of the Kingdom of Poland (SDKP), which in 1900 transformed into the Social Democracy of the Kingdom of Poland and Lithuania (SDKPiL). Luxemburg was the chief theorist of this party.

Unlike Plekhanov, Luxemburg showed little interest in philosophy and did not regard Marxism as a comprehensive, systematic worldview. Nevertheless, she was a gifted theorist, and her position within Marxism was markedly different from both the German orthodoxy and the dominant trends in Russia. Although she rarely wrote about freedom, almost all her interpretations of Marxism were related, directly or indirectly, to her understanding of human liberation. This applies also to her controversial views on the national question. Closer examination of these views will permit us to see one of the greatest weaknesses of the Marxist conceptions of both collective and individual freedom.

Because of the unsystematic and (usually) polemical character of Luxemburg's writings (except, of course, her economic writings, which concern us here only marginally), their inner logic and consistency is not easy to grasp. Hence, there is a need to present her views as forming a relatively coherent structure of meaning, a structure not always consistent on the level of scholarly theory but very consistent, as a rule, as a *Weltanschauung*, that is, on the axiological level. For the reasons of clarity, I have divided Luxemburg's ideas (those relevant to the problematic of freedom) into three groups: (1) general theory of historical development, (2) theory of the international workers' movement, and (3) the national question. Let us now turn to the first of these three subjects.

Freedom in History

According to Kolakowski, Luxemburg's thought was permeated by "an unshakable, doctrinaire fidelity to the concept of iron historical laws that no human agency could bend or break." [157] This view is, on the whole, quite correct, but needs additional interpretation; otherwise it might lead to grave misunderstandings, such as the standard accusation that Luxemburg's views are "fatalistic," or to mistakenly attributing to her the theory of "automatic progress."

In the usual interpretation, scientific knowledge of objective historical laws would lead the workers' movement to a guaranteed victory by helping it avoid premature "adventurist" actions, thus protecting it from defeat. Luxemburg, however, never thought about protecting herself, or her followers, from defeat; she needed only absolute certainty about the final goal. In a letter written in a German prison during the war, she wrote:

History itself always knows best what to do when conditions appear most desperate. I am not giving voice here to a comfortable fatalism. On the contrary: Human will must be spurred on to the utmost, and our job is to struggle consciously with all our might. But what I mean is: now, where everything seems so absolutely hopeless, the *success* of this conscious influence on the masses depends on the elemental, deeply hidden coiled springs of history. And I know from historical experience, as well as from personal experience in Russia, that precisely when on the surface everything seems hopeless and miserable, a complete change is getting ready, which to be sure will be all the more violent. Above all, never forget: we are tied to historical laws of development and these *never* break down, even when they do not exactly follow the plans we have laid.[158]

It is tempting to interpret this letter as an expression of the usual *nil desperandum* attitude—that is, as an attempt to derive solace from the conviction that the current defeat is not a final one. But the wider context shows that Luxemburg's attitude toward defeat was much more complex: she believed in the historical necessity of defeat and did not try to avoid it. Already in 1899, in her classic pamphlet *Social Reform or Revolution*, she dismissed the argument about the "ripeness" of the revolutionary situation, arguing that proletarian revolutions *must be* "premature" because only premature attacks of the proletariat on the bourgeois state create *political conditions* of the final victory. She made it mercilessly clear that "the proletariat is absolutely obliged to seize power 'too early,' " knowing in advance that the socialist transformation presupposes a long struggle in the course of which revolutionary workers "will be repulsed more than once." She prepared herself for all possible defeats and sacrifices and wanted the proletariat to accept this "Golgotha-road of its class liberation." [159] On the eve of the war she contemptuously rejected a friendly suggestion that she should flee Germany to avoid imprisonment: "I would not flee," she wrote, "even were the gallows threatening, for the simple reason that I consider it thoroughly necessary to accustom our party to the fact that sacrifice is part of the socialist craft and that this should be obvious." [160] And the last act of her life was active participation in the workers' uprising in Berlin in January 1919, an uprising she knew to be premature and doomed to be cruelly defeated. It has been argued that after defeat she did not flee to temporary safety for "petty-bourgeois reasons of honor." She paid for this decision with her life, but honor was a part of her philosophy of history and of her understanding of the proletariat's historical mission. In her last article, "Order Reigns in Berlin," she explained that "it was *a matter of honor* for the revolution" to repel the attack on it and to achieve thereby "the moral victory." She recalled previous defeats—from the defeat of the silk weavers of Lyons in 1831 to the crushing of the Paris Commune—and summed up her "philosophy of defeat" as follows: "The whole path of socialism, as far as revolutionary struggles are concerned, is paved with sheer defeats. And yet, this same history leads us step by step, irresistibly, to the ultimate victory! Where would we be today *without* those 'defeats' from which we have drawn historical experience, knowledge, power, idealism! Today, where we stand directly before the final battle of the proletarian class struggle, we are standing on precisely those defeats, *not a one of which* we could do without, and each of which is a part of our strength and clarity of purpose." [161]

Exactly the same arguments have been employed, and are still being used, in defense of the Polish national uprisings: all were defeated but nonetheless each embodied a moral victory and strengthened national self-consciousness, thus paving the way for national freedom. This reasoning is deeply rooted in the cultural legacy of Polish romanticism, whose greatest bard, Adam Mickiewicz, was Rosa Luxemburg's favorite poet.[162] He always rejected reasonable arguments advising caution, extolled heroic deeds irrespective of success, and argued that sacrifices were always useful, because it was necessary to throw more suffering on the scale of Providence in order to overweigh it and change God's verdict. Similar ideas were voiced by another romantic poet, Juliusz Slowacki, who was extremely popular in Poland at the turn of the century.[163] It is possible, therefore, that Luxemburg's "historiosophy of defeat" was culture bound and typically Polish. The explanatory value of such a hypothesis should not be too easily dismissed (although it is clear that it can provide only a partial explanation of the case).

Nonetheless, it should be evident that Luxemburg's unshakable belief in the necessity of the final goal had more in common with a messianic belief in the necessity of universal regeneration than with the positivistic determinism of Kautsky. Hence it is somewhat misleading to treat her conception of historical laws as a "more uncompromising" variant of the common belief of all Marxists of her time. Kolakowski rightly said that for Luxemburg, Marxism was a substitute for religion, "the universal key to the meaning of history." But he was also right in saying that Kautsky's evolutionist doctrine left "no room for eschatology or any belief in the general 'meaning' of history."[164] Plekhanov represented yet another case: unlike Kautsky, he deeply believed in the meaning of history, but Luxemburg's conception of the necessity of premature revolutions of course contradicted everything he stood for. Thus, as we can see, the notion of "historical necessity" was interpreted very differently in each case, although the awareness of these differences was not immediately obvious.

Seeing historical necessity as leading to a preordained goal aroused Luxemburg's interest in the meaning of historical process as a whole. In contrast to Plekhanov, who, owing to the Russian populists' example, was extremely suspicious of all attempts to attribute positive values to primitive agrarian communalism, Luxemburg enthusiastically endorsed the theory (very popular among the early Polish Marxists)[165] that saw the Marxist ideal as a dialectical return (on a higher level, to be sure) to the archaic model of society. Especially interesting from this point of view are her lectures on economics. She delivered these in 1914 at a party school and reconstructed them in written form in prison as *Einführung in die Nationalökonomie*, which was published posthumously in 1925. In them she devoted much attention to the significance of successive steps in the study of primitive communism and its various relics: from Maurer's discovery of the Teutonic *Mark*; to Haxthausen's description of the Russian *mir*; to the role of the Russian peasant commune in the ideologies of revolutionary populism (which she called "revolutionary Slavophilism"); to a number of studies of primitive communalism among Indians, Arabs, and Berbers; to the relevance of all these forms to a better understanding of the ancient Inca empire in Peru; and so on. She saw the scholarly literature on primitive communism and other forms of archaic property as the final refutation of the bourgeois view of the eternal character of private property and thus as a powerful foundation for Marx and Engels's work. Of course, she attributed an especially important role to Morgan in building this foundation. She readily agreed with those who called Morgan "the father of the German Social-Democratic Church" [166] and quoted with approval his words about reviving on a higher level the equality and brotherhood of ancient tribalism. Her concluding words in her discussion of Morgan's book summarize its contribution as follows: "The noble tradition of the ancient past gives a hand to the revolutionary aspirations of the future, the cognitive circle closes harmoniously and from this perspective the contemporary world of class domination and exploitation, seeing itself as the climax of history, turns out to be merely an insignificant transient stage in the great cultural march of humankind." [167]

As we know, the same view on the significance of Morgan's book was developed in Engels's *Origin of the Family*. The relative originality of Luxemburg's conception lies in her reinterpretation of Engels's triadic division of universal history in which she emphasized the role of planning in ancient society. The conception of the dialectical return to common ownership and classlessness was presented by her as a dialectical return to society based on planning; this idea strongly recalled Marx's conception of a return on a higher level to a "natural economy" (see chapter 1, section 7). She developed the following historiosophical trichotomy:

1. Primitive society: organization and planning based on collective instinct, similar to the "unconscious planning" that guides the bees in producing their honeycomb.

2. Class society: the increasing individualization and privatization of activities leading to the disappearance of "instinctive planning" in social life. The culmination of this tendency is capitalism, which brings about the complete anarchization of the economy.

3. The socialist society of the future: a return of planning but no longer "instinctive" and "unconscious." In other words, the establishment of a fully conscious, rational planning. This will be "the second exit from the animal kingdom," the passage to final humanization of humankind.[168]

It is easy to see that this trichotomy does not revolve around development through externalization and therefore has little in common with self-enriching alienation. But it strongly resembles two other historiosophical schemes, equally old and respectable: (1) the scheme of the "second salvation" through the "socialization of societies," and (2) the scheme of "paradise regained," or the conception of losing the primitive harmony ("unconscious paradise") and acquiring instead consciousness and passing through a long period of disharmonious development ("paradise lost") to the reestablishment of harmony on the conscious level. Both these schemes, which were very popular among socialists of the Romantic Epoch, had a distinctively millenarian tinge, since in both cases the third stage was a variant of the millenarian theme of collective salvation on earth.

Whatever we think about this historiosophy, its relevance for a better understanding of Luxemburg's views on necessity and freedom can hardly be denied. It shows us that the transition from capitalism to socialism was for her the radical breakthrough, the most important watershed in all of history, comparable only to "man's exit from the animal kingdom." It was to put an end to the rule of blind necessity symbolized by the uncontrollable laws of the market; political economy, as science dealing with these laws, was to disappear together with its subject. It was no wonder that Luxemburg saw this transition as a sudden leap, not as a gradual and smooth evolutionary process, and that she wanted this millennial dream to be guaranteed by iron laws of history. True, she used only conventional arguments, claiming that without objective necessity socialism could not be scientific. But it is evident that her deepest motivation was *axiological* in nature: it would have been impossible to believe in the immanent meaning of history if the final ideal was not firmly grounded in necessity. Salvation could not depend on accidents. Thus, Luxemburg needed the necessity of salvation, which was something quite different from the mechanistic necessity of evolutionary determinism. Necessity was for her a sort of secularized Providence, guaranteeing a happy solution to the drama of history.

This point of view helps us understand Luxemburg's theory about the inevitable collapse of capitalism, as developed in her main theoretical work, *The Accumulation of Capital* (1913). In it she argued that the capitalist system was doomed to collapse, not because of its inner contradictions (which, as Bernstein had shown, could be weakened), but because of its insoluble "external contradiction"—a contradiction between itself and its external markets. Capitalism, Luxemburg asserted, could not reproduce itself without a noncapitalist environment that served as a market and as an object of exploitation. At the same time, capitalism's universal expansion destroyed noncapitalist structures everywhere in the world, which meant destroying the necessary conditions of capitalism's existence.[169] In other words, the capitalist system depended on the noncapitalist environment (noncapitalist countries and noncapitalist strata still surviving under capitalism), but the destruction of this environment—the inevitable result of capitalism's inexorable expansionism—made its further continuance economically impossible.

The scientific value of this argumentation does not concern us here. But it should be stressed that Luxemburg did not see the collapse of capitalism as something that would take place automatically, independent of human will and consciousness. On the contrary, she energetically protested against such understanding of her work. She was sure that in fact capitalism would be overthrown by the revolutionary workers, who would not wait until its further existence became an economic impossibility. As a revolutionary leader she was always for heroism, never for quietism.

Freedom in the Workers' Movement

As a theorist of the workers' movement, Luxemburg developed organically, constantly enriching her conceptions but not subjecting them to a fundamental revision. Different aspects of her views developed, or simply came to the fore, in connection with concrete tasks that faced her at different stages of her life.

Her first great struggle, which made her name internationally known, was an unrelenting critical campaign against revisionism in the German movement. In one of her speeches to the Stuttgart Congress of the SPD (1898), she countered Bernstein's famous words, "The final goal, whatever it may be, is nothing to me; the movement is everything!" by saying, "The movement as an end in itself is nothing to me, the final goal is everything." By "final goal" she meant the seizure of political power and transition to socialism; the aim of "small steps forward" through legal reforms was for her not to adapt capitalism to the working class but to make the latter "strong enough to cast off its old shackles *by means of a social and political catastrophe*." In *Social Reform or Revolution*, she posed this question as "To be or not to be?" for the Social Democratic movement. If capitalism, as Bernstein claimed, was capable of adaptation and of saving itself from imminent ruin, then there was no objective necessity of socialism, and "the socialist transformation of society becomes a utopia." [170]

Luxemburg's concentration on the final end explains her dualistic approach to the problem of the relationship between scientific theory and the workers' movement. She stressed that "the entire strength of the modern labor movement rests on theoretical knowledge" but refused to use theory as an argument against "premature" revolution; she invoked theory only as a reminder about the proletariat's historical duty to struggle for a total transformation of society, not merely for more justice within the framework of capitalism. She ridiculed appeals to "the principle of justice," "that lamentable Rosinante on which all the Don Quixotes of history have galloped," and rejected the idea of identifying socialism with the "most just distribution." Social Democracy, she insisted, "does not struggle against distribution within the *framework* of capitalist production. It struggles instead for the suppression of commodity production itself." It followed therefrom that scientific theory was in full harmony with the workers' revolutionary activities but not with their reformist initiatives, which aimed merely at improving their lot within the existing system. Consequently, Luxemburg did not deny that her attitude toward trade unions was only "halfway friendly." In fact, this was a rather euphemistic expression, since she described trade unions as fostering in practice "the solidarity of capital and labor against the consuming society" and thus representing "the very opposite of class struggle." Her attitude toward consumers' cooperatives

254 "Necessitarian" Marxism

was equally critical. In a sense, both trade unionism and cooperatism were seen by her as essentially reactionary movements, aiming at "*a return to precapitalist conditions.*"[171]

The final liberation of the working class was guaranteed, in Luxemburg's view, by the objective necessity of the breakdown of capitalism. The "breakdown theory" (*Zusammenbruchstheorie*) was for her "the cornerstone of scientific socialism." At the same time, however, she forcefully rejected the conception of passively waiting for this breakdown, stressing instead (as already mentioned) the necessity and duty of seizing power "too early" and being "repulsed more than once."[172] Thus, "historical necessity," as interpreted by her, guaranteed the final victory of the working class without giving any assurances of success to the present generation of proletarian revolutionaries. This shows that her main concern was the liberation of the workers as a class, a collective subject, not as individuals, as now-living human beings. In this respect she was more faithful to Marxism in a deeper sense than were the empirically minded (and hence reformist) leaders of German Social Democracy.

A few years later Luxemburg's critique of the revisionist, or opportunist, wing of the workers' movement was supplemented by her critique of Leninism as a flawed and potentially dangerous attempt to counteract opportunism by an "ultracentralist" conception of the party.[173] In "Organizational Questions of Russian Social Democracy" (1904), she pointed out that the workers' movement must develop between two obstacles: the abandonment of its ultimate goal, on the one hand, and the loss of its mass character through becoming a sect, on the other.[174] In Russia—a country with a despotic government, ambitious intellectuals, and a young and still unorganized movement of the masses—"despotic centralism" was the easiest option. But precisely because of this, she argued, Leninism was in fact the Russian variant of "opportunism," if this word meant yielding to a "natural tendency" and choosing the easiest way. And since the easiest way was always the worst, from the point of view of the final goal of the movement, it logically followed that Lenin's organizational conception was the greatest danger for Russian Social Democracy: "Nothing will deliver a still young labor movement to the intellectual's thirst for power more easily than confining it in the straitjacket of a bureaucratic centralism which degrades the worker to a pliant tool of a 'committee.'"[175]

Luxemburg's critique of Leninism—probably the best, most farsighted critique of it at this early stage—has many aspects. One of them is the classical accusation of Blanquism. Lenin's two principles—"the blind subordination of all party organizations in the smallest detail of their activity to a central power which alone thinks, plans, and decides for all" and "the sharp separation of the organized kernel of the party from the surrounding revolutionary milieu"—were described by her as "a mechanistic transfer of the organizational principles of the Blanquistic movement of conspiratorial groups to the social democratic movement of the working masses." Lenin's answer to such censure stressed the difference between the two groups: despite their organizational form, the Bolsheviks, unlike the Blanquists, worked among the masses, mobilizing and channeling their revolutionary energy. But in Luxemburg's view—which she shared with syndicalism, otherwise foreign to her thought—this was even worse, because the masses should not remain under the tutelage of professional politicians, whether parliamentary leaders (as in Germany) or professional revolutionaries (as in Russia). Taking Lenin at his word, she wrote: "If, with Lenin, we say that opportunism is the attempt to cripple the independent revolutionary class movement of the proletariat in order to make it useful to the power-hungry bourgeois intelligentsia, then in the beginning stages of the labor movement this goal can most easily be reached not through decentralization but precisely through rigid centralism." [176]

The last part of Luxemburg's article provides an analysis of Leninism as a new form of "subjectivism," characteristic of the pre-Marxist revolutionary movement in Russia. Its brilliance and relevance for the problem of freedom merits the extensive quotation here:

In this anxious attempt of a part of Russian Social Democracy to protect the very promising and vigorously progressing Russian labor movement from error through the guardianship of an omniscient and omnipresent central committee, we see the same subjectivism which has already played more than one trick on the socialist movement in Russia. It is indeed droll to see the mad capers which the honorable human subject of history has thought it proper to carry out. The ego, knocked out and pulverized by Russian absolutism, takes its revenge in its revolutionary dreamworld by placing itself on the throne and declaring itself to be all-powerful—as a conspiratorial committee acting in the name of a nonexistent "people's will." The "object," however, proves itself to be stronger; the knout soon triumphs, proving itself to be the "legitimate" expression of the given stage of the historical process. Finally, another legitimate child of the historical process appears in the picture— the Russian labor movement, which makes a beautiful beginning at creating, for the first time in Russian history, the true will of the people. But now the "ego" of the Russian revolutionary quickly turns upside down and declares itself once again as the all-powerful director of history—this time as his majesty the central committee of the Social Democratic labor movement. However, the nimble acrobat fails to see that the true subject to whom this role of director falls is the collective ego of the working class, which insists on its right to make its own mistakes and to learn the historical dialectic by itself. Finally, we must frankly admit to ourselves that errors made by a truly revolutionary labor movement are historically infinitely more fruitful and more valuable than the infallibility of the best of all possible "central committees." [177]

The "People's Will" is, of course, an allusion to the populist party of that name, whose "subjectivism" was so strongly condemned by Plekhanov. But from Luxemburg's point of view, Plekhanov represented yet another form of subjectivism: he too wanted to keep the masses under the tutelage of theorists like himself. On the other hand, of course, he represented a doctrinaire "objectivism," trying, as he did, to impose dogmatic limitations on revolutionary activity. Luxemburg rejected this attitude in the name of the full independence of "the collective ego of the working class"—that is, in the name of the *collective subjectivism* of the revolutionary masses. The adjective *revolutionary* is extremely important in this context, because Luxemburg was very critical of such forms of mass activity as trade unionism, "purely economic" struggle, and so forth. She identified herself not with the masses as such, but with the *revolutionary* masses, aiming at "a goal that goes beyond the whole established order." [178] Spontaneity was important to her but not sufficient: it was important if opposed to external interference in the workers' movement, but insufficient and misleading if it was opposed to revolutionary will and fully developed class consciousness. Hence, she was not a theorist of "spontaneism." [179] She wanted to be a theorist of the workers' revolutionary self-emancipation.

One might say that there was nothing peculiarly original in this aspiration. And yet Luxemburg was unique in her "almost mystical belief in the revolutionary potential of the workers." [180] Original or not, her position was clearly distinguishable from all trends in Russian Marxism—"economism" and "vanguardism," "objectivism" and "subjectivism."

The next phase in Luxemburg's theorizing concerned the revolution of 1905–1906 in the Russian empire. Although she deliberately avoided distinguishing between Russian and Polish workers (treating the latter as part and parcel of the proletariat of Russia), it can safely be said that her views were strongly influenced by the situation in Poland in which "the basis of mass support from a revolutionary urban proletariat was admittedly greater than in Russia." [181] At the very end of 1905 she arrived (illegally) in Warsaw to take part in revolutionary events. Arrested at the beginning of March and released on bail after three months in jail, she went to Kuokkala in Finland (from where she could make brief visits to Petersburg); in September 1906, she returned to Germany.

Thus, her direct experience of the revolution was almost exclusively Polish. It is important to point this out because the element of spontaneity, very strong everywhere in Russia, was particularly strong in Poland—so strong, in fact, that it almost completely erased political divisions. "At the bottom, on factory floor or local cell, the often hazy distinction between PPS and SDKPiL seemed to lose all meaning in action." [182]

From the German point of view this looked like a relapse into anarchism. Luxemburg, however, resolutely rejected such an idea. In her important pamphlet *Mass Strike, Party and Trade Unions* (1906), she insisted that "the element of spontaneity plays such a prominent role in the mass strikes in Russia not because the Russian proletariat is 'unschooled' but because revolutions allow no one to play schoolmaster to them." She showed that mass strikes "originated for the most part spontaneously, in each case from specific and accidental causes, without plans or goals, and grew with elemental power into large movements."[183] And, to the dismay of the German party, she proposed the same way of struggle for Germany, arguing that one year of revolution was better training for the proletariat than thirty years of parliamentary and trade union struggles. The argument of anarchism was, in her view, totally obsolete. Mass strikes in Russia were not an alternative to political struggle (as the anarchists would have liked them to be) but an effective means of combining the economic and the political moment, the present interests of the workers with their future interests, thus making their class struggle one and indivisible.[184] From this perspective the very division between the political and the economic struggle, and the independence of each, appeared to be "nothing but an artificial, though also an historically conditioned, product of the parliamentary period."[185]

The German leaders remained skeptical. They argued that in any case the method of mass strikes could not be applied in Germany. Kautsky saw such an approach as uncontrollable, amounting in fact to the "strategy of overthrow," to which he opposed the "strategy of attrition."[186] Of course, he supported his view by invoking "Engels's Testament." Luxemburg, however, was inclined to reduce his argument to shameful cowardice. She made it plain that she opted precisely for the strategy of overthrow. Unlike Kautsky, and in accordance with her historiosophy of defeat, she believed that even a defeat of revolutionary masses should be treated not as a catastrophe but as a step forward in the realization of the great historical mission. And she correctly indicated that mass strikes were quite different from armed uprisings and struggles on barricades, and that "Engels's Testament" did not recommend "parliamentarism only."[187] Her convictions were so strong, and her language so sharp, that no compromise was possible. As a result, in 1910–11 she broke with Kautsky and became the ideological leader of the left-wing opposition to the social democratic orthodoxy in Germany.

In the Russian context she also placed herself on the extreme left. Although she criticized Bolshevik support for the armed uprising in Moscow,[188] she was much more critical of the Menshevik tactics of supporting the liberals and thus keeping the revolution within "bourgeois" limits.[189] At the London Congress of the Russian Social Democracy in 1907, she accused the Mensheviks of forgetting that Marxism meant not only "critical analysis" but also "active will."[190] Her own position was close to Trotsky's idea of a "permanent revolution."[191] But one element was unique to her: the conviction that even a crushing defeat might be admissible and acceptable as a necessary step toward final victory.[192] Because of this she could ardently advocate the proletariat's seizure of political power and still concede that it probably would not be possible to keep power for long. Needless to say, this way of thinking was utterly foreign to Lenin, for whom power, once seized, was never to be surrendered.

The socialists' vote for war credits in August 1914 was, in Luxemburg's eyes, a true "world-historical tragedy: the capitulation of Social Democracy." [193] Hence, the final stage of her intellectual evolution does not belong to the history of SPD. Like Lenin, she rejected the label "Social Democracy," embracing instead the old term *communism*. One can say even more: she also abandoned the spirit of "scientific socialism" and returned to a more uninhibited communist utopianism, as was evident even in the name "Spartacus League." (Marx and Engels saw the slaves of antiquity as incapable of creating a higher social order and, consequently, treated their uprisings as inevitably doomed to failure.)

An early document of the Spartacus League (April 1918) postulated creating a new International whose decisions would "supersede all other organizational duties." [194] It was to be a truly supranational body, effectively controlling its national sections and denouncing all nationalism as a tool of bourgeois domination. As a proposal to solve problems through purely organizational means, it was tinged by a certain authoritarianism, typical of Luxemburg's attitude toward the national question but totally absent in her attitude toward the working class. These two conflicting attitudes found full expression in her posthumously published pamphlet *The Russian Revolution*, which hailed the Bolshevik revolution as "the salvation of the honor of international socialism" but, at the same time, severely criticized the Bolsheviks for the lack of respect for democratic rights and too much respect for the rights of nations. She wrote: "While they showed a quite cool contempt for the Constituent Assembly, universal suffrage, freedom of press and assemblage, in short, for the whole apparatus of the basic democratic liberties of the people which, taken all together, constituted the 'right of self-determination' inside Russia, they treated the right of self-determination of peoples as a jewel of democratic policy for the sake of which all practical considerations of real criticism had to be stilled." [195]

The issue of Luxemburg's views on the national question is dealt with separately in this chapter. So, let us dwell now on her attitude toward democratic freedom, which a sampling of quotations characterizes better than any discussion:

To be sure, every democratic institution has its limits and shortcomings, things which it doubtless shares with all other human institutions. But the remedy which Trotsky and Lenin have found, the elimination of democracy as such, is worse than the disease it is supposed to cure; for it stops up the very living source from which alone can come the correction of all the innate shortcomings of social institutions. That source is the active, untrammeled, energetic political life of the broadest masses of the people. . . .

Public control is indispensably necessary. Otherwise the exchange of experiences remains only with the closed circle of the officials of the new regime. Corruption becomes inevitable. . . . Without general elections, without unrestricted freedom of press and assembly, without a free struggle of opinion, life dies out in every public institution, becomes a mere semblance of life, in which only the bureaucracy remains as the active element. . . .

Yes, we can go even further: such conditions must inevitably cause a brutalization of public life: attempted assassinations, shooting of hostages, etc. . . . yes, dictatorship! But this dictatorship consists in the manner of applying democracy, not in its elimination, in energetic, resolute attacks upon the well-entrenched rights and economic relationships of bourgeois society, without which a socialist transformation cannot be accomplished. But this dictatorship must be the work of the class and not of a little leading minority in the name of the class—that is, it must proceed step by step out of the active participation of the masses; it must be under their direct influence, subjected to the control of complete public activity; it must arise out of the growing political training of the mass of people."

And finally, her famous dictum: "Freedom only for the supporters of the government, only for the members of one party—however numerous they may be—is not freedom at all. Freedom is always and exclusively for the one who thinks differently."[196]

All these quotations substantiate the claim to impeccable democratic credentials. But in Luxemburg's case this impression is deeply misleading. Nobody knows what she would have done if she had to choose between communism and democracy; her "mythical, unshakable belief in the innate revolutionary character of the masses"[197] prevented her from admitting the possibility of conflict between the two. But anyway she cannot be counted among those who, like Kautsky, saw the problem clearly and condemned Lenin's policies consistently. Despite the sharpness of her critique, she admired Lenin's revolution and consciously imitated some of its characteristic features in her program for a communist revolution in Germany.[198]

This program, as set forth in Luxemburg's article "What Does the Spartacus League Want?" (December 1918) and in her speech to the Founding Congress of the Communist party of Germany (December 31, 1918), is quite detailed and deserves more careful attention than it can be paid in the present context. Its most salient characteristics are as follows:

No division into minimal and maximal programs. Socialism (or, rather, communism) is integral and must be realized at once.[199] Full freedom for "the great laboring mass," which must emancipate itself by giving its life "a conscious, free, and autonomous direction." No unprovoked terror, no killings, but "an iron fist and ruthless energy" in breaking the resistance of the bourgeois counterrevolution. The wage system and class rule must be replaced by common property and collective labor. Commodity production must give way to "planned production and distribution of the product in the common interest." The "inherited organs of the bourgeois class rule— the assemblies, parliaments, and city councils" must yield to the organs of proletarian class rule, namely, the workers' and soldiers' councils. In factories, "the highest productivity without slavedrivers, discipline without yoke, order without authority." This will be possible due to "the highest idealism in the interest of the collectivity." Of course, the protection of the revolution demands the dismantling of the old apparatus of repression, replacing the police by a workers' militia, establishment of a revolutionary tribunal, and "immediate confiscation of all foodstuffs to secure the feeding of the people"[200] (a measure modeled on Lenin's War Communism). In politics: a hierarchy of workers' councils within a unified German Socialist Republic. In economics, expropriation of capitalists (as well as large and medium-sized agricultural enterprises), confiscation of all wealth above a certain level (to be established),[201] election of enterprise councils to take over the direction of all enterprises, and "formation of socialist agricultural collectives under unified central direction in the entire nation" (to secure this the communists "must mobilize the landless proletariat and the poorer peasants against the richer peasants"). And, finally, the most important international task: to establish ties with fraternal parties in other countries in order "to secure the peace by means of international brotherhood and the revolutionary uprising of the world proletariat."[202]

All this was to be achieved not "with one blow" but by a "step-by-step" method. In every province, every village, every municipality, all the powers of the state were to be transferred "bit by bit from the bourgeoisie to the workers' and soldiers' councils." An attempt to take over governmental power could be made only "in response to the clear, unambiguous will of the great majority of the proletarian mass of all Germany."[203]

Luxemburg did not try to conceal that her program contradicted Engels's Testament; she claimed only that Engels wrote his introduction to Marx's *Class Struggles* under direct pressure from the Social Democrats in the Reichstag and did not predict the practical results of their application of his theory.[204] In her view, what was needed was the return to the revolutionary standpoint of the *Manifesto of the Communist Party*.[205] In fact, however, her program went beyond this; it was rather a return to an outright utopianism. She gave "historical necessity" a moral connotation (the necessity to save humankind from barbarism) and made it dependent on the will of revolutionary masses.[206] She endorsed the utopian features of Lenin's revolution (universal participatory democracy for the workers, as envisaged in *The State and Revolution*, and War Communism as a method of direct transition to the "final ideal"), while showing no trace of Lenin's cunning pragmatism. And it is quite clear that in many points, this program amounted to a withdrawal from her earlier criticism of the Bolshevik revolution (for instance, in conceding that parliaments and constitutional assemblies were by nature organs of bourgeois class rule).

Luxemburg was deeply convinced that the ultimate end of the revolution was human freedom. "Socialism," she explained, "is the first popular movement in world history to establish a conscious sense in the social life of man, a definite plan, and thus, free will. It is for this reason that Frederick Engels calls the final victory of the socialist proletariat a leap of humanity from the animal kingdom into the kingdom of liberty." [207] But she never explained how her revolutionary vision of universal liberation from the animal condition could be realized without destroying freedom in a more modest but, at the same time, more fundamental sense. Though not an ascetic person, she nonetheless did not understand that ordinary people, including workers, conceived freedom as living in accordance with their own individual plans, not as subordinating their lives to the pursuit of a collective utopian goal.

Having declared her readiness to lead revolutionary workers to a sure defeat, she did so and calmly awaited her fate. On the night of January 15–16, 1919, she was brutally murdered by *Freikorps* troops. On the eve of this tragedy there appeared an article in *Die Rote Fahne* (January 14) in which she assured her followers that "this 'defeat' is the seed of the future triumph." [208] She was great, no doubt, but being great does not always mean being right.

National Freedom

Now let us pass to Luxemburg's views on the national question. The arguments she used in the controversy over nationalism were drawn from the arsenal of the most narrow economic determinism. In her doctoral thesis *Die industrielle Entwicklung Polens* (Leipzig, 1898) she tried to prove that the independence of Poland was a reactionary utopia because Polish territory had allegedly become "economically incorporated into the Russian state." [209] In her programmatic article "Social Patriotism in Poland," she described Poland's economic integration with Russia in terms of truly mechanistic determinism: "It is an entirely objective historical process, independent of anybody's will, being the result of conditions of production and commercial exchange in Poland." [210]

In fact, however, Luxemburg's rejection of Polish independence was not a logical consequence of her commitment to economic determinism but rather the reverse: her one-sided approach to the national question inclined her toward a narrowly economic and objectivist interpretation of Marxism. [211] Characteristically, she did not even notice that her thesis was, in fact, self-contradictory. On the one hand, she took pains to present the bourgeoisie of the Congress Kingdom as a class deliberately created by the

Russian government in order to bind Poland economically to Russia.[212] On the other hand, she presented the same government as merely the obedient, passive instrument of objective economic forces.

However, Luxemburg's thesis should not be treated as the only justification of her views on the Polish question. Her arguments, in their entirety, were more prolific and could be summarized as follows.

First, she saw Polish lands as "organically incorporated" not only with Russia, but with Austria and Germany as well. This was the natural result of capitalist development, because capitalism, in her interpretation, could further the development of nationalism only in the case of a conflict between entirely different economic formations, which was not the case with Poland and its partitioning powers.

Second, to strive for the independence of Poland would be reactionary and doomed to failure even if Polish lands were not entirely involved in the economic life of the three alien states, because of the inevitable centralizing tendency of politico-economic progress. Luxemburg found support for this thesis in Marx and Engels's negative attitude toward the nationalist aspirations of the small "non-historical" Slavic nations. She was keenly aware, of course, that Marx and Engels saw Poland as a "historical" nation, having the "right to separate and independent existence" (see chapter 2, section 4), but she dismissed this view as obsolete, to say the least. National separatism, she thought, could be justified only in the precapitalist stage of development. This view enabled her to sympathize with nationalist movements in the Turkish empire without recognizing the political ambitions of the Poles.

Third, the idea of an independent Poland, although loudly proclaimed by the social-patriotic members of the Polish intelligentsia, had no support among the classes that provided the groundwork of Polish society. In Luxemburg's view it was a "feudal ideal," an ideal of a rebellious gentry that was never accepted by the multinational bourgeoisie of the Congress Kingdom. The bourgeoisie in Poland was an alien class, having no roots in Polish history, enjoying no prestige in Polish society; in fact, it was an imported class, artificially protected by the tsarist government and acting as "fetters binding Poland to Russia." [213] Under the influence of capitalist development, all propertied classes in Poland became reconciled to the lack of national independence; even the petty bourgeoisie, represented by the National Democracy party, abandoned this aim and, in this sense, ceased to be nationalist.[214] As for the modern industrial proletariat of Poland, it originated as a product of capitalist industrialization and could not be expected to embrace the libertarian aspirations of the feudal epoch.

Fourth, Luxemburg regarded the aims of the Polish national liberation movement as incompatible with pan-European revolutionary strategy. Marx and Engels had formulated their views on the Polish question at a time when the partition of Poland was the cornerstone of the reactionary Holy Alliance. Now, however, the international situation had radically changed.

Finally, she urged the socialist parties of subjugated countries—as a matter of principle, regardless of the international situation—to reject political nationalism in order to preserve the purity of the proletarian class consciousness. Otherwise socialism would lose its class identity and become a tool of nationalism, as had happened in the case of the PPS. The fear of such a development seems to have been decisive and accounts for Luxemburg's intransigence in combating all separatist tendencies, an attitude that sometimes blinded her to political and social realities. She condemned the Jewish Bund no less strongly than the PPS; Zionism was to her a comical phenomenon that deserved attention only as the most absurd consequence of a false principle.[215]

To hold such views it was necessary to assume that class consciousness could exist separately from and untainted by national consciousness and that the working class could fulfill its historical mission without becoming a "national class." Marx and Engels were very far from cherishing such illusions.[216]

Luxemburg's practice in combating national separatism was as extreme as her theory. She stubbornly clung to the view that as regards international congresses, Poles should be represented according to their formal citizenship, as part of the Russian, Prussian, and Austrian delegations (in Plekhanov's opinion the adoption of this principle would have constituted a new partition of Poland). She consistently opposed any all-Polish political programs and viewed with suspicion all collaboration between socialists from the three regions of partitioned Poland. Lenin rightly observed that she became unduly obsessed with her fight against the PPS, which made her unable "to see things from a viewpoint any deeper and broader than that of the Cracow anthill" (L, CW, 20:426).

It has been suggested from time to time that the psychological roots of Luxemburg's obsession lie in her Jewishness. In one sense this is obviously true, but in another it is obviously false.

It is obviously true that Luxemburg's "uncompromising rejection of nationalism can be understood only in the light of Jewish emancipation."[217] She represented a paradigmatic case of the so-called Red assimilation—that is, the act of liberating oneself from Jewishness through rejecting all national allegiances and embracing instead a cause of universal human liberation. She advocated assimilation and was strangely insensitive toward anti-Semitism, dismissing it as a necessary but transient by-product of capitalist development. She even demanded conscious severance of all special ties with the Jewish masses. In a letter Luxemburg rebuked Mathilde Wurm for being concerned with her "special Jewish sorrows," declaring that: "I feel just as sorry for the wretched Indian victims in Putamayo, the Negroes in Africa. . . . The 'lofty silence of the eternal' in which so many cries have echoed away unheard resounds so strongly within me that I cannot find a special corner in my heart for the ghetto. I feel at home in the entire world wherever there are clouds and birds and human tears." [218]

What is obviously false is the idea that Luxemburg's hostility toward Polish nationalism stemmed from her feeling that she was a hostile alien among the Poles. This was definitely not the case. Luxemburg's letters to Leon Jogiches—which provide the most intimate and authentic evidence of her feelings—testify that she considered herself to be a Pole and felt ill at ease among Germans; she loved Polish culture, the Polish language, and even the Polish landscape. The Polishness of Upper Silesia, where she was sent by the German Social Democrats to foment unrest among Polish workers, induced in her a truly euphoric mood. [219]

Yet the objective political purpose of her agitation was clear enough. She was sent to Upper Silesia by the secretary of the SPD, Ignaz Auer, whose attitude toward Silesian Poles was brutally outspoken: "We couldn't do the Polish workers a greater service than to Germanize them, only one mustn't say so." Luxemburg did not agree with this, but in practical terms her "opposition to the PPS and its policy of self-determination made her the most efficient ally of the SPD's policy of organizational integration for minorities in Germany." [220] In other words, her cultural Polishness did not prevent her from serving as an efficient instrument of the policy of Germanization. [221]

The most dangerous form of nationalism was, in Luxemburg's view, political nationalism—that is, the striving for national independence. She tried to sharply distinguish it from cultural nationalism, giving the latter a conditional and qualified support. Thus, in her foreword to the anthology *The Polish Question and the Socialist Movement* (Cracow, 1905) she wrote: "The cause of nationalism in Poland is not alien to the working class—nor can it be. The working class cannot be indifferent to the most intolerably barbaric oppression, directed as it is against the spiritual culture of society. To the credit of mankind, history has universally established that even the most inhumane *material* oppression is not able to provoke such a wrathful, fanatical rebellion and rage as the suppression of spiritual life in general, that is as religious or national oppression." [222]

There is no reason to question the sincerity of these words. It should be noted, however, that although Luxemburg felt national oppression to be "intolerably barbaric," it became "a drop in the ocean" when compared with the immensity of the injustice suffered by wage laborers in a capitalist society.

Like Engels, but with a diametrically opposite intention, Luxemburg distinguished between the terms *nation* (political) and *nationality* (cultural) (see chapter 2, section 4). In a series of articles (in Polish) entitled "The National Question and Autonomy" (1908–9), she denied the very existence of "the 'nation' as a homogeneous social and political entity."[223] Such a homogeneous whole could not exist in a class society, and therefore to speak of national self-determination amounted to a repetition of "metaphysical phrases." Nations have no will of their own, and if their will is identified with the will of the mechanical majority, such a principle cannot be accepted by revolutionaries who, as a rule, are in a minority.[224] Nations, she argued, were created as the result of economic processes and class struggles, not by democratic voting. Bowing to the principle of national self-determination was utterly un-Marxist, as Marx and Engels's negative attitude toward the national aspirations of the smaller Slavic nations clearly demonstrated. They were wrong in forecasting the extinction of the Czechs but right in disregarding abstract rights and other "metaphysical formulas."

In theory Luxemburg's approach to the "defence of *nationality* as a certain form of spiritual culture" was completely different. Unlike her conception of nation as a "homogeneous socio-political entity," she saw nationality not as a fiction but as a distinct cultural reality that was manifested in language, art, and literature. Acknowledging nationalities' right to existence does not involve recognizing the territorial delimitations and political sovereignty of each one. In this respect her position was similar to that of the leading Austro-Marxists, Karl Renner and Otto Bauer, who wanted to depoliticize the nationalities question by giving each nationality the right to extraterritorial cultural autonomy.[225] But this similarity in theoretical approach was coupled with different practical conclusions. Unlike the Austro-Marxists, Luxemburg did not intend to harness her Polish party to the defense of Polish schools and cultural institutions; in her view this would only distract attention from the main goal of international socialism. Under capitalism, she reasoned, national oppression could never be fully abolished, but under socialism there would be no need for a special protection of national cultures.

However, the hard realities of Polish life in the Russian empire unceasingly demonstrated that a solution of the national question could not wait for the final victory of socialism and that in solving it the principle of cultural autonomy could not be entirely separated from that of territorial autonomy. Because of this, after long hesitation, Luxemburg decided to accept the postulate of territorial autonomy for the lands of the Congress Kingdom, confessing privately that it was an unwilling concession on her part.[226] And she did her best to ensure that the proposed autonomy would serve only cultural purposes, without yielding to the obsolete principle of political decentralization.[227]

Characteristically, she disagreed with her own party in rejecting a similar

autonomy for Lithuania. Her main argument in favor of the Congress Kingdom was the fact that the latter possessed "its own bourgeois development,
urban life, intelligentsia, its own literary and scholarly life." [228] However,
historical Lithuania, a mixture of different nationalities culturally dominated by a Polish minority, lacked these prerequisites for autonomy. Even
harsher was Luxemburg's view of the Ukraine, which she saw as a country "without any historical tradition and without any national culture"
("except for the reactionary-romantic poems of Shevchenko"). She concluded from this that Ukrainian nationalism was "a mere whim, a folly of
a few dozen petty-bourgeois intellectuals." [229] Clearly, in this respect she
remained influenced by Marx and Engels's distinction between "historical nations" and "history-less peoples." During the war she treated small
nations as "merely pawns in the imperialist game" and condemned the
Wilsonian principle of "self-determination of all countries" as a hypocritical imperialist slogan. [230] And in her pamphlet on the Russian Revolution
she accused Lenin of bringing about the disintegration of Russia. [231]

It is obvious that Luxemburg's intransigent condemnation of all forms of
"social patriotism" did not help the cause of socialism in Poland. Neither
did it help the cause of socialism in Russia, since it created, paradoxically,
an insurmountable obstacle to the integration of the SDKPiL with Russian
Social Democracy. Her refusal to cooperate with the PPS Left because the
latter did not oppose Polish independence as basically wrong (although it
agreed, at the same time, to completely subordinate national to class tasks
in the workers' movement) [232] and her categorical demand that the Russian
Democrats should drop the slogan of national self-determination (although
Lenin made it perfectly clear that he would only welcome it if the Poles
decided not to secede from Russia) cannot be explained on purely rational grounds. [233] Small wonder that George Lichtheim, who did so much to
prove Marxism's compatibility with legitimate national aspirations, could
find no other word for defining her position than "insanity." In a review of
her biography he wrote:

It was the central issue of Rosa Luxemburg's political life. . . . It was the one issue
on which she stood ready to break with her closest associates and to fly in the
face of every authority, including that of Marx. Poland was dead! It could never be
revived! Talk of a Polish nation, of an independent Poland, was not only political
and economic lunacy; it was a distraction from the class struggle, a betrayal of
Socialism! . . . One thing only counted: fidelity to proletarian internationalism as
she understood it (and as Marx, poor man, had plainly not understood it). On this
point, and on this alone, she was intractable. . . . One of the strangest aberrations
ever to possess a major political intellect. [234]

J. P. Nettl, Luxemburg's biographer, sees it differently, in accordance
with Luxemburg's own views. For him it was a matter of transposing her
loyalties from nation to class. [235] His book ends with the words: "Rosa Lux-

emburg stands at the apex of the attempt to make operational the Marxist concept of class as the primary social referent, and to break once for all the old alternative stranglehold of nation. In this respect her contribution is second to none."[236]

I endorse this diagnosis, although I do not share the underlying regret about the failure of the attempted transposition of loyalties. It is fair to say that Luxemburg's intransigence on the national question stemmed from her desperate struggle for the souls of the Polish workers. She was proud of them, she could not believe that nationalism might be endemic to them, so she fought like a lioness to defend the purity of their class consciousness against the external influence of nationalist intellectuals. But she was deeply wrong in thinking that the development of class consciousness was bound to separate workers from their national community. On the contrary, the awakening of class consciousness narrowly conceived was, as a rule, a step toward a higher level of self-consciousness, which in turn led Polish workers to a deeper awareness of their national identity. This was correctly pointed out by Kazimierz Kelles-Krauz, the main Marxist theorist of the PPS and the best critic of Luxemburg's views on the national question. He was magnanimous enough to credit her party with positive, although unintended, contributions to the Polish national cause. By awakening the feeling of human dignity among the Polish workers, he argued, the SDKPiL also aroused their feeling of national dignity and thus, willy-nilly, served as a catalyst in making them into nationally conscious Poles.[237]

A similar observation has been made by Stanislaw Brzozowski, who wrote:

People have been at pains to show that the workers' movement can be, and is, a national movement. I do not know that their efforts were necessary. Poland is the field of action of the motive forces in Polish life and the resources which sustain it. To argue that the workers' movement can be independent of the nation's life and destiny is to say that it does not matter what range of forces and means of action it has at its disposal. As long as the Polish community is deprived of its rights, so long will our working class be an amorphous body of degraded paupers—not occupying the fourth rank in the social order, but the fifth, sixth, or even lower. What is the issue here? To renounce one's national existence is to give up hope of influencing reality; it means destroying one's own soul, for the soul lives and acts only through the nation. The so-called question of nationality does not arise, for it is the same as to ask whether we wish to lose our human dignity.[238]

Admittedly, Brzozowski's statement that the human soul "lives and acts only through the nation" went too far. It was not always so, not every-where, and not exclusively. But he was right in pointing out that national identity, once formed, is not something external to us, but a part of our innermost being.

Thus, the problem of national freedom should not be separated from the problem of general human freedom, or even individual freedom. Freedom is always intimately connected with identity; it assumes self-assertion and self-expression, that we act in accordance with what we perceive to be truly ours, what constitutes our identity.[239] If I feel myself to be a Pole, Polishness becomes a part of my identity, my area of identification. And the right to one's identity is universal and fundamental. Without identity, there is no freedom and no dignity. An individual deprived of his or her identity ceases to be a subject, an agent, becoming instead an atom, an empty shell. Luxemburg was quite close to understanding this when she wrote in 1905 that national oppression amounts to "the most intolerably barbaric" *spiritual* oppression.[240] But she failed to draw from this the necessary conclusions. Instead, she stubbornly supported the most unrealistic idea in the Marxist conception of human liberation: the idea of liberating people as species beings only—that is, as representatives of universal human nature, not as concrete individuals, shaped by different group affiliations and historical traditions (see chapter 1, section 1).[241] She was too attached to Marx's view of the proletariat as a class stripped from everything except its bare humanity and therefore striving only for universal human values (M, *SW*, 72–73). Unlike Marx and Engels, she interpreted this view too literally and fell victim to this grave error. Her biographer seems to exaggerate when he states that even the notion of "a special cultural home" was entirely alien to her.[242] If this were so, she would not have insisted that she must speak only Polish with her lover.[243] She had to work very hard to identify herself only with the "world brotherhood of workers." She succeeded in this heroic endeavor and became the closest approximation to this ideal. This was her area of identity, the foundation of her dignity, her conscious self-determination, and therefore the realization of her freedom. But she had no reason to expect that Polish workers, members of a divided and oppressed nation, would follow her example. Her stubborn struggle for keeping their class consciousness free from nationalist contamination was based on false assumptions. The Nemesis of history turned this struggle into an effort to impose dogmatic limitations on the freedom of the workers' movement in her native country.

4

Leninism: From "Scientific Socialism" to Totalitarian Communism

4.1 Lenin's Tragedy of Will and Fate

Writing about Lenin is not an easy task. In recent decades American historians, willing to overcome cold war attitudes toward communism, have made great efforts to present the founder of the Soviet State as a basically "acceptable" political figure, fully explicable in terms of Russia's historical development and bearing no responsibility for the unnecessary horrors of Stalinism.[1] The usefulness of the so-called totalitarian model as a heuristic device for explaining Soviet history was either called into question or restricted to the Stalinist epoch.[2] In both cases the Soviet Union under Lenin was not conceived as a totalitarian state, and Leninism as an ideology was not regarded as leading inevitably to a form of totalitarianism. Seeing Lenin as a totalitarian revolutionary was from this point of view a testimony of ideological bias and theoretical poverty. In the eyes of many progressively minded intellectuals, sharp criticism of pre-Stalin communism became even *morally* dubious, being seen as an expression of self-confident arrogance and philistine blindness.

One of the best expressions of this standpoint is, in my view, the short essay by Alasdair MacIntyre on "How not to Write About Lenin." The author does not indulge in preaching universal empathy; on the contrary, he soberly reminds us that for a truly historical approach "a certain lack of sympathy may indeed be necessary."[3] He stresses, however, that "it must be a lack of sympathy of the right kind" and that in writings about Lenin at least two prerequisites should be observed:

The first is a sense of scale. One dare not approach greatness of a certain dimension (and what holds of Lenin would hold equally of Robespierre or of Napoleon) without a sense of one's own limitations. A Lilliputian who sets out to write Gulliver's biography had best take care. Above all he dare not be patronizing. . . .

The second prerequisite is a sense of tragedy which will enable the historian to feel both the greatness and the failure of the October Revolution. Those for whom the whole project of the revolutionary liberation of mankind from exploitation and alienation is an absurd fantasy disqualify themselves from writing about Communism in the same way that those who find the notion of the supernatural redemption of the world from sin an outmoded superstition disqualify themselves from writing ecclesiastical history.[4]

In principle, I wholeheartedly endorse this view. I think, however, that the acknowledgment of Lenin's peculiar greatness should not paralyze our judgment on his sinister role in history. In particular I do not see why it should lead to the conclusion that "Stalinism was not in any sense the legitimate successor even of the negative sides of Lenin's work." Neither do I see why Lenin's "purity of heart," in the sense of "an overriding simplicity and certainty of revolutionary purpose," should be invoked as an argument against Lenin's opponents and critics.[5] On the contrary, such a purity of heart is, in my view, an unmistakably totalitarian feature. Nor do I not think that to call Lenin a totalitarian revolutionary amounts to adopting a patronizing attitude toward him or to denying him a certain greatness. The term *totalitarianism* should not be associated *only* with crimes. It might also be associated with noble causes, such as the revolutionary liberation of humankind.

Now, as to the sense of tragedy: I fully share the view that the history of the communist movement, as a project of human liberation, can and should be described as tragic; that communism was the most powerful modern incarnation of ancient millenarian hopes; and that the destruction of such hopes, no matter how unreasonable and dangerous in their practical application, should not be an occasion for facile celebration. But it does not follow from this that all individual representatives of this movement, even all its important theorists and leaders, were equally tragic: some of them were more tragic than others, and many were not tragic at all. Thus, for instance, Luxemburg was a tragic heroine par excellence, and Plekhanov can also be described as a tragic figure, but one can hardly talk of the tragedy of Engels.

Lenin's case is, from this point of view, a rather complicated one. On the one hand, he was too single-minded and single-hearted to experience genuine conflicts of values and thus to see his choices as tragic. On the other hand, his actions can certainly be regarded as tragic in an objective sense—that is, as an expression of heroic hubris facing a fateful power, intransigent in its aims but forced to acknowledge its defeat by the gods. Let us elaborate on these two aspects of a single phenomenon.

In his memoirs on Lenin, Trotsky pointed out the most striking feature of this great "machinist of the revolution." According to him, Lenin, in all his life and actions, "not only in politics but also in his theoretical works, in his philosophical and linguistic studies," was "irrevocably controlled by one and the same idea, the goal. He was probably the most extreme utilitarian whom the laboratory of history has produced."[6]

This all-consuming and unhesitating devotion to the goal, coupled with an extremely strong will for power (not contaminated, however, by a purely personal vanity),[7] struck all people who knew Lenin. Many of them saw it as almost superhuman and, therefore, somewhat inhuman; hence, they reacted to this by attempts to humanize Lenin by attributing to him softer (although duly suppressed) feelings. Such a tendency is clearly visible in Gorky's *Days with Lenin*. Nonetheless, this small book also provides important arguments to the contrary. Take, for instance, the following account of Lenin's words about his love for Beethoven: "I know nothing which is greater than the Appassionata; I would like to listen to it every day. . . . But I can't listen to music too often. It affects your nerves, makes you want to say stupid, nice things, and stroke the heads of people who could create such beauty while living in this vile hell. And now you musn't stroke anyone's head—you might get your hand bitten off. You have to hit them on the head, without any mercy, although our ideal is not to use force against any one. H'm, h'm, our duty is infernally hard!"[8]

Gorky's intention was obviously to convey the feeling that Lenin was a tragic figure, willing to subordinate everything to ultimate victory but aware of its price and regretting the yawning discrepancy between his goal and the means of struggle. The real Lenin, however, was remarkably free from such inner conflicts. He repeatedly stressed that a true revolutionary should be merciless, ruthless, guided by iron will, and free from all sorts of stupid sentimentality; he had the deepest contempt for the Hamlet-like hesitations of revolutionary intellectuals, and as we shall see, there can be no doubt that he himself fully succeeded in hardening his will and getting rid of moral scruples in revolutionary action. Using Turgenev's typology one may say that he had nothing in common with the tragic consciousness of a Hamlet whose "native hue of resolution is sicklied o'er with the pale cast of thought." He was much closer to Turgenev's Don Quixote: a narrow-minded fanatic, capable of resolute, even reckless action but seeing only "one point on the horizon," a point the nature of which is often not at all as it seemed to him.[9]

Men of action, however, can be tragic in an objective sense—that is, not experiencing the paralyzing conflict of values characteristic of tragic consciousness. We may call this the tragedy of will and fate, or the tragedy of unintended results. Thus, Turgenev's Don Quixote pursued ends that were utopian and achieved results different from those for which he had been striving. This ironic effect can be explained in terms of the Hegelian conception of "the cunning of the Reason of History" or, more pessimistically, as an illustration of the basic irrationality of historical processes in which powerful accidents always thwart conscious human endeavors. In both cases the heroic will faces inevitable humiliation and defeat.

In this sense Lenin was certainly a tragic figure. One can only wonder whether the concept of a tragedy of unintended results, or a tragic defeat, is not too broad. Would it not apply to *all* historical agents? In particular, would it not apply to Mussolini or Hitler, whose defeat was, after all, more abrupt and spectacular than Lenin's?

These rhetorical questions enable us to grasp the difference. Not all defeats, or other unintended results, deserve to be regarded as tragic. First, any concept of historical tragedy presupposes a value judgment. Lenin's failure withstands this test, since a failure of the communist utopia, the inheritor of humanity's old millenarian dreams, *cannot* be reduced to its criminal consequences or dismissed as merely an absurd fantasy. Second, Lenin's defeat, unlike Hitler's, was not a violent defeat caused by external military forces. He faced his defeat when he was in power as the undisputed leader of an outwardly victorious party and he became aware of it earlier and more bitterly than anybody else. It was instead a defeat by impersonal, fateful powers, and precisely because of this it bore some resemblance to classic tragedy.

In fact, this tragedy of will and fate also marked earlier phases of Lenin's revolutionary career. To present it in full would necessitate telling the whole complex story of Lenin's lifetime of struggle, which does not fall within the scope of this book. However, we must bring into relief its main ideological pattern, which grew out of the tensions between the deterministic assumptions of classical Marxism and the passionate voluntarism of a powerful revolutionary leader.

In his early works Lenin ridiculed the populist belief in "subjective factors," stressing the need for a purely objective analysis of social development and unambiguously rejecting "the absurd tale about free will." Following Plekhanov, he refused to see socialism in terms of an ethical option, quoting Engels's definition of freedom as "the appreciation of necessity," and solemnly pledged to subordinate revolutionary activities to the objective logic of social evolution (L, CW, 1:159, 420–21). This, of course, involved acceptance of the alleged inevitability of Russia's passing through capitalist phases of development, a conclusion that Lenin, like all Russian

Marxists of that time, fully endorsed. He clung to it even in the midst of the revolutionary events of 1905. Marxists, he wrote in *Two Tactics of Social Democracy in the Democratic Revolution*, "are absolutely convinced of the bourgeois character of the Russian revolution. What does that mean? It means that the democratic reforms in the political system, and the social and economic reforms that have become a necessity for Russia, do not in themselves imply the undermining of capitalism, the undermining of bourgeois rule; on the contrary, they will, for the first time, make it possible for the bourgeoisie to rule as a class. The Socialist Revolutionaries cannot grasp this idea, for they do not know the ABC of the laws of development of commodity and capitalist production" (L, *A*, 122–23).

And yet in April 1917, the same Lenin amazed his comrades and followers by proclaiming in "The Dual Power" the urgency of a struggle for full freedom—that is, for the revolutionary overthrow of the bourgeois Provisional Government and its replacement by "the undivided power of the Soviets of Workers', Agricultural Laborers', Peasants', and Soldiers' Deputies" (ibid., 303). A few months later, having achieved this objective and firmly installed his party in power, he unhesitatingly embarked on the realization of a direct transition to socialism—the favorite idea of Russian populists. He qualified this program by stressing that it could not be carried out too quickly: "For the success of socialism, in Russia," he said in 1918, "a certain period of time of *at least a few months is necessary*."[10] Trotsky, who quoted these words after the painful retreat represented by the New Economic Policy (NEP), anticipated the stupefaction of his readers. He commented:

Is it not a mistake? Are not years or decades meant? But no, it is no mistake. One could probably find a number of other statements of Lenin of the same type. I remember very well that in the first period, at the sessions of the Council of People's Commissars of Smolny, Ilyich repeatedly said that within a half-year socialism would rule and we would be the greatest state in the world. . . . He *believed in what he said*. And this imaginative half-year's respite for the development of socialism just as much represents a function of Lenin's spirit as his realistic hold of every task of today. The deep and firm conviction of the strong possibilities of human development, for which one can and must pay any price whatsoever in sacrifices and suffering, was always the mainspring of Lenin's mental structure.[11]

As we shall see, this was really so; Trotsky did not exaggerate at all. He did not, however, try to explain the relationship between this practical attitude and Lenin's obvious desire to remain true to the orthodox (i.e., necessitarian) account of Marxist theory.

At first glance it might seem that Lenin's practice glaringly contradicted his theories and that he was strangely unaware of this contradiction. It might also seem that Lenin often contradicted himself in theoretical statements, sometimes falling into strange inconsistencies. Thus, for instance, at the beginning of 1921 in "Once Again on the Trade Unions," he formulated the following view on the relationship between politics and economics: "Politics is a concentrated expression of economics. . . . Politics must take precedence over economics. To argue otherwise is to forget the ABC of Marxism" (L, CW, 32:83).[12]

How does this relate to the Marxist theory of economic base and political superstructure? Had Lenin simply forgotten the classical Marxist view on the centrality of economics to all social processes? Had he forgotten his own words (quoted above) on "the ABC of the laws of development of commodity and capitalist production" and on the need of respecting these laws in political action? How could he have arrived at such a strange reversal of the main thesis of historical materialism?

On close examination it turns out that this contradiction was in fact much less blatant than it seems. Lenin's view on the priority of politics over economics was not meant to be an alternative theory of historical development. The context makes it clear that this statement applied only to the theory of the workers' movement. In other words, it argued the priority of political forms of struggle over narrowly economic ones, or put another way, of the leading role of the party in relation to the trade unions. Of course, this did have an important bearing on the general theory, but it was not a direct negation of the centrality of the economic factor in history, being leveled against syndicalism and not aiming to question Marxist orthodoxy.

Second, we must realize that Lenin's interpretation of orthodox Marxism was from the very beginning remarkably free from the technological determinism so typical of the Second International. He criticized populist ethicism in the name of the "principle of causality," but by this he meant the laws of class struggle, not the quasi-automatic development of productive forces.[13] In his early polemic against Petr Struve, he rejected not only populist subjectivism but also the objectivism that in those years seemed to be an inalienable part of Marxism.[14] In his analyses of the development of capitalism in Russia, he claimed that the fully fledged capitalist formation was not a problem of Russia's future but rather something already "definitely and irrevocably established" (ibid., 1:495). He could claim this because he thought of capitalist development in rather different terms than other Russian Marxists, who stressed the economic and political backwardness of their country. For Lenin, the decisive criterion of capitalist development was not the level of productivity, still less a properly capitalist constitutional superstructure, but the prevailing class relationship, the nature of fundamental class antagonism. In other words, he defined capitalism in terms of class struggle and thus made its fate depend on the intensity of this struggle, on the will and consciousness of the working class under the able political leadership of its vanguard. This led him to almost imperceptibly put increasing emphasis on subjective factors—above all; the role of a well-organized, ideologically cohesive vanguard party.

This process of shifting the emphasis from economics to politics was neither simple nor unidirectional. It was conditioned not only by Lenin's thinking on social processes in terms of struggle, but also (as we shall see) by his deep pessimism about the economic forms of class struggle as practiced by the spontaneously developing workers' movement. In this context there is no need to follow all the twists in Lenin's revolutionary tactics and strategy. It suffices to say that these resulted from a constant tension between classical Marxist theory, which exerted a moderating influence, and revolutionary voluntarism, which was intensified by Lenin's "fanatical fear" that the revolution might be "missed." [15]

The final outcome of these tensions is known. At the decisive moment Lenin abandoned theoretical scruples and staked everything on the immediate victory of a socialist revolution. Although in 1914 he still thought that his generation might "not live to see the decisive battles of this coming revolution," by 1917 he had come to regard it as his most urgent immediate task. He consciously chose to take bold risks and to be guided by Danton's motto: *"de l'audace, de l'audace, encore de l'audace"* (L, A, 292, 414). To stress his intransigent radicalism and his unwavering commitment to the Marxist utopia, he changed the name of his party, rejecting the term *social democracy* as inadequate and compromised and unfurling instead the banner of communism (L, SW, 2:59–62). To begin with, he was almost completely isolated in his revolutionary resolve. In Plekhanov's eyes it was sheer madness; other Marxists, including the Bolsheviks, saw it as running counter to all tenets of "scientific socialism" and as leading to a victory of reaction. His only convinced supporter was Trotsky, hitherto a non-Bolshevik, who was armed with his theory of permanent revolution. Nevertheless, Lenin forced his party to act and appeared to have achieved his aim. His faithful follower, Trotsky, had no doubts that this was the rare case in which a single man proved capable of changing the course of history. He freely admitted that his own role was a secondary one. In 1933 (in exile) he put it as follows:

Had I not been present in 1917 in Petersburg, the October Revolution would still have taken place—*on the condition that Lenin was present and in command.* If neither Lenin nor I had been present in Petersburg, there would have been no October Revolution: the leadership of the Bolshevik party would have prevented it from occurring—of this I have not the slightest doubt! If Lenin had not been in Petersburg, I doubt whether I could have managed to overcome the resistance of the Bolshevik leaders. . . . But I repeat, granted the presence of Lenin the October Revolution would have been victorious anyway. The same could by and large be said about the Civil War.[16]

In the last year of his life, in the short article "Our Revolution" (January 1923), Lenin made an attempt to defend himself against the accusation of a voluntaristic departure from Marxism. He put forward two objective arguments that were reminiscent of Trotsky's theory of "uneven and combined development."[17] First, he presented the argument about the interconnectedness of all national economies in the epoch of imperialism and about the Russian Revolution as an outcome of the first imperialist war. According to this argument, the Russian economy, despite its backwardness, was part and parcel of world capitalism, which as a whole was already fully ripe for a socialist revolution. Second, he put forth the argument about the social and cultural peculiarities of national developments in peripheral countries. Such peculiarities, Lenin argued, were fully explicable within the general Marxist framework: "The idea that the development of world history as a whole follows general laws" does not preclude, but rather presumes that "certain periods of development may display peculiarities in either the form or the sequence of this development." Russia, for instance, "stands on the borderline between the civilized countries and the countries which this war has for the first time definitely brought into the orbit of civilization— all the Oriental, non-European countries" and therefore "she could and was, indeed, bound to reveal certain distinguishing features" (L, A, 704).

Both these arguments anticipate many recent theories about the peculiarities of economic, social, and cultural development in the backward, or unevenly developed, peripheral and semiperipheral countries of the interdependent world, countries unable successfully to modernize themselves in accordance with the classical capitalist model and therefore doomed to choose a noncapitalist road. This line of thought, supported on the theoretical level by Lenin's analyses of imperialism, greatly differs, of course, from Marx's classical thesis that underdeveloped countries must pass through the same phases of economic development that developed countries have already completed.[18]

Unlike Plekhanov, Lenin did not regard this thesis as the cornerstone of the entire edifice of Marxism. By finding the essence of Marxism in class analysis rather than in the theory of a necessary sequence of phases in socioeconomic evolution, he avoided the idea that socialist revolution in an underdeveloped country was doomed to failure through defeat or by bringing about unintended results. He hated to be reminded of the tragedy of premature revolution, as defined by Engels; he felt, not without reason, that it "smacks of doctrinaire thinking" and "sounds like desperation" (ibid., 717).[19] Otherwise, however, he shared the view that on the world scale, socialism must be the successor to capitalism, not an alternative to it, and that its fate would be decided only after its victory in the economically advanced capitalist countries. Therefore, he was inclined to regard his revolution as merely "the starting point for a communist development" in the West. In his *"Left-Wing" Communism* (1920) he openly declared that, once the proletarian revolution had triumphed in at least one of the advanced countries, "Russia will cease to be the model and will once again become a backward country" (ibid., 551).

In "Our Revolution" this important problematic was not touched on at all, hence it is not clear to what extent Lenin's remarks on Russian peculiarities can be seen as an argument for socialism in a single country. It seems rather that he wanted to provide retrospective justification for his past deeds without committing himself to any theory that might limit his freedom of action in the future. He ridiculed those who thought that "a textbook written on Kautskian lines" could foresee "all the forms of development of subsequent world history" and embraced instead the view that revolutionaries must act in an unpredictable world, constantly facing multiple uncertainties and knowing only too well that no theory of history could guarantee their success. Against deterministic dogmatism he set the maxim of Napoleon: "*On s'engage et puis on voit*, first engage in a serious battle and then see what happens" (ibid., 706).

At the same time, however, Lenin was only too well aware that his party had in fact failed to win, despite seizing unlimited political power for itself. At the Eleventh Party Congress, held in Moscow in March through April 1922, he defined the situation as the total defeat of the proud communist dream of consciously directing the course of history and thus realizing the ideal of positive collective freedom. The Communists, he said, "are not directing, they are being directed." They came under the influence of those whom they had conquered because the latter proved to be more "cultured." True, the culture of the bureaucrats of the old regime was not high; on the contrary, it was "miserable, insignificant," but nonetheless it was superior to the culture of the seemingly victorious Bolsheviks (ibid., 527, 527).

Even more spectacular was the Communists' utter inability to run the economy. In that respect, Lenin told them, they were inferior to the "ordinary capitalist salesman." In describing this humiliating defeat in the midst of victory, Lenin, characteristically enough, alluded to another sentence of Napoleon's—his famous words about the forty pyramids looking at the French army. He said: "Communists, revolutionaries who have accomplished the greatest revolution in the world, on whom the eyes of, if not forty pyramids, then, at all events, forty European countries are turned in the hope of emancipation from capitalism, must learn from ordinary salesmen. But these ordinary salesmen have had ten years' warehouse experience and know the business, whereas the responsible Communists and devoted revolutionaries do not know the business and do not even realize that they do not know it." These bitter words were followed by a simple, matter-of-fact statement: "We have everything you want except ability. We lack ability" (ibid., 521–22, 522, 522).

This expression of angry helplessness epitomizes Lenin's objective tragedy. At the height of apparently total victory, achieved at the cost of unheard-of sacrifices and titanic efforts, Lenin saw clearly that in fact he had not yet won, that his Grand Project of human liberation had been thwarted by uncontrollable forces and threatened to turn into a Grand Failure.[20] He tried to defend his millennial dream by attributing his retreat to a subjective factor—lack of ability, grounded in the notoriously Russian lack of culture. In fact, however, the truth was much more bitter.

Lenin was not a sophisticated philosopher of freedom. Nevertheless, all his revolutionary activities were undoubtedly aimed at the realization of the communist vision of human liberation—liberation from the blind necessities of economic and social life. Freedom, as presupposed by this vision, was essentially the *ability* to subject elemental forces to strict, conscious control and thus to become true masters of our collective fate. To achieve this sort of freedom Lenin mobilized tremendous energy, organized his party in a totalitarian way, and imposed on his country a boundless, truly totalitarian dictatorship. And yet, despite everything, he was forced publicly to confess that he and his followers had everything they wanted *except ability*. This was nothing less than a frank admission of total failure. True, Lenin did not despair; he tried to struggle, to mobilize his followers for new heroic efforts. But this struggle against destiny was tragically hopeless. The fate of communism in Russia has proved the essential accuracy of Lenin's diagnosis of 1922: Russian Communists were indeed unable to realize the communist vision. But was he right in attributing this inability to their Russian backwardness and lack of culture? The fate of communism worldwide indicates rather that the vision itself was inherently unrealizable. Hence, the enormous energy put into its implementation was doomed to be wasted.

Lenin's spectacular defeat in victory had two aspects, corresponding to the two sides of the Marxian conception of freedom: freedom as rational control over the economy and freedom as the conscious shaping of man's social forces. The experiences of both War Communism and the NEP made it clear that the Communist party was unable to run the economy and that its clumsy efforts to direct economic processes could only increase human dependence on uncontrollable forces. Even more telling was his experience with his own party as the ruling political body. Intended to be a perfect instrument of rational, conscious control, it turned out to be uncontrollable itself. Its mechanisms of organizational power came to be self-serving and independent of their original aim, and they imposed their will even on Lenin himself. In this way the party became manipulated and increasingly dominated by its first secretary, Joseph Stalin, who held in his hand the organizational strings of power. In the last year of his life Lenin, incapacitated by grave illness, observed the beginnings of this process with growing and entirely justified apprehension. In his so-called Testament he wrote: "Comrade Stalin, having become general secretary, has unlimited authority concentrated in his hands, and I am not sure whether he will always be capable of using that authority with sufficient caution." [21]

If Lenin had lived longer, he would have tried to stop Stalin's drive for power. But it is very doubtful if he could have prevented the party leadership from being corrupted by its unlimited political power. It is quite certain that even the least corrupt, most idealistically minded party leadership would not have been able to establish truly effective control over social developments in the Soviet Union. Neither would it have been able to prevent the emergence of different informal groups of special interests within the membership of the party. Sooner or later it would have emerged that its control was not vigilant or far-sighted enough, that certain actions brought about unintended results, and that social life could not be forced forever into an ideologically prescribed pattern.

4.2 Lenin's Critique of "Bourgeois Freedom" and the Russian Populist Heritage

It is clear that Lenin's vision of communism entailed a view of freedom as social emancipation that was defined negatively as freedom from capitalist oppression, and positively as the freedom to develop as human beings. Unlike Marx, however, Lenin did not indulge in thinking about the rich, all-round capacities of the human species. He concentrated instead on freedom to provide for the most basic needs of the masses, above all freedom from hunger. "Everyone to have bread; everyone to have sound footwear and whole clothing; everyone to have warm dwellings" (ibid., 431). These simple words conveniently summarize the first priority of Lenin's emancipatory program.

Lenin had always been deeply conscious of the difference between the social emancipation of the masses and liberal freedom—freedom in the sense of human rights and political liberty. He had always thought that "unless freedom promotes the emancipation of labor from the yoke of capital, it is a deception. . . . All freedom is deception if it is not subordinated to the task of emancipating labor" (L, CW, 29:352, 354). Before the Revolution, however, he stressed that "bourgeois-democratic freedom" was a great advance over autocracy and, formally at least, committed himself, like the other Russian Marxists, to this struggle. But in 1917 the situation drastically changed: the February Revolution, as Lenin himself admitted, had transformed Russia into "the freest of all belligerent countries in the world," but it did not go beyond "bourgeois freedom"—that is (to quote the well-known Marxist slogan), "freedom of capital to exploit the workers." This pushed Lenin into a sharp radicalization of his stand on "merely political" freedom. In *The State and Revolution* he came close to an outright denial of any substantial increase of freedom in the history of class societies. "Freedom in the capitalist society," he wrote, "always remains the same as it was in the ancient Greek republics: freedom for the slave-owners" (L, A, 296, 372). Soon afterward he ordered the freely elected Constituent Assembly to disperse, an extremely controversial decision even in the eyes of many of his followers and admirers. It would be idle to speculate on how difficult this decision was for him; apparently he saw it as the only correct choice, but who knows? Be that as it may, he felt obliged to explain and justify his harsh action in a number of passionately worded writings and public speeches. Some examples of his argumentation follow below.

Freedom is always class bound, all talk of freedom in general, or democracy in general, is nonsense, if not a deliberate fraud. The Bolsheviks know very well that they will be attacked in the name of liberty, but they are not afraid of this (L, CW, 29 : 352–53). True freedom will be realized only under communism and through communism; its time will come "when people have forgotten that it was possible for public buildings to be somebody's property." At the present stage of the class struggle, freedom is a catchword of the rich; anybody who opposes the Bolsheviks "with such catchwords as 'democracy' and 'freedom,' takes the side of the propertied classes, deceives the people, for he fails to understand that up to now freedom and democracy meant freedom and democracy *for the propertied classes* and only crumbs from their table for the propertyless." This is because the institution of private property is utterly incompatible with popular freedom; it enables property owners to control everything in social life, thus reducing the people's freedom to merely formal rights—"freedom on paper, but not in fact." Equality is "a much more profound subject," but it can also be merely formal and therefore fraudulent, running counter to the emancipation of labor from the yoke of capital. Like true freedom, true equality is incompatible with the existence of accumulated wealth. Overthrowing the political rule of the propertied classes is not enough; neither is it enough to nationalize the means of production. Exploitation continues to exist as long as money exists, because money is "congealed wealth," "a survival of yesterday's exploitation" (ibid., 355, 356, 353, 357, 358). Hence, to liberate the poor from the moneybags, it is necessary to abolish money and exchange (ibid., 359). As long as this is not done, formal freedom and equality cannot be granted. The dictatorship of the proletariat has to be "cruel, stern, bloody and painful" (ibid., 355). It cannot tolerate freedom of the press because this would mean "freedom of the rich to bribe the press, to use their wealth to shape and fabricate so-called public opinion" (L, SW, 3 : 101). Neither can it tolerate freedom of assembly: "To grant freedom of assembly to capitalists would be a heinous crime against the working people: it would mean freedom of assembly for counter-revolutionaries" (L, CW, 29:354).

All these reasonings were duly supported by invoking the authority of Marx. The author of *Capital*, Lenin argued, "ridicules the pompous and grandiloquent bourgeois-democratic great charter of liberty and the rights of man." He devoted "the greater part of his life, the greater part of his literary work, and the greater part of his scientific studies to ridiculing freedom, equality, the will of majority, and all the Benthams who wrote so beautifully about these things, and to proving that these phrases were merely a screen to cover up the freedom of the commodity owners, the freedom of capital, which these owners use to oppress the masses of the working people" (ibid., 427, 352)[22]

No doubt, Marx was often very brutal in his unmasking of "bourgeois freedom"; he contributed more than anyone else to its low reputation among socialists. But this should not prevent us from seeing that Lenin went much further in this direction and that some of his views did not derive from Marx. Take, for instance, Lenin's tirade against the moderate socialists who were concerned about freedom: "Less chatter about 'labor democracy,' about 'liberty, equality and fraternity,' about 'government by the people,' and all such stuff. . . . Fewer pompous phrases, more plain, *everyday* work, concern for the pood of grain and the pood of coal! More concern about providing this pood of grain and pood of coal needed by the hungry workers and ragged and barefoot peasants" (ibid., 428).

This is a comment on the freedom of workers, not on the freedom of the privileged. We should also note that here Lenin's arguments against freedom did not involve the threat of counterrevolution; they concentrated on crudely utilitarian considerations and were strongly reminiscent of the Russian "Enlighteners" of the 1860s. We cannot find such arguments in Marx, whose attitude toward human needs was aristocratic rather than populist.[23]

Another and even more telling illustration of the nihilistic tendency in Lenin's critique of "bourgeois freedom" is his passionate brochure *The Proletarian Revolution and the Renegade Kautsky*, which contains not only an unusually strong version of the Marxist view of bourgeois democracy as providing ample room for economic compulsion and therefore being "a paradise for the rich and a snare and deception for the exploited and the poor," but also develops a theory of bourgeois democratic institutions as hostile by their very nature to the workers and leading inevitably to the constant *increase* of exploitation and coercion. He calls this "the law of bourgeois democracy" and describes its functioning as follows: "The ruling party in a bourgeois democracy extends the protection of the minority only to another *bourgeois* party, while the proletariat, on all *serious, profound and fundamental issues*, get martial law or pogroms, instead of the "protection of the minority." *The more highly developed a democracy is, the more imminent are pogroms or civil war in connection with any profound political divergence which is dangerous to the bourgeoisie. . . . The more highly democracy is developed, the more the bourgeois parliaments are subjected by the stock exchange and the bankers"* (L, *A*, 468, 469).

This incredible theory cannot be regarded as a legitimate extension of Marx's views. Marx's prejudices against "bourgeois freedom" were very deep, but it is highly unlikely that he would have claimed that it led to pogroms. He saw it as involving the maximum increase of alienation, thus preventing a free self-realization of human higher capacities, but not as producing a steady and inevitable increase of direct coercion in social life. His views may have been wrong, but they were not absurd. And yet, Lenin's views should not be treated as an individual aberration. They were deeply rooted in the strong, wide current of Russian social thought—a current with which he was directly linked by Russian populism, broadly conceived.[24] Many aspects of Lenin's views on "bourgeois freedom" can be explained by his deep (although not fully conscious) indebtedness to the Russian populist tradition. It is justifiable therefore to devote some attention to this subject.

Lenin himself carefully distinguished between early Russian radicalism (the so-called Enlighteners of the 1860s) and its subsequent development into *narodnichestvo* (i.e., populism in a more narrow sense of this term).[25] He highly praised the first and severely criticized the latter, sharply disagreeing with *narodnik* theories of Russian exceptionalism and, above all, with their backward-looking economic romanticism. He felt that Russian Marxists must renounce the heritage of the *narodnik* theorists as idealizing archaic forms of economic and social life and must instead take up and develop the heritage of the early radicals—above all, of their greatest thinker, Nikolai Chernyshevskii. He even saw Chernyshevskii as a theorist who came remarkably close to "scientific socialism" and thus paved the way for Russian Marxism. This was certainly so for Lenin; he had been "transformed" by Chernyshevskii and had become a revolutionary before his introduction to Marxism.[26] The title of his most important early work, *What Is to Be Done?* was a deliberate reference to the title of Chernyshevskii's influential novel.[27]

One can agree with Lenin that Chernyshevskii was not a *narodnik*— that is, a populist in the narrower and specifically Russian meaning of the term. Nevertheless, he was a populist in the generic sense and also the true founder of populist radicalism in Russia. He was a populist (*sensu largo*) because he identified himself with the popular masses, being deeply suspicious of the liberals as representing the interests of the exploiters; because he tried to develop a political economy of the working masses, sharply distinguishing between national wealth and people's welfare;[28] and because his entire worldview was permeated with populist egalitarianism, which treated the satisfaction of people's elementary needs as the first and absolute priority. As befitted a populist from a backward country, he was, of course, very critical of capitalism and wished Russia to develop in a noncapitalist way. Capitalism, he thought, promoted national wealth at the expense of people's welfare; all "late comers to the avenue of history" should therefore hope for a direct transition to a form of socialism.

Lenin was particularly impressed by Chernyshevskii's criticism of the liberals and commented: "You can't find another Russian revolutionary who understood and condemned the cowardly, base, and perfidious nature of every kind of liberalism with such thoroughness, acumen and force as Chernyshevskii did."[29] Small wonder, therefore, that he deeply internalized Chernyshevskii's critique of the liberal conception of freedom, which runs as follows:

Freedom is a very pleasant thing. But liberalism understands freedom in too narrow and formal a way: it is conceived in terms of abstract rights, as a paper dispensation, as absence of legal restrictions. Liberals will not understand that juridical freedom has value for man only when he possesses the material power to take advantage of it. . . . Participation in the exercise of political power, or influence on social affairs depends not on whether certain people or certain classes have obtained the formal right to share in the formal acts of government: it depends on whether such people and such classes are so situated in the life of society as to be able to have a real significance in it.[30]

This view, apparently commonsensical but in fact confusing freedom with ability, was shared by Chernyshevskii and Western socialists, including Marxists. But the point is that in Russian conditions the contextual meaning changed: in the West it was a critique of the principles underlying the existing state of affairs (even if it was only a partial and inadequate realization of these principles), while in Russia it raised the problem of choosing an alternative road. Russian populist radicals quickly decided that political freedom on the Western model was a matter of indifference to them, because, as the young Chernyshevskii put it: "It does not matter whether there is a Tsar, or not, whether there is a constitution, or not; what really matters are the social relations, that is, how to prevent a situation in which one class sucks the blood of another." The next logical step was to conclude from this that for Russia, liberal freedom was positively undesirable. This view can also be found in the young Chernyshevskii, who wrote: "It would be the best if absolutism could retain its rule over us until we are sufficiently permeated with democratic spirit, so that, when a popular form of government comes to replace it, political power could be handed over—*de jure* and *de facto*—to the most numerous and the most unhappy class (peasants + hirelings + workers) and thus we skip all the transitional stages."[31]

An additional dimension was added by the fact that in the Russian language the word *democracy* had a social rather than political meaning—that is, it preserved its connection with the common people, or lower classes (the *demos*), but was not associated with a political system.[32] Hence, the adjective *democratic* was often used as a synonym for popular, and the expression *democratic autocracy* (in the sense of an antiaristocratic monarchy promoting the lower classes and relying on them) was not a contradiction in terms.[33] Combining this terminology with the populist commitment to "people's welfare" and with the corresponding contempt for "merely formal freedom" led to a course of reasoning that seems rather strange. A good example is Chernyshevskii's famous paradox about Siberia and England: "For a democrat our Siberia, in which the common people enjoy well-being, is far better than England, where the majority of the population endures great want."[34]

We should note that in later years Chernyshevskii changed his mind and arrived at different conclusions.[35] But his reversal had practically no influence on the development of Russian revolutionary thought. In the 1870s Chernyshevskii's disciples, having turned into full-fledged *narodniks*, came to see political freedom as antithetical to social emancipation, as a tool of bourgeois domination that would only worsen the people's economic slavery. This gave birth to the curious notion of the allegedly nonpolitical character of the Russian revolutionary movement.[36] This paradox really concealed a theoretically entrenched prejudice against liberal reforms and the sphere of politics in general. According to this view, Russian revolutionaries should concern themselves exclusively with economic and social changes while remaining indifferent to political struggle. It was even implied that they should actively oppose liberal political reforms, because constitutionalism and liberal parliamentarianism would give free rein to the propertied classes and thus only aggravate the economic plight of the poor.

This utterly negative attitude toward political liberty was not something exclusively Russian but should be seen in the context of the deep disillusionment with political freedom, especially with parliamentarianism, which was a common feature of European revolutionaries after the events of 1848–52 in France. The extreme variant of this tendency was represented, of course, by the anarchist movement, whose followers adamantly refused to participate in any political struggle; in their view, they should not fight for seats in a bourgeois parliament but should aim instead at the complete overthrow of all forms of political power. This total rejection of the political sphere as such was often, though somewhat misleadingly, described as indifference toward politics. What was really meant was, of course, not a lack of political will but a lack of interest in intrasystemic political struggles and a relative neutrality toward the question of forms of government.

The chief theorist of the anarchist movement was the Russian revolutionary Bakunin, but the importance of this fact should not be exaggerated. Anarchism was a pan-European, international movement, flourishing mostly in the Romance countries and well represented in the First International. As a part of the international workers' movement, it was the main rival of Marxism and of German socialism as a whole. As a rule, its ideologists tended to minimize the differences between Marxists and Lassalleans: both were accused of political opportunism and statism, of representing the interests of a well-to-do workers' aristocracy.

The Russian populists tried to avoid direct involvement in this controversy. They associated Marx and Engels with the moderate wing of the International, that is, with the policy of legal struggle clearly unsuitable in Russian conditions. Yet they saw Marx as the greatest theorist of socialism and believed that "Marxism as a theory—not as a membership in a Western Socialist party and espousal of its practical policy—does not exclude populism."[37] They did everything they could to propagate Marxism in Russia and achieved great successes in this field. Due to their efforts, and to Marx's surprise, the first translation of *Capital* came out in Russia (it was published in 1872, fifteen years before its English translation) and immediately became obligatory reading for all Russian radicals. Its influence had of course begun earlier, since its first German edition (1867) did not escape the attention of populist thinkers, and its importance can hardly be exaggerated. As I have attempted to show elsewhere, classical Russian populism (*narodnichestvo*) was not merely influenced but, in a sense, called into being by Marxism.[38] This was because the populist image of capitalism had been shaped by Marx and because the decision to treat capitalism as enemy number one was a reaction to Marx's vivid description of the horrors of capitalist development. The populists' understanding of Marxism was certainly inadequate, but in the reception of any theory "inadequate" interpretations often play a most important role. (The word *inadequate* is in quotes here to indicate that there is no such thing as a fully "adequate" transmission of ideas.) We must be aware of the one-sidedness and oversimplified character of the populist interpretation of Marxism, but nonetheless we are justified in treating Russian populism as one of the most important chapters in the history of a broadly conceived reception of Marxist ideas.

Paradoxically, this applies also to the issue of political struggle, which so sharply divided the First International. The populist attitude toward political struggle, as well as toward political freedom, was closer to international anarchism than to the Marxist wing of the workers' movement, but the main arguments for its theoretical justification were taken from Marx. The relevant reasoning ran as follows:

Marx has proved the existence of a necessary relationship between economic base and political superstructure, showing that the latter must serve the former. He has also demonstrated that liberal constitutions, parliaments, democratic republics, and all other forms of political freedom function as a superstructure for the capitalist economy, which means that they serve the interests of the bourgeoisie. The same Marx has insisted that bourgeois interests are antithetical to those of the working people—not only industrial workers, whose fate under capitalism is increasing immizerization, but also the peasantry, because the capitalist system produces inevitable expropriation and proletarianization. Hence, a party of the working people in a backward country must do everything to prevent capitalist development. Hence, it must not support the cause of political freedom, which is necessarily linked to the cause of capitalism.[39]

The logic of this seemed impeccable, not only to the Russian populists, but also to the anarchists. Bakunin, as the leader of international anarchism, fought against Marx politically but at the same time expressed the greatest respect for his theory of capitalist development, fully endorsing its implications for the working people. He called *Capital* a "magnificent work"[40] and saw his own program as more consistent with it than were the policies of Marx and Engels (who, in his view, had succumbed to the influence of their German background).

The emergence of Russian Marxism, as a separate, strongly antipopulist current of Russian revolutionary thought, was bound up with a thorough reexamination of the classical populist view on the relationship between socialism and political struggle (see chapter 3, section 2). Suffice it to say that the acceptance of political struggle against autocracy and the corresponding recognition of the value (relative, at least) of "bourgeois freedom" was in Russia, until 1917, an indispensable condition for being regarded a Marxist. All Russian Marxists duly emphasized that "the demand for liberty expresses primarily the interest of the bourgeoisie" but carefully avoided drawing populist conclusions from this statement. They seemed to agree that "there is not, nor can there be, any other path to real freedom for the proletariat and the peasantry, than the path of bourgeois freedom and bourgeois progress" (L, A, 139, 140). These are Lenin's words but we must not attribute to him a principled, unchangeable stand on this issue. His ideological evolution may be interpreted in many different ways, in sharp contrast to the unambiguous clarity of Plekhanov's standpoint. To understand the specificity of Lenin's Marxism, and particularly his views on freedom, we must examine some characteristic features of his conception of passing through the "capitalist phase."

First, Lenin did not expect that bourgeois progress would directly benefit the working people. He saw it as good for their struggle, but not as necessarily good for their welfare. The prospect of paying a heavy price for progress did not worry him, because he had always concentrated on the final goal and not on the immediate improvement of the people's lot; in this respect, he was a true Marxist, not Chernyshevskii's disciple. A good illustration of his readiness to accept human suffering can be seen in his refusal to help the hungry peasants during the great famine of 1891–92 on the Lower Volga. He decided that to counteract this famine would be unwise in view of its positive impact on the economy (speeding up the necessary proletarianization of the peasantry) and its revolutionizing influence on the masses. Yielding to humanitarian impulses would have been, in his view, "nothing but an expression of the saccharine-sweet sentimentality" characteristic of the Russian intelligentsia.[41]

Second, Lenin's acceptance of the struggle for political freedom was always combined with a deep hostility toward the liberals. He regarded them as part and parcel of the privileged classes about whom revolutionaries should have no illusions whatsoever. This linked his views strongly to the Russian populist tradition, from Chernyshevskii to the People's Will. From the very beginning this stance was a matter of controversy in his relations with Plekhanov. His first meeting with the "father of Russian Marxism" in the spring of 1895 induced the latter to comment: "You turn your back to the liberals, while we turn our faces to them."[42]

This was no mere tactical difference. In fact, it reflected two different interpretations of the very foundations of Marxist theory. For Lenin, Marxism was a theory of class struggle leading to the social emancipation of labor; for Plekhanov, historical materialism was a theory of progress through the development of productive forces. In the first interpretation, alliance between the workers' party and the liberals seemed to involve illogical cooperation between the exploiters and their victims, while alliance between the industrial workers and the poorer peasantry, as two parts of the exploited masses, seemed completely natural. In the other interpretation, this was the other way around: alliance between the industrial workers and the liberal bourgeoisie reflected a natural cooperation between two forces interested in the progress of capitalist modernization, while an alliance between the workers and the peasantry, *especially* the poor peasantry, threatened to involve dangerous concessions to the most backward forms of production. Lenin's interpretation was more in tune with the populist emotions of class hatred, but Plekhanov's views, though perhaps too cerebral in a revolutionary setting, were more consistent with classical Marxism. After all, the view of the reactionary nature of small-scale production was an essential part of the Marxist theory of economic development, and its antipeasant implications were quite obvious.[43] Marx and Engels's *Manifesto of the Communist Party* contained an explicit warning against a possible alliance between workers and all sorts of small producers, including the peasantry. "The lower middle class, the small manufacturer, the shopkeeper, the artisan, the peasant, all these fight against the bourgeoisie, to save from extinction their existence as fractions of the middle class. They are therefore not revolutionary, but conservative, for they try to roll back the wheel of history" (M&E, SW, 1:117–18). In their later works the authors of the *Manifesto* developed a detailed theory of decentralized small production as a relic of medievalism, doomed to be extinguished by progressive capitalist development; Plekhanov's conception of political alliance was a logical extension of this view. The practical consequences of this fundamental difference between Plekhanov's and Lenin's interpretations of Marxism were fully revealed during the revolution of 1905–1906.

Despite moments of hesitation caused by fears of a "rotten compromise" between the bourgeoisie and the government, Plekhanov remained faithful to the idea that bourgeois democratic revolution in Russia should aim at bringing the bourgeoisie to political power. By bourgeoisie he meant neither the petty bourgeoisie, which represented the most obsolete forms of production, nor the peasants, whom he saw as irrational, backward-looking, and having an "Asiatic" mentality, but rather the enlightened, Westernized, liberal bourgeoisie, which represented the most advanced section of the Russian economy and thus was capable of leading Russia toward thorough modernization. Hence, he offered critical but consistent support to the Kadet party, which placed him on the extreme right wing of Russian Social Democracy. Even the Mensheviks suspected him of attempts to reduce the role of the workers to that of an instrument of the bourgeoisie.[44]

Lenin took a diametrically opposite stand. He still agreed that the revolution had to be bourgeois democratic and that its ultimate result should be the establishment of bourgeois rule; in spite of this, however, he made stenuous efforts to justify the tactics of fighting *against* the bourgeois liberals and to prove that the Kadets were in fact the most dangerous enemies of the revolution. "There is bourgeois democracy and bourgeois democracy"—that is, "republican-revolutionary and monarchist-liberal bourgeois democracy," he argued. *In a certain sense* bourgeois revolution was not advantageous to the bourgeoisie as a class: "It is of greater advantage to the bourgeoisie for the necessary changes in the direction of bourgeois democracy to take place more slowly, more gradually, more cautiously, less resolutely, by means of reforms," relying on "certain remnants of the past." This, in Lenin's view, would inevitably lead to an alliance of the most privileged groups, old and new, and thus to a shameful betrayal of the revolutionary masses. The social basis of a *consistent* bourgeois democratic revolution in Russia was therefore not the bourgeoisie proper but

the small producers—"the revolutionary and republican petty bourgeoisie, and especially the peasantry." But the most radical revolutionary force
was "the Jacobins of contemporary Social Democracy"—the Bolsheviks.
"They want the people, i.e., the proletariat and the peasantry, to settle accounts with the monarchy and the aristocracy in the 'plebeian way'" and
were better equipped than anybody else to provide a firm, uncompromising
leadership in the revolutionary struggle (L, A, 126–27, 124–25, 132, 132).
In this way Lenin arrived at the conception of "a revolutionary-democratic
dictatorship of the proletariat and the peasantry." Such a dictatorship, he
reasoned, would represent the majority of the population while at the same
time putting the peasantry under the hegemony of the proletariat, thus
securing the decisive voice for his own party.

Clearly, this solution was a serious departure from the standard view
that the aim of political struggle against autocracy should be bourgeois
political freedom. True, Lenin still tried to pay lip service to this view,
arguing that his revolutionary dictatorship would simply be the most efficient means for establishing a democratic republic and complete political
liberty. But he had never explained how to reconcile his idea of installing
Bolsheviks in power with Plekhanov's view, hitherto treated as obligatory
for all Russian Marxists, that no socialist party in Russia should attempt
to seize political power for itself and that yielding to such a Blanquist
temptation could only bring about most undesirable results. Nor did he
explain how it might be possible to establish "complete political liberty"
while at the same time conducting "a ruthless and self-sacrificing struggle
for the direct and decisive path," using dictatorial powers not only against
outright reactionaries, but also, and above all, against the forces of moderation and compromise. Instead, he openly stated that "no one will be able
to blame the proletariat's representative [i.e., the Bolsheviks] if, when they
have done everything in their power, their efforts are defeated by the resistance of reaction" but that "everybody, and, above all, the class-conscious
proletariat, will condemn Social Democracy if it curtails the revolutionary
energy of the democratic revolution and dampens revolutionary ardor because it is afraid to win" (ibid., 140). This was virtually a declaration that
true revolutionaries must not be afraid of carrying the revolution *beyond*
the limits of bourgeois democracy.

In any event, it is quite clear that Lenin's "April Theses" of 1917, calling
for the immediate overthrow of the bourgeois democratic Provisional Government, were not a bolt from the blue without any previous theorizing. In
fact, the difference between Lenin's position in 1905 and his stand in 1917 is
the result of different circumstances. In both cases he opted for revolutionary voluntarism, contemptuously rejecting theoretical scruples. In 1905,
however, the main enemy was still the autocracy, which justified continued
usage of the slogan "political liberty." By contrast, in 1917 political liberty

had already been achieved, and it was therefore necessary to discredit it by invoking the entire arsenal of crudely socialist arguments against fraudulent "bourgeois freedom." The first drastic consequence of the Bolshevik seizure of power—the dispersal of the Constituent Assembly—made these arguments even more necessary, as an indispensable legitimation of Lenin's dictatorship. This explains Lenin's relapse into the crudities of the populist reception of Marxism.

A good example of this was his lecture "The State," delivered at the University of Sverdlovsk on July 11, 1919. In it he reached the typically populist conclusion that political freedom only increases the exploitation of the masses and is therefore in reality a shameless lie. Challenging the apologists of free states, Lenin wrote: "You say your state is free, whereas in reality, as long as there is private property, your state, even if it is a democratic republic, is nothing but a machine used by the capitalists to suppress the workers, and the freer the state, the more clearly is this expressed. Examples of this are Switzerland in Europe and the United States of America. Nowhere does capital rule so cynically and ruthlessly, and nowhere is it so clearly apparent as in these countries" (L, *SW*, 3:214).

The ease with which the Bolshevik leader returned to the populist tradition of violent denunciations of "bourgeois freedom" shows that his perception of the world was rooted in the Russian populist heritage more deeply than he himself had thought. This relapse into the older layers of revolutionary consciousness was reflected also in his language. Having defined their positions in the great debate against the populists, Russian Marxists prohibited the use of the vague terms like *people* (*narod*) or *toilers* as failing to indicate class characteristics and therefore unacceptable to "scientific socialists." For a long time Lenin observed this rule; because of this, he used to refer to the peasantry as the "petty bourgeoisie," stressing thereby that the peasants belonged to a class of people who *owned* their means of production. By 1917–18, however, he seemed to have forgotten such theoretical niceties. His articles and speeches of that time are full of class hatred but rather vague about class distinctions. They sharply divide the population into "working people" and "parasites," the "masses" and the "privileged," the "toilers" and the "moneybags," the "exploited" and the "exploiters," the "poor" and the "rich." Thus, for instance, in "How to Organize Competition" he wrote: "The rich and the crooks are two sides of the same medal, they are two principal categories of *parasites* which capitalism fostered. . . . The fate of the crook should, in justice, be the fate of the rich man" (L, *A*, 429, 431). And so on.

This is certainly not the language of "scientific socialism." Dichotomic division into the (good) poor and the (bad) rich characterizes the mentality of "primitive rebels."[45] Russian revolutionary populists and anarchists were, as a rule, greatly impressed by this mentality and tried to harness it to the service of their cause. Russian Marxists of Plekhanov's brand saw it rather as a repugnant and extremely dangerous obstacle on the way to a civilized, Western-type development. Lenin, in this respect, was always closer to the pre-Marxist revolutionary tradition. In his *State and Revolution* he openly declared that socialist revolution "is *impossible* without a certain 'reversion' to 'primitive' democracy" and that "under socialism much of 'primitive' democracy will inevitably be revived" (ibid., 340, 394). His crude campaign against *bourgeois* democracy was fully consistent with this view.

4.3   The Workers' Movement and the Party

There is widespread agreement that the most distinctive feature of Leninism is Lenin's theory of the party. There is also a well-established scholarly tradition that links this theory with the heritage of the so-called Jacobin (or Blanquist) wing of the pre-Marxist revolutionary movement in Russia. The origins of this tradition go back to Plekhanov and the Mensheviks, for whom the terms *Jacobinism* and *Blanquism* had a pejoratively voluntaristic meaning and who therefore treated Lenin's links with Russian Jacobinism as something that utterly compromised him as a Marxist. Curiously enough, this approach also characterized many Western scholars who otherwise had little in common with Marxism. Much light has been shed on the subject by Valentinov's memoirs, although he perhaps attributed too much importance to Lenin's casual personal contacts.[46] Many authors have pointed out a number of striking similarities between Lenin's revolutionary elitism and the ideas of Petr Tkachev, the main theorist of the Jacobin current within broadly conceived revolutionary populism.[47] With the passage of time, the wealth of accumulated evidence made it clear that Lenin's indebtedness to Russian Jacobinism was an obvious and undisputed fact. Tucker, for instance, summarized his views on this problem in a simple categorical statement: "Leninism was in part a revival of Russian Jacobinism within Marxism. Lenin himself must have been well aware of this" (ibid., xxxiii).

Indeed, Lenin was not slow to praise Tkachev, treating him as a great revolutionary and disagreeing with Plekhanov's attack on him.[48] Lenin distinguished between Blanquism and Jacobinism, defining the first more narrowly, as an exclusively conspiratorial tactic aimed at seizing political power by means of a revolutionary plot and completely neglecting mass support (an element of which he was, of course, strongly critical). But he was unhesitatingly positive about Jacobinism, which was to him a synonym for resolute, well-organized revolutionary action. Menshevik fears of Jacobinism roused him to anger and contempt. He categorically refused to regard Jacobinism as incompatible with Marxism. Taking up the challenge, he defined Bolsheviks as "Jacobins of contemporary Social Democracy" (ibid., 132).

On the whole, however, to stress Lenin's affinities with Jacobinism or Blanquism does not seem to be the best way of defining his place within Russian Marxism and his unique contribution to it. Jacobinism and Blanquism were old, deeply rooted tendencies within many revolutionary movements, and it is not true that Marx and Engels always and unconditionally opposed them; thus, for instance, they sympathized with the terrorist People's Will and would not listen to Plekhanov, who accused it of Blanquist heresy. They even tended to see his stand as too doctrinaire and as concealing, perhaps, a shrinking from real revolutionary activity.[49]

It seems, therefore, that the distinctive features of Lenin's contribution to Marxism cannot be reduced to a revival of either Jacobinism or Blanquism. True, his links with these currents were by no means unimportant. His way to Marxism was very different from Plekhanov's; Lenin was brought up to worship the heroes of the People's Will and, like his older brother, Alexander, wanted to continue its revolutionary tradition.[50] This basically positive attitude toward the People's Will, and even toward Tkachev, certainly influenced Lenin's ideological options. But his own version of revolutionary voluntarism did not consist of merely continuing old tendencies under new conditions, but rather of creating an original theory of a new type of revolutionary party, a theory that marked the beginning of revolutionary totalitarianism in the twentieth century. Tkachev can indeed be seen as Lenin's predecessor but mostly for reasons other than his Jacobinism: namely, because he linked the Russian revolutionary movement to the totalitarian tendency of Babouvist communism and because the vanguard party that he envisioned was to realize the communist utopia of totally regenerated humanity. In other words, he paved the way for Lenin as a Jacobin communist, not merely as a Jacobin.

To emphasize Lenin's links with the legacy of Tkachev usually leads to the conclusion that Lenin represented a uniquely Russian interpretation of Marxism. This suggests, in turn, that Leninism was merely a local, peripheral phenomenon, far removed from the mainstream history of communism. In reality, however, from the point of view of a universal history of communism, Lenin's most important predecessor was not Tkachev (who was merely a belated disciple of Babeuf and Buonarroti), but Babeuf himself. The same can be said of Lenin's relationship to the Jacobins. Like Babeuf, Lenin saw the Jacobin stage of the French Revolution as but the forerunner of a communist revolution, which would be (as Babeuf put it) "far more grand, far more solemn, and which will be the last." They both visualized the revolution as brought about by a self-appointed vanguard and followed by a period of revolutionary dictatorship under which private property and commerce would be replaced by wholesale nationalization and an all-embracing *planned* distribution of goods. Thus, the roots of Leninism should ultimately be seen not in the peculiarities of the Russian tradition but, rather, in the extreme, primitive communist, insurrectionary wing of the French Revolution.[51]

Let us turn now to Lenin's theory of the party, as set forth in *What Is to Be Done?* In writing this important work Lenin was not attempting an original contribution to Marxist theory. He only wanted to defend it against two newly emergent dangers: Eduard Bernstein's revisionism and the "economist" deviation in the Russian workers' movement, which he regarded as a Russian response to Bernstein's ideas.[52] He was horrified by Bernstein's neglect of final goals, as typified in his assertion that "the movement is everything and the final goal is nothing," by his appeal that Social Democracy should be transformed into a peaceful democratic party of social reform, and by his outright abandonment of revolutionary methods of struggle. Russian Economism—by which he meant different groups pushing the Russian workers' movement in the direction of everyday economic struggle at the expense of far-reaching political goals—represented, for him, not just a Russian version of Bernstein's opportunism, but also a dangerous relapse into classical populist apoliticism. The Webbs's *Theory and Practice of Trade Unionism* had convinced him that all workers' movements, if left to themselves, naturally tended toward a narrow-minded, politically indifferent trade unionism. Hence, the Economists' emphasis on working within trade unions seemed to him a particularly bad omen.

Faced with such threats, Lenin felt, the workers' party should first of all defend its Marxist identity, as defined on theoretical grounds. "The *role of a vanguard fighter*," he argued, "*can be fulfilled only by a party that is guided by the most advanced theory*." Engels was right, Lenin maintained, in recognizing "*not two* forms of the great struggle of Social Democracy (political and economic), *but three, placing the theoretical struggle on a par with the first two*." The most advanced theory, however, was not the product of a spontaneously developing workers' movement; it "grew out of the philosophic, historical, and economic theories elaborated by educated representatives of the propertied classes, by intellectuals." This theory was oriented toward the final goal of the movement, and therefore its priorities did not always harmonize with the current aims of the everyday economic struggle of the masses. Hence the guardians of theoretical purity must defend the theory against the constant pressure of trade unionist practice and also against the intellectual anarchy, lack of discipline, and love of pointless discussion characteristic of the intelligentsia. The party, unlike old-fashioned "circles," could allow "freedom of criticism." Its members should be clearly aware "that 'freedom of criticism' means freedom for an opportunist trend in Social Democracy, freedom to convert Social Democracy into a democratic party of reform, freedom to introduce bourgeois ideas and bourgeois elements into socialism." Freedom, Lenin continued, "is a grand word, but under the banner of freedom of industry the most predatory wars were waged and under the banner of freedom of labor, the working people were robbed. The modern use of the term 'freedom of criticism' contains the same inherent falsehood. Those who are really convinced that they have made progress in science would not demand freedom for the new views to continue side by side with the old, but the substitution of the new views for the old" (ibid., 20, 24, 14, 14–15).

This characteristic statement reveals the link between authoritarianism and belief in a nonrelative, objective truth. Those who possess true knowledge should not yield to the opinions of the ignorant majority. Lenin assumed, of course, that Marxism was the only vehicle of true knowledge and that party intellectuals, initiated into all the secrets of this world-transforming knowledge, were, potentially at least, a sort of gnostic aristocracy endowed with a superior capacity for finding correct, truly Marxist answers to the topical problems of the movement. Grass-roots workers' leaders could not compete with them, because the workers' perspective was necessarily too narrow, limited by a parochial sort of empiricism.

To add authority to this view, Lenin made use of Kautsky's theory of modern socialist consciousness as arising "only on the basis of modern scientific knowledge"—that is, "something introduced into the proletarian class struggle from without (*von Aussen Hineingetragenes*) and not something that arose in it spontaneously (*urwüchsig*)." He clung to the expression "from without," to which he gave a truly extremist interpretation. Kautsky only wrote of "scientific knowledge" with the intention of defending its autonomous status, while Lenin, posing as his disciple, extended the principle of "bringing consciousness from without" to all the operations of the movement, claiming for the vanguard the exclusive right of leadership and demanding the wholesale suppression of the workers' "spontaneity." He proclaimed "*a fierce struggle against spontaneity,*" (i.e., a fierce struggle against independent trade unionism). "The *spontaneous* development of the working-class movement," he wrote, "leads to its subordination to bourgeois ideology. . . . The spontaneous working-class movement is trade-unionism, is *Nur-Gewerkschaftlerei*, and trade-unionism means the ideological enslavement of the workers by the bourgeoisie. Hence, our task, the task of Social-Democracy, is *to combat spontaneity*, to *divert* the working-class movement from this spontaneous, trade-unionist striving to come under the wing of the bourgeoisie, and to bring it under the wing of revolutionary Social-Democracy." He maintained that the basic error of the Economists was "their conviction that it was possible to develop the class political consciousness of the workers *from within*, so to speak, from their economic struggle. . . . Such a view is radically wrong. . . . Class political consciousness can be brought to workers *only from without*, that is, only from outside the economic struggle, from outside the sphere of relations between workers and employers. The sphere from which alone it is possible to obtain this knowledge is the sphere of relationships of *all* classes and strata to the state and the government, the sphere of the interrelations between *all* classes" (ibid., 28, 30, 29, 49–50).

We may agree or disagree with this radically antisyndicalist view, but we should not fail to notice that it had no support in Kautsky's conception of the autonomous status of "scientific knowledge." Class political consciousness and "scientific knowledge" were obviously two different things. They could be confused only by someone who believed that class political consciousness could and should be derived from infallible scientific theory. Kautsky was too deeply steeped in the methodology of historical materialism and, more generally, in the historical approach to ideology to be suspected of such a confusion.

This point must be stressed because it is increasingly obscured in the literature on the subject. The widespread and correct interpretation of *What Is to Be Done?* as a forceful expression of Lenin's departure from Marxist orthodoxy has been challenged by Neil Harding, the author of an otherwise very useful two-volume account of Lenin's political thought. Harding has argued that this pamphlet was in fact "the reaffirmation of orthodoxy" and that all those who see it differently must also question Kautsky's position as the undisputed "guardian and oracle" of orthodox Marxism. Lenin's conclusions on the genesis of socialist consciousness were (allegedly) "but an exegesis of Kautsky," whose views on this subject were "very closely similar to those of the other orthodox within the Russian movement." *What Is to Be Done?* was read and discussed by all coeditors of *Iskra*, and there is no evidence of their disagreement on its main themes; "Plekhanov and Axelrod merely made minor suggestions in the draft which Lenin adopted."[53] Hence, it is, according to Harding, entirely unwarranted to regard Lenin's pamphlet as a manifesto of Bolshevism, as a separate current within Russian Social Democracy, or to derive this current from the Russian Jacobinist tradition and to attribute to it totalitarian features.[54]

This conclusion applies also to Lenin's views on the organizational question (i.e., to his theory of the party). Harding cannot claim, of course, that it was simply another side of Lenin's conception of socialist consciousness, otherwise he would have to explain why Kautsky failed to develop such a theory; neither can he claim that Lenin's views on this question represented Marxist orthodoxy in *any* meaningful sense of the term. Harding chose instead to minimize the importance of the organizational question, to explain the Menshevik attacks on Lenin as resulting from their "hurt pride and private resentment" and thus to suggest that the entire issue "was not one of principle but of personality."[55]

In one respect Harding is certainly right. In 1902 Lenin was not fully aware of the distinctive features of his thought and did not intend to cause a break in the party. He wanted to defend the old orthodoxy, which was threatened by Bernstein and the Russian Economists. In this he was supported by the entire *Iskra* camp, especially by Plekhanov, for whom the priority of political struggle was the basic tenet of Russian Marxism. It often happens that the visible presence of common enemies blurs the perception of divisions within one's own camp. This explains why the importance of some strikingly unorthodox features of *What Is to Be Done?* remained for a time either underestimated or simply unnoticed.

We may also agree that Lenin shared Kautsky's view on the autonomous status of Marxism as "scientific knowledge." It should be obvious, however, that he needed this thesis to stress the role of professional *revolutionaries*, not that of professional *scholars*. Unlike Kautsky, he had not the remotest wish to defend the autonomy of socialist intellectuals, who were trying to attain a fully objective, scientific understanding of necessity. Lenin's main concern was with revolutionary activism, which demanded, in his view, the strictest discipline and centralization. Focusing attention on the problematic of freedom enables us clearly to recognize this fundamental difference. Kautsky's defense of professionalism was a defense of the freedom of theoretical thinking; Lenin's advocacy of professionalism was a justification of his conception of a vanguard party cemented by an iron discipline and therefore possessing a single will.

All Lenin's reasonings revolve around this "organizational question." He wrote: "Give us an organization of revolutionaries and we will overturn Russia!" He did not see this as an easy task, because the Russian government was, in his view, a "purely military, strictly centralized organization, which is led in all its minutest details by a single will." This diagnosis naturally led to the conclusion that the revolutionary workers' party had to surpass its enemy in militarization, centralization, and resolute action. Developing this view in detail, Lenin particularly stressed that "the struggle against the *political* police requires special qualities; it requires *professional* revolutionaries." A dozen of the most experienced revolutionaries, "trained professionally no less than the police," should direct all activities of the party; it is they who "will centralize all the secret aspects of the work," it is they who will direct "the drawing up of leaflets, the working out of approximate plans," as well as "the appointing of bodies of leaders for each urban district, for each factory district, and for each educational institution, etc." The growth of legal mass organizations will not eliminate the need for such organizational principles; on the contrary, it will increase their importance, because broad organizations, if left to themselves, always choose the way of nonrevolutionary economic struggle; in addition, they "cannot apply methods of strict secrecy" and are therefore incapable of any resolute, effective action. "Broad democracy" within the party leads to the same consequences and should therefore be rejected as "a useless and harmful toy." A truly revolutionary organization should be based on "complete comradely, mutual confidence among revolutionaries," a confidence stemming from ideological unanimity, unity of purpose, and secured by a constant mutual control. Such control must be executed in the most ruthless way: "An organization of real revolutionaries will stop at nothing to rid itself of an unworthy member" (ibid., 79, 94, 66, 78, 78, 69, 88, 90, 90).

Thus, Lenin's model of the party envisaged a truly radical rejection of all sorts of "genuflections to spontaneity." Everything was to be directed from above, by police methods. All decisions should be made by the small central committee; local cells of the party should be fully subordinated to the central leadership and derive no authority from below.[56] It is evident that such a structure would not leave much room for that freedom of theoretical activity so dear to Kautsky's heart. Lenin needed intellectuals to legitimize his claim to "correct understanding of scientific socialism" and thus to resist the pressure of "bourgeois" tendencies within the workers' movement; otherwise, however, he held intellectuals in contempt, accusing them of inherent weakness, "oblomovism," and anarchic individualism.[57] It is totally wrong to credit him with the desire to see intellectuals as leaders of the workers' movement. He wanted a strong leadership composed of the toughest professionals, irrespective of their background, and he stated this clearly and explicitly: "We must have a committee of professional *revolutionaries*, and it is immaterial whether a student or a worker is capable of becoming a professional revolutionary" (ibid., 75).

This remarkable indifference manifested by a proletarian leader toward the genuine class roots of the proletarian party was one of the main differences between Lenin and Alexander Bogdanov, the man who was to become, for a short time at least, Lenin's rival within the Bolshevik party. In a recent discussion on Bogdanov's place in Russian Marxism, he was described as yet another theorist of the tutelary role of the social democratic intelligentsia in the workers' movement, a theorist whose views on this subject were in fact more consistent and extreme than Lenin's and who could therefore be used by those members of the intelligentsia who wanted, consciously or unconsciously, to constitute themselves as a "new class."[58] In reality, however, Bogdanov saw all ideas, including scientific knowledge, as deriving from the historically developing practice of collective work and thus could not endorse the conception of independent theorists bringing consciousness from outside into the workers' movement. Instead, he was sensitive to syndicalist views and saw intellectuals as merely *helping* the workers to articulate their inherent proletarian worldview.[59] He stressed the need to educate not just a "party intelligentsia" but a genuine "workers' intelligentsia" that would be capable of creating the necessary *cultural* premises of socialism.[60] In later years this led him to set forth the idea of cultural transformation as a separate road to socialism (alongside the political and economic roads) and to the founding of the Proletkult.[61] As might have been expected, Lenin's attitude toward Bogdanov's conception of "proletarian culture," and toward the Proletkult as well, was deeply suspicious and contemptuous. The origins of this important disagreement can be traced back to Lenin's distrust of a freely developing workers' movement as well as Bogdanov's exaggerated belief in its creative power.[62]

Despite his intention of defending established orthodoxy, Lenin was not blind to the novelty of his approach. He interpreted it as only a matter of emphasis but nonetheless saw his theory of the party as opening a new phase in the history of the workers' movement in Russia. He described its first period, covering approximately the years from 1884 to 1894, as one of "the rise and consolidation of the theory and program of Social Democracy." In the second period, from 1894 to 1898, Social Democracy appeared on the scene as a social movement and political party. In the third period, beginning in 1898, "the political consciousness of the leaders capitulated before the breadth and power of the spontaneous movement." Lenin hoped that his *What Is to Be Done?* would put an end to this state of affairs and thus open the fourth period in the history of the movement, a period in which "Russian Social Democracy will emerge from the crisis in the full flower of manhood" and in which "the opportunist rearguard will be 'replaced' by the genuine vanguard of the most revolutionary class" (ibid., 112–13, 114).

The first principled reaction to this vanguard theory was that of Trotsky, who took sides against Lenin at the Second Congress of the party. He pointed out the danger of an overconcentration of power, calling it "a process of self-devourment" in which "the modest [party] Council would be transformed into an all-mighty Committee of Public Safety" in order to enable Lenin "to play the role of an 'incorrupt' Robespierre."[63] Trotsky predicted that this would eventually lead to a state of affairs in which "the organization of the party takes the place of the party; the Central Committee takes the place of the organization; and finally the dictator takes the place of the Central Committee."[64] In a later work he described it as a system of "substitutionism": "a system of *thinking for* the proletariat, of the political *substitution* of the proletariat."[65]

Plekhanov's reaction, although somewhat delayed, was equally decided. As befitted one who thought of himself as the greatest authority on what orthodox Marxism really was, he concentrated on Lenin's "theoretical original sin," which consisted, in his view, of a relapse into a pre-Marxist (Left-Hegelian, or populist) "subjectivism."[66] Lenin, he argued, completely misinterpreted Kautsky, since the latter had never claimed that the working class, if left to itself, could produce only a trade unionist consciousness.

Kautsky's conception of "bringing consciousness from without" referred to socialism as *scientific theory*, not to socialist *class* consciousness or socialism on a pretheoretical, *instinctive* level;[67] hence, Kautsky was not claiming that the spontaneous development of the workers' movement could not produce socialist ideas. Lenin, however, credited Kautsky with a completely different conception, one that made a mockery of historical materialism and undermined the Marxist belief in the historical inevitability of socialism. Therefore, Plekhanov concluded, Lenin put himself beyond the pale of Marxism:

> According to Lenin, the working class, if left to itself, is capable only of struggling for better conditions of the sale of its labor force on the basis of the capitalist relations of production. According to Marx and Engels, the working class inevitably strives for the elimination of these relations, that is for the accomplishment of a socialist revolution.
> Who is right in this issue?
> Think as you please, but if you decide that Lenin is right, then do not call yourselves followers of Marx and Engels.
> Marxism is "an entirely different thing."[68]

The categorical tone of this statement was well justified. It would be difficult to deny that Lenin's theory of the origins of socialist consciousness was inconsistent with historical materialism and, furthermore, that it was also quite inconsistent with Marx and Engels's views on the workers' movement. After all, their *Manifesto of the Communist Party* solemnly proclaimed that "the Communists do not form a separate party opposed to other working-class parties. They have no interests separate and apart from those of the proletariat as a whole. They do not set up any sectarian principles of their own, by which to shape and mold the proletarian movement (M&E, *SW*, 1:119). In later years, when the First International was founded, they formulated the principle "The emancipation of the working class must be the work of the working class itself." They particularly emphasized that the task of the International was "to combine and generalize the *spontaneous movements* of the working classes, but not to dictate or impose any doctrinary system whatever" and indignantly rejected the idea that "the working class of itself is incapable of its own emancipation," flatly refusing to cooperate with people who held such views (ibid., 3:94; 2:81; 3:147).

Of course, we must take into account different circumstances, different polemical contexts, and so forth, but even so, the contrast between the statements quoted and Lenin's theory of the party can hardly be exaggerated. And if we compare Marx and Engels's view, quoted above, on the task of the First International with Lenin's famous 21 conditions for joining the Communist International,[69] we are forced to conclude that a greater contrast can hardly be imagined.

Nevertheless, there was a connection between Lenin's theory and the spirit of Marxism, namely, the connection between his idea of the party's total control over a spontaneous mass movement and the communist idea of emancipation as conscious control, as mastery over people's collective fate. True, when Marx described emancipated humanity as exercising rational, conscious control over its own social forces, he was thinking of the final ideal and not of the present tasks of a revolutionary movement; he meant the control over *economic* forces exercised by emancipated humanity as a whole, and not the control over a workers' movement exercised by a revolutionary minority; finally, he was concerned with the liberation of man's species being, not with matters of revolutionary expediency. Yet he thought of human emancipation in terms of conscious, purposeful activity, as overcoming the resistance of blind, natural necessity, and this way of thinking provided a powerful rationale for the criticism of chaotic spontaneity. In this sense Lenin's theory of the party was significantly linked to the Marxist ideal of establishing firm, conscious control over spontaneous, quasi-natural forces. The Economist deviation within the workers' movement could easily be seen as a surrender to blind market laws whose grip on the working class was to be destroyed by the Marxist revolutionary movement. Thus, it should be stressed that Lenin's conceptions were not unconnected with Marxism; it seems more appropriate to see them as extreme conclusions drawn from a one-sided interpretation of some important elements of the Marxist worldview. It should also be remembered that Lenin's theory of the workers' movement was not an entirely monolithic body of thought, free from all inner tensions and totally immune to change. It was subject to reinterpretations that reflected, as a rule, the ebb and flow of the revolutionary situation in Russia.

After the party split into two factions—Bolsheviks and Mensheviks—Lenin engaged in a ferocious campaign against his opponents. In *One Step Forward, Two Steps Back* (1904) he aimed at a clear-cut polarization in organizational matters. Instead of defending himself against Menshevik accusations, he took up the challenge and boldly confessed that he was indeed a social democratic Jacobin and a staunch supporter of "formal, 'bureaucratically' ordered rules." "Bureaucracy *versus* democracy," he wrote, "is in fact centralism *versus* autonomism; it is the organizational principle of revolutionary Social Democracy as opposed to the organizational principle of opportunist Social Democracy." Organizational unity, he asserted, was far superior to a merely ideological unity. Fear of factory discipline, of being transformed into the cogs and wheels of a machine, was a manifestation of aristocratic or intellectual anarchism, which should be totally alien to revolutionary Marxists. "Marxism, the ideology of the proletariat, trained by capitalism, has been and is teaching unstable intellectuals to distinguish between the factory as a means of exploitation (discipline based on fear and starvation) and the factory as a means of organization (discipline based on collective work united by the conditions of a technically highly developed form of production)" (L, CW, 7:383/393, 396, 391). In this way he linked his image of the party to the communist vision of society as "one great factory."

The revolution of 1905–1906 inspired Lenin with greater optimism about spontaneous tendencies in the workers' movement. His acceptance of mass strikes as a means of political struggle might have been expected; after all *What Is to Be Done?* contained references to "the elemental destructive force of the masses," which should be combined with and harnessed by "the conscious destructive force of the organization of revolutionaries" (L, A,108). The new element lay in his readiness to take the party closer to the mass movement and therefore to make it less hierarchical, giving it more autonomy for its local organizations.[70]

The years that followed saw the final separation of the two factions of Russian Social Democracy, paralleled by a visible growth of intolerance and sectarianism within Bolshevism. (The condemnation of Bogdanov's group was a milestone in this development.) The breakdown of the Second International provided Lenin with additional confirmation of the correctness of his original organizational plan. He accused Western socialists of being "degraded and stultified by bourgeois legality" and contrasted their organizations with his cherished vision of "organizations of *another* kind," consciously modeled on the army. He wrote: "Take the army of today. It is a good example of organization. This organization is good only because it is flexible and is able at the same time to give millions of people *a single will*. . . . When, in the pursuit of a single aim and animated by a single will, millions alter the forms of their communication and their behavior, change the place and the mode of their activities, change their tools and weapons in accordance with the changing conditions and the requirements of the struggle—all this is genuine organization" (L, CW, 21:252–53).

Despite this well-defined stand, Lenin's *State and Revolution* concentrated on the new, badly organized forms of *mass movement* without stressing the role of the party. This was necessary for many reasons: first, because the overthrow of the democratic Provisional Government had to be legitimized by a vision of a higher, participatory democracy, a true self-government of the masses; second, because the Bolshevik seizure of power would not have been possible without frantic attempts to get broad popular support; and finally, because the revolutionary events of 1917 turned Lenin's attention to the ultimate utopian goals of communism. But the successful seizure of power changed this situation almost overnight. "The elemental force of the masses" ceased to be useful as an instrument of revolutionary destruction, becoming instead a dangerous factor in economic chaos and political anarchy. This led Lenin to the forceful reassertion of his organizational principles. In the summer of 1918 he formulated his revolutionary credo as follows: "Our fighting method is organization. We must organize everything, take everything into our hands, keep a check on the kulaks and profiteers at every step, declare implacable war on them and never allow them to breathe freely, controlling their every move" (ibid., 27:517–18).[71]

We are told that in *What Is to Be Done?* that Lenin "*unconsciously* has sketched a blueprint for a dictatorship."[72] Whether this really was unconscious or not is a big question, but it is obvious that in 1902 he could only aim for dictatorship within his own party, which posed no visible threat to society as a whole. But in 1918, after the seizure of political power, followed by the violent dispersal of the Constituent Assembly, the story, of course, was different. With the Bolshevik party firmly in control, identifying its monopolistic rule with the dictatorship of the proletariat and deeply committed to a communist utopia, Lenin's organizational model of 1902 came to be seen as the consciously formulated blueprint for a new type of dictatorship, unlimited in scope (since the rulers were to take *everything* into their hands) and unrestrained by any rules. Lenin put it very succinctly: "The scientific term 'dictatorship' means nothing more nor less than an authority untrammeled by any laws, absolutely unrestricted by any rules whatever, and based directly on force. The term 'dictatorship' *has no other meaning but this*" (ibid., 10:246; see also ibid., 31:353).

Of course, this definition tells us more about Lenin than about political science. In fact the term *dictatorship* does not necessarily imply the rejection of *all* limitations of power. Lenin did not distinguish between the suspension of the political rights of citizens and completely arbitrary rule, between constitutional and other legal limitations, or between legal and traditional or moral limitations. He did not try to explain the relationship between his definition and the Marxian usage of the term, according to which the classical form of bourgeois dictatorship was the law-abiding democratic republic. He attempted instead to define and justify his own view of dictatorial rule, as exercised by his own party. He should have added that the aim of this dictatorship was an ideological one that involved forcing people to reeducate themselves, to abandon their individual and collective identities, to accept dictatorship as their own, and thus to conform to it not just externally but internally as well.

However, Lenin cannot be suspected of neglect of this ideological dimension of political commitment. Rather, as a dedicated communist, he took it for granted; it was implicit in his image of a militant party, as set forth in *What Is to Be Done?*

4.4   The Destruction of "Nomocracy" and
the Legitimization of Violence

Lenin's conception of dictatorship as authority "absolutely unrestricted by any rules whatever" was an extreme case of "teleocratic" thinking, of a resolute and contemptuous opposition to all sorts of "nomocracy."[73] It is therefore not enough to treat Lenin as "probably the most extreme utilitarian" in history:[74] utilitarianism as such does not necessarily involve contempt for all rules. The existence of some rules, on the contrary, may be justified on purely utilitarian grounds.[75] Neither does it suffice to define Lenin as a "legal nihilist"; typical legal nihilists, especially in the Russian tradition, condemned law in the name of morality,[76] whereas in Lenin's case contempt for all rules extended to morality as well. In his view, proletarian morality had to be strictly teleocratic, that is, consistently subordinated to the struggle for communism, as defined by the vanguard party. In "The Tasks of the Youth Leagues," he explained this with his usual precision and clarity: "We reject any morality based on extra-human and extra-class concepts. We say that this is deception, dupery, stultification of the workers and peasants in the interests of the landowners and capitalists. We say that our morality is entirely subordinated to the interests of the proletariat's class struggle. Our morality stems from the interests of the class struggle of the proletariat" (L, *SW*, 3:416–18).

Before the revolution, this class struggle consisted in "overthrowing the tsar, overthrowing the capitalists, and abolishing the capitalist class"—hence, everything that served this purpose was moral. After the revolution the immediate aim of the struggle was "to prevent the return of the old exploiters." The intensity of the struggle should not abate until its final goal was achieved—that is, until the new communist order was firmly established. The effectiveness of the struggle was incompatible with commitment to any fixed rules, since the justice of the cause legitimized the use of all possible means. Morality, therefore, should be defined in a purely instrumental way: "Morality is what serves to destroy the old existing society and to unite all the working people around the proletariat, which is building up a new, a communist society" (ibid.).

True, in the communist society of the future "the simple, fundamental rules of the community" were to be reestablished and become a *habit*. People were "to *become accustomed* to observing the elementary rules of social intercourse that have been known for centuries and repeated for thousands of years in all copy-book maxims." But this was to happen after the withering away of the state, in a society capable of maintaining itself "without force, without coercion, and without subordination" (L, *A*, 384, 303, 303). In other words, it was a utopian vision of the final goal, but not a program for the present or for the immediate, predictable future. Lenin made it absolutely clear that this final ideal should not influence in any way the struggle to achieve it. The means used in that struggle should be ruthlessly violent, unrestricted by any rules except one: disciplined subordination to the vanguard party. Thus, the final end of the movement was reduced in practice to a mere abstract, while the changing hierarchy of *practical* ends—ends really binding, to which everything else should be totally subordinated—was to be defined at each stage by a small, self-appointed revolutionary minority. In the period of postrevolutionary dictatorship, the end-governed structure of the revolutionary organization became the foundation of the party state and thereby of the entire social system.

Lenin's readiness to abandon all scruples for the sake of revolutionary expediency recalls the central idea of Sergei Nechaev's famous *Revolutionary Catechism*: "Everything that allows the triumph of the revolution is moral, and everything that stands in its way is immoral."[77] Admittedly, this is an incomplete parallel. Lenin was a man of much greater caliber than Nechaev; Lenin's intellect was vastly superior, his revolutionary experience much richer. Unlike Nechaev, Lenin was relatively honest in his personal relationships, was unwilling to resort to outright mystification, and did not indulge in the quasi-romantic demonization of professional revolutionaries in the fashion of the Blanquist conspiracies of the nineteenth century. Nevertheless, the outstanding features of his character as a revolutionary were anticipated in Nechaev's *Catechism*. He was "absorbed by a single, exclusive interest, a single thought, a single passion—the revolution"; he despised and hated "the existing social ethic in all its demands and expressions"; "revolutionary passion" became in him "a daily, hourly passion, combined with cold calculation."[78]

These Nechaevian features powerfully influenced Lenin's views on the revolutionary struggle and the proletarian dictatorship. Their relevance to the problem of freedom is obvious, although the tendency to minimize their importance, or to conceal their very existence, is still very strong. Progressive Marxologists, or Sovietologists, seemed to think that to draw attention to this ugly side of Lenin's legacy amounted to supporting the cold war and should not appear in respectable scholarly works. This climate of opinion enabled some authors to create an idealized and, in fact, falsified picture of Lenin. Even leading specialists sometimes yielded to this tendency. Thus, for instance, we read in Lewin's book that Lenin "hated repression" and thought that "it should be used only in the defense of the regime against serious threat and as a punishment for those who contravened legality."[79] Characteristically, the author did not bother to support these sweeping generalizations by any evidence whatever.

What is at stake is not merely Lenin's character as a person. Most attempts to tidy up his image have been part of a conscious effort to deny the continuity between Lenin and Stalin, to support the view that the founder of the Soviet state was not guilty of totalitarianism. Because of this we must consider this subject in more detail.

In "The Urgent Task of Our Movement" (1900) Lenin wrote: "With regard to questions of tactics, we shall confine ourselves to the following: Social Democracy does not tie its hands, it does not restrict its activities to some one preconceived plan or method of political struggle; it recognizes all methods of struggle" (L, CW, 4:371).

Truly, for Lenin anything was permissible so long as it profited the party. If he rejected certain methods (i.e., individual terrorism), he did so, as he himself admitted, "only on grounds of expediency" (L, A, 560). And when expedient, he was always ready to change his views. Thus, in 1905 the orthodox Marxist ban on individual terrorism did not prevent him from recommending such methods as the killing of spies, policemen, gendarmes, and members of the Black Hundreds gangs or the blowing up of their headquarters and so forth. He did not neglect such details as "getting on to the roofs of upper storeys of houses, etc., and showering stones or pouring boiling water on the troops, etc." (L, CW, 9:421–24).

Of course, revolution has its special rights. *A la guerre, comme à la guerre*. It is not our task here to distinguish between admissible and inadmissible forms of revolutionary struggle.

Let us assume for the sake of argument that in a struggle against autocracy many forms of revolutionary violence are justified and admissible. Let us even refrain from passing judgment on such unconventional methods as bank robberies, known as "revolutionary expropriations." The point is that all these concessions to the principle of revolutionary violence as such will not suffice to justify Lenin's understanding of revolutionary expediency as the highest law. It is not enough to place Lenin in the same category as all other revolutionaries; his implacable ruthlessness in subordinating everything to a single cause cannot be explained away by any reference to the revolutionary character of his tasks.

One of the best illustrations of this point does not involve the problem of revolutionary violence at all. I refer to Lenin's views on the use of deliberate slander against *other revolutionaries*, whose activities appeared to him detrimental to his own party. In 1906 he used violent language against the Mensheviks, calling them enemies of the working class and outright traitors. He was arraigned for this before an honorary jury of the Social Democratic party and seized this opportunity to challenge all "conventional" notions of morality. The wording of his attacks on the Mensheviks, he explained, was "calculated to evoke in the reader hatred, aversion and contempt." Such wording "is calculated not to convince, but to break the ranks of the opponent, not to correct the mistake of the opponent but to destroy him, to wipe his organization off the face of the earth. This wording is indeed of such nature as to evoke the worst thoughts, the worst suspicions about the opponent and indeed, as contrasted with the wording that convinces and corrects, it 'carries confusion into the ranks of the proletariat' " (ibid., 12:424–25).

Formally, the Bolsheviks and Mensheviks were still members of the same Social Democratic party. Lenin, however, saw the Mensheviks as the seceding section of the party, and for him this meant that all possible weapons must be used against them, including the deliberate deception of the workers. This, he argued, was because "it is one's duty *to wrest* the masses from the leadership of the seceding section." He proudly admitted that he had "purposely and deliberately carried confusion into the ranks of that section of the St. Petersburg proletariat which followed the Mensheviks," and concluded by demanding: "Are there any limits to a permissible struggle stemming from a split? No Party standards set limits to such struggle, nor can there be such limits, for a split implies that the Party has ceased to exist" (ibid., 425–28).

The memoirs of Angelica Balabanoff shed additional light on this remarkable reasoning. She asked Lenin how he could brand dedicated socialists as traitors and received the answer that he did not mean to say that the Mensheviks were "dishonest individuals"; he only wanted to point out that "*objectively*, through their attitude they became traitors." When she replied that ordinary workers understood only the literal meaning of the term, Lenin "shrugged his shoulders and left without a word."[80]

Let us briefly analyze this case. It shows that the cause of revolution was represented for Lenin exclusively by his own party; that other Marxist parties could legitimately be treated as deadly enemies; that for the true revolutionary party it was permissible to crudely manipulate and "confuse" (i.e., deceive) the workers; that any deviation from the "correct line" (as defined by Lenin) amounted to "objective treason" and put "objective traitors" beyond the pale. In other words, revolutionary expediency, which justified any measures, was to be defined only by one party or, more precisely, by its leaders. There was never any doubt, of course, that in the case of a split in the party leadership the right to represent the cause would belong exclusively to Lenin's supporters and that the other group would be treated in the same way as earlier deviationists and seceders.

These monopolistic claims, combined with the firm conviction that the leading force, the true carrier of the revolutionary cause, should be "absolutely unrestricted by any rules whatever," were a distinctively totalitarian feature of Lenin's revolutionism. If we add to this the notion of objective treason, we can easily recognize in this position the perfect justification for the Stalinist purges. After all, the infamous Moscow trials were based on the assumption that deviations from the "correct line" amounted (objectively) to crossing over to the enemy and that there was no difference between treason in the literal sense and so-called objective treason.

After the triumph of his revolution, Lenin repeatedly stressed that "not a single problem of the class struggle has ever been solved in history except by violence" (ibid., 26:458). Indeed, he hastened to confirm this view by his deeds, such as the Decree on the Suppression of Hostile Newspapers, the proclamation of the Kadet party as "the enemies of the people," the dispersal of the Constituent Assembly, the execution (without trial) of the deposed tsar and his entire family, and so forth. In the summer of 1918, after the collapse of his short-lived alliance with the Left Socialist Revolutionaries he unleashed a full-scale Bolshevik terror directed not only, not even primarily, against armed opponents, but especially against all sorts of "hucksters" and "idlers," including, of course, the grain-hoarding peasants. He prepared and justified this decision in a number of articles and speeches, all full of unrestrained class hatred and completely free of any "hatred of repression." His choice of words indicated that he enjoyed stirring up both organized terror and the most diverse forms of mass violence. His program of the "systematic application of *coercion* to an entire class (the bourgeoisie) and its accomplices" (L, A, 425) equated all the rich with "the crooks, the idlers and hooligans" and categorically demanded that they be subjected to every sort of humiliating repression. Despite his usual commitment to discipline and order, he particularly urged that the masses should be encouraged to manifest their class hatred in spontaneous pogroms and robberies, arguing as follows:

Variety is a guarantee of vitality here, a pledge of success in achieving the single common aim—to cleanse the land of Russia of all sorts of harmful insects, of crook-fleas, of bedbugs—the rich, and so on and so forth. In one place half a score of rich, a dozen crooks, half a dozen workers who shirk their work . . . will be put in prison. In another place they will be put to cleaning latrines. In a third place they will be provided with "yellow tickets" after they have served their time, so that all people shall have them under surveillance as *harmful* persons, until they reform. In a fourth place, one out of every ten idlers will be shot on the spot. (ibid., 431–32)

True, the article containing these practical recommendations never appeared in print. But in other articles and speeches Lenin preached revolutionary violence with equal force, refraining only from particularizing details. In his theses on "The Immediate Tasks of the Soviet Government" (April 1918), for instance, he praised "an iron hand," the "ruthless suppression" of the resistance of the exploiters, and the "salutary firmness" that manifested itself in "shooting thieves on the spot"; he also suggested in this context that the Soviet government was "excessively mild," resembling jelly rather than iron (L, SW, 2:607, 608). A little earlier (in January 1918) he had complained about the "monstrous inactivity" of the workers and proclaimed the need of *forcing* them to join the terror under the threat of hunger. "Each factory and company," he wrote, "must form contingents, not on a voluntary basis: it must be the duty of everyone to take part in these searches [for speculators] under the threat of being deprived of his bread card. We can't expect to get anywhere unless we resort to terrorism: speculators must be shot on the spot" (L, *CW*, 26:550).

An interesting element in Lenin's justification of violence was the view that petty bourgeois resistance to socialism had become especially danger- ous *after* the military suppression of the counterrevolutionary forces (L, *SW*, 2:608). This constant or increasing threat provided a rationale for his deep conviction that the dictatorship of the proletariat should not "fear any resort to compulsion and to the most severe, decisive and ruthless forms of coercion by the state." It is important to stress that the proclamation of the NEP did not involve political liberalization. On the contrary, the de- creasing role of direct compulsion in economic life was for Lenin a decisive argument for the strengthening of political control. He saw the NEP as a temporary retreat, not as a change of goals, and was therefore peculiarly suspicious of all those who wanted to give it another meaning. He stated his views on the real nature of his new policy quite bluntly: "The most important thing at such a moment is to retreat in good order, to fix the precise limits to retreat, and not to give way to panic. And when a Men- shevik says, 'You are now retreating; I have been advocating retreat all the time. I agree with you, I am your man, let us retreat together,' we say in reply, 'For the public manifestations of Menshevism our revolutionary courts must pass the death sentence, otherwise they are not our courts, but God knows what'" (L, *A*, 492, 524).

The idealization of the NEP period in Western literature on the subject is unfortunately so widespread that much work remains to be done to reveal the truth—both the truth about facts and the truth about intentions. The NEP cannot be seen as an anticipation of Gorbachev's *perestroika*, because *politically* it was a further step *toward* totalitarianism. It restored civil law to make possible commodity exchange relations between the cities and the countryside, while at the same time destroying the last remnants both of political pluralism in the country and of political freedom within the party. We should not perceive this as a contradiction, because it was a very logical development: in Lenin's view, economic retreat increased the dan- ger of a restoration of capitalism, which made it necessary to strengthen the dictatorship by suppressing all possible opposition, both outside and within the party. The peasants were allowed freedom to produce for the market, but for this very reason (according to Lenin's logic) they had to be prevented from becoming a self-conscious political force, a "class in itself."

The introduction of the NEP was preceded by a growing discontent among the workers, as reflected within the party in the increasingly strong workers' opposition and by the open revolt at the naval base of Kronstadt. In a sense the NEP was a direct response to these events: economic concessions and a strengthening of political control were equally necessary to save the Bolshevik dictatorship. Hence, it was entirely consistent that the inauguration of the NEP at the Tenth Party Congress (in early March 1921) was accompanied by the passing by the party of two resolutions that formally prohibited factionalism and opposition. The first condemned the Workers' Opposition as a syndicalist and anarchist deviation (ibid., 497–99). The second proclaimed all factions within the party to be "harmful and impermissible," defining the party as a fully monolithic structure based on "strict discipline" and "the maximum unanimity." The condemnation of syndicalism reflected Lenin's lifelong distrust of trade unionism, coupled with his deep conviction that only the vanguard party was "capable of uniting, training and organizing a vanguard of the proletariat" and of withstanding "the inevitable petty-bourgeois vacillations" of the workers. The ban on pluralism within the party was justified, because, as Lenin pointed out, "the enemies of the proletariat take advantage of every deviation from a thoroughly consistent communist line" (ibid., 500–502, 500). Thus, the party formally legislated that a proletarian dictatorship also had to be a dictatorship over the workers.

In terms of teleocracy versus nomocracy, the situation created by the NEP may be described as the difficult and hostile coexistence of two different types of social order. In the economic sphere there was room for the spontaneous, nomocratic order of the market, but the political sphere was totally dominated by a unitary and single-minded organization whose dictatorship was unhampered by any rules and whose declared aim was the replacement of the market economy by a consciously created and totally regulated economic system. Such a strange coexistence could not, of course, last forever.

4.5 The Partisan Principle in Literature and Philosophy

As we can see, the cornerstone of Lenin's theory of dictatorship was the legitimization of violence: "Dictatorship is a rule based directly upon force and unrestricted by any laws" (L, SW, 3:23). This brutal frankness excluded hypocritical attempts to embellish the proletarian state or to conceal its true functions. "The state," Lenin wrote, "is only a *weapon* of the proletariat in its class struggle. A special kind of *cudgel, rien de plus*" (L, A, 490).

The central problem of Lenin's theory of the dictatorship of the proletariat was, of course, the state and economy of the transitional period. But his vision of a fully regulated, teleocratic order was much broader and much more ambitious. True, his main concern was always the problem of power, of "*kto-kogo?*" (who-whom)—that is, of dealing with and crushing the enemy by physical force. Nevertheless, he was also a staunch defender of ideological orthodoxy, always ready to define "the only correct standpoint" and to press for unanimity. His favorite idea of disciplined partisanship applied also to philosophy and culture; his vision of a proletarian dictatorship included a distinctively "ideocratic" dimension (though less developed than under Stalinism, of course). We must not forget either that the revolutionary sailors of Kronstadt rebelled not only against the political dictatorship of Lenin's party, but also against its attempts to impose a *spiritual* tyranny. "The most hateful and criminal thing which the Communists have created" was, in their view, "moral servitude": "They laid their hands even on the inner life of the toilers and compelled them to think only in the Communist way."[81] Clearly, they perceived Lenin's state not merely as a cudgel but also as a *Weltanschauungsstaat*—that is, an *ideocratic* dictatorship trying to achieve total conformity, both external and internal.

This dimension of Lenin's thought was inherent in his theory of the party, conceived as the only legitimate channel of salvific revolutionary knowledge, which is why Pavel Axelrod called this theory "an organizational utopia of a theocratic character."[82] It must be stressed, however, that the totalitarian consequences of the organizational monopoly of "true knowledge" were not immediately obvious to Lenin himself but were revealed only gradually, under the pressure of events. Full realization of their destructive potential came only under Stalin.

Lenin's article "Party Organization and Party Literature" (November 1905) is perhaps the most drastic application of the partisan principle to the sphere of culture. Literature and the press, Lenin argued, cannot be free under capitalism, because "the power of money" excludes freedom. True freedom is not simply freedom from the police but also from capital, from careerism and from "bourgeois-anarchist individualism." Such freedom should manifest itself in the striving for great collective goals, as defined by the party. The socialist proletariat must therefore "put forward the principle of *party literature*, must develop this principle and put it into practice as fully and consciously as possible" (L, CW, 10:48, 47, 45).

Lenin made it plain that this meant nothing less than a complete politicization of literary art. He appealed to his followers: "Down with nonpartisan writers! Down with literary supermen! Literature must become *part* of the common cause of the proletariat, 'a cog and a screw' of one single great Social-Democratic mechanism set in motion by the entire politically-conscious vanguard of the entire working class. Literature must become a component of organized, planned and integrated Social-Democratic Party work" (ibid., p. 45). As may readily be imagined, this was a hard philosophy for Lenin's literary fellow travelers to swallow. Their only consolation was that Lenin's appeal was addressed to members or informal supporters of his own party—that is, only to those writers who had agreed to embrace his goals. In later years, the same qualification was often repeated by the theorists of socialist realism, who preferred, as a rule, more hypocritical wording. But the very principle of the party state deprived these declarations of any real meaning. Indeed, if the party is coextensive with the state and its declared aims are shared by all loyal, patriotic citizens, then, of course, the differences between party literature and national literature are reduced to differences of degree, not of kind.

The philosophic interpretation of the idea of the partisan principle underwent a similar evolution. At first it was no more than a sociologizing theory of philosophical knowledge stressing the class roots and content of philosophical ideas. Next, it gave rise to the demand that the Bolshevik party have a definite philosophy of its own, one that would be directly politicized and obligatory for all party members, while at the same time claiming a monopoly on "objective truth." Finally, of course, the official philosophy of the party became the official philosophy of the party state, being totally subordinated to the dictatorship of the proletariat and serving it as a powerful weapon of ideological uniformity and repression.

A good illustration of the transition from the first to the second stage is Lenin's conflict with Bogdanov. Bogdanov's view of all knowledge as the product and instrument of collective, historical, class-determined praxis led to a thorough sociologization of philosophical categories and to a programmatic rejection of the very notion of objective truth; in this sense he was even more committed than Lenin to a class theory of knowledge. However, he was an independent Marxist thinker and as such was unwilling to obey any prescribed orthodoxy; he sharply distinguished between a philosophy linked to class struggle and one subordinated to a political party— even his own Bolshevik party. A clash with Lenin was therefore inevitable, although both men hoped for some time to avoid the inescapable.

The story of this conflict, up to 1908, has been told in Lenin's long letter to Gorky of February 25. In it Lenin did not pretend to be an authority on philosophy; on the contrary, he posed as a rank-and-file Marxist (*riadovoi Marksist*) concerned with practical tasks and ready to leave philosophy to the philosophers.[83] He told Gorky that he had had doubts about Bogdanov's philosophy from the very beginning but sincerely wanted to disregard them for the sake of political alliance: "In the summer and autumn of 1904, Bogdanov and I reached a complete agreement, as *Bolsheviks*, and formed the tacit bloc, which tacitly ruled out philosophy as a *neutral field*" (ibid., 13:449).

From this it is clear that in 1904 Lenin had not yet reached the conclusion that all philosophy was necessarily partisan and that all talk of its neutrality was either an illusion or an outright deception. But he did reach this conclusion very soon, through his further exposure to Bogdanov's views. In the summer of 1906 he read Bogdanov's *Empiriomonism* and was roused to fury. It was now clear to him that Bogdanov "was on an absolutely wrong track, not the Marxist track." He gave expression to his rage in a letter to Bogdanov that took up three notebooks and was ironically called a "declaration of love" (ibid.).[84] The abusive language of these notebooks caused Bogdanov to return them to Lenin with a sort of ultimatum: if Lenin wanted to maintain personal relations with him, his letter must be treated as "unwritten, undispatched and unread."[85]

Of course, Lenin failed to comply with this demand. He thought, rather, of publishing his letter to Bogdanov under the title "Notes of an Ordinary Marxist on Philosophy" (ibid., 449).[86] Soon afterward Lenin read a collection of articles by Bogdanov's group entitled *Studies in the Philosophy of Marxism* and reacted vehemently against it: "Every article made me furiously indignant. No, no, this is not Marxism! Our empirio-critics, empirio-monists, and empirio-symbolists are floundering in a bog. . . . No, really, it's too much. To be sure, we ordinary Marxists are not well up in philosophy, but why insult us by serving this stuff up to us as the philosophy of Marxism! I would rather let myself be drawn and quartered than consent to collaborate in an organ or body that preaches such things" (ibid., 450).

Having reached this conclusion, Lenin decided on resolute action, which involved several interconnected tasks: the public denunciation and anathematization of the philosophy of Bogdanov and his group; the demonstration of the reactionary nature of empiriocriticism and the other philosophical currents that were influential among Russian Marxists; the elevation of the principle of partisanship in philosophy and its application to contemporary philosophical discussions; the narrowest possible definition of the orthodox Marxist position in philosophical matters; and, finally, the establishment of his own reputation in Marxist philosophy, thereby validating his claim to be recognized as the supreme philosophical authority in the Bolshevik party.

We should not see this claim as a testimony of Lenin's personal vanity, but rather as the logical consequence of his conviction that a fight against philosophical heresies was "absolutely inevitable" because there could be no neutrality in philosophical matters. In other words, Lenin came to see Marxist philosophy as part of his responsibility as a Bolshevik leader. He retained the highest respect for Plekhanov's philosophical authority while viewing him as unable, unwilling, or perhaps "too lazy" to effectively combat the views of Bogdanov's group—that is, to do so "simply, without unnecessarily frightening his readers with philosophical nuances." Besides, Bogdanov was a Bolshevik and should be disciplined by the leadership of his own faction. Lenin felt therefore that he himself must undertake this task, that he should do it "at all costs" and say everything "in his own way" (ibid., 34:388–89, 388, 388).

The result of this endeavor was Lenin's one and only philosophical book, *Materialism and Empiriocriticism: Critical Comments on a Reactionary Philosophy* (published in March 1909 under the pen name V. Ilyin). Its appearance marked the beginning of a new and much closer relationship between theory and practice: Marxist philosophy (as defined by Lenin) and Bolshevism. Lenin attached tremendous importance to this work and wanted to see it in print as soon as possible; he even considered offering the printer a bribe of 100 rubles to speed up his work.[87]

Let us try to summarize this book. We need not go into details because its content (in accordance with Lenin's intention) is simple and devoid of philosophical nuances. Its philosophical crudity is intensified by frequent use of abusive language (although Lenin's sister, A. I. Yelizarova, did much to tone this down)[88] and by constant repetition of the same arguments.

Nonpartisanship in philosophy, Lenin argued, does not exist. The entire history of philosophy is comprehended in the struggle between two principal alignments, two parties: materialism and idealism (ibid., 14:335–46). Nonpartisan knowledge is possible in empirical sciences but not in philosophy, which is thoroughly partisan. Therefore, bourgeois professors, who are "capable of making very valuable contributions in the special fields of chemistry, history and physics," cannot be trusted "*one iota* when it comes to philosophy." It is "for the same reason that *not a single* professor of political economy, who may be capable of very valuable contributions in the field of factual and specialized investigations, can be trusted *one iota* when it comes to the general theory of political economy. For in modern society, the latter is as much a *partisan* science as is *epistemology*. Taken as a whole, the professors of economics are nothing but learned salesmen of the capitalist class, while the professors of philosophy are learned salesmen of the theologians" (ibid., 342, 342–43).

The progressive camp in philosophy is materialism (ibid., 338). It must be "consistent to the end," since the slightest concession to idealism leads ultimately to fideism and clericalism, thus serving the cause of the exploiters and oppressors. Joseph Dietzgen, the German worker who independently arrived at dialectical materialism, justly said that the middle party in philosophy is the most repulsive (ibid., 339–40). His description of this party as "graduated flunkeys of fideism" accurately characterizes the Russian thinkers, who (following Bogdanov) try to combine Marxism with empiriocriticism (ibid., 341–42).

Materialism is incompatible with any doubts about the cognizability of the world. Agnosticism leads to subjectivism, that is, to subjective idealism, and finally to solipsism and reactionary fideism. For materialist epistemology (Lenin used the term *gnoseology*), the only legitimate position is therefore the copy theory of knowledge whereby our sensations are treated as "copies, photographs, images, mirror reflections of things." The notion of material objects and of their copies in the human mind are in fact two sides of the same concept: that of matter. "Matter," Lenin explained, "is a philosophical category which is given to man by his sensations, and which is copied, photographed and reflected by our sensations, while existing independently of them" (ibid., 232, 130). He was confident that such a concept could not become antiquated. All arguments to the contrary were in his view *"childish talk"* or reactionary wishful thinking. The struggle between materialism and idealism, between science and religion, between the assertion of objective truth and its denial, had not become out of date in the two thousand years of philosophy's development (ibid., 130); it could end only with the total victory of the right side.

As we can see, Lenin could not dispense with the notion of objective truth. He could not distinguish between "cognizability of the world" and "knowledge of the objective truth"; "to regard our sensations as images of the external world" and "to recognize objective truth" were for him "one and the same thing." Hence, he indignantly rejected Bogdanov's view of truth as the "organizing form of human experience." Religion, he argued, is also a form of "socially-organized experience"; therefore, Bogdanov's philosophy legitimized religion and thus led to "clericalism pure and simple" (ibid., 130, 229–30).

The same criticisms applied to all forms of historico-sociological relativism. Lenin conceded that an element of relativism was inherent in the dialectical method, but interpreted it not as a denial of objective truth but only "in the sense that the limits of approximation of our knowledge of objective truth are historically conditional." He even tried to rescue the notion of "absolute truth" and of "absolutely objective knowledge" (ibid., 137, 136). He feared, not without reason, that the relativization of truth would undermine his understanding of "scientific socialism" and "adequate consciousness," thereby destroying his favorite conception of the omnicompetent vanguard party. Without objective truth there can be no certainty, no firm guidelines, and therefore no resolute action.

The arguments supporting these views were crude and naive in the extreme. Thus, for instance, in his attack on "subjectivism," Lenin invoked the authority of Marx's son-in-law, Paul Lafargue, praising his correct understanding of Engels and his "left-wing criticism" of Kant. He quoted Lafargue's crudities at length and with obvious satisfaction, entirely approving of such reasonings as this: "The workingman who eats sausage and receives a hundred sous a day knows very well that he is robbed by the employer and is nourished by pork meat, that the employer is a robber and that the sausage is pleasant to the taste and nourishing to the body.

Not at all, say the bourgeois sophists, whether they are called Pyrrho, Hume or Kant. His opinion is personal, an entirely subjective opinion; he might with equal reason maintain that the employer is his benefactor and that the sausage consists of chopped leather, for he cannot know *things-in-themselves*" (ibid., 203).

To resort to such arguments was consistent with Lenin's conscious effort to reduce Marxist philosophy to a crude, commonsensical form of materialism, which was characteristic of his beloved teacher, Nikolai Chernyshevskii. Lenin supplemented *Materialism and Empiriocriticism* by a separate note on Chernyshevskii, presenting him as a great Russian thinker, a disciple of Feuerbach, whose criticism of Kantianism (and, by implication, of modern agnosticism and subjectivism as such) was "entirely on Engels's level" (ibid., 359–61). This amounted to saying that empiriocriticism, including Bogdanov's empiriomonism, could not withstand confrontation with the pre-Marxian materialism of the Russian radicals of the 1860s.

Lenin's virtual return to a pre-Marxian form of materialism is especially evident in his veneration of Feuerbach. Chernyshevskii's teacher is mentioned in *Materialism and Empiriocriticism* almost as frequently as are Marx and Engels and always in a positive context, as one of the greatest authorities on materialism and as an unsurpassed critic of Kantianism. Feuerbach's name often appears along with Marx's, as if the two represented the same philosophical standpoint—for instance: "All the great materialists—Diderot, Feuerbach, Marx and Engels," "this is what irrevocably divides the materialists Feuerbach, Marx and Engels from the agnostics," and so on. In one place Lenin even says that "the *entire school* of Feuerbach, Marx and Engels turned from Kant to the left, to a complete rejection of all idealism and of all agnosticism" (ibid., 48, 159, 204). Marx's criticism of Feuerbach in his "Theses on Feuerbach" was not mentioned at all; Lenin totally ignored Marx's intention of distinguishing his philosophical position from "all hitherto existing materialism (that of Feuerbach included)" (M, *SW*, 156 [Thesis 1]). Taking into account that the distinction in question consisted precisely in a different attitude toward the legacy of "subjectivism," as well as in a different conception of truth, Lenin's ignorance of this distinction is truly astounding.

According to Marx, reality should be conceived not only "in the form of the object or of contemplation" but as "sensuous human activity," as practice—that is, "subjectively." No previous materialism had understood this point, which was why the *active* side had to be developed, although only in an abstract way, through idealism. Hence, "the question whether objective truth can be attributed to human thinking is not a question of theory but is a practical question. Man must prove the truth, i.e., the reality and power, the this-sidedness of his thinking in practice" (ibid., 156 [Thesis 1–2]).

This was the Marxist justification of Bogdanov's belief that the classical definition of truth was untenable. To concern oneself with the concordance between the human intellect and things (*adaequatio intellectus atque rei*), to conceive cognition as merely "copying," or "photographing," external objects, was senseless because all human knowledge was a product of human collective practice. Man as knower was himself a product of this practice and could not raise himself to a superhuman observation point from which he might perceive reality in itself. It followed from this that the only criterion of truth was practice, that the truthfulness of thought was its power, and that the dispute about the reality or nonreality of thought isolated from practice was, as Marx put it, "a purely *scholastic* question" (ibid. [Thesis 2]).

Bogdanov thought that this praxis-derived and praxis-oriented theory of knowledge would help overcome the rigid determinism of the Second International and thus provide a philosophical foundation for a more activist variety of Marxism. Lenin, however, chose to defend an old-fashioned and utterly contemplative theory according to which "the world is matter moving in conformity to law" and "our knowledge is in a position only to *reflect* this conformity to law" (L, *CW*, 14:169). It is important to emphasize that he saw this option as entirely consistent with his political voluntarism, which culminated in his theory of the party. In order to resist the pressure of "spontaneity" and to bring "adequate consciousness" to the workers' movement, the Leninist party had to see itself as the only channel of "true knowledge," as revealed in "scientific socialism." The notion of "objective truth," or even "absolute truth," was needed to support its absolute self-confidence, its intolerance of any rivals, its claim to control and direct the workers, and, finally, its mandate to exercise dictatorial power untrammeled by any rules. Bogdanov's philosophy, even in conjunction with a Sorelian conception of an energy-creating collective myth, could not produce a comparable certainty.[89] The party of professional revolutionaries wanted to see its ideology as embodying and monopolizing the truth itself, not merely as a "socially organized experience" or a myth.

The authoritarian roots, as well as the consequences, of Lenin's commitment to "objective truth" did not escape Bogdanov's notice. In his critique of *Materialism and Empiriocriticism*, he pointed out that Lenin's use of the notion of absolute truth was deeply rooted in a precapitalist authoritarian structure of thought similar to the worldview of the clergy. This explained Lenin's fanatical intolerance, his belief in the absolute correctness of his views, and consequently his arrogant claim that these views should simply be imposed on the masses. Thus, despite all his sympathies with Bolshevism, Bogdanov saw the Bolshevik leader as a dangerous figure whose authoritarianism he compared to a vampire sucking the workers' blood and preventing them from achieving independence and cultural maturity.[90]

Bogdanov was, of course, well aware of Lenin's hatred of the clergy. The mentality of a blind believer could easily be combined with ardent atheism, and this was precisely Lenin's case. His hatred of religion was unbounded, and he was horrified by the idea of "God-building," as put forward by Gorky, Lunacharskii, and others of Bogdanov's circle. In a letter to Gorky of Nov. 13–14, 1913, Lenin wrote:

God-seeking differs from god-building or god-creating or god-making, etc., no more than a yellow devil differs from a blue devil. To talk about god-seeking, not in order to declare against *all* devils and gods, against every ideological necrophily (all worship of a divinity is necrophily—be it the cleanest, most ideal, not sought-out but built-up divinity, it's all the same), but to prefer a blue devil to a yellow one is a hundred times worse than not saying anything about it at all. . . .

Any flirtation even with a god, is the most inexpressible foulness, particularly tolerantly (and even favorably) accepted by the democratic bourgeoisie—for that very reason it is the most dangerous foulness, the most shameful "infection." A million *physical* sins, dirty tricks, acts of violence and infections are much more easily discovered by the crowd, and therefore are much less dangerous than the *subtle*, spiritual idea of god, dressed up in the most attractive "ideological" costumes. The Catholic priest corrupting young girls (about whom I have just read by chance in a German newspaper) is *much less* dangerous, precisely to "democracy," than a priest without his robes, a priest without crude religion, an ideologically equipped and democratic priest preaching the creation and the invention of a god. (ibid., 35:121–22)

Gorky tried to defend himself by defining God as "the complex of those ideas, worked out by the tribe, the nation, mankind, which awaken and organize social feelings, having as their object to link the individual to society and to bridle zoological individualism." This provoked Lenin to define God in his own way. God, he stated, is "first of all the complex of ideas generated by the brutish subjection of man both by external nature and by the class yoke—ideas which *consolidate* this subjection, *lull to sleep* the class struggle." It is not true, he continued in his letter, that the idea of God was needed to bridle zoological individualism: "In reality, 'zoological individualism' was bridled not by the idea of God, it was bridled both by the primitive herd and the primitive community. The idea of God *always* put to sleep and blunted the 'social feelings,' replacing the living by the dead, being *always* the idea of slavery (the worst, hopeless slavery). Never has the idea of God 'linked the individual with society': it has always *tied* the oppressed classes *hand and foot* with faith in the *divinity* of the oppressors" (ibid., 127, 128, 129).

Obviously, Lenin's hatred of religion had a peculiar intensity and quality that had little in common with the position of Feuerbach, who regarded religion as man's self-alienation and tried to transcend rather than destroy it. In fact Feuerbach's ideas of a humanized religion and a divinized humanity were one of the main sources of the philosophy of God-creation, and Lenin's violent criticism of this philosophy might easily be leveled against Feuerbach himself. Marx also defined religion in terms of human self-alienation, which was very different than reducing religion's role to that of a tool of class domination and oppression. What distinguished him from Feuerbach was principally Marx's emphasis on the *economic* roots of religious consciousness (M, *SW* [Thesis 4]). This meant in practice that the revolutionary workers' movement was to concentrate on the struggle with the economic system, not become involved in antireligious crusades, all of which were necessarily futile if not counterproductive.[91] He was attacked for this by Bakunin, Lenin's compatriot, who saw religion, along with the state, as one of the main pillars of the "old world" and therefore as the *direct* enemy of all genuine revolutionaries. Bakunin's aggressively antireligious stand, his categorical rejection of all flirtations with the idea of God, were fully consonant with Lenin's views on the matter. In his letter to Gorky, Lenin might have subscribed to Bakunin's antireligious tirades and repeated verbatim Bakunin's words: "Unless we desire slavery, we cannot and should not make the slightest concession to theology, for in this mystical and rigorously consistent alphabet, anyone who starts with A must inevitably arrive at Z, and anyone who wants to worship God must renounce his liberty and human dignity."[92]

Is it possible to regard Lenin's views on religion as directly influenced by Bakunin? An important argument for such a hypothesis is the way in which both men linked the origins of religion with the emergence of the state. Stressing the role of religion and of the state as two mutually dependent pillars of a class society, Bakunin seemed sometimes to have forgotten that religion had also existed in the prepolitical stage of social evolution. Lenin's view of the primitive herd as (allegedly) capable of preserving social unity without resorting to religious ideas is very reminiscent of Bakuninist conceptions.[93]

In this context, however, the intellectual genesis of Lenin's views on religion is a matter of secondary importance. More important is their relevance to a proper understanding of the antilibertarian nature of Lenin's revolutionary project.

It is evident that Lenin's extreme hostility toward religion stemmed from the same source as his fanatical intolerance of all unorthodox philosophical views—namely, his conception of the vanguard party. The Leninist party had to be monolithic and so could tolerate no ideological pluralism within its ranks. Its right to undisputed leadership derived from its alleged monopoly of the adequate consciousness of the workers' movement; hence, it could allow itself no deviation from the correct line. From the point of view of the class struggle, philosophy and religion were by no means neutral; on the contrary, all forms of philosophical idealism, as well as all forms of religious worldview, were the most dangerous ideological weapons of the class enemy. Total commitment to their destruction, therefore, was among the primary duties of all party members. In other words, all forms of ideological tolerance must be regarded as breaking party discipline and leading inevitably to betrayal.

Membership in such a party entailed, of course, severe restrictions on intellectual freedom, but it compensated for these restrictions by making choices clear and simple and by an intense feeling of participation in a sacred cause. Truly devoted party members should be able to identify fully with the party, to perceive it as a higher manifestation of their own identity, and thus to experience their subordination to it as a higher freedom. For this reason, the Leninist party was peculiarly attractive to people thirsting for faith and capable of behaving as true believers. But the secular religion of Leninism was very different from the universalistic religions of the world, being more like a militant chiliastic sect that saw signs of doom everywhere and felt itself to be the chosen instrument of earthly salvation.[94] Therefore, its quasi-religious character did not help it to sympathize with genuine religions but rather intensified its militant intolerance, its feeling of exclusive self-righteousness and intransigent hostility toward the entire "old world."

After the Bolshevik seizure of power, the practical consequences of this attitude were soon evident. There is no need to elaborate on the precise number of victims (including priests) or the exact scale of destruction (including churches); suffice it to say that repression was widespread, exceeding the record of all previous revolutions, although undoubtedly relatively modest compared with Stalin's terror. The arguments of the defenders of Lenin's party are well known: the magnitude of revolutionary events, the need to suppress resistance, civil war, the White Terror, foreign intervention, and so forth. Since a work on intellectual history cannot adequately deal with all these important issues, it seems best to suspend judgment and avoid hasty conclusions on this matter.

However, in 1922 the civil war was over, and Lenin was able to embark on a policy of national reconciliation.[95] His New Economic Policy seemed to be a step in this direction. True, economic liberalization was not followed by any increase of political freedom but was instead accompanied by "political terror against the Bolsheviks' recent allies in the struggle against the tsarist autocracy."[96] Nevertheless, the coercive terrorist methods of War Communism were abandoned, and arbitrariness and rampant violence gave way to an observance of market rules within the framework of civil law; all this resulted in a marked increase in nonpolitical civil freedom, including intellectual freedom. Was this the intended result of Lenin's policy or merely the unintentional and unexpected outcome of a forced retreat?

An optimistic reading of Lenin's intentions has become dogma for the revisionist school of American Sovietology. But the facts tell a different story. Lenin was not satisfied with dictatorship in the sphere of politics narrowly conceived. He clung to the idea of an ideological ("ideocratic") dictatorship capable of imposing its rule on human minds and consciences. Intellectual freedom under the NEP was not something he could tolerate for long. Even when mortally ill and confined to his bed, he planned to curtail it and to resume the ideological offensive.

A telling testimony to this is his role in forcibly banishing from Russia her most outstanding noncommunist philosophers (such as Nikolai Berdyaev, Lev Karsavin, Nikolai Losskii, Sergei Bulgakov, Semyon Frank, Ivan Lapshin, Ivan Ilyin), sociologists (Pitirim Sorokin), historians (Aleksandr Kizevetter), jurists, and other scholars, 160 in all.[97] Their banishment was preceded by a furious campaign in the Communist press, whose participants often urged harsher forms of repression; Trotsky, for instance, saw banishment as a "merciful" alternative to execution.[98] But the key role in the entire operation belonged to Lenin. In a letter to Feliks Dzierżyński of May 19, 1922, he demanded the following "preparatory measures": "Put the duty on the Politbureau members to devote 2–3 hours a week to looking through a number of periodicals and books, *verifying execution, demanding reviews in writing*, and securing the dispatch to Moscow of all non-Communist publications without delay. Add to this the reviews by a number of Communist writers (Steklov, Olminsky, Skvortsov, Bukharin, etc.). Collect *systematic* information about the political record, work and literary activity of the professors and writers" (L, CW, 45:555).[99]

A good example of a brief but decisive opinion on a non-Communist publication was provided by Lenin himself. In his view, the Petrograd magazine *Ekonomist*, published by the Eleventh Department of the Russian Technical Society, was "clearly a whiteguard center." Having noticed that a list of the members of this alleged center was printed on the cover, Lenin continued: "These are all patent counter-revolutionaries, accomplices of the Entente, an organization of its servitors and spies and corrupters of the student youth" (ibid., 555–56).

Evidently, the content of non-Communist publications (although otherwise legal) was, in his view, a sufficient basis for classifying their authors as spies and members of counterrevolutionary organizations. This was not just a transient aberration but an almost pathological obsession. The old conspirator saw conspiracies against his party everywhere. He assumed that scholarly or cultural activity *could not be* an end in itself but *had to be* directly connected to counterrevolution. In accordance with his understanding of the partisan principle of philosophy, he was particularly suspicious of philosophers. It is small wonder, therefore, that a collection of philosophical articles by Berdyaev, Bukshpan, Stepun, and Frank entitled *Oswald Spengler and the Decline of Europe* put him immediately on the alert. He saw this work as a "literary screen for a whiteguard organiza-tion" and wanted to take the matter up with I. S. Unschlicht, the deputy chairman of the Cheka (ibid., 500, 726 [n. 609]).

Thus, Lenin's commitment to the NEP did not weaken the totalitarian features of his ideology and mentality. Indeed, the loosening of the Com-munists' grip on the economy increased his fear of freedom and pushed him toward repressive policies in other spheres. He continually strove for total control, regarding this as inherent in the very nature of the dictator-ship of the proletariat. For him it was perfectly plain that a forced retreat in the economic field must be accompanied by a fiercer struggle for un-disputed ideological domination. The ultimate aim of this strugle was not merely the absence of active resistance, something that could be secured by sheer force, but also, and above all, a positive indoctrination, a posi-tive reeducation of the people (except, of course, avowed class enemies), a thorough, organized reshaping of their entire culture in accordance with the communist blueprint.

Lenin did not conceal that this involved an implacable struggle against national cultures, especially that of the Russians. In sharp contrast to Lux-emburg (see chapter 3, section 3), he approved (theoretically and tactically) the idea of national self-determination while remaining adamantly opposed to all manifestations of "cultural nationalism" (ibid., 19:503–7; 22:146–47). "Defense of national culture" was for him the battle cry of the worst obscurantists, the least acceptable form of nationalist aspiration. The dis-tinction he made between two cultures within every national culture broke all ties between the democratic culture (which was to be thoroughly inter-nationalist) and the *dominant* national culture. "Our task," he wrote, "is to fight the dominant, Black Hundred and bourgeois national culture of the Great Russians" (L, A, 655).[100] Accordingly, the postrevolutionary educa-tional policy of his party became resolutely antinational. Russian national traditions were criticized, ridiculed, or ignored. The teaching of Russian history (as the history of the Russian State) and the history of Russian literature was discontinued and replaced by the history of economic forma-tions and of the popular masses struggling for social emancipation. "The official thesis was that up to Lenin's birth and the rise of the labor move-ment Russian history had been all chaos, darkness and oppression and not worth being memorized." [101]

But there was also another, even more powerful enemy of the Com-munists' aspirations to rule over people's minds—namely, religion—espe-cially Christianity. Here it is important to remember Lenin's article "On the Significance of Militant Materialism" (March 1922), called sometimes Lenin's "Philosophical Testament".[102] In it he proclaimed the urgent need for "untiring atheist propaganda" and an "untiring atheist fight," including the mass distribution of militant atheist literature among the people. He indignantly rejected criticism of the atheist literature of the eighteenth century as "antiquated, unscientific and naive," castigating such views as either "pseudo-scientific sophistry" or a "complete misunderstanding of Marxism." All strivings for a greater philosophical sophistication in this matter were, from his point of view, the philosophy of the "graduated flunkeys of clericalism" (L, SW, 3:600–601).

In this way Lenin once again repeated the main thesis of his *Materialism and Empiriocriticism*, demonstrating that his studies of Hegelian dialectics from 1914 to 1916 had not changed his basic philosophical options at all.[103] He remained a crude materialist because he saw crude materialism as the best means of destroying the religious and philosophical culture of his class enemies. But this work of destruction was, in turn, only a means to a more ambitious end: the replacement of all existing religions and ideologies by a single centralized network of ideological controls. Commitment to this aim, as a necessary condition for the realization of a unified communist society, became one of the salient features of Leninism.

4.6 The Dictatorship of the Proletariat and the State

Clearly, it is difficult to treat Lenin as a philosopher of freedom. He approached the problem of freedom primarily in a negative way: as a justification of violence, systematic coercion, and authoritarian control. This narrowly conceived class approach to freedom made him uncompromisingly hostile to all conceptions of freedom in general. Unlike Marx (especially the early Marx) he did not try to counter the liberal conception of freedom with speculations about freedom as the disalienated, all-round development of the human species. Instead, he elaborated a theory of all-embracing dictatorship, which he called the dictatorship of the proletariat. He always insisted that this dictatorship was the only way for the mass of the people to achieve social emancipation and that to oppose its severity in the name of freedom could only serve the cause of capitalist slavery. As he said, "If freedom runs counter to the emancipation of labor from the yoke of capital, it is a deception" (L, CW, 29:351). For him this was an axiomatic truth and one of the fundamental tenets of Marxism.

Thus, Lenin's theory of the dictatorship of the proletariat was at the same time a theory of liberation, and its relationship to the problematic of freedom was not merely negative. The theory abandoned all scruples in dealing with rotten "bourgeois freedom" but retained a close relationship with the fundamentals of the Marxist view of communism as universal liberation. Its aim was to ensure the victory of communist freedom: freedom from all forms of class oppression and from the "anarchy of the market," freedom as rational control and conscious mastery over the collective fate of society. It upheld the uncontrolled use of coercion and violence while simultaneously proclaiming its adherence to the ideal of eliminating all institutionalized coercion, including the law and the state.

The central point of Lenin's theory in the transitional period was, of course, his view of dictatorship as "an authority untrammeled by any laws, absolutely unrestricted by any rules whatever" and his utterly authoritarian conception of the party (ibid., 31:353). But alongside this extreme and outspoken authoritarianism, we also find in Lenin a libertarian or, rather, quasi-libertarian strand that was manifested most strongly in his writings of 1917, especially in his *State and Revolution*.

Lenin's theory of the party, as developed in *What Is to Be Done?* and his theory of a universal participatory democracy, as presented in *The State and Revolution*, seem to belong to entirely different intellectual traditions. It is not surprising that many scholars have seen these texts as bluntly contradicting each other. As a rule, these scholars have tried to uphold the consistency of Leninism by minimizing the importance of *The State and Revolution*, treating it as nonrepresentative of Lenin's genuine political philosophy. Ulam, for instance, declared: "No work could be more *un*-representative of its author's political philosophy than this one by Lenin."[104] Bertram D. Wolfe was more cautious, seeing *The State and Revolution* as representative of a "strain of an insurrectionary anarchism" that had always been present in Lenin's thought. This caveat, however, did not prevent him from sharply contrasting this work with orthodox Leninism and calling it an "un-Leninist Leninist classic." He explained it as a utopian outburst, commenting:

Nothing in the resultant *State and Revolution* fits into the pattern of the orthodox Leninism that runs from *What Is to Be Done?* begun in the autumn of 1901, to the *April Theses*. . . . In *State and Revolution* there is no party to command and centralize all direction and control, no submissive mass to carry out the party's orders. In this Utopia it is the masses who are in command. An unwonted Lenin expressed complete faith in the soundness of their spontaneous reactions, their elemental moods and instincts. There is no need of *edinonachalie* or one-man rule, such as he was to advocate after a year or so of attempting to rule over mass chaos.[105]

There is a grain of truth in these opinions. *The State and Revolution* gives us a somewhat different insight into the nature of Leninism than *What Is to Be Done?* and there can be no doubt that its libertarian aspects were less characteristic of Lenin's legacy than his authoritarian theory of the party. Lenin himself made it clear that the foundations of Bolshevism as a school of thought and a movement within Russian Marxism had been laid in the years 1902–3, that is, as he was writing *What Is to Be Done?*[106] *The State and Revolution* was to be a careful *reconstruction* of Marx and Engels's views of the transitional period and therefore could not center on problems that were specific and distinctive to Bolshevism. Its purpose was to provide Bolshevism with a *legitimizing mythology*, while Lenin's other, more representative works concentrated on the problems of its practical implementation. It must also be stressed that the work was written under very specific conditions: Lenin was preparing himself for his ultimate test; he could not rule out defeat and wanted to leave a political testament—a work that "even after he might be gone, would rekindle the flame of the Revolution." [107] This explains the utopian dimension of this unusual text.

Incidentally, the same calculation can be found in the maximalist sweep of the Bolshevik revolution. In conversation with Boris Nikolaevskii, Bukharin claimed that their radicalism had developed, "because we didn't think we could actually succeed and we wanted to provide a monument, like that of the Paris Commune, to inspire the comrades of the future." [108]

However, exploring only the "exceptional" and "unrepresentative" character of *The State and Revolution* is not the most fruitful approach. The relationship between this work of Lenin's and the rest of his legacy should be analyzed in terms of dialectical tensions rather than mechanical contrasts. On closer examination *The State and Revolution* no longer seems such a strange and alien body in the corpus of Lenin's writings; the contrast between his authoritarianism and his (alleged) libertarianism becomes relative and misleading, while the importance of the utopian ingredient in *all* his writings becomes increasingly evident.

Before considering this point in detail, three preliminary observations are in order. First, it is not true that in *The State and Revolution* there is no reference to Lenin's theory of the vanguard party. This idea has been moved to the background, concealed, as it were, but *not* de-emphasized. The ever-present leading role of the party is revealed in a single very telling sentence: "By educating the workers' party, Marxism educates the vanguard of the proletariat, capable of assuming power and *leading the whole people* to socialism, of directing and organizing the new system, of being the teacher, the guide, the leader of all the working and exploited people in organizing their social life without the bourgeoisie and against the bourgeoisie" (L, A, 328).

Second, neither is it true that Lenin's utopia gave the masses full command and ignored, even if only briefly, the coercive apparatus of the state. On the contrary, in this utopia he envisaged and demanded "the *strictest* control by society *and by the state* over the measure of labor and the measure of consumption." The state that exercised this all-embracing and ubiquitous control was to be "not a state of bureaucrats, but a state of *armed workers*"; nevertheless, it was to be an apparatus of coercion, extending its power over the entire sphere of the economy and leaving little room for spontaneity. In fact, Lenin's view of the state of the Soviets presupposed "the conversion of *all* citizens into workers and other employees of *one* huge syndicate," i.e., the highest possible degree of organization, planning and supervision (ibid., 380, 380, 380). This idea of the strictest state control over the measure of labor was hardly compatible with complete faith in the soundness of the spontaneous conduct of the average worker; it suggested, rather, an efficient and ruthless dictatorship over labor. As Rudolf Bahro commented: "Here is the unmistakable voice of compulsion, and compulsion directed not against the former ruling classes, but one that can only be addressed to the 'backward elements' of the working class and the people itself." [109]

Finally, we should not see Lenin's utopian vision as in some way contradicting the totalitarian nature of his aims; we must not forget that a utopian-chiliastic ingredient is a necessary component of revolutionary totalitarianism. In contradistinction to traditional authoritarianism, totalitarianism must be equipped with a body of doctrine covering all vital aspects of human existence and projected toward a perfect final state of humankind; in other words, its legitimizing ideology must contain "a chiliastic claim, based upon a radical rejection of the existing society and the conquest of the world for the new one." [110]

The State and Revolution is the fullest elaboration of Lenin's chiliastic claim. Without it Leninism would have been merely a form of disciplinarian centralism in the service of power for power's sake, in which case, its impact would have been exhausted in the seizure and maintenance of political power. In fact, however, it was committed not only to establishing a system of total power, but also, and more significantly, to using this power to achieve the utopian goals of communism. [111] Lenin once said that the younger generation of the Soviet people "should know that the entire purpose of their lives is to build a communist society" (L, A, 674). This may have been an unrealistic expectation, but it was certainly true if applied to people like himself. Without this ardent belief in a communist utopia, Leninism would not have developed its distinctively totalitarian features. [112]

We now turn to a brief presentation of Lenin's views on the state in the transitional period. Naturally, he wanted to present them as the only correct reading of Marx and Engels's legacy and had therefore to pay tremendous attention to the occasional remarks on the dictatorship of the proletariat that occurred in their writings.

According to Lenin, the first formulation of the idea of the dictatorship of the proletariat was contained (although the term was not yet coined) in the *Manifesto of the Communist Party*, in the sentence describing the postbourgeois state as "the proletariat organized as the ruling class." The next significant passage was the famous argument from *The Eighteenth Brumaire of Louis Bonaparte* about the need to smash the previously existing state machine. Theoretical clarification of Marx's views on this matter comes in his famous letter to Weydemeyer (March 5, 1852) in which he wrote that "the class struggle necessarily leads to the dictatorship of the proletariat" and that this dictatorship constitutes "the transition of the *abolition of all classes* and to a *classless* society." Lenin quoted these words triumphantly, and to him they expressed with striking clarity the radical difference between Marx's theory and that of the foremost and most profound thinkers of the bourgeoisie, for "only he is a Marxist who *extends* the recognition of the class struggle to the recognition of the *dictatorship of the proletariat*" (ibid., 326, 333, 334).

To support this view Lenin made full use of Marx and Engels's analyses of the Paris Commune as the first form of proletarian dictatorship. The rich experience of the Paris Commune, seen in the light of Marx and Engels's writings, served Lenin as a historical and theoretical framework for speculation concerning its relevance to the cause of the Bolshevik revolution in Russia.

From the Marxist point of view this seemed quite legitimate, yet *The State and Revolution* should not be treated as a faithful, reliable reconstruction of Marx and Engels's position. Rather, it is a profound, although admittedly impressive, misinterpretation.[113] I shall not try to establish whether, and to what extent, it was a simple misunderstanding on Lenin's part (i.e., a genuine self-deception) or whether it was a deliberate manipulation or even a crude falsification. What really matters is not Lenin's personal character, his sincerity or cynicism, but the character of his theoretical and ideological contribution to the problem. As we shall see, his ardent desire to present himself as the only defender of true orthodoxy did not prevent him from developing what was in fact his own thoroughly revisionist interpretation of Marx and Engels's views on the question.

The suggestiveness of Lenin's interpretation was so powerful that most of his readers did not dare question its impeccably Marxist credentials. Its specifically Leninist features were concealed, as it were, and visible only from a greater distance. Hence, it is no accident that the most important observations on this issue have been made not by specialists on Lenin, but by a scholar, namely, Richard N. Hunt, who set himself the task of a detailed, painstaking reconstruction of the political ideas of Marx and Engels. This defense of classical Marxism proved to be a devastating criticism of Leninism.

Hunt's first observation is stunning in its simplicity: if the Paris Commune was to be the model for the dictatorship of the proletariat, then the latter could never be confused with the monopolistic rule of the one "truly Marxist" party. The Commune was firmly controlled by Marx and Engels's ideological rivals: a Blanquist majority and a Proudhonist minority. Hence, when Marx described it as "the most glorious deed of our Party," he meant *party* in the broadest sense, as pertaining to "the entire workers' movement, actual or potential, *regardless of present ideological affiliations.*" Similarly, when Engels wrote about the dictatorship of the proletariat, he meant "the revolutionary rule of the working-class majority, *regardless of present ideological affiliations.*"[114] In other words, the proletarian dictatorship was to be a dictatorship of the working class as a whole, not merely of its ideological vanguard, let alone a disciplined single party. As such, it would be compatible with a large measure of political freedom.

It is obvious that this idea ran counter to the very essence of Leninism. In *The State and Revolution* Lenin, for tactical reasons, preferred to concentrate on the rule of the revolutionary masses, but this was mostly lip service to the teaching of his masters; in fact, even in this unusual text he did not fail to mention that the party, "the vanguard of the proletariat," would direct and organize everything as the undisputed teacher, guide, and leader. In other texts of the same period he bluntly demanded that the masses should be "trained" (i.e., controlled and indoctrinated) by "class-conscious workers and soldiers," i.e., by his own people (ibid., 328, 404). Thus, universal participation in the revolution was to involve universal political control by the Bolshevik party.

Hunt's other observation is equally simple. He pointed out that in Marx's *Critique of the Gotha Program*, the time-span of the dictatorship of the proletariat was designated as preceding socialism, not as overlapping with socialism or constituting socialism as the first lower stage of a communist society: "Marx said very plainly that the dictatorship of the proletariat lies *between* capitalist and communist society generally; he did not say that it lasts until the end of its lower phase. Lenin's motives in restricting the label 'communist' to the higher phase are painfully transparent; what is harder to understand is the uncritical acceptance of this obfuscation by virtually everyone else."[115]

Certainly Lenin needed doctrinal legitimization for the use of dictatorial methods (in his own usage of the term) under socialism, since he did not really believe that the socialist construction could dispense with them. He had already made this plain in *What Is to Be Done?* and his *State and Revolution*, despite appearances, did not constitute a deviation from this line of thought.

Hunt adds to this an interesting terminological comment. Marx and Engels, according to him,

did seem to have a fairly clear idea of what they meant by dictatorship, proletarian or otherwise, when they spoke of something apart from individual dictators. They meant extralegal government, government outside or beyond the framework of normal law—thus most obviously revolutionary government and government under martial law. Lenin to the contrary, they did not regard all government as inherently dictatorial: they never referred to ancient or feudal governments in these terms, or even to the bourgeois governments of Britain and the United States. In fact they used the word most frequently to describe the post-June government of the Second French Republic that had labelled *itself* a 'dictatorship,' that is, a government of martial law, a government which—as Marx put it—declared the workers "*hors la loi*." Even the phrase "dictatorship of capital" followed the same logic, alluding to the private, *unrestricted* command power of the capitalist within the factory gates. Marx's early legal training, after all, could not but have left some trace.[116]

Here, however, I think Hunt goes too far. It would be more correct to say that Marx and Engels used the term *dictatorship* in two different senses: in its classic meaning (dictatorial methods, as described above) and in an enlarged sense, synonymous with domination and describing the "condition" or "state of affairs" (Kautsky's expressions; see chapter 3, section 1) in which a given class exercises a predominant influence. Engels made use of this latter sense when he wrote in "A Critique of the Draft Social-Democratic Program of 1891" of "the form of a democratic republic" as "the specific form of the dictatorship of the proletariat" (M&E, SW, 3:345). The context of these words leaves no doubt that dictatorship in this sense *did not mean* "extralegal government," or "government under martial law." We may wonder what has happened to "Marx's early legal training," but we must not forget that Lenin was also a trained lawyer. It is obvious that the extension of the term *dictatorship* served some purpose in Marx and Engels's thinking as well, otherwise they would not have allowed themselves to play with this dangerous word so carelessly. Hence they should not be too easily absolved from partial responsibility for the Leninist interpretation of their ideas.

The most powerful argument for defending Lenin's Marxist credentials is, of course, Marxist criticism of "bourgeois democracy." If the state as such is essentially organized violence, serving the interests of the exploiters, if only the most naive people could believe in its neutrality in the class struggle, if political freedom is fraudulent, merely formal, unable to liberate the oppressed from economic slavery, then it is logical to conclude that all forms of class rule are ultimately based on naked violence, that despite all possible embellishments they are inevitably dictatorial in nature, and that therefore from the point of view of their *class content* all forms of bourgeois regime are *essentially* identical. In *The State and Revolution* Lenin wrote: "The essence of Marx's theory of the state has been mastered only by those who realize that the dictatorship of a single class is necessary not only for every class society in general, not only for the *proletariat* which has overthrown the bourgeoisie, but also for the entire *historical* period which separates capitalism from 'classless society,' from communism. Bourgeois states are most varied in form, but their essence is the same: all these states, whatever their form, in the final analysis are inevitably the *dictatorship of the bourgeoisie*" (L, A, 334–35).

Hunt is right in claiming that such a crudely essentialist logic cannot be found in Marx and Engels, but it does not follow from this that they "held liberal-democratic values" and could be placed "squarely in the mainstream of the European liberal-democratic tradition." [117] It would be more correct to say that, in clear distinction to Lenin, their deep hostility toward liberal democratic values did not make them totally immune to the influence of liberal democratic political culture. Thus, they often preferred to avoid simplistic conclusions, even if this entailed some theoretical inconsistencies on their part. In political analyses they were not blinded by dogmatic search for "the essential" and took account of many more historical factors than their theory would have allowed them to acknowledge. In this sense Marx once said of himself that he was not a Marxist. The opposite was true of Lenin, who wanted to be "more Marxist than Marx" and deliberately concentrated on what seemed to him essential from the point of view of Marxist theory. In addition, his perception of Marxism was heavily influenced by the crude, nihilistic critique of "bourgeois freedom" characteristic of the Russian populists and anarchists, who (as already mentioned) had taken their theoretical arguments from a vulgarized version of Marxism. Thus, his dogmatic blindness found support both in his inadequate knowledge of Western realities and in his deep (though not fully conscious) indebtedness to the Russian populist tradition. This often led him into genuine, if mainly unintentional, departures from Marxism.

In analyzing Lenin's conceptions of the proletarian state, we must remember that he formulated them with the practical aim of providing theoretical legitimation for his program of action. His reconstruction of Marx and Engels's views on the state in general and the dictatorship of the proletariat in particular was, of course, the most important part of these efforts.

In Marxist terms the Russian autocracy could have been described as a variant of "the parasite state," estranged from society and possessing an autonomous power that it used to suppress *all* social forces.[118] As such, it might have served as an excellent, although somewhat extreme, illustration of Marx's thesis that the state as such represented the *alienation* of social power. Lenin, however, paid no attention to this important part of Marx's theoretical legacy; he chose instead to rely on Engels's view of the state as a mere *instrument* of class rule. Thus, the most important feature of the state was, in his view, direct class coercion, not alienation, caste egoism of the privileged, not the estrangement from civil society as a whole. He did not overlook the fact that officials of the state might sometimes enjoy a certain degree of independence but, following Engels, treated this as an exceptional case. *All* states were, in his view, organs of class rule for the oppression of one class by another. Like Engels, Lenin sharply contrasted the state with the "self-acting armed organization of the population" that had existed in classless societies. In this view, the state was a public power serving as an instrument for the exploitation of the oppressed classes and having at its disposal the professional apparatus of oppression. The essence of state power consisted therefore in "special bodies of armed men having prisons, etc., at their command" (ibid., 316).

Lenin's reliance on Engels reflects, no doubt, the enormous authority of the latter as the almost universally acknowledged interpreter and popularizer of Marx's theories, but it was also a deliberate theoretical and political choice. The view of the state as the alienation of social power seemed too close to the widespread perception of the Russian state as alienated but (for this very reason) standing above classes and capable of independent actions, often aimed against the interests of the rich and privileged. In Lenin's mind such ideas were firmly associated with liberal and populist illusions as well as with the conceptions of the "etatist school" in Russian historiography, which stressed the paramount and fully independent role of the state in Russian history. It is not surprising, therefore, that he chose the version of the Marxist theory of the state that emphasized the direct subordination of the state apparatus to the egoistic will of the exploiters and oppressors. Politically, this was a shrewd choice, since it mobilized more hatred, directed revolutionary efforts toward the complete destruction of the existing state, and most important, justified the view that the victorious proletariat should immediately organize *its own* apparatus of repression.

Of course, the end of class oppression was to be followed by the withering away of the state. On this point, however, the Engelsian account was somewhat unclear. On the one hand, it stressed that the proletarian seizure of power would result in the immediate nationalization of the means of production—that is, in the immediate abolition of "all class distinctions and class antagonisms" so that there would no longer be any need for the state. On the other hand, Engels explicitly denied that the disappearance of the state could take place at once. The state, he argued, would not be "abolished," it would "wither away." He hastened to add that the post-revolutionary state would be a qualitatively new phenomenon, genuinely representative of society as a whole. In other words, the most essential feature of the state—its class function—would disappear at once, although the form of state organization would only gradually die out. "The first act by which the state really comes forward as the representative of the whole society—the taking possession of the means of production in the name of society—is also its own last independent act as a state" (ibid., 321; see also Engels, *Socialism: Utopian and Scientific* in M&E, SW, 3:147).

These words were a flat denial of everything Lenin wanted to say about the need for dictatorial methods in the postrevolutionary period of transition, so he had to interpret them in his own way, or rather, interpret them away altogether. Engels, he explained, had directed this proposition against the opportunists, on the one hand, and the anarchists, on the other. Against the former, he emphasized that the proletarian revolution could not simply take over the bourgeois state; it had to abolish it in a revolutionary act. But this act would not be the direct transition to a stateless society the anarchists would like to have. The victorious proletariat would have to organize itself as a state, and this new state would gradually lose its oppressive function (i.e., would wither away). In the transitional period, however, it would remain a state, although no longer a *bourgeois* state, and this new state would be "the dictatorship of the proletariat."

In this way Lenin reconciled the two visions: the immediate abolition of the state and its gradual withering away. What was to be abolished was the *bourgeois* state; what was to wither away was the *proletarian* state, a view he boldly attributed to Engels. "According to Engels, the bourgeois state does not 'wither away,' but is 'abolished' by the proletariat in the course of revolution. What withers away after this revolution is the proletarian state, or semi-state" (L, *A*, 322).

This is, however, an extremely strained interpretation. In the passage cited, Engels said nothing about the dictatorship of the proletariat but simply asserted that the postrevolutionary state would represent the interests of society as a whole. Thus, it was to differ from the state in the proper sense of the term *by having no class function at all, not* by serving as a "special coercive force" for the suppression of the bourgeoisie by the proletariat. This provides a serious argument for the view that Lenin's theory of postrevolutionary dictatorship owed more to Tkachev than to the founders of Marxism.

To make his interpretation more plausible Lenin referred to Marx's criticism of the notion of a "free state" as presented in his *Critique of the Gotha Program*. Lenin used this as a basis for claiming that *every* state is essentially a special force for class suppression and consequently that "*every* state is not 'free' and not a 'people's state.' " Every state, even the most democratic one, is a form of dictatorship, based ultimately on naked force. "So long as the state exists there is no freedom. When there is freedom, there will be no state" (ibid., 323, 379).

In reality, however, this view of the state was Bakuninist rather than Marxist. It was Bakunin who wrote: "The existence of a state necessarily involves domination and, therefore, slavery; a state without slavery, overt or disguised, is unthinkable." [119] This assumption enabled Bakunin to play down the significance of the differences between forms of government and to argue that only anarchism was compatible with freedom. In Lenin's usage the same assumption led to a different but equally logical conclusion: if all forms of state are incompatible with freedom, then there is no reason to deplore the fate of freedom under the proletarian dictatorship. In this way Lenin, writing on the eve of the Bolshevik revolution, justified in advance its recourse to dictatorial methods. Libertarian critics of these methods were discredited in advance as blinded by bourgeois illusions or as paying tribute to bourgeois hypocrisy.

As I have tried to show, Marx and Engels greatly contributed to discrediting "bourgeois freedom." Nevertheless, their attitude toward the achievement of "bourgeois democracy" was far from the nihilistic approach of Bakunin and Lenin. In particular, *The Critique of the Gotha Program* provides no foundation for Lenin's conclusions. Marx's criticism of the idea of a "free state" was based *not* on the assumption that the very existence of a state excludes freedom, but on the view that "freedom consists in converting the state from an organ superimposed upon society into one completely subordinate to it" and that "the forms of the state are more or less free to the extent that they restrict the 'freedom of the state.'" He simply wanted to say that the freedom *of* the state should be distinguished from freedom *in* the state: the former is nothing less than absolute state power, and such power should be restricted for the sake of greater freedom for society. Marx was explicit that from this point of view a democratic republic was greatly preferable to a monarchy. He criticized the German workers' party for the illusion that its democratic program could be realized within "the present-day national state," that is, within the "Prusso-German Empire," but he *did not* imply that even a democratic republic could serve *only* the interests of the bourgeoisie (M&E, *SW*, 3:25, 26).[120] Neither did he imply that all forms of state are equally incompatible with freedom.

Clearly, the opinions on the "unrepresentative" "unLeninist" character of *The State and Revolution* are vastly exaggerated. This work has not abandoned, or revised, the basic tenets of Leninism. What it really offers is a thorough revision of Marx and Engels's view of the transition period— a revision stressing the need for the long-continuing use of organized violence and thus fully consonant with the general spirit of Leninism. It even argues that "until the 'higher' phase of communism arrives" (i.e., during the entire socialist phase), the proletarian state should not only make full use of its apparatus of repression but should also exercise the *strictest* control over the measure of labor and the measure of consumption. In short, it portrays a sort of "barrack communism" imposed on society by force and supported by the systematic use of dictatorial measures.

Nevertheless, most readers of *The State and Revolution* perceived Lenin's utopia as a "libertarian" vision, an attempt to show the ways of a genuine liberation of the masses and to prove that proletarian democracy would be "a million times more democratic than the most democratic bourgeois republic" (L, *A*, 471). We may (and should) not share this perception, but we must understand its reasons.

Lenin's "libertarian" program, first announced in his "April Theses," consisted in setting up against a bourgeois democracy the ideal of a direct participatory democracy based on a radical deprofessionalization of state functions. He did not really mean to abandon his favorite conception of the party as a hierarchical organization led by professionals. He instinctively understood, however, that parliamentary democracy might be effectively combated in the name of direct popular democracy, and that the revolutionary masses would give his party a better chance than would democratic voters. These practical considerations were supported by his deep-seated hatred of all "bourgeois" institutions and by his genuine wish to show himself a genuine Marxist, faithful to the ideas of his teachers and not given to the backsliding of Western social democratic parties. Hence, it was only natural that he should pay careful attention to Marx and Engels's views on the merits of the Paris Commune, above all, its commitment to direct democracy and nonprofessionalized government.[121] It was also natural that he should decide to set his hopes on the spontaneously created workers' councils (the Soviets),[122] seeing them as a possible power base in his forthcoming struggle against "bourgeois democracy."

A good summary of the "libertarian" ideas of *The State and Revolution* is the following passage from the "April Theses":

Not a parliamentary republic—to return to a parliamentary republic from the Soviets of Workers' Deputies would be a retrograde step—but a Republic of Soviets of Workers', Agricultural Labourers' and Peasants' Deputies throughout the country, from top to bottom.

Abolition of the police, the army and the bureaucracy.

The salaries of all officials, all of whom are elective and displaceable at any time, not to exceed the average wage of a competent worker. (ibid., 297)

All these ideas have been duly supported by references to the practices of the Paris Commune and/or their analyses in Marx and Engels. For instance, Lenin apparently quoted Marx's judgment that the Commune deprived judicial functionaries of their "sham independence" and made them "elective, responsible and revokable." He was equally approving of Marx's acceptance of the "abolition of parliamentarism." "The Commune," Marx wrote, "was to be a working, not a parliamentary, body, executive and legislative at the same time. . . . Instead of deciding once in three or six years which member of the ruling class was to represent and repress the people in parliament, universal suffrage was to serve the people constituted in communes, as individual suffrage serves every other employer in the search for workers, foremen and accountants for his business" (ibid., 339, 341–42; cf. Marx, *Civil War in France* in M&E, SW, 2:220–21). In summing up this passage Lenin sharpens its meaning: "To decide every few years which member of the ruling class is *to repress and crush the people through parliament*—this is the real essence of bourgeois parliamentarism" (L, A, 342). Here he is taking an essentialist position on the issue of parliamentarism—that is, he is assuming that the institution of parliament has a "bourgeois content" and can only serve bourgeois interests.

However, this was an illegitimate radicalization of Marx's position. Despite their fascination with direct popular democracy (especially pronounced, of course, in their writing on the Paris Commune), Marx and Engels did not see parliamentarism as a purely bourgeois institution completely useless for the workers. In *The Eighteenth Brumaire of Louis Bonaparte*, Marx developed the idea that parliamentary governments created by the bourgeoisie could become an instrument of socialism and that the bourgeoisie, in order to preserve its class rule, would have to resort to dictatorship (M&E, SW, 1:435–36). At the end of his life Engels developed this view even further. In his introduction to Marx's *Class Struggles in France*, Engels explicitly stated that his and Marx's revolutionary faith had proved to be wrong, that popular insurrections had become obsolete and that the workers' party should resort instead to the legal parliamentary way of struggle (ibid., 186–204).[123] Unlike Lenin, he had plainly lost much of his earlier faith in revolutionary violence and moved instead toward a reformist belief in the ballot box. Lenin, however, invoked Marx and Engels's authority without mentioning these inconvenient facts, simply passing over them in silence.

Furthermore, Marxist attitudes toward the Paris Commune had also been changing and were increasingly subject to political differentiation. German Social Democracy had become more and more committed to parliamentary methods of struggle and had "embarked upon a veritable offensive against the Commune."[124] Orthodox Marxists, including Engels, felt that the center of gravity of the European workers' movement had shifted from France to Germany and that the Commune as a positive model had therefore become irrelevant. But since they wanted to combat the rising tide of right-wing reformism, they still defended it, at least in public, as an important link in the workers' revolutionary tradition. This explains Engels's position in his programmatic text of 1895. While he praised the Commune as having revived the militant spirit of the proletariat, he yet insisted that after its defeat the historical initiative had passed to the hands of the German workers, who had proved capable of making "intelligent use of the universal suffrage" and so had promoted their cause without revolutionary bloodletting (ibid., 194). His conclusion was unambiguous:

With this successful utilization of universal suffrage, however, an entirely new method of proletarian struggle came into operation, and this method quickly developed further. It was found that the state institutions, in which the rule of the bourgeoisie is organized, offer the working class still further opportunities to fight these very state institutions. The workers took part in elections to particular Diets, to municipal councils and to trades courts; they contested with the bourgeoisie every post in the occupation of which a sufficient part of the proletariat had a say. And so it happened that the bourgeoisie and the government came to be much more afraid of the legal than of the illegal action of the workers' party, of the results of elections than of those of rebellion. (ibid., 196)

From this it is clear that Engels, so often quoted in *The State and Revolution*, did not share Lenin's conviction that the era of parliamentarism had come to an end (L, A, 514), but rather endorsed the methods of struggle the Bolshevik leader contemptuously condemned and rejected at the decisive moment. Lenin's praise of the Paris Commune for its rejection of "venal and rotten parliamentarism," for its vision of a "democracy without parliamentarism"—without representative institutions, without "division of labor between the legislative and the executive," and without a "privileged position for the deputies" (ibid., 343–44)—was designed to cut his party off from the German social democractic tradition of which Engels was an integral part.

Lenin's own attitude toward the Commune was also critical, but in an entirely different way. He accused it of what he saw as its excessive mildness, lack of a well-organized and resolute leadership, insufficient ruthlessness in dealing with enemies, and incomprehensible tolerance toward unreliable elements. In 1905 he even wrote that its government was "such as ours should not be" (L, CW, 9:80–81).[125] But it was natural that in 1917 he should concentrate on what he saw as the Commune's virtues. Despite all its weaknesses, it was valuable to him as a form of truly revolutionary authority not paralyzed by respect for bourgeois democratic institutions; not bound by any laws, rules, and procedures; deriving its power not from "a law previously discussed and enacted in parliament," but from direct "seizure," from "direct initiative of the people from below." He admired its efforts to replace the military and bureaucratic cadres of the old regime with new people whose proletarian class instinct and revolutionary zeal made up for their lack of professional experience. He found the same features in the Soviets of Workers' and Soldiers' Deputies, proclaiming, as early as April 1917, that their power was "of *the same type* as the Paris Commune" (L, A, 302, 302). He must have realized that to set his hopes on the workers' councils did not accord with his deeply ingrained pessimism about their spontaneity, that the support of such councils smacked of syndicalism, if not outright anarchy; but he was also keenly aware that the slogan "All Power to the Soviets!" was the only way to mobilize the masses against the Provisional Government. His suspicion of mass spontaneity was deep, but his hostility toward the bourgeoisie was much deeper. Moreover, he was confident that the workers would recognize the proletarian nature of his party and that the latter, in turn, would not become alienated from its class basis. He genuinely hoped to go down in history as a genuine proletarian leader and saw his party's task as the vindication of the revolutionary workers' cause, best symbolized by the Paris Commune.

All these reasons sufficiently explain the "libertarian" features of *The State and Revolution*. Lenin needed a "scientific," Marxist legitimization for his actions—hence, his attempt to present himself as the only interpreter of Marx and Engels's teaching on the dictatorship of the proletariat. He wanted to be seen as a truly *international* leader, fulfilling the promise of the Paris Commune and avenging its bloody suppression, so he chose to concentrate on its legacy at the cost of ignoring, for a time, the specific conditions obtaining in Russia and even disregarding the rich experience gained by the workers' councils in the revolution of 1905–1906. And, above all, he had to mobilize popular support for himself by promising the workers not only peace and bread, but also "full freedom" (ibid., 303).

But how was full freedom to be combined with the strictest discipline and control, a control embracing all spheres of life, from labor to consumption? Lenin did not see this as contradictory, because he was concerned with the *collective* freedom of the working class, not with freedom of individual workers; with freedom as *rational* self-mastery, not freedom in pursuit of different particularist aims; with freedom as *conscious* realization of a single aim common to the entire class and inherent in its historical mission, not with freedom as aimless pluralism and "unconscious" spontaneity. Workers were to be liberated as a collective entity, not as private individuals or members of different interest groups. Once free, they would crush their class enemies and take control of their fate. In this way capitalist slavery would be replaced by self-discipline and voluntary subordination. Workers were to be free, not from control and supervision as such, but from *bourgeois* control and supervision. As citizens, they were to be liberated from bourgeois rule but subject instead to a dictatorship of their own in which the repressive functions would be exercised by "the armed proletariat itself," or rather by its own "armed vanguard" (ibid., 345, 396).

Nevertheless, it is true that the political philosophy of *The State and Revolution* differs in some respects from the standpoint of orthodox Leninism as expressed in *What Is to Be Done?* As I have tried to show, Bertram Wolfe and Adam Ulam were mistaken in treating this difference as tantamount to a virtual abandonment of Leninism. It would be more proper to see it as an important shift of emphasis necessitated by circumstances and a change of focus. *What Is to Be Done?* is principally concerned with organizational questions, while *The State and Revolution* illuminates the utopian dimension of Lenin's thinking. The former criticizes reformist tendencies in the workers' movement and stresses the importance of a well-organized, disciplined, and professionalized revolutionary minority; the latter tries to discredit the basic principles of representative democracy as opposed to the ideal of a direct participatory democracy, presupposing, of course, the highest possible level of mass involvement. In other words, *What Is to Be Done?* represents the Jacobin side of Leninism, while *The State and Revolution* demonstrates a certain affinity between the Marxist and anarchist visions of the emancipation of the masses.[126] Like Engels, Lenin said so quite openly, declaring that Marxists "do not at all differ with the anarchists on the question of the abolition of the state as the *aim*" (ibid., 353). He agreed with both Marx and Engels that a proletarian dictatorship would not be "a state in the proper sense of the word," but rather a "communal state [*Gemeinwesen*]" (ibid., 256–57), or a "semi-state" and that the alienated "parasite state" would at once be abolished. The experience of the Paris Commune, as analyzed by Marx and Engels, convinced him that a proletarian dictatorship would be compatible with direct popular rule, entailing a radical deprofessionalization and (therefore) disalienation of political power. All these ideas were to be embodied in a completely new form of state: the Republic of the Soviets.

Let us briefly examine this political ideal from the point of view of the problem of freedom. Repressive functions in this new state were to be exercised by "a militia involving the entire population." Plainly, the scope of police control over the population would be greatly enlarged and, in fact would become unlimited, since there would be no legal safeguards of individual freedom. Why should such safeguards exist if the forces of order involve the entire population and see themselves as part and parcel of the people, a direct expression of its will? Direct popular democracy is hardly compatible with the rule of law but is perfectly compatible with organized violence. Lenin was very outspoken about this, describing "the organized, systematic use of force against persons" as a necessary function in a democratic state and contemptuously dismissing the liberal notion that political power might be limited and controlled by law (ibid., 382, 382).

Professional bureaucrats would be subject to control and supervision by *all*, which would result in the acquisition of the necessary administrative skills by the entire population; this would create conditions in which *all* would become bureaucrats for a time and *nobody* would be a professional bureaucrat (ibid., 389). The pay of a state official would never exceed that of a workman. In the course of time, socialism would shorten the working day and thus enable the entire adult population to take part "not only in voting and elections, *but also in the everyday administration of the state*." *Everybody*, without exception, would be able to perform state functions, and this would "lead to the *complete withering away* of every form of state in general" (ibid., 395, 395).

Many of Lenin's readers, including the libertarian-minded Marxist revisionists, were greatly impressed by this vision. They saw in it a powerful and consistent commitment to freedom as participation, as opposed to freedom as individual autonomy; to freedom in the public sphere, as opposed to freedom as privacy; and, of course, to positive freedom, as opposed to "merely negative" liberty. This point of view, however, ignores the other side of the coin. Lenin's idea of universal participation was inseparably bound up with his favorite conception of universal control, which in turn came very close to universal spying and "virtuous denunciations." Everybody was to control and supervise everybody, keeping account of one another's work, consumption, and daily conduct. This collective control was to be exercised not only over the former capitalists (now converted into employees), but also over the intelligentsia—"the intellectual gentry who preserve their capitalist habits"—as well as "over the workers who have been thoroughly corrupted by capitalism." All who failed to correct their ways would be quickly punished by armed workers. Their punishments would be severe because "the armed workers are practical men and not sentimental intellectuals, and they will scarcely allow anyone to trifle with them." The best summary of this truly Orwellian vision was Lenin's own: "This control will really become universal, general and popular; and there will be no getting away from it, there will be 'nowhere to go' " (ibid., 383, 384, 383).

Finally, an important aspect of Lenin's political utopia was the abolition of the division of power. Like Marx, he praised the Paris Commune for abolishing the independence of judicial functionaries and for being "a working not a parliamentary body, executive and legislative at the same time" (as quoted above). But he did not mention the fact that both the Paris Commune and the Russian Soviets allowed the activities of different political parties. This was no accident: everything indicates that even at this early stage Lenin's conception of the Republic of the Soviets was not compatible with political pluralism. He wanted the workers to be a single, homogeneous class, not divided into different strata and interest groups, having therefore a "single will" and becoming more and more united. Thus, his political philosophy excluded not only the liberal conception of limited government but also the democratic conception of political liberty. This aspect of the alleged libertarianism of Lenin's *State and Revolution* has been aptly characterized by A. J. Polan, who commented:

The text [of *The State and Revolution*], in all its moments—libertarian and authoritarian—is guilty of subsequent developments: that is, the features of the authoritarian Soviet regime are present within every line and concept of the text. . . . The central absence in Lenin's politics is that of a theory of political institutions. All political functions are collapsed into one institution, the soviet, and even that institution itself will know no division of labour within itself according to different functions. Lenin's state form is one-dimensional. It allows no distances, no spaces, no appeals, no checks, no balances, no processes, no delays, no interrogations and, above all, no distribution of power. All are ruthlessly and deliberately excluded, as precisely the articulations of the disease of corruption and mystification. The new state form will be transparent, monological and unilinear.[127]

But we have not yet exhausted the problematic of freedom in *The State and Revolution*. We have analyzed only Lenin's political ideas and should now turn to the application of these ideas to economic problems.

According to Hans Kelsen, the Marx-Engels view of the communist society of the future is characterized by a striking contradiction: the contradiction between political anarchism and economic authoritarianism. Politically, communist society was supposed to be "an individualistic anarchy," whereas economically it was to replace the "anarchy of capitalist production" by a "highly organized production on the basis of collective property in the means of production, necessarily concentrated in the hands of a central authority." [128]

I believe that to define Marx and Engels's political ideal as an *individualistic* anarchy is an obvious misinterpretation: their political philosophy was thoroughly collectivist, and the anarchic tendency in their thinking bears some resemblance to Bakunin's collectivist anarchism, but not to the individualistic varieties of anarchism. Kelsen's formula does, however, contain some truth. It helps us to understand the contradiction between the ideal of direct participatory democracy (as found, for instance, in Marx's writings on the Paris Commune or in Engels's praise of "ancient society") and the communist ideal of economic organization, which is based on a settled plan and completely eliminates "the anarchy of the market." It might also be formulated as a contradiction between the two conceptions of collective freedom: freedom as democratic self-government (presupposing decentralized decision making) and freedom as mastery over collective fate (presupposing rational planning and a highly centralized planning agency).

This truly striking contradiction is especially obvious in Engels's "scientific socialism." In *The Origin of the Family, Private Property and the State*, he enthusiastically endorsed Morgan's view that the society of the future would be "a revival, in a higher form, of liberty, equality and fraternity of the ancient gentes" (M&E, SW, 3:334). But in "Democratic Pan-Slavism" he asserted that historical progress consisted in the steady increase of centralization and proclaimed that in his own time, as a result of "the formidable advances in industry, trade and communications," political centralization was becoming more important than ever before and was bound to triumph everywhere: "What still has to be centralized is being centralized" (M&E, CW, 8:371). In his view, the authoritarian organization of work in capitalist factories was an enormous advance in comparison with the independence of small producers, which was for him a relic of medievalism. According to this logic, large-scale factories repre-

sented a mode of production based on planning and therefore prepared
the way for socialism, while the main obstacle to further progress was the
obsolete mode of exchange—the "anarchic freedom" of the market. He
even argued that the further development of monopolistic capitalism might
lead to a form of state capitalism—that is, capitalism based on planning,
liquidating the irrational, uncontrollable forces of the market. This was to
be a prelude to socialism, a society organized as one immense factory.

We must remember that this view of socialism was accepted by all orthodox Marxists of the Second International. The phrase describing socialist
society as "nothing more than a single gigantic industrial concern" figures
prominently in Kautsky's classic commentary on the Erfurt Program (see
chapter 3, section 1). The replacement of a horizontal chain of exchanges
by a vertical chain of command (later known as command economy) was
then seen as the very essence of Marxism, as a program for the future.[129]
Marxist intellectuals were convinced that this was the only way to true
liberation, the liberation of not just the workers from capitalist slavery
but, above all, of all humankind from its humiliating dependence on blind,
irrational, uncontrollable forces.

Lenin was one of the most ardent adherents of Marxist teaching on the
necessity and progressiveness of centralization. He was profoundly influenced by Engels's views on the development of monopolistic capitalism,
believing that he had foreseen, to some extent, the task of the workers'
movement of the imperialist epoch (L, A, 358). Lenin was fond of quoting,
in *The State and Revolution*, Engels's words about the planning character
of the trusts: "When we pass from joint-stock companies to trusts which
assume control over, and monopolize, whole industries, it is not only private production that ceases, but also planlessness"; but he hastened to
add that the capitalist trusts could not provide "complete planning." The
introduction of complete, nationwide planning was to be the task of postrevolutionary society, organized from top to bottom as the dictatorship of
the proletariat. He described this new society as follows: "*All* citizens are
transformed into hired employees of the state, which consists of the armed
workers. *All* citizens become employees and workers of a *single* country-
wide state 'syndicate.' . . . The whole of society will become a single office
and a single factory, with equality of labor and pay" (ibid., 358, 358, 383).

There were, however, some important differences between this vision
and Kautsky's idea of "a single gigantic industrial concern." In opposition
to the "Kautskyite renegades" (but in accordance with Russian populist and
anarchist tradition), Lenin committed himself to the cause of crude egalitarianism, minimizing the distinction between skilled and unskilled labor,
violently criticizing the material privileges of the "workers' aristocracy,"
and seeking warranties against bureaucratic place hunting and careerism.
He had to admit that such egalitarianism, along with the vindication of di-

rect participatory democracy, was in fact a reversion to "primitive" democracy, but he defended his position by distinguishing between primitive democracy in prehistoric or precapitalist times and primitive democracy on a higher level, based on capitalism and capitalist culture. Capitalism, he argued, "has *created* large-scale production, factories, railways, the postal service, telephones, etc., and *on this basis* the great majority of the functions of the old 'state power' have become *so simplified* and can be reduced to such *exceedingly simple operations* of registration, filing and checking that they *can be easily performed by every literate person*, can quite easily be performed for ordinary 'workman's wages,' and that these functions can (and must) be stripped of every shadow of privilege, of every semblance of 'official grandeur.' " The same solution, he thought, should serve for economic organization. As he wrote: "To organise the *whole* economy on the lines of the postal service so that technicians, foremen and accountants, as well as all officials, shall receive salaries no higher than 'a workman's wage,' all under the control and leadership of the armed proletariat—this is our immediate aim" (ibid., 340–41, 345–46).

Let us look more closely at this amazingly utopian program. First, it clearly expressed Lenin's commitment to a direct transition to socialism. He did not say that capitalism must be allowed to develop until objective conditions are ripe for the introduction of a nationwide and marketless organization of the economy. On the contrary, he defined this as his party's *immediate* aim.

Second, his egalitarian ideal was to be realized through a radical deprofessionalization of administrative and industrial functions. To convince his readers (as well as himself) of the feasibility of this aim, Lenin propounded a thesis about the alleged simplicity of these functions in modern industrial societies. In the interests of equality and participation, he wanted to emphasize horizontal cooperation rather than vertical command, and this directed his attention to the organizational achievements of modern communications services. Consequently, he chose to define the economy of the future not in Kautskian terms ("gigantic industrial concern"), but rather as organized "along the lines of the postal service."

However, the tension between centralization, implied by the notion of "a single country-wide state 'syndicate,' " and decentralization, inherent in the ideal of a radically egalitarian participatory democracy, was not removed thereby. To cope with this difficulty Lenin invoked the idea of "voluntary centralism," "voluntary amalgamation of the communes into a nation" (ibid., 348). But he could not sincerely believe that this could be achieved spontaneously. Had he done so, he would have had to revise all his views on the role of conscious leadership in the development of the workers' movement.

Of course, this was not the case. For tactical reasons Lenin had to play down, or even conceal, the role of the party, but he did not change his view that the proletarian masses, if left to themselves, would inevitably betray their own true interests and their historical mission. True, in the revolutionary year 1917 he was relatively more optimistic about the workers than before, but even then he continued to stress in *The State and Revolution* and elsewhere that the proletarian masses could not dispense with the workers' party as their leader, teacher, and guide; that they had to be *trained* by class-conscious workers; and that such training was a necessary precondition of their active participation in managing the state (ibid., 404). Thus, the activity of the party was to become less obvious in the everyday administrative sphere but at the same time more intense in the educational/ ideological sphere—in the *training* and active shaping of the minds and conduct of the masses.

This was Lenin's solution to the contradiction between centralism and decentralization, conscious leadership and mass participation. He wanted the party to become the collective teacher of the working class without alienating itself from its mass basis—hence his emphasis on strict egalitarianism, on the banning of all privileges, all forms of dubious place hunting and bureaucratic conceit. On the other hand, he expected that the masses would interiorize the ideas of their "conscious vanguard" so deeply that any resort to coercion would simply become unnecessary. Only class enemies would have to be coerced and repressed; the working masses would voluntarily observe the rules of communist conduct, becoming *accustomed* to them—that is, treating them as something natural, as an unreflectively accepted *force of habit* (ibid., 303). In the final result this would lead to the complete elimination of coercion from social life: "People will gradually *become accustomed* to observing the elementary rules of social intercourse that have been known for centuries and repeated for thousands of years in all copy-book maxims. They will become accustomed to observing them without force, without coercion, without subordination, *without the special apparatus* for coercion called the state" (ibid.).

Lenin's readiness to identify the elementary rules of communist conduct with the elementary rules of social intercourse that had been known (though not in fact observed) for centuries is hardly consistent with his categorical rejection of all extraclass concepts in morality. But more interesting in the present context is his view that becoming accustomed to the performance of certain roles and functions would provide the solution to the problem of mass participation in managing the state. The relevant passage deserves to be quoted in full:

We, the workers, shall organize large-scale production on the basis of what capitalism has already created, relying on our own experience as workers, establishing strict, iron discipline backed up by the state power of armed workers. We shall reduce the role of the state officials to that of simply carrying out our instructions as responsible, revocable, modestly paid "foremen and accountants" (of course, with the aid of technicians of all sorts, types and degrees). This is *our* proletarian task, this is what we can and must *start* with in accomplishing the proletarian revolution. Such a beginning, on the basis of large-scale production, will of itself lead to the gradual "withering away" of all bureaucracy, to the gradual creation of an order—an order without inverted commas, an order bearing no similarity to wage slavery—an order under which the functions of control and accounting, becoming more and more simple, will be performed by each in turn, *will then become a habit* [italics added] and will finally die out as the *special* functions of a special section of the population. (ibid., 345)

Thus, "iron discipline" at the start, plus the "training" of the entire population by the class-conscious vanguard of the workers, would create firmly established habits in the sphere of control and accounting, and in this way, the need for an apparatus of coercion, as well as the need for specialized officials, would disappear. The problem of centralized control and supervision of labor would also disappear, because the workers would perform their respective functions (assumed to become more and more simple) like perfect robots, needing no supervision and control from above.

It is difficult to understand how this dreadful utopia could have attracted so many often very humane and liberal-minded Marxist revisionists.[130] The main reason for this was probably the growing contrast between the deceptive grandeur of the utopian ideal and the misery of Soviet reality. Kelsen was right in treating *The State and Revolution* as "the first and basic work of the Soviet theory of the state";[131] its author was obviously the founding father of the Soviet state, so it was natural to see this text as containing a theoretical explanation of the Soviet experiment, an ideological legitimization of communist rule, and the binding promise to make the Soviet workers a truly emancipated class, true masters of their collective fate. But historical reality refused to follow the prescribed course, and the price for failure to realize the utopian blueprint proved to be unexpectedly and increasingly high. As often happens, the resulting frustration among ideologists of the new order took the form of blaming reality rather than the legitimizing ideology.

Lenin's own reaction was in one respect similar and in another drastically different. The similarity lay in his refusal to blame his communist ideal; the difference was that unlike the later revisionists, he was inclined to attribute its failure to a Russian "lack of culture," which he saw as a human imperfection that could be overcome by subjecting people to a thorough education—that is, a combination of coercion and persuasion, enforced discipline and skillfully organized ideological mobilization. This diagnosis justified a rapid and radical minimization of the "libertarian" features of his theory of the proletarian dictatorship. Of course, it was to be only a temporary retreat: the workers were to pass through a severely authoritarian training in order to become capable of true liberation.

The fact that a direct workers' democracy is incompatible with effective factory management (something Lenin should have known from Engels's article "On Authority") revealed itself immediately, and his reaction was also immediate. As soon as he realized that self-management did not work, that control by the workers brought chaos and inefficiency, he drastically changed his declared program. He proclaimed not only the necessity of terrorist methods against counterrevolutionary elements, but also the need for coercion in the workshop, since, as he put it, "*unquestioning subordination* to a single will is absolutely necessary for the success of processes organized on the pattern of large-scale machine industry." He even asserted that there was "absolutely *no* contradiction in principle between Soviet (*that is*, socialist) democracy and the exercise of dictatorial power by individuals" (ibid., 455, 454). In "Six Theses on the Immediate Tasks of the Soviet Government" he explained his position:

Dictatorship presupposes a revolutionary government that is really firm and ruthless in crushing both exploiters and hooligans [i.e., undisciplined workers], and our government is too mild. Obedience, and unquestioning obedience at that, during work, to the one-man decisions of Soviet directors, the dictators elected or appointed by Soviet institutions, vested in dictatorial powers (as is demanded, for example, by the railway decree), is far, very far, from being guaranteed as yet. . . . The proletariat must concentrate all its class consciousness on the task of combating this petty-bourgeois anarchy. (L, *SW*, 2:622)

These words were written in the spring of 1918. It had taken Lenin only a few months to abandon completely his vision of the proletarian dictatorship as a state in which the workers would be able to control and recall all officials and managers at any time. The former apologist of the Paris Commune as a direct participatory democracy had become an ardent advocate of iron discipline and "the exercise of dictatorial powers by individuals." It is not surprising that in January 1920 he supported Trotsky's demand for the "militarization of labor." [132] The fact that this demand was almost unanimously rejected proves only that Lenin's evolution in the direction of blatant authoritarianism was too rapid to be immediately acceptable and that some elements of democracy still lingered in the Bolshevik party.

In the same year, 1920, Trotsky wrote his reply to Kautsky, entitled *Terrorism and Communism*, in which he developed his view on the role and character of the state in the transitional period: "The road to Socialism lies through a period of the highest possible intensification of the principle of the State. . . . Just as a lamp, before going out, shoots up in a brilliant flame, so the State, before disappearing, assumes the form of the dictatorship of the proletariat, i.e., *the most ruthless form of State*, which embraces the life of the citizens authoritatively in every direction." [133]

This was, of course, a complete departure from Lenin's theory that the dictatorship of the proletariat would be, from the very beginning, not a state in the proper sense of the term, but a "communal state," or a "semi-state." At the same time Trotsky anticipated the views later developed by Stalin. But there is nothing to indicate that Lenin at that time held different opinions on this matter. He continued to believe that direct coercion would sometimes be replaced by the force of habit but was firmly convinced that the only effective method of habit forming was the all-embracing control of people's lives by "a party of iron" having at its disposal all the repressive apparatus of the state. Indeed, he boasted that his dictatorship possessed means of compulsion and persuasion such as no former rulers had ever possessed (L, *A*, 569, 492).

But this was not the last step in the hardening of Lenin's views. At the Tenth Party Congress in March 1921 (the same Congress that officially inaugurated the New Economic Policy), two important resolutions were adopted, both drafted by Lenin himself. The first, condemning the "syndicalist and anarchist deviation," defined experiments with direct workers' democracy, as well as the "bidding for or flirtation with the non-Party masses" as a "complete break with Marxism and communism" (ibid., 497). This was a radical rejection of the ideal of a Republic of the Soviets consciously modeled on the Paris Commune. Lenin's former attraction to the idea of "masses in command" had given way to the following solemn credo:

Marxism teaches—and this tenet has not only been formally endorsed by the whole of the Communist International in the decisions of the Second (1920) Congress of the Comintern on the role of the political party of the proletariat, but has also been confirmed in practice by our revolution—that only the political party of the working class, i.e., the Communist Party, is capable of uniting, training and organizing a vanguard of the proletariat and of the whole mass of the working people that alone will be capable of withstanding the inevitable petty-bourgeois vacillations of this mass and the inevitable traditions and relapses of narrow craft unionism or craft prejudices among the proletariat, and of guiding all the united activities of the whole of the proletariat, i.e., of leading it politically, and through it, the whole mass of the working people. (ibid., 498)

The second resolution condemned and prohibited all forms of factionalism within the party. The Kronstadt mutiny, it said, had proved that the enemies of the proletariat "take advantage of every deviation from a thoroughly consistent communist line." Therefore the Congress "hereby declares dissolved and orders the immediate dissolution of all groups without exception formed on the basis of one platform or another. . . . Nonobservance of this decision of the Congress shall entail unconditional and instant expulsion from the Party" (ibid., 500, 502).

In this way the working class was deprived not only of its right to political pluralism but also of its right to independent trade unions, and even within the ruling party political life was to be extinguished for the sake of "the maximum unanimity" (ibid., 502). The full implementation of these principles proved to be possible only under the Stalinist terror. But the dubious honor of their formulation and official proclamation undoubtedly belongs to the Founding Father of the Soviet State.

4.7   The Dictatorship of the Proletariat and the Law

Like the young Marx, the young Lenin was a student of law. He even practiced as a lawyer for some time. But unlike Marx, Lenin had not at any time treated law seriously or seen in it a means of human liberation.[134] He was indeed deeply steeped in the worst Russian tradition of contempt for law that characterized Russian revolutionary populism. Unlike Plekhanov, Lenin could never see the "juridical worldview" of the Enlightenment as an expression of the lofty aspirations, or at least honest illusions, of the progressive bourgeoisie or as an important dialectical phase in the unfolding of "Historical Reason." To him any belief in universal legal justice was simply absurd. He seems to have been deeply convinced that intelligent human beings could not honestly dispute the view that law, by its very nature, serves the interests of the stronger party; therefore, he was inclined to treat its lofty image as merely a contemptible expression of cowardly bourgeois hypocrisy. This explains why he sometimes showed "a certain tenderness for Anarchists";[135] he criticized them mercilessly but, unlike Plekhanov, treated them seriously, as brave and honest in their convictions, devoid of the cowardly spirit of bourgeois liberalism.

Lenin's contemptuous disregard for law comes out clearly in his view that every state is essentially a class dictatorship, that is, "rule based directly upon force and unrestricted by any laws" (L, CW, 10:246). This went beyond the usual Marxist view of the state and law as organs for the oppression of one class by another. The main thrust of Lenin's conception was directed against the view of law as an autonomous and indispensable element in the state, at least in the modern state. Unlike Engels or Plekhanov, Lenin was not content to assert that state power stands above the law and that every law is *in fact* a command of those in power; he wanted to add that the holders of political power could enforce their will directly, without the mediation of law and without putting their command in legal form.[136] The state, as the organized power of a given class, was for him essentially not a legal structure, but rather a phenomenon similar to the army. The same applied, of course, to the revolutionary party. He admired the military form of organization as maximally flexible, unrestrained by bureaucratic procedures, and therefore capable of "giving millions of people *a single will*" (ibid., 21:252). He grudgingly acknowledged the utility of specific laws or administrative regulations for controlling the population as well as state officials themselves, but always insisted that all such rules be flexible (i.e., not stable), subject to change at any time, and not allowed to restrain the power of the rulers. His phrase "unrestricted by any laws" should be understood literally. The dictatorship of the proletariat was not to be bound even by its own laws.[137] They were not to be used in defense of those who were destined to be suppressed and crushed. Consequently, this rule of the proletariat had to destroy the "bourgeois profession of advocates" that created obstacles to the unrestricted exercise of dictatorial power.[138] However, it also had to control everything, which it could not do without issuing an ever-increasing number of absurdly detailed legal regulations. Though it elevated direct coercion and the rule of terror, it also wanted to mobilize mass support for itself, so it tried to organize a participatory terror, a terror from below, exercised directly by the revolutionary masses. At different stages of its development, different tendencies of this terror prevailed, but each showed only different aspects, different possible forms of lawlessness.

There were three strains in what may be called Lenin's "legal nihilism": anarcho-populist, Babouvist-egalitarian, and Jacobin-centralizing. Their obvious common denominator was Lenin's outspoken contempt for such bourgeois notions as the independence of courts and procedural justice. In most cases these strains were ideologically interrelated and not easily distinguishable. Treating them separately, however, might help us understand the complex nature of Lenin's uncompromising hostility toward the liberal conception of freedom under law.

The anarcho-populist strain in Lenin's attitude toward law can be defined as an inclination toward direct popular justice, or rather, popular violence directed against the "enemies of the people." It is interesting to note that this motif appeared very early in his thought. In "Casual Notes" (1901), he was already praising "trial by the street" as "breathing a living spirit into the bureaucratic formalism" (ibid., 4:393). He made this remark in the context of defending the principle of trial by jury, but his argument clearly indicates that he was not really concerned with the jury as such; defending the jury principle was for him only a means for exposing the courts to direct political pressure from outside. In "Victory of the Kadets and the Tasks of the Workers' Party" (1906), he contrasted police dictatorship with a "dictatorship of the revolutionary people" and praised spontaneous outbursts of popular violence. In such acts of violence, he wrote, "we see the dictatorship *of the people*, because the people, the mass of the population, unorganised, 'casually' assembled at the given spot, itself appears on the scene, exercises justice and metes out punishment, exercises power and creates a new, revolutionary law" (ibid., 10:246–47).

After the revolution Lenin used the same words in "Contribution to the History of the Question of the Dictatorship" (1920) to describe the form of revolutionary justice characteristic of the dictatorship of the proletariat (ibid., 31:353).[139] He emphasized that the lynch law was exercised "without any police," which implied a negative judgment about police and a positive association with the process of the withering away of the state. Similar views on the superiority of direct, participatory people's justice are found, of course, in *The State and Revolution*. But these anarcho-populist ideas did not prevent the Bolshevik leader from giving close attention to the organization of a revolutionary police state. Six weeks after his coup d'état, the new state created the All-Russian Extraordinary Commission for Combating Counter-Revolution and Sabotage (colloquially called the Cheka), a highly centralized police organization unrestrained by any rules of procedure and responsible only to the very top of the party.

To organize the Cheka while at the same time encouraging and inciting direct popular violence was not a contradiction to Lenin. He honestly believed that terror from above (which he took for granted) would need active support and legitimization from terror from below; he genuinely hoped that the overthrow of the "bourgeois" government and the suppression of the opportunistic labor leaders would release the revolutionary energy of the masses and that his own party would be able to give direction to this energy in an indirect, concealed manner; in other words, he wanted to mobilize mass support for his revolution, and he was ready to pay for this by giving the workers' "spontaneity more room." The masses, however, did not live up to his expectations, being in Lenin's view often "monstrously" passive and too lenient toward their class enemies.[140] Consequently, he came to count less and less on direct action by the masses and instead relied more and more on revolutionary professionalism, military discipline, and centralization (as recommended in *What Is to Be Done?*).

The idea of the People's Court, one of the main components of the conception of "Soviet democracy," shared the same fate. The Bolshevik seizure of power was followed by the decree *On Courts* (December 7, 1917), which abolished all existing legal institutions and abrogated *uno actu* the entire legislation of the tsarist regime and of the Provisional Government. Lenin was very proud that Soviet power "immediately threw the old court on the scrap heap." In the "Third All-Russian Congress of Soviets" (January 1918), he praised this decision as paving the way for "a real people's court" and hoped that it would be implemented "not so much by the force of repressive measures as by massive example, the authority of the working people, without formalities" (ibid., 26:464). Indeed, this was a logical consequence of his ideas: his theory of the dictatorship of the proletariat, as developed in *The State and Revolution*, insisted that the entire machinery of the bourgeois state must be smashed and that the new state must seek support in different forms of direct participatory democracy. In accordance with his ideal of the Republic of the Soviets, the new, popular courts, composed of elected and "freely revocable" judges, were supposed to be guided not by any formal rules, but by the dictates of revolutionary conscious-ness, or the class consciousness of the working people. This class justice meant, among other things, taking into account the class background of the offender and the class character of the offense ("Was it or was it not committed with a view to restoring the oppressor class to power?").[141] Very soon, however, it turned out that the socialist character of the improvised courts could not be guaranteed, that their verdicts were very different from the expectations of the party leadership. Often, popular judges were too indulgent; in other cases, they were barbarically severe but at the same time far removed from the socialist hierarchy of values. (Thus, for instance, in rural areas "the death penalty was invoked for mere cases of theft and sometimes carried out on the spot.")[142] In view of this, the fate of decen-tralized popular justice was easily predictable: popular courts gave way to a highly repressive centralized system for the administration of justice, which was directly subordinated to the commands of the party leadership.

The Babouvist-egalitarian strain in Lenin's thinking about law is seen in his implacable hostility toward economic freedom: his conviction that commerce was (to paraphrase Babeuf's words) the worst poison in the social body,[143] that private production and trade could be tolerated only on the grounds of expediency, and that the organization of an equitable distri-bution should be one of the most important tasks of the revolutionary state. Thus far it was part of Lenin's communist ideal and had a place in both the populist and the Jacobin trends of his thought. Its distinctive feature was a preoccupation with the problem of redistribution: the problem of how to extract from the coffers of the rich all that had been amassed in them "through plunder over the years of ruthless criminal exploitation." This feature assumed a populist form of expropriations from below, carried out in popular pogroms under the slogan "Plunder what has been plundered," but was fully compatible with, and naturally inclined toward, centralized, Jacobin-style actions from above (ibid., 516, 516). Its best expression is, perhaps, Lenin's note to Dzierżyński of December 7 (20), 1917, which gave birth to the ill-famed Cheka (L, *PSS*, 35:156–58). It seems worthwhile, therefore, to summarize its content.

It was necessary, Lenin said, immediately to enact a decree "On the Struggle Against the Counter-Revolutionaries and Wreckers." This decree would require that all persons with an income of 500 rubles per month or more, as well as all owners of immovables or capital funds, be registered within three days with their house committees. (In the manuscript Lenin deleted the words *three days*, replacing them with *twenty-four hours* [ibid., 157].)[144] The penalty for failure to register was to be either a high monetary fine, imprisonment of up to one year, or sending the offender to the battle front. All registered individuals should provide themselves with special notebooks for keeping detailed accounts of their weekly incomes, expenses for private consumption, and services rendered to the community.

The proposed decree was passed immediately, and the Cheka (called into being the same day) was to enforce its implementation. In the next year the Fifth Congress of Soviets unanimously approved the Constitution of 1918, which deprived class enemies of the right to vote or to hold elective office. Among those deprived of political rights were persons hiring labor for profit, individuals living on nonlabor income, tradesmen, and clergymen of all religious denominations. In this way equality before the law was formally and triumphantly abolished in the name of material equality and class retribution.

The proclamation of the constitution coincided with the introduction of the policy known as War Communism, a policy involving the forcible requisition of farm produce, the banning of all private trade, the nationalization of most industrial concerns, and above all, the attempt to exercise total control over the allocation of goods. The period of toying with the conceptions of direct participatory democracy was over; the party renewed its commitment to Jacobin methods, liquidated workers' control, and substituted for it the exercise of dictatorial powers by individuals. But this abandonment of the anarcho-populist ingredient of Leninism was to be compensated for by another form of "flirtation with the non-party masses":[145] by mobilizing mass support for the party in the name of crudely communist (i.e., Babouvist) equality and class hatred.

The initial successes of this policy should not be underestimated. Lev Kritsman, a witness of this terrible time, described War Communism as "a heroic period of the Great Russian Revolution."[146] He pointed out that crude communism, with its violent rejection of "bourgeois legality," had already quite a wide and strong social base. In an eloquent passage he wrote:

The entire social system of this epoch was permeated with the spirit of a merciless class *exclusiveness*. . . . The bourgeois had become a contemptible and rejected creature. He was a *pariah*, deprived not only of his property but also of his honor. He was deprived of all civil and political rights. . . . He had no right to enter military service and possess weapons. He was fully crushed—not physically, but socially. . . . The stigma of belonging to the class of exploiters could lead to the concentration camp, to prison, or, in the best case, to a ramshackle house, left behind by those workers who had received better apartments for themselves. . . . This merciless class exclusiveness, this social annihilation of the exploiting classes, was a source of a great moral elation, a source of a passionate enthusiasm for the proletariat and all exploited people.[147]

The economic results of War Communism were truly catastrophic. Large-scale industry collapsed; labor productivity was reduced in 1919 to a mere 22 percent of what it had been in 1913.[148] Under these conditions the party had no choice but to allow a partial restoration of market forces, which could be done only at the expense of material equality. The explanation that the NEP was only a temporary retreat sounded unconvincing to all who had been mobilized for the communist cause. The party could no longer rely on the moral elation of the masses; many of its own members felt bitterly disappointed, if not actually betrayed. In addition, economic liberalization, institutionalized by the reinstatement of a civil code, increased the pressure for a measure of political freedom, while at the same time, the Kronstadt revolt provided the party with an additional argument for an undisputed monopoly of power. Lenin reacted to this obvious defeat of the communist utopia by seeking salvation in his favorite ideas of iron discipline and hierarchical centralization, which, of course, brought to the fore the Jacobin strain in his attitude toward law.

At this stage, however, his Jacobinism contained a new element: the emphasis on legal culture as a necessary condition for a successful struggle toward socialism. In his letter to Stalin on "Dual Subordination and Legality" (dictated by telephone on May 20, 1922), he complained about the Russian "lack of culture," about "living amidst an ocean of illegality," and concluded that the "fundamental task" of the party consisted in "constantly introducing respect for the law" (L, CW, 33:364–65).

Taken literally, this might be interpreted as a total revision of Lenin's view that the dictatorship of the proletariat should not be restricted by any laws, but this interpretation would be quite false. In fact, Lenin was always consistent in insisting that law must be a docile servant, never a master.[149] In this respect, he agreed with those highly placed bureaucrats of imperial Russia who espoused the ideal of a police state and therefore regarded law as "an instrument of administration rather than a higher principle binding both rulers and ruled."[150] It did not even occur to him that "respect for law" might involve anything other than the principle of strict subordination. He instructed Stalin and the Politburo that local procurators must be subordinate *only* to the central government, not to the local authorities. In his letter on "Dual Subordination," any form of decentralization in the administration of justice was condemned as incompatible with the (truly Jacobin!) ideal of the absolute uniformity of law throughout the state. Viewed in this way, local influence appeared as a source of corruption and hence "one of the greatest, if not the greatest obstacle to the establishment of law and culture." The only remedy against this evil was strict control exercised from the top by "half of a score of reliable Communists who possess an adequate legal education and are capable of resisting all purely local influences" (ibid., 33:365, 365). It is evident, therefore, that in this context law meant vertical relationships of command, not horizontal relationships between free and equal persons.

A telling confirmation of this view of Lenin's conception of legal culture and respect for law is his letter to the Commissar of Justice, Dmitry Kursky, written on May 17, 1922 (almost exactly at the same time as his letter to Stalin about dual subordination). The principal passage reads: "The courts must not ban terror—to promise that would be deception or self-deception—but must formulate the motives underlying it, legalize it as a principle, plainly, without any make-believe or embellishment. It must be formulated in the broadest possible manner, for only revolutionary law and revolutionary conscience can more or less widely determine the limits within which it should be applied" (ibid., 358).

Thus, terror was to be *legalized* and applied in the broadest possible manner. Reference to revolutionary law and revolutionary consciousness were in fact a justification for arbitrariness, since in Lenin's view revolutionary law should be flexible—that is, totally politicized, dispensing with formalities, rejecting procedural rules (often equated by him with sheer bureaucracy),[151] and reduced thereby to a matter of naked expediency. The scope of the application of terrorist measures was indicated in a postscript saying that all forms of anticommunist activity, including mere propaganda, should be treated as "an offence punishable by death." In another letter to Kursky (of the same time) Lenin was even more specific, saying that "the application of the death sentence should be extended (commutable for deportation) . . . to all forms of activity by the Mensheviks, SRs *and so on*" (ibid., 359; 42:419).

Even more instructive is his view on the criteria for selecting people for such savage punishment. The postscript to his letter to Kursky proposes two variants of the definition of counterrevolution. The first describes different forms of activity (beginning with propaganda and agitation) that *assist* the counterrevolutionary deeds of the international bourgeoisie; the second proposes using the formula about "objectively serving the interests" of the counterrevolutionary bourgeoisie. To make this formula as flexible as possible Lenin even suggested that the words "objectively serving the interests" might be replaced with yet more imprecise wording: "is likely to serve" (ibid., 33:359). And he had no doubt that the mere *likelihood* of *objectively* serving the interests of his political enemies was sufficient to warrant the death penalty.

According to Piers Beirne and Alan Hunt, Lenin indicated his preference for the second alternative.[152] This was logical and consistent, since he had never been concerned with safeguarding the basic human rights of his class enemies. It is deplorable that so many Western scholars share the view that "the origins of authoritarianism in general, and of authoritarian penal practices in particular, were intrinsic neither to the early Bolshevik project nor to Lenin's discourse as its major exponent."[153] Attempts to present the Bolshevik terror as purely defensive, based on "the heroic assumption" (E. H. Carr's words)[154] that the harshest penalties applied to class enemies were justified as temporary measures necessitated by the mortal struggle, may seem convincing but are, in fact, missing an essential point. As Lenin expressed it in "To the Moscow Revolutionary Tribunal" (October 20, 1921), the purpose of terror was mostly educational (ibid., 45:348). Fear was necessary for educating not only his enemies but also, and above all, his own party. This is why he insisted that drastic penalties for corruption (no less than ten years' imprisonment in addition to ten years' compulsory labor) be tripled for party members (see his letter to Kursky, February 20, 1922, ibid., 36:562). In 1922 he was not threatened by the white terror; indeed, he had a unique chance to achieve a degree of national reconciliation. The Mensheviks and SRs praised the NEP and declared their willingness to cooperate. But just because of this it was necessary, in Lenin's view, to teach the Communists that their ideology must not become diluted, that economic liberalization must not involve political concessions, and that any attempt to soften the proletarian dictatorship would be treated as the gravest crime.

An integral part of this theory of crime and punishment was the concept of *objective* guilt—that is, guilt undefinable in juridical terms and consisting solely in the so-called objective results of one's activity, as seen and defined by one's ideological enemies. As a rule, this concept applied to unintended results; otherwise, guilt would have been classified as "subjective" as well. Thus, one could be guilty objectively by the mere fact of being classified as such by those who had usurped for themselves the monopoly on truth and justice. A variant of this peculiar conception of political crime was Lenin's notion of "objective treason," which he applied in 1906 to the Mensheviks (as discussed earlier). The most horrible thing about this was the possibility that ideologically minded party members would interiorize it to the extent of sincerely believing that (as Trotsky put it) "it is impossible to be right against the party." [155] This combination of external terror with extreme and (partially, at least) interiorized ideological pressure created the conditions leading to the Stalinist Moscow trials.

It remains to characterize Lenin's attitude toward the increased role of civil law under the NEP. He was aware that market relations could not develop without a certain amount of stability and predictability in law; hence, he himself insisted that greater legality was needed to improve relations with the peasantry and to promote trade.[156] But his views on Soviet civil law sharply differed from those of Evgeny Pashukanis, the most talented Marxist legal philosopher of his day, who was to become the main theorist of the NEP legal culture.[157] For a long time these differences remained almost unnoticed. Lenin was unaware of them because Pashukanis's *General Theory of Law and Marxism* (1924) appeared only after his death; Pashukanis, in his turn, did, all he could to pass for an orthodox Leninist. Nevertheless, a brief comparison of the relevant views of the two men may be helpful in elucidating the two possible Marxist approaches to the problem of civil law in the transitional period.

Pashukanis liked to quote Lenin's opinion about jurists as "the most reactionary people on earth." [158] Like Lenin, he was convinced of the essential incompatibility of communism and law. Law, he argued, is needed only in conditions of bourgeois society in which individuals confront one another as isolated, egoistic, and mutually competing subjects. In other words, "the juridical element in the regulation of human conduct enters where the isolation and opposition of interests begins." [159] Pashukanis supported this thesis by quoting Marx's early article "On the Jewish Question" in which the concept of a person as entitled to legally guaranteed rights was treated as specific to bourgeois civil society. [160] For Marx, the very idea of right was "the justification of egoistic man separated from his fellow men and the community" (see chapter 1, section 2). Pashukanis extended this view to morality, which he saw as "a necessary supplement to juridic life." According to him, "egoism, freedom and the supreme value of personality" were in fact three expressions of the same social relationship: "The egoistic subject, the subject of a right and the moral personality are the three basic masks under which man appears in commodity production." [161]

If this was so, what would replace morality and law in the communist society of the future? Pashukanis answered this by pointing out that morality and law characterized the individualistic society of commodity producers and would disappear in a true community that was based on genuine social instinct and that bound individuals by "close emotional ties which erase the boundary of the I." Following Engels, he indicated that such a community, embodying heroic virtues and capable of "intensified social enthusiasm," had existed in "the earlier periods of organic, and particularly tribal, existence." [162] It would reappear in a communist society in which market relations would be replaced by directly socialized production. Members of this society would also be "directly socialized" and therefore have no need of either external legal regulation or individualized moral conscience.

As we can see, Pashukanis's hostility toward law was deeply rooted in Marxist tradition. He visualized the communist society of the future as one in which the communal cohesiveness of tribal societies would coexist with comprehensive rational planning, thus combining a capacity for further technological and industrial development with the advantages of primitive harmony. In such a perfectly collectivist society people would be directly and totally socialized but no longer individualized and independent; they would be free as "communal beings" but not as "egoistic individuals." Their individual interests would be identical with the interests of society as a whole; hence they would be able to settle their disputes simply, without courts or professional lawyers. [163] They would share the same values, strive for the same collective aims, and cooperate with one another without conflict. Their cooperation would depend on many technical rules, presupposing a unity of purpose, but not on legal regulation, presupposing the opposition of private interests. The application of these rules might involve coercion, but "so long as this coercion is considered from the perspective of the same single purpose (both for the rulers and the ruled), it remains solely a technically expedient act." Pashukanis illustrated this reasoning by comparing the task of economic and social planning to the task of a doctor in curing a sick person. He assumed that the content of the rules of medical treatment was established by medical science alone and had nothing to do with law. From this he concluded that "the application of these rules may be accompanied by coercion with respect to the patient" and that the joint purpose of both sides—the restoration of the patient's health—provided a satisfactory justification for coercive treatment.[164]

In this way Pashukanis justified the use of coercive methods even under communism (i.e., after the withering away of law and the state). This socially acceptable and directly exercised coercion was to be legitimated by a "unity of purpose," and decisions about its application were to be made on the basis of objective science. This was, of course, a very attractive vision to all who espoused the conception of "scientic socialism" and saw their mission as organizing all social life on the basis of scientific planning.

The view of the basic incompatibility between communism and law was common to the whole communist tradition, so it is hardly surprising that in many respects Lenin's attitude toward law agreed with Pashukanis's theory. Both indignantly rejected the idea of the legal protection of private individual interests, seeing it as an expression of egoistic individualism incompatible with the unity and unanimity of the collectivist communist society of the future. Both also stressed the essential incompatibility of rights, especially property rights, with the principle of rational planning. Both saw law not as a safeguard of human freedom but rather as a divisive and enslaving device that served the interests of the exploiters, preventing those exploited from combining forces and so achieving their social and economic liberation.

A distinctive feature of Pashukanis's legal philosophy was his commodity exchange theory of law. This claimed that law emerged as an integral part of commodity production, that legal relationships were essentially market relationships, being constituted by the exchange of goods, and that only private law (i.e., laws regulating the relationships between separate individuals, the subjects of egoistic interest) was law in the true sense of this term.[165] This view somewhat contradicted the usual Marxist explanation of the origins of law that, following Engels's classic account, stressed the inseparability of law and state, seeing both as forms of the collective will of the ruling class, but it found firm support in Marx's conception of the close relationship between law and commodity exchange. As he said: "At first there is *commerce*, and then the legal order develops out of it. . . . In a developed trade the exchangers recognize each other tacitly as legal persons and owners of the goods to be exchanged respectively by them. . . . This practical relation, arising through and in exchange itself, only later attains a *legal form* in contracts, etc." (M, *TOM*, 210).

These two accounts of the genesis of law coexisted in classical Marxism. On the purely theoretical plane they could be seen as complementary rather than mutually exclusive. What was often overlooked, however, was that they led to very different practical conclusions. The commodity exchange interpretation implied that law was an expression of economic relationships that could not be changed by an act of political will; that its source should be seen in the economic base rather than in the ideological superstructure; that legislation must express "the will of economic relations" (to use Marx's awkward expression),[166] not merely the political intentions of the rulers. In other words, this aspect of Pashukanis's theory was directed against "the view that law is capable of voluntaristic manipulation by dominant social classes."[167] At this point this theory was not consistent with the voluntarist spirit of Leninism. It clearly implied that Lenin's formula about the dictatorship of the proletariat as "unrestricted by any laws" was not felicitous, since no form of government could be independent of its economic base.

The full importance of this difference was revealed in Pashukanis's attitude toward the code of civil law introduced under the NEP. From his point of view, the Soviet civil law of this period could only be bourgeois law, which served the needs of the market economy and therefore created very tangible limitations for the voluntarist policies of the state. He supported this opinion by references to Marx's *Critique of the Gotha Program*, according to which "right can never be higher than the economic structure of society" (M&E, *SW*, 3:19). Soviet society, Pashukanis argued, was still in the transitional stage. It was bound to tolerate, and even encourage, the development of commodity exchange relationships; hence, the Communist party had no choice but to introduce bourgeois private law and to treat it seriously. The possibility of transcending the "narrow horizon of bourgeois right" would appear only at the higher, fully marketless phase of communist society (ibid.).[168] Therefore, as long as the NEP remained in force, the Soviet state must respect its private law even while being aware of its "bourgeois" character.

From this it followed that the state should temporarily refrain from arbitrary interference in the private sector and from the use of terrorist measures. This suggestion, however, was not acceptable to Lenin. His long letter to Kursky of February 20, 1922, is a clear warning that such an interpretation of the NEP would not be tolerated (L, *CW*, 36:560–65). It therefore provided powerful arguments against the idealization of the NEP, as well as of Lenin's intentions, that so frequently appear in the literature on the subject.

Let us try to summarize this most important document. The People's Commissariat for Justice, Lenin wrote, should not limit its activities to "reprisals against the political enemies of the Soviet power." Its fighting role was equally important in the sphere of the NEP. "There is no evidence of any understanding of the fact that we recognize and will continue to recognize only *state* capitalism, and it is we—we conscious workers, we communists—who are the state" (ibid., 560, 561). A tendency to restore bourgeois civil law had emerged, but the task of the People's Commissariat was to swim *against* the tide:

Its task is to create a new civil law, and not to adopt (rather not to allow itself to be duped by the old and stupid bourgeois lawyers who adopt) the old, bourgeois concept of civil law. . . . We do not recognize anything "private," and regard *every-thing* in the economic sphere as falling under *public* and not *private* law. We allow *only* state capitalism, and as has been said, it is we who are the state. Hence, the task is to extend the right of the state to annul "private" contracts; to apply to "civil legal relations" not the *corpus juris Romani* but *our revolutionary concept of law*; to show systematically, persistently, with determination, through a series of model trials, *how* this should be done wisely and vigorously; to brand through the Party and expel those members of revolutionary tribunals and people's judges who fail to learn this or refuse to understand it. (ibid., 562–63)

These statements are so unambiguous that it is hardly necessary to comment on them. But the question of Pashukanis is more puzzling. How could he have risen so high in the Soviet legal profession when his views on private law under the dictatorship of the proletariat were so glaringly different from Lenin's? There are, I think, two possible explanations, partial ones, certainly, but mutually supporting each other.

First, we must remember that Lenin's letter to Kursky was strictly confidential.[169] Lenin was well aware that "it is stupid to disclose our strategy to the enemy" and therefore asked that all careless talk about it be prohibited "on pain of Party responsibility." He attached such importance to this that he repeated his request in the postscript: "There must not be the slightest mention of my letter in the press. Let anyone, who so wishes, write in his own name, without any mention of mine" (ibid., 563, 565). The reasons for Lenin's insistence on secrecy are obvious. He did not want to compromise the NEP; he wanted the peasants and other small producers, as well as native merchants and foreign capitalists, to believe that honest economic activity in the private sector could count on genuine legal protection, that the period of legal nihilism was definitely over, and that the new civil code offered a necessary minimum of legal stability and predictability. In other words, he wanted to deceive his peasant allies by not disclosing to them the true nature of the NEP. So the People's Commissariat for Justice could only be glad that a talented Marxist jurist had developed a theory of law that (irrespective of the author's intentions) contributed to the strengthening of the useful illusion about current economic liberalization.

Second, Pashukanis himself was a sworn enemy of the market and supported the NEP only as a necessary, temporarily-to-be tolerated evil. He was not free from revolutionary impatience and certainly not immune to careerist considerations. So he was prepared to adjust his theory to changing circumstances and the party line. In 1925 he supported the "revolution of the law" program, that is, the second Soviet experiment with the "withering away of law."[170] Writing in 1927, he claimed that the withering away of law in the period of the construction of socialism was being achieved through the struggle between the principle of equivalent exchange (i.e., the market) and that of socialist planning, leading to the victory of the latter.[171] Consequently, he modified his view of Soviet civil law, conceding that it was "fundamentally different from genuine bourgeois law,"[172] and stressed that it should be seen from the perspective of the victory of the socialist elements of the Soviet economy over capitalist ones.[173] Elsewhere he related these conceptions to Engels's vision of the "leap to the kingdom of freedom."[174] This vision, he argued, should not be interpreted as a *sudden* change; in fact, the passage to freedom was a process of gradual but steady replacement of "objective economic regularities" by "the conscious will of the collective."[175] It followed from this that legal relationships had already begun to disappear (together with the laws of the marketplace) and that the revolutionaries should do all they could to hasten the process. The subsequent voluntaristic turn in Stalin's policy was thus theoretically approved and politically supported.

All this shows once again that early Soviet Marxism was deeply hostile to law and that the NEP was simply "a retreat in order to make better preparations for a new offensive against capitalism" (ibid., 33:184). Lenin remained faithful to the convictions that had justified his seizure of power: that only power was the source of law, never vice versa; that the proletarian dictatorship would not be bound even by its own laws; and that its final aim was to create a communist society in which individuals would have no rights against the collective and in which legal regulation would be replaced by deeply internalized collective habits. To adopt the Lenin of the NEP period as a sort of patron saint for Gorbachev's *perestroika*,[176] or to see Gorbachev's advocacy of the rule of law as fulfilling Lenin's ideological testament, is unspeakably naive, a complete misunderstanding, if not a conscious falsification, of history.

4.8 The Dictatorship of the Proletariat
and the Economic Utopia

In Lenin's view, the main difference between bourgeois revolutions in the past and his own socialist revolution was the constructive character of the latter's principal task. In bourgeois revolutions the task of the revolutionary forces was limited to "the negative or destructive work of abolishing feudalism, monarchy and medievalism"; the positive task of organizing the new social order was left to the spontaneous economic activities of the property-owning minority of the population. In contrast to this, a socialist revolution could not end with the overthrow of the old regime: its principal task was the constructive work of setting up a new organizational system, based on "the planned production and distribution of the goods" (L, *A*, 439, 440).

This was to be the main *immediate* task of the Soviet government. In his other articles at this time (early spring 1918), Lenin defined the immediate tasks of his party as *socialist* reforms but stressed the need to have "a clear conception of the goal toward which these reforms are in the final analysis directed." This goal was defined as *communism*, not merely socialism; as implementing the principle "From each according to his ability, to each according to his needs" (L, *CW*, 27:127, 127). The name "Communist party" was the only one that was scientifically correct for a truly proletarian party (ibid.). The Bolsheviks had already realized this in April 1917. Now they must do everything to prove that they were genuine communists who had broken off all connection with European official socialism, which had utterly compromised itself during the war. They must in fact struggle for the eradication of the very root of capitalism—commodity production (ibid., 129). Nor must they postpone the realization of this task under the pretext of lacking well-trained communist cadres: the construction of communism must begin "now, in two months and not in twenty years' time." If there were not enough communist experts, bourgeois experts must be compelled to work for the communist cause. Trotsky's experience with officers of the old tsarist army had shown how to compel those opposed to communism to help build it. There was no alternative to communism and communism could not dispense with violence. "The only alternative is either violence against Liebknecht and Luxemburg, the murder of the best leaders of the workers, or the violent suppression of the exploiters; and whoever dreams of a middle course is our most harmful and dangerous enemy" (ibid., 29:70, 71).

Thus, Lenin's openly declared aim was to lead Russia to communism as quickly as possible. He understood that this goal would not be immediately attainable, but he believed in the possibility of passing through several

transitional stages in the space of a few months.[177] His mood was hero-
ically triumphalist even at the time of signing the humiliating Brest-Litovsk
Treaty. The Bolshevik party, he explained, must not behave like the Polish
szlachcic (nobleman) who would choose a gallant death in a hopeless fight
(ibid., 27:161). It chose the harsh peace with Germany to save itself for the
realization of its historical mission, which was "of immense significance
for the emancipation of the world." The past achievements of the party had
been glorious (a "victorious triumphal march of Bolshevism from one end
of the country to another"); its revolutionary will was inflexible, unbroken. Only the Communists could "ensure that at any price Russia ceases to
be wretched and impotent and becomes mighty and abundant." But it was
necessary to fight "with clenched teeth," "mustering all forces and straining every nerve," realizing that "the road of world socialist revolution"
provided the only salvation (ibid., 159, 160, 160, 161).

This was the language of a leader fanatically devoted to his cause and
refusing to deviate from his chosen path. Lenin's realistic acceptance of
Russia's defeat in the war with Germany was not accompanied by readiness
to make internal concessions to noncommunist forces. On the contrary, he
was then at the height of his revolutionary utopianism. All his writings of
this time express the spirit of the heroic period of the Russian Revolution;
a willingness consciously and deliberately to realize Marx's communist
utopia and so to achieve full communist freedom.

What Lenin meant by this is summarized in his outline of the draft
program of the party, written in March 1918. The relevant parts of this
revealing document contain the following proposals:

• Socialist organization of production on the scale of the whole state: management by *workers' organizations* (trade unions, factory committees, etc.) under the
general leadership of Soviet power, which alone is *sovereign.*

The same for transport and distribution (at first state monopoly on "trade,"
subsequently replacement, complete and final, of "trade" by planned, organized
distribution through associations of trading and industrial office workers, under
the leadership of Soviet power).

• Compulsory organization of the whole population in consumer and producer
communes.

While not (for the time being) abolishing money and not prohibiting individual
purchase and sale transactions by individual families, we must, in the first place,
make it obligatory by law to carry out all such transactions through the consumer
and producer communes.

• An immediate start to be made on full realization of universal compulsory
labor service, with most cautious and gradual extension of it to the small peasants
who live by their own farming without wage labor.

The first measure, the first step towards universal compulsory labor service must
be the introduction of consumers' work (budget) books (compulsory introduction) for all the well-to-do people (= persons with an income over 500 rubles per

month, and then for owners of enterprises with wage-workers, for families with servants, etc.).

Buying and selling is also permissible not through one's commune (during journeys, at markets, etc.), but with compulsory entry of the transaction (if above a definite sum) in the consumers' work book.

- Complete concentration of banking in the hands of the state and by all financial operations of trade in the banks. Standardization of banking current accounts; gradual transition to the compulsory keeping of current accounts in the bank, at first by the largest, and later by *all* the country's enterprises. Compulsory deposit of money in the banks and transfer of money *only* through the banks.

- Standardization of accounting and control over all production and distribution of output; this accounting and control must be carried out at first by workers' organizations and subsequently by *each and every* member of the population.

- Organization of competition between the various (all) consumer and producer communes of the country for steady improvement of organization, discipline and labor productivity, for transition to superior techniques, for economizing labor and materials, for gradually reducing the working day to six hours, and for gradually equalizing *all* wages and salaries in *all* occupations and categories.

- Steady, systematic measures for (transition to *Massenspeisung*) replacement of the individual domestic economy of separate families by joint catering for large groups of families. (ibid., 156–57)

As we can see, at this early stage Lenin's program envisioned not only a countrywide socialist organization of production, coupled with the forced allocation of labor, but also a complete and final replacement of trade by "planned, organized distribution" to be followed by the gradual abolition of all forms of monetary exchange; it demanded strict collective control over individual consumption of all well-to-do people and postulated that individual households should be replaced by communal catering for large groups. In other words, it was a program for a drastic collectivization of all spheres of life, including private consumption. It did not, as yet, demand the expropriation of the bourgeoisie but made up for this by abolishing the market, introducing universal control, and compulsorily organizing the whole population into consumer and producer communes.

The context of this program reflected the practice of the Bolshevik dictatorship. From the very beginning it was a systematic assault on the capitalist system of ownership, production, and exchange. As early as December 1917, urban real estate was withdrawn from commerce; in the spring of 1918, it was expropriated on behalf of the state. A series of other decrees in early 1918 forbade the selling or leasing of enterprises, required the registration of securities and bonds in private possession, and outlawed inheritance of property. From the very beginning, formally private enterprises were subject to "compulsory syndication, i.e., compulsory amalgamation in associations under state control" (L, A, 402). In addition, flats, furniture, and other personal property of the rich were taken away from their owners and redistributed among the workers.[178] Money was seen as a survival of "bourgeois robbery," and catastrophic inflation was welcomed as a step toward a future economy without money.[179] Trade was treated as the greatest evil, and every effort was made to replace it with direct allocation of goods and organized barter. Lenin insisted that this should take the form of "*exchange of products in kind* between the towns and the small-peasant consumers' societies" (L, *SW*, 2:486).[180] The purpose of this exchange was not to "enable the rich peasants to obtain goods" (and so to stimulate production for the market), but only to help the poor peasants, in order to win their support in beating the kulaks and taking their surplus grain (L, *CW*, 29:78). From the very beginning, therefore, the Bolshevik party embarked on the brutal suppression of the market in the name of the communist ideal of a consciously regulated marketless economy; this was its ideological option, its "conscious and deliberate attempt to realize Marx's utopia."[181]

This conclusion, however, is far from being universally accepted. On the contrary, in the literature on the subject there abound more-or-less ingenuous attempts to present the problem in a different light.[182] First, it is often argued that during the first months of their dictatorship the Bolsheviks tried to realize a moderate economic policy modeled on the German war economy and anticipating the NEP, and that the harsh, coercive policies of so-called War Communism only began in the middle of 1918. Second, it is widely believed that the economic program of War Communism was not ideological in origin; it is alleged instead that it was only a matter of expediency, a reaction to the outbreak of civil war that (as E. H. Carr put it) "removed all hesitations by driving the regime willy-nilly at breakneck speed along the socialist road."[183] Finally, many respectable scholars have done all they could to present the crude communism of these years as having nothing, or very little, in common with Marxism. Thus, for instance, Moshe Lewin has claimed that War Communism (as well as the NEP) was merely a pragmatic adaptation to circumstances and had no connection at all with "pre-Revolutionary preoccupations and theories."[184] Richard Stites stresses the utopian aspects of the Bolshevik policies of this period but argues that the roots of this utopianism lay in indigenous "Russian traditions rather than in Marxism."[185] Even Richard Pipes does not recognize War Communism as an attempt to realize Marx's communist utopia; in his view, the spirit of War Communism "resembled most the patrimonial regime (*tiagloe gosudarstvo*) of medieval Russia."[186]

All these viewpoints, different as they are, have in common a refusal to take seriously the Marxist inspiration of Russian communism.[187] In many cases this refusal is bound up with a programmatic neglect of the role of ideas in shaping history; this attitude especially characterizes economic historians, some of whom (e.g., A. Gerschenkron and A. Nove) have not hesitated to claim that almost nothing in Soviet history needs to be explained in terms of Marxism.[188] Many left-wing scholars have a tendency to absolve Marx of responsibility for the cruelties of Russian history and, whenever possible, to diminish Lenin's responsibility for them as well; hence, the shockingly harsh, proto-Stalinist policies of War Communism are now being interpreted as necessitated by circumstances (such as lack of food in the cities or counterrevolutionary activities) and as having nothing to do with Lenin's original intentions. In other cases we have an exaggerated emphasis on the indigenous Russian tradition, often combined with an insufficient knowledge of Marxism.

I do not intend to dismiss all these approaches as totally unproductive. It is obvious that great historical movements are rarely able to follow the inner logic of their ideologies, that they have to respond to the exigencies of the changing situation and consequently change themselves, sometimes losing their original identity completely. (I shall try to show that this was the case with Russian communism after Lenin.) It is no less obvious that great international ideologies cannot avoid being influenced by the indigenous traditions of the various nations. But all this does not undermine the legitimacy of interpreting the Bolshevik experiment in direct transition to communism as the culminating phase in the history of Marx's communist utopia. From this point of view (i.e., from the point of view of intellectual history), the first three years of Soviet power (1918–21) essentially constitute one period:[189] the period (to quote Lenin) of "a direct transition from the old Russian economy to state production and distribution on communist lines," of "attempting to go over straight to communism" (ibid., 33:61, 63). This period was characterized by the domination of utopian blueprints over all sorts of pragmatic considerations and so may justly be called militant communism rather than War Communism. It was undoubtedly "one of the more interesting utopian experiments in comparative political and economic history,"[190] a time of unprecedented attempts to change the entire course of history by achieving *ex ante* coordination of economic activity through the substitution of production for direct use in place of production for the market. For this book, this experiment is of crucial importance: after all, it was the only attempt to realize the Engelsian idea of the leap from the "kingdom of necessity" to the "kingdom of freedom."

The three different approaches to this problem give us the opportunity of beginning with a discussion and so removing a number of lingering misunderstandings. First, the division of the first three months of Soviet power into a period of alleged moderation (resembling the NEP) and War Communism (necessitated by the civil war) is one of the Stalinist falsifications of history. The "heroic period of the Russian Revolution" described by Kritsman embraced the entire period before the NEP. He did not deny that the civil war and foreign intervention strengthened the Bolshevik determination to expropriate the bourgeois element and finally to suppress the market,[191] but he saw these military interventions as mere catalysts in the great heroic process of proletarian liberation inaugurated immediately after the Bolshevik seizure of power. Other veterans of the revolution were equally direct. Bukharin wrote: "War communism was seen by us not as military, i.e., as needed at a given stage of civil war, but as a universal, general, so to speak 'normal' form of economic policy of a victorious proletariat."[192] Trotsky stressed that the revolution had started with a violent assault on the very foundations of the old system: "How did we start? We began . . . in economic policy by breaking with the bourgeois past firmly and without compromise. Earlier there was a market—we liquidate it, free trade—we liquidate it, competition—we abolish it, commercial calculation—we abolish it."[193] The same view was expressed by Lenin on the occasion of the fourth anniversary of the October Revolution. He explained the policies of militant communism as due to an excess of revolutionary enthusiasm, not to the economic situation or pressure from enemies (ibid., 58). In another article of the same time he said explicitly that choosing such policies had nothing to do with sound, pragmatic considerations: "In attempting to go over straight to communism we, in the Spring of 1921, sustained a more serious defeat on the economic front than any defeat inflicted upon us by Kolchak, Denikin or Pilsudski" (ibid., 63).

Elsewhere, however, Lenin described War Communism as forced on his party "by extreme want, ruin and war" (ibid., 32:342). Strictly speaking, these two interpretations are not mutually exclusive. War Communism as an attempt at a direct transition to communism should be distinguished from War Communism in the narrower sense, as referring only to acts of brutal and economically irrational violence, such as taking from the peasants not only their surpluses but their necessities as well in order to meet the requirements of the army and to sustain the workers (ibid.). What is important is that this terminological confusion came to be used by Lenin deliberately to cover up the fact that the catastrophic failure of War Communism as an economic policy was connected with communist principles as such and that the NEP was nothing but the capitulation of communist ideology before harsh realities. Nevertheless, Lenin himself saw the NEP as a forced and temporary ideological retreat; if this was so, then the policies preceding it must have been an ideological advance, not merely a matter of expediency. True, Lenin was now ready to admit that these extreme measures were counterproductive and needed some additional justification; for just this reason, to put the part of the blame on external factors, the party at that time began to use the term *War Communism*.[194] But this terminological manipulation did not entail the absurd view that the NEP was in fact a return to the correct, truly Marxist policies of the end of 1917 and the first half of 1918.

The Hungarian scholar László Szamuely has recently observed that this strange interpretation of the relationship between the NEP and Bolshevik policies before the summer of 1918 originated with Stalin himself. In a speech delivered in July 1928, Stalin authoritatively declared that, contrary to widespread opinion, the proletarian dictatorship in Russia "began its constructive work not with War Communism, but with the proclamation of the principles of what is called the New Economic Policy. Everyone is familiar with Lenin's pamphlet: *The Immediate Tasks of the Soviet Government*, which was published in the beginning of 1918, and in which Lenin first substantiated the principles of the New Economic Policy. True, this policy was temporarily interrupted by the conditions of intervention, and it was only three years later, when war and intervention had been ended, that it had to be resumed." [195] This view was soon made canonical and survived many twists and turns in the Stalinist and post-Stalinist policies of the party. Until very recently it was repeated almost verbatim in all textbooks and other writings on the political and economic history of the Soviet Union. [196]

Szamuely did not explicitly explain why Stalin chose to insist on this particular distortion of historical events. It may seem strange, considering the fact that by 1928 the NEP had lost its usefulness for him. Nevertheless, it was certainly not mere caprice on his part. Having identified himself for so long with the NEP, he was vitally interested in stressing that it was a correct Marxist policy, not merely a forced retreat; in other words, he preferred to see himself during the years of the NEP as a truly Marxist leader realizing the original policies of Lenin, not as the main organizer and ideologist of a retreat.

But this is not all. What is truly intriguing is that Stalin chose to present Lenin's *Immediate Tasks of the Soviet Government* (April 1918) as a text substantiating the principles of the NEP, when it would be more accurate to say that the opposite was true. The essence of the NEP consisted in allowing market forces some freedom, while the essence of Lenin's policies in the *entire* period before the NEP was a fanatical commitment to the principles of comprehensive planning of production and distribution realized through detailed accounting and pervasive control of everything. In his *Immediate Tasks* Lenin forcefully proclaimed these principles, reminding the workers that their task consisted in "taking the entire management of the society and the supervision of the consumption of the rich in their own hands" (L, SW, 2:600). [197] This was to be achieved through strict control of the *supply organizations*, that is, through full suppression of the market. In this way the whole population of the country was to be organized into "a single co-operative society under proletarian management" (ibid.). How was it possible to associate these ideas with the NEP?

From Stalin's point of view it *was* possible. He saw an essential similarity in the *antilibertarian* features of both periods. In *The Immediate Tasks* Lenin proclaimed the principle of "personal dictatorship," of "*unquestioning subordination* to a single will" (ibid., 611), as opposed to the practice of workers' self-management; this policy, bitterly opposed by the workers' opposition,[198] was resumed and continued under the NEP. For example, the proclamation of the NEP was accompanied by condemning and outlawing the anarcho-syndicalist deviation in the party. In the spring of 1918 Lenin tended to define his policy as aimed at the introduction of state capitalism, by which he meant, among other things, a conscious and deliberate return to such capitalist methods of exploitation of labor as the notorious Taylor system (see ibid., 603; see also L, A, 448–49, 622). The same policy was systematically applied to the workers under the NEP. In *The Immediate Tasks* Lenin set out his aim of ending the anarchy of factory management by the workers; similarly, the NEP put an end to the disorderly practices of War Communism in pursuing ultraegalitarian objectives. In both policies, therefore, there was (from Stalin's point of view) an emphasis on order (as opposed to petty bourgeois anarchy) and a tolerance of certain aspects of capitalism (as opposed to the voluntarist adventurism characteristic of the extreme Left). According to this logic, both policies ensured that the Soviet Union should not be "something absurd, anarchistic and savage" (L, A, 454).

However, the presence of an inner logic in one person's opinion does not guarantee that the opinion itself is right. Stalin's views on the parallels between Lenin's early state capitalism and state capitalism under the NEP contained a grain of truth but were nonetheless seriously misleading. This was because for Lenin, as for all consistent communists of his time, the decisive criterion was the attitude toward the market, and in *this* respect the two policies were diametrically opposed to each other. In Lenin's original understanding, state capitalism had nothing to do "with the reintroduction of market methods of production as under the NEP."[199] It was to be a system that would replace the market with a unified plan and so be able to achieve the *ex ante* coordination of production and distribution. The capitalist features of this system would consist only in the widest possible utilization of capitalist methods of organization (especially the banking system), in ensuring the maximum discipline and productivity of labor, in employing capitalist cadres, and in tolerating, to a certain extent, capitalist inequalities of income. It was to be modeled on "'the last word' in the modern large-scale capitalist engineering and planned organization," i.e., on the German war economy, which Lenin saw as totally "*subordinated to Junker-bourgeois imperialism.*" As he said, "Cross out the words in italics, and in place of the militarist, Junker, bourgeois, imperialist *state* put *also a state*, but of a different social type, of a different class content—a *Soviet* state, that is a proletarian state, and you will have the *sum total* of the conditions necessary for socialism" (L, *CW*, 27:339, 339).

In other words, Lenin's original idea of state capitalism was based on the assumption, central to his theory of imperialism, that at the highest stage of capitalist development, not just in the West but also in Russia,[200] market relations would give way to conscious planning and that what remained of them would be supported only by the small commodity producers, a class representing an obsolete mode of production and stubbornly fighting for its survival. Hence, he saw this group (mostly the more affluent peasants) as the chief enemy of socialism—an enemy whose "habits, customs and economic position" stood in the way of the centralizing tendency of economic progress and were the main obstacles in transforming the country into a single economic unit (ibid., 29). Although it may seem cynical in light of all his political slogans about the need for an alliance between workers and peasants, he wanted to make use of state capitalism—its organizational forms, management, and technology—to eliminate the peasants as a class of market-oriented small producers.

The NEP was, of course, something completely different. It was a major (if only temporary) concession to small commodity producers, a restoration of the market exchange between town and country, a conscious retreat from the program of a direct transition to the marketless economy of socialism. Thus, the NEP should not be interpreted as a return to the policies of the first months of the Bolshevik dictatorship. The entire period before the NEP was a period of militant communism, an attempt to go straight over to communism at all costs, and it is rather naive to see this period mainly as a reaction to the brutalities of civil war. More convincing is Medvedev's view that the civil war was provoked by the brutality of Bolshevik policies, that, as he put it, "the historical responsibility for civil war falls not only on the Russian counter-revolution and on intervention, but on the Bolsheviks themselves who, through a premature introduction of socialism, raised against themselves a large part of the population."[201]

We may therefore conclude that even a very brief summary of the basic facts of the first three years of Soviet power seriously undermines two conventional views on the relationship between Leninism and what has been called War Communism. These facts show that it is simply not true that the course for going straight over to communism was chosen by Lenin only in mid 1918 and that War Communism was something very different from the policies of the first months of his dictatorship. It also shows that interpreting the militant communism of these years as a matter of expediency, a defensive reaction against external threats, is not sustainable; militant communism was undoubtedly an ideologically motivated option.

Next we must deal with the argument that this option had almost nothing to do with Marxism. Most advocates of this view try to substantiate their thesis by a simple denial of the ideological character of Leninist practice, which adds nothing to the argument about the allegedly pragmatic character of Bolshevik policies after the revolution. More interesting, and more relevant for our purposes, are the arguments of those critics of Lenin who seek to question the Marxist character of his practice on theoretical grounds. How was it possible (they ask) to be a Marxist and to believe in the possibility of constructing communism in a backward country? And once this risky choice had been made, why did the Bolsheviks put so much emphasis on the control of distribution while obviously neglecting the need to increase productivity? Why did they concentrate on the struggle against the market without formally expropriating the bourgeoisie?[202] Was it not a version of a primitive communism of consumption, deeply alien to the spirit of historical materialism, that had always stressed the priority of production over distribution?

These are serious arguments indeed. They have been leveled against Lenin not only by the Mensheviks but also by the Socialist Revolutionaries, who, because of their populist heritage, might otherwise have been expected to sympathize with historical shortcuts and distributive justice. But due respect for the theoretical and historical weight of this argument should not prevent us from trying to look at the issues involved from a different perspective.

The first objection, characteristic of the determinist Marxism of the Second International, has already been dealt with elsewhere in this book and there is no need to return to it in the present context. Suffice it to say that we are now more aware than ever that Marxism as a theory of history is allowing of different interpretations and that the possibility of a socialist revolution in an underdeveloped country can well be explained in Marxist terms.

However, the subject matter of this book is not Marxism as a socioeconomic theory or a theory of history, but the Marxist conception of communism as universal human liberation. From the point of view of *this* problematic, the scientific side of Marxism is much less important than Marxist utopianism, as expressed in the vision of "scientific communism," and it was just this utopianism that was at the heart of Lenin's Marxism. Despite his constant preoccupation with practical, organizational matters, Lenin's specific contribution to the history of Marxism was not limited to his theory of the party; his place in the history of socialism, as well as in history in general, is assured by the fact that *he was the first Marxist leader to seize political power in order wholeheartedly to commit himself to a practical realization of the Marxist utopia.* The same can be said of the Bolshevik party in the period of its militant communism. The first three years of Bolshevik power represent the first, as well as the most serious and instructive, attempt to mobilize all its unlimited political power toward the practical realization of a communist utopia. Hence, it is vitally important to answer the question about the Marxist character of Lenin's utopianism. Was it a legitimate interpretation of Marxism or merely a distortion of it? It is clear that in the first case the responsibility for the outcome of the Bolshevik experiment with communism would have to be shared, to some extent, by the founders of "scientific communism" and by all who helped codify this utopian blueprint and establish its legitimacy as the final end of the workers' movement.

Szamuely thinks that the main culprits were the Marxist theorists of German Social Democracy. It was they who drew from Marxism, and turned into a dogma, the absurd conclusion that a socialist economy excludes market relations and realizes a natural economy on a higher level.[203] It was they who made this view the cornerstone of their Erfurt Program of 1891—a document that for so long defined the theoretical position of the international Marxist movement.[204] It was Kautsky, in particular, who developed the theory of a socialist society as "nothing else but a single huge industrial plant" in which everything is rationally planned and the allocation of resources takes place without market transactions; it was he who authoritatively endorsed such stupidities as, for instance, the superiority of barter over monetary exchange and the need to pass from "money services" to "services in kind."[205] In other words, the German Social Democrats bear the chief responsibility for the perpetuation for over half a century, in various more-or-less refined forms, of the ideal of a marketless economy in Marxist thought, which caused immense damage to the economic development of socialist societies.[206]

There is much truth in Szamuely's observations. As I have tried to show, it is perfectly true that Kautsky saw the precondition of socialism in the liquidation of the market and that this view was shared by all orthodox Marxists of the epoch of the Second International. The Social Democrats of that time were committed to communism as the final goal of the workers' movement. It is useful to remember this, if only to eliminate ahistorical views on the relationship between German Social Democracy and Leninism. Despite all the differences that divided them, the image of the communist society of the future was something they held in common. Hence, Lenin could for a long time define his party as social democratic and sincerely believe that Bolsheviks and German Social Democrats belonged to the same international movement.

But this is only part of the story. The main purpose of this book is to show that classical Marxism was not only historical materialism—that is, a theory of history, a critique of the capitalist political economy, and a set of methodological proposals for historiography. It was also the most modern and apparently "scientific" version of the old communist utopia, a version whose distinctive feature was its view that the main source of evil existed not only, or even primarily, in the institution of private property, but rather in the uncontrollability of economic life that resulted from production for sale. Therefore, communism, which for Marx and Engels was synonymous with freedom, had to establish conscious rational control over blind economic forces, thus putting an end to the subjugation of the human species by its own alienated products. In this way humanity was to acquire the ability consciously to control the processes of its own self-objectification and so to raise itself to genuine self-determination. The necessary precondition of this final achievement was the ability to exercise control over nature, which explains Marx's emphasis on productivity and technology—the development of productive forces even at the cost of increasing alienation—which culminated in a capitalist world market. But the realization of communism was a very different task. It was directed toward reappropriating man's alienated forces by establishing conscious rational control over man's social forces, toward liquidating man's enslavement by his own alienated powers, as embodied in the capitalist market. This was to be achieved by the organization of labor in society as it had been organized in separate capitalist workshops, "in accordance with an approved and authoritative plan" (M, C, 1:337). The old division of labor in society, determined by spontaneous market forces, was to be replaced by the new division of labor—the "division of labor upon a *definite plan*, as organized in the factory" (M&E, SW, 3:136). Market relationships were to be completely eliminated as incompatible with rational control over exchange. In this way commodity fetishism would disappear, production would be directly socialized, and human relationships would become simple and transparent as in the natural economies of the past. As we remember, Marx even compared the social economy of the future to the economic activities of Robinson Crusoe: in both cases, he reasoned, there was a single subject of economic activity (in one case, simply an individual; in the other, a unified collective) working in accordance with his own settled plan, producing only for use, not for sale, and so enjoying full control over his products (M, C, 1:81–83).

It is quite logical that from this point of view the capitalist system of exchange was a greater evil than the capitalist organization of production. After all, capitalism not only enormously increased the productive capacity of the human species, but also paved the way for the planned economy of the future by rationally organizing large-scale production. The division of labor in big capitalist factories was based on an "*a priori* system" (i.e., a system of planning) and not on the "*a posteriori*, nature-imposed necessity" of market forces (ibid., 336). In contrast to this, the lack of such rational organization in society as a whole, as well as on a global scale, made the capitalist system irrational and anarchic, depriving people—both workers and capitalists—of any capacity to control their fate and making them utterly dependent on the caprice of blind market forces. The quintessence of this dehumanizing, alienating, and enslaving power of the market economy as such, and the capitalist market economy in particular, was trade. The young Marx wrote:

Trade, which after all is nothing more than the exchange of products of various individuals and countries, rules the whole world through the relation of supply and demand—a relation which, as an English economist says, hovers over the earth like the fate of the ancients, and with invisible hand allots fortune and misfortune to men, sets up empires and wrecks empires, causes nations to rise and to disappear—whereas with the abolition of the basis, private property, with the communistic regulation of production (and, implicit in this, the abolition of the alien attitude [*Fremdheit*] of men to their own product), the power of the relation of supply and demand is dissolved into nothing, and men once more gain control of exchange, production and the way they behave to one another. (M&E, CW, 5:48)

It is no accident, however, that the control of exchange is mentioned in this quotation before the control of production. Engels went even further in this direction; in some of his late works the presence or absence of market relations was treated as a process independent of the emergence and abolition of private property. But in his analysis of tribal societies he pointed out that the destructive role of trade among different tribes generally preceded the emergence of private property relations within each tribe (see chapter 2, section 6). The appearance of intertribal commerce, he argued, played a progressive role in "revolutionizing the whole hitherto existing society" but at the cost of destroying ancient freedom, equality, and harmony. This was, in Engels's view, the beginning of the long and cruel period of civilization in which economic development depended on blind and increasingly uncontrollable economic forces. On the other hand, he also suggested that the liquidation of the market economy and of monetary exchange as such would take place *within* the framework of monopolistic capitalism, thus creating a ready-made basis for socialism. Incredibly, he believed that the centralizing tendency of economic development would bring into being a form of capitalism without market relations, without competition (within a given country), and without money. In *Socialism: Utopian and Scientific* he described this as the final victory of the mode of production (large-scale factories) over the mode of exchange, leading to the actual capitulation of capitalist production to "the production upon a definite plan of the invading socialist society" (M&E, SW, 3:144).

It is therefore clear that Lenin's plan for setting up communism in Russia was not a madman's deviation from the "scientific" spirit of Marxism. His conception of state capitalism as the first step toward socialism was merely a variation on the Engelsian theme of marketless capitalism. His definition of the main task of his party as "the transformation of the whole of the state economic mechanism into a single huge machine, into an economic organism that will work in such a way as to enable hundreds of millions of people to be guided by a single plan" was entirely in accord with Marx and Engels's view on comprehensive planning as the necessary premise, the stepping-stone, for socialist construction (L, CW, 27:90–91). Lenin's stubborn insistence on planning, accounting, and control as well as his emphasis on planned distribution had very little in common with the notion of planning as an economic technique used to promote industrial growth and compatible, in principle, with a monetary exchange economy (although limiting the freedom of market forces). For Lenin, planning was not a pragmatic device, not simply a means of overcoming Russia's backwardness; it was for him a matter of principle, the realization of the original intention of socialism. The aim of planning was not the increase of production but the abolition of the market and the establishment of full political control over the entire range of economic life.[207] This aim was to be realized at all costs, even at the cost of ruining the productive forces of the country and drastically reducing the population's standard of living. Even economic collapse was theoretically justified by claiming that "the proletarian revolution is inevitably accompanied by an extremely profound decline in the productive forces."[208] Militant communists of that time readily accepted this theory as a welcome explanation of the catastrophic state of their country. Planning was firmly associated in their minds not with industrialization or other forms of increasing productivity, but with the communist utopia of a totally rationalized and totally controlled marketless economy.

The state capitalism of the first months of Bolshevik power (i.e., state capitalism on the German model) was undoubtedly an attempt to *combine* the elimination of the market with capitalist efficiency. But it soon became apparent that, while these two goals could be treated as equally important, one of them must be given absolute priority. The choice was obvious: the decree of June 28, 1918, expressed the communist determination to concentrate on the struggle against the market. In the view of communist militants, it was a decision entirely justified by Engels's theory of the historical mission of capitalist large-scale production. If this mission consisted in the elimination of the market, and if small commodity producers represented a relic of the past, then it was necessary to fulfill this historical task in Russia; if it appeared, however, that in Russian conditions the reactionary class of small commodity producers (mostly kulaks) was too strong, and that therefore the liquidation of the market could not be completed by politically controlled capitalist trusts and syndicates, then it could only mean that this task had to be fulfilled by communists alone. "In its work on constructing the planned natural economy of socialism," wrote Kritsman, "the proletariat is merely continuing and completing the historical task of capitalism: the overcoming of the market."[209]

This view was shared by all communist theorists in these years. "The socialist organization of the economy," explained Trotsky, "*begins* with the liquidation of the market, and that means the liquidation of its regulator—namely, the 'free' play of the laws of supply and demand."[210] We must admit that there was a certain logic in this viewpoint, since the decision to "go straight over to communism" was incompatible with free market forces and the liquidation of the market could only be achieved through the centralized, nationwide organization of consumption. Despite their readiness to resort to really drastic measures, such as compulsory labor conscription and the forced allocation of productive tasks, Russian communists could not begin with the socialist organization of production: such an organizational and technical task was then simply beyond their capacity. Hence, they had to choose the alternative course of suppressing the market, the way of planned distribution and consumption. What this meant in practice is well known: it was the nightmare of dictatorship over needs,[211] realized by means of a consistent policy of abolition of all commodity and money relations. Private trade was banned, and all free-market transactions were prohibited; the market supply of food was replaced with the forced requisitioning of farm products by the urban workers and poor peasants (the famous decree on "food dictatorship" of May 9, 1918); market distribution was replaced by "class rationing" and other forms of allocation in kind, the population being divided into four consumer categories. The realization of this policy was far from perfect, because even the most brutal tactics proved insufficient to suppress the illegal exchange of goods.[212] But the principles were clear, ideologically pure, and therefore capable of arousing genuine enthusiasm among communist believers.

It should be remembered that the communists at that time were well prepared to accept and actively promote the military forms of the organization of labor. Lenin was not alone in seeing the army as the highest form of organization, capable of "giving millions of people a *single will*" (ibid., 21:253). This was indeed a typical feature of those forms of communist utopianism that stressed the need of economic centralization. The use of "industrial armies, especially for agriculture," was suggested by Marx and Engels in their *Manifesto of the Communist Party*. A very good example of a communist utopia making use of military analogies is Edward Bellamy's *Looking Backward from the Year 2000*. In this book, once extremely popular and influential, the communist vision of the wholesale abolition of the monetary exchange economy by organizing the entire nation as "one great business corporation"[213] was combined with an enthusiastic support for militarism. Bellamy recognized in the modern military system "not merely a rhetorical analogy for a national industrial service, but its prototype, furnishing at once a complete working model for its organization, an arsenal of patriotic and national motives and arguments for its animation, and the unanswerable demonstration of its feasibility drawn from the actual experience of whole nations organized and maneuvered as armies."[214] For him military organization was a model for rational, consciously planned, "scientific" organization, as opposed to the notorious irrationality of the market. In this sense he contrasted the "scientific manner" in which modern nations went to war with the "unscientific manner" in which they went to work.[215]

Bellamy's book was well known and very popular in Russia. Its first translation into Russian was organized by no less a figure than Tolstoy, and the book's success was immediate. A Russian critic noted in 1906 that it was "more effective propaganda for the ideas of socialism among the broad masses than any other book during the past thirty years."[216] Maxim Gorky assured an American audience that Bellamy's theories in *Looking Backward* were "known to all Russian students."[217] It may justly be assumed that Bellamy owed his success in Russia to the fact that the Russian intelligentsia saw his vision of the future as remarkably consistent with socialism in general and with Marxist "scientific socialism" in particular.

But let us return to War Communism. Its ideological climate provides a strong argument against the view that it was merely a matter of expediency. This is how it was seen by one of the early theorists of Soviet planning:

Money circulation gradually dies away, supplanted by natural exchange, indeed, by the direct allocation of products. Foreseeing this, the People's Commissariat of Finance deliberately aims at the doing away with money and transforms the issue of money merely into a tool of the expropriating of private economy, into a kind of tax levied on the not yet socialized economic relations, this being one of the sources from which to finance the revolution.

Human relations are becoming transparently natural, the fog of money fetishism, of commodity fetishism, is dissipating before our very eyes and discloses the real economic substance of the relations between town and countryside, consumer and producer, buyer and seller.

Every pillar of the old world is shaken, the whole old socio-economic system is breaking up and from its constituents entirely new socio-economic combinations have emerged.

There can be hardly any doubt that with more advanced industrial technologies and with an agriculture which had been more loosened by the capitalist plough and thus suited in bulk for collectivization, a country in conditions of emergency similar to that prevailing here could have evolved towards true communism.[218]

This nostalgic view based on hindsight was endorsed and supplemented by countless testimonies from other participants in the Soviet experiment with militant communism. A prominent place among them belongs to

Lenin. His language during these years was not that of a pragmatic states-man. He was driven by deep emotions when he described trade in grain as a hideous crime, "*a crime against the state*," something that Bolshe-viks should "fight against at all costs" (ibid., 30:149). He proclaimed a life-and-death struggle against "the accursed old gospel of everyone for himself and God for all," setting against it the ideal of "each for all, and no God"; and he made everything dependent on the heroic virtues of those "who have sacrificed everything for the victory of socialism" (ibid., 238/ 305, 515). Sometimes his tone became almost hysterical:

We are prepared to perish to a man rather than yield our territory, rather than yield our principle, the principle of discipline and firm policy for the sake of which everything else must be sacrificed. At the time when the capitalist countries and the capitalist class are disintegrating, at this moment of crisis and despair, this political factor is the only decisive one. Talk about minority and majority, about democracy and freedom, decides nothing, however much the heroes of a past historical period may invoke it. It is the class-consciousness and firmness of the working class that count here. If the working class is prepared to make sacrifices, if it shows that it is able to strain every nerve, the problem will be solved. . . . The determination of working class, its inflexible adherence to the watchword "Death rather than surrender!" is not only a historical factor, it is the decisive, the winning factor. (ibid., 454)

Obviously class consciousness and heroic will were to decide the ulti-mate fate of the proletarian revolution. Nothing more was heard of the objective laws of history, and nothing was left to the operation of material incentives. The old (economic) sources of discipline and unity were sup-posed to have weakened or to no longer exist, and the new discipline and unity were to be based entirely on noneconomic factors: on enthusiasm and/or coercion, mobilization and/or compulsion (ibid., 454, 414).[219] From such a point of view even the socialist principle of remuneration according to work done had to be considered as something to be overcome and re-placed by the higher, communist (not merely socialist) principle of unpaid work, as manifested in the communist subbotniks (ibid., 284–88). It was to be "labor performed gratis for the benefit of society, labor performed not as a definite duty, not for the purpose of obtaining a right to certain products, not according to previously established and legally fixed quotas, but voluntary labor, irrespective of quotas . . . labor performed without ex-pectation of reward, without reward as a condition, labor performed as a conscious realization (that has become a habit) of the necessity of working for the common good" (ibid., 517).

It is characteristic that the most important feature of the new type of labor was, for Lenin, *not* its voluntary character but simply its indepen-dence of any material rewards. Therefore, he was able to write: "Subbotniks, labor armies, labor conscription—these are the practical realization of socialist and communist labor in various forms" (ibid.). He probably did not even notice that this statement virtually equated labor motivated by communist enthusiasm with compulsory labor conscription and the compulsory allocation of labor tasks. In other words, he stressed approvingly the existence of a common denominator between communist heroism and communist slavery.

Lenin, however, was not the main communist theorist of these years. The idea of "a direct transition from the old Russian economy to state production and distribution on communist lines" was certainly his, but a comprehensive elaboration of the theory of a transition period belongs to others, who all expressed the official party line of that time (ibid., 33:61). Three books are of special importance for our topic: Bukharin and Preobrazhenskii's commentary on the 1919 program of the party entitled *The ABC of Communism*, Bukharin's *Economics of the Transition Period* (1920), and Trotsky's *Terrorism and Communism* (1920).

The first of these has been described as not "merely a commentary on the Program, but rather the most complete and systematic compendium of Marxist-Leninist theory produced until that time," "a veritable Bible of communism, enjoying greater currency and authority than any of the works of such well-known figures as Lenin and Trotsky."[220] Under Stalin, however, it became a rare document, not only because of the purge and execution of its authors. Even if the authors had survived and become staunch Stalinists, this book would have sunk into oblivion. It was natural that Stalinists wanted to forget the ideas they had abandoned and the promises their party had not been able to fulfill. They had outgrown the stage of naive hopes, wanted to acquire instead some semblance of bourgeois respectability, and did not like to be reminded of the crusading spirit and unashamed utopianism of the early period of communist construction.

There is no need in this context to discuss *The ABC of Communism* in detail. I shall concentrate only on those features of this remarkable document that shed light on the communist utopia, that is, the communist program of universal liberation. The tone of the book is triumphalistic. The authors are confident that communism will win everywhere: "Within a few decades there will be a quite new world, with new people and new customs." The destruction of capitalism is inevitable because it is simply "a badly constructed machine in which one part is continually interfering with the movements of another." It will soon be replaced by an *organized* society, free from the anarchy of production, from competition, and from war and crises. In this society "the factories, workshops, mines and other productive institutions will all be subdivisions, as it were, of one vast people's workshop, which will embrace the entire national economy." Everything will be produced in accordance with a "general plan," all details will be thought out beforehand, and the work will be guided in conformity with these calculations. Production for the market will be replaced by production for use; hence, there will be no *commodities* but only *products*. "These products are not exchanged one for another: they are neither bought nor sold. They are simply stored in the communal warehouses, and are subsequently delivered to those who need them. In such conditions money will no longer be required." [221]

Following Engels and Lenin, the authors stressed that contemporary capitalism had also moved in the direction of liquidating the market economy. The economy of the advanced capitalist countries had been united into syndicates and trusts that could force prices up to any figure they pleased.[222] "At the head of the whole economic life there is a small group of great bankers who administer industry in its entirety. The governmental authority simply fulfills the will of these bankers and trust magnates." Thus, contemporary capitalism was also an organized society. Nevertheless, it was torn by inner contradictions and would never be able to provide solutions for its grave social problems. It was moving toward "complete disintegration, hell broth, further brutalization and disorder." The only alternative to this "*absolute* chaos" was communism. "And since communism can be realized only by the proletariat, the proletariat is today the true saviour of mankind." [223]

However, the road to final victory would not be easy. On the contrary, the authors insisted that under a proletarian dictatorship the resistance of the bourgeoisie would intensify, becoming sterner, harsher, and more and more threatening and would compel the proletariat to resort to terrorist methods.[224] They also stressed that rich peasants were by their very nature intensely hostile to socialism and would inevitably prove irreconcilable enemies of the agrarian policy of a proletarian state, and that the Soviet power "may eventually be compelled to undertake a deliberately planned expropriation" of the rich peasants as a class. As to the middle peasants, they might save themselves from the onslaughts of world capitalism by a frank acceptance of the leadership of the proletariat. But this would not save them as a class of small commodity producers. "The system of petty agriculture is in any case doomed. It must inevitably be replaced by a more advantageous and more productive system, by the system of large-scale cooperative agriculture." [225]

As we can see, this earliest "systematic compendium of Marxist-Leninist theory" formulated the ideas later taken up and realized by Stalin: the idea of the intensification of the class struggle after the overthrow of the bourgeois regime, the idea of the liquidation of the kulaks as a class, and the idea of imminent, wholesale collectivization.

The authors presented the communist society of the future in an imaginative way, with much interesting and characteristic detail. It was to be a thoroughly collectivistic society, one proclaiming the principle that "the individual human being does not belong to himself, but to society, to the human race." This entailed a complete program that eliminated the individualizing influence of the family. Children would not be treated as belonging to their parents; their upbringing and education would be directed and controlled by society as a whole. "The barbaric methods of individual cookery" would be replaced by the preparation of meals in large communal canteens in which the same meal would be served to hundreds of people. Of course, there would be no trade and no money; these would be replaced by a purposive distribution of goods, and the apparatus for its mass distribution would be "more perfect than any known to the history of capitalism."[226] Humanity would no longer be divided into fatherlands and nations.[227] It would become ideologically unified, and this newly acquired unanimity would be maintained through a unified and compulsory system of education, as well as by other means for the conveyance of communist ideology and the enforcement of proper conduct.[228] In this context the authors mentioned such means of social reeducation as the "unified popular law-court" guided by "a socialist sense of equity," "comradely courts of law," "social censure as a penal method," and last but not least, "compulsory labor." They particularly stressed the importance of Lenin's ideas on "*the strictest mutual control,*" as well as on the need of "an extensive propaganda of communist ideas, and the utilization to that end of all the apparatus and means of State Power."[229]

The expected result of all these measures was to be entirely new human beings, who would work less and devote their free time to cultural creativity, who would no longer need alcohol (an artificial need imposed on workers by greedy capitalists)[230] but would develop instead a thirst for culture:

The working day will grow continually shorter, and people will be to an increasing extent free from the chains imposed on them by nature. As soon as man is enabled to spend less time upon feeding and clothing himself, he will be able to devote more time to the work of mental development. Human culture will climb to heights never attained before. It will no longer be a class culture, but will become a genuinely human culture. Concurrently with the disappearance of man's tyranny over man, the tyranny of nature over man will likewise vanish. Men and women will for the first time be able to lead a life worthy of thinking beings instead of life worthy of brute beasts.[231]

In other words, the highest aim of communism was conceived as the realization of the Marxian idea of freedom: freedom as the creative self-realization of the human species, which had previously liberated itself from dependence on nature as well as from its own class divisions. It would have been more sophisticated had the authors also said something about liberating the human species by overcoming and reappropriating its own alienations. But as a popular explanation of the communist program of the period of War Communism, it was good enough and indeed remarkably consonant with the spirit of classical Marxism as well as with the writings of Marx and Engels. The vision of the communist collectivism of the future especially was based on Engels's "Speeches in Elberfeld" (see chapter 2, section 3).

The Marxist credentials of *The ABC of Communism* are beyond doubt, and so too are its Bolshevik credentials, which were endorsed by Lenin, who wrote: "We have a Party program which has been excellently explained by Comrades Preobrazhensky and Bukharin in the form of a book which is less voluminous but extremely useful" (L, A, 493). In one respect, however, the ideas developed in this book differed in emphasis from Lenin's. While he was by then concentrating on preaching "unquestioning subordination to a single will," Bukharin and Preobrazhenskii continued to toy with the "libertarian" variant of the Leninist utopia, with the concepts of self-management; deprofessionalization; abolition of the state, police, and prison; and the organization of divisional work as one might an orchestra.[232] They conceded that in reality the instruments of Soviet power had to be organized "on militarist lines" but still thought this a temporary deviation from the general rule. This state of affairs, they explained, "is due to the military situation of the Soviet Republic. What exists today in Russia is not simply the dictatorship of the proletariat; it is a militarist-proletarian dictatorship. The republic is an armed camp."[233]

To some extent this position reflected the authors' left-wing sympathies, though these were not deep enough to lead them toward anarcho-syndicalist ideas. Indeed, in the following year Bukharin published his *Economics of the Transition Period*, which offered a general theoretical (and not merely circumstantial) justification for the harsh realities of the regime. His basic assumption was that the main task of the transition period was the complete elimination of commodity production, thus definitely ending human enslavement by the "blind laws of the market." "*Unorganized* social economy" would be replaced by a "teleological" system consciously guided and possessing a definite plan. Following Luxemburg, Bukharin concluded that in this planned system, political economy as a science would no longer be needed. Political economy, he reasoned, was the science of the self-regulating market; in a consciously regulated society there would be no place for it, for "the market itself will no longer exist."[234]

The rationalization of economic processes through conscious planning had made great advances under capitalism. In fact the growth of finance capitalism had converted the capitalist national economy from an irrational system into a rational organization, from an economy without a (conscious) subject into an economic subject. At the highest stage of this development, that of state capitalism, the commodity market had been eliminated and replaced by a nationwide organization of production in which money was merely a "unit of account." But for two reasons this achievement had not been able to provide a stable solution to the socioeconomic problems of the day. First, state capitalism was only "the rationalization of the production process on the basis of antagonistic social relations and under the dominance of capital, which is manifested in the dictatorship of the bourgeoisie." Second, capitalism as a world economic system had remained subject to the blind irrational forces of the market, and this entailed "the subordination of the entire 'national economic' mechanism to the goals of international competition, i.e., mainly to war." [235] Thus, the rationalization of capitalist economies on a national scale had been accompanied by a sharp intensification of both class antagonisms and international conflicts. This had created a situation in which the only alternative to communism was universal disintegration and the destruction of culture.[236] Only communism could organize humanity into "a classless, stateless, and fully harmonious structure in all its parts"—"the very first instance of an absolutely unified, organized 'whole.'" [237]

The construction of communism, however, could not be achieved by merely economic methods. It presupposed the conscious destruction of market forces and therefore also vastly greater use of extraeconomic compulsion. This was not just because of the inevitable resistance of the petty bourgeoisie (especially the rich peasantry) but was principally due to structural reasons: the replacement of market-regulated horizontal relations by a conscious decision making in accordance with a definite plan required the establishment of a vertical structure of command, that is, a chain of personal orders from the top down.[238] If Bukharin had known Marx's *Grundrisse*, he could have supported his argument by referring to Marx's theory of the inversely proportional relationship between "personal dependence" and "objective (reified) dependence." According to this theory the elimination of objective, impersonal dependence (culminating in the "commodity fetishism" of classical capitalism) entails a proportional increase of personal dependence, and vice versa: "The less social power the medium of exchange possesses . . . , the greater must be the power of the community which binds the individuals together. . . . Rob the thing [i.e., money] of this social power and you must give it to persons to exercise over persons" (M, G, 157–58).

There remained the question of the subject of this power of command. In the first stage of a proletarian dictatorship, this power was given to workers' collectives. This system of collective management and control proved to be not only very effective in destroying the old capitalist relations, but also equal to coping with constructive economic tasks. This was not only because of external circumstances (such as civil war), but also mainly for structural reasons, since the principle of the broadest collegiality involved decentralization and divided responsibility, which was incompatible with rational planning. Hence, the introduction of "militarized production" represented a necessary organizational progress. The construction of communism, Bukharin explained, required "the utmost punctuality and precision, unconditional and unquestioning compliance with orders, rapid decisions, and unity of will. These requirements mean there must be a minimum of discussion and chatter, a minimum of collegial decision making, and a maximum of one-man responsibility." [239]

In his short preface Bukharin had promised consistent thinking and to not fear any conclusions, and he certainly kept his promises. This is especially true of the chapter entitled "Non-Economic Compulsion in the Transition Period." Noneconomic coercion, he reminded his readers, was to Marx the midwife of every old society pregnant with a new one. [240] In the transition to communism, however, the role of coercion was more important than ever, because a consciously regulated system could not emerge spontaneously. It needed the action of conscious forces, and revolutionary compulsion was precisely that, "a conscious force of cohesion, bringing together the different parts of the working class." From the proletarian point of view this was not an external compulsion, but rather "self-compulsion," a "compulsory self-discipline within its own ranks," a "method of compulsory, accelerated self-organization." This involved the abolition of "labor freedom," but under capitalism this so-called freedom was merely "a conditional right to choose one's own master." Individual freedom to choose one's work was "incompatible with a properly organized, 'planned' economy"; consequently, it was incompatible with the true interest of the working class as a whole. [241]

From a broader point of view, Bukharin concluded, "all forms of proletarian compulsion, beginning with executions and ending with obligatory labor service, are methods of forging communist mankind out of the human material left by the capitalist epoch." These were needed not only for crushing physical resistance but also, and primarily, as a means of social regeneration. "The former bourgeoisie, now defeated, smashed, subdued, deprived of their wealth and schooled in physical labor, undergoes spiritual reform and reeducation." The same was true of the intelligentsia and of the peasantry. Even the proletariat itself "remakes its own nature," becoming more and more worthy of its mission. In this way, executions and compulsory labor paved the way for "gathering humanity together" in a classless and stateless communist society, a society in which "compulsion, in all its forms, will disappear forever." [242]

Lenin read Bukharin's *Economics of the Transition Period* carefully, and his reactions are indicated by marginal notes in his copy. Characteristically, he was especially impressed by the chapter on noneconomic compulsion. "This is an excellent chapter!"[243] he noted, and he underlined many phrases, adding such comments as "very good," "correct," or "exactly." Among others, he endorsed the phrases quoted above about "forging communist mankind out of the human material left by the capitalist epoch" and "gathering humanity together." He liked Bukharin's conception of proletarian self-compulsion, that is, "both self-regulation and coercion, the latter being established by the working class, as a class for itself, and extending to all of its sections," and also agreed with his pessimistic view of the peasants (not only rich peasants, but the peasantry as a whole) as being opposed to the state monopoly on grain and inclined toward free trade. He doubly underlined the phrase equating free trade with speculation, noting in the margin: "correct!"[244]

Soon afterward Lenin and Bukharin changed their views and developed the ideas of the NEP, and after Lenin's death Bukharin became its most consistent defender. Because of this he is sometimes presented as the chief ideologist of the genuinely moderate, pragmatic wing of bolshevism, a force that in principle could be seen as a possible alternative to Stalinism.[245] However, this view cannot be accepted without serious qualifications. Like Lenin, Bukharin saw the NEP as a retreat and therefore defended it only as a necessary and temporary concession, not as a matter of principle. His views on socialism as a marketless society remained basically unchanged. Convincing proofs of this are to be found in his interesting study on Marx written in 1933.[246] This work is especially important to our point because it contains a direct and detailed comment on the relationship between Bukharin's (and Lenin's) theory of proletarian dictatorship and Marx's conception of freedom.

The dictatorship of the proletariat, Bukharin argued, is characterized by not being bound by its own laws. This naked power increases its "freedom of action," which is necessary for the transformation of society into a purposive, teleological order.[247] This is precisely the historical task of the proletarian dictatorship, which consists in the *rationalization* of all spheres of social life, in the transformation of a disintegrated subjectless society into a conscious collective subject.[248] (See Marx's parallel between a socialist society and Robinson Crusoe in chapter 1, section 7). The objective regularities of development are not eliminated thereby, but radically change their character: they cease to be blind external forces standing above people and thwarting their actions. This is what Marx meant when he wrote: "Freedom in this field can only consist in socialized man, the associated producers, rationally regulating their interchange with Nature, bringing it under their common control, instead of being ruled by it as by the blind forces of Nature. . . . But it nonetheless still remains a realm of necessity" (M, C, 3:820).[249]

In fact, as Bukharin pointed out, the transition from capitalism to socialism does not mean replacing necessity with pure contingency, or the reign of "free will" on a social scale. Socialist planning, or rational control of the economy (Marx's "common control"), will not eliminate the laws of necessity, but it will change their character, since necessity will no longer manifest itself as a "blind force": instead, it will be perceived as freedom, as "necessity understood." In other words, blind necessity will indeed be eliminated, but not necessity as such. Marxism must therefore beware of two wrong tendencies in its interpretation: a voluntaristic tendency to ignore necessity as such, on the one hand, and a tendency to forget about the main task, the replacement of blind necessity by conscious planning, on the other. The first expresses itself in subjectivist, arbitrary decision making, ignoring the scientific character of Marxism; the second capitulates before causal necessity, thus representing a "bourgeois-liberal caricature of Marxism." [250] The proper solution of the problem is scientific planning—that is, a conscious control over economic forces based on objective science and so avoiding the errors of subjectivism. Comprehensive scientific planning is an expression of freedom, because freedom is nothing but a scientific understanding of necessity. [251]

As we can see, Bukharin, politically defeated, marginalized, and increasingly insecure, tried to counter the dangers of arbitrary dictatorship by pointing out that the dictatorship of the proletariat should be based on the objective, impersonal authority of science. But this attempt showed only the vulnerability of Marx's conception of freedom, which Bukharin invoked to support his view, as well as his own helplessness in defending freedom. Science cannot tell us anything about a choice of values, let alone a choice of policy. It can help us to find the proper means for realizing our ends, but it says nothing of their moral acceptability; in other words, science can to some extent protect us against errors, but it offers no safeguards against crimes. It is well known that the most inhuman policies, including genocide, can be implemented by resorting to scientific methods, or can even be legitimized by invoking the authority of "science," as happened with the Soviet dictatorship. "Scientific Marxism" could be used (and *was* used by Stalin) to warn that excessive zeal in implementing the policy of "dekulakization" might prove counterproductive; at the same time, however, it provided this same policy with a quite convincing "scientific" justification. The only safeguard against tyranny is the institutionalization of the rule of law; Bukharin, however, stubbornly persisted in rejecting all forms of "nomocratic" order, seeing lawlessness as a positive feature, as increased freedom of action necessary for the establishment of the communist "teleocracy." His interpretation of Marx's conception of freedom was entirely compatible with his earlier advocacy of coercion as a means of replacing the blind laws of the market by a consciously regulated "teleocratic" order. [252]

Let us pass now to Trotsky's *Terrorism and Communism*. Like another horrible document from the time of War Communism—Lenin's *Proletarian Revolution and the Renegade Kautsky*—it was written in reply to Kautsky's critique of Bolshevik practices. The historical importance of *Terrorism and Communism* lies in the author's frank assertion that the construction of communism requires terror and unrestrained coercion and that contrary views are hopelessly naive, sentimental illusions. There is nothing morally wrong with terrorist methods as such, Trotsky argued; it all depends on *who* is applying these methods against *whom*.[253] Communists "were never concerned with the Kantian-priestly and vegetarian-Quaker prattle about the 'sacredness of human life.' " In spite of Kautsky's slanders, "Marx had nothing in common with the view of democracy as the last, absolute, supreme product of history"; as a true revolutionary, he wanted, first and foremost, a revolutionary victory and never regarded democracy as "something standing above the class struggle."[254] His resolution was demonstrated, for example, in his opinion that the Paris Commune should not have hesitated to take hostages or, if necessary, kill them.[255]

Revolutionary victory, however, is not the whole story, Trotsky maintained. Terrorist, coercive methods must still be applied, and even intensified, after the revolution, because the construction of socialism cannot dispense with them. It is necessary to reject the Kautskian and Menshevik views of the transition to socialism as "a milky-way, without the bread monopoly, without the abolition of the market, without the revolutionary dictatorship, and without the militarization of labor." Man is a "fairly lazy animal"; he always needs to be compelled to work, and it is not true that extraeconomic compulsion can yield only unproductive labor. Slave labor and serf labor were productive and (originally) progressive forms of labor. The capitalist principle of the so-called freedom of labor has become historically obsolete, being incompatible with rational planning. Therefore, it has been abolished forever: "The principle itself of compulsory labor service has just so radically and permanently replaced the principle of free hiring as the socialization of the means of production has replaced capitalist property." Under a proletarian dictatorship workers must be organized as freely movable "labor armies" subject to harsh military discipline, thus combining capitalist methods of labor discipline (such as piecework and the Taylor system) with the advantages of militarization.[256]

Why "militarization"? Trotsky's answer to this question deserves to be quoted in full:

Of course, it is only an analogy—but an analogy very rich in content. No social organization except the army has ever considered itself justified in subordinating citizens to itself in such a measure, and to control them by its will on all sides to such a degree, as the State of the proletarian dictatorship considers itself justified in doing, and does. Only the army—just because in its way it used to decide questions of life and death of nations, States and ruling classes—was endowed with powers of demanding from each and all complete subordination to its problems, aims, regulations, and orders. And it achieved this to the greater degree, the more the problems of military organization coincided with the requirements of social development.

The question of the life and death of Soviet Russia is at present being settled on the labor front; our economic, and together with them our professional and productive organizations, have the right to demand from their members all that devotion, discipline, and executive thoroughness, which hitherto only the army required.[257]

Like Lenin, Trotsky also encouraged "labor voluntarism" in the form of voluntary unpaid labor on Saturdays (subbotniks);[258] he agreed with Lenin that enthusiasm and compulsion complement each other in enabling the state to organize labor on communist lines (i.e., without the labor market). He therefore wanted to combine "communist voluntarism" and "state compulsion," using both to mobilize the masses for the construction of communism.[259] But he was not trying to foster illusions. He made it plain that in the last instance everything would depend on the apparatus of compulsion (i.e., the state) and grandiloquently proclaimed that under the dictatorship of the proletariat, state compulsion would be more powerful and all embracing than ever. "The road to socialism," he argued, "lies through a period of the highest possible intensification of the principle of the State. And you and I are just passing through that period. Just as a lamp, before going out, shoots up in a brilliant flame, so the State, before disappearing, assumes the form of the dictatorship of the proletariat, i.e., the most ruthless form of State, which embraces the life of the citizens authoritatively in every direction. . . . No organization except the army has ever controlled man with such severe compulsion as does the State organization of the working class in the most difficult period of transition." [260]

The idea that communism cannot be constructed without maximum development of the coercive apparatus of the "proletarian" state was to become the main theoretical justification of the Stalinist dictatorship. Trotsky, in his turn, became the first Marxist theorist to accuse Stalin of transforming Bolshevism into totalitarianism.[261] In reality, however, the view that the dictatorship of the proletariat must be the strongest and most ruthless form of the state had become commonplace much earlier. As I have shown, it was openly supported by all theorists of War Communism, and its harshest formulation was Trotsky's. It would be difficult to deny that Trotsky's insistence on the *all-embracing* character of control and compulsion gave his theory of the proletarian dictatorship a distinctively totalitarian flavor.

Abramovich, one of the Menshevik leaders, compared this Bolshevik socialism to "Egyptian slavery." Trotsky, of course, indignantly rejected this comparison and ridiculed Abramovich for having forgotten a "little insignificant fact," namely "the class nature of the government": "He has forgotten that in Egypt there were Pharaohs, there were slaveowners and slaves. It was not the Egyptian peasants who decided through their Soviets to build the pyramids; there existed a social order based upon hierarchical caste; and the workers were obliged to toil by a class hostile to them. Our compulsion is applied by a workers' and peasants' government, in the name of the interests of the laboring masses." [262]

But this was sheer hypocrisy on Trotsky's part. Everything he ever wrote on democracy leaves no doubt whatsoever that he cared very little about democratic legitimation and democratic procedures. He never recommended that the construction of communism should be made dependent on the will of the laboring masses, as expressed through their Soviets. On the contrary, he held the average worker in contempt (as "a lazy animal") and advised that the masses be subjected to the most severe, all-embracing control and compulsion, which was to be modeled on the army and exercised by the revolutionary minority. So only one part of his answer to Abramovich can be taken seriously: his belief that the *final* goals of the Bolshevik dictatorship coincided with the interests of the working class and, more important, its historical mission. It is quite obvious that by the interests of the working class he did not necessarily mean the interests of the *present* generation of the workers. Like all true Marxists, he concentrated entirely on the *ultimate* goal, readily sacrificing the present for the sake of the future. Naturally, it was politically expedient not to state explicitly that the workers, as living human beings, might not see the fruits of their labors, that they were merely instruments in solving great historical tasks, and that their well-being here and now was of no significance whatever in comparison with the final end of the movement.

In *Their Morals and Ours* (1938)—written in Mexico, his last place of exile—Trotsky gave a more credible account of his justification of coercion and terror. Here he did not refer to the (alleged) will and interests of the masses, but invoked only "the laws of history" and the communist ideal, which is consonant with these "laws" and thus enables us to discover a deep human meaning in the seemingly absurd cruelties of history. [263] Like Marx, he defined this ideal not in terms of class interests or of distributive justice, but in terms of freedom; not individual freedom, it is true, but species freedom, which consists in the power of humanity over nature, on the one hand, and in the abolition of social oppression and exploitation, on the other (see chapter 1, section 3). For him, this, and *only this*, ideal justified all means of action, even the cruelest and least acceptable from a conventional moral point of view. For a Marxist, he explained, every action is justified "if it leads to increasing the power of humanity over nature and to the abolition of the power of one person over another." In other words, everything is permissible if it *"really* leads to the liberation of humanity."[264]

Thus, in accordance with Marx, communism was identified with true freedom, and vice versa. It should be stressed that Trotsky's understanding of this Marxian conception was quite remarkable, being far superior to the current Marxist views of his time. He understood, much better than either Lenin or Bukharin, that the establishment of conscious, rational control over both nature and society was merely a necessary condition of true freedom, because the latter (according to Marx) would reveal itself in the unhampered development of the creative capacities of the species. It is not surprising that Trotsky's best comment on freedom was part of his reflection on the artistic creativity of the communist future, a creativity no longer dependent on blind economic forces, free of any class interests, and for the first time in history genuinely an end in itself.

I am referring, of course, to Trotsky's *Literature and Revolution*, a valuable collection of articles first published in 1924. In it he argued that the Bolshevik revolution had to save society "by means of the most cruel surgery," concentrating all forces in politics and revolutionary struggle and trampling everything else underfoot.[265] Therefore, the dictatorship of the proletariat cannot become culturally productive. It is not "an organization for the production of the culture of the new society" but only "a revolutionary and military system" laying the foundations of the new social order in which a new, fully liberated culture will be possible.[266] The Bolshevik revolution was indeed the beginning of a new historical era. Engels was right when he spoke of the socialist revolution as a leap from the kingdom of necessity into the kingdom of freedom. Nevertheless "the Revolution itself is not as yet the kingdom of freedom." On the contrary, it "carries the class struggle to its highest tension,"[267] applying ruthless coercion to its enemies and demanding boundless sacrifices from its supporters. This cruel revolutionary period will last many years, perhaps half a century.[268] But all these cruelties will be justified by the final result: the full liberation and regeneration of humanity in the creation of an entirely new and superior man. In the last pages of *Literature and Revolution*, Trotsky described this vision thus:

Communist life will not be formed blindly, like coral islands, but will be built consciously, will be tested by thought, will be directed and corrected. . . . Man, who will learn how to move rivers and mountains, how to build people's palaces on the peaks of Mount Blanc and at the bottom of the Atlantic, will not only be able to add to his own life richness, brilliancy and intensity, but also a dynamic quality of the highest degree. . . . More than that. Man at last will begin to harmonize himself in earnest. He will make it his business to achieve beauty by giving the movements of his own limbs the utmost precision, purposefulness and economy in his work, his walk and his play. He will try to master the semiconscious and then the subconscious processes in his own organism, such as breathing, the circulation of blood, digestion, reproduction, and, within necessary limits, he will try to subordinate them to the control of reason and will. Even purely physiologic life will become subject to collective experiments. The human species, the coagulated *homo sapiens*, will once more enter into a state of radical transformation, and, in his own hands, will become an object of the most complicated methods of artificial selection and psycho-physical training. . . . Is it not self-evident that the greatest efforts of investigative thought will be in that direction? The human race will not have ceased to crawl on all fours before God, Kings and capital, in order later to submit humbly before the dark laws of heredity and a blind sexual selection! Emancipated man will want to attain a greater equilibrium in the work of his organs and a more proportional developing and weaving out of his tissues, in order to reduce the fear of death to a rational reaction of the organism toward danger. There can be no doubt that man's extreme anatomical and physiological disharmony, that is, the extreme disproportion in the growth and weaving out of organs and tissues, give the life instinct the form of a pinched, morbid and hysterical fear of death, which darkens reason and which feeds the stupid and humiliating fantasies about life after death.

Man will make it his purpose to master his own feelings, to raise his instincts to the heights of consciousness, to make them transparent, to extend the wires of his will into hidden recesses, and thereby to raise himself to a new plane, to create a higher social biologic type, or, if you please, a superman. . . .

Man will become immeasurably stronger, wiser and subtler; his body will become more harmonized, his movements more rhythmic, his voice more musical. The forms of life will become dynamically dramatic. The average human type will rise to the heights of an Aristotle, a Goethe, or a Marx. And above this ridge new peaks will rise.[269]

Trotsky saw this idea as perfectly Marxist, and he was basically right. True, Marx did not indulge in fantasies about a future superman able consciously to control even his own biology. This was, however, merely an extension of Marx's view of freedom as conscious self-mastery and autocreation of the species; it would be logically difficult to deny that such freedom, freedom as conscious control and creative engineering, should include eugenics as well. It was perfectly Marxist to expect that communism would bring about a total regeneration of humanity and thus raise man to an entirely new and vastly superior level of existence. Trotsky's vision of the liberated man of the future as harmonized within himself and capable of previously unheard-of creativity was fully consonant with Marx's view of communism as the positive overcoming of alienation. Trotsky's expectation that the average human type of the future would rise to the heights of an Aristotle or Goethe was merely the logical consequence of Marx's conception of communism as the reappropriation by each individual of the previously alienated creative capacities of the entire species (see chapter 1, section 5). Moreover, it was unmistakably Marxist to assume that the necessary precondition of this miraculous transformation of humanity was the exercise of a conscious collective control over extrahuman nature, on the one hand, and over the blind quasi-natural forces of society, on the other.

It was an axiom for all Marxists that man cannot be free if his own products escape his control and acquire an independent life of their own. Hence, it was obvious to all that the construction of communism first of all necessitated the liquidation of the market. In spite of conventional opinions, this was for them a more urgent and imperative task than the abolition of private property, since private property without freedom of exchange could be amenable to control and even compatible with rational planning (as, for instance, in natural economy or in "state capitalism"). Trotsky would certainly have been very surprised had he been told that Western scholars would interpret the antimarket crusade of War Communism as merely an emergency policy, a practical response to external circumstances. For him, as for Lenin, it was the first and most important step toward communist freedom.

The Nietzschean, or quasi-Nietzschean, flavor in Trotsky's vision may appear to reflect the ideas of Russian "Nietzschean Marxists."[270] In fact, however, there is no need to assume any direct influence. Trotsky himself knew Nietzsche well; as a young man he had even written a perceptive essay on the Nietzschean "superman."[271] The parallels between Marx and Nietzsche as Promethean visionaries ready to sacrifice their miserable and contemptible contemporaries to the splendid, powerful, creative man (or superman) of the future, were quite obvious to Russian intellectuals of Trotsky's generation. Both Marx and Nietzsche were praised, or condemned, for providing convenient justification for those who wanted to substitute "the love for the far-off" (Fernstenliebe) for the love of one's poor and imperfect neighbor (Nächstenliebe). This willingness to sacrifice the present generation for the sake of a bright future was rightly regarded as one of the most conspicuous features of Marxism, and it was just this aspect that provided theoretical justification for the ideology and practice of War Communism. Because of this, Lenin, Bukharin, and Trotsky could sincerely believe that their policies of terror and extermination, of physical violence and unprecedented moral intimidation, as well as the ruthless self-compulsion applied by the party to its own members and to the working class itself, were legitimate means of action that ultimately served the cause of human freedom.

It must be stressed that such beliefs were by no means exclusive to Russian Marxists. The glorification of violence was also a distinctive feature of the philosophy of Lukács, the "father of Western Marxism." In mid 1919, when War Communism in Russia was at its most violent and brutal, he gave a lecture in Budapest praising the Bolsheviks for their use of violence and condemning the old Kautskian orthodoxy for its neglect of the role of extraeconomic compulsion in history.[272] In his view, the very essence of the "vulgar Marxist economism" typical of the Second International lay in its denial of the role of violence in the transition from one economic system to another and in substituting for it the so-called natural laws of economic development. In fact, however, "the demand that socialism be realized by virtue of the immanent laws of economics without recourse to 'extra-economic' violence is effectively synonymous with the eternal survival of capitalist society."[273] The "leap from the realm of necessity into the realm of freedom" would be merely an empty phrase if historical materialism proved unable to change its function, taking account of the fundamental difference between the nature of capitalist society, in which everything was economically determined, and the nature of socialist revolution. "Men," wrote Engels, "make their history themselves, but *not as yet* with a collective will according to a collective plan." For Lukács, this meant that Engels had foreseen the time when history would be made consciously, according to a collective plan. Now this time had arrived, and therefore the importance of the role of extraeconomic compulsion must be clearly recognized. For revolutionary Marxists "the question of violence takes precedence over the question of economics. . . . And this violence is nothing but the will of the proletariat which has become conscious and is bent on abolishing the enslaving hold of reified relations over man and the hold of economics over society."[274]

In this manner Lukács, emphasizing the concept of reification and consciously opposing the social democratic Marxism of the Second International, gave his full support to the Russian theorists of militant communism. In this he was *not* deviating from Marx's teaching (although he did so on many other questions). He had merely discovered a discrepancy between the classical version of historical materialism and the Marxist vision of the communist ideal, between the necessitarian account of the Marxist philosophy of history and the commitment to the ultimate goal of the socialist revolution. Kautsky remained faithful to orthodox historical materialism, and this led him to abandon the communist ideal. Lenin, Bukharin, Trotsky, and Lukács chose to be faithful to the orthodox vision of communism, which led them to a conscious (in Lukács's case) or unconscious (in Lenin's case) reversal of the classical Marxist view on the relationship between economics and politics, on the immanent laws of development and conscious action.

As we know, the attempt to achieve a direct transition to communism proved a total failure. Neither revolutionary enthusiasm nor absolutely ruthless coercion could save the country from economic catastrophe. The deliberate destruction of the market did not lead to its replacement by a rationally planned and equitable economic order; in fact, it created a chaotic state of affairs in which almost everything was unpredictable and uncontrollable. The forced requisition of grain and other foodstuffs gave rise to an increasing number of peasant uprisings without preventing starvation in the cities. The shock methods (*udarnost'*) and the communist subbotniks may have been successful as means of political mobilization but not as means of counteracting, or even containing, the catastrophic industrial decline. The Kronstadt revolt of the elite sailors, formerly staunch supporters of the regime, added a real threat to the Bolshevik monopoly of power.

The Bolshevik leaders could easily reconcile themselves to economic disasters (after all, as Bukharin explained, economic collapse was a necessary price for the construction of communism) but were not prepared to risk their political power. Lenin therefore decided to save the political dictatorship through economic liberalization, an extremely difficult and painful decision for him. He himself asked the question: "Is it another 'Brest' "? (L, CW, 32:320). It certainly was, since in both cases absolute political power was saved at the cost of making humiliating concessions to the enemy. In Brest-Litovsk they were territorial losses; in March 1921 it was the postponement of the realization of communist ideals.

Such was the genesis of the NEP. Its direct connection with the Kronstadt revolt, showing a concern for the fate of the dictatorship rather than the population, is shown by the fact that on the eve of the revolt Lenin was firmly convinced that " 'freedom to trade' will not return" (ibid., 36:503). He even continued to support such extreme War Communism measures as the grotesque "national plan of obligatory sowing," which had established special sowing committees to control in detail the productive activity of the peasants.[275]

The arbitrary character of the NEP and its inconsistency with communist principles were not camouflaged. In his justification of the proposed policy, Lenin made it clear that free exchange amounted for him to a return to capitalism and therefore to "a revival of capitalist wage-slavery." He defended the NEP not as a matter of principle but as a necessary concession that, if kept within proper limits, would not endanger "the political power of the proletariat." He allowed free exchange on a *local* scale only, giving a variety of reasons for this, such as "the vastness of our agricultural country with its poor transport system, boundless expanses, varying climate, diverse farming conditions, etc." He did not promise the peasants fair terms of trade; indeed, he stated that "the peasant will have to go hungry for a while in order to save the towns and factories from famine" (ibid., 32:218, 219, 219, 188). This shows that the main reason for the decision to substitute a tax in kind for the ineffective "surplus appropriation system" was simply the urgent need for radical improvement of the food supply in the cities and avoidance of political unrest among the workers.

Nevertheless, despite the limited character of its original objectives, the NEP soon became "a surprising negation and complete reversal of the 'war communism' policies . . . a remarkable *volte-face*, which astonished the world as well as the Bolsheviks." Lenin quickly became aware that palliative measures, such as a "socialist goods-barter,"[276] would not do, that a "regular commodity exchange" was needed, and that the Communists themselves would have to engage in business and learn market techniques (ibid., 322). He came to see trade as "the only possible economic link between the scores of millions of small farmers and large-scale industry" in Russia. Consequently, he declared War Communism policies to be based on erroneous assumptions while continuing to treat the NEP as a retreat, both material and moral, and he tried to console his followers by promising "to stop the retreat in time and revert to the offensive." He urged Communist managers to engage in commerce, as a necessary condition for constructing communism in a backward, peasant country. He even wrote of the need not to surrender to "the old Russian, semi-aristocratic, semi-muzhik and patriarchal mood, with their supreme contempt for trade" (L, A, 515, 517, 516). But in the very same article he demonstrated his own contempt for commercial values: after the final victory of communism, he declared, gold would be used to build public lavatories in the streets of the largest cities.[277] This would be the most "just" and educational way of expressing the communist attitude toward the symbol of commercial greed, for which humanity had paid so dearly.

Some scholars see these statements as contradictory and confusing. According to Lewin, Lenin "did not explain in what sense the NEP was a 'retreat' if 'War Communism' was not an advance."[278] How could Lenin define the NEP as a retreat if, at the same time, he defined his previous policies as an error? A retreat from error is obviously a contradiction in terms. So Lenin should have answered the question: "A retreat from what?"

In fact, however, Lenin and the other Bolshevik theorists had a clear answer to this question. They defined the notions of "retreat" and "advance" not in terms of empirical indicators of economic success, but in relation to the ideological principles and final goal of the communist movement. Hence, an economically successful policy could represent an *ideological* retreat, and this was precisely the case of the NEP. Despite all its errors, War Communism was a communist offensive, a policy consistent with communist principles, while the NEP was by definition a retreat—a retreat from the communist ideal, a pragmatic compromise, a forced and reluctant acknowledgment of the need to slow down the march toward communism. For the leaders of the communist movement, it was so self-evident that they did not even suspect that sometime in the future additional explanations would be required.

This book is concerned not with the fate of the communist movement, but with the fate of the communist ideal of universal human liberation. Hence, historical details about the Soviet Union under the NEP are not directly relevant here. The party's commitment to the NEP did not involve any change in its view of its final goal. Despite their readiness to make concessions to market forces, Lenin and his direct successors remained dogmatic Marxists in their vision of the communist future. Differences between them might be important in practical matters but had no impact on their conception of communism as the final goal, as legitimizing all their activities. Even Bukharin, who became a theorist of "organic development" and the chief advocate of the "plan and market" approach to the construction of socialism, was no exception. He saw the NEP as a long-term policy, but (as his 1933 study on Marx shows) he remained faithful to the Marxian view of communist freedom as presupposing full conscious control over the economy, that is, the complete elimination of a spontaneous market order. Perhaps he would have revised this view if the NEP had lasted longer and developed in accordance with his policy recommendations, but this is mere speculation about what might have been. The fact remains that neither Trotsky nor Bukharin dared to revise the ideological foundations of Marxist communism. In fact, they did everything to persuade both the party and themselves that the advocacy of market methods in the transition period was a matter of expediency that could be justified in Marxist terms but should not entail any revision of the communist ideal.[279] Because of this, economic debates of the NEP period, unlike the theories of War Communism, were loosely related to the communist utopia and revealed nothing new about its nature.

As it is not necessary to analyze these debates in this context, let us instead conclude this chapter with a few remarks about the problems of the NEP in Lenin's last works. Lenin's commitment to the NEP was not as deep or as stable as some authors want us to believe. The view that Bukharin in his NEP period was the best interpreter of Lenin's intentions seems very doubtful if not plainly wrong. From the very beginning Lenin treated the NEP as a *short-term* policy and anticipated its termination impatiently. In November 1921 he already saw "visible signs that the retreat is coming to an end," that his party would be able "to stop this retreat in the not too distant future" (L, *A*, 517). In March 1922 he assured the communist metal workers that the NEP would soon come to an end: "*We can now stop the retreat we began, we are already stopping it. Enough!* . . . I hope the Congress will confirm the fact that we shall not retreat any further. *The retreat has come to an end*." In the same speech he told the "NEP men" that the party would no longer tolerate illegitimate profits and would "adopt terror again, if necessary" (L, *CW*, 33:219/223, 218/220). This was the language of hysterical threats, not that of a responsible statesman trying to create conditions for honest business and peaceful "organic development."

Lenin's theoretical explanation of the need to terminate War Communism was, to put it mildly, quite inadequate. At the Tenth Congress of the party he said: "Direct transition to communism would have been possible if ours was a country with a predominantly—or, say, highly developed—large-scale industry, and a high level of large-scale production in agriculture" (ibid., 32:233). This shows that he continued to share Engels's view that highly developed large-scale production makes possible, even requires, the abolition of the market. He used this view to argue that the main reason for the failure of "direct transition" was the insufficient centralization of Russian industry and, especially, the absence of large-scale agricultural production. In other words, he was as far as ever from understanding the indispensability of the market to a complex, highly developed industrial society. Clearly, this diagnosis, as well as explaining the need for the NEP, could also provide (and in fact did so) theoretical arguments for the Stalinist policy of forced industrialization and collectivization.

The first year of the NEP was economically successful. Agriculture, as well as the retail trade and small private enterprises, recovered rapidly, food shortages in the cities ceased, and, real wages in industry increased. For Lenin, however, there was no cause for rejoicing. At the Eleventh Congress held in March to April 1922, he spoke of the results achieved in a somber, alarming tone, presenting the recovery of the private sector as a humiliating defeat for his party, a defeat in "the last and decisive battle," the battle against Russian home-grown native capitalism, "the capitalism that is growing out of the small-peasant economy." His main conclusion was that the party, despite its monopoly of power and a host of economic and other resources, had proved unable to compete successfully with private capital or to control it, thus showing its lack of culture and economic incompetence. The party, Lenin argued, had "everything you want except ability." Its capacity to run the economy proved inferior to that of "the ordinary capitalist salesman" (L, A, 522, 520/522, 522). Even the 4,700 Communists in responsible positions could not establish effective control of the economy, or of the huge bureaucratic state machine. In reality they were not directing, but rather being directed (ibid., 527), even though the economic power in their hands was "quite adequate to ensure the transition to communism." What was lacking was "culture." "If the conquering nation is more cultured than the vanquished nation, the former imposes its culture upon the latter; but if the opposite is the case, the vanquished nation imposes its culture upon the conqueror." This was just what happened to Russian Communists in the role of conquerors. Capitalist Russia represented a "miserable, insignificant" cultural level, but, as the NEP showed, this miserable culture was still superior to the culture of the Communist elite. Because of this, the party had to retreat. Many devoted Communists reacted by falling into despair or panic; several even "burst into tears in a disgraceful and childish manner." On the whole, however, the party "retreated in good revolutionary order." Now it had learned the lesson and decided "to halt the retreat" (ibid., 527, 527, 523, 532, 532). But this, Lenin stressed, should not involve a return to previous militant methods. The party would advance slowly and cautiously, without risking the alienation of the peasantry and fully aware of its own shortcomings. It would concentrate on educating and remolding itself, on acquiring the skills that would enable it to work with the peasants, to assist them and to lead them forward (ibid., 533).

This brief summary of Lenin's Congress speech shows that his attitude toward the NEP was very ambivalent, to say the least. He wanted the Soviet economy to evolve into an orderly state capitalist system, no longer a centralized and marketless one (as in his early conception of state capitalism in Russia) but at least a system in which everything, including the market, would be firmly controlled by the party state. He was deeply disappointed that the party elite was unable to cope with this task and saw a lack of culture as the only reason for this. Otherwise, the party had, he thought, enough political and economic power to ensure the transition to communism. In other words, for Lenin the main obstacle to Russia's transition to communism was the subjective factor, the inadequate cultural level of the communist cadres. Plainly, the experience of both War Communism and the first year of the NEP had taught him nothing. He remained an unreformed communist and Jacobin: the former, because of his uncritical belief in the feasibility of a communist utopia; the latter, because of faithfulness to his old conviction that ultimately everything depended on the quality of the revolutionary vanguard.

It should also be noted that the NEP, to Lenin, gambled on the peasantry rather than on the market. He treated freedom to trade as equivalent to the freedom of capitalism (L, CW, 36:535), a necessary evil, the price to be paid for an alliance with the peasantry (L, A, 515). This alliance was to be a long-term policy, but, as his last article made it clear, freedom to trade was to be terminated as soon as possible.[280] In his article "On Cooperation" (January 1923), Lenin offered a "radical modification" of his whole outlook on socialism: "shifting to peaceful, organisational, 'cultural' work" (ibid., 712). The aim of this was to transform the Russian peasants into civilized cooperators, so winning them to the cause of socialism (ibid., 710–12). In other articles of the same time he stressed the difference between the peasants (whom, as we know, he saw as having two souls; that of a petty bourgeois proprietor and that of a laborer) and the new bourgeoisie (the "NEP men"), doing so with the aim of strengthening the workers' alliance with the peasant masses and setting them against the "NEP men" (ibid., 733). His growing concern about "uncontrollability" found expression in different proposals for improving the work of the Central Control

Commission and of the Workers' and Peasants' Inspection, through famil-
iarizing their staff with "the principles of scientific organization of labor
in general, and of administrative work, office work, and so forth, in particular" (ibid., 730). This was fully consistent with the idea of conscious,
scientific planning, as opposed to the alleged anarchy and irrationality of
the market.

Lenin's last articles are also a vivid testimony to his deep dissatisfaction
with the apparatus of the party state. In "Better Fewer, But Better," he described it as truly "deplorable, not to say wretched," reflecting in its defects
the worst features of the Russian past (ibid., 735). The harshness of this
judgment demonstrated Lenin's fear that the huge bureaucratic machine
was not only utterly inefficient in controlling market forces, but also increasingly uncontrollable in itself. Instead of looking to the public good, as
defined by the leadership of the party, it was pursuing its own particularist
interests in a way that smacked strongly of old-style corruption. But his
only remedy for this was the establishment of more effective, more centralized, and more elitist control: to "select a few dozen and later hundreds of
the best, absolutely honest and most efficient employees" (L, CW, 33:354),
and to entrust them with the task of controlling not only the peasants and
the "NEP men" but also the entire state apparatus and even the highest
party echelons. Neil Harding, otherwise Lenin's loyal defender, has rightly
classified this method as Jacobin: "It was a plan which rested entirely upon
the exemplary qualities of what he recognized to be a tiny handful of able,
devoted, totally uncorruptible men grouped in one exemplary all-powerful
institution. Here, at the last, was the Jacobin solution, the rule of the men
of Virtue." [281]

Lenin's last article "Better Fewer, But Better" (February 1923) contains
very revealing details about the tasks of the proposed Central Control
Commission. Its members should carefully investigate the routine work of
all institutions, "from the very small and privately-owned offices to the
highest state institutions," including the Politburo, whose papers and documents should be systematically examined (L, A, 740). But it was not enough
to use the usual methods of administrative control. The members of the
Central Commission should also resort to "special ruses to screen their
movements" in order to catch suspects red-handed. For this they should
make use of their "sociability," or the ability to penetrate into circles that
are not always open to administrative officials (ibid., 739). In studying the
conduct of people under control, they should have no scruples in resorting
to such unconventional methods as "some semi-humorous trick, cunning
device, piece of trickery or something of that sort." In other words, the
supreme controllers should not be bound by any procedural rules; they
should "abandon what the French call *pruderie*" and feel themselves free
to behave as spies and provocateurs (ibid., 740, 740).

Lenin's deep conviction that "bourgeois decency" was merely a convenient fiction did not prevent his recognition of the shockingly unusual character of these proposals. He readily conceded that "if such proposals were made in West-European government institutions they would rouse frightful resentment, a feeling of moral indignation, etc." But he was confident that his followers had not "become so bureaucratic as to be capable of that." The NEP, he argued, "has not yet succeeded in gaining such respect as to cause any of us to be shocked at the idea that somebody may be caught. Our Soviet Republic is of such recent construction, and there are such heaps of the old lumber still lying around that it would hardly occur to anyone to be shocked at the idea that we should delve into them by means of ruses, by means of investigations sometimes directed to rather remote sources or in a roundabout way." Any reluctance to use such methods would be a "ridiculous primness," or "ridiculous swank," playing into the hands of the Soviet and party bureaucracy (ibid., 740, 740, 740).

To sum up, the NEP, as conceived by Lenin, could not provide a reliable model for a market-based socialist state. Freedom for market forces was recognized not as a principle or even a long-term policy orientation, but simply as the only available means (apart from naked violence) for creating an economic link (*smychka*) between the cities and the multitude of small and scattered farms. Lenin did not reject command economy as such; he saw the abandonment of militant communism as a retreat and hoped to resume the anticapitalist (read: antimarket) offensive as soon as possible. He decided to *tolerate* some freedom of the market, but it never occurred to him to see market mechanisms as compatible in principle with the construction of socialism, let alone communism. Thus, the "radical modification" of his whole outlook on socialism did not involve a renunciation of the communist economic utopia.

Politically, this allegedly radical modification was rather insignificant. It contained a promise to avoid direct coercion but involved no change in Lenin's understanding of the dictatorship of the proletariat as *unlimited* by any laws. He defined the problem of fighting the evils of bureaucratization as one of choosing the proper people and raising their cultural level, not as providing checks on the system.[282] Furthermore, he saw *economic* liberalization as a means of avoiding *political* concessions. The introduction of the NEP made him more nervous than ever about political instability and led him to silence all opposition, even within the party. As a result, he eliminated all possible checks on the abuse of power. Instead of considering acceptable *rules* of the game, he once again gambled on the revolutionary vanguard.

5

From Totalitarian Communism to Communist Totalitarianism

5.1 Leninism and Stalinism: The Controversy over the Continuity Thesis

The last part of this book must be different from the rest. Stalin's contribution to the Marxist theory of freedom was virtually nonexistent, and his use of Marxism as ideological, or scientific, justification for the suppression of freedom was based entirely on Leninism. What was really novel in this respect was the Stalinist *political practice*, but this is obviously a separate subject that does not fall within the scope of intellectual history. The criminal, terrorist aspects of Stalinism are so widely known and universally condemned that there is really no need to dwell on these horrors in the present context. Our general view of Stalin does not depend on establishing the precise number of his victims, because there is no moral difference between killing twenty million, or twice as many.[1] Anyway, we must agree with Roy Medvedev that "not one of the tyrants and despots of the past persecuted and destroyed so many of his compatriots."[2] We may legitimately wonder if the ideas of such a man can be meaningfully related to the problems of human freedom, no matter how conceived.

Nevertheless, Stalinism is directly relevant to our topic, for it was the closest approximation yet achieved to totalitarianism in the Orwellian sense of the term—that is, as not only a system of *external* coercion but also, and primarily, as a system that attempted to coerce people *from within*, through control of their thoughts and feelings. It is important to add that this control was to be not merely negative—that is, limiting freedom of thought—but also positive—that is, dictating to people what they should think, changing their innermost identity, and thus depriving them of the most elementary freedom, the freedom to be themselves.[3] In this way total unanimity was to be created—"the moral and political unity of society," as Stalinists used to call it. To this end the Stalinist state mobilized all possible means, from naked terror to organized ideological pressure. Hence, it is not enough to describe Stalinism as a system lacking even the minimal safeguards for individual and group freedom. We should rather define it as a system mobilizing all the means at its disposal *against* such freedoms and doing so in the name of replacing spontaneity and "anarchy" with an all-pervasive conscious control from above, a control seen as a necessary condition for raising society to the level at which it could consciously plan its historical future.

As discussed earlier, the conscious control of "man's social forces" to achieve "mastery over human collective fate" was essential to the Marxist ideal of freedom. Because of this, Marxism provided an excellent justification for the totalitarian strivings of Leninism and Stalinism. For this reason alone Stalinism should not be seen as a merely local phenomenon unrelated to genuine Marxism and having nothing in common with the Marxist ideal of the communist future.

Of course, this is not to say that Stalinism was the inevitable outcome of Marxism, or even of Leninism. I do not share the view of history as predetermined in its course and thus lacking any alternatives; neither do I believe that the history of great ideologically inspired movements is totally predetermined by the content of their respective ideologies. In the development of Marxist communism in Russia and elsewhere, there were both continuities and discontinuities. The evaluation of their respective importance depends, above all, on existential factors such as the researcher's historical experience, relation to the communist movement, and sympathy (or lack of it) with its goals. Thus, for instance, Alexander Solzhenitsyn denied the very existence of Stalinism as a distinct historical phenomenon; in his view, it was indistinguishable from Leninism, which in turn was nothing but a practical implementation of Marxism.[4] Trotsky took a view completely opposed to this continuity thesis, maintaining that Stalinism was not a logical development of Bolshevism but rather its counterrevolutionary negation, being divided from Leninism by a "whole river of blood."[5]

In American Sovietology disagreements about the relationship between Leninism and Stalinism have been closely related to different views of the concept of totalitarianism as applied to Soviet history. In the mid 1950s the totalitarian model seemed to be established as the dominant paradigm in the field. Yet a reaction against it soon appeared that, with the passage of time, yielded a number of alternative "revisionist" interpretations of the Soviet system, its genesis and evolution. The main reason for this was Khrushchev's literary "thaw" of 1956 and his de-Stalinization campaign. Despite all its limitations, these events showed that the Stalinist system was not immune to change, whether intentional or not, and that the concept of totalitarianism was too static to explain these processes. There were also domestic reasons for challenging this concept. A growing number of American scholars felt that to conceptualize the rival world power in terms of a rigid totalitarian model served the aims of the cold war and justified, albeit indirectly, the anticommunist hysteria and the corresponding practices of McCarthy while at the same time strengthening the attitude of arrogant self-righteousness among Americans. Alfred Meyer wrote of this passionately and, on the whole, convincingly.[6] Whatever we think of the scholarly value of the totalitarian model, we should be aware of its functions in the political struggle. It is natural that in the period of the cold war, people committed to the same or similar values but living in different countries should see these functions in a different light: American liberals, concentrating on combating McCarthyism, naturally differed from East European liberals, for whom enemy number one was the continuing and unbearably repressive Stalinist system.

It is arguable, of course, that the real cause of the cold war was simply Stalinism, that the greatest threat to liberal values on a global scale was the Stalinist Soviet Union, and that therefore the perspective of the East European liberals was relatively less ethnocentric and more valid. As may be expected, I fully share this view, but just because of this I should like to stress that acceptance of the totalitarian model as a heuristic device explaining those features of Soviet communism that culminated in the Stalinist system does not, and *should not exclude* sharp criticism of this model when applied to the *post-Stalinist* period. It is obvious that stubborn attachment to this model fostered a deeply prejudiced and flawed perception of the post-Stalinist reality in the Soviet Union and other countries of "actually existing socialism." Convinced believers in the unchangeable nature of totalitarianism refused to accept the evidence that these countries were really changing, moving away from their totalitarian past and at the same time becoming more and more independent of the basic tenets of communist ideology. Thus, for instance, the anticommunist Polish intellectuals firmly believed that their country remained totalitarian as late as 1989.[7] They were supported in this self-imposed blindness by some right-wing Sovietologists, who seriously claimed that the Soviet Union was totalitarian to the last and that Gorbachev's *perestroika* was merely a clever ploy for deceiving the West while in fact strengthening the Soviet Empire and preparing a new communist offensive. Incredible as it now seems, this was really their belief.

At any rate, there were many legitimate reasons for challenging the totalitarian model and for revising at the same time many established views of the communist past. The revisionists were right to argue that the classic totalitarian interpretation was increasingly inadequate to explain "actually existing socialism," too monolithic and too pessimistic about its possible evolution. Therefore, it might have been expected that the peaceful collapse of Soviet communism would be perceived as decisive proof that the revisionist school had a better grasp of Soviet reality than its totalitarian opponents, that the ahistorical notion of the unchangeably totalitarian nature of the Soviet system would be finally discredited, and that revisionist appeals for a less "essentialist" and more empirical approach to this system would be regarded as historically vindicated. Yet this did not happen. "The advent of *perestroika* and *glasnost'*, and the final collapse of Soviet communism, have led not to the victory for revisionism and defeat for the totalitarian model, but nearly to the opposite."[8]

The author of these words, Terence Emmons, sees this outcome as "not a small irony." At the same time, however, he himself points out that this ironic result was politically predictable, because the revisionist school was perceived as contributing to a cover-up of the horrors of the Soviet system and even giving it moral succor.[9] In other words, the revisionists were seen, rightly or wrongly, as representing a leftist, soft-line approach to communism, and such an approach could hardly avoid sharing the fate of the defeated communist system.

The correctness of this perception, as well as the wisdom of politicizing knowledge, is, of course, a matter of dispute. In the present context I shall refrain from discussing this issue. I need only stress that the revisionists themselves greatly weakened their position by attempts to eliminate the notion of totalitarianism altogether or, at least, to prove that it was not applicable to the pre-Stalinist period of Soviet history. In fact their struggle against the rigid dogmatism of the totalitarian school would have been more successful had they accepted the notion of totalitarianism as an important typological category while at the same time supplementing it with a theory of "detotalitarianization." Such an approach would justify concentration on the positive changes in the countries of "actually existing socialism" while avoiding the temptation to embellish their totalitarian past. At the start of Gorbachev's *perestroika* I wrote:

The term "totalitarianism" should be reserved for socio-political systems characterized by revolutionary dynamism, genuine commitment to a messianic ideology, the ability to exercise ideological control over the population and the corresponding capacity to mobilize the masses for active, though strictly controlled participation in the "building of a new life." It should be evident to objective observers that these features of totalitarianism are now greatly weakened in the USSR. In the other countries of "really existing socialism," especially in Hungary and in Poland, this process of detotalitarianization is, of course, much more advanced. This means that there is no such thing as an "unchangeable nature of totalitarianism." The theory of totalitarianism is useful in explaining a certain phase in the history of "really existing socialism" but is too static to explain its further development.[10]

The present book is an attempt further to clarify the totalitarian phenomenon and to show that the notion of communist totalitarianism should be preserved and used to explain two historical processes: that of totalitarianization and the reverse process of detotalitarianization. Such usage of the term *totalitarianism* historicizes its content and avoids the error of seeing totalitarianism as a stable system, a viable alternative to liberal democracy, let alone a system capable of effective control over everything and therefore virtually immune from change. At the same time, it helps us distinguish and conceptualize different phases of the totalitarian movement: the phase of its revolutionary offensive, the establishment of a full-blown totalitarian state, the short period of its relative stabilization, and the long period of gradual detotalitarianization that paved the way for the final collapse of the system. Stalinism is, from this point of view, the closest approximation to the totalitarian model; the year 1956, in which communist mythology received a mortal blow, marks the beginning of a slow and convoluted, but nonetheless steady and continuous, retreat from the totalitarian ideal. It is therefore clear that this position differs from both the rival schools in American Sovietology. It differs from the totalitarian school because it rejects the view that totalitarianism survived in the countries of actually existing socialism until the Communist parties surrendered their political power.[11] But it differs also from the revisionist interpretations of communism *before* Stalin and *under* Stalin. In this respect I endorse Kolakowski's view that Stalinism was a logical (though not inevitable) and ideologically legitimate result of Leninism. Hence, I cannot accept Tucker's opinion that "a matter of decisive importance in the rise of Stalinism" was simply Stalin's personality, and that without this accidental factor "the post-Leninist development would have been definitely different."[12] I should be happy if it were so, but it is not. Stalinism, as Kolakowski put it, "is not an incidental evil which somehow superimposed itself on an otherwise benign vision."[13] The present book unfortunately provides additional arguments for relating Stalinism not only to Leninism, but also to the very essence of Marxist communism, as formulated in the utopian vision of the "leap to the kingdom of freedom."

Having said this, let us examine the main arguments for the thesis that Stalinism was in fact a radical departure from Leninism and Bolshevism as a whole. These arguments are worthy of serious examination because, as Cohen has correctly pointed out, the aprioristic assumption of an unbroken continuity between Leninism and Stalinism "has largely obscured the need for study of Stalinism as a distinct phenomenon with its own history, political dynamics, and social consequences." [14] This is quite true but does not undermine the validity of the continuity thesis as such. This thesis should not be interpreted as excluding the existence of discontinuities. Careful examination of these discontinuities is undoubtedly greatly needed for a better understanding of the specific features of Stalinism, its specific task, and its place in the history of Soviet communism.

Of course, I cannot deal here with all the authors who contributed to this important discussion. For the sake of convenience and clarity, I shall concentrate on three major scholars and two basic arguments (or rather, lines of argumentation). The first, advanced by Tucker and by Cohen, says that the Stalinist regime established itself through a "revolution from above," which allegedly could not be accepted by Lenin and amounted in fact to "a radical departure from Bolshevik programmatic thinking." [15] The second, put forward by Jerry F. Hough, stresses the lack of continuity between the two phases of Stalinism: the phase of revolutionary mobilization (the cultural revolution of 1928–31 and the Five Years' Plan) and the phase of the Great Retreat of the 1930s. Hough sees the second phase as representing mature Stalinism and concludes from this that Stalin's aim had not been the ideologically motivated radical transformation of man (which was the first distinguishing feature of totalitarianism); he was satisfied to institute "an ever-tightening and all-encompassing network of controls," but this was merely an authoritarian ambition free from genuinely totalitarian aspirations. [16] In this manner Hough wants to undermine not only the continuity thesis but also the validity of interpreting both Leninism and Stalinism in terms of the totalitarian model. [17] On his own interpretation Leninism was not totalitarian because, unlike full-blown Stalinism, it did not succeed in establishing a truly all-encompassing network of controls; Stalinism, on the other hand, was not totalitarian in a deeper sense, as a system that had, in fact, given up the totalitarian aims of its legitimizing revolutionary ideology. In addition, this analysis undermines the validity of the totalitarian model in general. Hough concedes that "the model's emphasis upon ideologically determined drive to transform society applies reasonably well to the first Five Years' Plan"; he also agrees that "the emphasis upon tightening of control fits well with the authoritarianism and ideological rigidity of the later Stalin years." He insists, however, that these two major aspects of the model are "an anachronistic combination" and, more important, that "they are essentially an inconsistent combination in human terms, for the type of person necessary to administer and carry through a continuous revolutionary transformation is too undisciplined and disrespectful to fit easily within—or be tolerated by—a system with rigid controls and an abhorrence of experimentation." [18]

We now turn to a critical examination of these views. Cohen's and

Tucker's version of the discontinuity thesis depends mostly on their inter-pretation of Leninism as allegedly culminating in the NEP and genuinely renouncing the possibility of a return to a revolutionary approach to the solution of the peasant question. "The transcending of the NEP," wrote Tucker, "was to take place within the framework of the NEP, by evolution, not revolution." Stalinism, however, at least in its time of self-assertion and triumph, represented "a revolutionary approach in exactly the sense that Lenin had defined it in warning against a revolutionary approach to the further building of Soviet socialism. . . . Instead of transcending the NEP evolutionarily, Stalinism abolished it revolutionarily, by decree and by force." In doing this Stalin consciously embraced the model of a state-building and modernizing Russian autocracy; hence his revolution from above should be understood "in terms of a reversion to a revolutionary pro-cess seen earlier in Russian history." No wonder, therefore, that the result of the Stalinist revolution "recapitulated in essentials its tsarist predecessor's pattern. The latter involved the binding (*zakreposhchenie*) of all classes of the population, from the lowest serf to the highest noble, in compul-sory service to the state." Similarly, the Stalinist revolution brought about a "neo-tsarist version of the compulsory-service state, an entity that may properly be called 'totalitarian.' "[19]

This conception, further developed and substantiated in Tucker's monu-mental *Stalin in Power*,[20] has a certain explanatory value and deserves to be treated as a contribution to a deeper understanding of the multiplicity of factors that influenced the complex phenomenon of the Stalinist state. But it must not be regarded as a refutation of the basic truth that Stalin was above all a revolutionary Marxist, a Bolshevik, and a faithful disciple of Lenin. It represents an interesting and legitimate point of view on Stalin as a state builder and autocratic modernizer, but it does not substantiate Tucker's and Cohen's defense of Leninism and of the pre-Stalinist Bolshe-vik tradition. It is simply not true that the Stalinist revolution from above was a radical departure from Bolshevism, that the idea of a terror-enforced collectivization of the peasantry never entered Lenin's mind,[21] that the "heart of Lenin's thinking" was the idea of achieving consensus through persuasion, and that this "politics of persuasion" had been the essence of Leninism since 1902 (i.e., since *What Is to Be Done?*)[22]

It is very embarrassing to read such statements. Obviously, some major American scholars went much too far in their attempts to defend Leninism from being equated with Stalinism. But just because of this their argu-mentation provides a useful stepping-stone for a brief discussion of the relationship between Leninism and Stalin's revolution from above. So let us try to deal with these arguments point by point.

The idea of "persuading people to change their minds"[23] has very little in common with the Leninist conception of introducing adequate consciousness into the workers' movement from without. To put it simply, genuine persuasion assumes free dialogue, while Lenin's conception laid the foundation for a program of organized and unscrupulous indoctrination: a program for liquidating the autonomy of the spontaneously created manifestations of the workers' movement by subjecting them to the tight organizational and ideological control of the party, or rather of its vanguard, and usurping unto itself the monopoly on truth. The difference between persuasion and ideological pressure from a position of alleged infallibility—a pressure, moreover, supported by the brutal suppression of deviation and dissent—should be evident.

This was certainly evident to Stalin, who was in this respect a faithful and remarkably consistent disciple of Lenin. From the very beginning of his political involvement, he had no doubt that only the vanguard could adequately represent socialist consciousness. He may even be credited with having anticipated—in order to substantiate Lenin's conception—the Lukácsian distinction between the empirical consciousness of the workers and their potential, adequate consciousness. As Stalin wrote in 1905: "The point is that owing to my *position* I can be a proletarian and not a bourgeois, but at the same time I can be unconscious of my position and, as a consequence, submit to bourgeois ideology."[24] Concerning Leninist "persuasion," as opposed to Stalinist "coercion and violence," we may happily turn to Lenin's own discussion of the issue. Lenin wrote:

We, of course, are not opposed to violence. We laugh at those who are opposed to the dictatorship of the proletariat, we laugh and say that they are fools who do not understand that there must be either the dictatorship of the proletariat or the dictatorship of the bourgeoisie. Those who think otherwise are either idiots, or are so politically ignorant that it would be a disgrace to allow them to come anywhere near a meeting, let alone on the platform. The only alternative is either violence against Liebknecht and Luxemburg, the murder of the best leaders of the workers, or the violent suppression of the exploiters; and whoever dreams of a middle course is our most harmful and dangerous enemy. That is how the matter stands at present. Hence, when we talk of utilizing the services of the experts we must bear in mind the lesson taught by Soviet policy during the past year. During that year we have broken and defeated the exploiters and we must now solve the problem of using the bourgeois specialists. Here, I repeat, violence alone will get us nowhere. Here, *in addition to violence, after successful violence*, we need the organization, discipline and moral weight of the victorious proletariat, which will subordinate all the bourgeois experts to its will and draw them into work.

Some people may say that Lenin is recommending moral persuasion instead of violence! But it is foolish to imagine that we can solve the problem of organizing a new science and technology for the development of communist society *by violence alone*. (L, CW, 29:71–72)

As we can see, Lenin advocated persuasion "in addition to violence" and "after successful violence." Stalin's position was exactly the same. He had learned from Lenin that violence should be supplemented by persuasion and persuasion be backed by the ever-present threat of a return to violence. Like Lenin, he was well aware that violence alone was not enough to secure the cooperation of bourgeois specialists, and also like Lenin, he became the chief critic of the party's baiting of experts. We may even say that he put *more* emphasis than Lenin on persuasion because Stalin wanted not only the cooperation of the old technical intelligentsia but also the positive reeducation (i.e., the successful indoctrination) of the old humanistic intelligentsia—historians, writers, artists, and so forth. It has also and rightly been noticed that he did much to create the conditions for persuading them more effectively: "The immediate improvement—not only in comparison with the period of cultural revolution, but *also in comparison with NEP*—was that the 'bourgeois' non-Party intellectuals were no longer subject to attack within their professions by organized Communist groups, or to harassment on grounds of social origin. In many fields, the old professional 'establishment' won back its previous authority." [25]

But what about the sweeping generalizations concerning the alleged incompatibility between Leninism and "the idea of construction of socialism as a revolution from above" through the "terror-enforced collectivization of the peasantry"? What about the categorical statement that before Stalin the idea of collectivization was completely alien to the Bolshevik party and that its implementation by Stalin was a radical departure from Bolshevism? [26] Nobody can deny that Stalin carried out collectivization as he did everything else, in the name of Leninism. He reminded the party that Lenin saw the peasantry as "the last capitalist class," that he regarded a peasant economy ("small commodity production") as "*engendering* capitalism and the bourgeoisie continuously, daily, hourly, spontaneously and on the mass scale," and that he therefore "called on the party to organize collective forms from the very first days of the October Revolution." Stalin quoted Lenin's words defining the NEP as merely a temporary retreat, made "in order to prepare for a longer leap forward," and stressed that "the policy of eliminating the Kulaks as a class could not have dropped from the skies." "It was prepared for by the whole preceding period of restricting and, hence, of squeezing out the capitalist elements in the rural districts" (that is to say, during the entire period of the NEP). Stalin was deliberately using Lenin's own words in referring to kulaks as "bloodsuckers, spiders, vampires." Above all, Stalin carefully explained the Leninist, and indeed the Marxist, rationale for collectivization. Small peasant farming, he reasoned, was a relic of the past, incompatible with both capitalism and socialism and doomed to extinction. It was a general economic law that small commodity production must be centralized and transformed into a large-scale production. This could be done in the capitalist way—that is, through the expropriation of the poor and middle farms and the creation instead of large capitalist enterprises in agriculture—or in the socialist way—that is, through "the amalgamation of the small peasant farms into large collective farms, technically and scientifically equipped" and through "squeezing out the capitalist elements from agriculture." The first solution, whatever its purely economic merits, was unacceptable for both ideological and practical reasons. The state of the proletarian dictatorship could not for long be based on two different foundations, "on the foundation of the most large-scale and concentrated socialist industry and on the foundation of the most scattered and backward, small-commodity peasant farming." [27] The urgent need to secure a regular food supply to the cities, especially in view of the grain crisis of 1928 and the ambitious aims of the first Five Years' Plan, made the second solution an imperative task for the party, one whose fulfillment could no longer be delayed. [28]

The theoretical part of this reasoning was based on firm Marxist foundations. In *Capital* Marx described small peasant farming as incompatible with the centralizing tendency of economic development and therefore doomed to extinction. Attempts to save it were for him reactionary efforts to perpetuate "universal mediocrity." The decentralized mode of production as such, he argued, must and would be annihilated by the action of "the immanent laws of capitalistic production." "Its annihilation, the transformation of the individualized and scattered means of production into socially concentrated ones, of the pigmy property of the many into the huge property of the few, the expropriation of the great mass of the people from the soil, from the means of subsistence, this fearful and painful expropriation of the mass of the people forms the prelude to the history of capital. The expropriation of the immediate producers was accomplished with merciless Vandalism, and under the stimulus of passions the most infamous, the most sordid, the pettiest, the most meanly odious." Nevertheless, it was a historical inevitability, a necessary stage in historical progress. In the long run it was not only necessary but also beneficial, as creating preconditions for the economic system based on "the possession in common of the land and of the means of production" (M, C, 1: 713–14, 714, 714, 715).

This theory, also elaborated by Engels, became obligatory dogma for all orthodox Marxists. To treat small producers as doomed to extinction without appeal and without mercy came to be seen as a distinctive feature of "scientific socialism," a proof of liberation from populist sentimentalism and bourgeois illusions. [29] The Erfurt Program of German Social Democracy confidently proclaimed that the days of small commodity production were numbered (see chapter 3, section 1). Russian Marxists fully shared this view, treating the merciless expropriation of the peasantry as a necessary price for capitalist development. Because of this their populist opponents routinely accused them of a readiness to sacrifice the peasantry on the altar of industrial progress, or even of betraying the popular masses in the interests of the rising bourgeoisie. These accusations were not entirely misplaced, because the hard-line Russian Marxists really believed that small farming had to disappear, no matter at what cost, and that populist attempts to counteract this natural process were reactionary and stupid.

Plainly, such habits of thought about the peasantry were bound to influence Bolshevik postrevolutionary policies. The fact that revisionist historians and Sovietologists have failed to take this into account reflects their deep skepticism about the importance of ideas as factors of historical change. They countered ideological explanations with empirical ones; some of them even claimed that the evolution of Soviet communism could be interpreted in terms of responses to situational and personal factors, without paying too much attention to the final goal of the movement.[30] I do not deny that such a change of focus may sometimes be commendable and useful, but I do not see any justification for a programmatic neglect of ideology in the study of thoroughly ideologized revolutionary movements. For the understanding of Bolshevism as a militant communist movement, communist ideology *is* of paramount importance. Nor should we forget that this ideology defined the peasants, and other small commodity producers, as relics of the past and the main obstacle on the way to the communist millennium. Lenin's wager on the alliance with the poor and middle peasantry should not obscure his deeply ingrained fear of the peasantry as an independent force, a "class for itself," free from proletarian hegemony, a fear expressed even in those of his articles that recommended the policies of the NEP. Here, for instance, is his description of the market-oriented peasants: "We know that the million tentacles of this petty-bourgeois octopus now and again encircle various sections of the workers, that instead of state monopoly, profiteering forces its way into every pore of our social and economic organism" (L, SW, 3:528).

There was, of course, a major difference between the Bolshevik attitude toward the peasantry before and after the Revolution. Once the Bolsheviks had become the ruling party, endowed with unlimited dictatorial powers, they could no longer rely on the spontaneous working of the "immanent laws of capitalistic production." If Russian capitalism had not finished its centralizing mission, this mission should be carried out to the end by the conscious activity of the proletarian dictatorship. But the proletarian party had to solve this task in its own, socialist way: through the expropriation not of the poor but of the rich peasants and through deliberately organizing agricultural production in large collective farms strictly controlled by the state.

This is the ideological genesis of the idea of collectivization. It is really absurd to attribute it to Stalin alone and to maintain that it never entered Lenin's mind. In reality it was from the very beginning a part of the ABC of Bolshevism. In Bukharin and Preobrazhenskii's *ABC of Communism* we read: "The Soviet Power may eventually be compelled to undertake a deliberately planned expropriation of the rich peasants. . . . The system of petty agriculture is in any case doomed. It must inevitably be replaced by a more advantageous and more productive system, by the system of large-scale cooperative agriculture."[31] It is true that under the NEP Lenin preferred to collectivize the peasants through voluntary cooperation, but the difference was in the method rather than in the aim, in tactics rather than in principle.[32] It is also true that the final decision belonged to Stalin, that the other Bolshevik leaders of that time were not prepared to launch a new revolution (even from above), and that even Evgeny Preobrazhenskii, whose conception of the "law of primitive socialist accumulation" (parallel to the "law of primitive capitalist accumulation") was so important in linking collectivization to the industrialization of the first Five Years' Plan, did not dare to propose such a quick and radical solution.[33] But this does not mean that Stalin had radically departed from Bolshevism, only that he alone among the Bolshevik leaders was unbending and vigorous enough to make practical use of the ideas of the left wing of the party and to initiate the long-awaited new socialist offensive. It cannot be denied that the declared aim of this offensive was a further approximation to the Leninist ideal of total control by the conscious vanguard, presupposing a forceful elimination of individual profiteering and the anarchy of the market. Hence, fanatical communists, as well as their fellow travelers, saw the results of the Stalinist revolution not as a sort of industrial feudalism based on new serfdom, but as a Promethean victory over blind forces and therefore a new long step toward the "kingdom of freedom."

Striking evidence of this is provided by the ideologists and leaders of the former Left opposition. Despite his deep personal hostility toward Stalin, Trotsky "seemed eager to associate himself with policies that most historians consider Stalinist, in particular the destruction of the kulaks."[34] In his *Revolution Betrayed* he wrote proudly of the Soviet regime's "gigantic achievements in industry" and "enormously promising beginnings in agriculture," trying to prove that a large part of the credit for these developments belonged to himself, that Stalin had for long been too cautious, "wholly imbued with the mood of spiteful disbelief in bold economic initiative,"[35] firmly allied with the Bukharinite right wing, and had even seriously considered the denationalization of the land.[36] Collectivization, from this perspective, seemed the right decision, though left until too late, implemented too hastily and clumsily, and ending unfortunately in a disorderly retreat.[37] Preobrazhenskii, the chief economic theorist of the Left, also severely criticized Stalin's initial leniency toward the kulaks and later endorsed collectivization as the only solution for the grain collection crisis. In essence, this solution consisted in doing away with the peasants' "freedom to choose the time and the terms at which to dispose of their surpluses."[38] In other words, the new enslavement of the peasantry was yet another victory over the chief enemy of communist freedom—the notorious "anarchy of the market."

Bukharin's case was, of course, different. He became indeed a consistent opponent of collectivization and supporter of the further extension of market relationships in agriculture. But just for that reason Trotsky saw him as the main danger, in comparison with which Stalin was the lesser evil.[39] The whole conduct of the left-wing opposition was governed by this principle: "With Stalin against Bukharin?—Yes. With Bukharin against Stalin?— Never!"[40] In his classic trilogy on Trotsky, Deutscher treated the Bukharin of that period as a neopopulist rather than a Bolshevik.[41] Although Bukharin would never have accepted this classification, there was some truth in it, because his support of the market directly contradicted the basic ideological commitment of communism. Trotsky had good reason to argue that the realization of Bukharin's program would result in "a 'connection' not between peasant economy and the socialist industries, but between the kulak and world capitalism." Every genuine Bolshevik would have agreed that "it was not worthwhile to make the October Revolution for that."[42]

This gives us the chance briefly to reflect on Cohen's thesis that Bukharinism might have provided a viable alternative to Stalinism.[43] I do not intend to question this thesis from the point of view of the alleged historical inevitability of Stalinism, neither do I wish to deny the possibility that the Bolshevik party could have evolved in such a way as to abandon its communist character. Given the intensity of its ideologization at that time, I see such an outcome as very unlikely, but I would gladly accept evidence to the contrary. I only insist that the victory of the Bukharinist line would have entailed a factual surrendering of some basic tenets of communism and would thus have resulted in a quick *decommunization* of the party. If so, our attitude toward Cohen's thesis will ultimately depend on terminological clarification. If we define Bolshevism very broadly and loosely as a party that (like, say, the German Social Democrats) happened to embrace the communist ideal for a time but could in principle discard it at any moment, then the very fact of Bukharin's prominent position within the party must be regarded as an important argument for Cohen's thesis. But if Bolshevism is treated as inseparable from Leninism, and the essence of the latter is seen in its passionate, militant communism (and this is certainly how it should be defined as a *current of thought*), then the eventual victory of the Bukharinist line would have to be regarded as involving a deep transformation of the Bolshevik identity, as a *departure* from Bolshevism and not its legitimate continuation. From such a perspective, a perspective characteristic of intellectual historians who *have* to treat ideas more seriously than other members of the historical profession, Stalin appears as a leader whose personal ruthlessness was closely allied to the ruthless logic of Leninist ideology and who therefore was best qualified to represent the Bolshevik cause and to ensure for it new victories.

We can now pass to the problems raised by Jerry Hough in connection with the stabilization of the Stalinist regime in the 1930s. His argumentation has been greatly influenced by the emigré Russian sociologist Nicholas S. Timasheff's work *The Great Retreat: The Growth and Decline of Communism in Russia*, published in 1946. Therefore, it is proper to begin with a brief presentation of the content of this rich and undeservedly forgotten book.

According to Timasheff, the Bolshevik revolution shared the fate of other social movements inspired by utopian ideals. The utopians, once in power, were always faced with a yawning discrepancy between their program and the objective needs of the nation, which even under dictatorship offered a passive resistance to their utopian blueprints. Hence they sometimes had to retreat in order to preserve their political power and continue to cultivate at least some parts of their utopian garden.[44] In the Bolshevik revolution this regularly took the form of a series of socialist offensives followed by periods of retreat. The first offensive was the period of revolutionary explosion and War Communism (1917–21). This was followed by the retreat of the NEP (1921–29), which ended in 1929 with the Second Socialist Offensive, the Stalinist "revolution from above" (1929–34). The periods of militancy resulted in a "conspicuous malfunctioning of society," while the period of the mitigation of communist rule brought very positive results. According to Timasheff, this was especially true of the Stalinist 'Great Retreat.' It gave the Russians the notion of "increasing crops, expanding herds, increasing population, progress in the output of heavy and light industry, advance in education, and recession of crime."[45] In return the regime received a measure of popular legitimacy that enabled it to survive the war and loosen its dependence on the dogmas of the utopian doctrine. Instead of the withering away of monetary exchange, law, and the state, it was the communist faith itself that began to wither away.[46] The author conceded that nothing precise could as yet be said about the degree of actual de-ideologization, but he was inclined to be optimistic in this matter. "Very probably," he wrote, "even within the inner circle, faith in the Doctrine has substantially declined. Perhaps there is no longer any faith, but merely stereotyped repetition of formulas which have been associated with the days of struggle and victory. In the beginning, the regime was of the type of an 'ideocracy'; today it is much more the exertion of power on the basis of a newly acquired legitimacy."[47]

This state of affairs augured well for the future. Timasheff thought it reasonable to expect that the Stalinist regime would restore "the system of free enterprise relating to small industrial and commercial units" and grant Soviet authors and artists genuine freedom of creation. Certainly, he did not expect a return to militant communism. He wanted to believe that the revolutionary cycle had been completed and was currently giving way to organic development. Being properly cautious, he formulated this view in a conjectural form: "It is, therefore, rather probable that the Russian Revolution will remain a four-phase process—in other words, that no Third Socialist Offensive will follow The Great Retreat."[48]

Timasheff was well aware that the new policy of concessions did not create any room for political liberty. Nevertheless, he saw these concessions as extremely important not only for the national welfare, but also, and primarily, for national freedom. Such a judgment on the Stalinist system sounds very unusual today, but it cannot be denied that Timasheff's argumentation is impressive and worthy of serious consideration.

In the economic sphere, Timasheff argued, the policy of concessions was started on March 26, 1932, when the Central Committee condemned the practice of collectivizing all the cows, pigs, sheep, and poultry.[49] Soon afterward the new Kolkhoz statute allowed the peasants to possess small individual allotments. This essentially changed the very meaning of collectivization: "In the framework of mitigated communism, a peasant was both a member of a collective (indirectly, State) enterprise, and an independent producer."[50]

The next step was the gradual abolition of the system of ration cards and a partial restoration of monetary exchange. Taking into account the original aims of communism, this was a complete retreat. The new system of distribution was "identical with that used in capitalist society, except for the fact that the shops were mainly State agencies." Some people gained, others lost by this move, but in general "everybody was pleased, because after the reform one of the basic freedoms was returned to the population—the liberty of consumption, or the ability to choose freely the way of spending one's income."[51]

The logical consequence of this reform was to encourage state enterprises to produce for profit, that is, to engage in "commodity production." Timasheff, with some exaggeration, called it "the commercialization of the Revolution."[52] Parallel to this was the encouragement of the spirit of competition among the workers. This was promoted under the patriotic banner of Stakhanovism but in fact was really inviting workers to work better and earn more. Consumerist attitudes were no longer condemned as expressions of counterrevolutionary petty bourgeois individualism. When a big meeting of prominent Stakhanovites took place in the Kremlin, Stalin did not try to persuade them (as Lenin did on the occasion of "communist subbotniks") that genuine communists should work "without expectation of reward, without reward as a condition" (L, CW, 30:517). On the contrary, he argued that there was nothing wrong in earning money to buy phonographs and records, nice dresses and silk stockings, or even a little house in the country. He told the audience that in Soviet society workers should be given the chance to enjoy life as they never could in bourgeois countries.[53]

This new system did not apply only to workers. Large differences in income were now approved as a socialist principle, and egalitarian attitudes characteristic of the period of "socialist offensives" came to be regarded as petty bourgeois. In the report to the Seventeenth Congress of the party, Stalin declared:

Every Leninist knows (that is, if he is a real Leninist) that equality in the sphere of requirements and individual life is a piece of reactionary petty-bourgeois absurdity worthy of a primitive sect of ascetics, but not of a socialist society organized on Marxian lines; for we cannot expect all people to have the same requirements and tastes, and all people to live their individual lives on the same model. . . . By equality Marxism means, not equalization of individual requirements and individual life, but the abolition of classes. . . . Marxism has never recognized, nor does it recognize, any other equality. To draw from this the conclusion that socialism calls for equalization, for the levelling of the requirements of the members of society, for the levelling of their tastes and of their individual lives—that according to the plans of the Marxists all should wear the same clothes and eat the same dishes in the same quantity—is to deal in vulgarities and to slander Marxism.[54]

This passage reveals a quite substantial difference between Stalin and Lenin, for whom the tradition of Babouvist radical egalitarianism was a precious part of the communist heritage. Many interpreters of Stalinism saw this break with egalitarianism as merely a crude attempt to justify the privileges of the higher echelons to the bureaucracy. One of the original features of Timasheff's interpretation is that he pointed out that Stalin's antiegalitarianism was designed above all to justify the difference of incomes among workers. But the main difference, of course, lay in a value judgment. Unlike the left-wing critics of Stalinism, Timasheff regarded Stalin's views on equality as breaking with the oppressive spirit of leveling down and therefore as enlarging the sphere of individual freedom, allowing individuals the free use of their capacities for the pursuit of their individual happiness.

Equally important from this point of view were the changes in the regime's attitude toward the family, the educational system, and the church. The period of socialist offensives was accompanied by cultural revolution, that is, aggressive and well-orchestrated attacks on all traditional values. The traditional family was treated as the mainstay of bourgeois egoism and a prison for women; marriages could be canceled by sending a postcard; the distinction between legitimate and illegitimate children, as well as the right of inheritance, was abolished; sexual promiscuity (despite Lenin's personal puritanism) was tolerated; and militant feminism made slow but steady progress.[55] The old educational system was deliberately destroyed: the authority of the teachers was constantly challenged and the methods and content of teaching were subject to arbitrary and risky experimentation; a decree of 1918 allowed all boys and girls over the age of sixteen to enroll in a university irrespective of their previous education; another decree was designed to dismantle the universities from within by abolishing academic degrees and removing professors from controlling positions on the university councils.[56] This struggle for control over education continued under the NEP. For instance, in 1922 the communist National Council of Science began to supply its own detailed programs of lectures to be delivered by professors, and students belonging to the party were instructed to check how far these lectures conformed to the prescribed programs.[57] As for religion, it was declared quite incompatible with socialist values and systematically persecuted, although with varying degrees of intensity.

The Stalinist Great Retreat brought conspicuous changes in all these areas. The family suddenly became the fundamental cell of Soviet society, marriage was treated as "the most serious affair in life," divorce was made much more difficult, and abortion was officially condemned.[58] School experiments were ended, and the prerevolutionary educational system was almost completely restored. Changes in attitudes toward religion came last, beginning in 1939 with directions to propagandists and teachers to acknowledge the contribution of the Orthodox church to the historical advancement of Russia. (Paradoxically, the carrying out of these directions was to be supervised by the Union of the Godless.) In 1940 Sunday was chosen as the official day of rest, and finally in September 1943, Stalin asked the church for moral support in the struggle against the Germans and in return allowed the election of a Patriarch.[59]

According to Timasheff, all these changes deserved to be regarded sui generis as a "return to normalcy." He saw them as symptoms of a weakening of ideological pressure and therefore as an increase in freedom. Equally optimistic was his evaluation of the new attitude toward national values. The abandonment of the national nihilism characteristic of the 1920s, the rehabilitation of the Russian past, the fact that Russian history, which "for many years had been taught only in terms of mass activity, reappeared as a sequence of magnificent deeds performed by Russia's national heroes" was for him "tantamount to a liberation from a foreign yoke." He concluded, somewhat hastily, that Russia had rediscovered her national identity, that "the disruptions in the national structure effected by the shock of the Communist Revolution have been, in the main, healed," that Russian history was once more *Russia's history*, and "not that of an anonymous body of international workers."[60]

It is rather odd to see such views expressed by an emigré Russian scholar. Today only the so-called national Bolsheviks could endorse them; noncom-

munist Russian patriots share Solzhenitsyn's view that Stalinism, together
with the entire Bolshevik tradition, was the imposition of an alien doctrine
incompatible with the Russian spirit and preventing Russians from feeling
at home in the Soviet state. But in the 1930s the perspective was different:
the very fact that it had become permissible to regard Soviet Russia as part
of Russian national history, to treat the Five Years' Plan as a great national
task, and to openly to admit the importance of patriotic motivation for its
fulfillment brought a feeling of tremendous relief to noncommunist Russians. Stalin was well aware how important it was to harness this feeling
and to use it to build the socialist state. He was eager to do so because
he himself saw no contradiction between the construction of socialism in
one country and the building of a patriotic state; he therefore was able to
make quite spirited appeals to Russian patriotism. At the First All-Union
Conference of Managers of Socialist Industry in 1931 he made the classic
connection between patriotism and speedy industrialization:

To slacken the tempo would mean falling behind. And those who fall behind get
beaten. But we do not want to be beaten. No, we refuse to be beaten! One feature of
the history of old Russia was the continual beating she suffered for falling behind,
for her backwardness. She was beaten by the Mongol Khans. She was beaten by the
Turkish beys. She was beaten by the Swedish feudal lords. She was beaten by the
Polish and Lithuanian gentry. She was beaten by the British and French capitalists.
She was beaten by the Japanese barons. All beat her—for her backwardness: for
military backwardness, for cultural backwardness, for political backwardness, for
industrial backwardness, for agricultural backwardness. She was beaten because
to do so was profitable and could be done with impunity. Do you remember the
words of the pre-revolutionary poet: "You are poor and abundant, mighty and impotent, Mother Russia"? These words of the old poet were well learned by those
gentlemen. They beat her, saying: "You are abundant," so one can enrich oneself
at your expense. They beat her, saying: "You are poor and impotent," so you can
be beaten and plundered with impunity. Such is the law of the exploiters—to beat
the backward and the weak. It is the jungle law of capitalism. You are backward,
you are weak—therefore you are wrong; hence, you can be beaten and enslaved.
You are mighty—therefore you are right; hence, we must be wary of you.

This is why we must no longer lag behind.

In the past we had no fatherland, nor could we have one. But now that we have
overthrown capitalism and power is in the hands of the working class, we have a
fatherland, and we will defend its independence. Do you want your socialist fatherland to be beaten and to lose its independence? If you do not want this you must
put an end to its backwardness in the shortest possible time and develop genuine Bolshevik tempo in building up its socialist system of economy. There is no
other way.[61]

This perfect manifesto of national planning struck a new note in the
history of Russian communism: for the first time, socialist planning was
openly employed for patriotic state building.[62] Under Lenin (especially

under War Communism) the obsession with control, accounting, and planning had nothing to do with the task of national modernization. Indeed, the ideological rationale for planning was its role in suppressing market forces and so realizing the communist ideal of a totally controlled economy, *irrespective* of productivity. Of course, these crude planning techniques could also be used to deal with the urgent tasks of distribution and redistribution. It was only under Stalin that socialist planning came to be regarded as a means of overcoming national backwardness.

It is clear that this new emphasis on national tasks necessitated a corresponding change in the highest law of the country: the Constitution of 1936 adopted with great ceremony the general principles of democracy. Communist sympathizers in the West welcomed this with excessive enthusiasm, quite failing to notice that the constitutional guarantees of all possible freedoms were in fact empty declarations creating a deceptive facade for a regime of terror. Some Russian emigrés, however, pointed out that even the hypocritical adoption of the principles of law-based democracy could have positive value for the future.[63] In this context, Stalinist "rehabilitation of law," following on the brutal suppression of Pashukanis's legal nihilism, had some positive significance, if not for the lawlessness then current, at least for the possibility of further evolution.

Timasheff himself did not express such a view. Indeed, although a theorist of law, he was strangely insensitive to these developments and did not pay them due attention. It may even be argued that he failed to analyze one of the most characteristic features of the Stalinist regime: the peculiar coexistence of extralegal coercion, culminating in the Great Terror, with the new emphasis on the security of law.[64] This was probably the result of a somewhat aprioristic assumption that in this respect the communist regime could not really have changed, either for the worse or for the better. His high opinion of the Great Retreat was based not on any illusions about democracy or the rule of law under communism but simply on the conviction that the communist faith was eroding and that communism was abandoning its utopian ambition to create a totally new man, a man culturally transfigured, liberated from all identities inherited from the past, incarnating a perfect conformity with the communist ideal.[65] In other words, in the Great Retreat Stalin's regime continued to subject people to extremely rigid, authoritarian controls but no longer forced them to change their nature, to abandon their genuine identities in order to realize the Orwellian idea of absolute and totally internalized conformity.

Hough accepted this analysis and concluded from it that mature Stalinism did not meet the requirements of the totalitarian model. It was extremely authoritarian but not totalitarian; its cultural conservation had little in common with the revolutionary aspirations attributed to totalitarianism.[66] Other contributors to *The Cultural Revolution in Russia* claimed in turn that Russian communism before the Great Retreat did not fit the totalitarian model either and that this was especially true of its periods of greatest revolutionary dynamism; it was then (allegedly) too deeply rooted in the spontaneity of the masses, too iconoclastic, and not likely to subject itself to a militaristic discipline of the totalitarian type.[67] In this way an attempt was made to show that the concept of totalitarianism was inapplicable to Soviet communism in all phases of its evolution.

Obviously, the denial of the totalitarian character of mature Stalinism depends heavily on Timasheff's argumentation. Hence, the supporters of the opposite thesis (i.e., all those who see Stalinism as the closest approximation to totalitarianism) should carefully examine this argumentation and precisely define its errors. To be effective, such criticism should not assume that Timasheff simply knew too little about Stalin's Russia and yielded to the temptation of wishful thinking. His perspective, though very one-sided, was yet helpful for a deeper understanding of the Stalinist phenomenon, and the developments highlighted were real and important. True, it is now evident that these developments did not represent a return to normalcy, but Timasheff rightly saw them as a departure from communist ideals. So it must be conceded that his book really did provide some serious arguments against Kolakowski's thesis that Stalinism was "*the* perfect embodiment of the spirit of Communism."[68] To assess the validity of these arguments we must disentangle them from Timasheff's preposterously overoptimistic general view of Stalinism. To do so, it will be useful to compare *The Great Retreat* with another contemporary book on Stalinism that deals with the same facts but illuminates them from a diametrically opposite ideological position, namely Trotsky's *Revolution Betrayed*.

According to Trotsky, Stalin's retreat of the 1930s represented the Thermidorian phase of the Russian Revolution. Stalin revealed himself "as the indubitable leader of the Thermidorian bureaucracy" and in this capacity "conquered the Bolshevik party."[69] It was necessary for the ruling stratum to prevent the discontent of the masses from finding coherent political expression through the party;[70] it was necessary to deprive the working class of its vanguard and to transform the Communist party into "the political organization of the bureaucracy."[71] But this betrayal of the Revolution did not mean the overthrow of the system; the latter had a great power of resistance, and the ruling stratum could not overthrow it at will.[72] Having subjected the party to its own officialdom, the ruling bureaucratic stratum created a *totalitarian* regime (Trotsky's expression)[73] standing halfway between capitalism and socialism.[74] Its socialist side was a planned economy based on the nationalization of the means of production; its capitalist side was the replacement of planned distribution (i.e., ration cards) by trade, accompanied by a conscious support of inequality.[75] Hence it was a transitional regime characterized by a deep contradiction between socialist norms of production and bourgeois norms of distribution.[76] As such, it could develop in either direction, depending on the relative strength of its social forces. It could slip back into capitalism, which would be to the advantage of its upper stratum, or it might give rise to a new proletarian revolution, which would overthrow bureaucratic totalitarianism and open the way to genuine socialism. Trotsky hoped, of course, that the achievements of the proletarian revolution would prove irreversible and that Soviet workers would not fail to save socialism from its temporary bureaucratic degeneration. "A socialist state," he wrote, "cannot peacefully merge with a world capitalist system. . . . If the bureaucracy was compelled in its struggle for a planned economy to dekulakize the Kulaks, the working class will be compelled in its struggle for socialism to debureaucratize the bureaucracy."[77]

As we can see, Trotsky quite agreed with Timasheff about the restorationist character of the Stalinist regime, while completely disagreeing with his value judgments. For Trotsky, the restoration of trade meant not freedom of consumption, but a strengthening of the main enemy of communist freedom: the enslaving power of money and the blind irrationality of market forces. He accused the Stalinist bureaucracy of becoming "the carrier of the most extreme, sometimes unbridled, economic individualism" while at the same time "ruthlessly suppressing the progressive side of individualism in the realm of spiritual culture." He indignantly condemned "the triumphal rehabilitation of family, taking place simultaneously with the rehabilitation of the ruble,"[78] and he warned that this would lead to a gradual rehabilitation of religion as well.[79] The return to home dining was in his view a shameful betrayal of the communist commitment to liberate women through the destruction of the so-called family hearth.[80] He was most dissatisfied with the concessions to collective farms, because he believed that allowing peasants to have their own cows and gardens was socially wasteful ("a terrible robbery of human power") and enslaving, since it imposed on farm families "the burden of medieval digging in manure."[81] He was horrified by the sharp increase in material inequalities, by the restoration of the old hierarchies and caste privileges, as symbolized by ranks and uniforms as well as by the pursuit of such items of conspicuous consumption as fur coats, bathrooms, and (above all) cars.[82] He was utterly scandalized that houses built for Soviet dignitaries often had rooms for "houseworkers" (i.e., domestic servants). The regime's tolerance of the acquisitive spirit and consumerist attitudes was for him not a "return to normal," but a symptom of the degeneration of the ruling stratum, aggravated by the fact that many of its members chose to marry ladies of aristocratic or bourgeois background. He was no less severe toward the individualistic and acquisitive spirit among the workers, especially as represented by the Stakhanovite movement. Socialism, he explained, was not ascetic, but it still could not accommodate too much concern with individual prosperity: "Human prosperity begins for socialism not with the concern for a prosperous life, but on the contrary with the cessation of this concern."[83] For this reason, even a partial restoration of market relations posed a mortal threat to socialist values.

Somewhat paradoxically, Trotsky seemed to have been more aware than Timasheff of the completely repressive character of the Stalinist state. The latter saw its denial of personal freedom and self-government as comparable to conditions in the Russian Empire at the end of the eighteenth century.[84] Trotsky was much more exact in describing the Stalinist state as "a hitherto unheard of apparatus of compulsion."[85] He defined it as totalitarian and stressed its similarity to fascist states in its demand for unconditional obedience and absolute personal loyalty to the leader.[86] But he also stressed its uniqueness, pointing out that "in no other regime has a bureaucracy ever achieved such a degree of independence from the dominating class." He explained this by an ingenious reinterpretation of the Leninist idea of a "bourgeois state without bourgeoisie."[87] Such a state was to be an organ of the proletarian dictatorship, which meant that in its relations with the workers it was to be only a "semi-state" whose state functions properly so called were expected gradually to wither away. In reality, however, the Soviet state did not fulfill this expectation. On the contrary, its functionaries developed into a privileged stratum that had no social support for its authority and therefore could rely only on the apparatus of state compulsion. To support the bourgeois norms of distribution fitted in with its egoistic interests but contradicted the socialist principles of the Revolution. Hence, these people developed bad consciences and a truly bourgeois fear of the masses.[88] At the same time, they owed their very existence to the nationalization of the means of production and therefore were unable, at least for a time, to constitute themselves into a genuine social class firmly rooted in the social structure and relatively unafraid of the future. Because of this the Stalin regime developed into "a Bonapartism of a new type"—a regime "rising above a politically atomized society, resting upon a police and officers' corps, and allowing of no control whatever."[89]

The Constitution of 1936 was an important step toward strengthening the bourgeois side of the regime. While protecting by law the peasant's hut and cow, it also legalized the town house, summer house, and car of the bureaucrat.[90] By enshrining the principle of the "universal, equal and direct" vote of an atomized population it liquidated *eo ipso* the juridical foundation of the dictatorship of the proletariat.[91] It was, in fact, "an immense step back from socialist to bourgeois principles" and at the same time a reinforcement in law of "the absolutism of an 'extra-class' bureaucracy." Its multiple concession to the bourgeois principle of private property created "the political premises for the birth of a new possessing class."[92]

Trotsky's analysis of Stalin's "betrayal of the Revolution" is in entire agreement with Timasheff's view of mature Stalinism as the Great Retreat, but Trotsky also presents convincing arguments against treating Stalinism as a form of traditional authoritarianism rather than totalitarianism. For this reason Trotsky should be regarded as one of the pioneers of a totalitarian interpretation of the Stalinist regime. He deserves credit for being able to rise above a narrowly conceived class analysis and to see that "Stalinism and fascism, in spite of a deep difference in social foundations, are symmetrical phenomena."[93]

The unmistakably and *extremely* totalitarian character of the Stalinist dictatorship is convincingly demonstrated in Trotsky's description of Stalinist aspirations to exercise full control in the sphere of thought and artistic creativity. He does not deny that the imposition of "severe limitations upon all forms of activity, including spiritual creation" was a practice legitimized by Lenin's conception of proletarian dictatorship but argues that before Stalin the Bolshevik leaders were extremely cautious in such matters and never pretended to the role of commanders in the spheres of science, literature, and art. It was (Trotsky holds) only under Stalin that the ruling stratum began to consider itself called "not only to control spiritual creation politically, but also to prescribe its roads of development."[94] Trotsky presents the results of this far more clearly and exactly than Timasheff. The importance of this aspect of Stalinist totalitarianism—as distinct from mere authoritarianism and more oppressive than fascism—warrants a long quotation:

The method of command-without-appeal extends in like measure to the concentration camps, to scientific agriculture and to music. The central organ of the party prints anonymous directive editorials, having the character of military orders, in architecture, literature, dramatic art, the ballet, to say nothing of philosophy, natural science and history. . . .

Taught by bitter experience, the natural scientists, mathematicians, philologists, military theoreticians, avoid all broad generalizations out of fear lest some "red professor," usually an ignorant careerist, threateningly pull up on them with some quotation dragged in by the hair from Lenin, or even from Stalin. To defend one's own thought in such circumstances, or one's scientific dignity, means in all probability to bring down repressions upon one's head.

But it is infinitely worse in the sphere of the social sciences. Economists, historians, even statisticians, to say nothing of journalists, are concerned above all things not to fall, even obliquely, into contradiction with the momentary zigzag of the official course. About Soviet economy, or domestic or foreign policy, one cannot write at all except after covering his rear and flanks with banalities from the speeches of the "leader," and having assumed in advance the task of demonstrating that everything is going exactly as it should go and even better. Although this 100 percent conformism frees one from everyday unpleasantness, it entails the heaviest of punishments: sterility.

In spite of the fact that Marxism is formally a state doctrine in the Soviet Union, there has not appeared during the last twelve years [i.e., since 1924] one Marxian investigation—in economics, sociology, history, or philosophy—which deserves attention and translation into foreign languages. The Marxian works do not transcend the limit of scholastic compilations which say over the same old ideas, endorsed in advance, and shuffle over the same old quotations according to the demands of the current administration conjuncture. Millions of copies are distributed through the state channels of books and brochures that are of no use to anybody, put together with the help of mucilage, flattery and other sticky substance. Marxists who might say something valuable and independent are sitting in prison, or forced into silence. . . . Facts are distorted, documents concealed or fabricated, reputations created or destroyed. A simple comparison of the successive variants of one and the same book during the last twelve years permits us to trace infallibly the process of degeneration of the thought and conscience of the ruling stratum.

No less ruinous is the effect of the "totalitarian" regime upon artistic literature. The struggle of tendencies and schools has been replaced by interpretation of the will of the leaders. There has been created for all groups a general compulsory organization, a kind of concentration camp of artistic literature. . . .

The life of Soviet art is a kind of martyrology. After the editorial orders in *Pravda* against "formalism," there began an epidemic of humiliating recantations by writers, artists, stage directors and even opera singers. . . . The impressions made by the new opera upon high-up auditors are immediately converted into a musical directive for composers. The Secretary of the Communist Youth said at a conference of writers: "The suggestions of Comrade Stalin are a law for everybody," and the whole audience applauded, although some doubtless burned with shame. As though to complete the mockery of literature, Stalin, who does not know how to compose a Russian phrase correctly, is declared a classic in the matter of style. There is something deeply tragic in this Byzantinism and police rule, notwithstanding the involuntary comedy of certain of its manifestations.[95]

This long quotation is in fact economical as not just the best but also the most *concise* presentation of the subject. It powerfully demonstrates that attempts to question the totalitarian character of Stalinism on the basis of its alleged similarity to "more traditional types of authoritarian regime"[96] are not only misguided but also reveal a strange insensitivity to the fundamentals of human freedom. In addition, the fact that the quotation refers to the early period of Stalin's rule ("the last twelve years") helps to dissipate many misconceptions about the late 1920s and especially the years of the "revolution from above," which are presented by some scholars as a time of spontaneous and creative cultural revolution.

We may now draw some preliminary conclusions. Timasheff represented the restorationist tendency of the Stalinist regime as bringing about an increase of freedom. Trotsky represented it as part of the consolidation of the totalitarian state. These interpretations are not, however, absolutely mutually exclusive.

For all who wanted to preserve their noncommunist identities—that is for the overwhelming majority of the Soviet population—the cessation, or weakening, of the communist offensive against family, national consciousness, market distribution, and personal property was indeed an increase of freedom, although only in this particular respect. Timasheff (for whom the culmination of communist tyranny was obviously the period of War Communism) was right to point this out, although wrong to see it as a symptom of a general mitigation of communism. He completely overlooked, or grossly underestimated, two other aspects of the Stalinist regime: the unmitigated terror and equally exhaustive efforts to ensure the effective indoctrination of the entire population. He was therefore totally wrong to see Stalinism as a virtually deideologized system that allowed increasing freedom from ideological oppression. His notion of the Great Retreat revolved exclusively around the restorationist side of Stalinism and obscured the fact that in other respects the Stalinist regime was militantly ideological and aggressively offensive.

Despite all differences, almost the same can be said of Trotsky's notion of the "Revolution betrayed." Unlike Timasheff, he was clearly aware of the militantly totalitarian character of Stalinism, but nonetheless he also chose to concentrate on its restorationist tendencies. This was because he wanted to explain the Stalinist horrors as ultimately deriving from the betrayal of the Revolution and thus as unrelated to genuine Bolshevism.

Both books—*The Great Retreat* and *The Revolution Betrayed*—therefore supply arguments against the continuity thesis in interpreting the historical fate of Russian communism, or communism in general. But the continuity thesis, as I understand it, does not exclude discontinuities, sharp policy changes, bloody conflicts, or the possibilities of alternative developments. It is not just a simple theory of a straight line between Bolshevism and Stalinism, or between Marxism and communist totalitarianism.[97] If such a theory was indeed inherent in the totalitarian model, the revisionist Sovietologists would have had a very easy task. Trotsky's indignant reminder of "a whole river of blood" that divided Stalin from his Bolshevik past has a purely emotional value; it cannot explain away the fact that Trotsky himself did all he could to put unrelenting struggle above morality and to legitimize unrestrained terror. Robert Conquest, Arthur Koestler, and Leszek Kolakowski knew more than enough about this "river of blood," but none of them regarded it as a valid argument against the existence of a destructive inner logic connecting Stalin's Bolshevism with the Bolshevism of his victims; on the contrary, they saw it as a paradoxical and tragic, but *not unpredictable*, consequence of Bolshevism as an ideological and moral phenomenon. This shows that they conceived the question of continuity in a dialectical manner, which ruled out reducing it to a search for straight lines.

A more detailed discussion of different variants of the continuity thesis does not fall within the scope of this book. As mentioned above, my own way of accepting this thesis, as well as my partial endorsement of the totalitarian model, does not involve a belief that ideas have *inevitable* consequences or that only one interpretation of a given set of ideas is historically possible. Nevertheless, I support the view that ideas *do* have consequences, that great historical movements need ideological legitimization, and therefore that their historical fates depend to a certain extent on their ideology. This is especially true of movements that define their goals in terms of secular salvation, of which the most striking, at least in our century, has certainly been Russian communism.

As I tried to demonstrate, the existence of a close, meaningful relationship between Marxist communism and Lenin's revolutionary totalitarianism cannot, and should not, be denied. This does not mean that Marxism inevitably passed into Leninism; as Kautsky's example clearly shows, the mainstream Marxism of the Second International developed in the opposite direction. But the point is that this development involved, first, the conscious abandonment of Marxist communism and, at a later stage, the abandonment of Marxist theory in general. Hence it is arguable that only Leninism, supported by the enormous authority of the Bolshevik revolution, prolonged and greatly intensified the life of the Marxist utopia. It can also be said that without Lenin as unquestioned leader of the Revolution, the Marxist claim to a monopoly of truth, as well as the Engelsian ambition to transform Marxism into an all-embracing, quasi-scientific view of the world, would have shared the fate of the Marxist utopia of a totally controlled, marketless economy.

There was no straight line between Marxism and Marxism-Leninism for the simple reason that Leninism emerged as a specific solution to the "organizational problem" to which Marx and Engels had paid very little attention. Furthermore, as I have emphasized, Lenin's conception of the vanguard party—a conception solving the organizational problem in a truly totalitarian manner—had no antecedents in Marx and Engels's views. The same holds true of Lenin's totalitarian reinterpretation of the Marxian dictatorship of the proletariat. Nevertheless, it is obvious that Leninism would have been impossible without an arrogant self-confidence based on an unshakable belief in its absolute historical legitimacy—a belief grounded in the ideological and scientific authority of Marxism. "Scientific socialism," with its contemptuous dismissal of all bourgeois authorities in social science, created a firm foundation for Leninist confidence in the virtual infallibility and magic omnipotence of "the only correct theory."

Especially striking is the close (although not immediately visible) connection between the Leninist advocacy of tight, repressive control over everything spontaneous—both in the workers' movement and in society at large—and the Marxian ideal of freedom as conscious, rational control over economic and social forces. The identification of true liberation with total control deserves to be regarded as the philosophical cornerstone of the Leninist edifice of oppression. The specifically communist side of this peculiar vision of human liberation was Lenin's fanatical commitment to the Marxist utopia abolishing forever the "blind forces" of the market. The NEP did not signify a weakening of this commitment; it was merely a tactical retreat made with a bad conscience in order to resume the communist offensive as soon as possible. In a sense the entire history of the Bolshevik party resolves itself into a series of desperate efforts to achieve full control: political control through the seizure of power and elimination of all real, possible, and imagined opponents, and then economic control through meticulous accounting and planning, extending even to the sphere of personal consumption. In order to mobilize itself for these tasks, the party had to legitimize in advance all sorts of extralegal coercion and naked violence. The Marxist view of law as merely a weapon in the class struggle, the Marxist unmasking of the "fraudulent bourgeois democracy," the Marxist view of human rights as merely the safeguards of bourgeois egoism, and finally and significantly, the Marxist conviction that historical necessity must pave the way regardless of human costs, gave plausibility to the claim that such legitimization of violence had already been provided by the founders of Marxism.

In this way the theory and practice of Leninism prepared and justified the theory and practice of Stalinism. This is true of almost all Stalinist practices, including that of treating dissenters within the party as "outright traitors" ("objective" traitors) and of using "deliberate slander" against them with the aim not to convince them but to destroy them and wipe their faction off the face of the earth (see chapter 4, section 4). Of course, Stalinist totalitarian practices were much wider in scope and even more ruthless than was possible under Lenin. This book, however, deals not with practices but with ideas, and in this respect Stalin was merely Lenin's faithful disciple.[98] Stalin identified himself completely with Lenin and always justified his actions by invoking Lenin's authority. He wanted to be a "man of steel," more resolute in crushing enemies than Lenin himself, but since Stalin was at the helm, he seldom dared call things by their true names, preferring instead sanctimoniousness, hypocrisy, and mendacity. Lenin, like Hitler, was as a rule much more frank about his real intentions.[99] He proudly laid the foundations for totalitarian practices without caring about the opinion of the world or bourgeois respectability. His writings therefore provide a frank and solid ideological justification for communist totalitarianism.

Nevertheless, the relation between Leninism and Stalinism was more complex than simple continuity suggests. There *was* a continuity, a very essential one, but with a difference. Timasheff and Trotsky were not wrong to point out the existence of some restorationist (or quasi-restorationist) tendencies in the Stalinist regime after 1934. These were, however, bound up with the introduction of the principle of absolute personal loyalty (*Führerprinzip*, as the Nazis called it) and with an unprecedented intensification of ideological propaganda. We may therefore say that Stalinist totalitarianism moved toward right-wing totalitarianism at the expense of its specifically communist objectives. However, Stalin did not intend and could not really afford to repudiate the communist utopia entirely, even if its realization made his task more difficult and demanding. He did not intend to get rid of the utopian ideal, because he wanted to go down in history as the savior of the Russian Revolution and the greatest hero of the international working class. He could not afford to abandon this idea because he was acutely aware that his absolute power had no other legitimization than Marxism-Leninism and the communist cause.

To conceptualize all these differences it is useful to distinguish between (1) the totalitarian potential of certain ideas, (2) the totalitarian character of an organized revolutionary movement, and (3) the totalitarian character of a state. Several of Marx and Engels's crucial ideas, in fact their entire conception of human liberation as well as their "scientific socialism," come under the first rubric. Leninism, which was formed as a current of revolutionary movement, is the best exemplification of the second, while Stalinism, formed in the process of state building, represents the third.[100] Hence Stalin did not betray his task when he traduced and murdered the entire old guard of the Bolshevik party. He saw them as a potential source of revolutionary ferment in his state and dealt with them in accordance with totalitarian logic.

It is important therefore to see Leninism and Stalinism as two forms and two stages of communist totalitarianism. Lenin, who remained to the end a communist revolutionary, subordinated everything to the ultimate goals of communism. Since his methods were unabashedly totalitarian, fully realizing the totalitarian potential of Marxist communism and adding to it the totalitarian zeal of older Babouvist origin, he deserves to be regarded as representing "totalitarian communism." Stalin, who decided to concentrate on the construction of socialism in a single country and so became a state builder, had to change his priorities. For him the maintenance and strengthening of totalitarian controls in the state actually became more important than the communist ideals. Leninism remained the sole legitimization of his rule but with a notable shift in emphasis: totalitarian power came to be the first concern, while communist ideology was reduced in practice to the role of an obedient instrument of this power. Goals and means changed places; totalitarian *communism* became transformed into communist *totalitarianism*—that is, totalitarianism using communist ideas as *a means* of its own justification.

5.2   Stalinist Marxism as a Total View of the World

Unlike Bukharin and Trotsky, Stalin was not a talented Marxist theorist. He himself was dimly aware of this lack and because of this longed for recognition in the theoretical field.[101] At the height of his power he achieved this ambition in excess, being hailed as the greatest genius of humanity and therefore the supreme authority in all spheres of knowledge. Millions of people, not only in the Soviet Union and not only Communist party members, blindly believed in his unique, unequalled knowledge of the laws of history and saw this (alleged) knowledge as justifying his absolute power at home as well as his claims to the position of undisputed authority for progressive forces everywhere in the world. He was described as "the great engine-driver of history's locomotive,"[102] as understanding the laws of historical necessity and confidently leading humanity to the kingdom of freedom: "He who knows the laws of social development may foresee the future and possesses the best possible tool for the transformation of the world."[103]

When this collective hypnosis passed away, Stalinist Marxism came to be generally seen as unworthy of serious examination. This was a perfectly understandable but not very rational reaction. It is not enough to dismiss the past; it is necessary also to understand it. Stalinist Marxism deserves close attention as the most widespread and successful form of mass indoctrination, as the most powerful and effective means of establishing control over people's minds and feelings, and consequently as a masterly achievement in transforming Marxism into the official ideology of a consistently totalitarian state. Failure to reflect more deeply on these functions of Stalinist Marxism has resulted in many false conclusions about both totalitarianism and Marxism. Stalinist totalitarianism was reduced to a system of institutionalized violence, although in fact the Stalinist regime never relied on force alone.[104] This neglect of the ideological side of communist totalitarianism naturally helped those historians and political scientists who wanted to sever all connections between Marxist theory and totalitarian practice.

An instructive illustration of the emerging confusion was the intellectual fascination with Antonio Gramsci that characterized the revisionist Marxists of the early post-Stalinist period. Gramsci's views on intellectual and cultural hegemony as a precondition of genuine political victory were interpreted as representing a democratic and humanist tendency in Marxism that was consciously opposed to the Leninist conception of the proletarian dictatorship (as "based directly upon force") and of course to Stalin's uninhibited use of terror and violence. This idealization of the Italian thinker found expression even in Kolakowski's *Main Currents of*

Marxism, in which he endorsed the widespread view that the Gramscian vision of "cultural hegemony achieved by purely ideological means" was incompatible with ultimate reliance on force.[105] Gramsci's conception of collective historical praxis was, for Kolakowski, at the opposite extreme to Lenin's conception of the vanguard party and of bringing consciousness from without into the workers' movement. Kolakowski even credited Gramsci with the conscious rejection of the idea of "scientific socialism."[106] In conclusion he suggested that Gramsci "provided the ideological nucleus of an alternative form of communism, which, however, has never existed as a political movement, still less as an actual regime."[107]

I do not intend to deny the multiple merits of Gramscian Marxism. The philosophical foundations of his theory of praxis, which differed greatly from the crude Engelsian Marxism of Lenin and Stalin, are discussed elsewhere in this book (see chapter 2, section 1). I should only like to point out, first, that Gramsci's interpretation of Marxism was not as innocent as the revisionist Marxists wanted it to be and, second, that his stress on intellectual and cultural hegemony should not be regarded as incompatible with Leninism and Stalinism. The need to achieve such hegemony, that is to establish effective control from within over intellectual life and culture, was neither disregarded nor neglected by the Bolshevik leaders and because of this their conception of the dictatorship of the proletariat deserves to be seen as truly totalitarian. This is especially true of Stalin, for whom control over thought, through the wholesale indoctrination and consequent cultural transformation of society, became at least as important as the system of external controls.[108] Of course Gramsci's conception of cultural hegemony was much more articulated than its crude Stalinist equivalent. But this is a good argument for using its conceptual apparatus for a better understanding of those aspects of Stalinist totalitarianism that consisted in systematic ideological persuasion and not merely physical intimidation.

Gramscian Marxism has been described as a form of millenarian gnosticism, that is, an absolutely certain, salvationist knowledge of good and evil.[109] Its aim was to establish a perfect social order—perfect, that is, in the sense of excluding egoism, particularistic pluralism, and lack of unanimity. Gramsci's vision of this ultimate earthly salvation combined the Promethean ideal of conscious control over the collective fate of humanity with nostalgia for premodern communal relationships (Tönnies's *Gemeinschaft*, as opposed to the pluralist "open society" based on a market economy).

The idea of replacing market mechanisms by conscious direction raised the question of who was to do the directing. In answering this question Gramsci did not deviate from Lenin: the leading role in the new society was to be taken by the Communist party, the "Modern Prince," endowed with indivisible and unlimited power. To ensure for itself the position of ideological and cultural hegemony, the party should become a "collective intellectual" able to influence the traditional, autonomous intellectuals and at the same time educate its own "organic intellectuals," who were wholly devoted to its cause. The task of the latter would be to penetrate the masses and endow them with an all-embracing worldview, a sort of popular religion ensuring ideological unanimity and indicating directions of collective praxis. In this way, as Gramsci said, "the Prince takes the place, in people's consciousness, of the divinity or the categorical imperative." [110] The masses would become ideologically subordinated to the disciplined sophocratic rule of party intellectuals initiated into the Marxist gnosis and exercising a spiritual power (the Saint-Simonian and Comtean *"pouvoir spirituel"*) over the rest of the population.[111] This would enable the party to exercise its power in the form of a *pedagogical* dictatorship, relying on organized persuasion and thereby minimizing the need to resort to violence. This dictatorship would be based on the conquest of souls, not merely on the coercive apparatus of the state.

Gramsci's insistence that the attainment of cultural hegemony should precede the seizure of political power was of course deeply alien to Leninism and Stalinism. Similar ideas had been propagated within the Bolshevik party by Bogdanov, but he had been quickly and firmly condemned by Lenin (see chapter 4, section 5). Nevertheless, Gramsci's emphasis on persuasion and unanimity had nothing to do with pluralist democracy; rather, it was an attempt to promote a consensus-seeking form of totalitarianism. It should be noted that Gramsci himself used the term *totalitarianism* in a positive sense, making a distinction between the reactionary and progressive varieties.[112] In his view, the virtue of progressive totalitarianism was that it restored wholeness to the political universe and meaning to history. One may properly say, therefore, that he saw totalitarianism as "the specific form that religion has assumed in the era of secularization." [113] He conceived of communist totalitarianism not as a police state but as an essentially *ideocratic* power. He expected the masses voluntarily to submit to the rule of the "Modern Prince," being rewarded for this by the comforts of moral unanimity and confidence in the future. The party elite was to enjoy not only the prestige of power but also the glory of a salvationist mission. But the price for this was acceptance of Leninist "iron discipline," a total submission to the legitimating doctrine, and consequently the total politicization of culture.

It is obvious that this idea was in fact very close to the hearts of the Bolshevik leaders. Neither Lenin nor Stalin wanted their dictatorship to rely only on naked force; both justified it in ideological terms and did everything to promote consensus based on common commitment to the ideology. For historical reasons Stalin put even more emphasis on this task than Lenin. This was because as a totalitarian state builder he needed to persuade the entire population, not just the workers' movement (which had lost the last vestiges of its autonomy) or the party (which had been crushed as a political body distinct from the apparatus of the state). It was therefore natural that under his rule an unprecedented intensification of terror was combined with an equally unprecedented indoctrination crusade, all done in the name of creating a new man and a new culture.[114]

For all these reasons the Gramscian theory of the Modern Prince, which exercised power through the organized, systematic conquest of people's consciences, minds, and culture, should not be treated as offering a genuinely democratic alternative to Stalinism. On the contrary, "it is legitimate to argue that there is no significant break in continuity between the Gramscian alternative and the Stalinist and neo-Stalinist praxis."[115] This is because Stalinism aimed at establishing a totalitarian ideocracy, and Gramsci's theories were nothing less than a sophisticated explanation and justification of this newest and most consistent form of an absolute monopoly on power.

Within this common denominator there were, of course, differences, both theoretical and political, that were more or less relevant to the problem of freedom. Two were especially important and deserve to be mentioned in the present context. First, the Stalinist ideocratic dictatorship was exercised in the name of science—the "only correct" and "most advanced" scientific theory of Marxism-Leninism. We may agree with Gramsci that this science was in reality a sort of "popular religion" or a Sorelian myth; nevertheless, it was a myth claiming to represent the authority of objective science and so not subject to different interpretations or tolerant of any deviation from the "correct, truly scientific standpoint." The Gramscian antiscientific conception of knowledge as a product and instrument of historical praxis was in harmony with the antinaturalist revolt in philosophy and with the activist anti-Engelsian currents within Marxism (see chapter 2, section 1). Hence it was philosophically superior to the crudities of old-fashioned "scientific socialism." In a sense, it was also a better philosophical justification of ideocracy: after all, it helped to dismiss empirical evidence, deliberately undermined common sense, blurred the distinction between science and ideology, and thereby paved the way for unrestrained ideological manipulation. On the other hand, however, it contained an element of historical relativism that could be used to legitimate doubts. It is no wonder, therefore, that the Stalinist regime preferred to rely on the tested authority and certainty of "science." If the Gramscian theories had been known to its ideologists, they would have been treated as a variety of Bogdanovism and dealt with in the Leninist manner. Stalinism could not abandon its grotesquely pseudoscientific pretenses. It had to legitimize itself "scientifically," to justify its claims to total control by invoking at every step the authority of an all-embracing, "truly scientific" theory containing ready-made and absolutely valid answers to all possible problems.

Second, the Stalinist regime could not allow any weakening of the apparatus of external coercion. Indeed, it had to strengthen this control as much as possible. Stalin's was a mobilization regime using the methods of ideological campaigns together with the methods of naked violence, organizing collective enthusiasm (sometimes genuine, sometimes half real, half faked) but always ready to crush the faintest resistance by the most violent means of extralegal coercion. It preferred voluntary submission but was not satisfied with a half-hearted, resigned subordination; it demanded active support and obtained this by a combination of ideological pressure and physical intimidation. Its ideocratic side was not meant to develop into a merely pedagogical dictatorship or to eliminate in the foreseeable future the need for a monstrously developed apparatus of coercion; the latter was to remain in force until the final victory of socialism on a global scale. In other words, ideological domination was conceived by Stalin not as an alternative to violence but as its necessary legitimation and justification. Such domination was to serve not only as a means of enforcing "the political and moral unity of society," but also as a means of strengthening the apparatus of coercion by endowing it with a feeling of absolute self-confidence and ideological self-righteousness unknown to police forces in ordinary authoritarian states.

A telling Soviet testimony about a typical official of the People's Commissariat for Internal Affairs (NKVD) illustrates this point:

What would a Pryrogov say if he were required to defend himself in a court of law? He would not, we believe, refer to superior orders, but to the teachings of Marxism and Leninism, as he understood them. Pryrogov was as loyal and obedient as an SS man. But his faith was founded on a conviction that it fully accorded with the demands of reason and conscience. He was fully convinced that his was no blind faith but was founded on science and logic. He was brutal because the general line required him to be brutal. The general line, so long as it accorded with the fundamental principles of Marxism, was everything to him. Without the allegedly "scientific" foundation of the general line, which was the backbone of his faith, all the instructions of the party authorities would have lost their significance for him. He was convinced of the logical and ethical correctness of his Marxist principles, and on this conviction his faith depended.[116]

Stalinist Marxism was perfectly adapted to satisfy the needs of such a faith, as well as the need of believing in its "scientific" foundation. It was a distinctly nonelitist Marxism, a Marxism for the masses. Its peculiar combination of blind faith with quasi-scientism can be explained in the light of Gramsci's views on the "philosophy of praxis" adapted to the mentality of the popular masses. "In the masses *as such*," wrote Gramsci, "philosophy can only be experienced as a faith."[117] This is normal, because human conduct in general is determined not by reason but by faith. Nevertheless, and especially in a secularized society, the people need to be convinced that there are reasons behind their faith. They are unable to remember these reasons and cannot repeat them but feel comfortable if they know that reasons exist, that they have heard these reasons expounded by their intellectual superiors and were convinced by them.[118]

However, the new conceptions acquired through reasoning "have an extremely unstable position among the popular masses." For them to be thoroughly internalized and stable, several conditions must be fulfilled. It is necessary to unite the converts in an organized community that will nourish its faith "permanently and in an organized fashion, struggling at all times and always with the same kind of arguments, and maintaining a hierarchy of intellectuals who give to the faith, in appearance at least, the dignity of thought." The content of the faith must be appropriately simplified, because the populace can digest only its "crude, unsophisticated version." The method of maintaining the faith will consist in the endless repetition of the same arguments, because "repetition is the best didactic means of working on the popular mentality." The task of indoctrinating the masses and thereby "giving a personality to the amorphous mass element" will be consigned to "intellectuals of a new type" specially produced for this purpose, intellectuals who "arise directly out of the masses, but remain in contact with them to become, as it were, the whale-bone in the corset."[119]

Gramsci did not omit to add that to ensure effective control of the "intellectually subordinate strata," the "superior groups" would have to set "the limits of freedom of discussion and propaganda." He believed that these limits could be conceived of, not "in the administrative and police sense, but in the sense of a self-limitation which the leaders impose on their own activity." He stressed, however, that individual initiatives in pursuit of knowledge "should be disciplined and subject to an ordered procedure, so that they have to pass through the sieve of academies or cultural institutes of various kinds and only become public after undergoing a process of selection."[120] Stalin's Marxism was more than adequately simplified and more than adequately institutionalized to meet all these requirements.

First of all, it was necessary to prepare a manual of basic ideology, a digest of the essentials of Bolshevik mythology popular enough to be studied by all citizens and to be treated as binding for all of them. This project materialized in 1938 as the *History of the Communist Party of the Soviet Union: A Short Course*. As Kolakowski put it, this was "not merely a work of falsified history but a powerful social institution—one of the party's most important instruments of mind control, a device for the destruction both of critical thought and of society's recollections of its own past."[121] Published in millions of copies, it served both as a bible and as the main prayer book of the secular religion of Marxism-Leninism; its formulae had to be memorized and virtually repeated on every possible occasion by party members and nonparty members alike. It is no exaggeration to say that this one book laid the solid foundations of a consistently totalitarian "propaganda state." It is ironic that the original Bolshevik party, whose ideology and history provided the unshakable legitimation of this state, had been crushed and physically destroyed by it.

Written for mass readers, the *History* offers an excellent illustration of the authors' views on what the popular mentality could assimilate and how it should be shaped and controlled. The book's basic assumption was that readers must not be allowed any freedom of interpretation. The ideological creed must be simple and unambiguous, sharply contrasting good and evil, reducing all colors to black and white, and thus leaving no scope for doubt. This purpose was accomplished by endless repetition (as recommended by Gramsci), the drawing of a clear moral from all historical events, and the ending of each chapter with a set of "correct" and binding conclusions. The party was presented as virtually omniscient and infallible, heroic and wise, guided by "the most advanced scientific theory," and therefore capable of consciously shaping historical processes, planning them in advance, and with occasional exceptions, avoiding unintended results. All of the party's successes were shown as historically inevitable, and the possibility of alternative developments was confidently excluded. At the same time, however, the party would not have achieved anything without the extraordinary wisdom of its two great leaders: Lenin and his best and favorite pupil, Stalin. Other leaders were divided into two categories: those who died before the Great Purge and those who underwent trial and repression. The first were mentioned either briefly or not at all; the second were presented as engaged from the very beginning in all sorts of antirevolutionary conspiracies, sabotage, and outright shameful treachery. Class enemies were treated as the incarnation of all human vices and weaknesses—cowardice, baseness, cruelty, and stupidity. These individuals were doomed by the objective laws of history but nonetheless remained personally responsible for all casualties of the class struggle. Needless to say, any differences between noncommunist political parties were almost totally ignored; readers were to be convinced that the Bolshevik party had a monopoly of "political correctness" and that all other parties were in fact equally reactionary, vying with one another in their common struggle against revolution and progress.

Although the authorship of the book was officially anonymous, it was known that it was composed under the personal and most scrupulous supervision of Stalin. Its most important theoretical part, the section on "Dialectical and Historical Materialism," was written by Stalin himself, and for this reason was immediately proclaimed to be a work of genius, the best possible account of Marxist philosophy, and the cornerstone of the entire edifice of communist education.

The theoretical sources of this work are obvious: Engels's *Anti-Dühring*, Plekhanov's *Development of the Monist View of History*, and Lenin's *Materialism and Empiriocriticism*. Hence it was a *naturalistic* and quasi-scientistic account of Marxism based entirely on the Engelsian conception of materialist dialectics, Plekhanov's necessitarian version of historical materialism, and Lenin's "copy theory of knowledge." Stalin's own contribution lay mostly in the manner of presentation, which was characterized by a tendency toward simplistic systematization, a strict ordination of the three parts of Marxism (dialectical method, philosophical materialism, historical materialism), and of course, an intrusive, importunate didacticism. Dialectics, despite being called a method, was treated as the most general part of Marxist theory, dealing with the four universal laws of all movements in nature: the law of universal interconnectedness, the law of continuous change, the law of passing from quantitative (evolutionary) to qualitative (revolutionary) change, and finally, the law of the "unity and struggle of opposites."[122] (The law of "negation of negation," although recognized by both Engels and Lenin, was omitted for obviously political reasons.) Philosophical materialism, being a materialist interpretation of these laws, was characterized as upholding three principal theses: that the world is by its nature material and "the multifold phenomena of the world constitute different forms of matter in motion"; that matter is "an objective reality existing outside and independent of our mind"; and finally, that "the world and its laws are fully knowable." Historical materialism was defined as "the extension of the principles of dialectical materialism to the study of social life, an application of the principles of dialectical materialism to the phenomena of the life of society."[123] From these theses the following logical deduction was drawn:

If the connection between the phenomena of nature and their interdependence are laws of the development of nature, it follows, too, that the connection and interdependence of the phenomena of social life are laws of the development of society and not something accidental.

Hence social life, the history of society, ceases to be an agglomeration of "accidents," and becomes the history of the development of society according to regular laws, and the study of the history of society becomes a science.

Hence the practical activity of the party of the proletariat must not be based on the "good wishes" of "outstanding individuals," not on the dictates of "reason," "universal morals," etc., but on the laws of development of society and the study of these laws.

Further, if the world is knowable and our knowledge of the laws of development of nature is authentic knowledge, having the validity of objective truth, it follows that social life, the development of society, is also knowable, and that the data of science regarding the laws of development of society are authentic data having the validity of objective truths.

Hence the science of the history of society, despite all the complexity of the phenomena of social life, can become as precise a science as, let us say, biology, and capable of making use of the laws of development of society for practical purposes.[124]

The specifically materialist element of this "science of the history of society" is, of course, the peculiar status of the "mode of production of material values." The first aspect of each mode of production—an aspect expressing people's relation to the objects and forces of nature—is the *productive forces*; the second aspect is "the relation of men to each other in the process of production," that is, the *relations of production*. Following his favorite method of enumeration, Stalin distinguished three principal features of the mode of production in general and five main types of relations of production. The first feature of production is constant and inevitable change; the second is the crucial role of the productive forces as the most mobile and revolutionary element of production; the third is the necessary adjustment of the relations of production to the rise of new productive forces. The five historical types of the relations of productions are: primitive communal, slave, feudal, capitalist, and socialist.

The most striking feature of this account of Marxism is its closed character, dogmatically authoritarian tone, and obsessively didactic tendency. Stalin's text leaves the impression that Marxism is a closed and neatly codified system in which nothing can be changed or subject to different interpretations. The questions it raises are merely rhetorical; it is evident that they have been formulated for merely didactic purposes and that each will immediately be followed by a ready-made, correct, and binding answer. It is equally clear that any doubt deserves to be treated as a testimony of intellectual immaturity, if not outright class hostility; hence there is no place for further scrutiny. Readers are invited not to solve problems, but rather to participate in practical, world-changing activity under the command of those who have mastered Marxist science and know how to apply theory to practice. Each formula of dialectical and historical materialism is therefore immediately translated into a practical directive or instruction. For instance:

Hence, in order not to err in policy, one must look forward, not backward. . . .

Hence, in order not to err in policy, one must be a revolutionary, not a reformist. . . .

Hence, in order not to err in policy, one must pursue an uncompromising proletarian class policy, not a reformist policy of harmony of the interests of the proletariat and the bourgeoisie, not a compromisers' theory of "the growing of capitalism into Socialism." . . .

Hence, if it is not to err in policy, the party of the proletariat must both in drafting its program and in its practical activities proceed primarily from the laws of development of production, from the laws of the economic development of society.[125]

The first three of these directives derive from the laws of dialectics; the fourth illustrates a practical conclusion from the general assumptions of historical materialism. The complete set of directives was to provide a reliable theoretical foundation for the struggle toward socialism and so convert it "from a dream of a better future for humanity into a science." [126]

It is somewhat surprising that such general and imprecise directives could be seen as guidelines to infallible political activity, but Stalin had no real illusions about their praxeological value. He correctly relativized them by stressing that "everything depends on the conditions, time and place," [127] making it clear enough that their concrete application was to be decided every time by the supreme leader, the philosopher king who had penetrated all the arcana of salvationist "science." He did not intend to provide people with a set of praxeological rules that they could use in accordance with their own understanding of the situation. The formulation of all these principles of unerring political activity was to serve a completely different purpose.

The derivation of Bolshevik policy from the most general laws of the material and social world was above all a primitive but powerful legitimating device.[128] It was a stunning attempt to demonstrate that the activity of the party was grounded in the innermost structure of the universe, that it accorded with the universal laws of nature and history, and that therefore it could not be wrong. This emphasis on the laws of dialectics, understood as the most general laws of the material universe, was to create the impression that all decisions of the party leadership had not only a historical sanction, but also a cosmological sanction. Thus, for instance, Stalin's determination to crush right-wing deviation within the party was entirely consistent with the dialectical law of uncompromising struggle between opposites, while Bukharin's theory of equilibrium and his gradualist strategy of growing into socialism contradicted this law in the interest of a metaphysical standpoint. Consequently, Stalin represented the authority of a universal law, while Bukharin, who tried to oppose this law, was rightly condemned and sentenced by the tribunal of history.

This obsession with legitimizing arbitrary behavior by a reference to "higher laws" was not peculiar to Stalin. Hannah Arendt has shown in her classic book that this was a common feature of both Stalinism and Nazism, as two forms of totalitarian rule:

It is the monstrous, yet seemingly unanswerable claim of totalitarian rule that, far from being "lawless," it goes to the sources of authority from which positive laws received their ultimate legitimation, that far from being arbitrary it is more obedient to these suprahuman forces than any government ever was before, and that far from wielding its power in the interest of one man, it is quite prepared to sacrifice everybody's vital immediate interests to the execution of what it assumes to be the law of History or the law of Nature. Its defiance of positive law claims to be a higher form of legitimacy which, since it is inspired by the sources themselves, can do away with petty legality.[129]

Hence, what is really important is not the legality of individual conduct but its conformity with the objective laws of Nature or History, the interpretation of which is, of course, the monopoly of the totalitarian leaders.

This way of thinking explains Stalin's peculiar understanding of political responsibility. There were two aspects of this problem: the political responsibility of those who (like Stalin) acted in accordance with the inexorable laws of history, and the political responsibility of those who (like Bukharin) slid away from the "correct line" and obstructed further progress. As a rule, a deterministic emphasis on objective laws supports the view that human conduct depends on causes largely beyond the control of individuals and that therefore one should be extremely cautious in judging it in terms of individual responsibility (if the notion of individual responsibility can be retained at all). Stalin, however, did not seem to agree with this conclusion. On the one hand, he endorsed Plekhanov's view that "world-historical individuals," as defined by Hegel, had to be unfettered by ordinary morality or law. This he interpreted as absolving people like himself from any responsibility for their cruelties and violence; ruthlessness was in their case a great merit, and the "tribunal of History" was above the ordinary courts of justice. On the other hand, he did not believe that people like Bukharin could invoke in their defense the notion of historical necessity. On the contrary, he was convinced that to oppose the necessary course of history was a criminal action deserving the most severe punishment from the appropriate organs of the "workers' state." As a result he had to define all such actions as punishable crimes for which each individual should be made personally responsible and brought to justice, and he did so without any scruples whatever. His theory of a historical development, whose interests were represented by only one party (a party headed by leaders who had "correctly understood" the laws of the universe), justified him in equating any opposition with outright treason, with selling out to the enemy. It remained only to translate this view into the language of a public prosecutor, and this was done by Andrei Vyshinskii, the chief prosecutor of the USSR, who was unconstrained by any rules of procedural justice. It is not necessary to believe literally in the details of these accusations, because the really important thing (as Lenin had already explained in 1906) was "*objective* treason" (see chapter 4, section 4). It was necessary to extract the absurd confessions in order to crush the opposition not only physically but morally as well. The official trial was a mere formality that had to be performed in order to convince the politically immature masses.

It should be noted here that Bukharin himself did not dare deny that by opposing the policy of the party he had committed a "crime" against the Revolution and "degenerated" into an enemy of socialism. To his credit, he did all he could to refute the charges of direct complicity in assassinations, spying, and wrecking, while at the same time categorically accepting his political and legal responsibility for all the crimes of the "bloc of Rights and Trotskyites." [130] In this way he hoped to save his reputation for personal honesty, in the old-fashioned legal sense of the word, while accepting his complicity in crimes in the broader sense—political crimes against socialism, the Revolution, and the party. Irrespective of the internal consistency or otherwise of this position (a point we shall return to later), it was a testimony to the party's success in creating feelings of guilt in all who tried to oppose its leadership. The supreme self-confidence of Stalin's philosophical credo was an efficient means of intimidating all opponents, actual and potential, who wanted to remain faithful to revolutionary Marxism.

The first paragraph of Stalin's text explains that dialectical and historical materialism (in Stalin's interpretation, of course) was "the world outlook of the Marxist-Leninist party." At the same time it was proclaimed as the official ideology of the Soviet party state. This was the most important article of the *unwritten* constitution of the Stalinist state: like Nazi Germany, the Soviet Union was to be a *Weltanschauungsstaat*, deriving its legitimacy from a total view of the world and dedicated to the goals prescribed by its legitimating ideology. Thus, Stalin's summary of the communist world outlook was to perform at least three functions: legitimating, disciplining, and mobilizing. The concept of objective and implacable laws of development directing history toward a scientifically predetermined goal was an excellent legitimation of Stalin's dictatorship: it made it clear that the activity of the party was consistent with universal laws of development, that its cause was therefore invincible, that all its opponents were doomed to perish, and that skeptical hesitations could only lead to outright betrayal. The claim to a monopoly of scientific truth justified in its turn the strictest control over thought. In this way all potential dissidents were mercilessly condemned in the name of the highest authorities of the secular religion: the authority of History and Science. The slightest disobedience was to be punished by intellectual and moral annihilation in the proverbial "rubbish-bin of History."

It is more difficult to explain the mobilizing function of Stalin's digest of Marxist philosophy. Mobilization for heroic deeds usually requires a powerful vision of the social ideal, of the great collective aim to be realized in the immediate future. Such a vision, however, is conspicuously absent from Stalin's catechism, which contains no inspiring blueprint for a communist society. In presenting the problems of capitalist development, *Dialectical and Historical Materialism* avoids the language of moral indignation; neither does it employ the concept of alienation. Since all the relevant texts of the young Marx would have been easily accessible to Stalin, these omissions were probably the result of a conscious decision.[131] Instead, it employs the language of technological determinism, warning sternly that heroic effort can achieve nothing unless supported by an adequate development of productive forces.[132]

This strongly antivoluntarist tendency may appear inconsistent with the voluntarist character of Stalin's program of constructing socialism in a single country. Stalin, however, combined a necessitarian emphasis on objective laws with a dogmatic belief in the miraculous power of a "scientific understanding" of these laws and did not see this as a contradiction. He simply followed the logic of Engels's reasoning, according to which the scientific understanding of historical necessity makes it possible to achieve complete mastery over the blind forces of history. Needless to say, Stalin arrogated such miracle-working knowledge to himself and wanted to realize the Engelsian ideal of transforming social forces "from master demons into willing servants" (see chapter 2, section 6). In pursuit of this aim he needed discipline and control above all; hence, he preferred to be silent about the libertarian and egalitarian aspects of the communist utopia. He had to avoid mass voluntarism in the form of a revolution of rising expectations and therefore had to stress that the construction of socialism requires above all the development of productive forces—that is, the puritan ethic of hard work and the ability to cope successfully with the Herculean task of forcible industrialization. In other words, the emphasis on objective laws and on the primacy of productive forces was, for Stalin, a means of educating the masses for maximum productivity, an argument explaining the need for sacrifice and for keeping utopian impulses under strict control. There was to be no immediate gratification, no "paradise now"; the "habit of dreaming" that had been allowed to flourish in the first stage of the Stalinist "revolution from above" had to be taken away and replaced by "scientific leadership" and "scientific planning," leaving no place for subjectivist fantasies.[133]

However, the emphatically "scientific" and "objectivist" character of Stalin's Marxism had little in common with the genuinely antivoluntarist Marxism of the Second International. It involved no danger of belief in automatic progress and therefore did not invite a wait-and-see approach; Stalin rightly assumed that under socialism the economy would not function automatically and that the objective laws of the productive processes would not be confused with the laws of the market. It probably did not occur to him that his endorsement of technological determinism (including the classical thesis that "men are not free to choose one mode of production or another")[134] might be used to point out the premature character of the Bolshevik revolution in Russia and so cast doubts on its historical legitimacy. For him this problem was conclusively solved by Lenin's theory of the "weakest link" and by the victory of the conception of "building socialism in one country." Stalin assumed (no doubt correctly) that nobody would dare to return to the old argument about Russia as "not yet ripe for socialism," since Lenin had dealt with this by arguing in "Our Revolution" that backwardness did not necessarily exclude the socialist option: "If a definite level of culture is required for the building of socialism . . . why cannot we begin by first achieving the prerequisites for that definite level of culture in a revolutionary way, and *then*, with the aid of the workers' and peasants' government and the Soviet system, proceed to overtake the other nations?" (L, *SW*, 3:707).

What Lenin said about the level of culture, Stalin could have said about the level of the development of the productive forces. But the choice of expressions is no accident. *Culture* is a much broader term, nonreducible to mode of production, let alone its technological side. Lenin's use of this term involved, as a rule, criticism of bureaucratic inefficiency and corruption, complaints about the lack of adequate organizational experience among the masses, and so forth. In contrast to this, the term *productive forces* refers only to the technological element of production, as distinct from relations of production, (i.e., the relations of people to one another in the process of production). Stalin's emphasis on productive forces was therefore an indication that productive capacity or technological modernization as such, should be given absolute priority, that it was more important for the development of socialism than interhuman relations (i.e., the distinctively socialist element of the new mode of production). Hence, we may conclude that Stalin's penchant for technological determinism was not a genuine concession to the necessitarian spirit of classical Marxism, but rather the expression of a narrowly technocratic attitude, overshadowing the humanist dimensions of the communist vision.

Despite its theoretical crudities, Stalin's treatment of "voluntarism" and "utopianism" seems to be quite consistent with the "scientific socialism" of classical orthodox Marxism. His scientific program was directed against the voluntarist impatience and utopian dreams of undisciplined individuals; at the same time, however, his unshakable belief in the magic power of Marxist "science" justified all sorts of voluntarist experiments with human beings, if backed by the authority of the "most advanced scientific theory." Indeed, if the laws of history had at last been "scientifically understood," and if those who possessed this understanding had seized political power,

then nothing could prevent them from the realization of the further prescriptions of revolutionary science. The victory of their cause was doubly
guaranteed: by history itself and by the infallible knowledge of its laws.

Thus, Stalinist Marxism was antiutopian in style but not in substance. It
rejected and ridiculed utopian extravagances in the name of rigid scientific
(i.e., antiutopian) socialism, but "scientific socialism" of course contained
a quite extravagant utopian blueprint whose realization was mandatory
for all its followers. Stalin did not and could not reject this scientific utopia,
since such a move would have deprived him of all appearance of historical
legitimacy. He tried instead to curb communist utopianism, to control it,
to suppress its revolutionary ardor while providing it with a number of
bureaucratically supervised and routinized forms of expression. But the
state he was building could not evolve into a nonideological authoritarian
system: it had to be a "utopia in power." [135] Stites was therefore right in
stressing that "Stalinism was not simply a negation of utopianism. It was a
rejection of 'revolutionary' utopianism in favor of a single utopian vision
and plan, drawn up at the pinnacle of power and imposed on an entire
society without allowance for autonomous life experiments." [136]

It is instructive to compare Stalin's catechism, as well as the whole *History of the Communist Party of the Soviet Union*, with Bukharin and
Preobrazhenskii's *ABC of Communism*, a book that was also written for
mass consumption and was for many years the most popular systematic
compendium of Marxist-Leninist theory. The propagandist functions of
these two texts were completely different. The *ABC of Communism* appealed to revolutionary emotions and the utopian imagination, concentrating almost entirely on an elaborate vision of the communist society of the
future. In contrast, problems of future communist freedom are conspicuously absent from Stalin's text. He indoctrinated and motivated his readers
in a different way, not by showing them a grandiose blueprint for the
revolutionary transformation of society, but by persuading them that the
cause of his party was historically legitimate and scientifically grounded,
that the party leadership was endowed with unique infallible knowledge
of the laws of the natural and human universe, that to build socialism in
the Soviet Union was to be in the van of universal history, and that victory in this task was historically inevitable. In both works Marxist theory
performed the function of Gramscian "popular religion": in the *ABC of
Communism* Marxism was still a millenarian religion of imminent earthly
salvation, while in Stalin's credo it had become a predestinarian religion
of implacable destiny.

To define dialectical materialism (together with its subdivision, historical materialism) as "the world outlook of the Marxist-Leninist party" implies that Marxism was not enough and had to be supplemented by Leninism. Such a conclusion, however, faced Stalin with a difficult dilemma. On

the one hand, he needed the support of the internationally acknowledged authority of Marxism and was afraid that to emphasize the original features of Leninism might reduce the meaning of the Russian Revolution to a merely local event, thus putting in question its universal significance and the right of its leaders to a commanding position in the international communist movement. On the other hand, he firmly believed that the center of the revolutionary movement had been transferred to Russia, that Lenin had created a universally applicable theory of the proletarian revolution, and that he had therefore become the undisputable leader of the international proletariat (a position inherited, of course, by his worthy successor).[137] Stalin therefore had to emphasize Lenin's contribution as much as possible while at the same time presenting him as the most orthodox of Marxists, one who had never intended to change anything in the world outlook of his teachers. Stalin also had to reject all attempts to define Leninism in terms of the specific conditions obtaining in Russia as well as all theories limiting the relevance of Lenin's ideals to the problems of economically underdeveloped or peripheral countries. Stalin felt that any concession to such theories would inevitably entail the marginalization of Leninism and a considerable weakening of the international standing of his own regime.

The solution to this dilemma was the definition of Leninism as "Marxism in the epoch of imperialism and of the proletarian revolution . . . the theory and practice of the proletarian revolution in general, the theory and tactics of the dictatorship of the proletariat in particular." Defined in this way Leninism was a sort of "philosophy of action," a theory for the practical implementation of the general principles of Marxist philosophy, a bridge between the Marxist theory of communism and the actual practice of the proletarian revolution. Its main contribution was therefore the theory and practice of the "party of a new type" and (after the seizure of power) of the dictatorship of the proletariat. In both these areas problems of strategy and tactics were of course of paramount importance. For this reason Stalin referred to Leninism as constituting "the science of leadership in the revolutionary struggle of the proletariat."[138]

In his views on the party Stalin was an exemplary Leninist from the very beginning of his revolutionary career.[139] He repeatedly stressed the urgent need to raise the "unconscious, spontaneous and unorganized" workers' movement to the level of adequate class consciousness represented by the compact, centralized party,[140] which was equipped with the most advanced scientific theory and capable of directing its actions according to a single plan. He went even further in this direction by interpreting the party in quasi-biological terms as a living organism endowed with only one will.[141] He had no doubt that in his time only two ideologies could exist: bourgeois and socialist.[142] He maintained that the slightest deviation from the latter (as defined by the party) inevitably would lead to union with the former. In an article of 1905 he defined the main duty of the vanguard as combating "spontaneity," *diverting* the working-class movement from spontaneous trade unionist tendencies and *imbuing* it with truly socialist consciousness.[143] Even then he did not see such policies as expressing a voluntarist standpoint, exaggerating the role of subjective factors, and in fact reversing the relationship between consciousness and being. Indeed, he visualized the revolutionary vanguard as "standing at the head of science," armed by scientific knowledge and able "deeply to investigate the laws of historical development."[144] From this perspective it was the ignorant masses who were likely to commit subjectivist errors, not their enlightened leaders.

In his two attempts to codify the principles of Leninism—*Foundations of Leninism* (1924) and *Problems of Leninism* (1926)—Stalin described the party as the "vanguard of the working class," the elite of knowledge, heroism, and sacrifice, the political leader of the proletariat and its military staff. Elsewhere he even compared it to the medieval military religious Order of the Knights of the Sword: in his view the party was "a kind of order of sword bearers within the Soviet State, guiding the latter's organs and giving inspiration to their activity."[145] He did not try to conceal that "the dictatorship of the proletariat is *in essence* the 'dictatorship' of its vanguard." At the same time, however, he argued that the party was *not only* the vanguard and that its dictatorship in relation to the working class was not "dictatorship in the actual sense of the term ('power based on violence')" but simply political leadership. In order to rule, the party "must from day to day win the confidence of the proletarian masses . . . it must secure the support of the masses . . . it must not command but above all convince the masses and help them to realize by their own experience the correctness of the policy of the Party . . . it must, therefore, be the guide, the leader and teacher of its own class." In this context Stalin allowed himself to correct Lenin's terminology: the latter, he warned, "uses the word *dictatorship* of the Party not in the strict sense of the word ('power based on violence') but uses it figuratively, in the sense of leadership." Therefore "anyone who attributes to the Party the function of employing violence against the working class, which is not one of its attributes, violates the elementary requirements of correct mutual relationships between the vanguard and the class, between the Party and the proletariat."[146]

The foregoing provides an ironic commentary on the view that Lenin "stressed the importance of persuasion" while Stalin allegedly preferred to rely on coercion alone (see above, Section 1). In reality Stalin exceeded Lenin in both organized coercion and organized persuasion but paid more attention, as well as greater lip service, to persuasion than did his teacher. This was because only under Stalin had the communist dictatorship achieved the ability to penetrate all spheres of social life from within and thus deprive them of any semblance of autonomy. This could not have been done without intimidation, but massive ideological pressure, called peaceful persuasion, was also involved.

The general principles guiding these policies were undoubtedly Leninist. Stalin described them as follows: The party is not the vanguard only, because its total membership also consists of the party masses. The vanguard leads, guides, and teaches; the party masses act in accordance with received instructions and thus implement "correct policy" in all walks of life. Apart from the party, the working class possesses other organizations, all penetrated by party members and therefore serving the party as auxiliary bodies, as levers and belts in the system.[147] Hence proletarian dictatorship is a complicated system in which the party vanguard rules not directly, but through cooperation with mediating bodies (or transmission belts) linking it with its class and with other toilers. Of course, the number of such organizations has to be strictly limited and their functions narrowly defined. To be precise, Stalin authorized the existence of four mass organizations and defined their aims thus:

The *trade unions*, as the mass organizations of the proletariat, linking the Party with the class primarily in the sphere of production; the *Soviets*, as the mass organizations of all toilers, linking the Party with these latter, primarily in the sphere of the state; the *co-operative societies* as mass organizations, mainly of the peasants, linking up the party with the peasant masses, primarily in the economic field, and serving to draw the peasantry into the work of socialist construction; the *Young Communist League*, as the mass organization of the young workers and peasants, whose mission is to help the proletarian vanguard in training young reserves.[148]

The function of the party was to *combine* the work of all these organizations and "to *guide* their activities toward a single goal." But what if a conflict arose between the party and a nonparty organization of the workers? Stalin did not need to discuss such a possibility. He took for granted the Leninist dogma that only the vanguard party, the party of conscious communists, was "capable of fulfilling the role of chief leader in the system of the dictatorship of the proletariat"; that otherwise "the unity of the struggle of the proletariat and the leadership of the proletarian masses in their fight for power and for the building of socialism is impossible." [149] This being so, clearly if the leaders of a nonparty organization refused to be persuaded and to accept (not merely to obey, but to accept) the decisions of the party, they automatically revealed themselves as traitors and wreckers and should be dealt with accordingly. In other words, the communist vanguard should organize support for itself in mass organizations of the workers, without allowing them even the slightest degree of genuine independence and categorically excluding any form of power sharing.

The same principle was to operate in the party's relationships with other classes. Stalin would have agreed with Gramsci that the Communist party

should seek support for itself in a system of alliances with the nonproletarian classes of the people. Stalin stressed that proletarian dictatorship did
not signify that the proletariat did not need "an alliance with the toiling
and exploited masses of other classes for the attainment of its objectives."
He was eager to emphasize that this dictatorship of a single class "can
be firmly established and exercised to the full only by means of a *special
form* of alliance between the class of proletarians and the toiling masses
of the petty-bourgeois classes, especially the toiling masses of the peasantry." The only things he absolutely refused to accept were democratic
principles. His "special form of alliance" was to be an *unequal* alliance,
one in which the leading force was to be the proletariat, or rather, "the
party of the proletariat, the party of communists, which *does not and cannot share* that leadership with other parties."[150] This was a truly Leninist
principle. For instance, the alliance between the proletariat and the peasantry never allowed the peasants to create their own party: they were to
remain a "class-in-itself," deprived of their own political leadership and of
any means of legally defending their specific interests and values.

This policy of unequal alliances was sometimes very flexible. As mentioned above, Stalin even extended it (although rather halfheartedly) to the
Orthodox church—that is, to a historical force that for him, as for Lenin,
represented the most reactionary bastion of the anticommunist world. It
would be fair to say that the aim of this pseudoalliance was not only to
make it easier to co-opt religiously minded people or to arouse patriotic
feelings in the war with Nazi Germany. Stalin did not intend to give the
church a stable, respectable place in the Soviet system. His concessions to
the church were designed in the long run to bring about its destruction,
by breaking its spirit of resistance, demoralizing and corrupting the clergy,
penetrating their ranks with police agents, and thus effectively destroying
it as an independent moral authority.

The most far-reaching manifestation of Stalin's Machiavellian flexibility
in dealing with the nonparty masses was his flirtation with Russian nationalism. At first he simply rejected the previous policy of "national nihilism"
and thus enabled Russian patriots to see Soviet Russia as a continuation of
their historic motherland (see above, section 1). Soon afterward the next
step was taken: Russia came to be regarded as a hero nation, first among
equals in the Soviet family, but this entailed official condemnation and
penalization of excessively critical views of her past.[151] This glorification
of Russian virtues was further strengthened during the war with Germany.
At the close of the war Stalin raised his glass in a toast to the Russian
people as "the most outstanding of all the nations that constitute the Soviet
Union."[152] He also paid the Russians a rather doubtful compliment by
thanking them for the extraordinary patience with which they had endured
his rule. In the first postwar years this pro-Russian trend (properly com-

bined with a brutal crushing of the slightest manifestation of genuinely national feeling among the non-Russian nationalities of the Union) was codified by Andrey Zhdanov in his ill-famed "struggle against cosmopolitanism." This most powerful ideological campaign of Stalin's last years was terrifying in its crudeness although at the same time unintentionally comic.[153] The Russians were accorded primacy, or the highest achievements, in all branches of scholarship and culture. Almost all pre-Zhdanov Soviet scholarship, especially in philosophy and history, was condemned as "self-prostration" (niskopoklonstvo) and "kowtowing" (kolenopreklonenye) to the West; even Plekhanov was put in this category because of his reverence for classical German philosophy. In the name of historical truth, allegedly distorted by the "graduated flunkeys of the bourgeoisie," the uncontrolled and systematic falsification of well-established facts took place. Russian imperial conquests were presented as wars of liberation, acts of exceptional brutality (as, for instance, Suvorov's massacre of the civilian population of Warsaw's eastern suburb in 1794) were shown as acts of remarkable humanitarianism, and so forth. It was strictly prohibited to study Western influences on Russian thought and culture; even comparative studies of Russian folklore, which led inevitably to the discovery of many borrowings from the folklore of other nations, were outlawed as "cosmopolitan" and "antiscientific."[154] Quoting from the Marxian classics was obligatory but highly selective. Even quotations from Lenin were strictly controlled: thus, for instance, it was obligatory to quote his praise of Chernyshevskii as a great Russian materialist, but the rest of the paragraph describing him as a Hegelian and a disciple of Feuerbach was always omitted, as diminishing his greatness. Russian progressive thinkers had to be shown as virtually immune to Western influences (apart from Marxism) and "standing four heads higher" than all pre-Marxist thinkers of the West.[155]

The most dreadful thing about this ideological offensive was precisely its thoroughly organized and controlled character. It left no room for anything spontaneous and unpredictable. All Soviet books published at that time, especially those on Russian culture and history, were as alike as peas in a pod: the same contents, the same thunderbolts launched against "Western falsifiers" and native "cosmopolites," the same quotations from Lenin and Stalin, and the equally significant omission of those statements that did not fit in with the currently binding indoctrination program. The Russian cultural legacy was divided in two: the culture of the popular masses, which included all great writers and artists of Russia, irrespective of their social backgrounds and political affiliations, and the culture of the ruling classes, reduced to a small number of half-forgotten reactionary figures. The first group was regarded as reflecting in a mysterious way the spiritual greatness and the invariably progressive ideas of the Russian nation, while the second was presented as having no deep roots in the national culture, as hostile (if not subjectively, then at least objectively) to truly Russian values, and as not deserving of serious consideration. The legacy of Russian thought was also dichotomized in two ways: by materialist versus idealist criteria or progressive versus reactionary criteria. However, the accepted part of this legacy was much smaller, since idealist and religious Russian thinkers were treated, with only a few qualified exceptions, as nonpersons unworthy of being published and studied and necessarily isolated from the general reader. In contrast to this, Russian "progressive" thinkers, especially the so-called "revolutionary democrats," were praised to the skies and published in countless popular editions. But genuine interest in their thought was effectively killed by subjecting them to an extremely schematic, teleological interpretation that ignored their historically important individual features and concentrated instead on their (alleged) progressiveness in overcoming their "historical limitations" and drawing ever closer to Marxism. But when Russian Marxism appeared on the scene, all non-Marxist or insufficiently Marxist thinkers, even those as left wing and representative of the Russian mind as the revolutionary populists, came to be seen as lagging behind and creating obstacles to true progress and therefore as not deserving inclusion in the accepted intellectual canon.

Obviously, the point of the "struggle against cosmopolitanism" was not to defend the authentic values of the native culture, nor was it some new edition of the struggle between Slavophiles and Westernizers. The point was to cut Russian culture off from the rest of the world in order to make it easier to destroy this culture as an independent wellspring of spiritual values; the point was to intimidate and paralyze all enlightened people in Russia, to bring to the fore the crude upstarts, to play on their primitive xenophobic reactions and anti-intellectual resentments in order to make them an instrument of the systematic destruction of all authentic spiritual life, which by its very existence offered resistance to Stalinism. It was quite a diabolical attempt to extend complete control over human thought and feeling. Last but not least, it compromised the cause of Russian patriotism by suggesting that cosmopolitanism was identical in practice with Zionism, and Zionism with Jewish nationality.[156]

In view of all this, it is impossible to see Stalin as a genuine Russian patriot. He may have been quite sincere in his pro-Russian feelings (although there is no unanimity on this point), but what he wanted above all was to succeed in "adjusting Russia to himself, that is, to his globally conceived Bolshevik cause."[157] In his plans Russia was an instrument of communism, not vice versa. This was necessary for the simple reason that his totalitarian rule could not be legitimated by Russian national tradition. He could consciously utilize some elements of Russia's autocratic legacy, but was well aware that his claim to unlimited power depended wholly

on the communist cause. He realized that he embodied the collective charisma of the communist movement while lacking a personal charisma of
his own.[158]

This brings us back to the crucial problem of Stalinism: the problem of
its communist legitimacy. As we have seen, Stalin's account of dialectical
and historical materialism was intended to provide a scientific and ideological legitimation of his rule—scientific because derived from an unerring
understanding of the most general laws of nature and history, and ideological because of its perfect agreement with the most progressive aspirations
of humanity. The same assumptions sustained Stalin's theory of effective
action—that is, his reconstruction and development of the Leninist conception of the dictatorship of the proletariat. At the same time, however,
he remained remarkably reticent about the final goals of the communist
movement. Some of his actions, especially his Great Retreat of the 1930s,
might even be interpreted as a deliberate retreat from communist utopianism or as a willingness to consolidate his power at the expense of its
legitimating ideology. But could he really afford to abandon his utopian
aims? Was it possible for him to maintain and strengthen his totalitarian power while increasingly playing down its revolutionary character and
communist goals?

For a while it seemed that such a possibility could not be excluded. In
his report to the Seventeenth Party Congress (the so-called Congress of
Victors), Stalin expressed his deep satisfaction that all anti-Leninist groups
had been crushed and that his leadership was now unchallenged: "There is
nothing more to prove and, it seems, no one to fight." [159] This comfortable
situation enabled him to indulge in ridicule of "Leftist chatter" about the
inherently evil character of all trade and the need to abolish money and
to organize a direct exchange of products.[160] He argued eloquently that if
the communist ideal of the complete liquidation of all vestiges of a market
system were to be realized, it must be preceded by the establishment of
a "perfectly organized system of Soviet trade" and that to cope with this
task the party had "to give a drubbing to the 'Left' freaks" and "to scat-
ter their petty-bourgeois chatter to the winds." [161] Nor did he conceal that
his reluctance to implement communist economic ideals stemmed from his
awareness of their impracticability and irrelevance as far as the needs of
the state were concerned. He warned the Left that a direct exchange of
products was far more difficult and complicated than simply relying on
a state monopoly of trade,[162] and he stressed that the total abolition of a
monetary exchange relationship should be realized only at the higher stage
of communist development.

Timasheff interpreted this policy as "a complete retreat," the first decisive step toward the restoration of a normal market. Trotsky was more
cautious; he allowed the possibility that the Soviet regime might "backslide

to capitalism" but saw this as unlikely, because the Soviet bureaucracy, headed by Stalin, had not consolidated and legalized its rule and was therefore "compelled to defend state property as the source of its power and its income."[163] He clung to this position to the end of his days and based his principle of standing for the defense of the USSR on it.[164] The totalitarian character of Stalinism seemed to him to show that Stalin's regime, like all "naked dictatorships" in history, was transitional and that its beneficiaries were incapable of transforming themselves into a "stable ruling class."[165]

There is no doubt that Trotsky's diagnosis was more realistic than Timasheff's, although Trotsky's argument leaves much to be desired. He apparently failed to recognize that political systems stand or fall together with their legitimations and that the Soviet system was no exception to this rule. The Stalinist bureaucracy, or more precisely, the managing strata of Stalinist society, could not openly constitute themselves a "stable ruling class" because this would destroy the legitimacy of their social power. Similarly, Stalin's personal dictatorship was not and could not be "naked"; he was keenly, almost nervously aware of the need for ideological legitimation and did all he could to strengthen it and ensure its effectiveness. That is why he laid so much stress on the total ideological control of people's minds. But the other side of the coin was the fact that he himself became a prisoner of communist ideology and did not dare openly to abandon its utopian goals.

A telling testimony of this is his last work, *Economic Problems of Socialism in the USSR* (1952). This text, too often neglected in the literature on the subject,[166] sheds light on Stalin's views on the communist future of the Soviet Union and therefore warrants analysis here.

Economic Problems deserves to be called Stalin's ideological testament. Unlike his other works, it contains a direct discussion of the Marxist conception of freedom. The ailing dictator wanted to oppose the voluntarist approach to economic planning and therefore stressed yet again that economic laws have an objective character and cannot be disregarded even under socialism. In doing this he naturally referred to Engels's conception of freedom and necessity, presenting it as follows:

Reference is made to Engels' *Anti-Dühring*, to his formula which says that, with the abolition of capitalism and the socialization of the means of production, man will obtain control of his means of production, that he will be set free from the yoke of social and economic relations and become the "master" of his social life. Engels calls this freedom "appreciation of necessity." And what can this "appreciation of necessity" mean? It means that, having come to know objective laws ("necessity"), man will apply them with full consciousness in the interests of society. That is why Engels says in the same book:

"The laws of his own social activity, which have hitherto confronted him as external, dominating laws of nature, will then be applied by man with complete understanding, and hence will be dominated by man."[167]

The end of this paragraph from *Anti-Dühring* contains the famous formula about "humanity's leap from the kingdom of necessity to the kingdom of freedom" (E, *AD*, 344). Stalin, however, did not repeat these words: he preferred to emphasize the necessitarian aspect of Engels's conception. Engels's formula, Stalin argued, "does not speak at all in favor of those who think that under socialism economic laws can be abolished and the new ones created. On the contrary, it demands, not the abolition, but the understanding of economic laws and their intelligent application." [168]

By choosing such an interpretation Stalin sought to defend his policy of preserving some forms of commodity production and trade under socialism. Certain comrades, he explained, "affirm that the Party acted wrongly in preserving commodity production after it had assumed power and nationalized the means of production in our country." [169] They argued that production for the market (and the market itself) should have been abolished, together with the nationalization of the means of production. To support this position they cited Engels, who had said: "The seizure of the means of production by society puts an end to commodity production, and therewith to the domination of the product over the producer." [170]

Stalin did not deny that this was indeed the final goal of communism as a program of economic liberation, a program that was binding for his party and for himself as the supreme communist leader. He seemed however to sense that to embark on the realization of this program might bring about a dangerous political and social destabilization. Hence he wanted to delay it as much as possible, justifying this policy by reference to the objective character of economic laws. In this way he hoped to defer the difficult transition to the Marxist millennium in the name of Marxist "science" and to avoid committing himself to the risky experiments prescribed by Marxism, while preserving his Marxist credentials.

To do so, it was, of course, necessary to give a suitable interpretation to the paragraphs cited from *Anti-Dühring*. He could not claim that Engels did not really mean what he wrote, nor openly disown his economic utopia; the only alternative was to argue that his formula was not "fully clear and precise" and therefore needed dialectical concretization.[171] This Stalin did by pointing out that Engels had failed to indicate whether his words referred to the seizure by society of *all* or only part of the means of production. In his own interpretation Engels had in mind the nationalization of all means of production, not only in industry but also in agriculture.[172] It followed from this that a necessary precondition for the complete abolition of the market was the expropriation of all small producers, which, according to Stalin, had not occurred in Soviet Russia. The Russian peasants were not expropriated but collectivized, and collective property should be clearly distinguished from nationalized property. Hence, the nature of the existing property relations precluded the immediate realization of the final communist goal. Excessive zeal in the transition to the higher phase of communism would also endanger the existing "alliance" with the peasantry: "At present the collective farms will not recognize any other economic relation with the town except the commodity relation—exchange through purchase and sale. Because of this, commodity production and trade are as much a necessity with us today as they were thirty years ago, say, when Lenin spoke of the necessity of developing trade to the utmost." [173]

Having said this, however, Stalin hastened to reassure his readers that there was no question of a restoration of capitalism and that the final ideals of communism were not being betrayed. Soviet commodity production, he argued, was "a commodity production without capitalists." [174] Collective farmers did not own machinery and land and could not develop in a capitalist direction. In theory they owned only their products, and their unwillingness to alienate these products in other form than the form of commodities was not a danger to the socialist state. The preservation of monetary exchange and hence of the law of value was still useful, because it trained Soviet business executives to conduct production on rational lines.[175] However, there was no danger of a reemergence of the capitalist relationship, because the sphere of operation of the law of value was "strictly limited and placed within definite bounds." Because of this the Soviet economy was developing in a "balanced" way, without productive chaos or permanent crises. This agreed with Marx's description, in his *Critique of the Gotha Program*, of the first stage of communism, a stage that should not be arbitrarily shortened but that would not last forever. The coexistence at this time of publicly owned production and collective farm production was a transitional phenomenon. At the higher stage "there will be only one all-embracing production sector, with the right to dispose of all the consumer goods produced in the country," and then "commodity circulation, with its 'money economy,' will disappear." [176]

The logic of these arguments now seems very strained, if not bizarre. Stalin did not explain why the will of the peasantry should have been so important or why the collective farmers, totally dependent on the administrative and party authorities, could not have been "persuaded" to agree to the direct nationalization of land. After all, such a move could have been combined with a guaranteed minimum income for them (similar to the income of industrial workers), with freedom for the peasants to leave their villages, and with a system of medical insurance coverage (from which up until then they had been excluded on the pretext of not belonging to the public sector), and so forth. We may surmise that the existing system of collective farms was to be preserved just because it was an effective way of exploiting the peasantry, but this aspect of the problem was of course passed over in silence. Stalin's arguments about the "law of value" under socialism were equally unconvincing. He himself gave some examples of an absurd arbitrariness in price-fixing policy,[177] which clearly demonstrated that the system was in fact a standard form of command-administrative economy based on central planning. Since all market-type self-regulation had been successfully eliminated, the elementary rules of economic alculation could now be ignored. The vestiges of commodity production remaining under this system were only money and trade, as means of accounting and distribution. Nevertheless, Stalin obviously felt that even these residual forms of a market economy might appear illegitimate under socialism and that their continued existence required a cautious defense.

To make sense of all this, we must realize that Stalin was neither a democratic leader trying to secure his reelection by promoting the material welfare of the electorate, nor merely a nationalist dictator interested primarily in the power and prestige of his state. He was acutely aware that the communist doctrine was the only justification of everything he had done in its name and that his place in history depended on his role in the realization of the final goals of communism. He was, in fact, a prisoner of this ideology, often wanting more freedom of action though he neither dared nor could afford to ignore the fact that Marxist communism was the only legitimation of his bloody dictatorship. His common sense and his acute political instinct warned him against adopting Marxist economic utopianism and compelled him to engage instead in a cautious reinterpretation of Marxist dogma. This explains his rather clumsy attempt to convince his readers that Engels's thesis on ending commodity production and seizing the means of production should not be understood literally. Again, in discussing the abolition of the antithesis between town and country, he allowed himself even greater license, stating flatly that Engels was wrong to proclaim that "the great towns will perish."[178] But he never dared to question the Marxist vision of communism as a dialectical return to a natural economy. Indeed, at the end of his booklet he pledged his devotion to this goal and promised to prepare for a gradual transition from commodity exchange (i.e., monetary exchange through the market) to an exchange of products (i.e., simple barter). This revealed that he had not conveniently forgotten the true meaning of Marxist communism and that he was well aware that from a Marxist point of view the abolition of capitalism was not enough, since the final goal was the abolition of all forms of market economy (commodity production) as such. As he frankly said, "We, Marxists, adhere to the Marxist view that the transition from socialism to communism and the communist principle of distribution of products according to needs preclude all commodity exchange, and, hence, preclude the conversion of products into commodities, and, with it, their conversion into value."[179]

The goal therefore was clear, and the first step toward its realization was raising collective property to the level of public property. Stalin promised to implement this policy by extending the existing rudiments of product exchange to the whole of agriculture and developing them into a broad system of direct exchange of products between town and country. The merit of this system would be in reducing the sphere of operation of commodity circulation and so facilitating the transition from socialism to communism.[180]

In Western literature on the subject, as well as in the political thought of most of the Western Left, it has become customary to defend Marxist communism by arguing that all the disasters caused by the Soviet regime were in fact the work of one man, Stalin. For instance, in a recent collection of articles on the failure of communism, we read that "Marxism has nothing to do with it." Even Lenin should not be blamed for single-party monopolistic rule: "The real architect of the model of the rule which came to prevail in all Communist regimes was in fact Stalin, who first established it in the Soviet Union, and then had it copied by other communist leaders."[181] Another article in the same collection denies any relationship between Stalinism and "the utopian impulse."[182] In this way Marxist communism is exonerated from blame not only for the unprecedented political repression under Stalinist totalitarianism, but also for the economic failure of "actually existing socialism."

My own interpretation of Stalinism presented here is of course completely different. I have supported it by a careful reconstruction of Marx and Engels's views on the communist ideal, which they saw as the final victory of human freedom. Nevertheless, the provocatively self-confident tendentiousness of the statements quoted is reason enough for going a little further and assuming the otherwise thankless role of devil's advocate. It is useful, I think, to ask a different question about what might have been in history: not the question of how communism might have developed if Stalin had not succeeded Lenin, but rather what Stalin's historical role might have been had he not been so dependent on communist ideology.

The economic order as consolidated under Stalin was not unrelated to the image of communism in Marx and Engels's writings. Indeed, its main principle, the conscious regulation *ex ante* of all economic processes, was quite consistent with the Marxist economic utopia and based on the principal tenets of "scientific socialism." One of the best (although too little-known) analyses of the subject describes this incontestably Marxist foundation of Stalinism as consisting in three sorts of certainty: (1) in the sphere of social interaction, the certainty that spontaneous market processes could be entirely replaced by organized, teleological activities; (2) in the normative sphere, the certainty that the abolition of classes makes it possible to eliminate conflicts of social interest and other forms of divisive pluralism; (3) in the epistemological sphere, the certainty that "scientific socialism" will help people to be guided by a rational understanding of the possible and will enormously increase their freedom, making them true masters of their fate.[183]

Stalin, even more than Lenin, was not a philosopher of freedom. But he was a communist and was willing to pass into history as a great leader of the movement, as a second Lenin if not more; he was also acutely aware that his legitimacy as a communist leader was conditional on his active commitment to the realization of the Marxist vision of universal human liberation. The more crimes he committed in the name of communism, the more he needed ideological legitimation for his actions. The extraordinarily intense ideological indoctrination of the entire population of his country was for him necessary not only as a means of raising people to the level of the "most advanced scientific theory" and "socialist consciousness," but also as a way to legitimate his rule and justify its cruelties by the greatness of its ultimate goal.

If communism can be imagined without Stalin, then we can also imagine Stalin without communism. Let us make a mental experiment by trying to visualize him as a nonideological dictator. Is it not obvious that he would not have needed such genocidal and economically ruinous experiments as collectivization? Is it not evident that he would not have been able, or even willing, to impose an all-embracing and universally binding "scientific ideology" on the population, that it would not have occurred to him to regard himself as possessing a monopoly of the correct view on everything or to extend his political control to all spheres of the social and private lives of his subjects? Surely he would have been satisfied with Hitler's methods of economic control—that is, he would not have totally suppressed private property and the market economy, nor would he have considered a return to the primitive exchange of products to be his mission and sacred duty. Very probably he would have been just as cruel as the real Stalin in wars with foreign powers, but it seems certain that he would have had no interest in exterminating twenty million or more of his countrymen.

Some people might be inclined to say that such a naked dictatorship, deprived of higher ideological justification, would be harder to bear than the dictatorship of the proletariat, which, though merciless, claimed to represent the verdict of history and promised terrestrial salvation. They would certainly add that cooperation with a communist dictatorship might be ideologically motivated and therefore morally acceptable, even laudable, while supporting a nonideological, repressive regime would merely be shameful, cynical opportunism. This might be true, but historical experience has shown that beliefs in earthly salvation are little more than collective illusions and that from the point of view of the number of likely victims, nonideological dictatorships are as a rule greatly preferable to ideological ones. Last but not least, it is arguable that ideological, *ideo-*

cratic dictatorships are the most destructive of human freedom in that they deprive people of their spiritual freedom, their innermost identity. As we shall see, the case of Stalin's Russia, and of Stalinism in general, gives ample reasons for such a judgment.

5.3 "Dual Consciousness" and Totalitarian "Ideocracy"

By now it should be evident that totalitarianism is not a subject for political scientists only and cannot be defined as merely a certain system of institutions. The years 1989–91 have demonstrated beyond any doubt that institutional systems created by totalitarian regimes can remain formally intact while in reality being no more than empty shells, houses of cards on the brink of total collapse. The existence or nonexistence of totalitarianism depends ultimately on the totalitarian will of a disciplined elite inspired by a messianic creed, on the one hand, and on the regime's ability to impose on the population an *ideocratic* rule, that is, a rule based on ideological control of thoughts and feelings, on the other. Arendt was right in stressing that one-party dictatorships are not necessarily totalitarian (although she was wrong in thinking that in the Soviet case one-party dictatorship became totalitarian only under Stalin).[184] A totalitarian party is not simply a party intolerant of dissent and having a monopoly on political power; it must be a "party of a new type," one that firmly believes in its sacred mission and its exclusive right to leadership, a party that imposes an iron discipline on its activists, demanding from them total devotion and giving them instead powerful collectivist compensations—namely, organic fusion with a supraindividual force realizing the highest collective purpose. Obedience to such a party is not based on physical coercion alone; it must include an element of inner enslavement, of yielding to ideological pressure, resulting in dual consciousness, "ideocratic fear," and the elimination of "the distinction between truth and falsehood, fact and fiction."[185]

The most essential and distinctive features of totalitarianism are, first, the existence of mechanisms for creating the extraordinary, inhumanly strong discipline of the elite and, second, the ideological control of people's inner life—not dictating to people, not just in a negative sense but also in a positive one, what they should think, trying to govern their emotional lives, and establishing a code of behavior.[186] The history of the communist experiment in the Soviet Union, and its powerful influence in the affluent, noncommunist countries of the West, provides most instructive examples of these features. They must be discussed in this book, because Marxism-Leninism, whether we like it or not, was the most influential form of Marxism as well as the most effective challenge to liberal views on freedom in our troubled century.

The Party Mystique and the Moscow Trials

At the Thirteenth Party Congress (May 1924), the first after Lenin's death, Trotsky delivered a speech that combined a defense of the opposition with an attempt to define its (and his own) attitude toward the party. He said:

None of us wants to be or can be right against his own party. The party in the last analysis is always right, because the party is the only historical instrument given to the proletariat to resolve its fundamental tasks. . . . I know that it is impossible to be right against the party. One can be right only with the party and through the party, for history has not created any other way of determining what is right. The English have a saying: My country, right or wrong. With much more historical justification we can say: Right or wrong on any particular, specific question at any particular moment, this is still my party.[187]

These words clearly formulated the principle of absolute loyalty based ultimately on belief in the party's collective infallibility. It was somewhat paradoxical that it was formulated by the man who had once been so clearsighted about the dangers of Lenin's conception of partisan discipline. Stalin, who was certainly no less convinced of the necessity of unconditional loyalty, reacted to this statement critically and suspiciously. The party, he said, "not infrequently makes mistakes. Ilyich taught us to teach the Party, on the basis of its own mistakes, how to exercise correct leadership. If the Party made no mistakes there would be nothing from which to teach it. It is our task to detect these mistakes, to lay bare their roots and to show the Party how we came to make them and how we should avoid repeating them in the future. . . . It seems to me that this statement of Trotsky's is a kind of compliment, accompanied by an attempt—an unsuccessful one it is true—to jeer at the Party."[188]

Arendt treated Trotsky's statement as a theoretical explanation of the amazing fact that during the Great Purge the overwhelming majority of the accused proved willing to help in their own prosecution.[189] In reality, however, Trotsky's view was inadequate as a principle of unconditional obedience and for that reason had to be corrected by Stalin. The latter did not intend to undermine the party's confidence in the absolute rightness of its cause; he wanted rather to stress that the "correct point of view" was the monopoly of those who (like himself) represented the scientific, Marxist knowledge of the objective laws of development and were therefore qualified to teach other members of the party. Trotsky's view of the collective wisdom of the party as such failed to emphasize the role of the party's leaders and teachers; hence, it could be used to legitimize the ideas of the opposition within the party. If the party as a whole were ultimately always right, there would be no reason to fear deviations and no justification for the suppression of democracy within its ranks. We may add that such a view of the party would not provide a convincing rationale for the purge and execution of the overwhelming majority of its oldest, most experienced, and devoted cadres.

The most elaborate and best-known attempt to explain the mystery of the "sincere confessions" and recantations of the Great Purge show trials is Koestler's *Darkness at Noon*. Koestler, himself an ex-Communist who was personally acquainted with a number of victims of the Moscow Trials, gave a dramatic account of the psychic mechanism that caused the Bolshevik old guard publicly to confess that they had joined "the accused ranks of the counterrevolution" and were guilty of "the most heinous of possible crimes" against their socialist fatherland.[190] The manner of thinking of Koestler's hero, Rubashov, was modeled on Bukharin, although his personality and physical appearance were a synthesis of Trotsky and Radek.[191] According to Robert Conquest, the most authoritative expert on the Stalinist terror, "Koestler's account is in fact extremely well founded on the facts."[192] Hence, it is a good starting point for a discussion of some of the mechanisms of the mental captivity of the old Leninist vanguard.

The state of mind that prepared Rubashov to accept the reasonings of his interrogators is reflected in the extracts from his diary on the fifth day of imprisonment. Its motto, taken from the works of a medieval Catholic bishop, is that "the individual must be sacrificed to the common good." Rubashov develops this idea in the light of the merciless logic, or dialectic, of Marxist historical necessity and its bearing on the problem of individual responsibility. He reasons as follows:

It is that alone that matters: who is objectively in the right. . . . For us the question of subjective good faith is of no interest. He who is in the wrong must pay; he who is in the right will be absolved. That is the law of historical credit; it was our law.

History has taught us that often lies serve her better than the truth. . . . We have learned history more thoroughly than the others. We differ from all others in our logical consistency. We know that virtue does not matter to history, and that crimes remain unpunished; but that every error has its consequences and venges itself unto the seventh generation. Therefore we concentrated all our efforts on preventing error and destroying the very seeds of it. Never in history has so much power over the future of humanity been concentrated in so few hands as in our case. Each wrong idea we follow is a crime committed against future generations. Therefore we have to punish wrong ideas as others punish crimes: with death. We were held for madmen because we followed every thought down to its final consequence and acted accordingly. . . . We resembled the great Inquisitors in that we persecuted the seeds of evil not only in men's deeds, but in their thoughts. We admitted no private sphere, not even inside a man's skull. We lived under the compulsion of working things out to their final conclusions. Our minds were so tensely charged that the slightest collision caused a mortal short-circuit. Thus we were fated to mutual destruction.

I was one of those. I have thought and acted as I had to; I destroyed people whom I was fond of, and gave power to others I did not like. History put me where I stood; I have exhausted the credit which she accorded me; if I was right I have nothing to repent of, if wrong, I will pay.[193]

As we see, these words endorse the Leninist conception of objective guilt and objective treason (see chapter 4, section 4). Lenin, however, well knew that the word *objective* should be dropped, since the difference between subjective and objective or legal crime and political crime is too difficult for the masses. Besides, subjective motivation and formal legality must be ignored in political struggle. Rubashov, as a good Leninist, agrees with this as well. He formulates the golden rule of mass propaganda, well known to both the Bolsheviks and the Nazis (and also recommended by such humanist Marxists as Gramsci): "It is necessary to hammer every sentence into the masses by repetition and simplification. What is presented as right must shine like gold; what is presented as wrong must be black as pitch."[194]

Gletkin, Rubashov's second interrogator, skillfully uses these theories. He quotes Rubashov's own words in order to persuade him to accuse himself and thus to render "the last service to the Party." Rubashov's faction, he argues, is beaten and destroyed, which means that its policy has proved to be wrong. Nevertheless, there are still great dangers: a split in the party ranks may lead to civil war, which may easily lead to an international catastrophe. Hence, the imperious need for the party to be united, "filled by blind discipline and absolute trust." Rubashov has made a rent in the party; if he wants to remedy this, he must publicly condemn himself and do it in such a way as to make the opposition contemptible. So he must not explain the political motives of its conduct; his task is to gild what is right and blacken what is wrong. He must use simple language and tell the masses that opposition is a crime and that its leaders, including himself, are simple criminals.[195]

Rubashov has no arguments against this logic. He admits that history has proved him wrong and knows that he has to pay for it with his life. He is ready to reconcile himself to this but cannot bear his severance from the organization that gave meaning to his entire life. Gletkin understands this and therefore appeals to Rubashov as a party member, for the first time calling him not Citizen but Comrade. He hastens to stress that Rubashov cannot expect any reward for his "last service." The party can promise him only one thing: that sometime in the future, when it can do no more harm, the secret archives will be opened and then Rubashov, with other victims of the purge, will be given the sympathy and pity denied them today.[196] This proves to be enough; Rubashov surrenders and signs the required statement of his crimes.

Koestler did not assert that all "confessions" were extracted in the same way. Indeed, Gletkin mentions the fact that some of the accused were "made amenable" by other methods, such as physical pressure, promises to save their heads, or threats to extend repression to their relatives.[197] Koestler's Rubashov (Bukharin) obviously represents a rather extreme case. Nevertheless, he is no exception, since (to quote Conquest) "in many cases the idea of being useful to the Party was a component of the intellectual and psychological conditions of surrender."[198] This fact is confirmed by many sources, some stressing its decisive importance. Thus, for instance, Beck and Godin, two minor victims of the purge who managed to survive and publish in the West an account of their experiences, testified: "It is true that the interrogation methods, particularly when applied for months or years, are capable of breaking the strongest will. But the decisive factor is something else. It is that the majority of convinced Communists must at all cost preserve their faith in the Soviet Union. To renounce it would be beyond their powers."[199]

And yet, Koestler's explanation of the communists' readiness to sacrifice themselves not only physically but morally as well is far from being universally accepted. Most people find it extremely difficult to believe that human beings could be forced to slander themselves—and in such a grotesquely absurd manner—by the application of ideological pressure, as distinct from torture or threats of physical repression of their loved ones.[200] But there are other reasons for radically questioning Koestler's explanation. It may be useful to point out the ideological and/or political nature of these reasons.

The first group of reasons has been put forward by traditional anticommunists who lack personal experience of participation in the communist movement. From their point of view, Koestler's interpretation idealized the Communists, showing them as motivated by enormously strong convictions and capable of heroic selflessness, instead of stressing their wickedness, base personal ambitions, and demonic lust for power. Thus, he presented communism as a powerful "New Faith" and, contrary to his intentions, helped to make it attractive to people suffering from spiritual emptiness or longing for absolute certainties. The acceptance of Koestler's account by many ex-communists is easily explicable: he provided them with a conveniently self-justifying explanation of their communist past, one, moreover, that made simple things look complicated and so prevented people from passing a straightforward, unambiguous judgment. If the communists had been blindly obedient to the party and ready to transgress all norms of elementary human decency, then it was their own personal fault, not to be justified by reference to a party mystique. If they agreed to take part in show trials and accused themselves of the most heinous and utterly absurd crimes, then this could only be explained as their having yielded to physical torture, not as morally motivated conduct. A typical representative of this view is Gustaw Herling-Grudziński, author of *A*

World Apart, one of the best first-hand accounts of the Soviet Gulag before Solzhenitsyn.[201]

Similar views are held by anticommunist intellectuals and politicians in postcommunist countries. In their cases, however, additional ideological reasons and psychological mechanisms are involved. Most of them are too young to have experienced communism in its militantly ideological phase; they associate it not with the party mystique, but rather with party corruption; not with the rule of ideological fanatics, but rather with the rule of the *nomenklatura*—that is, people seeing power as a means of pursuing their own group interests and generally far removed from heroic fanaticism. At the same time the intransigence of their anticommunism rests on the assumption that communism has an unchangeable essence and that therefore the communists known to them cannot be radically different from the communists of the time of the Great Terror. This assumption, however, can hardly withstand confrontation with Koestler's analysis of the communist mentality. Hence, the dismissal of this analysis is the easiest way of avoiding cognitive dissonance.

Anti-anticommunist Western intellectuals, including the majority of American Sovietologists, rejected Koestler's account for completely different reasons.[202] In their view, Koestler presented Stalin's annihilation of the original Bolsheviks as the logical triumph of Bolshevism itself, thus endorsing an extreme version of the continuity thesis.[203] If his interpretation of Bukharin's confession and his view of its paradigmatic importance for the understanding of the Bolshevik old guard were credible, then (they felt) it would be necessary to agree that Bolshevism did not contain a democratic alternative and therefore that hard-line anticommunists were right to deny the possibility of a peaceful evolution of the Soviet regime in the direction of a genuine socialist democracy. The latter conclusion could easily have been avoided, because the evolution of the Soviet regime might have been conceived as dependent on the erosion of Bolshevik communism, not on discovering an alternative tradition within it. Nevertheless, some leading American scholars set their hopes on overcoming the Stalinist legacy through a return to the policies of the NEP as represented by Bukharin (who, in their view, "had special claim to represent the original Bolshevik heritage").[204] Taking issue with Koestler and offering a completely different interpretation of Bukharin's trial was the logical consequence of this position.

Clearly, this issue is of crucial importance to our understanding of Soviet communism, its past and its recent dissolution, and is particularly important in all attempts to analyze the fate of freedom under communist totalitarianism. However, this matter has obviously too many facets and dimensions to be adequately dealt with in a book on intellectual history. Therefore, what I offer here is not a full historical interpretation, but merely an attempt to explain why I regard Koestler's book as consistent with what we know (or should have known) about the extreme forms of totalitarian communism as a secular faith. I shall naturally concentrate on Bukharin's depositions and on the remarkable confirmation of Koestler's account in the former's recently published "Letter to the Future Generation of Party Leaders." But in order not to view Bukharin's case as individual and unique, I shall preface my analysis of it by a brief presentation of the case of another old Bolshevik, Yuri Piatakov. Although less well known than Bukharin, he too was a very representative figure in the Bolshevik movement. In his "Testament" Lenin mentioned these two as those younger members of the Central Committee who might be considered for the office of general secretary of the party.

At the end of 1927 the Left Opposition, of which Piatakov was a prominent member, was expelled from the party. This punishment, although not immediately followed by more severe punitive measures, broke the spirit of the group and induced a mood of repentance that soon found expression in a number of official recantations. One of these, published in *Pravda*, was by Piatakov, by then the Soviet trade representative in Paris. His friend, a former Menshevik N. V. Volsky (Valentinov), could not understand such a sudden repudiation of long-held views and interpreted it as lack of moral courage. In a private conversation with Valentinov, Piatakov defended himself in a long and extremely emotional tirade, explaining the peculiar nature of membership in the Bolshevik party.[205] The main points of this proud, sincere, and profoundly revealing statement follow:

Non-Bolsheviks could not understand Lenin's party, because it was a truly miraculous and miracle-working body. Its dictatorship, exercised in the name of the proletariat, had been described by Lenin as "based directly upon force and unrestricted by any laws" (see chapter 4, section 4). The most essential part of this formula was not the emphasis on force, but the idea of freedom from any man-made laws, either legal or moral. Piatakov argued:

A law is a limit, a ban, a definition of one phenomenon admissible and another inadmissible, one action possible and another impossible. When thought holds to violence in principle and is psychologically free, unbound by any laws, limits or obstacles, then the field of possible action expands to gigantic proportions and the field of impossible contracts to the points of zero. The essential feature of the Bolshevik Communist party is the limitless extension of the possible. . . . This feature distinguishes it from all other parties and makes it a party of miracles. Bolshevism is a party whose idea is to bring into life that which is considered impossible, not realizable and inadmissible. . . . For the honor and happiness of being in its ranks we must sacrifice our pride and self-esteem and everything else. Returning to the party, we put out of our heads all convictions condemned by it, even though we defended them while in opposition. . . . I agree that non-Bolsheviks and the category of ordinary people in general cannot make any instantaneous change, any reversal or amputation of their convictions. But the true Bolsheviks are people of special temper, without any equivalents in history. We are different from all others. We are a party of men who make the impossible possible. Steeped in the idea of violence, we direct it against ourselves, and if the party demands it and if it is necessary and important for the party, we can by an act of will put out of our heads in twenty-four hours ideas that we have cherished for years. It is absolutely incomprehensible for you because you are unable to go beyond your narrow "self" through subordination to the severe discipline of the collective. But a true Bolshevik can do it. His personality is not limited by the boundaries of individual self, it fuses with a collective named the party. I do not lie, I tell the truth when, asking for my reinstatement in the party membership, I repudiate my former views and my resistance, stemming from selfish pride, and declare my submission to the party. And my agreement with the party should not be merely external. This would be double-dealing [*dvurushni- chestvo*].[206] In suppressing one's convictions or tossing them aside, it is necessary to reorient oneself in the shortest possible time in such a way as to agree, inwardly, with one's whole mind. Is it easy to put out of mind something that only yesterday you considered to be right and which today you must consider to be false in order to be in full accord with the party? Of course not. Nevertheless, through violence directed against oneself, the necessary result is achieved. . . . This sort of violence against the self is acutely painful, but such violence with the aim of breaking oneself so as to be in full accord with the party constitutes the essence of a truly principled Bolshevik Communist.

Someone objected to this argument, pointing out that the party may be absolutely mistaken and call something black that is clearly and indisputably white. Piatakov saw this objection as philistine and mean spirited and declared: "Yes, I shall consider black something that I felt and considered to be white, since outside the party, outside accord with it, there is no life for me."[207]

Valentinov saw Piatakov's self-disclosure as extremely important for the understanding of Bolshevik-communist psychology in general and the Great Purge trials in particular.[208] At the end of his article Valentinov quoted a long paragraph from the self-criticism Piatakov had published in 1936 on the eve of his arrest. This monstrous but not untypical document contains praise of Stalin as the beloved leader of all the toilers of the world and violent denunciation of the former leaders of the Left Opposition (Trotsky, Zinoviev, Kamenev) as simple bandits motivated by insatiable personal ambitions and bestial hatred of the victorious Leninist party. All of them, Piatakov concluded, should be exterminated as dangerous vermin polluting the clean, fresh country of the Soviets and capable of murdering its leaders.[209] In Valentinov's opinion this was not just Piatakov's desperate bid for his own life. Piatakov had written "his monstrosities, made his confessions and went to his death with the conviction that all these things were necessary for the victory of communism."[210]

Let us pass now to Bukharin's confession. It is true that he categorically denied the most absurd charges, such as being connected with foreign intelligence services or preparing a series of assassinations of important political figures (including Lenin, Kirov, and Gorky).[211] In doing this he demonstrated some residual attachment to old-fashioned notions of truth and dignity. Nevertheless, he also frankly admitted his political and legal responsibility for the "defeatist orientation and all its grave and monstrous crimes" against "the Socialist fatherland and the whole international proletariat," including even "the dastardly plan of the dismemberment of the USSR," declaring that it was obvious to him that the gravity of these crimes would justify the severest sentence. "A man deserves to be shot ten times over for such crimes. This I admit quite categorically and without any hesitation at all."[212]

The most illuminating part of Bukharin's confession is a remarkably self-conscious attempt to explain his conduct. The crucial element here is the reference to "a peculiar duality of mind" characteristic of a Bolshevik oppositionist like himself.[213] The logic of the factional struggle drove such people to counterrevolutionary positions close (in Bukharin's own case) to "a kulak praetorian fascism." This struggle, however, took place "amidst colossal socialist construction, with its immense scope, tasks, victories, difficulties, heroism," which must profoundly impress even the most degenerate members of the party. Hence "a dual psychology" arose among them.[214] Torn between their counterrevolutionary tendencies and the awareness of "the objective grandeur of socialist construction," their state of mind came to resemble the Hegelian "unhappy consciousness," inwardly split and divided. Their faith in the counterrevolutionary cause could therefore not be complete, and their will remained semiparalyzed.[215] Bukharin presented this process as a triumph of socialism, a testimony to its superior capacity to dominate even the will of its opponents: "The might of the proletarian state found its expression not only in the fact that it smashed the counterrevolutionary bands, but also in the fact that *it disintegrated its enemies from within, that it disorganized the will of its enemies.* Nowhere else is this the case, nor can it be in any capitalist country."[216]

Having said this, Bukharin attempted to explain the Moscow Trials to Western observers, who attributed the repentance of the accused to "diverse and absolutely absurd things" like "Tibetan powders," hypnotism, or the proverbial "Slavic soul" of Dostoevskyan characters. All such explanations, he stressed, revealed a complete failure to understand the fact that in the Soviet Union "the antagonist, the enemy, has at the same time a divided, a dual mind."[217] In other words, the defendants in the Moscow Trials were not convinced of the rightness of their cause; indeed, deep down they admitted the rightness of the cause of the party, as represented by their accusers. This, and nothing else, made them capable of sincere repentance.

Passing from general explanation to his own case, Bukharin clarified his repentance thus: "For three months I refused to say anything. Then I began to testify. Why? Because while in prison I made a revaluation of my entire past. For when you ask yourself: 'If you must die, what are you dying for?'—an absolutely black vacuity suddenly rises before you with startling vividness. There was nothing to die for, if one wanted to die unrepented. And, on the contrary, everything positive that glistens in the. Soviet Union acquires new dimensions in a man's mind. This in the end disarmed me completely and led me to bend my knees before the Party and the country." [218]

The meaning of these words is quite clear. Bukharin knew that he must die but desperately wanted to save the meaning of his life. A non-Bolshevik would have chosen to die protesting against the orgy of terror and thus turning his trial into Stalin's trial. Tucker did all he could to attribute such an intention to Bukharin, but the results of his complicated and extremely strained argument are utterly unconvincing. [219] For Bukharin the party was the whole meaning of his life, and Stalin, whatever one might think of his personality and his policies, became "a sort of symbol of the party." [220] Bukharin was well prepared to surrender before his imprisonment, when he still continued to believe that a change of policy was badly needed. During his trips abroad in 1935 and 1936 he had explained his position to the emigré Mensheviks, Theodore Dan and Boris Nikolaevskii. He told Dan that loyalty to the party left people like himself without a choice: "We all put our heads in his [Stalin's] mouth . . . knowing for sure that one day he will gobble us up." [221] And in a conversation with Nikolaevskii, Bukharin justified this attitude by a historicist argument: "One is saved by a faith that development is always going forward. It is like a stream that is running to the shore. If one leans out of the stream, one is ejected completely." In this view, Stalin was the personification of the stream of history, and the old Bolsheviks could only console themselves that this stream "still goes forward in the direction in which it must." [222]

This duality of mind—seeing Stalin as a monster, on the one hand, and yet regarding him as the legitimate incarnation of the party and its socialist cause, on the other—was not a stable equilibrium, of course. Sooner or later one element had to prevail and suppress the other. Bukharin's imprisonment catalyzed this process. Facing inevitable death he (as he himself put it) raised himself above "everything personal, all the personal incrustation, all the rancor, pride" and recognized "the complete internal moral victory of the USSR over its kneeling opponents." Bukharin mentioned in this context Feuchtwanger's *Moscow 1937*, which he had read in prison and which helped him to see the Soviet Union as the strongest bastion of all antifascist forces in Europe. While greatly praising this book, he also criticized it for stopping halfway and failing to acknowledge that "world history is a world court of judgment."[223] According to Tucker, this amounted to claiming that his (Bukharin's) trial was taking place before the bar of history and that it would pass to history as a trial of Stalin.[224] In reality, however, this is (unfortunately!) a completely groundless interpretation. Bukharin reproached Feuchtwanger for being insufficiently Stalinist and too lenient to Stalin's opponents, especially to Trotsky, whom Feuchtwanger placed on the same plane as Stalin. In Bukharin's view Feuchtwanger was absolutely wrong in this, because world history had vindicated Stalin and unequivocally condemned the opposition: "In reality the whole country stands behind Stalin; he is the hope of the world; he is a creator."[225]

The following two paragraphs, summarizing the whole speech, contain a sentence that has been construed as implying that the trial was a sort of medieval witchcraft trial and therefore should not be taken seriously. The apparent plausibility of this contention makes it necessary to quote the relevant sentence in context. Bukharin said:

I am explaining how I came to realize the necessity of capitulating to the investigating authorities and to you, Citizens Judges. We came out against the joy of the new life with the most criminal methods of struggle. I refute the accusation of having plotted against the life of Vladimir Ilyich, but my counter-revolutionary confederates, and I at their head, endeavored to murder Lenin's cause, which is being carried out with such tremendous success by Stalin. The logic of this struggle led us step by step into the blackest quagmire. And it has once more been proved that departure from the position of Bolshevism means siding with political counter-revolutionary banditry. Counter-revolutionary banditry has now been smashed, we have been smashed, and we repent for our frightful crimes.

The point, of course, is not this repentance, or my personal repentance in particular. The court can pass its verdict without it. The confession of the accused is not essential. The confession of the accused is a medieval principle of jurisprudence. But here we also have the internal demolition of the forces of counter-revolution. And one must be a Trotsky not to lay down one's arms.[226]

As the context clearly shows, Bukharin, in full accordance with Lenin's conception of "objective treason," saw himself as guilty *irrespective* of his subjective motives and regarded the verdict of the court as justified *irrespective* of his admission of guilt. For him the real significance of the public trial was its role in the internal demolition of the forces of counterrevolution, of which he was an important part, an attitude quite consistent with the explanation of the Moscow Trials (i.e., their methods of extracting confessions and the need of these confessions for the political "education" of the masses) in Koestler's *Darkness at Noon*. The reference to Trotsky indicated Bukharin's negative judgment on the strength of Trotsky's personal ambitions, setting him apart from the collectivist spirit of genuine Bolshevism.

At the end of his last plea Bukharin called Trotsky the main motive force in the parallelogram of counterrevolutionary forces, the main source of their criminal methods, such as terrorism, espionage, the dismemberment and wrecking of the USSR. Not surprisingly, he also declared his rejection, in principle, of Trotsky's endeavors to defend him, as well as similar endeavors by the Second International, because he was "kneeling before the country, before the Party, before the whole people."[227]

The *New York Times* (March 13, 1938) described Bukharin as "the first of the fifty-four men who have faced the court in the last three public treason trials who has not abased himself in the last hours of the trial."[228] Indeed, compared to the other defendants he made an effort to defend his personal decency, to appear a tragic figure rather than a common criminal. But apart from this comparison and seen from a greater historical distance, he must be regarded as having morally capitulated, albeit in a less abject way than required by Stalin, but abject and humiliating enough. It is therefore hardly surprising that the posthumous rehabilitation of Bukharin under Gorbachev's *glasnost'* did not make him a cult figure in the Soviet Union; it was too late to extol his unbending, self-denying loyalty to the party.[229]

One of the revelations of *glasnost'* was the publication of Bukharin's "Letter to the Future Generation of Party Leaders."[230] This was dictated by him to his young wife, Anna Larina, memorized by her, submitted to the party authorities in 1961, but only published in 1988.[231] In it Bukharin stated that he had always been an honest revolutionary, never a traitor, that despite his mistakes he had never wanted to destroy the achievements of socialism, and that for many years he had had no disagreements with the leadership of the party.[232] He asked therefore that a new generation of party leaders reexamine his case and restore him posthumously to party membership.

This was precisely what happened, and it is proper to note that both Bukharin's "Letter" and the belated fulfillment of his last request are a telling corroboration of the accuracy of Koestler's insights. Rehabilitation in the unspecified future was the only thing Gletkin promised Rubashov for his "last service to the party"; it may seem very little, but for a communist like Rubashov (Bukharin) it was desperately important.

The amount of space I have devoted to Piatakov and Bukharin is justified, I believe, by the fact that they may be considered paradigmatic cases of the totalitarian communist mentality. They provide an excellent illustration of the party mystique (Conquest's expression)[233] that survived the period of the Great Terror and later slowly eroded under the influence of both Khrushchev's "thaw" and Brezhnev's stagnation. Arendt might have used their stories in perfect corroboration of her thesis that as long as a totalitarian movement holds together, its "fanaticized members can be reached by neither experience nor argument."[234]

It is important to stress that Piatakov, Bukharin, and countless other Bolsheviks of a similar mentality were products of Leninism, not Stalinism. This simple observation provides an additional and decisive argument for the view that whatever we think of the character of the Soviet state under Lenin, the totalitarian nature of the Leninist party cannot be seriously questioned. The so-called democracy within the party that, within certain limits existed under Lenin had nothing to do with individual freedom, since the defeated minorities were forced to submit to the general will of the party, not just externally but internally as well, by renouncing their own separate opinions in the name of the fetishized "unity of the party."[235] With the passage of time these obligatory conversions were supplemented by obligatory self-criticisms and recantations of previous errors. The public confessions at the Moscow Trials were an extreme but otherwise logical development of these practices.

Of course, the bloody extermination of the old party cadres would not have occurred under Lenin, but the party mystique, together with the cult of the Great Leader, developed in his lifetime. Let me quote, for example, a few verses from Mayakovsky's long poem "Vladimir Ilyich Lenin," written on the occasion of Lenin's death and dedicated to the Russian Communist party:

> The Party—
>   is a million-fingered hand
> clenched
>   into one
>   gigantic fist.
> The single—is nonsense,
>   the single—is nil.
>   . . . .
>
> The Party—
>   is the backbone of the working class.
> The Party—
>   is the immortality by which our work lasts.
>   . . . .
>
> The Party and Lenin—
>   are brother-twins—
>   who's more valuable
>   to mother-history then?
>   We say—Lenin,
>   and the Party
>   we mean,
>   We say—the Party,

and Lenin
is meant.[236]

It seems to me that this quotation may be helpful for a better understanding of at least three problems: the Bolshevik contempt for a single individual, which of course involves contempt for individual freedom; the identification of the party with its leader and consequently Stalin's successful attempt to achieve the status of a "new Lenin"; and finally, Bukharin's ardent and desperate desire not to be excluded from the party's collective immortality.

Stalinist Communism and Western Intellectuals

Owing to Gorbachev's *glasnost'*, Koestler's *Darkness at Noon* has finally been published in the Soviet Union. In the discussion following this event, one critic pointed out that Stalinism was an international phenomenon, not something unique to Russia, and that its influence on many Western intellectuals warranted its treatment as a part of Western intellectual history.[237]

There is much truth in this opinion. It applies to the entire communist experiment in Russia, and the reasons for it can easily be identified. The world of global capitalism and bourgeois society seemed to have collapsed in 1914 and (as Eric Hobsbawm recently put it) "even intelligent conservatives would not take bets on its survival." [238] This widespread insecurity deepened during the time of the great economic crisis in the West and Stalin's "revolution from above" in the Soviet Union: in the eyes of many people world capitalism seemed to be inevitably doomed, while Stalin's Five Years' Plan was perceived as remarkably successful, a decisive proof of the viability and dynamism of the Soviet system. An additional and extremely important circumstance was the rise of fascism and Nazism in Europe, which led many Western intellectuals to despair of Western liberal values and thus prepared them to accept Soviet communism as the only salvation.

The reception of Stalinism in the West took many forms. The Soviet leader could be praised from many different standpoints: from a purely "bourgeois" position, seeing his Five Years' Plan as comparable to Roosevelt's New Deal (Wells),[239] from the position of communist fanaticism, and of course from many intermediate positions characteristic of many different sorts of fellow travelers and communist sympathizers. This book is certainly not the place for a comprehensive analysis of this rich and important problematic, but we cannot ignore it altogether. Otherwise, Stalinism will be conceived of as a merely local phenomenon, a peculiarity of Russian political culture, and its appeal to Westerners will be conveniently forgotten.

It is necessary therefore to present the essentials of the problem without pretending to exhaust it. The success of such a task depends on a representative selection of sources. For the sake of brevity I have decided to limit this section to a short review of three books only. The first, *Soviet Communism*, written by the veterans of British socialism, Sidney and Beatrice Webb, documents the extraordinary illusions of the Western Left about the alleged grandeur of Soviet achievements. The second, Merleau-Ponty's *Humanism and Terror*, is a sophisticated effort to reinterpret the issues raised by Koestler and by Bukharin's trial, with the intention of defending Stalinist justice or at least giving it the benefit of the doubt. The third, Crossman's *The God That Failed*, provides, in my opinion, an extremely important account of the experiences of six Western intellectuals who had once been infatuated with communism, either as "initiates" (i.e., party members) or merely as "worshippers from afar."

The Webbs's two fat volumes (more than eleven hundred pages altogether) were the result of intensive research and several visits to the USSR. Their content is well summarized in the introduction to the new edition, written by Beatrice Webb and dated 1941, the argument of which runs as follows.

Stalin is not a dictator but "the duly elected representative of one of the Moscow constituencies to the Supreme Soviet of the USSR." He was for long content to be simply a member of the Presidium; he took over the office of prime minister only after the outbreak of the war and did it "in exactly the same way" as Winston Churchill. He does not have "anything like the autocratic power of the President of the U.S.A." [240]

The USSR is a political democracy; its Constitution of 1936 makes it clear that it is "the most inclusive and equalized democracy in the world." Unlike the Roman Catholic and Anglican churches, the Communist party is not an oligarchy; "it is democratic in its internal structure." Stalin has never claimed "the position of a dictator or fuehrer." [241] The one-party system does not contradict the democratic nature of the state, because the special interests of the Soviet citizens are continually expressed in the public organizations to which they belong (such as trade unions, cooperative associations, cultural and scientific societies, and so forth). [242] Most important, there is no alternative to this system, because a revolutionary government, confronted with the task of educating a mass of illiterate and oppressed people of diverse races and religions, cannot afford the existence of an organized political opposition. [243]

The superiority of the Soviet democracy over the democracies of the West consists in securing full racial equality and the democratic control of the instruments of production, distribution, and exchange. The Soviet peoples are free from the yoke of "the all-powerful governing class of landlords and capitalists"; hence, they are not divided into "a nation of the rich and a nation of the poor."[244] They are also free from the egoistic pursuit of profit and do not work for the pecuniary gain of an entrepreneur but for the welfare of the human race.[245] This applies also to the collective farms, which represent a higher type of mixed economy. Every Soviet citizen has numerous rights: not only traditional civil rights, such as the right to protection against arbitrary arrest, but also social rights, such as the right to remunerative work and paid holidays, the right to education of every kind and grade, the right to a special provision for motherhood, and finally and most important, "the right to full economic provision, according to need, in all the vicissitudes of life."[246]

The group of men responsible for this splendid transformation of their country—the Communist party—is characterized by intense faith and a puritan ethic of self-restraint, which is manifested in the penalization of homosexuality, the limitation of the right to abortion, and "most reactionary of all," the "outspoken approval of the lifelong attachment of husband and wife." Interestingly, in writing this description in the introduction, Beatrice Webb ignored the fact that the relevant section of the book did not stress any of these points. She also gave a completely different assessment of the nature of the party than appeared later, stating: "In fact, in the nature of its mentality, as in the code of personal conduct, the Communist Party resembles more a religious order than the organization of the learned professions of Western Europe." Elsewhere, however, we read: "In fact, in the nature of its mentality, as in the direction of its activities, the Communist Party reminds us less of a religious order than of the organization of the learned professions of Western Europe."[247]

This contradiction (reflecting some hesitations in judgment or, perhaps, some differences between Beatrice and her husband) did not, however, affect the optimism of the overall diagnosis. In the view of both authors, the communist ideology put "no limit to the growth of knowledge" and in fact counted "on a vast and unfathomable advance of science in every field."[248] The party was *outside* the constitution and therefore could act only by persuasion.[249] Having no legal right to enforce its decisions, it simply could not abuse its power.

The Webbs conceded that not everything was perfect in the Soviet Union. But it was only natural that Soviet communism should suffer from some "infantile diseases." One of these was the "idolization of the Leader"— something deeply embarrassing for both Lenin and Stalin—which reflected the backwardness of the masses and was bound to die out with the spread of education.[250] Another shortcoming was the "disease of orthodoxy" and the absolute prohibition of any antisocialist propaganda.[251] But this was justified in a country threatened with foreign invasion or domestic upheaval and would disappear with the increased prosperity of the Soviet Union and its security in the world at large. Even now the Soviet government was "singularly open-minded," as was shown, among other things, by the publication in Russian of the complete works of Ricardo.[252] Moreover, the disease of orthodoxy was not wholly absent in capitalist political democracies, as shown, for instance, by the intolerance toward Jesuits in Switzerland.[253]

Finally, the Moscow Trials: Beatrice Webb refused to see them as a scandalous event (which would have undermined her optimistic view of the Soviet Union). She had no doubts about the crimes of the defendants. Treason trials, she argued, were a normal event in all countries that had undergone a violent revolution. Britain was no exception to this general rule: "Even our own limited revolution of 1689 in Great Britain, whereby a Protestant king by Parliamentary statute was substituted for a Catholic king by Divine Right, was followed, for nearly a hundred years, by generation after generation of conspirators to whom treason and rebellion, spying and deceit, with or without the connivance of a foreign power, were only part of what they deemed to be a rightful effort to overturn an even worse state of home and foreign affairs than they had joined as rebels to destroy." Hence, the Soviet government did not discredit itself by liquidating the conspiracies inspired by Trotsky. On the contrary, "the success of the Soviet government in instituting not only a political but an industrial democracy, and thereby enormously increasing the health, wealth and culture of the inhabitants, and the consequent recognition of the USSR as a Great Power, discredited the Trotsky movement."[254] This reasoning, of course, applied to Bukharin as well.

The final conclusion of this exercise in procommunist apologetics was the view that the USSR had achieved a fundamental transformation of the social order, one "so conducive to the progress of humanity to higher levels of health and happiness, virtue and wisdom, as to constitute a new civilization."[255] Western countries, particularly Britain, should learn from the experience of the Soviet Union and follow its example in raising civilization to new heights.

In fairness to them one must say that on the whole the Webbs's book is a striking example of the particular blindness that results from looking at everything through the prism of one's own culture-bound standards and failing to understand that these standards might be totally inapplicable: that, for instance, extraconstitutional power might be the only real power, thus making most constitutionally guaranteed rights no more than a fiction. Nevertheless, the authors were vaguely aware that the Soviet system could not be adequately described by such traditional categories as democracy, oligarchy, or dictatorship. They pointed out that "history records also theocracies, and various other 'ideocracies,' in which the organized exponents of particular creeds or philosophic systems have, in effect, ruled communities irrespective of their formal constitutions, merely by 'keeping the conscience' of the influential citizens."[256] In this respect they showed more insight than those Sovietologists who tended to reduce Stalinism, and totalitarianism as such, to a system of power.[257] At the same time, however, they proved totally incapable of realizing that an effective "ideocracy" or "creedocracy" allows no room for freedom of conscience and thus liquidates individual freedom at its deepest source. In their view the dominance over conscience could be exercised only by persuasion, and this in its turn could pose no threat to liberty.

In his *Humanism and Terror* the French phenomenologist Merleau-Ponty approached "the communist problem" from a more philosophical standpoint. His main concern was the overall meaning of human history and human responsibility for making history meaningful. Marxism was, in his view, the only philosophy of history—that is, the only philosophy capable of vindicating the idea of history as a meaningful process.[258] Hence, it was superior to all other humanisms; it was the only critique of the present world order that did not lead to nihilistic despair, and in this respect it could not be surpassed.[259] Its project of general human emancipation was subject, however, to the test of practice—that is, to the test of the proletarian revolution, whose birthplace was Russia and whose directing center continued to be located in Moscow. The question of the meaning of universal history was dependent therefore on the fate of the Russian Revolution.

Koestler's book suggested that the Russian Revolution had failed and had entered a phase of wanton self-destruction. Merleau-Ponty did not want to agree with this because so much was at stake for him, but what he knew about the Soviet Union made it impossible to rid himself of grave doubts. He described his situation as inextricable: "It is impossible to be an anti-Communist and it is not possible to be a Communist."[260] This was a good description of a "peculiar duality of mind" not dissimilar to that of Bukharin. So arises a peculiar parallel between Bukharin's efforts to save a belief in the meaning of history (and the meaning of his own life) and Merleau-Ponty's attempt to refute Koestler. In both cases historicist arguments have been used to prove that the worst moral evil might be historically justified and that therefore it was still possible to believe in communism, *despite* the Moscow Trials.

The same arguments were employed by Koestler's heroes—Rubashov and his interrogator, Gletkin. This enabled the French philosopher to reinterpret Koestler's book in such a way as to use it for a historico-philosophical justification of the Stalinist terror.

Revolutionary violence, Merleau-Ponty argued, is a necessary part of historical progress. Hence, it does not make sense to condemn it from an abstractly moralist position. The struggle for justice always involves violence, and thus "he who condemns all violence puts himself outside the domain to which justice and injustice belong."[261] A wholesale condemnation of violence is always hypocritical, because violence is a necessary part of the rules of the game in the human world.[262] Nobody understood this better than Marx, and this was what made Marxism "a theory of violence and a justification of Terror."[263]

The rejection of abstract moralism and rationalism (attributed to Trotsky) profoundly influenced Merleau-Ponty's understanding of individual responsibility. He historicized this notion and claimed that "historical responsibility transcends the categories of liberal thought—intention and act, circumstances and will, objective and subjective." It followed from this that what really mattered were the objective consequences of any given conduct and that in certain situations individuals could be condemned and sentenced in the name of history, irregardless of procedural justice. Revolutions cannot afford to distinguish between legal and illegal forms of counterrevolutionary activity or between subjective and objective opposition to revolutionary policy. Indeed, "in a period of revolutionary tension or external threat there is no clear-cut boundary between political divergences and objective treason." In such a situation it is normal that "Humanism is suspended and government is Terror."[264]

Thus, an evaluation of the Moscow Trials depended above all on the reading of the general situation obtaining by then in Russia, on whether it was seen as revolutionary, or no longer so. Merleau-Ponty chose the first interpretation, observing that the Moscow Trials "only make sense between revolutionaries, that is to say between men who are convinced that they are *making history* and who consequently already see the present as past and see those who hesitate as traitors." Hence, the Moscow Trials were in fact "revolutionary trials presented as if they were ordinary trials."[265] This was well understood by Koestler's Rubashov, and so he had to declare himself guilty of treason. The same applied to his prototype. It is evident that Bukharin was no fascist, but the objective logic of the struggle linked him with White Guard emigré cossack circles. He was politically interested in the kulak opposition and therefore kept himself informed on the kulak revolts, using (indirectly) the information coming from cossack circles. Consequently, he had to accept responsibility for these revolts.[266] Had his policy been successful, its consequences would have been disastrous for the cause of socialism in the Soviet Union. They would have been disastrous for the whole world, because to undermine socialism in the USSR would have done Hitler a service and significantly changed the balance of power during World War II.[267]

After the war Stalin declared: "All the Trotskyite and rightist machinations against the Party and their entire wrecking 'activity' directed against our government's policies had only one aim: to destroy the Party's program and delay the task of industrialization and collectivization."[268] Merleau-

Ponty agreed with this, proposing only different expressions: "Instead of saying 'had only one aim,' let us say 'could have only one result,' or 'one meaning,' and the discussion is closed."[269] This was as much as to say that from the point of view of the highest tribunal—the tribunal of history—Stalin's terror was justified and his opponents (as they themselves admitted) only got what they deserved. Koestler commented: "Professor Merleau-Ponty, the successor to Henri Bergson's chair at the Collège de France, published a remarkable book to prove that Gletkin was right."[270]

Humanism and Terror has been described as an expression of the attitude of "the classical fellow-travelling intellectual, offering fellowship (but not allegiance) on the assumption that, whatever the appearances, Official Communism was (or might be) travelling, albeit by 'dialectical detours,' towards true Communism."[271] In other words, it was the work of an outside spectator trying to elaborate for himself a comfortable understanding of history. In contrast with this, the first part of *The God That Failed* explains the experiences of those Western intellectuals who joined the various national Communist parties and thus became communist insiders.

The most important of these testimonies belongs to Koestler, who had been a member of the German party. He described himself as a member of the "pauperized bourgeoisie," a class displaced by history and reacting by joining the rebels of the Right or Left. Reading the *Manifesto of the Communist Party* and other works by Marx and, even more, by Engels was a new revelation for him and resulted in a total conversion. It was like a mental explosion and a true initiation into a redeeming knowledge: "To say that one 'had seen the light' is a poor description of the mental rapture which only the convert knows. . . . The new light seems to pour from all directions across the skull; the whole universe falls into pattern like the stray pieces of a jigsaw puzzle assembled by magic at one stroke. There is now an answer to every question, doubts and conflicts are a matter of the tortured past—a past already remote, when one had lived in dismal ignorance in the tasteless, colorless world of those who *don't know*."[272]

Joining the party (in January 1932) was a unique experience of the fraternal comradeship of the righteous. "Both morally and logically the Party was infallible: morally, because its aims were right, that is, in accord with the Dialectic of History, and these aims justified all means; logically, because the Party was the vanguard of the Proletariat, and the Proletariat [was] the embodiment of the active principle in History."[273] Membership in it was therefore equivalent to being one of the elect. At the same time, however, this chosen status was blended with an atmosphere of mutual distrust and constant exposure to collective supervision. Not only the thinking, but also the vocabulary of party members were strictly controlled. Certain words were taboo, as indicative of a philosophical, strategical, and tactical fallacy.[274] For instance, there could not be such a thing as a "lesser evil," since such a notion implied a relativistic departure from absolute certainty. Everything had to be clear and unambiguous in accordance with the dichotomized black-and-white vision of the world that expressed the deep inner need of rank-and-file party members. They "craved to become single- and simple-minded" and therefore willingly subjected themselves to "intellectual self-castration."[275]

As we can see, this was a simple, unreflective faith, defending itself at all costs from any shadow of doubt. Of course, it could not preserve itself forever in this virgin state. In Koestler's case the first doubt arose during his visit to the USSR in the autumn of 1933. As a result, his naive faith was replaced by mental reservations; he accepted the notion of a "lesser evil" and developed in the direction of a dual consciousness. At this stage his membership in the party required additional, increasingly dialectical justifications. One was the view that communism, despite all its distortions, was the historical force best prepared to end the rise of Nazism. Another was the conviction that "the party could only be changed from inside, not from outside." One could not leave the party, because in spite of everything, it was "the incarnation of the will of History itself. Once you stepped out of it you were *extra muros* and nothing which you said or did had the slightest chance of influencing its course."[276]

The authors of two other testimonies were writers: the Italian writer Ignazio Silone and the black American writer Richard Wright. Both underwent a complete communist conversion, described by Silone as changing his entire internal world.[277] For both the party became everything, and "the world that lay beyond it was to be destroyed and built anew." However, both suffered greatly from its iron discipline, especially from its attempts to impose rigid intellectual control. Wright modestly confessed that it was not courage that made him oppose the party: he "simply did not know any better." It was inconceivable to him that "a man could not have his say." He had come North "just to talk freely, to escape the pressure of fear," and now, as a member of the Communist party in Chicago, he faced fear again—and could not stand it.[278]

A peculiarly interesting episode in Wright's story is his account of a party trial at which a black comrade named Ross was accused of a number of political crimes. Nobody was compelled to give information against him, and yet almost everybody gave it willingly, citing dates, conversations, scenes. In this way "the black mass of Ross' wrongdoings emerged slowly and irrefutably." The accused stood trembling, unable to defend himself. "His personality, his sense of himself, had been obliterated." And yet he could not have been so humbled unless he had shared and accepted the vision in the name of which he was being condemned. Finally, he pleaded guilty of "all the charges, all of them."[279]

The author, as he sat there, thought of the people who had been skeptical of the Moscow Trials, and commented:

They could not have been skeptical had they witnessed this astonishing trial. Ross had not been doped; he had been awakened. . . . The Communists had talked to him until they had given him new eyes with which to see his own crime. And then they sat back and listened to him tell how he had erred. He was one with all the members there, regardless of race or color; his heart was theirs and their hearts were his; and when a man reaches that state of kinship with others, that degree of oneness, or when a trial has made him kin after he has been sundered from them by wrongdoing, then he must rise and say, out of a sense of the deepest morality in the world: "I am guilty. Forgive me."[280]

For Wright this was a spectacle of horror but at the same time a spectacle of glory.[281] The yielding to ruthless collective pressure may sometimes appear a sublime expression of oneness, of the strength of the inner ties that bind together the oppressors and their victims.

The ambiguity about absolute collectivism characterized both writers. Having extricated themselves from their parties, they felt nostalgic about their communist past. Silone wrote: "The truth is this: the day I left the Communist Party was a very sad one for me, it was like a day of deep mourning, the mourning for my lost youth. . . . It is not easy to free oneself from an experience as intense as that of the underground organization of the Communist Party." And Wright was nostalgic about the days when he had been able to paint everything in black and white and to assign a role of honor and glory to the Communist party. For he knew in his heart that he would never be able to write in that way again, "should never again express such passionate hope, should never again make so total a commitment of faith."[282]

In the second part of *The God That Failed*, the most interesting piece is the autobiographical essay by the English poet Stephen Spender.[283] Although classified as a "worshipper from afar," he had been very close to the leadership of the British Communist party and even joined its ranks for a brief period in the late 1930s. He was therefore an intellectual fellow traveler who knew the party from the inside while preserving the cognitive advantages of an outside observer.

His main motive for joining the communist movement was a sense of social and personal guilt and a desire to purge himself of an abnormally developed individuality.[284] This confirmed the observation of the French writer André Gide that the triumph of the individual consists in renouncing individualism.[285] But after joining the party Spender let himself be forced to feel guilty not only about his bourgeois indecisions but also about the original humanitarian motives that had brought him close to Communism—and which the Communists saw as bourgeois sentimentalism, incompatible with the virtues of ruthless decisiveness and single-mindedness in pursuit of the goal. He saw this process as typical: "The Communist, having joined the Party, has to castrate himself of the reasons which have made him one."[286]

Among the reasons for this peculiarly communist anesthetization of humanitarian feelings, two were of decisive importance: an exclusive fixation on the future, which made party members completely indifferent to what happened in the present,[287] and a self-righteous identification of the actual policy of the party with the cause of historical progress and moral justice in general. Spender came to see very clearly that "the self-righteousness of people who believe that their 'line' is completely identifiable with the welfare of humanity and the course of history, so that everyone outside it exists only to be refuted or absorbed into the line, results in the dehumanization of the Communists themselves."[288]

Of course, it was not easy for a "bourgeois intellectual" to achieve this state of absolute certainty. He had to be torn by contradictions, which led to a characteristic "duality of mind." But this struggle of conscience helped Spender understand the psychology of the communist true believer, which he described thus: "Communists, who act in ways which may seem to the non-Communist unscrupulous, may nevertheless be perfectly sincere. Such Communists are like ships doubly anchored fore and aft, amid crosscurrents which swing all other craft. The two anchors are: the fixed vision of the evils done by capitalism, and the equally fixed vision of the classless society of the future." Contrasted with this were the "crosstides disturbing liberal conscience": "scruples about the methods necessary to achieve the ends of communism and awareness of events such as the suffering of thousands of people who do not happen to be Communists."[289]

Like the Polish poet Czeslaw Milosz (whose views on communism are presented below), Spender could not succeed in persuading himself that the communist cause justified the destruction of artistic freedom. He understood, however, that the communist intolerance of this freedom was not an accidental misunderstanding. "The destruction of this freedom," he wrote, "is justified by a slogan: that freedom is the recognition of necessity. The political freedom of necessity is the necessity of the state version of the needs of generalized, collectivized man." This was incompatible with artistic freedom, because "art speaks for the individuality of each human being."[290] Since it was necessary to choose between communism and art, the British poet chose the latter.

In his review of *The God That Failed*, Deutscher firmly rejected Koestler's view that only ex-communists really knew what communism was about. He risked the assertion that the opposite was true: "Of all people, the ex-Communists know least what it is all about." Ex-Communists, he argued, were incapable of detachment; their thinking was too emotional, and consequently their view of communism was "pure demonology." A good example of their lack of objectivity was their attitude toward Stalin. For Deutscher, Stalin should be compared to Napoleon. "An honest and critically minded man could reconcile himself to Napoleon as little as he can now to Stalin"; nevertheless, one must realize that Stalin, like Napoleon, was a great historical figure whose violence and frauds ultimately served the cause of the revolutionary transformation of the world.[291]

This was written in 1950. Today these words sound rather odd, and the testimonies of the authors of *The God That Failed* strike us as philosophically detached, rendering justice to the communists' intentions and their ardent, unshakable faith. In postcommunist countries, however, the dominant view of Communists is quite different: they are presented, as a rule, as corrupt, cynical individuals who have always cared only about their own group interests, privileged status, and monopoly of power. Reading *The God That Failed* is a good antidote to such oversimplification. It reminds us that Communism was once a god, although a god that was doomed to fail. The Communist *nomenklatura*, so often demonized today and presented as the very essence of Communism, had never aspired to such divine status.

The same can be said about Merleau-Ponty's *Humanism and Terror*. It helps us understand the ideological legitimation and rationale of Stalinism, demonstrating thereby how childish it is to explain the Communist problem merely in terms of "a 'lust for power' or the Party interests."[292] The monstrousness of Merleau-Ponty's historicist justification of Stalinist crimes is extremely instructive, reconstructing in detail and with a great philosophical sophistication the intellectual and moral mechanisms of Bukharin's surrender. Both books convincingly show that the Communist mechanisms of intellectual captivity were the same everywhere and not unique to Russia, that the West also had its Stalinist experience, although, happily, on the intellectual and moral level only. Both prove that Western intellectuals did not consider Soviet Communism as something alien to Western culture and that it is unjust to describe Soviet Communism as a phenomenon whose "parentage was obscure."[293]

The Webbs's book, despite its incredible naiveté, is also an important document of its time. It shows us that the Soviet Union could be a symbol of hope and a legitimate development of civilization not only for Marxist Communists, but for noncommunist leftists as well. The rulers of Stalinist Russia had no reason to feel themselves condemned and isolated pariahs of the world. On the contrary, they saw themselves as the vanguard of universal History. This was one of the necessary conditions of their ability to exercise an ideocratic tyranny.

The Dual Consciousness of the Soviet Intelligentsia

As we have seen, the "dual mind," or "dual consciousness," was a common characteristic of those communists, or communist sympathizers, who became acutely aware of the discrepancy between their ideals and reality. Bukharin formulated this problem by referring to the Hegelian conception of the inwardly split "unhappy consciousness"; Orwell applied to it his famous conception of "doublethink." But these two conceptions should be distinguished from each other. Bukharin was trying to explain the tragedy of a Communist true believer attempting to save what gave meaning to his life, while Orwell's purpose was to lay bare the mechanisms of totalitarian control over people's minds. We may say that the first elaborated a secular theodicy, while the second unmasked the mendacity of a secular theocracy. In practice this difference was often blurred: the Communist "unhappy consciousness" assumed the presence of powerful ideocratic pressure, while doublethink contained, as a rule, an element of voluntary accommodation. Nevertheless, the tragedy of Communist true believers was something different from the sufferings of those people who were simply the victims of ideological oppression—even if they were forced actively to participate in maintaining this oppression, as was the case of the Soviet intelligentsia.

Valentin Turchin, a Soviet liberal democratic dissenter, made a useful distinction between the three forms, or stages, of totalitarian enslavement: physical enslavement through terrorist measures; enslavement through blinding (i.e., through the pressure of false information); and finally, enslavement through subjecting people's minds to an ideological operation that changes their identity and paralyzes their will to resist, even without cutting off their access to true factual information.[294] In the first stage, actual or potential dissenters are simply imprisoned or killed; in the second, they are ideologically disarmed and reduced to helplessness; in the third, they accept the system as an alleged necessity that may not be perfect but cannot possibly be changed.[295] According to Turchin, this third stage, characteristic of "stationary totalitarianism" (that is, of Brezhnev's USSR), represented the final victory of the totalitarian enemies of freedom: an effective transformation of the human consciousness, an effective suppression of the will for freedom, enabling the system substantially to reduce its reliance on physical force and outright intimidation.[296]

An interesting feature of this conception is its emphasis on the ideocratic aspect of totalitarianism. Unlike Tucker and many other Western scholars, Turchin does not reduce totalitarianism to a system of power. He stresses instead the importance of its ideological props and argues, quite logically, that perfect totalitarian control of people's minds would make physical repression superfluous. However, he goes too far in this direction. His conception assumes that the Soviet Union was more totalitarian under

Brezhnev than under Stalin or Lenin, which is obviously not true. Accepting the system as merely a necessity, historically inevitable but otherwise alien to people's values, was a rather shaky form of internalization of the official ideology, a form whose survival depended ultimately on the conviction that the system was strong, that is, that it had enough force at its disposal. Under Stalin ideological pressure was infinitely stronger, and it was not considered good enough to go along with the regime on the assumption of its necessity; this attitude was seen rather as demonstrating a certain mental reservation and thus indicating a lack of genuine enthusiasm or (which was in fact the same) an insufficiently internalized conformity. People accepting the regime as a historical necessity (that is, not on the basis of its intrinsic goodness) risked being classified as "two-faced persons" or double-dealers (dvurushniki) and accused of using the mask of loyalty to conceal their true feelings.[297]

Another weak point in Turchin's conception is the assumption that the use of ideological controls was inversely proportional to the use of physical coercion. In reality the time of the greatest terror was also the time of the greatest intensity of organized ideological pressure. Physical intimidation increased the effectiveness of "ideocratic fear," and vice versa. Soviet history provides ample evidence of this.

Let us take, for example, the testimony of a Russian historian who was arrested at the time of the Great Purge. He had been regarded as a loyal Soviet scholar, yet he was prepared for arrest. Why? He himself explained it thus: "Like all other Soviet citizens, I carried with me a consciousness of guilt, an inexplicable sense of sin, a vague and indefinable feeling of having transgressed, combined with an ineradicable expectation of inevitable punishment. Thus each one of us had been shaped by sifting and checking, criticism and self-criticism. The arrest of acquaintances, colleagues, and friends who felt just as guilty—or guiltless—as ourselves intensified this state of mind."[298]

It is not surprising that such a man "had not the courage to fight for truth alone" and yielded to the demands of his interrogators.[299] He felt himself guilty, because the pressure of Stalinist indoctrination deprived him of any deeply rooted convictions of his own, but had not succeeded in eliminating all his doubts and potentially subversive feelings. In other words, he felt guilty in being unable to live up to the ideal of total conformity with official Soviet values, and he expected to be duly punished for this. He was divided between a passive acceptance of the official ideology and the remnants of his authentic identity, which had somehow survived the indoctrination process but at the same time proved to be too weak to resist it effectively. In his view the same was true of all other Soviet citizens.

The assertion that all Soviet people, or all members of the Soviet intelligentsia, were exactly the same in this respect is of course an exaggeration.

We know that there have always been some enclaves of "inner freedom" in the Soviet Union. But on the other hand, it would be an exaggeration to say that the inhabitants of these enclaves—or rather the lonely people whose inner world constituted an enclave of freedom—were completely immune to ideological pressure and unacquainted with the phenomenon of "dual consciousness." As a rule, their inner freedom was defensive, rather than self-assertive, and vulnerable to threats. The case of the great Russian poet Osip Mandelstam is very instructive on this point. He managed to preserve his identity, his unique creative individuality, and did not become a "Soviet writer." Nevertheless, in 1937, at the height of terror, he did what was required of him and wrote an "Ode to Stalin." His widow, Nadezhda Mandelstam, comments: "Many people now advise me not to speak of it at all, as though it had never existed. But I cannot agree to this, because the truth would then be incomplete: leading a double life was an absolute fact of our age, and nobody was exempt. The only difference was that while others wrote their odes in their apartments and country villas and were rewarded for them, M. wrote his with a rope around his neck. Akhmatova did the same, as they drew the noose tighter around the neck of her son. Who can blame her or M.?"[300] This passage suggests that Mandelstam's writing of the "Ode" was protective mimicry. This was certainly true, but it was not done out of cynicism. This point was emphasized by the poet's widow:

To write an ode to Stalin it was necessary to get in tune, like a musical instrument, by deliberately giving way to the general hypnosis and putting oneself under the spell of the liturgy which in those days blotted out all human voices. Without this, a real poet could never compose such a thing: he would never have had that kind of ready facility. M. thus spent the beginning of 1937 conducting a grotesque experiment on himself. Working himself up into the state needed to write the "Ode," he was in effect deliberately upsetting the balance of his mind. "I now realize that it was an illness," he said later to Akhmatova.[301]

Thus, physical terror combined with organized ideological pressure pushed people not only into outward pretense but also toward deliberate attempts to force themselves into the mood of a total inner conformity. For people like Mandelstam, it was a torture of self-denial, but nevertheless they often succeeded in killing their true selves. Undoubtedly, the repetition of such "grotesque experiments on themselves" involved the risk of losing the capacity to recover.

After Stalin's death, as a result of Khrushchev's de-Stalinization campaign, physical coercion in the Soviet Union was greatly reduced. Soon afterward, under Brezhnev's "actually existing socialism," the forward-looking ideological zeal of the leadership began to give way to a conservative attitude toward ideological control: "continuous mobilization" for the construction of communism was replaced by a concentration on maintaining the system as it was, which of course gradually weakened the ideological pressure. Yet the interiorized collective memory of the physical and ideological terror of Stalin's day was so strong that the liberation from mental restrictions proceeded at a much slower pace than in other countries of the Soviet bloc. In addition, the monstrously developed apparatus of ideological control had vested interests of its own and could not readily be dismantled. Hence, it was natural for the question of ideological compulsion to appear as one of the main problems on the agenda of the dissident movement in the USSR.

The nature of this problem was best shown by two *samizdat* writers who used the pseudonyms of O. Altaev and Dmitrii Nelidov. The former presented the dilemma of the Soviet intelligentsia in an essay on "The Dual Consciousness of the Intelligentsia and Pseudo-Culture"; the latter, referring directly to Orwell, analyzed the Soviet version of "doublethink" in an article on "Ideocratic Consciousness and Personality." [302]

According to Altaev, there was a pervasive duality in the whole existence of the Russian intelligentsia in the Soviet Union.[303] The majority of the intelligentsia, he asserted, did not accept the regime, tended to shun it, or even held it in contempt. Yet there existed also a peculiar symbiosis between them, because the members of the intelligentsia were actively engaged in producing the tools of their intellectual enslavement, and the regime rewarded them for performing this task. Awaiting the collapse of the regime and hoping this collapse would come sooner or later, the intelligentsia nevertheless collaborated with the regime, fed it, and fostered it. It was not enough to call it conformism, because conformism is a normal compromise of interests by means of mutual concessions; neither was it simple opportunism. It was servility of a peculiar kind: "An ostentatious servility with suffering, with a 'Dostoevskiian touch' to it. Here we have at the same time a horror of the fall and enjoyment in it; no conformism, no opportunism knows of such refined torments. The existence of the intelligentsia is painful for itself, irrational and schizophrenic." [304]

Thus, the Russian intelligentsia was characterized by a painful inner dualism: a dualism in the cognitive subject itself, a split between the subject and its ethos. But it was not a case of simple clinical pathology, as the term *schizophrenic* might suggest: "The dualism of the intellect, though it causes incalculable suffering and palpably destroys the individual, still, as a rule, leaves the subject within the bounds of the normal; it cannot be described in clinical terms because above all the fact is that the phenomenon of dual consciousness characterizes an entire social class, it is the property of a large group, and is not exclusively individual." [305]

An important factor in keeping "within the bounds of the (clinically) normal" were the different forms of mental adjustment to the situation.

These consisted mostly in persuading oneself that the double life and the dual consciousness were somehow justified by higher reason, or necessity. The simplest form was the rationalization of one's conduct by attributing to it a higher hidden meaning: thus, for instance, joining the party might be justified on the grounds that "it is necessary to increase the percentage of decent people in the party." Or one might console oneself that the hated regime had yet some historical justification: "The Bolsheviks are bad, but without them Russia would have perished anyway. Hence, in their appearance there is a certain conformity to law." The most comprehensive and tragic form of this self-enforced reconciliation with reality was a voluntary rejection of freedom in the name of the Engelsian "understanding of necessity." But the effects of choosing necessity as the ruling principle were actually suicidal rather than salutary: "When man rejects his own freedom, he also denies his own individuality. He ceases to see any prevailing value in himself, and, irrespective of what he thinks, becomes only a link in the natural chain, only a little bridge to succeeding generations, only an element, a necessary one of course, but still only an element in the system." [306]

In the last part of his essay the author described the different successive disappointments of the intelligentsia, its different temptations, and its growing awareness that "evil will never collapse by itself. It will take on the most refined and sophisticated forms, but it will never lose its identity, never will it cross the boundary to the humane." In his view, everything depended on the intelligentsia's next move: Would it finally separate itself from the regime, or find a new form of accommodation within it? This conclusion explained his initial suggestion that "today, in one way or another, the intelligentsia again clearly holds the fate of Russia in its hands, and with it the fate of the whole world." [307]

Nelidov's article differs from Altaev's in that it reflects a greater pessimism about the chances of liberation from ideocratic tyranny. In Nelidov's view, the intelligentsia's submission to "boundless ideological rule" had little to do with its corruption by material rewards and could not be terminated by an act of will. Neither did he agree that this submission assumed a conscious rejection of freedom. Ideocratic consciousness, he argued, existed in an atmosphere in which the very word *freedom* was "senselessly outside the habitually mastered reaction." This was because ideocratic consciousness assumed "a rejection of personality, a rejection in the presence of which nothing can be done with freedom, and wherein freedom is conceived to be an indecency, an outrage." [308]

Nelidov did not see the official Soviet ideology as merely a tool in the hands of an individual or collective dictator. Indeed, he declared that "no personality, in essence, can rule over totalitarian society. It was not Stalin who was the absolute dictator, but the deified truth which welded people together by its mystery." But this did not mean that the official creed had become deeply internalized by the Soviet people and should be regarded as part of their genuine identity. It was rather an "alienated consciousness" external to individuals and belonging "to everybody together, but to no one in particular." Its acceptance had little to do with the psychological mechanism of adjustment, because it was "simply an 'objective reality given to us in an idea' that each citizen must, in some measure, pay heed to." The Marxist-Leninist catechism was not something in which the Soviet people really believed, but it was rooted in each of them "in the form of coded knowledge, emotions, and impulses." In this way, paradoxically, Marx's discoveries led to the creation of a "pneumocratic state" estranged from any individual consciousness and transforming truth into "coercive objectivity."[309]

Of course, it was necessary to develop an appropriate culture of social adaptation, and here the Russian author saw the relevance of Orwell's theory of doublethink as "the power of holding two contradictory beliefs simultaneously, and accepting both of them."[310] He defined doublethink as submission to "the socio-ideological mannequin" installed in everybody's mind through "ideocratic" pressure, which allowed people to separate themselves from this mannequin by stepping back, as it were, and looking at themselves from the outside. In Soviet conditions every person (unless "blessed with a special inner power of resistance") was forced in some measure to accept this mannequin, "to make it one's self," at the cost of repudiating his or her genuine identity. But there were different degrees of possible separation from it. At one pole there was "ideological infantilism"—the minimal degree of separation—at the other, cynicism—the maximum degree of distancing oneself from the externally accepted rules of the game. Cynics usually felt themselves to possess inner freedom but in fact were also held on an ideological leash, though a longer one than in the case of others. They too saw no alternative to the official ideology and in fact served it more effectively than the "infantile believers." Despite their ability to indulge in irony, they voluntarily submitted to the "ideological mannequin," becoming accustomed to it and correcting themselves in accordance with "the mechanics of reflexes elaborated in it."[311] Nelidov's conclusion was predictable: the first priority of the democratic movement in Russia must be *inner, spiritual* liberation. Inner freedom was of the first importance; without it one could not successfully fight for external legal or political liberty.[312]

The article was dated September 1973. By a curious coincidence it was in this same month that Alexander Solzhenitsyn completed his *Letter to the Soviet Leaders*, a passionate plea for spiritual freedom.[313] In it he tried to convince the leaders that it would be in their own best interests to break the ideological shackles and to allow people to live with the truth. He wrote:

Cast off this cracked ideology! Relinquish it to your rivals [i.e., the Chinese leaders], let it go wherever it wants, let it pass from our country like a storm cloud, like an epidemic, let others concern themselves with it and study it, just as long as we don't! In ridding ourselves of it we shall also rid ourselves of the need to fill our lives with lies. Let us all pull off and shake off from all of us this filthy sweaty shirt of Ideology which is now so stained with the blood of those 66 million that it prevents the living body of the nation from breathing. This Ideology bears the entire responsibility for all the blood that has been shed. Do you need me to persuade you to throw it off without more ado? Whoever wants can pick it up in our place.[314]

This belief in the healing, salutary effect of getting rid of the iron grip of ideology was based on Solzhenitsyn's deep conviction that "universal, obligatory force-feeding with lies" was the most agonizing aspect of existence in the Soviet Union, "worse than all our material miseries, worse than any lack of civil liberties."[315] "Our present system," he wrote elsewhere, "is unique in world history, because over and above its physical and economic constraints, it demands of us total surrender of our souls, continuous and active participation in the general, conscious *lie*."[316] From this perspective a traditional, nonideological authoritarianism seemed to him to be incomparably better, to be compatible with inner freedom. He even saw such authoritarianism as a better exit from totalitarianism than the struggle for political democracy would be, because (as he argued) external freedom would be worthless and dangerous without full spiritual liberation.

Unfortunately, his encounter with the West led Solzhenitsyn to a moralistic critique of "merely external" freedom and to the unreserved idealization of nontotalitarian forms of authoritarianism. This compromised him in the eyes of the great majority of Western intellectuals, and as a rule his views ceased to be taken seriously. This was an overhasty and undiscriminating reaction: the conservative crudeness of some of his views on Western democracy should not overshadow the depth and force of his diagnosis of the main evil of the Soviet totalitarian system. As I have tried to show, this diagnosis reflected the deeply felt experiences of a wide spectrum of the Russian intelligentsia. Solzhenitsyn's appeal: "Do not take part in the lie! Do not support the lie!"[317] made a profound impression not only in the USSR, but also in the socialist countries of East-Central Europe. His views on the primary importance of spiritual liberation therefore deserve serious consideration. To do them justice, they must be presented in the context of existing accounts of the horrors of spiritual enslavement, not only in Russia and the USSR, but also in all countries that have passed through a period of genuine totalitarianism.

Solzhenitsyn's conviction that the worst evil of the Soviet regime was omnipresent ideological coercion is in complete agreement with Orwell's view on the most essential and distinctive feature of totalitarianism. According to Orwell, totalitarianism tries to coerce people from within by controlling their thoughts and feelings. "It is necessary to understand," he stressed, "that the control of thought is not only a negative feature, but a positive one as well. It not only forbids you to express, or think, certain thoughts; it also dictates to you what you have to think, it provides you with an ideology, it tries to govern your emotional life and it establishes a code of behavior."[318] This is, I think, an unsurpassed description of the totalitarian suppression of freedom, and to my knowledge, it has not been seriously questioned. If so, Solzhenitsyn's view on the paramount importance of inner freedom deserves respect as well. It should be noted that the Russian writer knew Orwell's vision and accepted it as an accurate description of Soviet life. He wrote: "Where did Orwell light upon his *doublethink*, what was his model if not the Soviet intelligentsia of the 1930s and 1940s? And since that time this doublethink has been worked up to perfection and become a permanent part of our lives."[319]

Part of this Orwellian world were, of course, the Moscow Trials. Solzhenitsyn (who had little emphathetic understanding of Marxist true believers) would probably not have agreed with this, but it is fair to say that the old Bolsheviks were also victims of ideocratic coercion: they too were forced to lie, although in their case participation in official lies could not ensure their survival. In a sense, Bukharin's confession was the reverse of the usual doublethink: he yielded to ideological pressure in the name of ideas that were truly his own, his participation in the Great Lie was not self-protective but tragically self-destructive. Nevertheless, it was also a telling—and terrible—exemplification of the ideocratic nature of totalitarian tyranny.[320]

The Polish Case: The Captive Mind Revisited

Poland's experience with totalitarian communism is often neglected. It is widely believed that a strong national feeling did not allow Stalinism to take root in Poland, that the majority of Poles saw the Stalinist government as a mere puppet regime, a tool of Poland's traditional enemy, and that the Catholic church, so powerful in Poland, saved its believers from internalizing communist ideology.

This was not always so. It is true that Poland is the only country of the Soviet bloc "in which Sovietization was not fully implemented."[321] But it is not true that Polish Stalinism completely failed to impose its rule on people's minds or that Polish Stalinists lacked the will radically to transform Poland's national identity. Jakub Berman, the veteran of the Communist party of Poland who in 1948 became responsible for ideology and culture as well as foreign affairs and security matters in the People's Poland, tried to establish Communist ideological hegemony in a mild Gramscian way but had no hesitation about the final goal. Even at the very end of his life, after the Solidarity revolution and the martial law that followed, he remained firmly convinced that history was on his side, that it was a historical law that the minority, the vanguard, always rescued the majority, and that the Polish nation would, sooner or later, "mould itself into its new shape." He ended a long interview with Teresa Torańska by saying: "I am nonetheless convinced that the sum of our actions, skillfully and consistently carried out, will finally produce results and create a new Polish consciousness. . . . It may happen in fifty years or it may happen in a hundred, I don't want to make prophecies, but I am sure it will happen one day." [322]

If one takes into account the hostile atmosphere in the country and the deliberate moderation in the reeducation of the intelligentsia by means of physical terror, the success of Polish Stalinism in the mass production of captive minds was quite impressive. This is now regarded as incomprehensible and as a "domestic shame," [323] but it was especially true of the intelligentsia. After the full-scale ideological offensive following the crushing of Gomulka's "right-wing nationalist deviation" in 1948, most of the Polish intelligentsia fell under the spell of the "New Faith." Admittedly, some intransigent enemies of the regime remained unbroken; some intellectual circles (mostly Catholic) accepted the regime as a sort of "geopolitical necessity" while remaining immune to its ideology; many, indeed probably most, were intimidated rather than convinced. But it was unfortunately a fact that at least two especially important groups—the majority of the so-called creative intelligentsia and of the students—proved susceptible to Stalinist indoctrination. In the early 1950s, Czeslaw Milosz (author of *The Captive Mind* and a future Nobel Prize winner in literature) was right to see Poland as one of the "converted countries." [324]

The Captive Mind (1953), a semiautobiographical book written primarily for Western readers, was once hailed by philosophers (including Karl Jaspers), sociologists, and political scientists as an enormously important contribution to the understanding of communist totalitarianism. With the passage of time, however, some of its theses have come to be seen as controversial or simply not credible. This applies, above all, to its central thesis about the Communists' aspirations to control thought and their ability to produce captive minds. This growing skepticism reflects the increasingly critical, sometimes frankly hostile, attitude toward the very concept of totalitarianism, as (allegedly) coined for cold war purposes. So we cannot omit an analysis of *The Captive Mind* from this chapter.

Milosz was a left-wing Polish intellectual who hated right-wing nationalism and had serious doubts about capitalist democracies. After the defeat of Nazi Germany he accepted the new regime in Poland and became a Polish cultural attaché, first in Washington and later in Paris. The increasingly aggressive Stalinist cultural offensive, however, finally led to his decision in 1951 to break with the regime and to remain in the West. In "Nie [No]," an article explaining this move, he confessed that he had never been a communist.[325] If the communists could be called "the new Christians," his relation to them was that of a "good pagan"—somebody attracted by the "New Faith" and willing to serve it, but not a true convert. He believed in the historical necessity of the "New Christianity" but refused to become "baptized." The old pagan values were a part of himself, and he was unable and unwilling to renounce his identity. The priests of the "New Faith" solved all problems for the writers, both material and moral. They offered them great prestige and a carefree, privileged existence.[326] But in exchange for this they demanded a renunciation of freedom and truth. Their dialectical method (which Milosz otherwise found very convincing) proved that lies could serve the cause of truth and that true freedom consisted in the understanding of necessity. Milosz did not object to this theory; he was simply unable to cross this threshold in practice. He chose the West, fearing that he was committing suicide as a poet and anticipating only feelings of loneliness. The alternative, however, was a worse sort of moral suicide: speaking with an alien voice and thus ceasing to belong to himself.[327] In this situation, he chose the West as the proverbial lesser evil.

The historical parallel between the breakdown of European civilization under the onslaught of communism and the catastrophe of ancient Rome indicates that Milosz did not think of history in terms of the linear theory of progress.[328] His position might be defined as a peculiar variety of dialectical catastrophism. What made it dialectical was the perception of catastrophe not merely as a disaster, the end of one's world, but also as a regenerative event, a "new beginning." And what made it peculiar was the fact that this catastrophe was not a matter of historical prophecy, but an accomplished fact, the reality of the present.

Such a stance, although not yet a commitment, was by no means value free. To define the situation as a "dialectical catastrophe" was to see it as historically legitimate, as something deserved by the sinful "old world," and necessary for earthly salvation. Nazism could never claim such a status, at least outside Germany. In Poland nazism was perceived as only an episode, a most terrifying one, but inescapably temporary and short lived. This is an important argument against the view that the Stalinist "New Faith" was simply a rationalization of interiorized terror. Not every terror gives birth to an ideocratic fear; the content of its legitimating ideology also counts. The strength of communism as an ideology of expansionist totalitarianism was inseparable from its appeal to universalist values. On the other hand, Polish intellectuals of Milosz's generation as a rule knew too much about the cruel history of their part of Europe and cherished no naive illusions. Hence, they faced the task of *explaining the contrast* between ideals and reality. This task, similar to that of theodicy (or rather, historiodicy), led them to think in historiosophical terms and especially to the widespread use of the Hegelian category of "historical necessity." Milosz called it "the Hegelian bite"; the young Kolakowski, in his revisionist stage, referred to it as "the opiate of the demiurge."[329] The exoteric aspect of the "New Faith" was represented by ideas of a better world and a radiant future, but on a deeper level it stressed the Engelsian (and Hegelian) "conscious recognition of necessity." The ideological functions of the idea of necessity were many. As a rule, it combined therapy with intimidation: people in its grip were "paralysed with fear" of finding themselves "on the wrong side" and landing in the "rubbish heap of history."[330] In all cases it provided powerful arguments, not merely opportunistic, but historical, philosophical, and moral, for swimming with the current and thus accepting the power of those who seemed (and pretended) to embody historical reason. As Milosz later wrote:

> He who has power, has it by historical logic.
> Respectfully bow to that logic.[331]

However, the victory of socialism was not to be the result of the Hegelian cunning of historical reason, which acts behind our backs and achieves its ends irrespective of our will and consciousness. The doctrine of necessity understood, especially in its Leninist-Stalinist interpretation, made it dependent on a subjective factor: the *correct understanding of,* and *active cooperation with,* necessity. A merely passive, philosophical acceptance of socialism was not enough. Milosz was afraid of this when he asked himself: "If we swim with the current, what kind of conditions must be met?" It turned out that these conditions included not only the recognition of necessity, but also acceptance of and active participation in the crudest and most mendacious propaganda, since ideological mobilization could not be based on a frank admission of the truth or by explaining it historiosophically as the necessary price for progress. Such ideological commitment required concealment of truth, enthusiastic support for propagandist lies, and active participation in collective brainwashing. It aimed at creating "social and political conditions in which man ceases to think and write otherwise than necessary." The means for achieving this were a combination of physical and psychological terror, the first, "to destroy the fabric of human society" and to change "the relationships of millions of individuals into channels for blackmail,"[332] and the second, to subject atomized individuals to a system of ideologically conditioned reflexes that would control them from within, thus depriving them of their own minds and consciences.

Milosz had seen all this in Poland. He felt the hostility of the terrorized population, took part in congresses of artists and writers, saw them surrender to the doctrine of socialist realism imposed on them under pressure, and realized that his own fate might be the same. At this point he said his "no" and wrote *The Captive Mind*.

Twenty years after the publication of this book, when the issues it raised had long ceased to be relevant in Poland, the phenomenon of mental captivity, and of the doublethink resulting from it, came to be scrutinized by Russian *samizdat* writers (as mentioned earlier). Against this background, we can see the originality of Milosz's contribution, reflecting as it did the relative weakness of totalitarianism in Poland. Unlike either Orwell or the Russian *samizdat* writers (especially Nelidov), Milosz focused attention on a form of dual consciousness in which the separation from the automatic reflexes of the imposed ideological self (or to use a Freudian term, the totalitarian superego) is not merely passive (observing oneself from outside) or cynical, but involves a form of *active, although disguised, resistance*—a "game played in defense of one's thoughts and feelings." He found an analogy to it in the Islamic civilization of the Middle East, where this form of consciousness had developed into a sophisticated technique called Ketman, a technique of dissimulation and deception combined with a form of positive self-assertion that functioned by interpreting the obligatory faith in one's own special way and thus preserving one's separate identity. According to Milosz, a similar Ketman developed in the people's democracies, where the response to totalitarian indoctrination was "a conscious mass play rather than automatic imitation."[333] In his analysis of what happened to the intellectuals in these countries, Milosz employs three crucial terms: the New Faith, the Murti-Bing pill, and Ketman.

The Murti-Bing pill was the invention of S. I. Witkiewicz, a Polish catastrophic writer who committed suicide when the Soviet army invaded Poland in 1939. In his fantastic novel *Insatiability* (1932), he described two contrasting worlds, a decadent Western world, with intellectuals tormented by "the *suction* of the absurd," and a Sino-Mongolian Empire, whose inhabitants had swallowed the pill invented by a Mongolian philosopher, Murti-Bing. They had thereby acquired an organic worldview making them "serene and happy," or if not entirely so, Milosz suggested, at least helping them to attain "a relative degree of harmony."[334] The incompatibility of the two worlds led to a war in which the Western army quickly surrendered. The Sino-Mongolian army occupied Europe and helped build "the new life" there. The Western intellectuals, eager to get rid of their tormenting problems, offered their services to the new society: instead of dissonant music and abstract paintings, they now produced marches, odes, and socially useful pictures. But they did not succeed in changing themselves completely and so became schizophrenic.[335]

Milosz saw this vision as a prophecy that was being fulfilled in much of Europe. In his view, the cultural revolution in East-Central Europe, that is, the adoption there of Soviet Marxism and socialist realism, could not be explained in terms of physical coercion alone. For many reasons (such as disappointment with right-wing ideologies and regimes, disappointment with the West, fear of nihilism, social alienation, and a desire to feel useful), the intellectuals and artists of these countries were generally prepared to accept the "New Faith." Nevertheless, they proved to be too firmly rooted in their cultures to accept it *entirely* in its primitive Soviet form. Their conversions, however sincere, did not lead them to swallow the Murti-Bing pill in its *entirety*, and so they were able to protect their identities by playing the game called Ketman.

The possible variations of this game were practically unlimited. The most typical seem to be the following:[336]

• "National Ketman," widespread among the masses and appearing even in the upper brackets of the party. Genuine commitment to the "New Faith" combined with "an unbounded contempt for Russia as a barbaric country." A means of secretly qualifying the obligatory allegiance to Soviet communism by pledging loyalty to one's national identity.

• "Ketman of Revolutionary Purity," a variety more common in Russia than in the people's democracies. Hatred toward the Great Leader as the butcher of nations, combined with a fatalistic conviction that in the given circumstances it was necessary to support him. A means of combining loyalist behavior with independent moral judgment.

• "Aesthetic Ketman," or loyalty to the "New Faith" combined with the preservation and cultivation in private of one's own aesthetic taste.

• "Professional Ketman," or paying lip service to the official ideology while not allowing it to interfere with one's professional work.

• "Metaphysical Ketman," characteristic of countries with a Catholic past, especially Poland. Justifying the "New Faith" on the grounds of the old, Christian faith ("perhaps the New Faith is an indispensable purgatory; perhaps God's purpose is being accomplished through the barbarians," etc.); trying to penetrate it, influence its evolution, and so on. In other words, trying "to swindle the devil who thinks he is swindling them." [337]

It is somewhat surprising that Milosz's list does not include the form of Ketman that was particularly important in his own case: the "Hegelian" or "historiosophical" Ketman. Probably he could not have written about it without giving away his friend, whom he named "Tiger," a philosophy professor in Warsaw who would not have liked to be unmasked in this way.[338] After Tiger's premature death, Milosz lost no time in writing of him in his *Native Realm*, thereby providing an important supplement to *The Captive Mind*. He portrayed Tadeusz Kroński as a master of dialectics, a true Hegelian for whom the notion of historical necessity was a two-edged weapon justifying existing reality but also revealing it as historically transient and distinguishing its essential and inessential features. By holding this notion, he remained free "in his inner self" and saw a positive mission for people like himself: "to carry the precious values of our European heritage across the dark era." But he was also "filled with a great dread,"[339] which was to increase after his visit to Moscow (in 1950), where he saw the most advanced stage of the Orwellian world. Unfortunately, even the Polish thaw of 1956 did not liberate him from this fear, but instead added another to it: the fear of setting free Poland's reactionary forces.

The intellectual portrait of Tiger provides a better understanding of Ketman as a general phenomenon, correcting, as it were, certain passages in *The Captive Mind*. It defines Ketman as similar to the Jesuit *reservatio mentalis* and quite different from mere hypocrisy or cynicism. This in turn modifies the statement that "he who practices Ketman lies."[340] In his remarks on Kroński's speeches, Milosz is careful to indicate that Kroński was not simply a liar: his words carried a double meaning—the literal meaning and the meaning for the initiated—and thus aimed at expressing what he saw as truth.[341] This shows that Ketman is not just dissimulation, but such a form of dissimulation as allows for resistance and self-expression.

Nevertheless, Ketman was a risky game. Although it was intended as a cunning way of defending one's identity, it also involved some yielding to ideological pressure and an attempt to adapt oneself to the system. There is no doubt that for many readers of Milosz's book, this second aspect of Ketman overshadowed the first. *The Captive Mind*, as its title suggests, is most commonly perceived as a book about surrendering to "mental captivity," not about defending oneself against it. This assumption is not entirely false: the stories of the four Polish writers who became victims of "playing with the devil" show Milosz's profound pessimism about the chances of living under a communist regime and avoiding the fate of the "captive mind." But it does not follow that he saw Ketman as a mechanism of cowardly self-surrender. Rather, he saw it as an insufficiently effective means of self-protection. He distinguished between Ketman and swallowing the Murti-Bing pill: the very existence of the former was for him proof that the struggle for the defense of inner freedom had not yet been lost. If he criticized Ketman, he did it from within, not from an external, ahistorically moralistic position.

The young Polish intellectuals of the Solidarity generation, who wanted to see Milosz as a paradigmatic moralist and intransigent anticommunist, could hardly understand how such a man could have played Ketman and apparently have become "insensible to totalitarian atrocities,"[342] how he could regard communism as a historical necessity, and why he saw a refusal to recognize this necessity as a symptom of madness.[343] But Milosz did not conceal these facts. He analyzed them in depth in his *Native Realm* in the chapters on his friendship with Tiger, emphasizing that: "We were firmly lodged inside a totalitarian system."[344] This, of course, could not please the many who accepted no excuse for any form of collaboration with the Communists. For them Milosz's Ketman was merely a "self-justifying mechanism of capitulation."[345] The extreme version of this view was the charge that the real purpose of The Captive Mind was to provide a complicated philosophical justification of Milosz's opportunistic conduct, which could in fact be explained by simpler and more earthly reasons.[346]

This severe judgment is both morally and historically unjust. Ketman was a form of dual consciousness that combined a partial yielding to ideological pressure with an active concern for preserving one's genuine identity. As long as the process of ideological mobilization was countrywide, people who played this game had little chance of winning; from the point of view of the militant anticommunists, Ketman players certainly seemed to be on the way to total mental indoctrination. But the situation changed with the gradual weakening of ideocratic pressure. In Poland the real milestone was the year 1956. Thereafter, communist ideology was always on the defensive, and all mechanisms of dual consciousness, especially Ketman, came to function as mechanisms of communism's disintegration. For a long time these mechanisms were much more efficient than external attacks on communism. Efforts to preserve in private life a measure of intellectual independence and genuine cultural identity were transformed into a conscious, public struggle to liberate intellectual and cultural life, piece by piece, from the deadening grip of official doctrine.[347] Given the dual consciousness of Ketman players, it was possible to pretend, or even sincerely believe, that this important inner liberation would ultimately serve the regime by improving its image and providing it with a national legitimation. The actual results, whether intended or not, were very different: the regime lost its original ideological legitimation without obtaining another. A situation emerged in which even Communist hard-liners ceased to be convinced of the intrinsic merits of the system; they too came to have second thoughts and justified the regime for other reasons than Communist goals. In the party as a whole, ideological self-confidence was replaced by ideological timidity or nonideological pragmatism, often combined with a sense of guilt and vulnerability to the ideological and moral pressure of its opponents. Marxism became a liability rather than an asset, and all references to it were tacitly abandoned. In its struggle with Solidarity, the party no longer presented itself as the vanguard of history but merely as a force representing "the lesser evil."[348] The ideological legitimation of its power ceased to be important, because its communist identity had disintegrated and collapsed long ago. This explains its ineffectual resistance to its enemies and its rapid disappearance after losing political power.

It was far otherwise in Russia, where Marxist-Leninist indoctrination had gone much deeper and lasted longer. Nevertheless, there were some important similarities and analogies. It is true that most Russians, unlike the majority of Poles, had swallowed the Murti-Bing pill and that their ideocratic consciousness (as described by Nelidov) seemed completely to suppress their genuine identities. But it would not be fair to claim that Ketman, as a means of defending one's separate identity, was specific to East-Central Europe and unknown in the USSR.

Greater familiarity with Soviet literature and intellectual life makes it clear that many intellectuals and writers adapted themselves to the Soviet regime by the means described by Milosz as "historiosophical Ketman" or/and "national Ketman." [349] This applies even to the so-called National Bolsheviks, who supported the regime as a new incarnation of the historical Russian Empire: their ideology was also a form of mental dualism that contributed, in the final analysis, to undermining the regime's original ideological legitimation.

An important milestone in the process of Russian intellectual liberation was Solzhenitsyn's appeal "to live without lies." A few years later a similar fundamentalist reaction against all remaining forms of dual consciousness, as involving too many concessions to official lies, emerged in Poland and from there spread to the other people's democracies. Even fully conscious intrastructural opposition (i.e., activities consciously undermining the system but using the cover of loyalty) was condemned as a relic of accommodationist attitudes and replaced by an ostentatiously public, sometimes intentionally provocative, opposition. [350] After the proclamation of martial law, Polish intellectuals and artists achieved impressive results in realizing Solzhenitsyn's program of "nonparticipation in lies" and organized an effective boycott of the mass media and official cultural institutions, including most theaters and publishing houses.

Finally, a parallel can be drawn between the final stages of the struggle for ideological and moral delegitimization of the system. In Poland the agent was the anticommunist crusade in the numerous underground publications of the 1980s and in some officially published newspapers and journals (mostly Catholic ones); in the USSR it was Gorbachev's *glasnost'*. In both cases the legitimation of the respective regimes was completely destroyed, and soon afterward they inevitably collapsed.

These brief remarks on the historical events of 1989–91 are relevant here for one reason: these events proved that the well-known truth that no regime can long survive without ideological legitimation is especially true of the so-called communist regimes. Such regimes, lacking both democratic mechanisms for the transfer of power and automatically functioning market mechanisms, *have* to rely on ideological controls and ideological legitimation to a much greater extent than do capitalist democracies. An exaggerated awareness of this need for ideological consensus resulted in attempts to establish that "ideocratic" dictatorship, which was a *distinctive feature* of communist totalitarianism. Despite all their differences,

Solzhenitsyn and Milosz, the two Nobel Prize winners, were in agreement about this.

However, communist "ideocracy" failed to achieve its end. Ideological pressure paralyzed people but did not produce genuine unanimity. Even in the Soviet Union, the communist indoctrination proved incapable of becoming firmly internalized. The Soviet people, including the increasing number of party members, reacted to the ideocratic tyranny by developing different forms of dual consciousness that enabled them to accommodate the system but failed to make them feel truly "at home" in it. The New Man of the communist utopia did not appear; the older, precommunist loyalties and identities were brutally suppressed but not killed, being frozen, as it were, but capable of reasserting themselves with the weakening of external ideological controls.

6

The Dismantling of Stalinism: Detotalitarization and Decommunization

6.1 Preliminary Remarks

It is a well-established tradition in European thought to classify political regimes from the point of view of their relationship to liberty. Measured by this yardstick, totalitarianism, of course, means a total suppression of individual freedom. As I have tried to show, this is because of its ideocratic nature, its successful attempts to subject people to all-pervasive ideological control, a control *from within* that deprives people not only of their external freedom but also, and principally, of their innermost identity, of their freedom to be themselves. Totalitarianism tries to achieve a "coerced unanimity of the entire population"[1]—a unanimity based on an all-embracing ideology that subordinates everything to an ideologically prescribed Final Goal.

The classical theorists of totalitarianism were unanimous in this. George Orwell defined totalitarianism as coercing people from within, through ideological control over their thoughts and feelings. Arendt stressed that "totalitarianism is never content to rule by external means, namely, through the state and a machinery of violence: thanks to its peculiar ideology and the role assigned to it in its apparatus of coercion, totalitarianism has discovered a means of dominating and terrorizing human beings from within."[2] Waldemar Gurian wrote about "the ideocratic or pseudo-religious charac-

ter of totalitarianism."[3] Carl Friedrich pointed out that the most characteristic feature of totalitarianism is "an official ideology, consisting of an official body of doctrine covering all vital aspects of man's existence, to which
everyone living in that society is supposed to adhere at least passively"—
an ideology that "is characteristically focused in terms of chiliastic claims
as to the 'perfect' final society of mankind."[4] Leonard Schapiro saw theocracy as a salient feature of totalitarianism, in the sense of extending state
control to the most private spheres of a person's life.[5]

However, monolithic ideocracy is not an end in itself. In contrast to the
traditionalist, custom-based unanimity of primitive tribal society, it is to be
a *revolutionary* unanimity, a unanimity of the revolutionary collective will,
subordinating everything to the not-yet-achieved, positively formulated,
ultimate goal. It possesses such features of premodern agrarian communalism as "the demands of constant orthopraxy, the infectious display of
loyalty to unit by comportment in all aspects of life," but combines these
with a revolutionary dynamism inspired by a "persuasive messianic secular
promise"[6]—hence the importance of the utopian element in totalitarian
regimes and societies. Totalitarian ideology is not merely a secularized religion; it is a secularized form of *chiliastic* religiosity. It derives its legitimacy
from a commitment to aggressive action, aiming at the total transformation of society; it even aims to transform the very nature of man. To
abandon these ambitions, to yield to the temptations of a stable existence,
in fact amounts to desertion of the totalitarian ideal and entails a long and
tortuous retreat from totalitarian aspirations.

Unfortunately, with the passage of time the term *totalitarianism* lost its
original meaning and "came to be simply an insult, a pejorative term useful
in identifying movements, governments, and countries to be blacklisted."[7]
Especially widespread was a tendency to use it in a narrowly political sense
as denoting merely a system of total power exercised by means of institutionalized intimidation and repression. Thus, a well-known Sovietologist,
David Lane, was able to write that "legitimacy and support were concepts
that were absent from the vocabulary of totalitarianism."[8]

In reality, of course, nothing can be less true. Legitimacy and support—
or, to be more precise, ideological legitimacy and ideologically motivated
mass support—are constitutive parts of the totalitarian model.[9] Without these essential components there would be no difference between a
totalitarian regime and an unrestrained dictatorship, and so the notion of
totalitarianism would be superfluous. The usefulness of totalitarian theory
consists precisely in its ability to explain the phenomenon of a modern,
revolutionary dictatorship deriving its legitimacy from a powerful secular
faith and capable of mobilizing the masses for the realization of a single,
ideologically prescribed collective goal.

This is particularly true of militant communist totalitarianism—the most consistent, paradigmatic form of the totalitarian phenomenon.[10] Happily, some of the best scholars in the field can still recall its features and distinguish it from the "actually existing socialism" of the later period. Thus, for instance, Ernest Gellner has recently expressed the view that Marxism was a more total system of belief than Islam, that it was, in fact, "too total, too all-embracing a religion" and that this was the reason for its undoing. Marxist civilization collapsed because it could not surmount the inevitable weakening of ideological zeal. It could afford the "initiatory, purificatory terror" but not "squalid, corrupt inefficiency in the productive sphere. In other words, faith can survive Stalin but not Brezhnev."[11]

It may justly be said, therefore, that communist totalitarianism cannot be adequately understood without a careful study of its intellectual roots and that intellectual history perhaps provides better tools for its understanding than does empirically oriented social history. Communist totalitarianism legitimized itself by the Marxist theory of history and sought to realize the Marxist vision of communism. It is irresponsible to consider communist totalitarianism in all its varieties as a *misinterpretation* or deliberate *distortion* of the true meaning of Marxist doctrine. One must explain how it was possible for the Marxist conception of universal human liberation to give rise to and serve the cause of totalitarian tyranny.

6.2 Marxist Freedom and Communist Totalitarianism

It goes without saying that totalitarianism was not a necessary consequence of Marxism. It is the ABC of intellectual history that every ideology or trend of thought is subject to different interpretations and that the practical consequences of these interpretations depend on concrete historical circumstances. There is no such thing as one true Marxism; the search for a correct and binding account of Marx and Engels's legacy is an infantile disease afflicting true believers. The richer a given doctrine is, the greater the number of its historically legitimate and logically coherent interpretations.

Nonetheless, it is a fact that Marxism proved to be very well suited to the legitimization of the most consistent and long-lived form of totalitarian regime known, that the crimes of this regime were meant to serve the cause of the Marxist utopia, and that almost all Marxists in the world supported this regime without questioning its ideological legitimacy. We can readily concede that it was not unavoidable but not that it was accidental. Leninism and Stalinism, both as theory and as practice, were not the products of an erroneous reading, much less a deliberate distortion, of Marxism; they were the dominant form of Marxist thought in the twentieth century. The significance of this fact is overwhelming, and attempts to deny its relevance for the understanding of Marxism are either naive or intellectually dishonest.

We can go even further. Marxist totalitarianism was the *predictable* outcome of a Marxist-inspired revolutionary communist movement. It is quite obvious that Marxism as a theory of socioeconomic development contained many reasonable warnings against reckless revolutionism and utopianism; hence, it could evolve (and did evolve in the West) in the direction of a democratic socialism that was increasingly compatible with bourgeois democracy and capitalist economy. However (as shown in chapter 3, section 3.1), the inevitable price of such evolution was to abandon the essential elements of Marxist identity: its commitment to revolutionary radicalism and its communist ideals. Marxist historical materialism could be easily separated from the Marxist utopian ideal and serve as a critical weapon against all forms of its practical realization. Eduard Bernstein was among the first to oppose the scientific (evolutionary) side of Marxism to its utopian (revolutionary-dialectical) side, supporting the former and rejecting the latter. Undoubtedly, this decommunization of Marxism marked the beginning of a gradual but steady de-Marxization of German social democracy. It is not surprising, therefore, that all who saw the heart of Marxism in revolutionary radicalism and communism felt bound to sympathize with the Russian Bolsheviks, who in 1917 contemptuously rejected the compromised term *social democracy* and proudly adopted the older name, "the Communist party." Lenin had then good reason to see himself as the savior of integral Marxism and the only legitimate inheritor of Marx's legacy.

In this way the Marxist workers' movement split between the old social democracy, which avoided revolution and relinquished communist ideals, and Leninist communism, which in fact represented an early stage of the totalitarian revolutionary movement. Its totalitarian features have often been explained as something specifically Russian—as characteristic of Russian tradition and political culture or simply of the specific conditions obtaining in the Russian revolutionary movement. There is an element of truth in this explanation, but more important in the present context is the fact that revolutionary communism, from Babeuf onward, was never free of totalitarian aspiration.

Despite Marx's conscious attempts to dissociate himself from "primitive communism" and to identify the cause of communism with the cause of universal species freedom, Marxist revolutionary communism was no exception to this general rule. Indeed, Marx and Engels's vision of communist freedom was in many respects inherently (although unconsciously) totalitarian—hence, the relevance of this vision to a proper understanding of communist totalitarianism, and vice versa.

The current use of the term *communism* does not help us understand what communism really is or was. In capitalist countries this term generally denotes all countries ruled by people who call themselves communists, irrespective of the degree of socialization of the countries' economies or of the actual policies of the ruling elites. In the countries of "actually existing socialism," the word *communism* became an increasingly meaningless label, used in a positive sense to express loyalist attitudes, or in a pejorative sense to express disapproval of the system and negative feelings toward its beneficiaries. In postcommunist states, *communist* is a derogatory label applied to all ex-members of the overthrown political establishment, or even to all ex-members of the Communist party, despite a widespread awareness that most of these people are thoroughly de-ideologized, knowing very little, if anything, of communism and quite often sincerely hostile to communist ideas. One characteristic of this terminological confusion is a readiness to see communism as compatible with capitalism: if former communists (or, more precisely, those who failed to change their political allegiance before the collapse of the system) become capitalist entrepreneurs, they are called "communist capitalists" and regarded as a symptom of the vitality and perfidy of the communist forces.

This strange amnesia concerning the proper meaning of the term *communism* is the result not just of the recent collapse of communism, but also of the longer period in which this term underwent, as it were, a process of dilution and virtually ceased to be related to the communist ideal. The term was used simply to name one of the competing world systems, irrespective of the degree of its development in individual countries or of the actual direction of their evolution. Attempts to replace *communism* by a more adequate and less ideologically loaded term, such as *state socialism*, have failed to be accepted in official political discourse. This is because both sides of the political conflict have been equally interested in presenting their struggle as an ideological crusade either for or against communism. The communist countries of the Soviet bloc, as well as Communist parties of the West, were in fact retreating from their original commitment to communist goals but did not want to admit this for fear of losing their ideological legitimation and their right to lead the anti-imperialist forces of the Third World. The militant anticommunists, in turn, exaggerated the vitality and ideological intransigence of Communism in order to mobilize their countries for the anticommunist crusade. In other words, both were afraid of the ideological delegitimation of their respective causes and of a consequent erosion of their supporters and followers.

But let us return to the period covered in this book—the period when Marxists firmly believed in their communist utopia.

The Russian critics of the Soviet past, both the radical supporters of Gorbachev's *perestroika* and the outright enemies of socialism as such, have rightly noticed that the "original sin" of the Bolshevik vision was the belief that the first requirement of socialism is the abolition of the market, as representing "blind, natural forces" utterly incompatible with the dignity of man as a rational creature.[12] In their view, this nonmarket conception of socialism became central to Soviet ideology and fatally distorted the entire Soviet development.

The value of this diagnosis lies in demonstrating the close connection between the Marxist idea and a totally administered command economy brought into being and maintained by totalitarian methods. This thesis, with which I entirely agree, is of course difficult to accept for those Western Sovietologists who have tried to explain the Soviet system by reference to historical circumstances rather than utopian blueprints. Moshe Lewin, for instance, has rejected with disgust the bare idea of any "original sin" in the Soviet system.[13] In his *Stalinism and the Seeds of Soviet Reform* he has done all he can to minimize the role of orthodox Marxism in the shaping of Stalinist economic policies. In his foreword (1990) he even suggests that the idea of a marketless economy was a peculiarly Bolshevik fallacy, not a generally accepted tenet of classical Marxism.[14] The introduction of the NEP proves for him that "the anti-market obsession was not an incurable disease."[15] Lenin's conception of the NEP as merely a temporary retreat is conveniently passed over in silence. Consequently, Stalin's elimination of the NEP can be shown not as "resuming the socialist offensive" but as an arbitrary decision, ignoring the (allegedly) promarket evolution of Bolshevik thought and unrelated to Marx's vision of communism.

Another curious statement appears in Lewin's discussion of War Communism. He writes: "It should be remembered that *the doctrine of market relations in socialism*, best expressed in the Bolshevik theoretical literature by Bukharin's *Economics of Transition Period*, was an old socialist doctrine clearly stated by Marx and Engels and later accepted by the entire Marxist movement."[16] The footnote to this sentence says that this was well shown by W. Brus in a book published in Warsaw in 1964.[17] Brus, however, expresses views completely opposed to Lewin's, stressing that Marxism was by no means free of utopian ideas and that the salient feature of Marx's economic utopia was the abolition of the market and the replacement of market mechanisms by an economy "regulated *ex ante*," that is "consciously directed from a central point of control."[18] He maintains, first, that the Bolsheviks in this respect faithfully adhered to the letter and spirit of Marxism; second, that their unchanging commitment to the abolition of market relations is made clear by the virtual identity of the relevant formulae in two programmatic documents—the program of the Russian Communist party of 1919 and the program of the Communist International of 1928 (i.e., of the period "when the five-year plan offensive was opened and the collectivization of agriculture was started"); and, finally, that it is impossible to conclude from Lenin's writings that he saw the system of War Communism as basically erroneous—the mistake was not in the actual premises of the system but simply in the fact that "it was introduced prematurely before the conditions were ripe."[19] In other words, Brus sees Stalin's revolution from above as consistent with both Lenin's and Marx's vision of the construction of communism. Unlike Lewin, Brus explains it not as "imposed by circumstances,"[20] but as motivated by the doctrinal standpoint, derived from classical Marxism, and "independent of strictly economic conditions and needs."[21]

The literal meaning of the passage quoted about "the doctrine of market relations in socialism" (i.e., of *the existence* of market relations in socialism) as "an old socialist doctrine, clearly stated by Marx and Engels" is simply absurd and therefore cannot be attributed to a scholar of Lewin's caliber. Analysis of his text indicates that this passage was intended to explain the practices of War Communism and that the words "the doctrine of market relations in socialism" should be read as "the doctrine of *the absence* of market relations in socialism." Most probably the author meant the doctrine *concerning* market relations in socialism and chose a shorter, unintentionally misleading formula. Still this is not just a matter of stylistic awkwardness, but reveals Lewin's unwillingness to state plainly and clearly that Marxian socialism presupposed the total abolition of the market. He was looking for a formula that would suggest that the word *abolition* was too strong, that Marx would not seriously have contemplated the total elimination of a monetary exchange economy, that the "antimarket obsession" was not a basic, essential feature of his vision of a socialist future, and that therefore it was possible for a Marxist to opt for a mixed economy combining rational planning with a genuine market system. Unfortunately, this is simply not true. Marx made it absolutely clear that market relations must be eliminated in the first (socialist) stage of communist construction. He was more extreme in this respect than Stalin because he also demanded the immediate abolition of money and the replacement of trade by a planned distribution of products. There cannot be any doubt that he would have regarded a "socialist mixed economy" or "market socialism" as a philistine, petty bourgeois illusion.

This utterly negative attitude toward a market economy cannot be dismissed as a curable affliction or an irrational obsession having little to do with the essential features of Marx's communist vision. Rather, it was at the heart of Marx's communism, the very foundation of his axiology. His highest value was species freedom consisting in the conscious, rational control of human collective fate, in the liberation of man's communal nature, and the unfettered, nonalienated development of his species powers. The market was the opposite of all these values: it was the embodiment of the uncontrollable, of the blind natural forces thwarting human plans and creating a situation in which people are enslaved by their own products. The market symbolized the radical dehumanization of man through the suppression of his communal nature and the victory of egoistic individualism, which reduced people to isolated economic subjects. As such, the market was of course the most powerful cause, as well as the final result, of human alienation. Hence, the abolition of the market was even more important in the construction of communism than the socialization of property. According to Marx, individual property could be nonalienated, or de-alienated, and therefore compatible with the human essence, while market relationships were identical with dehumanizing alienation, necessary as a stage of development but contradicting in every way the communist view of human freedom and dignity. Even capitalist private property, despite its alienated and exploitative character, was in some respects more compatible with communist values than was the capitalist market. Its centralization, culminating in monopolistic capitalism, created ever more room for rational planning, thus progressively eliminating the spontaneous (i.e., blind and unpredictable) mechanisms of the market and paving the way for the planned economy of the future. In this way the "old" market-regulated division of labor characteristic of a society of small, independent commodity producers would gradually be replaced by the "new" consciously planned division of labor characteristic of a capitalist factory. Engels carried this reasoning to its logical conclusion by arguing that the capitalist mode of production increasingly contradicted the market form of distribution and therefore that the monetary exchange economy would be eliminated *within* capitalism as a result of the immanent development and centralization of its productive forces. The socialist economy, in its turn, would be run as a single factory, not just consciously controlled but centrally planned, directed, and managed by a board of socialist directors.[22]

This clarification of Marxist views on the relationship between communism (including socialism, as its subordinate stage) and the market is directly relevant to recent discussions about market reforms in the socialist countries. Contemporary socialists, and left-wingers in general, insist as a rule on the basic compatibility of socialism and the market. They carefully distinguish capitalism from a market economy, condemning the former but cautiously endorsing the latter and postulating different ways of controlling and regulating it while definitely not advocating its abolition. Such an attitude, however, should not be attributed to Marx and Engels; attempts to do so (unfortunately very numerous) reveal either a complete lack of understanding of Marxist communism or, more often perhaps, a purely manipulative approach to Marxism and an unwillingness to treat its principles seriously. If Marx and Engels could join in our discussions of the market economy, they would certainly say that it is incompatible with socialism, that attempts to perpetuate its mechanisms are totally reactionary, and above all that while socialism has much to learn from the capitalist organization of production, it has nothing to gain from the anarchy of the market. After all, socialist society was to be organized like a capitalist factory, while the market economy and the commodity fetish-ism associated with it were to disappear completely, giving way to fully conscious collective self-determination. Engels further stressed that this victory over chance and natural blind forces would not weaken the severe regime of factory work; neither would it diminish people's dependence on the authorities. On the contrary, their liberation from the impersonal forces of the market would proportionately *increase* their dependence on public authorities, "no matter how delegated." In *Grundrisse* Marx said the same thing: dependence on the market ("objective dependence") is in-versely proportional to personal dependence. "The less social power the medium of exchange possesses . . . the greater must be the power of the community which binds the individuals together " (M, G, 157–58).

Clearly, Lenin was much more faithful to classical Marxism than is usually believed. True, he departed from the established interpretation of historical materialism by undertaking to build socialism in a relatively backward country. But we must not forget that classical Marxism was more than historical materialism. It also contained a vision of the com-munist future, and from *this* point of view Lenin was certainly Marx and Engels's most faithful disciple. He knew everything they had written on this subject and tried to adhere to it as closely as possible. He was certainly following his teachers faithfully when he pictured the socialist society of his dreams as a single factory run from a single office. He was also true to their ideas when he set his hopes on "state capitalism" and saw his main enemy not in centralized, large-scale capitalist production but in the millions of small commodity producers. He was following the orthodox version of Marxist communism in suppressing market exchange and replacing it by the strictly regulated distribution of goods. The deep frustration felt by his party at the introduction of the NEP is readily understandable in Marxist terms: the Mensheviks, academic Marxists, and other evolutionary social-ists might welcome a partial return to a market economy as consistent with the Marxist "theory of stages," but the Bolsheviks, as deeply committed revolutionary communists, could only see it as a tragic, humiliating re-treat from the communist ideal of Marx and Engels. Almost all of them were waiting impatiently for the termination of the NEP and enthusiasti-cally supported Stalin's "revolution from above." It is quite true, therefore, that this strongly held view of socialism as a marketless society was the "original sin" of Bolshevism and the main ideological factor that pushed it toward Stalinism. But it is equally true that this "original sin" was an essential, constitutive part of Marx and Engels's communist utopia.

It follows from this that the market and communism are fire and water. If communism is treated seriously, if it signifies a definite social doctrine or utopia, not just something associated with a certain country, political party, or group of people, then it is self-contradictory to advocate its "marketization." It is not possible to remain a communist and at the same time to argue, as Gorbachev did in his "Political Report of the CPSU Central Committee to the 27th Party Congress" of February 1986, that it is time "to overcome prejudices regarding *commodity-money* relations and underestimation of these relations in planned economic guidance."[23] Prejudices against market relations belong to the very essence of communism, and planned economic guidance without these prejudices has nothing to do with Marx's communist ideal. If a party calling itself communist seeks salvation in marketization and privatization, it must be seen as abandoning communism, irrespective of the reformers' intentions. We should not be deceived by outward appearances of continuity; neither should we interpret promarket declarations as a sudden volte-face. As a rule, marketizing reforms are the result of a long and painful process of "de-utopianization" by the Communist party in question—a process inevitably leading to the loss of its communist identity.

The Russian experiment with communism was initially recklessly utopian. The circumstantial explanations of War Communism contain an element of truth but ignore the most important and decisive factor: the profoundly communist character of the Bolsheviks' ideological commitments, their euphoric mood after their seizure of power, and the inevitable impact of the unprecedented success of revolutionary Marxism on the radicalization (read: utopianization) of their program. In short, it was decided to reject the "opportunistic," social democratic account of Marxism and to follow instead the precepts of the Marxist communist utopia, ignoring both hard social reality and the democratically expressed will of the people. This ideologically motivated historic choice, made by the charismatic leader of a disciplined, militarily organized, and deeply indoctrinated vanguard party, predetermined the increasingly totalitarian character of the Soviet "dictatorship of the proletariat." True, the road to totalitarianism was not straight and undeviating. It involved experiments with a workers' participatory democracy, a limited tolerance of ideological pluralism, and above all the period of enforced retreat from the initial antimarket crusade. But in the last resort, the will to build socialism (conceived as the first stage of communism) always prevailed, and ideological thinking proved stronger than pragmatic considerations. When the experiment with a workers' democracy failed to produce economically positive results, it was decided that a planned economy must be based on authoritarian command and direct compulsion. When it became obvious that the overthrow of capitalism had failed to liberate man's "communal nature" or to produce a new and satisfactory class consciousness in the workers, it was decided that the "new man" must be created through a system of comprehensive, total indoctrination carried out by interminable propaganda, organized ideological pressure, and an appropriate system of penalties and rewards. If achieving such aims required the elimination not only of political freedom but also of all other freedoms as well, thus abolishing all areas in which individuals could do as they liked or be themselves without ideological direction and control, then it could only mean that the system had to develop in this direction. It is hardly surprising that this ultimately produced the justification of mass terror and the enthusiastic acceptance of the virtual deification of the Leader.

In this way the Marxist communist utopia gave birth to communist totalitarianism. This system set a definite order of political priorities and subordinated everything to the great final goal, which meant in practice that the political authorities arrogated to themselves the right of moral, intellectual, and cultural leadership. This system wiped out civil society and established the strictest control over the private lives of citizens. Not content with passive obedience, it demanded and effectively enforced active support for its policies. It knew how to organize mass enthusiasm and how to mobilize the masses for the march "toward the radiant future." It would not confine itself to external limitations of freedom, because it saw itself as the only legitimate source of all activity. It had to be ideocratic because its aim was to establish a "politically correct" moral and intellectual unanimity. At the same time, it set itself the task of creating the "new man," that is, of changing the individual and collective identities of its subjects in accordance with its utopian blueprint. It was therefore a system of "institutionalized revolution,"[24] a permanent ideological crusade, an unceasing struggle for the control of people's minds, moral impulses, imaginations, and language. It did not always win the struggle, and its victories did not last, but for many years it was on the whole amazingly successful in "the conditioning of man on the basis of its ideological assumptions."[25]

Obviously, Marx and Engels had not envisaged such a realization of their ideas. But it is generally true that ideas have consequences that are not always intended, and it can hardly be questioned that the study of these unintended consequences, with the goal of explaining how they came about, is an important and perfectly legitimate task of intellectual history. So the question arises, To what extent was the totalitarian development of the Soviet Union a consequence of its Marxist ideology? To what extent was it inspired and justified by Marx and Engels's theory of the necessary laws of history and by their vision of the ultimate communist liberation?

In the first place, Marx and Engels were by no means totally unaware of what their ideal of "humanity's leap from the kingdom of necessity to the kingdom of freedom" really entailed. It was to result in a "systematic, definite organization" in which everything would be firmly controlled and no natural, irrational spontaneity would be allowed to contradict the rational unanimity of liberated human beings and the rational collective planning of their lives (see chapter 2, section 6). This ideal of collective self-mastery involved not only the abolition of the market, but also the abolition of civil society in the Hegelian sense (i.e., as the sphere in which different autonomous groups interact with one another in freely pursuing their particular interests). It has become fashionable to treat civil society as the foundation of liberal freedom and a necessary condition for overthrowing the totalitarian legacy. There is of course much truth in this view, and precisely for this reason it is most important to remember that the founders of Marxism intended something completely different. True, they opposed the attempts of "parasitic" states (of the absolutist or Bonapartist type) to subject social life to bureaucratic control, but this applied only to class societies, not to the socialist society of the future in which public authorities would represent the general interest of the species. In particular, this opposition did not indicate sympathy for a pluralist society, in which different private interests conflict and compete with one another within the framework of the general formal rules of the civil law. In his early essay "On the Jewish Question" Marx treated such civil society with contempt and hostility, seeing it as the triumph of antisocial bourgeois egoism and postulating its total suppression in the name of harmonious species life (see chapter 1, section 2). It is not possible to see this conclusion as characteristic only of Marx's early views. His idea of species freedom, which inspired his communism, presupposed the restoration of universal human identity and the rational control of social forces in the name of the common interests of the species; hence it was altogether opposed to particularistic pluralism, to the fragmentation of humanity into multiple autonomous groups and to the freedom of spontaneous social forces. The spontaneous order, regulated by the "invisible hand" of the market, was for Marx the order of alienation, the victory of blind natural forces that dominated people by means of a reified "objective dependence," and as such was incompatible with the rationality and universality of human beings. From this perspective it is evident that the "leap to the kingdom of freedom" must consist in restoring man's "communal nature" by abolishing the pluralist *bürgerliche Gesellschaft* and eliminating the distinction between public and private; that it must ensure the victory of collective rationality by completely suppressing uncontrollable natural spontaneity and thus, as Engels put it, transforming the active social forces from "master demons" into "willing servants" (E, AD, 339). This view of socialism as a totally administered society—one in which the "invisible hand" of the market and the chaotic pluralism of civil society are replaced by the "visible hand" of benevolent public authorities and the rational order of a single, systematic, and definite organization—was therefore entirely consistent with the Marxist vision of the "leap to the kingdom of freedom."

It remained only to clarify two things: first, *who* were to be in control, entitled to represent the general interest of humanity and to deprive social forces of their egoistic and anarchic autonomy; and second, *who* were to be reduced to the role of willing servants, obedient instruments of those who embodied the rational self-mastery of the species. The most general answer to this question was, of course, that the interests of humanity were adequately represented by the working class. However, Engels, with Marx's consent, was more specific in his conception of "scientific socialism." He made it clear that the workers could liberate themselves, and thereby humanity as a whole, only by mastering Marxist teaching and thus acquiring a scientific knowledge of the laws of social development and of the objective direction of historical processes. As I have shown, this conception became the philosophical foundation and "scientific" legitimation of Stalinism. By dismissing all "bourgeois" scholarship in the social sciences as profoundly class biased, idealist, and unscientific, "scientific socialism" justified the claim that Marxists had a monopoly on truth. By treating the laws of social development as objective and guaranteeing the victory of communism, it provided the Marxist party (especially the Leninist vanguard) with a more complete legitimation than the popular vote—namely, it provided an unrivaled feeling of self-righteousness, a messianic sense of purpose, and an unbending will to power. The Marxist vision of a communist utopia inspired this party with a powerful quasi-religious faith, the Marxist theory of historical necessity legitimized the use of the most brutal violence, and the Marxist critique of liberalism justified its unscrupulous undermining and crushing of the legal and political achievements of "bourgeois democracy." The interpretation of Marxism as an all-embracing, "scientific" worldview added to this an ideocratic dimension and laid the foundations for what the Nazis called a *Weltanschauungsstaat*. It was a perfectly logical and consistent development: if ultimate liberation is dependent on mastering "true knowledge," then the spread of this saving knowledge through universal indoctrination is a precondition of final victory.

Of course, I do not mean to say that the emergence of communist totalitarianism can be explained by its ideological sources alone. There were obviously other reasons as well—economic and social, political and cultural. I do not deny the usefulness of circumstantial explanations, and I am ready to recognize the relative importance of accidents and purely personal factors. The arguments presented in this book aim only to show that *without* its ideological component, provided by the revolutionary communist account of Marxism, communist totalitarianism is hardly conceivable and would not have appeared in its Leninist-Stalinist form. The connection between revolutionary Marxism and Soviet communism is incomparably closer and more direct than the selective affinity between Protestantism and capitalism to which Max Weber drew attention. For the citizens of postcommunist states, it is something immediately evident, so that to write a large book about it may seem rather superfluous. But this is not true of the West, where a great many attempts have been made to dissociate Marxism from the communist experience, resulting in an idealized misreading of the former and a flat, unphilosophical interpretation of the latter.

My aim in this book has been to reconstruct the Marxist theory of freedom in the light of its totalitarian consequences and also to demonstrate the relevance of the history of ideas for a deeper understanding of the totalitarian phenomenon. One of my main tasks has been to show the paramount importance of ideological factors in the emergence of the Soviet totalitarian system. The other side of this argument makes it clear that the inevitable ideological demobilization, followed by an outright "de-ideologization," played a particularly significant role in the gradual disintegration and final dismantling of this system.

6.3   The Phases and Factors of Detotalitarization and Decommunization

The classical theories of totalitarianism, as elaborated in the 1950s, all stressed that a totalitarian system effectively suppressed all germs of internal opposition and therefore could not be overthrown from within. This was often taken to be a decisive argument for the view that totalitarianism is virtually immune to internal change. But this radical version of the totalitarian model rapidly proved untenable. Despite its partial setback, Khrushchev's de-Stalinization campaign proved that the Soviet system would not remain frozen in its Stalinist form. Brezhnev's policy of conservative stabilization, though partially rehabilitating Stalin, also moved the country away from Stalinist totalitarianism, exposing the exhaustion of the regime's revolutionary impetus and the weakening of its commitment to communism. It was increasingly difficult to deny that this system was subject to change and that it had never been as monolithic as had been assumed in extreme versions of the totalitarian model. It is not surprising that this gave rise to serious doubts about the continuing usefulness of this model as an explanatory device. "Within the confines of the so-called totalitarian model," wrote Chalmers Johnson, "it is hard to conceptualize development and its consequences. . . . It is even harder to conceptualize the resulting unintended changes in the social structures and the consequences of those changes."[26] As a result, most scholars concluded that "totalitarianism as a concept had lost its explanatory power; that it is oversimplified; that it is too narrow in focus; that it unduly magnified Soviet peculiarities, such as Marxist ideology."[27] Some went even further, treating the theory of totalitarianism as a product of the cold war and rejecting it altogether.

Of course, wholesale rejections of the notion of totalitarianism were (and are), as a rule, politically motivated: for left-wing scholars it was convenient to get rid of a concept that had, in their view, too often been used for right-wing purposes. But the same is generally true of right-wing defenders of this concept, at least of those for whom the main thing was to prove that the Soviet Union and its allies remained unchangeably totalitarian and that all the changes emphasized by the left were inessential, merely cosmetic if not simply fraudulent and consciously aimed at deceiving the West. Disappointment with the détente of the 1970s and later with the suppression of Solidarity in Poland visibly increased the number and intensity of such efforts. Their authors assumed that the Soviet Union, the paradigmatic exemplification of totalitarianism, could not really change its "totalitarian essence," and so they had to ignore or minimize the significance of the changes, on the one hand, and constantly to redefine the concept of totalitarianism, on the other. In this way the original meaning of totalitarianism became diluted and almost forgotten, although the term remained associated with the greatest political crimes of the century and thus preserved its utterly negative connotation. It is hardly an exaggeration to say that finally the term *totalitarian* came to be applied to every country in which a party calling itself communist remained in power.

All these developments created great intellectual confusion. The younger scholars just entering the field seemed faced with the choice either of recognizing the importance of the changes in the Soviet system and treating them as a refutation of the totalitarian model, or of accepting the model together with the sterile idea of the impossibility of real change. In fact, however, this was a false alternative, created by the cold war uses of the totalitarian model but having no logical connection with the original content of the totalitarian theory. The thesis that totalitarianism effectively eliminates all opposition and therefore cannot be *overthrown* from within does not mean that it cannot lose its dynamism, disintegrate, and collapse. Indeed, the greatest theorist of totalitarianism, Hannah Arendt, was the first to coin the term *detotalitarization*. She maintained that Soviet totalitarianism had not survived the death of Stalin, that Khrushchev's "thaw" was not a temporary crisis of succession but the beginning of "an authentic, though never unequivocal, process of detotalitarization," and that the Soviet Union of the 1960s could "no longer be called totalitarian in the strict sense of the term."[28] Her readiness to recognize the importance of change could not be attributed to a "softness on communism": it was rather the result of treating the totalitarian model seriously and applying it rigorously. Unlike many shallow popularizers, Arendt did not define totalitarianism as simply a "one-party dictatorship"; she stressed that one-party dictatorship in the Soviet Union had ceased to be totalitarian and that Khrushchev's own attempt to reverse the process of detotalitarization proved a complete failure.[29] For her, totalitarianism was not a static notion but an ideal type— that is, a heuristic device enabling us to explain sociopolitical reality by measuring the degree of its approximation to the model (which was closest under Stalin) as well as the degree of its departure from it (which characterized post-Stalinist detotalitarization). Her totalitarian model was not merely a particularly oppressive form of government; it was the product of a totalitarian movement legitimated by a totalitarian ideology. Hence it could not be a static model, since it was dependent on the dynamism of the movement and the strength of its ideological faith, taking it for granted that the energy of the movement might exhaust itself, that its legitimating ideology might lose its mobilizing force. Thus, it was not the model of a system immune to any essential change; it was rather a model requiring maximum mobilization and, just because of this, containing in itself the seeds of its own destruction.

It should be noted that other serious theorists of totalitarianism, including those of the right wing of the political spectrum, proved equally open to the idea that totalitarianism might evolve or disintegrate. Schapiro, for instance, stressed that totalitarianism "is not a fixed and immutable form: it can change and evolve, as well as end in collapse and overthrow." In his view the Soviet Union under Brezhnev (in 1972) was a country "in a state of transition," waiting, perhaps, for a new leader of Stalin's caliber to restore the original form of totalitarianism or drifting away from totalitarian rule toward a different form of oligarchic dictatorship.[30] More recently, on the eve of the momentous events of 1989 in East-Central Europe, Zbigniew Brzezinski outlined an ambitious theory of the three phases a country might go through to retreat from communist totalitarianism: (1) communist authoritarianism, (2) postcommunist authoritarianism, and (3) postcommunist pluralism.[31] According to this scheme, in 1988 communist totalitarianism survived only in Albania, North Korea, and Vietnam; Romania, East Germany, and Czechoslovakia represented the transition to communist authoritarianism; the Soviet Union had already accomplished this transition; and Poland and Hungary were heading for the pluralist phase. Some of these classifications may be questioned (for instance, the Soviet Union under Gorbachev was as far on the way to postcommunist pluralism as was Hungary) but what is important is Brzezinski's disagreement with the widespread view that East-Central Europe was totalitarian until 1989, and the Soviet Union, until 1991. It should be added that Brzezinski's theory did not envisage the immediate revolutionary overthrow of then-existing communist regimes. It implied rather that the transition to postcommunist pluralism would result from the increasing weakness and demoralization of the various Communist parties, forcing them to make ever more room for the pluralization of political life but without a quick and total surrender of political power.

Obviously, endorsement of the classical totalitarian model does not necessarily entail a static view of Soviet and Soviet-type regimes and societies.

Rather, as I have argued elsewhere in this book, this model can and should be used to explain the two historical processes: totalitarization, culminating in Stalinism, and the long, multifaceted, and convoluted process of detotalitarization (see chapter 5, section 1). Used in this way the totalitarian model provides a yardstick for measuring the changing degree of the suppression of freedom in the Soviet system. I quite accept that this is not the only legitimate approach to a study of the Soviet system, let alone Soviet society, but I think that all whose primary interest is the fate of freedom and repression in history are intellectually and morally entitled to study political phenomena in their relationship to freedom, giving special attention to a system that aimed at the total suppression of freedom. And it is simply a fact that among many competing approaches in the literature of Western Sovietology, the totalitarian approach is the only one that concentrates on the problem of freedom. The totalitarian model, in its original, undistorted version, provides the best available explanation of modern attempts to totally suppress freedom in the name of collectivist values (including "collectivist freedom") and for this reason alone deserves to be given "a permanent place in the typologies of political science."[32] Its applicability to social or economic history is a different matter, which need not concern us in the present context.[33]

For the same reasons, however, the concept of totalitarianism should not be made too broad, too inclusive. We should either treat it seriously, or reject it altogether. It is simply useless if it is treated as defining the nature of the Soviet system irrespective of the stages of its development, but it is very useful if we treat it as a model, an ideal type, and "try to ascertain how far the Soviet Union has deviated from that model."[34] Attempts to conceptualize the changes in this system as development toward a more mature form of totalitarianism are flawed, because communist totalitarianism was not a system capable of organic development in which its nature would reveal itself ever more clearly. It was a special type of "politically forced development,"[35] the result of a clash between utopian project and resistant reality, the not entirely intended (although not entirely unintended) product of an extraordinary mobilization of conscious effort to force social life into the Procrustean bed of the utopian blueprint. Hence, its development could consist only in detotalitarization—that is, not in the process of maturation but *in the gradual loss of its constitutive features*—leading ultimately to complete disintegration. In addition, to see post-Stalinist changes in the Soviet system as mere mutations of totalitarianism inevitably leads to a minimization of their importance and diverts attention from totalitarianism in its heyday; thus, it (unintentionally) prevents students from fully understanding the horrors of a truly totalitarian regime. It also prevents us from understanding that the so-called collapse of communism was not a sudden, miraculous event but only the last link in a long chain of less spectacular, sometimes hardly visible events and processes. If the main communist regimes in East-Central Europe and Gorbachev's Soviet Union had remained totalitarian until the very end, their sudden collapse in 1989 and 1991, respectively, would have been theoretically inexplicable and practically impossible.

This is not the place to present or analyze the complex process of the gradual disintegration of communist totalitarianism as manifested in the internal history of the Soviet Union and East-Central Europe after Stalin. It seems useful, however, to summarize the relevant analyses in the existing literature on the subject and to compare them with my own experiences over four decades in observing the changing Soviet scene from my vantage point in neighboring Poland, where the process of change was deeper and quicker. The aim of this endeavor is to point out the main factors and phases of detotalitarization. In doing this I shall keep to the classical totalitarian model and try to demonstrate its usefulness for an understanding of the general direction of the post-Stalinist evolution of communism.

The first phase of the detotalitarization process began with a conscious political decision and a corresponding political action: Nikita Khrushchev's de-Stalinization campaign. Most historians and memoirists agree that the cultural "thaw" that this bold move produced represented "the beginning of a spiritual renewal" for Soviet society.[36] Not only did Khrushchev's secret speech at the Twentieth Party Congress of 1956 deal a powerful blow to the cult of Stalin and to his reign of terror, it was also a mighty contribution to the delegitimation of the whole structure of communist totalitarianism, as a result of which the role of the terrorist features of the system was greatly reduced. The use of slave labor in concentration camps was partially dismantled, and most political prisoners were rehabilitated and freed. Members of the political elite were assured that changes of political line would no longer involve a threat to their physical security. The rigid criteria of ideological conformity, as well as the corresponding practice of official and unofficial censorship, were sufficiently relaxed to allow the appearance of a number of literary works, memoirs, and publicist writings that expressed a longing for simple decency and truth; exposed at least some of the official lies; condemned the repressiveness of the regime; and showed its deadly effect on human creativity, initiative, and personal responsibility. Terrible facts about the recent Soviet past, widely known but never mentioned even in private—facts that people wanted to forget in order to be able to live but that nevertheless shaped the suppressed, ideologically outlawed part of their "dual consciousness"—rose to the surface of the Soviet collective memory and became the subject of heated discussion, mostly in private but sometimes semipublic. This led to the emergence of overt dissidents and gave rise to the circulation of uncensored writings known as *samizdat*. The authorities observed these processes with mixed feelings and reacted to them in a somewhat haphazard way, hesitating between limited tolerance and repression but not daring to resort to terrorist measures. There were many setbacks in this process of "spiritual renewal," the most spectacular of which was the campaign against Boris Pasternak, who was mercilessly hounded not only by the entire Soviet press but also by his fellow writers. But there were also great victories, such as the liberal policy of Tvardovskii's magazine *Novyi mir*, which were crowned by the publication of Solzhenitsyn's story set in a labor camp, *One Day in the Life of Ivan Denisovich*, a publication made possible only by Khrushchev's personal authorization. On the whole, there is no doubt that despite everything it was a period remarkable for its increase of freedom, and very few would deny that Khrushchev deserves credit for this.

But there is another, less widely known side to Khrushchev's period in power that is particularly relevant to our topic. Khrushchev is often regarded as the grave digger of communism as a living faith. Leszek Kolakowski, for instance, describes Khrushchev's secret speech as the "moral funeral of the communist mythology."[37] There is much truth in this description, for if the year 1956 did not see the death of the communist gods, it certainly marked the beginning of their agony. But this was not Khrushchev's intention. Paradoxically, he was the last Soviet leader who truly believed in the utopian goals of communism, and this fact had an important impact on his policies.[38] He wanted to make the Soviet state less repressive and in this narrow sense, less totalitarian, but he hoped by doing this to speed up the ultimate triumph of communism. He loosened ideological controls but did not abandon the utopian goal of an essentially unanimous society. At the Twentieth Congress he proclaimed the "full scale construction of communism" (*razvërnutoe stroitelstvo kommunizma*), as distinguished from the previous "gradual transition" to communism.[39] In the party program of 1961 he prophesied that within ten years the Soviet Union would have achieved final victory in economic competition with the United States and within a further ten would have reached the stage of full communism in which people would be rewarded according to their needs. His de-Stalinization was not intended to put an end to utopian experimentation. He shared Stalin's belief that communism requires a single form of property and that the party must take steps to eliminate both the private plots of collective farmers and collective farms themselves, thus transforming all peasants into hired workers.[40] Consequently, he tried to persuade the farmers "voluntarily" to sell their private cattle to the collective and gradually to move from their villages into new central "agro-towns," thus realizing the communist ideal of "the abolition of the antithesis between town and country."[41] Unlike Stalin, he sympathized with the egalitarian aspects of communism and planned to reduce wage differentials, even encouraging the view that such items of personal use as dachas (country homes) should become the public property of the Soviet people as a single united whole.[42] In short, he was driven by a restless utopian dynamism that impelled him to constant reorganization and to the endless vain pursuit of universally applicable solutions. Therefore, he could not offer the country the stability for which both the people and most of the apparatchiks longed. Neither could he offer the world at large a convincing prospect of peaceful coexistence. As a true Communist he saw foreign policy as an extension of the class struggle, which was to end with the total elimination of the enemy. He did not try diplomatically to conceal this arrogant self-righteousness, in this respect preferring Lenin's frankness to Stalin's hypocrisy. It is not surprising that on a visit to the United States his peaceful intentions did not prevent him from bluntly informing his American hosts, "We will bury you."

An important part of Khrushchev's plan for the revitalization of the communist utopia was his emphasis on the withering away of the state. Needless to say, he did not mean by this a weakening of the Soviet state machine nor the abandonment of aspirations to become the world's leading great power. What he really meant can be summarized under three heads. First, following Lenin's *State and Revolution*, he sought a debureaucratization, and thus de-alienation, of the state through the expansion of political participation—that is, by involving ordinary citizens in the daily work of state organs.[43] Second, to promote the withering away of law, he wanted to replace the legal norms of socialist society by nonjuridical, *social* norms.[44] Finally, he envisaged and supported a steady increase in the role of public organizations, whose functions were to parallel those of state institutions, thus inspiring Soviet society with initiative and gradually transforming it into a self-managing community. In other words, the bureaucratic state agencies would gradually be replaced by self-organized groups of mature citizens taking their affairs into their own hands and so raising themselves to the level of collective self-mastery.

This vision had solid Marxist credentials but, just because of this, had little to do with liberalization in the sense of greater individual freedom. A close examination of Khrushchev's ideas, taking account of proposals for their practical realization, reveals that his vision was really a very instructive caricature of the Marxist ideal—instructive, because it is significantly related to its source and naively exposes all the dangers of communist collectivism. It shows that the Soviet leader was very far from moving toward a pluralist civil society; his aim was to create a voluntarily conformist society free of conflicting interests, ideologically unanimous, and leaving no room for individualist options. He genuinely wished to reduce the role of fear and violence in his state, but only on condition that state-enforced conformity would be replaced by a deeply internalized conformism capable of mobilizing the masses for the active, enthusiastic, and voluntary pursuit of centrally prescribed goals.[45] In his view, the moral and political unity binding Soviet society to the Soviet state would become steadily stronger, thus ensuring ever broader support for the authorities. Meanwhile, the increasing role of citizens' initiatives and public organizations in the construction of communism would exemplify the dialectical character of the Soviet march to utopia: active popular participation would *strengthen* the Soviet state in the very process of its withering away.[46]

A specifically Leninist element of Khrushchev's vision, developed in detail by the official Soviet ideologists of the period, stressed the need to steadily increase the leading role of the party. This was because the party was treated not as a part of the state but as the vanguard of society, representing its most advanced consciousness, and the role of consciousness would of course increase in the process of communist construction. In addition, the party, as distinct from the coercive apparatus of the state, was supposed to act by persuasion, and as the state (i.e., direct administration and repression for noncompliance) withered away, the role of persuasion would increase in importance. Therefore, it was logical to claim that "the further along the road to communism our country advances, the stronger will grow the guiding role of the Party in the life of our society."[47]

Admittedly, this paternalistic guidance was not to last forever. It was assumed that after the final victory of communism all members of society would be raised to the level of the most advanced communist consciousness. At that stage the party itself would wither away, transforming itself into "an all-inclusive organization, merged with organs of self-management."[48] Full control over the economy would then pass to a planning agency that operated on the basis of democratic consensus and social science. Conflicts between science and popular demand would not arise, because the common communist consciousness would be based on a scientific understanding of economic and social laws. All members of society would have the same interests, the same aspirations, and the same scientific understanding of what is possible. The public power would continue to exist, but without its "political," specifically governmental features. People would submit to it voluntarily and consciously, just as musicians submit to the direction of their conductor.[49]

Obviously, all these prognoses and promises depended on successful communist indoctrination. J. M. Gilison has shrewdly observed that communism was to consist in unquestioning submission, "born of an inner, well-indoctrinated belief that the leadership at all echelons is infallible."[50] In such a situation, politics in the usual sense would indeed be superfluous, and the state and law could safely wither away.

In their practical application the most ominous of these prognoses and promises proved to be the gradual replacement or supplementing of existing state laws by nonjuridical social norms and ideological relationships.[51]

The enforcement of these norms, essentially a policing function, was entrusted to different public organizations, such as the so-called *druzhiny* (or people's guards), to apartment committees, comradely courts, and so forth. All these became instruments for denunciation, blackmail, or even (in the case of the overzealous *druzhiny*) physical intimidation and harassment of fellow citizens considered to be not adequately socialist or Soviet in their private morality and life-style. For example, the people's guards were used to force people to denounce one another, to exercise unscrupulous control over the private lives of their neighbors, and even to forcibly remove unauthorized exhibitions of paintings.[52] The comradely courts had the power to sentence people for violating socialist morality and did so without any procedural rules and only rudimentary legal knowledge (let alone respect for the constitution). Most important, they were used to implement the infamous law against so-called parasites (i.e., people without a permanent place of work or regulated social status). One of the victims of this socialist justice was the poet Joseph Brodsky (the future Nobel laureate for literature), who was classified as a parasite and deported from Leningrad to a remote northern village.

But these forms of the accelerated march toward communism in fact proved difficult to combine with another part of Khrushchev's program: the search for a more genuine consensus, which allowed the emergence of public opinion and some freedom of expression. Because of this a number of Soviet jurists dared to oppose the most drastic extrajuridical innovation planned for 1957: the authorization of mass meetings of residents of a given area "to sentence a neighbor to banishment at compulsory labor if he was found to be socially unproductive."[53] Their protest, unimaginable under Stalin, achieved its aim; the regime drew back, and the proposed legislation was withdrawn. Arendt rightly saw this as demonstrating that the detotalitarization process was genuine and, at least in the main, irreversible.[54]

Nevertheless, this attempted revitalization of communist utopianism was just as characteristic of Khrushchev's rule as the de-Stalinization campaign, the literary "thaw," and other liberalizing measures. In the beginning Khrushchev promoted the idea of imminent communism, which precipitated an almost volcanic eruption of utopian enthusiasm among Soviet Marxists.[55] Numerous books, mostly very schematic and repetitive, described the communist future in detail, presenting it as a complete victory of the New Man over the egoistic instincts of the unregenerate. Their authors praised collective education of children and public catering as effective remedies against family egoism and a means of liberating women from domestic slavery. The well-known economist Stanislaw Strumilin proposed that parents should be allowed to visit their children only after working hours and hoped that reducing the role of the family, accompanied by cor-

respondingly increased participation in public collective life, would eliminate occasions for domestic quarrels.[56] The problem of permissible limits
for personal property was the subject of heated discussion, and the idea
that everything, including underwear, should belong to the collective was
treated with all due seriousness as one possible solution.[57] It was taken for
granted that money would be abolished and that the collective, or rather its
bureaucracy, would plan everybody's consumption and organize the distribution of goods, thus "freeing the citizens from the nuisances of daily
care." Leisure time was also to be used in a "conscious and purposeful"
way. Interference in the personal lives of citizens was not merely allowed
but was regarded as the moral duty of the collective.[58]

The general content of these visions of the imminent future has been
aptly characterized as the realization of total voluntary conformity, the
substitution of collective nurture for individual freedom, and the "virtually
complete submergence of the self in collective values."[59] A rather striking
feature of this idea was the absence of the Marxian theme of the "Man
of the Future" as a virtual superman embodying all hitherto dispersed
and alienated power of the species and thus incomparably stronger, more
intelligent, and even more physically beautiful than the human beings of
the imperfect present. This was hardly accidental; the idea of a superior
man of genius was by then firmly associated with the cult of personality,
which Khrushchev opposed with a populist and egalitarian version of the
communist ideal.

A general evaluation of Khrushchev's contribution to detotalitarization
is not simple and cannot be reduced to giving him credit for his pathbreak-
ing attack on the personality cult while eliminating the most repressive
features of communist totalitarianism. He did his best to revitalize totalitarian *communism* as an ideology, a way of life, and a unifying Final Goal.
He weakened the repressive machine of the totalitarian state but tried to
strengthen the internalized mechanisms of conformity and submission. He
departed from both Stalin and Lenin in optimistically stressing the end of
class conflict in the Soviet Union, but in a certain sense he was right to
describe his intentions as a sui generis return to original Leninism. Like
Lenin, and in contrast to Stalin, he treated the totalitarian state machine as
merely a means for the achievement of communist goals. Hence, his role in
the detotalitarization process may be defined as an attempt (relatively) to
de-emphasize the apparatus of coercion while at the same time reempha-
sizing the role of persuasion, the integrating, ideological mission of the
party, and the crucial importance of the ultimate goal of the communist
movement.

Despite appearances, the situation in Poland was by then very different. There the uncompleted totalitarization process suddenly turned into a
wholesale retreat that resulted in a deep legitimation crisis for the regime

and brought about its quickly increasing de-ideologization, accompanied by a considerable loosening of ideological controls. The Polish "thaw" of 1955–56 shook the very foundations of communist ideology; it was greatly encouraged, of course, by Khrushchev's secret speech but went much further and deeper than the "thaw" in the Soviet Union. Wladyslaw Gomulka, who resumed the leadership of the party after a few years' imprisonment for his "nationalist deviation," was a loyal Communist who nevertheless greatly contributed to the process of de-ideologization by emphasizing purely Polish problems and deliberately diverting attention from the final goals of the movement. He derived the legitimacy of communist rule in Poland less from Marxist doctrine than from his conviction that Polish communists had the merit of saving the political existence of Poland that prewar bourgeois parties had put in mortal danger and finally lost. He was aware that communism was, to put it mildly, very unpopular in Poland and that his party could gain nothing by stressing its commitment to the communist utopia; consequently, his "Polish road to socialism"—unlike Khrushchev's "full-scale construction of communism"—was to be as long as possible, and its final destination was never clearly defined. While Khrushchev saw collective farms as not sufficiently communist and planned the transformation of cooperative property into fully socialized property, in Gomulka's Poland existing collective farms were allowed to disband, and the predominance of the private sector in agriculture was treated as a praiseworthy distinctive feature of the Polish economic model. Communist old-timers were removed from the leadership as having been responsible for Stalinist excesses, and the party as a whole quickly became increasingly pragmatic, putting expediency above principles and dogma. Even the hard-liners were often more cynical than dogmatic and quite uninterested in accelerating the march toward utopia. Lack of interest in "constructing communism" also characterized the revisionists, who as a rule tried to combine a vaguely defined socialism with liberal democratic values. Marxism, interpreted ever more critically, became for them a historical theory or method but certainly not a blueprint for the perfect society of the future.

Ideological retreat was not followed by the development of greater political freedom. The party clung firmly to its monopoly on power, to the inevitable disappointment of the revisionists and other politically minded intellectuals. But the period of the communist offensive was clearly over, and there was no real danger of its return. The scope of enforced conformity contracted as a demoralized party lost its ability to exercise ideological and moral pressure and to keep people in the state of "mental captivity" described by Milosz (see chapter 5, section 3). Apart from a few areas of peculiar sensitivity, the regime was forced to considerably water down its totalitarian ambition of positively shaping intellectual and artistic life. "Socialist realism" was immediately discredited; publicists continued, though within limits, to enjoy their newly acquired right to their own judgment; humanists, if daring enough, could produce books free from the taint of official ideology (sometimes even subtly subverting it), reflecting instead the creative contact with Western thought and increasingly differing from the works of their Soviet colleagues.[60] The remaining taboos and external limitations of freedom were most effectively justified on geopolitical grounds, such as the imperative need to maintain friendly relations with Big Brother of the East. While this might be humiliating to Polish national pride, it would not be seen as an imposition of alien ideology and was therefore more compatible with the inner freedom of the intellectuals.

However, it would be quite erroneous to think that all these changes mattered only to intellectuals. The literature on Stalinism in Poland has recently been enriched by a comprehensive, well-documented sociopsychological study of the subject based on systematic participatory observation of different social strata in the years 1948–56.[61] Hanna Świda-Ziemba, the author of this revealing work, concludes that in Polish conditions Stalinism was a distinct phase of "really existing socialism" and that the year 1956 marked its final demise. The peculiar feature of this phase was not the party's monopoly on power, since this survived the year 1956, thereby supplying an element of continuity. What characterized Stalinism, and disappeared from Polish life in 1956, was a system of organized ideological pressure ruthlessly exercised by people situated *within* society and having at their disposal not merely the state apparatus of coercion, but also *social* mechanisms of control by which they tried to force the population to "reeducate" itself into surrendering and destroying its former individual and collective identity. The means employed sharply distinguished totalitarianism from a merely authoritarian regime and included the total ideologization and politicization of society, the programming and control of all spheres of life, a refusal to respect the right to privacy, strict thought control, and constant interference in private morality. There was a deliberate, skillful destruction of spontaneously emerging group ties and even of bonds of personal friendship, with the aim of replacing these ties by artificially created collectives that had the right and duty constantly to "educate" their members by means of criticism and self-criticism, in addition to the frequent use of secret and public denunciations. This system of intimidation and quasi-moral collective pressure was organized from above but proved equally capable of maintaining and reproducing itself on a local level. In accordance with the classical analyses of totalitarianism,[62] it did not tolerate strict lines of authority and kept everybody, including its ideologists and beneficiaries, in a state of social instability and personal insecurity. This whole system, however, could not survive the emancipating power Polish society developed between the "thaw" and October 1956. As Świda-Ziemba comments: "All these facts enjoin the revision of the now popular view, according to which October 1956 changed very little and was quickly followed by a return of totalitarian darkness. This thesis might be politically correct but is, nevertheless, fundamentally mistaken from a sociological viewpoint. In the sociological sense the period after 1956 was qualitatively different. It changed the character of the *everyday life* of the people. The horrifying darkness, the paralyzing fear and the ideological shackles were finally gone. Life became full of colors again. People could immerse themselves in the secure sphere of privacy." [63]

My own analysis supports this conclusion and takes it even further. I do not think that Poland after 1956 can justifiably be called a totalitarian country in the narrow sense of the term. Using Brzezinski's typology, we may rather define Gomulka's regime as basically posttotalitarian communist authoritarianism: posttotalitarian in that it substantially departed from the classical totalitarian model while still preserving its institutional structure; communist because it clung to communist ideology in spite of having a certain degree of national support and seeking more secure national legitimation; and authoritarian because it firmly defended the party's monopoly on power and, despite fierce factional struggle, refused to institutionalize pluralism within the party. Therefore Gomulka's Poland had advanced much further on the way to detotalitarization than Khrushchev's Soviet Union. I do not mean to diminish Khrushchev's historical role: his termination of the reign of terror made possible the cultural "thaw," and his public (or rather semipublic) exposure of Stalin's crimes gave impetus to the process of detotalitarization and made it irreversible. But he cannot be given credit for replacing Soviet totalitarianism with a basically nontotalitarian form of authoritarianism. His regime, still deeply committed to totalitarian goals, kept the population under constant ideological pressure and aimed only at replacing the highly repressive "totalitarianism from above" by a less oppressive, more consensual, populist "totalitarianism from below." In contrast to this, Gomulka's regime, supported in 1956 by most of the population and by the Church, was forced to accept an unwritten contract with Polish society: it retained its monopoly on political power but paid for it by abandoning the "communist offensive" and reducing to a minimum its totalitarian ambitions.

The suppression of the student disturbances in March 1968, followed by the infamous "anti-Zionist" (i.e., anti-Semitic) campaign, does not change this evaluation. On the contrary, the fact that the police faction of the party, represented by General Mieczyslaw Moczar, decided to appeal to nationalist feeling is proof of how far communist totalitarianism in Poland had disintegrated, both ideologically and organizationally. The short-lived victory of the hard-line faction strengthened the hand of the police at the expense of the political authority of the party without really intimidating the active sections of the population. The party's flirtation with nationalism backfired: the unintended result was a genuine national revival, which soon became powerfully allied with the noncommunist opposition.

Let us turn now to the Brezhnev period in the USSR. Most people, especially in postcommunist countries, see this period primarily as a partial return to Stalinism under a rigidly conservative gerontocratic rule. From this point of view it undoubtedly represents the relative consolidation of a stagnating, oligarchic form of totalitarianism. But this solid totalitarian and static facade concealed a far more complex reality, which was steadily moving away from the totalitarian model. Most of the changes were unintended but, even when deliberate, had unintended consequences that contributed to the slow but unceasing inner disintegration of the totalitarian system.

A comprehensive presentation and analysis of the Brezhnev period does not, of course, fall within the scope of this book, but it will be proper to summarize briefly the observations of the various competing schools of Western Sovietology that justify the thesis that despite appearances the Brezhnev era was in fact an important phase in the detotalitarization process.

First of all, Brezhnev was the first Soviet leader to silently abandon the utopian dream. This was implicit in the new team's condemnation of Khrushchev's "voluntarism" and "adventurism," in their dropping of the slogan about the "full-scale construction of communism,"[64] and a few years later, in the introduction of the phrase, "really existing socialism," which suggested that the existing system, such as it was, was valuable in itself, not just as a transition stage to the ultimate goal. Marxist theory on the laws of history was still used as an ideological legitimation of Soviet past and present, but the Marxist vision of communism was rarely mentioned and was de-emphasized as a "teleological legitimacy doctrine."[65] This significant shift of emphasis, accompanied by a trend toward the de-ideologization of current policies, was warmly welcomed by those bureaucrats and managers who longed for tranquillity and had had enough of "the restless, unpredictable fluidity" of Khrushchevism.[66] Brezhnev's open course toward stability allowed them to treat the ideologically prescribed final goal much less seriously and to concentrate instead on current tasks in the running of the state, as well as on consolidating their position within the existing system. According to an ex-Soviet scholar, this represented in practice a considerable weakening, if not a total abandonment, of their commitment to communism: "Having completely relinquished, even at the mythological level of their consciousness, the idea of building a communist society, they enthusiastically accepted the thesis of Brezhnev's regime that maintenance of the existing order is the highest State wisdom."[67]

Soviet communist totalitarianism was now entering a postutopian and postrevolutionary stage while simultaneously taking a long step on the way to detotalitarization.[68] Revolutionary dynamism and a chiliastic vision are, after all, central to a genuinely totalitarian system. According to Richard Löwenthal, whose contributions to the understanding of twentieth-century communist movements seem to me especially convincing, communist totalitarianism is essentially "institutionalized revolution." In this view, postutopian and postrevolutionary communist regimes must also be post-totalitarian.[69] They may still be very oppressive, more so than nontotali-tarian (as distinct from posttotalitarian) forms of authoritarianism. Never-theless, having exhausted their revolutionary energy, they must beat a steady retreat, must abandon (whether knowingly or not) their totalitarian aspirations, and must provide (whether willingly or not) greater room for individual and group freedom.

The most visible step in this direction was the consolidation of the Soviet *nomenklatura*, which for the first time in Soviet history "succeeded in emancipating itself from the subservience to higher authorities"[70] and constituted itself as a stable privileged stratum enjoying not only physical security (which it had obtained under Khrushchev) but also job security, regardless of performance—in effect a status similar to that of a new ruling class.[71] To see this development as a positive contribution to detotalitar-ization may seem strange, since it has become fashionable, especially in postcommunist countries, to view the *nomenklatura* as a central feature of communist totalitarianism.[72] However, the logic of this "new class theory of totalitarianism" would require us to see the Soviet Union under Brezh-nev as more totalitarian than under Stalin, which is obviously absurd. The high-water mark of totalitarianism was the period of the permanent purges, which aimed at the absolute elimination not just of all possible deviations, but also of stable interest groups whose very existence might endanger ideological purity and undermine the monolithic structure of power.[73] Arendt emphasized that instability was "a functional requisite of total domination," and she had no doubt that to end "the terror of perma-nent instability" would result in detotalitarization.[74] The same view was developed by Löwenthal, who described the emergence and function of the *nomenklatura* in dialectical terms: as a necessary result of totalitarian, "politically forced" modernization of the nation, and at the same time, as a mortal threat to monolithic unity and to the final goal of the com-munist totalitarian system.[75] In this view it was logical to claim that the fully fledged, socially entrenched *nomenklatura* could only have emerged in the postrevolutionary, postutopian, and indeed, posttotalitarian stage of Soviet history.

This aspect of the new class was highlighted and almost enthusiastically welcomed by Alexander Yanov, the emigré Soviet historian. He described it as an "aristocratizing elite" interested in security and gradual Western-ization, and thus as a powerful potential ally of the West. True, this was not meant as a positive assessment of all members of the emerging new class; indeed Yanov sharply distinguished the inept, nationalistically minded party bureaucrats, or "little Stalins," from the skilled managers, as well as a "vast stratum of central officials" represented, as he thought, by Brezhnev. But this was a division within the *nomenklatura* and an attempt to set one part of it against the other.[76]

Yanov's views, of course, contained much wishful thinking, which is especially striking in his estimate of Brezhnev, who in fact represented the conservative, bureaucratic side of the Soviet elite. Nevertheless, Yanov was not alone in setting his hopes on the evolution of a ruling stratum in the USSR.[77] The emancipation of the *nomenklatura* did have many consequences, all more or less destructive of the totalitarian system.

First, there was now more room for different interest groups, which theoretically had no right to exist in the Soviet State, being seen as incompatible with its alleged monolithic unity and the "single will" of the ruling party. Removing the threat of mass purges and giving more voice to the managerial cadres made it immediately obvious that different enterprises, different branches of industry, and different organs of the state have different conceptions of the common interest, which are linked to particular corporate interests of their own, and are no longer willing to treat the center as omniscient, as having a monopoly on the correct and binding interpretation of what is good for all. This introduced an element of pluralism into the Soviet system, which although not officially recognized, substantially affected Soviet decision making, especially in the field of economic planning.[78] Arbitrary intervention by the leader and ideological prescriptions yielded in practice to collective bargaining, which reflected the influence of the various groups.[79] In this way the Marxist ideal of planning as the rational instrument of man's species freedom was in fact rejected and buried.

Second, the emergence of the element of institutional pluralism diminished the role of direct vertical command and created instead an opportunity for settling disputes according to firmly established legal rules. This led under Brezhnev to an increased role for law, which sharply contrasted with Khrushchev's emphasis on the gradual replacement of legal norms by nonjuridical social norms. Another element in this trend toward legality was of course the corporate interest of the *nomenklatura* in protecting themselves against political arbitrariness and the tyranny of personal rule. Thus, it is perfectly legitimate to argue that "socialist legality" under Brezhnev was not meant to equally protect all citizens, irrespective of their social and political status. The Brezhnev Constitution of 1977, like the Stalin Constitution of 1936, contained a number of articles impossible to observe under the existing system, serving really only as a sort of verbal embellishment. But the tendency of the Brezhnev regime to replace arbitrary command with legal regulation and to legitimate its rule by basing it on law was indubitable. And this tendency, however limited, supported detotalitarization, because "if there is one thing which is incompatible with the totalitarian way of rule it is legal order of any kind." This increased reliance on law gave the *nomenklatura* more freedom of action (in itself a breach of the totalitarian system) but also necessarily extended the basic security of the law to the entire population, which thus strengthened the position of the dissident civil rights activists. As Schapiro has commented: "If you go on pretending for long enough that your rule is based on law, and not on arbitrary and unpredictable will, someone someday will take you seriously." [80]

Third, it was natural for an emancipated *nomenklatura* to use the relaxation of monocentric control for the pursuit of its private interests at the expense of its public duties. This "privatization of the bureaucracy, of the party and of the state apparatus" was immediately initiated from below.[81] In this way the elimination of mass terror combined with a stabilization and pluralization of the ruling stratum gave rise to almost universal corruption and to the emergence of a powerful countereconomy—that is, economic activities that were formally illegal but in fact tolerated, or even encouraged, by the authorities as providing them with additional sources of income and also as supplying the population with necessary commodities, thus serving as a substitute for the inherent inefficiencies of socialist planning.[82] This large network of illegal enterprises, owing its existence to corruption and run by different mafias personally linked with the *nomenklatura*, has been viewed as morally disgusting and as helping the rotten system survive. But it is equally legitimate to regard it as a form of "negative intrastructural dissent," that is, a factor in the internal disintegration of the system.[83] John Gray has even described it as a nascent form of civil society that, though greatly distorted by the totalitarian environment, nevertheless created "a space within which quasi-autonomous institutions could exist and in which resources could be diverted from the control of the state to private ends." [84] The use of the positive term *civil society* does not seem appropriate, but nonetheless the gist of this observation is true; the "second economy" was indeed a powerful factor in detotalitarization. It was also an *outcome* of detotalitarization, because its emergence on such a scale would not have been possible in a fully totalitarian system. Furthermore, it is evident that its very existence deeply compromised and undermined the ideological legitimation of the system. In the Soviet Union under Brezhnev it was no longer possible to cherish idealistic illusions about creating a New Man, free of bourgeois egoism and consciously shaping his destiny.

Finally, some members of the lower ranks of the *nomenklatura*, or people close to them, became involved in a positive, constructive form of intrastructural dissent. Alexander Shtromas, who introduced this useful term, meant by it all forms of opposition to the multiple irrationalities of the system from within, exclusive of taking an openly confrontational stand.[85] The simplest and most modest form of such conduct consisted in trying to circumvent the ideologically motivated dictates of the "partocracy" in the rational exercise of one's profession; in this it was essentially identical with Milosz's "professional Ketman" (see chapter 5, section 3). A more ambitious form, adopted by informal groups of technocrats, lawyers, and other professionals, consisted in jointly promoting constructive goals and publicly advocating the need for specific intrasystemic changes. Sometimes even entire offices consciously engaged in such activities. The first important case of such institutional intrastructural dissent had already appeared under Khrushchev, namely, Tvardovskii's magazine *Novyi Mir*, which consciously promoted the cause of cultural liberalization. The erosion of the official ideology under Brezhnev enabled the penetration of intrastructural dissent into some scientific institutions. The most important result of this was the so-called Novosibirsk Memorandum, prepared in April 1983 by academician Tatyana Zaslavskaya, which contained a program of reforms whose realization would amount to a revolution from above. This time, however, it would not be a revolution in the name of the communist ideal, but one producing greater efficiency and rationality at the expense of the system's ideological commitments.

The consistent de-ideologization of the system (a necessary condition of its further detotalitarization) was, however, an extremely difficult matter. The overwhelming majority of the ruling stratum might be tired of the "struggle for communism" and wishing for nothing but "to increase its power, to increase its privileges, and to enjoy both in tranquility."[86] Yet the regime badly needed ideological legitimation and so could not afford to surrender, totally and irrevocably, its utopian pretensions.[87] It had to base its legitimation on a utopian goal because it was afraid to loosen ideological controls and to allow the masses to think for themselves. Selectively applied terror was obviously not enough to counter the challenge of the overt "extrastructural" dissidents, who included such towering figures as Alexander Solzhenitsyn and the academician Andrei Sakharov. True, their real influence was still very limited, but their existence was known, their moral authority untainted, and their voice heard and listened to in the West. This was more than enough to convince the regime that the original promise of the Revolution must not be questioned. This, therefore, was the peculiar paradox of Brezhnev's "really existing socialism": although the "construction of communism" was shelved in practice and de-emphasized in theory, it could not be formally abandoned. Until 1985 Soviet social science had to pay tribute to it by repeating the relevant passages from Stalin's *Economic Problems of Socialism*.[88]

Foreign policy considerations were another reason for upholding the commitment to communism.[89] Brezhnev's regime, especially in view of its conflict with the militantly ideological Maoist China, could not follow Solzhenitsyn's advice and get rid of its "internationalist" obligations. To do so would have meant abandoning its claim to global leadership of the "anti-imperialist" forces, leaving this role to China and thus reducing Russia's Third World image to that of a social imperialist superpower no better, if no worse, than the United States. This would also have destroyed the remnants of Soviet prestige with the Western Left and would have significantly undermined the ideological legitimation of Soviet domination in East-Central Europe. This explains another paradox of Brezhnev's policy: the need constantly to prove its communist credentials by helping various "progressive forces" worldwide while at the same time presenting itself as the mainstay of responsible wisdom and peaceful intentions. This contradiction appears even in the text of Brezhnev's Constitution of 1977, which bound the Soviet State consistently to follow "the Leninist policy of peace" while also formally declaring the Soviet commitment to reinforcing the position of world socialism and to supporting national liberation (i.e., "anti-imperialist") struggles.

Clearly, the Soviet rulers remained, in a sense, prisoners of their legitimating ideology. They could not simply abandon it, because (as Shtromas put it) nothing but that upheld their claim of an exclusive and inalienable right to absolute power.[90] Therefore, they continued to depend on it, regardless of their steadily increasing mistrust of its dogmas, a point Shtromas made in his intelligent controversy with Löwenthal. In his view Löwenthal was wrong in claiming that after Khrushchev the Soviet system entered a postutopian, postrevolutionary, and therefore posttotalitarian stage of its development. He was wrong even from the point of view of his own conception of totalitarianism as "institutionalized revolution," to which the Soviet Union remained committed, because its international politics could be called "institutionalized revolution" on a global scale.[91]

There is some force in this reasoning, but it should not obscure the fact that the USSR under Brezhnev had moved a long way from the classical totalitarian model. Foreign policy arguments cannot be decisive, because foreign policy is not the sole determinant of any particular regime; one may readily imagine an Orwellian regime pursuing a policy of isolationism or a nontotalitarian revolutionary state zealously committed to revolutionary internationalism. The weakest point of Löwenthal's argument is his assumption that the Soviet system had outgrown totalitarianism while retaining its capacity to advance the economic modernization of the country. This was quite wrong, because the command-administrative economy created by totalitarianism could not function adequately without totalitarian mechanisms of "revolutionary mobilization." Hence, the evolution of the Soviet system was not a process of positive growth but rather one of wholesale disintegration. Notwithstanding all the efforts of the various representatives of "positive intrastructural dissent," what was happening was not the positive overcoming or outgrowing of the totalitarian inheritance, but instead the unintended and uncontrolled collapse of totalitarian structures. In this sense, however, the Soviet system under Brezhnev undeniably represented a very advanced stage of detotalitarization, which in conjunction with its emphasis on security and legality deserves to be recognized as a change for the better.

I am well aware that most of the Soviet intelligentsia saw matters differently, and with good reason. The Stalinist terror was over but its memory remained in the form of a deeply interiorized fear. The cultural excesses of Zhdanovism were not repeated, but neither were they officially condemned; indoctrination was conducted in a less demanding, more routine way, but there was still no safe space for cultural and intellectual freedom. The regime seemed to fear that the relaxation of ideological controls would lead to a loss of its communist identity and thus destroy its legitimacy; the intellectuals, for their part, appeared paralyzed both by fear of repressions and by the still unimpaired system of mental captivity. Socialist realism, therefore, remained the obligatory norm for art, and Marxism-Leninism, the only idiom of legally permitted intellectual discourse. The utopian goal of "building communism" ceased to exert much pressure on people's daily lives but (to paraphrase Andrei Siniavskii) continued to have a hypnotic effect on their minds.[92] Greater personal freedom and access to dissident underground publications only made the intelligentsia more aware of their lack of freedom. Dual consciousness, as described by Altaev and Nelidov, gave ever more pain to those who suffered it, and only a very few were brave enough to recover their integrity by openly challenging the system. For this reason it is understandable that most intellectuals perceived the detotalitarization process only as an increase in corruption but not as an increase in freedom.

The attitudes and perceptions of the other strata of the population seem to have been rather different. The collective farmers, for instance, whose material and legal status had undergone considerable improvement, could hardly fail to appreciate the changes. Members of the *nomenklatura*, especially on the managerial side, also appreciated their newly acquired rights to privacy and greater wealth, but the most enterprising of them wanted much more. They were no longer satisfied with a situation in which everything was dispensed from above, as a right to use but not as private ownership.[93] They also sought a greater role in economic decision making and thus more openings for market relations. According to Wolfgang Leonhard's perceptive analysis, this laid the foundations for a "rapprochement

528 Dismantling Stalinism

between the *nomenklatura* officials and the increasingly self-confident representatives of the 'second economy.'"[94] Both groups were working for the "commercialization" of the system:

The *nomenklatura* officials are striving for personal property and wealth, and the representatives of the second economy are striving for unhindered freedom of enterprise. In the event of a "commercialization" of the system, the first step would be the legalization of private enterprise in agriculture, small industries and the private sector. This would very probably lead to a quick increase in the scope of private economic activity. *Nomenklatura* officials would get, or simply take, the right to participate in these private ventures as a reward for having legalized them. The integration of both strata might even go both ways, as representatives of the second economy might be brought into the apparatuses of Party and State.[95]

These words, written before *perestroika* and shedding much light on some of its aspects, show the difference between the de-Stalinization of the period of the "thaw" and the less spectacular, as well as less attractive, detotalitarization processes of the so-called period of stagnation. Khrushchev's de-Stalinization campaign aimed to make the Soviet state less oppressive, though also more committed to the communist ideal. Brezhnev's rule was marked by a partial retreat from the "construction of communism," but also by a completely new phenomenon, a tendency toward marketization, that is, in fact, decommunization. This trend of course had to disguise itself to save the ideological legitimation of the system. Nevertheless, it paved the way for the imminent undermining and rejection of that system.

Under Gomulka's successor, Edward Gierek, Poland was in many respects very like the USSR under Brezhnev. It also witnessed the emergence of almost universal corruption, the consolidation of the *nomenklatura*, and the visible presence of different informal groups, which were organized on the basis of "clientelism" and furthered their interests through notorious "connections." Central planning in Poland too had ceased to represent the will of a unified center, becoming in fact a matter of decentralized decision making that took particular account of the bargaining power of different interest groups. The leadership of the Polish party had also abandoned communist ideals, encouraging instead the *nomenklatura*'s tendency toward "embourgeoisement" and even tolerating some forms of obvious corruption. The party itself, like its Soviet counterpart, had become a mass organization supporting the regime as it was and caring little for its declared ideological goals. The Soviet party under Brezhnev has been described, with some exaggeration perhaps, as a nonideological Union of Soviet Patriots;[96] *mutatis mutandis* the same was true, without any exaggeration at all, of the Polish United Workers' Party (PUWP) under Gierek. Most party members in Gierek's Poland openly despised Marxism, disliked being called communists, and justified their political options on the ground of expediency-oriented patriotism.

The net result of all this was just as in the Soviet Union. The economy became an arena of conflicting particular interests, often pursued in a semilegal, if not quite illegal, way. Central planning lost its ability to control general development; the fulfillment of plans was, as a rule, little more than statistical fiction. A constantly growing and changing multiplicity of bureaucratic rules, often completely impractical or contradicting one another, made the situation even worse, since the economy was adjusting itself to bureaucratic absurdities at the expense of both efficiency and legality. In short, the command-administrative economy had become unworkable without making room for genuine market mechanisms.

Yet, despite these important similarities, the situation in Poland differed from that in the Soviet Union in that it reflected a much more advanced state of detotalitarization. A significant number of these differences were the result of the well-known peculiarities of the "Polish road to socialism," that is, of *incomplete* totalitarization. Some (for example, private agriculture) could not be justified on doctrinal grounds and came to be seen as proof of Poland's relative backwardness. Gierek's team, however, did not plan to bring Poland rapidly to the stage of "developed socialism." On the contrary, it regularly pointed out that Poland was not ripe for consistent sovietization.

Other differences reflected the erosion of ideology and a corresponding crumbling of totalitarian practices and structures. The Polish leadership was able and eager to base its legitimacy not on ideological grounds but rather on a conveniently pragmatic interpretation of Poland's national interest. It openly declared that the party must remain in power solely because Poland's continued existence as a separate state within its existing boundaries was impossible except as part of the Soviet bloc and with the support of the Soviet Union, which would tolerate only a communist-run Polish state. The system as such, it was argued, could not be overthrown because its existence was guaranteed by postwar agreements concerning the division of Europe; hence, the performance of the government, and the ruling party, should be assessed on the basis of its ability to protect Polish interests and freedoms in existing conditions, thus allowing Poland to be as different as possible from the other countries of "really existing socialism." This implied that pragmatic and tolerant communist rule, though not ideal, would be the lesser of two evils as far as Poland was concerned. This view, while not inspiring party members with healthy self-confidence, did allow them to present themselves as a patriotic force and consequently to appeal to "constructive patriotism" and "rationally conceived" national solidarity. This process of de-ideologization in fact removed many psychological barriers dividing party from nonparty members and thus brought about a partial disalienation of the party. In this way the party under Gierek succeeded in getting rid of its ideological legitimation, which under Polish conditions had become practically worthless anyhow, and acquired instead a measure of national legitimation and some genuine, if relative and conditional, popular support.

The cost was a further weakening of ideological controls, but this was less a voluntary concession than the unintended consequence of de-ideologization. Despite its increasing indifference or even cynicism toward ideology, the party tried to retain some control over literature (which could now be apolitical though not politically hostile), journalism, and such politically sensitive areas of scholarly activity as philosophy or history. This control, while limited enough to ensure good relations with intellectuals, was to be sufficiently strict to prevent the emergence of active political dissent and nonconformist attitudes among the younger generation, with special emphasis on the control of education in schools. However, the authorities had seriously underestimated the strength of "positive intrastructural dissent" in Polish intellectual and cultural life. A significant number of intellectuals and artists proved nonconformist or honest enough to fight for the broadening of intellectual freedom, making use of all cracks in the system, ignoring official lies whenever possible, and isolating the party propagandists disguised as scholars. Inevitably, the party lost most of the battles in this undeclared war because the intellectuals were better placed and equipped; after 1956 there were no "captive minds" among them, their contacts with the West, including Polish emigré circles, were regular and steadily increasing, and opinion polls showed their social prestige in the nation to be very high. Consequently, Poland became the most detotalitarianized socialist country, one in which the Communist party lost not only its ideological monopoly but even its competitive position in the market of ideas. Its efforts at indoctrination were substantially reduced, and those that remained were plainly counterproductive. The exile of a number of influential intellectuals after the events of March 1968 was certainly a great loss to Polish culture, but a general comparison of intellectual life under Gomulka with that under Gierek shows a marked increase of freedom and a rapid lessening of the authority of Marxism. The best achievements of the "thaw" and the period immediately following were outstanding, but in the next decade intellectual liberalization was broader in scope, less elitist, and more pluralist. Exclusive concentration on the vindication of the true, universal values of the Left gave way to a general vindication of the non-communist legacy of national and European culture and to a spectacular resurgence of different forms of national patriotism. In the 1960s Marxist true believers were still influential in the party and had the ear of the general secretary himself, while in the 1970s the party as a whole cared very little about ideological principles, trying instead to discount politically its pragmatic and pro-Western orientation. In the early 1960s the prestige of Marxism was sustained by Marxist revisionists, whereas in the 1970s revisionism, as an influential current of oppositional thought, had ceased to exist: the last hour of its prolonged agony struck in 1968. Official Marxism had also ceased to exist as a coherent doctrine; any sort of eclectic ideology could be called Marxist so long as it made use of quotations from the Marxist classics and especially if its author declared his support for the existing system. This state of affairs was bound to have a devastating effect on the system's ideological legitimation.

Thus, despite some similarities, Gierek's Poland was a very different place from Brezhnev's Soviet Union. The latter was still a country of all-pervasive indoctrination, of "dual consciousness," "captive minds," and a handful of heroic dissidents trying to morally arouse a largely indifferent, intimidated, or ideologically hypnotized population—a country whose intellectual life was still paralyzed by Marxism-Leninism, where party control of journalism and the humanities included not only uniform obligatory interpretations of past events but detailed rules for quotation from the "classics of Marxism" and from the "bourgeois writers." Unlike Poland, with its openness to Western ideas and relatively easy and frequent travel to the West, the USSR was a closed society in which all contact with foreigners was feared and avoided and travel to capitalist countries was virtually impossible, except in organized groups led by official guides and penetrated by informers. The two countries were two different worlds, and the Russians were more aware of this than the Poles. Many Polish newspapers and journals were strictly prohibited in the Soviet Union; many Polish books could be found only on the closed shelves or "special divisions" of Soviet libraries. Those Polish publications whose circulation, although limited, was legally allowed, were eagerly read as important vehicles of liberalization and Westernization. Indeed, quite a few Russians learned Polish just to have access to literature in Polish, including Polish translations of forbidden thinkers and writers.

Obviously, the Soviet Union and Poland by now represented two different stages of detotalitarization. It is difficult to conceptualize this difference in terms of Brzezinski's theory of the "retreat from communism,"[97] since both countries were already posttotalitarian, in the sense that they had substantially departed from any very close approximation to the totalitarian model, though both were still in the stage of oligarchic authoritarianism. But this equation only shows the inadequacy of the existing conceptual apparatus of political science. Authoritarian regimes may differ radically in the scope of their authoritarian control, as well as in the intensity and depth of sociopolitical pressure to conform. Certainly, the USSR under Brezhnev had departed from totalitarianism in the profound disintegration of the monocentric and mono-organizational mechanisms of its command economy, in the emancipation of the *nomenklatura* and its division into different interest groups (which often cooperated with the illegal second economy), and finally, in its erosion of ideology and consequent loss of revolutionary dynamism. It preserved, however, the totalitarian mechanism of ideological control and the associated model of a closed society—both sustained by living memories of terror and by a deeply interiorized, conscious or subconscious, fear of repressions. Poland under Gierek, on the other hand, was already a semi-open society, notably in the intellectual and cultural spheres, a country whose younger citizens, making up most of the population, had neither memories of terror nor experience of "mental captivity." Brezhnev's regime retained some ideological legitimacy and could stand on its own feet. In Poland the main pillar of the existing system was the country's political dependence on its Russian "elder brother," and this fact, humiliating but incontestable, was paradoxically the rulers' main excuse.

Within systemic limits, the legitimacy of Gierek's government depended on its capacity to improve the economic situation. In the middle of the 1970s, however, economic conditions began to deteriorate. In spite of the vivid memory of the powerful protest of shipyard workers in December 1970—a protest that led to popular riots and their violent suppression by armed police forces, and consequently to the fall of Gomulka's government—the authorities once more resorted to the risky operation of price raising. Predictably, the 1970 scenario repeated, and in 1976 Gierek's government used police force to brutally suppress popular unrest in Radom. This created a new political situation, since earlier methods of pacifying workers by means of promises, changes in the ruling team, and selective economic concessions were now neither credible nor available.

The main factor in this new situation was the emergence of an organized and overt opposition, no longer intrastructural but ostentatiously extrastructural, determined to organize social forces and to mobilize them to exert continuous powerful pressure *from without* on the communist rulers. The most spectacular step in this direction was the activity of the KOR (Committee for the Defense of Workers), an organization that provided legal and material support for the repressed workers of Radom and so forged an anticommunist alliance between the intellectual opposition and the working class. There emerged also other overtly oppositional organizations (for instance, the nationalist Confederation of Independent Poland), and a number of uncensored underground (though as a rule not anonymous) publications sprang up, ranging from political newspapers to books and creating a powerful alternative culture. To a certain extent these publications were consciously modeled on the Russian *samizdat*,[98] but their political effect was more far-reaching; by publishing the real names and even the addresses of their authors and editors, they presented the authorities with the dilemma of either resorting to repression and so destroying their benevolent "liberal" image, or of accepting the situation and so demonstrating their weakness. The same tactics were employed by the Society for Scholarly Courses, a sort of alternative university lecturing in private apartments on politically sensitive subjects, and of course by the KOR, which challenged the regime by subjecting it to openly hostile politicomoral pressure. The authorities reacted inconsistently, in some cases using intimidation through different forms of malicious harassment (including acts of violence by "unknown perpetrators"), but did not dare to crush the movement. In this way they quickly became neither feared nor respected, while the independent social organizations grew in power, mobilizing the active and critically thinking sections of the population for open, nonviolent but intransigent, political struggle. The aim of this struggle, moreover, was no longer yet another form of socialism. By the mid 1970s even the left wing of the democratic opposition broke with the notion of "true" socialism as too reminiscent of revisionist illusions.[99]

Obviously, this open and increasingly successful struggle against the system would have been impossible without the long process of internal detotalitarization. But the leaders of the democratic opposition saw it differently. In their view, totalitarianism had remained virtually unchanged, and the process of its destruction in Poland only *started* in the later 1970s— that is, when the opposition organized itself to attack the system from without.[100] On a purely intellectual level, this was of course a very naive view, but its adoption was very useful for political purposes.[101] To see the regime as unchangeably totalitarian enabled the opposition to blame it for all the crimes of communist totalitarianism everywhere and so to deprive it of any remaining semblance of legitimacy. On the other hand, to demonize the enemy in this way boosted the morale of the opposition and enormously increased its prestige, since visible success in the struggle against totalitarianism, the most powerful system of total domination so far known, counted for much more than success in combating "really existing socialism" in a stage of highly advanced disintegration and decline. So the antitotalitarian and anticommunist crusade in the uncensored publications was a sort of counterindoctrination that helped the opposition to build up its authority and to destroy the authority of the party state.

The outcome of this struggle is well known. When the next great outburst of worker discontent occurred, its leaders were well prepared to formulate political demands, particularly the independent, self-governing trade unions. August 1980 saw the birth of Solidarity and the beginning of sixteen months of self-limiting, nonviolent, anticommunist revolution. Its leadership did not aim at a total overthrow of the system because of the well-grounded fear of Soviet intervention, but the radicalization of the masses could not be kept within rational limits and made confrontation practically inevitable. This time the party leadership faced the dilemma of either openly discarding the remnants of its communist identity, and so provoking intervention, or openly embracing the Soviet position and abandoning all hope of a national reconciliation. General Jaruzelski's martial law, proclaimed on December 13, 1981, was an attempt to find a middle way. It was intended to be a self-limiting counterrevolution, freezing the revolutionary movement but not strangling it and solemnly promising a continuation of reform.[102] As we now know Jaruzelski indignantly rejected the hard-line proposal to cancel Solidarity's registration forthwith, as well as all agreements with it, and to bring its leaders to military trial, followed by severe sentences, forcible banishment, and so forth. Instead, he stressed that the party must cling to legalism, that its moral capital was a willingness to compromise, the assumption of humility, and the capacity for self-purification.[103] This was hardly the language of a convinced Marxist-Leninist.

The Polish underground and emigré press, as well as many in the West, described Poland after martial law as a country with a particularly oppressive totalitarian regime, but this reasoning was deeply flawed. It stemmed from what I call the "democratic fallacy" in understanding totalitarianism—that is, from seeing totalitarian regimes as founded on "naked force" and thus openly contradicting the "popular will." In reality, as Arendt and Milosz have explained, totalitarian rule cannot be reduced to the rule of force as applied in ordinary police states. Lack of consent is not a totalitarian feature; the relationship of "open hostility" means that the ruled have liberated themselves from both fear and indoctrination, and this marks the end of totalitarianism.

Totalitarianism, therefore, is not merely the opposite of political democracy. Even a drastic curtailment of nonpolitical civil liberties is not necessarily a step toward the reestablishment of totalitarian rule. "The extinguishing of civil liberties in order to maintain and strengthen the regime," wrote Kolakowski, "does not amount to totalitarianism unless accompanied by the principle that every activity—economic, cultural, etc.—must be completely subordinated to the aims of the state; that not only are the acts against the regime forbidden and ruthlessly punished, but no political actions are neutral and the individual citizen has no right to do anything that is not part of the state's purpose; that he is the state's property and is treated as such."[104]

Jaruzelski did not try to justify martial law in terms of Marxist ideology. His government repeatedly stressed that it did not want to be loved but only to be recognized as a "lesser evil," a geopolitical necessity, thus deriving its legitimacy from a certain understanding of the national interest at the given moment, not from any universalist ideology. The utopian vision of the "radiant future" completely disappeared, giving way to a rather gloomy realism; the authorities carefully avoided excessive optimism in assessing the situation, because they had learned how dangerous it could be to allow popular expectations to rise and then prove unable to fulfill them. "Really existing socialism" was no longer praised as the best possible system; the ruling group instead tried to exculpate itself by putting all the blame on anonymous systemic mechanisms. The totalitarian aim of "political and moral unanimity," reinterpreted under Gierek as "national solidarity under the leadership of the Party," was officially replaced by a policy of so-called "socialist pluralism" that required only a necessary *minimum* of national consensus. The political mobilization of the masses became conceivable only as a popular crusade against the regime; hence, paradoxically, the party began to encourage depoliticization. Associations of artists and writers were not expected to support the regime politically; they were dissolved for refusing to be apolitical. Underground publishers and distribution networks, as well as the support of the church, enabled intellectuals and artists to engage in active delegitimization of the system both in the political content of their works and in an ostentatious refusal to cooperate with official institutions, especially the mass media. The ideological legitimization of the system ceased to be treated seriously even by its otherwise staunch supporters; isolated attempts to revive it appeared ridiculous, and public declarations in favor of communism required more civic courage than did public attacks on it.[105]

Thus, in contrast to totalitarian regimes, the Polish regime of the 1980s did not derive its legitimacy from an all-embracing ideology, nor did it commit itself to "a single positively formulated goal";[106] it did not attempt to politicize all spheres of life, especially the cultural and intellectual spheres; and finally, it did not try to encourage and organize the controlled political activization of the masses but clung instead to the traditional policy of keeping them away from politics. It emphasized not only "socialist legality" but also "socialist constitutionalism," supporting its declared intentions by introducing such institutions as the constitutional tribunal and the ombudsman, or independent guardian of human rights. In short, this represented the final abandonment of totalitarian aspirations in favor of a self-limiting, consensus-seeking authoritarianism. In a sense it was the final outcome of a process that had begun as long ago as 1956. But it is important to stress that this was not just a largely unintended result of the inner disintegration of the system, but a consciously adopted policy. One is tempted to say that it was no longer the government tolerating the increasing independence of social forces, but rather the reverse: liberated social forces tolerating, temporarily, an authoritarian government while continually trying to limit its actual power. Nor can there be any doubt that this was the result of Solidarity's challenge. After all, every restoration assimilates aspects of the preceding revolution. If the underground activists of

Solidarity called Jaruzelski's regime totalitarian, this made sense only as an act of political struggle. In reality the other side of Solidarity's defeat was not merely a moral victory, but the final blow to the totalitarian aspirations of "really existing socialism" in Poland.

The fact that Jaruzelski's government, weak and unpopular as it was, remained in power for so long cannot be explained by fear of its apparatus of repression. True, naked force played a crucial role, but it was the force of Poland's eastern neighbor. Fear of this force created a silent understanding between the government and the opposition; both were convinced that as long as Brezhnev's doctrine concerning the "limited sovereignty" of Soviet socialist allies remained in force, the revolutionary overthrow of communist, or rather pseudocommunist, rule in Poland was out of the question. Then, at this juncture, a new factor appeared: Gorbachev's "new thinking" about international relations. In his *Perestroika* of 1987, this thinking was not yet sufficiently clear: the "absolute independence" of socialist countries might have meant the independence of separate states on the basis of a common acceptance of the premises of the socialist system.[107] But the following year Gorbachev made it plain that his "new thinking" also included "freedom of choice," i.e, the freedom to choose, or not to choose, socialism and that this new principle was to be *universally* applicable.[108] Polish Communists were the first to take this message seriously and to react accordingly. At the beginning of 1989 they invited the Solidarity leadership to round-table talks about power sharing. Despite carefully negotiated precautions, the half-free election of June 4, 1989, brought a landslide defeat of the PUWP and its allies and in the final result called into being the first noncommunist government in postwar Poland. This was an instructive precedent and set in motion a chain reaction. Very soon—in the same year—communist-run governments disappeared in almost all the countries of East-Central Europe.

6.4   Gorbachev's *Perestroika* and the Final
Rejection of Communist Freedom

The story of Gorbachev's *perestroika* is too rich, too recent, and too controversial to be briefly summarized here. There is no agreement either about its causes or its overall historical significance. Some Western scholars minimize its ideological dimension, preferring to see it as just another attempt to "salvage the whole Leninist enterprise" through belated and inadequate reforms,[109] an attempt, moreover, necessitated by the economic and social crisis in the Soviet state and/or by the Soviet defeat in the cold war. In this view Gorbachev appears as a dedicated Leninist, or even as the defender of "a worn-out totalitarianism," and his prestige in the West is presented as totally unjustified, as part of a strange and irrational "Gorbomania."[110] Other scholars, closer to mainstream liberal opinion, supported Gorbachev to the end and even boldly defended him against his numerous domestic critics. Cohen, for example, in an article published in March 1991 in the official organ of the Soviet government, argues that Gorbachev's achievements were enormous: in 1985 no one could have dared to suppose that the Soviet Union would change so much. But great reforms of a whole system, he adds, cannot be expected to produce immediate positive results. America's *perestroika* (i.e., the New Deal) took thirty years, and Gorbachev faced much greater challenges; therefore, he deserves to be seen as the great reformer whom nobody could replace.[111]

The weak point of this argument is the assumption that Gorbachev's restructuring would eventually bring about positive results comparable to Roosevelt's New Deal—that is, that it would surmount the crisis through successful *intrasystemic* change. As we know, this was not to be Gorbachev's fate. The failed coup of August 1991 discredited the Communist party and catalyzed the final collapse of the system. Martin Malia, one of the most energetic critics of "Gorbomania," interprets this as empirical proof of the "intrinsic irreformability of communism."[112] Communism, he wrote, "cannot be reformed or given a human face; it can only be dismantled and replaced." This is because the communist system "was no ordinary despotism, but the world's premier and most total totalitarianism," which did not allow any significant change: "There is no middle way between the integral preservation of such a system and its collapse."[113] Hence, the period of Gorbachev's *perestroika* and *glasnost'* was, as Malia has written elsewhere, merely "six wasted years of failed reform communism."[114] The real change came about only with "an unambiguous and revolutionary break with communism" symbolized by the Russian president, Boris Yeltsin.[115]

This strong reassertion of the old thesis about the unchangeably totalitarian essence of the Soviet system is a good starting point for the formulation of a quite different view of the consequences, intended and unintended, of *perestroika*.

The weakness of Malia's reasoning consists not merely in its one-sided presentation of facts, but primarily in its logic. There are several obvious non sequiturs in it. The August coup might have provided an argument for Malia's thesis had it been successful and had its success brought about a return to communist totalitarianism. However, its rapid collapse, its amazing halfheartedness, its avoidance of drastic measures, and its strenuous efforts to preserve some semblance of legality can hardly be treated as proof that the Soviet system, or the Soviet political elite, remained unchanged. Similarly, the fact that the "19-million-member Communist Party was dissolved by simple decree, without offering the slightest resistance" is hardly evidence of its unalienably totalitarian nature.[116] The theory that the centrally planned command economy could not be reformed but only dismantled and replaced may have been true (here I have *treated it as true*), but it does not follow that Gorbachev wanted to preserve it or was trying "to reform the irreformable"; indeed, he often declared that *perestroika* was not just a reform but a *revolution* aimed at *replacing* the existing system with a different one based on market mechanisms and multiple forms of ownership. Gorbachev's ideal of combining a market economy with democratic socialism was not shown to be either inherently feasible or unfeasible; the collapse of the system after the August coup is irrelevant in this matter, since its reasons were political, not economic. Finally, and most important, the failure of Gorbachev's economic reforms does not validate the view that his *perestroika* was not successful in changing the Soviet system by making it more compatible with moral, intellectual, and political freedom and so giving it a human face. From the point of view of this book, this is of fundamental importance. As far as freedom is concerned, Gorbachev's achievements were in fact much greater than mere intrasystemic change— they *were changing the system itself* by removing its totalitarian features, destroying its legacy of fear and mental bondage. A country having a fully free press, tolerating extremes of opinion, and publishing such ostentatiously anticommunist authors as Orwell, Koestler, Solzhenitsyn, Hayek; a country with leaders dedicated to the rule of law and accepting political pluralism, including the principle of contested elections; a country where political opposition, represented by a multiplicity of parties, was legally recognized while the former ruling party was officially deprived of its constitutional right to a monopoly of power; a country where the head of state was not protected against political and personal, sometimes deliberately provocative, attacks [117] and where to support him, let alone his government, required more civil courage than supporting his unrelenting critics did—such a country did not deserve to be called totalitarian in any acceptable sense of the term. This was a tremendous, truly epochal change, even though the frustrated masses failed to appreciate it as a change for the better. [118]

Interestingly, Gorbachev himself saw it in this light. At a meeting with cultural leaders he explained his actions by referring to a scale of values that presupposed the priority of freedom: "If it is socialism, that means it is, above all, democracy. If it is democracy, that means freedom. Or maybe freedom comes first of all, and then democracy follows. Political freedom, human and spiritual freedom, economic freedom." [119] Somewhat earlier, in late 1989, he told the Congress of People's Deputies: "We are estimating the results of *perestroika*. It is true that it has not brought us economic results on the whole, but it has provided freedom of expression and creativity and freedoms in the political sphere. Only recently we all said that we had been suffocating under paralyzed ideas and deeds. Didn't we dream of freedom as the most cherished thing?"[120]

This is not an isolated and accidental statement, but an expression of Gorbachev's personal credo. On the eve of the August coup, when it was perfectly clear that the Soviet state was on the brink of political disintegration and economic catastrophe, he declared that, were it possible to return to the spring of 1985, he would unhesitatingly follow the same path—the path of reforms that would not bring people happiness "from above" but instead "offer them in free movement to create their own well-being" and to be guided in this not by dogma but by "simple and universal human values." In his book on the coup he emphasized that from the very beginning the main aim of *perestroika* was to create a situation in which "freedom of the individual, his honor and dignity" would become the moral and legal foundation of the state.[121]

It is clear that the notion of freedom underlying these statements of intention was a commonsense, liberal notion having nothing in common with the Marxist concept of freedom as rational, collective control over spontaneous forces. The very fact that the head of the Soviet party state used the words *freedom* and *democracy* in their ordinary "bourgeois liberal" sense was striking testimony to the failure of Marxist-Leninist indoctrination. Without this failure the "Gorbachev phenomenon" would have been impossible, and without Gorbachev (as he himself has stressed)[122] a semitotalitarian Soviet regime might have survived for much longer. Gorbachev's reforms led to the full disclosure of the ideological bankruptcy of the system, to its thorough delegitimization, and thereby to its final collapse. The disintegration of the Soviet system under Brezhnev had shown that without ideological militancy, communist totalitarianism would lose its dynamism, self-confidence, and sense of purpose. Gorbachev's *perestroika* demonstrated, in turn, that the Soviet system as such could not survive without ideological hypocrisy. His reforms, especially *glasnost'*, destroyed the last remnants of the system's ideological legitimation, thus revealing the truth about the historical record of the Communist party and the Soviet state. So Gorbachev prepared his own defeat as the president of the Soviet Union. But if freedom—ordinary human freedom—was his main aim, he was right in refusing to regard his cause, and in this sense himself, as defeated.

This interpretation is not designed to neglect the economic and social causes of the Gorbachev revolution. It only claims that many of them, such as the degeneration of the cadres, the demoralization of the people, and "mafia feudalism"[123] were significantly related to the ideological crisis and that the general situation of the Soviet Union in the first half of the 1980s was not catastrophic enough to be held to have forced the general secretary of the CPSU to embark on highly unorthodox and risky changes.[124] Adam Ulam is right in his contention that the main cause of the collapse of the Soviet system was "the collapse of Soviet ideological mission." In the past "the Soviet regime had demonstrated a resilience unmatched in history." It was able to survive such catastrophes as collectivization, followed by famine and the death of millions, mass terror, and the most atrocious, genocidal war in modern history. "How trivial in comparison with its past disorders were the ailments that afflicted it in the beginning of the 1980s as far as the domestic scene was concerned: a lowered rate of growth of the GNP for the past decade, still at 1.5 to 2 percent per year, which does not compare so badly with that of the United States; an elderly and somnolent ruling oligarchy; active dissent by just a tiny segment of the intelligentsia, which the regime semitolerated as a sort of safety valve."[125] In Ulam's view, such flaws and deficiencies were no more serious than those afflicting many other societies and can explain neither Gorbachev's actions, nor their catastrophic consequences for the system.

Elsewhere in the same book Ulam recalls that long ago, in connection with the détente of 1972, Western observers of the Soviet scene asked: "Could communism remain in power after jettisoning a crucial part of its ideological baggage?" It was widely believed then that it could, because the real instruments of power "did not depend on ideological incantations." But as he observes: "What happened under *perestroika* provides a vivid proof that those instruments of power at the disposal of a Communist regime by themselves were unable to save it from internal erosion. Those ideological incantations scorned by pragmatic politicians would be thus shown to have been vital in preserving the system as long as the rulers who recited them did so with some conviction."[126]

Indeed, had the ideological legitimation of the system not been destroyed, as it was under Gorbachev, the whole scenario of the events of August 1991 would have been unimaginable. This shows the absurdity of the view that the Soviet system remained totalitarian until the "August revolution." Had this been true, there would have been no need of a coup. Even had it been only partially true—that is, had the country only begun to deviate from its totalitarian norm, had the Communist party preserved a part of its earlier self-confidence, had the army and the KGB not been influenced by independent, democratically inclined public opinion—there would have been no difficulty in forcibly removing Yeltsin and his followers from the political scene.[127]

Therefore, we may justifiably say that the process of detotalitarization of the Soviet Union paralleled the erosion and gradual dismantling of its official ideology and was completed when Marxism-Leninism, as a legitimizing device, ceased to hold sway over people's minds. This interpretation is not derived from idealistic exaggeration of the role of ideologies in history. I quite agree that *in general*, that is, in the case of most sociopolitical systems, the role of ideological legitimation (let alone ideological mission) is much less important. It was much less even in the People's Poland, where the communist regime after 1956 legitimized itself not so much in ideological terms but rather (and increasingly) in terms of a certain conception of Poland's national interest in the existing constellation of powers in postwar Europe. In the Soviet Union, however, the role of ideology was crucial and decisive, because it was the country that had given birth to genuine and consistent totalitarianism as a system of a thoroughly *ideocratic* nature, one constructed in accordance with an ideological blueprint and therefore utterly dependent on its ideological legitimation and capable of maintaining and reproducing itself only with the help of omnipresent, all-pervasive ideological controls. This was the unique character of the Soviet system,[128] which was adequately described by the first theorists of totalitarianism but unfortunately increasingly neglected, or even altogether denied, by more recent schools of political science. Unlike Malia, I see many positive contributions by these schools (especially the so-called revisionist school) to the explanation of changing Soviet reality.[129] Nevertheless, I remain convinced of the relevance of the classical, *ideocratic* model of totalitarianism (if coupled with a coherent conception of change, i.e., of detotalitarization) for an adequate understanding of the emergence, disintegration, inevitable crisis, and final collapse of the Soviet system. My interpretation of the significance and historical fate of Gorbachev's reforms is closely related to my emphasis on the crucial importance of the ideological factor in the communist movement and communist totalitarianism, as well as their evolution, decomposition, and finally, rapid decline.

If we look from this perspective at Gorbachev's *perestroika*, it immediately becomes obvious that it was a true "moral revolution," or a "revolution in consciousness," and it is equally clear that, regardless of his original intention, it was in fact not only an antitotalitarian but also an anticommunist revolution.

To substantiate this view as briefly as possible, let us try to summarize the net results of *perestroika* under the following four points.

First, let us consider the problem of the marketless economy, which is, as I have tried to show, of the very essence of Marxist communism. In this matter Gorbachev formulated his position very early on, before assuming the post of general secretary. For instance, in December 1984, at an ideological conference of the Central Committee, he stated matter-of-factly that "commodity-money relations" (i.e., market mechanisms) were not alien to socialism and, therefore, should be properly developed."[130] He was probably not fully conscious of contradicting Marx's views on this subject, as set out in *The Critique of the Gotha Program*; after Khrushchev the theme of the opposition between "commodity relations" and communism (including socialism, as its lower phase) had been deliberately, and with some embarrassment, avoided in party propaganda; thus, ignorance of its crucial importance was perfectly possible. In any case, it is very instructive to see what the new general secretary recommended for the Soviet economy and what he wanted to de-emphasize. In the revised 1986 version of the party program, the stages by which communism was to be achieved had entirely disappeared, and the very concept of the "building of communist society" had given way to the "planned and all-round perfection of socialism."[131] At the same time, at the Twenty-Seventh Party Congress, the classical communist view of the need to eliminate "commodity-money relations" was presented as a prejudice to be overcome in the interests of the country's economic development. At the next stage of *perestroika* Gorbachev presented the market as the best, most effective, and most democratic mechanism of economic cooperation, a necessary instrument of civilization without which a planned economy was quite impossible.[132] In June 1989 his closest advisor, Alexander Yakovlev, said explicitly that Marx's utopian vision of a marketless economy had simply not justified itself and that attempts to realize it would only create a basis for dictatorship.[133] This frank rehabilitation of the market was accompanied by support for the many forms of social and personal property, which opened the way to the idea of privatization.

It has become customary to present Gorbachev's economic reforms as "an effort to return to the spirit, if not the precise institutions, of the NEP."[134] Gorbachev himself contributed to this misunderstanding by his strenuous attempts to link his policies with the final phase of Lenin's thought, that is, with the Lenin of the NEP period. It is hard to say whether this arose from genuine conviction or was merely a tactical maneuver; to some extent it was probably both. In any event it is a misleading parallel. For Lenin the NEP was a forced, temporary retreat from the building of communism, while *perestroika* was to be an advance, a revolution. Gorbachev would never agree that his reforms constituted a retreat, and in his "Crimean Article" he proudly asserted that in his six years as leader he had "never yielded to the temptation of retreat."[135] His use of the word *retreat* was indeed the exact opposite of Lenin's, which makes plain the fundamental incompatibility between their views on the desired direction of the movement.

The failure of Gorbachev's economic policy was not due only to its theoretical inconsistencies and the lack of resolve in its practical implementation. Malia has rightly noticed that Gorbachev was in a much more difficult position than was Lenin in 1921.[136] The peasants, demoralized by several decades of collectivization, failed to respond to changes offered by marketization. The industrial workers had no stake in economic *perestroika* and, not surprisingly, saw it as promoting the interests of the hated "mafia." But "mafia" members also opposed it, because a civilized market would put a stop to the enormous profits to be made from a corrupt shadow economy.[137] In short, the market reforms had no social basis, but many enemies, who were able surreptitiously to sabotage, or cleverly circumvent, the new rules of the game so that they could be implemented only by authoritarian methods in the interests of the state as a whole, but no social group in particular. Such a policy, however, if realized by the general secretary of the Communist party, would have been perceived as an unacceptable increase of state coercion, contradicting Gorbachev's promise of decentralization and democratization.[138] Hence, Gorbachev's commitment to marketization undermined the ideological legitimation of the system without being able to provide a constructive alternative to its command economy.

The second point concerns *perestroika* in international relations. The subtitle of Gorbachev's book *Perestroika* is *New Thinking for Our Country and the World*, which indicates the close relationship between his international and domestic policies. For some time, however, the ideological importance of this policy change was more obvious to those in the West than in the Soviet Union itself. This was because the Soviet people, and citizens of other communist-ruled countries, were accustomed to propaganda about peaceful coexistence, while Westerners, especially political leaders, were very uneasy about the Soviet claim to be "a part of a historical process toward a definite end," an end that could only signify the complete victory of communism on a global scale.[139] As Ulam has observed, Soviet confidence in the ultimate and universal triumph of their cause greatly undermined the morale of Western politicians: "It was the ominous self-imposed isolation of the USSR and the awesome figure of Stalin that more than compensated for the Soviet weakness and mesmerized the West with fear." The claim that the Soviet regime represented the class interests of the proletariat worldwide, and so the will of history itself, was also important on the domestic front, since only a great world-historical mission could justify countless deprivations and sacrifices at home. This powerful support would be lost if the Soviet Union became not the "vanguard of humanity," but just one country among many others, one, moreover, whose achievements, if measured by the welfare of its citizens, were not very impressive and one that, after deviating from the mainstream of universal human civilization, urgently needed to rejoin it. Therefore, one must agree with Ulam that Gorbachev's renunciation of the universal claims of Soviet communism had "stripped it of its last line of defense."[140] From an ideological point of view, this was a sort of moral self-disarmament; if Stalin's "socialism in a single country" sounded like heresy, then Gorbachev's abandonment of the confrontation with capitalism in the name of universal human values was total surrender.

As we have seen, Gorbachev was consistent and courageous enough to concretize his new thinking on international affairs by openly proclaiming that each country had an inalienable right to freely choose its political and economic system. The unintentional, though hardly surprising, consequence of this frankness was the collapse of communism in Poland and, soon afterward, in the other countries of East-Central Europe. The Soviet leader wisely refused to regard this as an unacceptable setback but found it harder to accept another result of preferring free choice to the interests of socialism, as stronger efforts toward national self-determination were made in the Soviet Union itself. These separatist tendencies, long suppressed by fear or paralyzed by communist indoctrination, proved much stronger than he had expected. The final result of this process for the Soviet state is only too well known.

The third point is Gorbachev's complete rehabilitation of the general principles of "formal" "bourgeois liberal" democracy. In 1988 he declared a need for profound changes in the Soviet political system,[141] rejecting the "command-and-pressure mechanism" operated by the party and replacing it by a system based on sovereignty of law, competitive elections, the transfer of executive authority from the party to the state, and a constitutional division of powers. In the following year the Soviet Union witnessed the first competitive elections for the Congress of People's Deputies, as well as a number of competitive elections at the republican and municipal levels. These resulted in a revolutionary transformation of the Soviet political landscape. The Communist party split up into different factions whose ideology, as a rule, had little in common with communism as a system of ideas. A number of openly noncommunist political parties emerged, often represented in the Congress of People's Deputies and in republican and municipal bodies. They ran their own press organs, reflecting all shades of the political spectrum from monarchism and conservative nationalism to liberalism and democratic radicalism, as well as various, often bizarre mixtures of Russian nationalism with communist ideas. Municipal councils in many cities, including Moscow and Leningrad, were controlled by noncommunist democrats, or even (as, for instance, in western Ukraine) militantly anticommunist non-Russian nationalists for whom "Soviet power" was simply foreign occupation. This was not just political pluralism in public opinion, but the beginning of a genuine and increasingly uncontrollable power sharing. In February 1990 the Communist party was officially deprived of its constitutionally guaranteed monopoly on power (the notorious Article 6). Soon afterward Boris Yeltsin proclaimed the sovereignty of Russia's laws over those of the Soviet Union. In the Russian elections of June 12, 1991, Yeltsin won the post of the first president of the sovereign Republic of Russia. One of his first moves in this office was to banish all party organizations from the workplace and from state institutions in Russia.

The fourth and final point is that of increasingly uncontrolled *glasnost'*. This was, of course, a precondition for and part of the general movement toward democracy, but because of its paramount importance it deserves a separate analysis. It is indubitable that *glasnost'* was Gorbachev's greatest achievement and at the same time the main reason for his political defeat. At first it was only to be another intellectual/cultural "thaw," but it soon became clear that this time small doses of freedom of expression would not be enough to mobilize intellectual support for reform. Unexpectedly, Gorbachev was prepared to accept this fact and to draw the necessary conclusions. At the end of 1988 he proclaimed that in the interests of socialism, *glasnost'* would have no limits.[142] The new law on the press, published in draft in December 1989,[143] abolished censorship except for reasons of state security; true, it also contained an article prohibiting advocacy of the overthrow of the existing system, but this caveat had almost no practical importance. Freedom of expression, including political expression, had been restored, triggering a domino effect that quickly destroyed the last remnants of ideological legitimation of the system. After this, the final collapse of the system was only a matter of time.

The role of *glasnost'* in the final dismantling of "really existing socialism" is so obvious that there is no need to explain it. What does need to be explained is rather its spectacular failure to produce the desired results—namely, popular support for Gorbachev's restructuring or at least popular recognition of its significance for the cause of freedom. In this respect *glasnost'* proved totally counterproductive. In the last three years of Gorbachev's tenure, successive waves of criticism of the Soviet system, as well as revelations of its past crimes, failed to produce any general recognition that totalitarianism was finished. On the contrary, the dramatic increase of liberty was, as a rule, scorned or ignored, and when foreigners noted it, Soviet citizens, especially Russians, treated this as a manifestation of Western "Gorbomania." This widespread and stubborn refusal to give Gorbachev credit for this newly acquired intellectual and moral freedom was coupled with a profound disbelief in the possibility of changing the system for the better. A typical expression of this nihilistic attitude toward all Gorbachev's reforms appeared a few days before the failed coup in the radical weekly *Stolitsa*. The relevant passage runs as follows:

The conclusion is unambiguous: despite all "excesses" of democratization we are living now in a much more Soviet and much more socialist society than six years ago. This outcome forces us to think that *perestroika* was never a retreat: from the very beginning it was an attack, cloaked under deceptive maneuvers. The context of Gorbachev's revolution, criticized by radicals of all camps, revealed itself in a wholly "dialectical" manner: more democracy for some, more socialism for others. For people at the top more economic independence and more freedom from political dogma. For "people at the bottom" more humiliation, poverty and death. In this way this grandiose political provocation, worthy of Ulyanov and Dzhugashvili, has completed its cycle.[144]

The absurdity of the view that socialism under Gorbachev became stronger and more pervasive seems patent, but we must try to understand the reasons for such thinking.

The first was an inability to separate the cause of freedom from the general dissatisfaction with Gorbachev's policies stemming mostly from their increasingly disastrous economic effects. In March 1991 *Nezavisimaia Gazeta* published the results of a public opinion poll entitled "It Is Worse Every Day," which showed that only a minority would support "the change achieved in 1985." The positive results of Gorbachev's policies included, for most people, the withdrawal from Eastern Europe, the political independence granted to the republics, and the support for private ownership. Yet as many as 50 percent of respondents saw as the principal cause of the fall in living standards the toleration of the second economy (i.e., "the mafia system"), and as many as 48 percent favored a stronger government. The proportion opposed to both price increases and the second economy (65 percent) was almost twice as high as the proportion demanding that the land and the means of production be restored to the peasants (34 percent). The overwhelming majority had no confidence in public authorities and held extremely pessimistic views on the future of the country: 54 percent predicted economic disaster, and only 7 percent thought that the existing political system would survive until the year 2000.[145] The radicals from *Stolitsa* reflected the prevailing gloom in their own way by attributing all the dissatisfaction to Gorbachev's continuing loyalty to socialism. According to this logic, the feeling that it was getting worse every day could only mean that the evil-producing force—socialism—was becoming more pervasive and stronger.

Another reason for the negative dismissal of the liberating aspects of *perestroika* was a moralistic fundamentalism that precluded an appreciation of freedom as an autonomous value distinct from moral or material satisfaction. This mentality attached such importance to rejecting the system emotionally and morally that rational analysis was impossible. In this frame of mind, many came to believe that nothing had changed in Russia: totalitarianism continued to function because life was harder and harder, both materially and morally.

This mind-set is familiar from the history of the nineteenth-century Russian intelligentsia, especially those of a populist socialist persuasion. Members of this group who visited the West were, as a rule, quickly disappointed with the freedom they saw there and even denied its very existence, because they confused individual liberty with a moral order and social justice that provided everybody with opportunities for unlimited self-realization. In this sense, of course, there was no freedom in the West. Yet liberal freedom, which begins with freedom of conscience and of speech, is *the* most fundamental freedom, valuable and irreplaceable even if not accompanied by moral harmony and material welfare. This was not understood by the Russian populists and anarchists, but it *was* clearly understood, for instance, by Alexander Herzen, an otherwise merciless critic of liberalism. In his opinion, the "bourgeois" West in the midnineteenth century had not solved the "social question," offering no answers to questions about the meaning and value of life; it did not even practice the purely formal demands of political democracy. But nevertheless, unlike Russia under Tsar Nicholas I, it endowed the individual with fundamental freedoms, above all the priceless gift of freedom of speech.[146] This is just the sort of argument that can be used in support of the immense and too often underestimated difference between Gorbachev's Russia and the Russia of a mere decade ago.

Finally, the main result of *glasnost'* was the collapse of all possible consolations and justifications, all illusions about the ultimate meaning of those terrible sufferings the Russian nation had inflicted on other nations and (above all) on itself. Hence many people perceived *glasnost'* as utter disillusionment rather than an increase of freedom. Gorbachev had been wrong to expect that to reveal the horrible truth about the Soviet past would help mobilize popular support for his *perestroika*. The actual result of *glasnost'* was a total delegitimation of the communist claim to rule, which fostered the demand for a radical and morally unambiguous dissociation from the entire communist tradition. Gorbachev, however, unlike Yeltsin, was not prepared to take this step. Consequently, the results of his policies turned against him as general secretary of the CPSU and president of the Union. By destroying the last remnants of communist legitimacy, he destroyed his own title to power. Because of this the very fact that he remained in power came to be felt as a truly intolerable oppression. The people of Russia needed now a leader who would dare to break with the entire legacy of communism and boldly proclaim the "new beginning." This historic role fell to the lot of Yeltsin.

This brief analysis reveals the contradictory character of *perestroika*: the tension between its evolutionary and revolutionary sides, its continuity and discontinuity. This tension, or rather unresolved contradiction, characterized all Gorbachev's ideas. On the one hand, he saw his task as inaugurating a new epoch in the thousand-year development of Russia;[147] on the other hand, he defined himself as a Leninist, unwilling to break radically with the entire Soviet past, including Russia's "socialist option" in 1917. He was split, as it were, between two persons: one deeply aware that "everything was rotten through and through" and that his country "couldn't live that way" any longer; the other "profoundly committed to socialism," unable to give it a precise definition but nevertheless treating it as the most significant thing in his life.[148]

A revealing illustration of this personal split, as well as proof of the impossibility of solving this existential contradiction on a theoretical level, is Gorbachev's article "The Socialist Idea and Revolutionary Restructuring," published in November 1989. It is undoubtedly Gorbachev's most outspoken comment on the meaning and final aim of his life's task. As such, it deserves attention in the present context. To emphasize the contradictions in Gorbachev's thought I shall sharply distinguish his anti-Leninist and (objectively) anticommunist aims from his clumsy attempts to reconcile them with Russia's Leninist legacy and his own "socialist idea."

T. H. Rigby has rightly pointed out that the ideal of communism as a utopian endpoint of history was replaced in Gorbachev's article by "that of a humane socialism as an evolving order." [149] Furthermore, the general secretary of the CPSU readily recognized that there were many legitimate forms of socialism, some of them developing in the West and therefore somehow compatible with a capitalist economy. The main error of Soviet thinking on socialism was, in his view, to see it in terms of a "confrontational, absolute, metaphysical opposition" between two contemporary world systems.[150] Happily, this metaphysical opposition has been overcome by life itself. The most important element in the new thinking on socialism is the notion of universal civilization, whose achievements must be protected and preserved for future generations. This notion includes "the simple norms of universal morality," the principles of formal law and of the rule-of-law state, as well as the principles of commodity production and market exchange.[151] The idea of socialism in its contemporary sense is, above all, the idea of freedom.[152] In other words, democracy and freedom are the great values of universal human civilization, values that the Soviet people must inherit and fill with "socialist content." [153] In practice Gorbachev interpreted this postulate as a renewal of Soviet socialism through the introduction of mechanisms of civil society: formal democracy, the rule-of-law state, and a market economy.[154] From the Leninist (and Marxist!) point of view, this was of course total ideological surrender. Even from a purely logical standpoint it was not a program that filled bourgeois institutions with socialist content, but rather the reverse, a program that transformed "really existing socialism" in accordance with "bourgeois" ideals and values. This aspect of Gorbachev's vision does substantiate the view that "Gorbachev is an anti-Lenin who initiated a movement in reverse." [155] We can go even further and say that the head of the Soviet Communist party also became an "anti-Marx," because his interpretation of the idea of socialism essentially outlawed communism in the name of civilization.

But the point is that Gorbachev himself did all he could to avoid such conclusions. He defined his stand as a rejection of Stalinism in the name of Leninism and Marxism.[156] He tried to defend Marx's theories but did it in the clumsiest way, continually contradicting himself. Thus, for instance, he absolved Marx from any responsibility for the Soviet experiment with the idea of a centralized marketless economy by arguing that, in Marx's view, the abolition of the market was possible only at the highest stage of industrial development, far above anything achieved in Russia.[157] Gorbachev failed to notice, however, that in Marx's conception socialism ("the lower phase" of communism) *presupposed* the abolition of the market and that therefore either Lenin's decision to embark on building socialism in Russia was totally wrong even in Marxist terms (which Gorbachev refused to admit), or if not, then in order to be consistent with Marx's views, it *had* to involve attempts to dispense with the market (in which case Marx could *not* be altogether absolved from responsibility for the outcome). Elsewhere Gorbachev attributes "lasting significance" (*neprekhodyashchee znachenie*) to the Marxist conception of socialism as a legitimate consequence of the laws of historical development, but in the same sentence he light-heartedly relativizes this view by adding that it should not be treated as something "done once for all."[158] Similarly, he supports the idea of "scientific socialism," which claimed to enable its followers to create history in a conscious way (i.e., without producing unintended results), while at the same time defending the Bolshevik revolution on the grounds that all historical experience clearly shows that no revolution can be planned in advance and avoid unintended consequences, thus refuting the claims of "scientific socialism."[159] He praises Marx's idea of building "the kingdom of freedom" as a still-unsurpassed achievement of social thought,[160] without apparently noticing that this freedom presupposes full suppression of the "blind forces of the market" and without attempting to reconcile this objective with his own view of the market as a precious, universally accepted achievement of civilization. His attempts to defend Lenin are equally strained, inconsistent, and lamentably unconvincing. Lenin deserves sympathy, Gorbachev maintains, not so much for what he did in accordance with his communist blueprint, but rather for being a pragmatic leader, allegedly with no definite program, whose main virtue was his ability to constantly correct himself as he learnt by experience.[161] In this perspective Lenin's greatest achievement was the NEP; a parallel achievement in the sphere of theory was his discovery that enthusiasm alone was not enough, since economic activity cannot ignore the role of personal interests and calculations.[162] As might have been expected, Lenin's justification of terror and violence, coupled with his utter contempt for law and universal norms of ethics, is passed over in silence. Instead, Lenin, together with Marx, is presented as a convinced supporter of the Kantian principle that each human being must always be treated as an end, and never as a means.[163]

What were the reasons for these strange contradictions, inconsistencies, and empty verbalism? One obvious reason was, of course, the general state of Marxist theory at the stage of democratization. As the various Communist parties became increasingly de-ideologized, Marxist tenets were treated less and less seriously, though lip service to them was still an obligatory ritual. Especially destructive of the inner coherence of Marxist theory were all attempts to give socialism a human face by presenting Marxism, which had originated as an instrument of class struggle, as a philosophy that fostered universal human values together with attitudes of partnership and dialogue. The Polish and Czech experiences have shown that such intentions, if not combined with a readiness to make an open break with Marxism, were in fact the surest way to replace the crudeness of Stalinist Marxism with various forms of humane eclecticism.[164] Now it was the turn of Soviet Russia.

Another reason was Gorbachev's plan constantly to reassure the party that *perestroika* had some Marxist-Leninist credentials and should not be regarded as a betrayal of the communist cause. This was because he saw the party as a sclerotic but still dangerous monster that had to be lulled asleep rather than provoked to more active resistance to change. As we now know, Yakovlev had a different view on this matter, arguing that "the monster had long since turned into a rabbit" and urging Gorbachev to distance himself from it more decisively.[165] A similar view, more radically expressed, was advanced by V. Shostakovskii, former rector of the Higher Party School and vice chairman of the Republican Party of the Russian Federation. In an article published early in 1991 he wrote of communist dictatorship in the past tense, arguing that the so-called communists had in fact long since ceased to be communists and Marxists. They had rejected all the ideas of Marxian communism: class struggle, worldwide revolution, the withering away of the state, and a marketless economy. In fact, communism had died with no chance of resurrection.[166]

There was much truth in these arguments. Nevertheless, some caution on Gorbachev's part, especially in ideological matters, was a reasonable tactical requirement. Responsible statesmen must sometimes act in disguise.

However, and this seems to be the crucial point, Gorbachev's attempts to give his *perestroika* some Marxist-Leninist coloring could not be explained on tactical grounds alone. Nor should they be attributed, as Shostakovskii seems to have suggested,[167] to Gorbachev's personal narrow-mindedness or political cynicism. Gorbachev's frequent references to Russia's socialist option and the communist perspective expressed his deeply felt desire to preserve some continuity in Soviet history and so to save his own identity as one of its products. He was quite explicit about this when he wrote: "We cannot renounce our history."[168] These simple words were neither an attempt to give a new, more human face to Marxism, nor a tactical maneuver. They reflected his need, and the need of most Soviet people of his

generation, to save the meaning of their lives as Soviet citizens and to preserve their Soviet identity—not the abstract, purely ideological communist
identity, but Soviet identity as a product of common experiences and a
common historical fate. He could not simply reject this identity, nor did
he want to. His dilemmas were similar to the problems of the great nationalist reformers who hoped to radically reconstruct their nations without
disowning their past, without infringing their innermost collective identity.

If this is true, then Gorbachev was equally sincere in his resolve to
change the system radically, in his desire to preserve a sense of continuity,
in his awareness that it was impossible to continue "living that way," and
in his feeling that "socialism is ingrained in the people, ingrained in all
of us." [169] He was equally sincere in his yearning for freedom—political,
human, spiritual, and economic—and in his determination to combine this
freedom with some form of the socialist idea, as well as with the continued
existence, in some form, of the Soviet Union. There was an often dramatic
tension between these two ambitions, but *both* were part of his identity,
with deep roots not just in his individual makeup, but also in his family
history. In a rare moment of self-disclosure Gorbachev explained the radical reform program as the result of the conclusion that people could not go
on living in the way they had been living.[170] He mentioned a conversation
with E. A. Shevardnadze and went on to comment:

We hadn't taken a simple path to our conclusions. We weren't boys any more;
we had lived through a good deal, and if you consider that we had been through
the war as well, we had seen and knew a great ideal. Take my two grandfathers.
One was convicted for not having fulfilled the sowing plan in 1933, when half the
family died of starvation. He was sent to Irkutsk to cut timber. And there was that
tormented family, half of it dead in 1933. My other grandfather was an organizer
of collective farms, and at that time was the local representative of the Ministry
of Procurements. That was a pretty important personage in those times. He was
from a peasant family, a peasant of average means. He was put in prison, too, and
interrogated for 14 months—they tried to make him admit to something he hadn't
done. He survived, thank goodness. But he lived in that "plague house," in the
house of an "enemy of the people," and his relatives and friends couldn't enter it.
Otherwise, they would have gone where my grandfather had been. So, we had been
through everything, we had seen it from the inside, we knew that life and know it
today, we could make comparisons and can make them today.

I think that most of the people sitting here have that irreplaceable experience
that awakens one's thinking, impels a person to make comparisons and look for
answers, and doesn't let one's conscience rest easy.[171]

This irreplaceable experience of self-awakening resulted in a firm decision
that everything must be changed "in such a way that a person in this society
would feel like a human being." [172]

But this was not to be a simple negation. Using a Hegelian term we may say that Gorbachev sought an *Aufhebung* of the Soviet system. It was to be negated dialectically, that is, radically changed but in such a way as to preserve and raise to a higher level everything good in it. Such a program ruled out nihilistic attitudes toward the past, which brings us to the other part of Gorbachev's self-explanation:

Yes, we had to bid farewell to the past. An agonizing process! But what and whom are we supposed to renounce? Am I to renounce my grandfather, who was totally committed to all this? In his time, he was the chairman of a collective farm for 17 years. I never heard that he had any doubts about what was being done on that land. On the land where he was born and where all the others lived: some had come from Voronezh, others from Chernigov. I can't go against my grandfather. I can't go against my father, who fought at the Kursk battle and was in a forced crossing of the Dnieper when the river ran with blood. He made it to the border and was wounded in Czechoslovakia. In cleansing myself and renouncing all the barrack-style system of Stalinism, am I supposed to renounce my grandfather, my father and what they did? To renounce whole generations? Did they live their lives in vain, then? No, I have said more than once that we did not just grow up out of a swamp; we have a firm footing beneath us.[173]

Gail Sheehy, the author of an illuminating biography of Gorbachev, explains the duality in Gorbachev's feelings and thinking in terms of Orwellian doublethink, or "thinking on two levels," as a typical product of Soviet totalitarianism.[174] The constant ideological pressure characteristic of this system created conditions under which publicly confessed truth had to be different from private experience while usually being internalized to a certain extent and so forming a distinct part of an individual's genuine identity. In this way the Soviet people have learned through "the conflict of holding two mutually antagonistic ideas in mind at the same time."[175] In this view, Gorbachev represented a typical case of this peculiarly Soviet type of dual consciousness; on the one hand, he was "entirely open to seeing the evils of communism as they translated into everyday Russian life," but on the other hand, he was capable of behaving like a sincere and true believer. To an outside observer this indicated a fundamental uncertainty as to what he really stood for; to Gorbachev himself, however, it was simply the ability to see both sides of a question and to approach it *dialectically*.[176]

There is much truth in this interpretation, since, as I have tried to show, duality of mind was indeed a typical product of totalitarian ideocracy (see chapter 5, section 3). Nevertheless, it is not an adequate explanation of Gorbachev's case; the category of dual consciousness is too broad, while the Orwellian notion of doublethink is too narrow, suggesting a sort of mental captivity that was remarkably absent in Gorbachev's thinking. Unlike the communists of Bukharin's generation, he was no longer a prisoner of communist ideology. He did not declare an inability to renounce communist dogmas, only to renounce the countless Soviet people who had truly

believed in communism and for whom their Soviet fatherland was inseparable from its ideological mission. This was obviously something different,
allowing more room for intellectual freedom.

But why indeed should he feel required to renounce those people? A
patriotic Frenchman, even of a conservative persuasion, does not have to
renounce the legacy of the French Revolution; contemporary Americans
from the South may feel attachment to its distinctive traditions without defending the institution of slavery; similarly, modern, Westernized Turks do
not have to renounce the Ottoman empire. Therefore, why was Gorbachev
so afraid of betraying his father and grandfather? Why did he feel that a
radical and outspoken break with communism would have been equivalent
to a renunciation of Soviet history itself?

These questions are, of course, only rhetorical, because the answer is
self-evident: it was because Soviet patriotism was incurably ideological,
because the Soviet Union represented an extreme case of an "ideological
fatherland" incapable of surviving de-ideologization. It is only too obvious that this was so because of the inherently ideocratic character of the
Soviet state. Unlike national patriotism, Soviet patriotism could not become ideologically neutral—hence, the inevitable tension between the two
parts of Gorbachev's identity, between his loyalty to his Soviet inheritance
and his awareness of the need for change. He proved unable to separate the
history of his country, including even the battle of Kursk, from the history
of communism, and this forced him to pay verbal tribute to an ideology in
which he had ceased to believe. He felt it necessary to legitimize his task in
Leninist terms, fearing that otherwise the older generations of Soviet patriots would treat him as a traitor. His fear of being seen as a renegade shows
that he was still a prisoner of the ideological fatherland despite his own
factual rejection of communist principles and his emphasis on the need to
join "the mainstream of civilization." Although he had destroyed the very
foundations of communist ideology and the communist utopian blueprint,
he continued to overestimate the moral strength of communist tradition.[177]
He saw it as capable of maintaining the cohesiveness of the supranational
Soviet peoples, and this acted as a powerful brake on his endeavors as a
radical reformer. In this sense he himself needed more enlightenment from
glasnost', more liberation from the Soviet past. He needed to thoroughly
rethink Leninism and to dare to reject it freely and frankly. Very probably he would have done so had he been given more time. But the course
of unconcealed decommunization, released by his own efforts, ran out of
control and proved quicker than his own, otherwise astonishingly rapid
ideological evolution.

Gorbachev's dilemmas were similar in some degree to the problems of
those French patriots of the early nineteenth century who welcomed the
end of revolutionary experiments while trying at the same time to interpret

the Revolution as an integral, inseparable part of French history. Pierre Simon Ballanche, for instance, responded to this challenge by developing a theory of "social palingenesis" that explained how France might have radically changed its institutions while preserving its essential identity. But the point is that a national fatherland like France is much more inclusive and much more likely to preserve its identity in the process of change than is an ideological fatherland like the Soviet Union. It was therefore predictable that the Soviet Union might not be able to survive the general collapse of communism.

Gorbachev, however, greatly underestimated this possibility. He continued to believe that the Soviet Union had found an adequate solution to national questions, that it had become a genuine and irreplaceable fatherland for most of its citizens, and that existing economic interdependencies would prove much stronger than separatist movements. He failed to foresee that Soviet citizens would react to the crisis of communist power not just as individuals but as peoples as well, that their search for freedom would reawaken their national identities and so make personal freedom inseparable from national self-determination. He also failed to appreciate that for people like himself, Soviet-Russian patriots unwilling to betray their fathers and grandfathers, the only way of preserving continuity with the past was to treat the whole Soviet period as a chapter of Russian national history—a closed chapter, of course, but nonetheless part of Russia's national heritage. Only thus was it possible to break with communism while at the same time paying tribute to those who, like his grandfather, had once sincerely embarked on the communist utopian romance or those who, like his father, had bravely defended their socialist fatherland in the war against Nazi Germany.

Notwithstanding all these failures, Gorbachev's contribution to the final dismantling of Soviet communism can hardly be overestimated. The inertia of the system was so great that without energetic initiatives from the very top, it would not have set out on the road of serious structural reform. Hence it is perfectly true that "without Gorbachev (or a similar Soviet first secretary with another name) we would still sit awaiting the end of communism."[178] True, the intended result of *perestroika* was not the collapse of the Soviet Union but rather to make it more humane, more economically effective, and therefore more internationally competitive. But it is a big mistake to assert that Gorbachev's aim was to preserve and strengthen the Soviet Union as the mainstay of communism. On the contrary, his Soviet patriotism and attachment to a broadly conceived socialist idea should not conceal the fact that the real aims of his revolutionary reconstruction were not communist in any meaningful sense of the term. As he himself repeatedly stressed, his main purpose, indeed his mission, was *to replace* the existing system with one consonant with freedom—not with communist freedom (i.e., freedom conceived as rational mastery and conscious control, or the liberation of man's species powers), but ordinary freedom, as established and practiced in the liberal democratic countries of the world. In this case his main objective has been achieved, though in a form different from what he had hoped for. He was defeated as Soviet president and defender of the Soviet state, but not as a reformer whose priority was freedom for the Soviet people. His *perestroika* was not "six wasted years of reform communism,"[179] but an incredibly quick and peaceful dismantling of the entire edifice of communist tyranny, and *this* he declared to be an *intended* result of his reforms.

Georg Soros, one of the most discriminating and otherwise very pessimistic observers of the Soviet scene, observed that "Gorbachev regards the transformation of the Soviet Union into an open society as his primary goal, one that takes precedence over all other objectives including his own survival, let alone the survival of the Soviet empire."[180] These words were written in 1989, and what has happened since then confirms, on the whole, this diagnosis.

I do not think that the collapse of "really existing socialism" in the former Soviet Union and Eastern Europe can be interpreted as the final victory of capitalism or, correspondingly, the final defeat of all socialist movements. I hope, however, that it marks the end of Marxist communism. If so, it is a historical event of the greatest significance for the whole world, East and West, North and South. The Russian nineteenth-century thinker Peter Chaadaev once wrote that the meaning of Russian history would involve teaching the world a great lesson. The tragic fate of the Russian Revolution has indeed been a great lesson for the world at large.

It has been pointed out that after this lesson "the critique of market rationality in the name of social justice and the social consensus concerning 'the public purpose' of economy must never assume the form of suppressing or substituting market economy."[181] Very few people will disagree with this, but it is only part of the moral of the fable. We should add that the wish to improve the world must never pretend to represent "scientific" certainty based on alleged knowledge of the laws of history. Those with such a goal must consciously and consistently renounce all forms of arrogant, undemocratic self-righteousness inherent in claiming a universalist saving mission, and the legitimation of political movements and sociopolitical systems must never rest on the authority of an allegedly infallible doctrine, or any other form of monopoly on truth. Finally, nobody must be allowed to define freedom for others, to "liberate" them in accordance with *his own* views on the matter or to sacrifice whole categories of people, or entire generations, for the sake of the triumph of some "true freedom," or "higher freedom," in the future. Never again.

Reference Matter

Notes

For full forms of works cited by author or author and title only in the Notes, see the Works Cited, pp. 619–35.

Introduction

1. In principle such a work should also deal with the fate of communist ideas in Asia—at least in China. I regret being unable to address this task.

2. A good example of someone obviously uneasy about Marx's idea of a market-less society is Perry Anderson, one of the main theorists of British Marxism, who welcomed with relief Alec Nove's views on the "economics of feasible socialism." (See Anderson, *In the Tracks*, pp. 100–101.) Attempts to ignore the centrality of the antimarket stand in socialism are well reflected in a recent book on modern ideologies described by its author as a product of a long-standing undergraduate course on political ideas. It simply plays down the importance of Marxism (especially Soviet Marxism, which it does not discuss at all) and says that the widespread opinion "that socialism is always critical of free markets and capitalism" is an "odd view," a part of "the popular myth about socialism" (Vincent, p. 109).

3. Balibar, pp. 33, 36.

4. A recent example of this attitude is Graham's *Karl Marx, Our Contemporary*—a book trying to prove that Marx's philosophy has contemporary relevance and that the collapse of communism was in fact merely a collapse of Leninism. Another recent book, Gottlieb's *Marxism, 1844–1990*, voices the same view but with much less knowledge of Marx's ideas. Graham, whose approach is that of "analytical Marxism," knows at least that Marx's image of the future society presupposed the abolition of money (see pp. 118–19), while Gottlieb describes Marx's social ideal as (among other things) "a just exchange of labor for money" (p. 34), showing thereby his total ignorance of Marx's well-known views on this subject.

5. See Merquior, *Western Marxism*.

6. Dostoevsky, pp. 384–85.

7. The expression is T. H. Rigby's. See "Stalinism and the Mono-organizational Society."

8. For an elaboration of this view, see my essay "The Intellectual Tradition of Pre-Revolutionary Russia."

9. See Löwenthal, "Development vs. Utopia in Communist Policy."

10. I do not endorse this theory because of fundamental differences between the economic mechanisms of Stalinist Russia and Nazi Germany. These two countries were economically and socially different, though similar in their power structures and in their ruthless pursuit of genocidal policies.

11. See Arendt, new preface to Part 3.

12. Rupnik, p. 210. In another place the author calls Poland "the laboratory for political change for the whole of the Other Europe" (p. 150).

13. My experiences with Marxism, Stalinist totalitarianism, and the "really existing socialism" of the post-Stalinist period have been described in my auto-biographical book *Spotkania z Miloszem*. See also my essay " 'The Captive Mind' Revisited."

14. See the following articles of mine: " 'Meaning of History' and 'Meaning in History' " (1982); "The Marxian Conception of Freedom" (also in Japanese trans-lation, 1983); "Marx and Freedom" (1983); "Karol Marks: emancypacja ludzkości a wolność indywidualna" (1984); "The Marxian Conception of Freedom" (1984); "Karl Marx as Philosopher of Freedom" (1988).

Chapter 1

1. See Kamenka, p. xii.

2. See Moore, p. 56.

3. The importance of such an understanding of Marxism has been emphasized in recent years by some American scholars. Thus, Wood argues that freedom and self-actualization, as values directly dependent on the development of labor, have a transcultural significance, while justice has a meaning or content only within a given mode of production (see Wood, "Marx on Right and Justice," in M. Cohen, pp. 121–22). A similar view is ably developed by Brenkert.

4. Lukács, *History and Class Consciousness*, p. 315.

5. Dworkin, p. 34.

6. This antipersonalist character of Marxism has been stressed in Berdyaev's characterization of "Socialism as Religion." He wrote about it thus: "The person is never a goal and always a means. The person himself possesses no worth and is valued only according to his usefulness in winning the proletarian-socialist para-dise. With respect to person, all is allowed in the name of the benevolent goals of socialism. The person can be deprived of his freedom and his rights. His dignity does not have to be respected; it can be suppressed if necessary for just social goals. The evil principle of Marxism is nowhere so manifest as in this atheistic and in-human attitude toward the human face, toward individualism, and in this respect Marx himself sinned more than anyone" (p. 112).

7. Dewey, p. 41.

8. For an able presentation of the view that "freedom is no more than action from (or with) identification" see Bergmann, p. 64.

9. Osborn, p. 13.

10. Simmel, *On Individuality and Social Forms*, pp. 220, 221, 221/286.

11. See O'Rourke, p. 6.   12. Brenkert, p. 98.

13. O'Rourke, p. 185.   14. See G. Cohen.

15. See Gouldner.

16. The most comprehensive presentation of the "anti-Engelsian" interpretation of Marx is presented by Levine. See chapter 2, section 1.

17. O'Rourke, p. 184.

18. Merleau-Ponty, pp. 129, 153.

19. Kolakowski, *Światopogląd i życie codzienne*, p. 194.

20. Hunt, *The Political Ideas of Marx and Engels*, vol. 2, pp. 211, 361.

21. See Kuhn.

22. The term *liberalism* is employed here in its continental European meaning, which is different from its current American usage. For a good presentation of the ideal model of "classical liberalism," see Hayek's "Liberalism," in *New Studies*.

23. Ibid., p. 134.

24. Hayek, *The Constitution of Liberty*, pp. 11–12.

25. Locke, p. 244.

26. For a brilliant philosophical analysis of these two notions, see Berlin's "Two Concepts of Liberty," in *Four Essays on Liberty*.

27. Ibid., p. 131.

28. For a good summary of Fichte's conception of freedom, see R. Hausheer, "Fichte," in Pelczynski and Gray, pp. 123–49.

29. See Berlin, *Four Essays*, p. 130.

30. Ibid., pp. 162–66.

31. See Constant, 308–28.

32. In a sense, an opposition to modernity in the name of classicism characterized the entire socialist tradition. Lomasky has shown that "socialism incorporates motifs central to the study of politics that germinated in Greece and were preserved throughout the Middle Ages, but which were superseded by the modern revolution in political theory" (p. 115).

33. See Tönnies.

34. Buchanan, *Marx and Justice*, pp. 163, 51.

35. By way of digression, it seems worthwhile to add that this conception was taken up and developed by the outstanding Soviet legal theorist Evgeny Pashukanis in his book *The General Theory of Law* (1924) in Pashukanis, *Selected Writings on Marxism and Law*, pp. 101–2. Kamenka and Erh-Soon Tay have shown that it is possible to agree with some of Pashukanis's views without sharing his (and Marx's) value judgments. (See especially their *Law and Social Control*.)

36. Hayek, *New Studies*, p. 143.

37. See Lukács, *The Young Hegel*, ch. 1. The similarity between the young Marx and the young Hegel does not extend, of course, to the "Napoleonic utopia" propounded by the latter.

38. Quoted in Yu. Steklov, vol. 1, pp. 448–49.

39. See Walicki, *The Controversy over Capitalism*, pp. 80–107.

40. Chernyshevskii, vol. 5, pp. 106, 217.

41. Berlin, *Four Essays*, p. 125.

42. See, for instance, D. F. B. Tucker, *Marxism and Individualism*.

43. See Wood, *Karl Marx*, p. 235.

44. Green, *Works*, vol. 3, p. 371. Quoted in Gaus, p. 163.

45. Quoted in Gaus, p. 172.

46. See the distinction between end-connected and rule-connected societies in Hayek, *Law, Legislation, and Liberty*, vol. 2, pp. 38–39. From this point of view, both tribal society and socialist "teleocracy" represent the end-connected type of society, while liberal welfare states, at least in principle, can still be classified as rule-connected open societies.

47. See John Gray, "Mill's Conception of Happiness," in Mill, pp. 201–3. The same position has been taken by Bergmann, who wrote: "Even if there were a universal human nature, freedom according to our definition still would not be the expression of it, but would be action from our individual identification" (p. 91).

48. Mill, "On Liberty," in Mill, pp. 33, 33.

49. Kolakowski, *Main Currents of Marxism*, vol. 1, ch. 1, "The Origins of Dialectic."

50. See Schaff, *Alienation as a Social Phenomenon*, pp. 24–29. Probably the most comprehensive treatment of the theme of alienation in Marx is found in Calvez.

51. Kolakowski, *Main Currents of Marxism*, vol. 1, p. 116.

52. Such a notion of freedom was, of course, deeply rooted in Hegelianism. It has been rightly observed that in Marx's critique of Hegelian legal philosophy, "le véritable ennemi de Marx, c'est le libéralisme, et non pas la *Rechtsphilosophie*." (See Haarscher, p. 88.)

53. See Lukács, *The Young Hegel*, pp. 497–502.

54. For an analysis of these important texts see Walicki, *The Controversy over Capitalism*, pp. 185–94.

55. Berlin, *Karl Marx*, p. 138.

56. See Bulgakov, "Karl Marks kak religioznyi tip," in Bulgakov, pp. 326–35.

57. Feuerbach, p. 14.

58. On Cieszkowski's "philosophy of action," see Lobkowicz, pp. 193–206, and Walicki, *Philosophy and Romantic Nationalism*, pp. 127–51. Hess discussed Cieszkowski's *Prolegomena* in his *European Triarchy* (composed between 1839 and 1841), attributing to Cieszkowski the merit of having positively overcome not only orthodox Hegelianism but also the Hegelian Left.

59. Hess, pp. 223–24.

60. Ibid., p. 335.

61. Ibid., p. 336.

62. Ibid., p. 337.

63. Ibid., p. 342.

64. Ibid., p. 343.

65. Ibid., p. 345.

66. Ibid., p. 346.

67. Ibid., pp. 346–47.

68. See Misrahi, and Weyl, and also Wistrich.

69. See Cornu, vol. 2, ch. 3.

70. Fragments from this book have been published in English in Stepelevich, *The Young Hegelians*, pp. 335–53.

71. See Stepelevich, "Max Stirner and Ludwig Feuerbach," pp. 461–63.

72. See Hamowy, pp. 249–59.   73. M&E, CW, 5:33, 35.

74. Ibid., pp. 47–48, 51.   75. Ibid., pp. 51–52.

76. Ibid., pp. 80–81.

77. See Brenkert, Marx's Ethics of Freedom, pp. 88–89.

78. See R. Tucker, Philosophy and Myth in Karl Marx, p. 63.

79. See Hamilton, Madison, and Jay, p. 78.

80. See Walicki, A History of Russian Thought, pp. 256–57. Mikhailovskii differed from Marx in rejecting the necessity of capitalist development, but nonetheless his social philosophy was, in a sense, a populist reinterpretation of Marxism. (See ibid., pp. 224–25, 259–61, 406–7.)

81. Kolakowski, Main Currents of Marxism, vol. 1, pp. 161–62.

82. Hayek, Law, Legislation, and Liberty, vol. 2, p. 30.

83. Kolakowski, "The Myth of Human Self-Identity," p. 33.

84. See Simmel, On Individuality and Social Forms, p. 169.

85. Novgorodtsev, pp. 199–200. For a more detailed discussion of Novgorodtsev's views on Marx, see Walicki, Legal Philosophies of Russian Liberalism, pp. 329–37.

86. Kolakowski, "The Myth of Human Self-Identity," p. 35.

87. See Tönnies.

88. On "wealth" or "abundance" as Marx's fundamental value, see Heller, "Toward a Marxist Theory of Value."

89. Heller, The Theory of Needs in Marx, p. 46.

90. Selucký, pp. 23–24.

91. In this sense, Hayek pointed out that the market is a sort of "discovery procedure" and that the "dispersed knowledge" contained in its self-regulating mechanisms is infinitely greater than the amount of information any one person or agency can possess. (See Hayek, Law, Legislation, and Liberty, vol. 2, p. 71.)

92. See Lavoie, p. 76.

93. This is the expression Berlin used in his essay "Historical Inevitability." See Berlin, Four Essays on Liberty, p. 77.

94. Lunacharskii, vol. 1, pp. 186–89.

95. O'Rourke, p. 84.

96. Mikhailovskii, "Karl Marks pered sudom," pp. 171–73. For a historical comment, see Walicki, The Controversy over Capitalism, pp. 132–47.

97. See also Walicki, The Controversy over Capitalism, pp. 185–92.

98. This can already be seen in Marx's polemics against Proudhon in The Poverty of Philosophy (1847).

99. See Mehring, pp. 196–97. In later years, Mehring changed his views and became a Marxist.

100. In the quoted edition the word Fremdheit is translated, quite wrongly, as "independence." Terrell Carver, who quotes this passage from Capital in his preface to Marx's "Notes on Adolph Wagner," has corrected this obvious error (M, TOM, 171).

101. For an analysis of the drafts of Marx's letter to Zasulich, see Walicki, The Controversy over Capitalism (pp. 188–92), and also Shanin. Shanin's work con-

tains three introductions (by Shanin, by Wada, and by Sayer and Corrigan) and a selection of relevant texts, including the Marx-Zasulich correspondence.

102. Gellner, *State and Society in Soviet Thought*, p. 53.

103. Neurath, *Wesen und Weg zur Sozialisierung*. As we shall see, many Soviet economists took up these views and continued to defend them even after the death of Stalin. (See Temkin, pp. 266–301.)

104. Dunayevskaya comments: "So hostile was Marx to labor under capitalism, that at first he called, not for the 'emancipation' of labor, but for its 'abolition'" (*Marxism and Freedom*, pp. 60–61).

105. Rainko, *Świadomość i historia*, p. 301. Despite the author's commitment to Marxism-Leninism, this book provides an interesting reconstruction of Marx's theory of freedom. The same can be said about Rainko's book *Świadomość i determinizm*.

106. According to Engels, "juridical world view," i.e., belief in the omnipotence of rational legislation, was the classical worldview of the bourgeoisie. (See Engels and Kautsky, "Juridical Socialism," p. 204; originally published as "Juristen-Socialismus," *Die Neue Zeit*, no. 2 [1887].)

107. This has been strongly stressed by Temkin (see note 103 above). His book, in spite of verbal declaration of loyalty to the party line, seems to have been written with the deliberate aim of exposing the presence and vitality of the utopian elements in Marxism.

108. In *Stalinism and the Seeds of Soviet Reform*, Lewin wrote, for instance, that the "anti-market obsession" was "one of the fallacies of Bolshevik (and some other socialist) thinking which they had begun to cure themselves of during the NEP" (p. xxiv). I do not dare suspect that authors of Lewin's caliber know so little about Marx's communism; hence, I must assume that statements of this kind are misguided attempts to conceal the truth about the ideological origins of the Bolshevik experiments in Russia. For a fuller discussion, see chapter 6, section 1.

109. Mandel, "Economics," in McLellan, ed., *Marx: The First Hundred Years*, pp. 234–35.

110. In his preface to Marx's *Civil War in France*, Engels wrote: "Look at the Paris Commune. That was the Dictatorship of the Proletariat" (M&E, *SW*, 2:189).

111. See Hunt, *The Political Ideas of Marx and Engels*, vol. 2, pp. 194–95, 198–99.

112. As we can see, Marx's understanding of "the very nature of right" excluded all sorts of affirmative action.

113. Hayek, *Law, Legislation, and Liberty*, vol. 2, pp. 36–39.

114. Moore, pp. 50–51.   115. See note 35 above.

116. Moore, pp. 66–67.   117. Ibid., pp. 29, 90.

118. Ibid., p. x. A telling example of the horrible consequences of communist utopianism is seen by the author in the genocidal policies of Pol Pot's government in Kampuchea (p. vii).

119. Ibid., p. 44.

120. See Rainko, *Świadomość i determinizm*, p. 105.

121. Lukács, *History and Class Consciousness*, p. 229. The radical break between Marx's historical materialism and his communist ideal is emphasized also

by Calvez, who distinguishes between "communism as an act" and "communism as a state of affairs," seeing them as mutually exclusive:

> Le communisme comme *acte* et le communisme comme *état* s'excluent réciproquement. Le communisme, comme acte de supprimer l'aliénation, se trouve situé dans l'histoire selon l'explication du matérialisme historique: il est un acte révolutionnaire fondé dans la contradiction entre forces de production et rapports de production, elle-même explicable par les rapports dialectiques essentielles que l'homme entretient avec la nature at avec les autres hommes. *Le communisme comme acte est dans les conditions générales de l'histoire* définie par Marx. . . . Au contraire, le communisme comme société communiste réalisée, suppose que toute l'histoire antérieure soit considérée comme préhistoire, donc comme n'ayant pas de sens humain, ne pouvant pas être comprise: ce communisme est une telle réussite qu'il n'a de rapport avec aucun passé et que bien plutôt c'est lui seul que commence l'histoire. Le communisme comme état échappe aux conditions générales de l'histoire définies par Marx. (pp. 533–34)

This analysis shows the usefulness of interpreting Marx's general historiosophy in terms of self-enriching alienation. Only such interpretation enables us to see the meaningful relationship between historical materialism (as a theory of history at the stage of alienation) and Marx's vision of communism as man's final destiny.

122. Moore, p. 36.

123. Habermas, p. 5.

124. Durkheim, p. 41.

125. Ibid., pp. 116–17.

126. Berger, p. 109. Similar observations have been made by Soviet sociologist L. G. Ionin (pp. 87, 92–94, 114).

127. Simmel, *The Philosophy of Money*, p. 285.

128. Ibid., pp. 285–86, 286.

129. Ibid., pp. 288–89.

130. Ibid., pp. 289–90, 291.

131. Ibid., p. 292.

132. Ibid., p. 294.

133. Ibid., p. 297.

134. Ibid., p. 298.

135. Ibid., p. 299.

136. Ibid., p. 313.

137. Ibid., pp. 302–3.

138. Ibid., p. 307, 307, 307.

139. Simmel, "The Metropolis and Mental Life," in Simmel, *On Individuality and Social Forms*, p. 325. A similar view was developed by Karl Mannheim, although he did not put special emphasis on the role of money. According to him, the genesis of the "formal quantitative approach" characteristic of modern rationalism was bound up with the search for forms of knowledge that "appealed to what is common in all human beings" and thus could be "knowable by all and communicable to all" (Mannheim, p. 149). The connection between this capacity for abstract, formal, quantitative thinking and the development of a money economy can be easily grasped.

140. For a comparative analysis of the views of Marx and Weber on capitalism and freedom, see Löwith, *Max Weber and Karl Marx*.

141. Hayek, *The Constitution of Liberty*, p. 38.

142. Simmel, *On Individuality and Social Forms*, pp. 233–34.

143. Lukes, p. 149.

144. I mean, of course, *Marx's* conception of freedom, which centered around

the problems of alienation and reification, not Lenin's theory of social and national liberation.

Chapter 2

1. That is, in the epoch of the Second International. See Kolakowski, *Main Currents*, vol. 2, *The Golden Age*.

2. This has been recently stressed by Carver, who believes that Engels wanted to become the "foremost authority on a comprehensive and universally valid *Weltanschauung*" (p. 157).

3. Ibid., p. 96.

4. See G. S. Jones, "Engels," in Bottomore, p. 151.

5. Kolakowski, *Main Currents*, vol. 1, p. 261.

6. Lichtheim, p. 241.

7. Anderson, *Considerations*, p. 60.

8. Sartre's essay was later included in his *Critique of Dialectical Reason* under the title "The Problem of Method."

9. British Marxist historian E. P. Thompson reacted to this by writing "An Open Letter to Leszek Kolakowski" (*The Socialist Register*, 1973), which ended with the words: "In any case, can we meet one day and have a drink? I owe you more than one. And can we still drink to the fulfillment of that moment of common aspiration: 1956?" (p. 95).

10. See Anderson, *Considerations*, p. 46.

11. The expression is Milosz's (see his *The Captive Mind*).

12. Carver, pp. 118–32.

13. See Trotsky, *On Engels and Kautsky*, p. 24.

14. See Jay, ch. 2, and Merquior, p. 87.

15. Lukács, *History and Class Consciousness*, pp. 3, 3, 132.

16. Ibid. Lukács obviously forgot that Marx himself, in his preface to the first German edition of *Capital*, chose to stress that his method was similar to that of the physicist who "either observes physical phenomena where they occur in their most typical form and most free from disturbing influence, or, whenever possible, he makes experiments under conditions that assure the occurrence of the phenomenon in its normality" (M&E, *SW*, 2:87).

17. Lukács, *History and Class Consciousness*, p. 128.

18. Ibid., p. 14.

19. Ibid., pp. 10, 49, 43.

20. See Jacoby, pp. 53–57.

21. Kolakowski, *Main Currents*, vol. 1, p. 400.

22. For a comprehensive analysis of Brzozowski's views and his intellectual evolution, see Walicki, *Stanislaw Brzozowski*.

23. Brzozowski, *Kultura i życie*, p. 48.

24. Brzozowski, *Idee*, pp. 7–8. This chapter from Brzozowski's *Ideas* was originally published in *Neue Zeit* (no. 31 [1907]: 153–60) under the title "Geschichtsmaterialismus als Kulturphilosophie: Ein Philosophisches Programm."

25. Brzozowski, *Kultura i życie*, p. 358.

26. Brzozowski, *Idee*, p. 136.

27. Lukács, *History and Class Consciousness*, p. 130.

28. Lukács, *Political Writings, 1919–1929*, p. 144.

29. Brzozowski, *Idee*, p. 397.

30. Gramsci, *Selections from the Prison Notebooks*, pp. 445, 448.

31. Ibid., p. 446.

32. Ibid., p. 401.

33. Ibid., p. 426.

34. See Brzozowski, *Legenda Mlodej Polski*, pp. 278–79.

35. Gramsci, "The Revolution Against '*Capital*,'" in *Selections from Political Writings (1910–1920)*, p. 34.

36. Gramsci, *Selections from the Prison Notebooks*, p. 342.

37. Some of the similarities between Brzozowski's, Lukács's, and Gramsci's critiques of classical Marxism can be explained by their common indebtedness to Georges Sorel (which was the greatest in Brzozowski's case).

38. MacIntyre, *Marxism and Christianity*, p. 88.

39. Levine.

40. Kolakowski, *Main Currents*, vol. 1, p. 405.

41. Ibid., pp. 401–2.

42. Ibid., vol. 3, p. 238; vol. 1, pp. 403, 402. The chapter on Brzozowski in Kolakowski's *Main Currents* (vol. 2, pp. 215–39) is entitled "Marxism as Historical Subjectivism."

43. Kolakowski, "Le marxisme de Marx," pp. 412–14.

44. Levine, pp. xv, 183.

45. Lichtheim, p. 237.

46. According to Levine, "Unilinearism was foreign to the very spirit of Marx" (p. 176). Such a categorical assertion is, of course, a great exaggeration.

47. Ibid., pp. 151–52, 215.

48. See Meikle, p. 44.

49. See Wood, *Karl Marx*, p. 23.

50. Meikle saw Marxian materialism as much closer to genuine Aristotelianism than the idealistic essentialism of Hegel (p. 43).

51. Levine, pp. 211, 213, 213. It should be noted that concerning essence Levine's interpretation differs from Gramsci, who saw the Marxian "philosophy of praxis" as "absolute historicism." Brzozowski's "anti-Engelsism" was also programmatically antiessentialist: he thought that the concept of human essence entailed reducing human history to a mere unfolding of a given content that would contradict the idea of man's autocreation. See Walicki, *Stanislaw Brzozowski*, pp. 118–21.

52. In reality things were more complicated. As we shall see, the concept of alienation *was* present in the writings of young Engels. It could not have been otherwise, because in Germany (to quote Engels's own words) almost everybody who arrived at communism did so "by way of the Feuerbachian dissolution of Hegelian speculation" (Engels's preface to *The Condition of the Working Class in England*, in M&E, CW: 4, 303).

53. Levine, pp. 216–17.

54. Gouldner, pp. 253, 159.

55. It is very easy, therefore, to juxtapose short quotations from their works in such a way as to create the impression of a full concordance between their ideas. See Bekerman.

56. The best recent book on this is by Toews.

57. See Niebuhr's article on Schleiermacher, pp. 316–19.

58. See Blackwell, pp. 83–84.

59. Berlin, *Four Essays on Liberty*, p. 77.

60. A pantheistically tinged love for nature and a peculiar fascination with the sea remained with Engels until the end of his life. When he died, his body, in accordance with his will, was burned in a crematorium and the urn with his ashes dropped into the sea.

61. Paul Tillich defined philosophical romanticism (which he derived from neo-Platonist mysticism, especially from Nicholas of Cusa) as a view according to which the finite includes the infinite, and vice versa (p. 77).

62. See K. Löwith, *From Hegel to Nietzsche*, pp. 113–14, and Hayner, pp. 98-100.

63. The name "Feuerbach" means literally "fiery stream."

64. This peculiar, prepositivist sense of the term *positive*, characteristic of the German philosophical tradition, has been preserved by Marcuse.

65. See Engels's article "Schelling on Hegel," published in December 1841 under the pseudonym "Friedrich Oswald" (M&E, CW, 2:181–87).

66. According to Levine, Engels was, in fact, "a right-wing Hegelian who made man the victim of universal motion, who saw in man something that did not act, but rather was acted upon and shaped by forces totally external to him and totally beyond his control" (pp. 151–52). Classifying Engels as a right-wing Hegelian is, of course, formally and historically untrue, but otherwise the point is well taken.

67. Carver, p. 22.

68. Mayer, p. 26.

69. For an analysis of the Jewish sources of Hess's millenarianism, see Avineri, and also Zlocisti.

70. For an analysis of Cieszkowski's "philosophy of action," including its influence on Hess, see Walicki, *Philosophy and Romantic Nationalism*, pp. 127–51.

71. See Mayer, pp. 31–33.

72. The first of these was published in the *Deutsch-Französische Jahrbücher* (1844). The other two were placed, with Marx's help, in the German emigré newspaper *Vorwärts!* (Paris, Aug. 31 to Oct. 19, 1844).

73. See Y. Talmon.

74. Feuerbach, pp. 14, 230. Feuerbach's views greatly impressed Dostoevsky, who became acquainted with them in his youth as a member of Petrashevsky's circle. In his great novels and in his *Diary of a Writer*, Dostoevsky developed the conception that socialism is an attempt to substitute the idea of "Man-God" (or "Man-Godhood") for the Christian idea of "God-Man" ("God-Manhood") and thus to save a humankind without God. See Walicki, *A History of Russian Thought*, pp. 159–61, 315–20.

75. See Rodrigues, pp. 154–55; Bazard and Enfantin, pp. xx–xxii, 269–82; and Leroux. For a study of the influence of these ideas in Germany, see Butler.

76. See especially Leroux and the Saint-Simonians (who took this idea from Lessing). In my *Philosophy and Romantic Nationalism*, I directed attention to the fact that both millenarian ideas and the belief in reincarnation express the yearning for terrestrial salvation: "The importance of the romantic rediscovery of this an-

cient belief [reincarnation] consisted in the fact that it enabled the reconciliation of the millenarian idea of collective salvation with romantic individualism, claiming immortality for the individual. The future Kingdom of God on earth was thus made open for each individual spirit, who through the long chain of his incarnations had achieved the highest level of perfection" (p. 257).

77. The conception of such an alliance with French thinkers was discussed in the *Deutsch-Französische Jahrbücher*. At the end of 1843 Arnold Ruge went to Paris to make contact with the French socialists. His mission, however, ended in a fiasco because the French firmly rejected the German critique of religion while Ruge could not accept the French ideas of a "new religion." See Cornu, vol. 2, ch. 3.

78. As expressed in his first book, *The Sacred History of Mankind* (1837) (see *Philosophische und sozialistische Schriften*).

79. See Carver, pp. 44–50.

80. I consciously allude here to the title of the excellent book on actually existing socialism by Fehér, Heller, and Márkus.

81. Carver, p. 48.

82. Despite the similarity to the philosophical vocabulary of young Marx, this is Engels's expression. (M&E, CW, 3:424).

83. As an illustration of the "separation of interests" within the family, Engels mentioned wage-earning children: "It is common practice for children, as soon as they are capable of work (i.e., as soon as they reach the age of nine), to spend their wages themselves, to look upon their parental home as a mere boarding house, and hand over to their parents a fixed amount for food and lodging" (M&E, CW, 3:423–24).

84. Engels was so impressed by Fourier that he translated the relevant fragments from his works and wanted to publish them in Germany in a "Library of the Best Foreign Socialist Writers." See "A Fragment of Fourier's *On Trade*" (M&E, CW, 4:612–44, 713n).

85. "In Marx's interpretation," explains Agnes Heller, "alienation is not some sort of long-standing 'distortion' of the species or of human nature; the essence of man develops within alienation itself, and this creates the possibility for the realisation of man 'rich in needs.'" (*The Theory of Needs in Marx*, pp. 46–77).

86. Ironically, the reactionary circles in Germany highly appreciated Engels's book as a warning against capitalist modernization. Of course, they tried to prove that Engels's critique of the condition of England did not apply to Germany. (See Cornu, vol. 4, summary of ch. 3.) It is worthwhile noting that reaction to Marx's *Capital* in the governmental circles of imperial Russia was identical. *Capital* was permitted to be published in Russia on the ground that Marx's denunciations of capitalism were directed only against Western countries and did not concern Russia, whose government never espoused the principles of laissez-faire. See Reuel, pp. 234–35.

87. See Marx, Engels, and Lenin, pp. 10–16.

88. See Hunt, *The Political Ideas*, vol. 1, pp. 147–61.

89. Ibid., pp. 157, 156.

90. In his *Statism and Anarchy*, (1874–75), Bakunin used against Marx and Engels the same arguments as their opponents in the Communist League.

91. Children's education was to be "combined with production" (M&E, CW, 6:351).

92. Quoted in Hunt, *The Political Ideas*, vol. 1, p. 155.

93. "As soon as possible" did not mean that the bourgeois government could be overthrown immediately. Marx and Engels were unanimous in stressing that the period of bourgeois domination would be at least "several years." See Hunt, *The Political Ideas*, vol. 1, p. 181.

94. McLellan, *Friedrich Engels*, p. 99.

95. See especially Wolfe, *Marxism*, pp. 19–20, 152–54. "The *Circular*," the author has asserted, "is noteworthy both for the extremism of the methods advocated to secure its aims and the highly statist and centralist formulation of those aims. It is doubtful if there is any other document from the hands of Marx in which Lenin, Stalin, Khrushchev, and Mao Tse-tung could find so much evidence for the claim to be the faithful heirs and so large a heritage to claim" (p. 19).

96. Hunt, *The Political Ideas*, vol. 1, p. 248.

97. See ibid., pp. 244–45.

98. See ibid., pp. 281–83.

99. These words are a part of Engels's reflection on the unification of Germany.

100. This has been convincingly stressed by Moore (see chapter 1, section 8).

101. Engels returned to this idea in his articles on "The Housing Question" (1872–73). See M&E, CW, 23:330, 347.

102. See especially Strumilin's "Rabochii byt i kommunizm," "Zakon stoimosti i planironvanie," and "Kommunizm i razdelenie truda."

103. Quoted in Gilison, pp. 106–7.

104. On the dangers of combining "scientist prejudice" with Hegelian historicism and utopian eagerness to predict the future, see Hayek, *The Counter-Revolution in Science*.

105. It seems strange, I should add, not from the point of view of Marx and Engels's intellectual development but only from the point of view of latter-day left-wing Marxists, like Luxemburg or Lenin, for whom the fact that the leading parties of the Second International supported in 1914 the war efforts of their respective governments was something totally unexpected and absolutely disastrous. Szporluk is right in claiming that Marx and Engels had little understanding of the importance of national features as part of human identity (see Szporluk, pp. 57–60). Nevertheless, they did not underestimate the strength of national allegiances in the class struggles of their time.

106. See Nicolaevskii and Maenchen-Helfen, p. 167.

107. For this reason some authors have even tried to present Engels as an ideological predecessor of Hitler. See Watson, pp. 100–24. Watson complains that "Hitler's debt to Marxism has been so largely neglected" (p. 123).

108. Rosdolsky, p. 160.

109. This has been properly stressed by Molnár. Unfortunately, in many recent books on Marxism, this fundamental feature of Marx and Engels's theory of history is played down, ignored, or even outrightly denied.

110. Engels's Hegelianism was "vulgar" because Engels (unlike Marx) had never tried to critically understand the epistemological foundations of Hegel's absolute idealism (see chapter 2, section 1).

111. On the Jacobin conception of nation and "Jacobin nationalism," see Hayes, and also Kohn. In its application to Hungary or Poland, the "Jacobin conception of nation" (or simply, "the French conception") meant above all a *unitarist* conception, as opposed to federalism or "multiculturalism." This was quite natural and historically justified; after all, modern nationalism was essentially a species of patriotism that favored cultural homogeneity (see Gellner, *Nations and Nationalism*, p. 138). Anyhow, Lajos Kossuth and other leaders of the Hungarian uprising of 1848 firmly believed in the possibility of applying to Hungary, in its historical frontiers, the French model of nation building (i.e., in the transformation of a historical, multilingual, decentralized Hungary into a modern unified nation). Polish opinion was more divided, because many Poles, especially poets, were strongly tempted to romantically idealize the diversity of the old Polish-Lithuanian Commonwealth. Nevertheless, the majority of politically active Poles of the Romantic Age embraced the unitarist conception of the nation. Like the reformers of the Age of Enlightenment, they were fairly united in their support for the integration of the historic territories of the commonwealth, and after the emancipation and education of the peasants, they expected swift results in polonization. See Walicki, *The Enlightenment and the Birth of Modern Nationhood*, pp. 77–81, and *Philosophy and Romantic Nationalism*, pp. 69–72.

112. For a detailed presentation and analysis of Marx and Engels's view on the Polish question, see the chapter "Marx, Engels, and the Polish Question" in Walicki, *Philosophy and Romantic Nationalism*, pp. 358–91.

113. Engels's letter contains an unfavorable characterization of Poles and an unashamedly cynical conclusion. "The more I think about it," he wrote, "the more obvious it becomes to me that the Poles are *une nation foutue* who can only continue to serve a purpose until such time as Russia herself becomes caught up into the agrarian revolution. . . . Conclusion: To take as much as possible away from the Poles in the West, to man their fortresses, especially Posen, with Germans on the pretext of defence, to let them stew in their own juice, send them into battle, gobble bare their land, fob them off with promises of Riga and Odessa and, should it be possible to get the Russians moving, to ally oneself with the latter and compel the Poles to give way" (M&E, CW, 38: 363–64). The quoted letter is not representative of Engels's view on the Polish question, because in a few years he returned to his pro-Polish standpoint. It shows, however, how cynical he could be as a politician.

114. Stalin reversed this proposal by giving the Poles "extended territories" in the west, thus compensating them for territorial losses in the east. In this manner Engels was duped by the very Hegelian "irony of history" he wanted to eliminate through his idea of a scientifically controlled human universe.

115. Rosdolsky, pp. 129, 159.

116. Molnár, p. 10.

117. Molnár, pp. 320–21.

118. Ibid., p. 324. In a letter to Engels of Oct. 8, 1858, Marx wrote: "The proper task of bourgeois society is the creation of the world market, at least in outline, and of the production based on that market" (M&E, CW, 40:347). Colonialism was fulfilling this task and thus paving the way for socialism.

119. See Bloom, p. 49.

120. For a detailed analysis, see Walicki, *The Controversy over Capitalism,*

pp. 179–94 (chapter entitled "Marx and Engels in Confrontation with Russian Populism").

121. See Molnár's ironic remark: "Les 'nations historiques' les plus exemplaires selon Engels étaient donc celles où la noblesse sauvegardait les plus ses privilèges seigneuriaux" (p. 82). This remark, however, is not historically accurate. In the central part of Poland feudalism in the sense of seigniorage had been already abolished by Napoleon (although he gave no land to the peasants). Using the term *feudalism* in the broad Marxist sense, we can say that feudal, or half feudal, relationships remained in existence; nonetheless, nobles were merely landowners, not feudal seigneurs. We must also remember that a large portion of the Polish nobility was poor and landless, thus, "having nothing to lose and everything to gain" in the struggle for national independence.

122. Marx and Engels paid homage to the Cracow revolution in their speeches in Brussels on Feb. 22, 1848 (see M&E, CW, 6:545–52), and mentioned it also in the *Manifesto of the Communist Party* (M&E, CW, 6:518).

123. Rosdolsky, p. 63. Interestingly, Marx and Engels believed that Szela was a Ruthenian (which was not the case).

124. See, for instance, Engels's remark: "The Ruthenians had belonged to Poland for a long time and learned only from Metternich that the Poles were their oppressors" (M&E, CW, 8:230). This remark reflects Engels's mistaken belief that the Galician massacre was perpetrated by the Ruthenian peasants.

125. See Lichtheim, p. 74.

126. This solution, based on the democratization and autonomous status of different nationalities within the monarchy, would have transformed Austria into a state no longer ruled by the German minority.

127. Rosdolsky, p. 130.

128. Rudnytsky, pp. 40–41, 41–42. Another Ukrainian historian who uses the conception of historical versus nonhistorical nations is Himka, the translator and editor of Rosdolsky's book. See Himka, pp. 3–8.

129. See Walicki, *The Enlightenment and the Birth of Modern Nationhood*.

130. Because of this, Bronislaw Szwarce, one of the leading Polish radicals of that time, defined himself as an "ultraconservative" in political matters. Obviously, he felt it compatible with being "red" in social matters.

131. Marx fully endorsed Engels's reasoning, thus showing that the widespread view that "Marx and Engels left nothing that could be called a theory of the nationality question" (Kolakowski, *Main Currents*, vol. 2, p. 88) is not entirely correct. We should rather say that they supported the traditional historico-political conception of the nation and strongly opposed the emerging ethnolinguistic conception.

132. Rosdolsky, p. 133. Rosdolsky quotes Engels's article "Germany and Pan-Slavism" (M&E, CW, 14:156–57).

133. Wolfe, *Marxism*, p. 380.

134. "For philosophy, which has been expelled from nature and history, there remains only the realm of pure thought, so far as it is left: the theory of the laws of the thought process itself, logic and dialectics" (M&E, SW, 3:375). However, Engels himself interpreted dialectic as dealing with the universal laws of motion, not merely the laws of the thought process. This provided him with a back door through which philosophy could return. Despite Engels's claims to the contrary,

many features of his dialectic of nature were quite similar to the old speculative *Naturphilosophie*.

135. According to Carver, this review marked the beginning of the Engelsian interpretation of Marxism (pp. 96–117). This is correct if what is meant is the beginning of the peculiar combination of Hegelian dialectic with the materialism of the natural sciences that came to be known as dialectical materialism. Unfortunately, Carver phrased this as the invention of dialectics: "In August 1859 Friedrich Engels invented dialectics" (p. 117). Thus Carver transformed his valuable observation into a wholly untenable thesis.

136. Carver, pp. 114–15. (The extravagant nature of this claim does not demand any special comment.)

137. See Walicki, *Stanislaw Brzozowski*, p. 157.

138. See Carver, p. 122.

139. For the quotation from Hegel, see Hegel, *Encyclopedia of Philosophical Sciences*, par. 147, addendum.

140. See Engels and Kautsky, p. 204.

141. Engels and Kautsky, pp. 205, 205, 209, 209, 212–13, 212.

142. Spinoza, *Ethics*, bk. 1, def. 7. See G. Parkinson, "Spinoza on the Freedom of Man and the Freedom of the Citizen," in Pelczynski and Gray, p. 43.

143. My account of Spinoza's philosophy of freedom is based mostly on Kolakowski, *Jednostka i nieskończoność*. See also Parkinson, note 142.

144. See Schacht, pp. 71–90.

145. Toews, pp. 89–90. Toews offers also a good analysis of the similarities between the integrating function of Hegel's philosophy and the philosophy of Schleiermacher (who also defined freedom as the "understanding of necessity" and whose influence on young Engels was so important). See ibid., pp. 56–67.

146. Kolakowski, *Main Currents*, vol. 1, pp. 386–87.

147. See Levine, pp. xvi, 24.

148. See Berger, pp. 103–14.

149. See Pelczynski.

150. In Marx's case, such a substitution was warranted by his utopian belief in the possibility of a full harmony and virtual identity between individual existence and general human essence. This position, however, presupposed an essentialist conception of human species nature, which Engels had rejected in the name of historicism and scientific evolutionism.

151. See Hunt, *The Political Ideas*, p. 93.

152. See Levine, p. 216.

153. See Panasiuk, pp. 284–303.

154. See Walicki, *The Controversy over Capitalism*, pp. 179–94.

155. Morgan, p. 552. Quote from Engels (M&E, *SW*, 3:266).

156. Interestingly, in the *Manifesto of the Communist Party* the most progressive epoch in history—that of bourgeois progress—was characterized quite differently: as putting an end to all embellishments of exploitation. The bourgeoisie, as described in the *Manifesto*, "has pitilessly torn asunder the motley feudal ties that bound man to his 'natural superiors,' and has left remaining no other nexus between man and man than naked self-interest, than callous 'cash payments.' It has drowned the most heavenly ecstasies of religious fervour, of chivalrous enthusi-

asm, of philistine sentimentalism, in the icy water of egotistical exploitation. It has resolved personal worth into exchange value, and in place of the numberless inde-feasible chartered freedoms, has set up that single, unconscionable freedom—Free Trade. In one word, for exploitation, veiled by religious and political illusions, it has substituted naked, shameless, direct, brutal exploitation" (M&E, CW, 6:487). It has to be noted that Marx and Engels stressed the positive side of this evolu-tion. In their view it made possible a truly radical and fully self-conscious social revolution.

157. For instance, see above, note 46.

158. Moore, p. 56.

159. "Where the ancient communities have continued to exist, they have for thousands of years formed the basis of the cruelest form of state, Oriental despo-tism, from India to Russia. It was only where these communities dissolved that the peoples made progress of themselves, and their next economic advance consisted in the increase and development of production by means of slave labor" (E, AD, 222).

160. An alternative conception of the state—as an alienation of man's commu-nal essence—has been outlined in Marx's early works (especially "On the Jewish Question").

161. The quoted part of Anti-Dühring (pt. 3: "Socialism," ch. 2: "Theoretical") is identical (except for a few small alterations) to Engels's pamphlet Socialism: Utopian and Scientific, pt. 3 (as reprinted in M&E, BW, 131–52).

162. The existence of these differences needs mentioning in view of the fact that Engels's account of capitalist development was treated by most readers as exactly following Marx's in Capital. In a letter to F. A. Sorge (1882) Engels himself sug-gested that his Socialism: Utopian and Scientific might be read instead of Marx's Capital: "Most people are too idle to read thick books like Capital, and so a little pamphlet does the job much more quickly" (quoted in Carver, p. 132).

163. In this book the utter misery of the industrial proletariat in England was contrasted with an idyllic picture of the life of preindustrial workers. According to Engels, preindustrial workers "vegetated throughout a passably comfortable existence, leading a righteous and peaceful life in all piety and probity; and their material position was far better than that of their successors. They did not need to overwork; they did no more than they chose to do, and yet earned what they needed. They had leisure for healthful work in garden or field, work which, in itself, was recreation for them, and they could take part besides in the recreations and games of their neighbors, and all these games—bowling, cricket, football, etc., contributed to their physical health and vigor. They were, for the most part, strong, well-built people, in whose physique little or no difference from that of their peas-ant neighbors was discoverable. Their children grew up in the fresh country air, and, if they would help their parents at work, it was only occasionally; while of eight or twelve hours work for them there was no question" (M&E, CW, 4:308). This shows that Engels had changed his views about the epoch of "primitive har-mony" and its place in historical evolution. In the 1840s he placed this harmony in a relatively recent past—before the industrial revolution. In later years he moved this period to the remote, prehistoric past.

164. To be precise, the entire problematic of the human cost of "primitive accu-

mulation" was summarized by Engels in two sentences: "The number of these permanent wage workers was further enormously increased by the breaking up of the feudal system that occurred at the same time, by the disbanding of the retainers of the feudal lords, the eviction of the peasants from their homesteads, etc. The separation was made complete between the means of production, concentrated in the hands of the capitalists, on the one side, and the producers, possessing nothing but their labor power, on the other" (E, *AD*, 328–29; cf. M&E, *BW*, 136).

165. In *Anti-Dühring* the italicized sentence is longer: "The mode of production is in rebellion against the mode of exchange, the productive forces are in rebellion against the mode of production which they have outgrown" (pp. 334–35). The removal of the second part of this sentence in *Socialism: Utopian and Scientific* cannot be satisfactorily explained by a claim that Engels simply desired to avoid repetition. This change also reflected Engels's conviction that the main contradiction of late capitalism was the alleged conflict between the mode of production and the mode of exchange. It was a logical conclusion that the mode of production had already become "socialized" and represented (in a sharp contrast to the mode of exchange) the principle of planning.

166. In *Socialism: Utopian and Scientific*, the phrase "humanity's leap" is changed into "the ascent of man" (M&E, *BW*, 150).

167. The adjective *analogous* appears in the following sentence: "Thus the conflicts of innumerable individual wills and individual actions in the domain of history produce a state of affairs entirely *analogous* to that prevailing in the realm of unconscious nature" (M&E, *SW*, 3:336; italics added).

168. Vogel, p. 182.

169. Ibid., p. 195.

170. It is important to note that this article was written during Marx's lifetime, in connection with the split at the Hague Congress of the First International. Small wonder that Bakunin and his followers in the First International termed the supporters of Marx and Engels "authoritarians" or "authoritarian communists." See Haupt, pp. 2–7.

171. This conclusion differs from Vogel's analysis. According to Vogel (pp. 160–68), Engels elaborated two different explanations of the relationship between society and nature: the deterministic explanation, which assumed the ontological identity between the two realms, and the "second nature thesis," which pointed out the potential ontological distinction between them. According to my interpretation, there is no difference between these two explanations, because both refer to the laws of commodity production—laws that, according to Engels, are only "analogous" to the laws of nature. The continuity between nature and society was seen by Engels elsewhere: in the sphere of material production, in the sense of humans' intercourse with nature, whether direct (by means of their hands) or mediated by technology. At this point there is, I think, a certain (limited) analogy between Engels and John Stuart Mill, who distinguished between "the laws and condition of the production of wealth" and "the laws of the distribution of wealth." Unlike the second, the first "partake of the character of physical truths. There is nothing optional, or arbitrary in them" (*Principles of Political Economy*, bk. 2, ch. 1, p. 243).

172. Buchanan, *Ethics, Efficiency, and the Market*, p. 96.

173. See Haupt, p. 12. In spite of this, Rubel accused Engels of tolerating the increasingly widespread usage of this term, for if he had vetoed it "this universal scandal would never have seen the light of day" (M. Rubel, *Marx critique du Marxisme*, pp. 20–21; quoted in Haupt, p. 1).

174. See Haupt, p. 18.

175. See Marx's letter to Domela Nieuwenhuis, Feb. 22, 1881, quoted in Haupt, p. 39.

176. See Haupt, "The Commune as Symbol and Example," in Haupt, pp. 23–47. According to Haupt, "this rejection of the Commune was set in the overall context of the reformist offensive at the end of the nineteenth century" (ibid., p. 41).

177. Haupt, p. 42.

178. On the eve of the Paris Commune (letter of Sept. 4, 1870) he wrote to Marx: "*La Terreur* is for the most part useless cruelties perpetrated by people who are themselves frightened, for the purpose of reassuring themselves. I am convinced that the blame for the Reign of Terror, Anno 1793, falls almost entirely on the over-nervous bourgeois acting as the patriot" (quoted in Wolfe, *Marxism*, p. 166).

179. Quoted in Mayer, *Engels*, p. 312; see also Wolfe, *Marxism*, p. 79.

180. See Haupt, pp. 136–38.   181. See Mayer, pp. 313–16.

182. Wolfe, *Marxism*, pp. 73, 73.   183. Mayer, pp. 315–16.

184. Ibid.

185. Ibid., pp. 315–16 (cf. Wolfe, *Marxism*, pp. 73–74). Mayer points out that Engels's support for war credits was qualified: "Next year he spoke no more of such concessions, when the controversy flared up about the army estimates in which it was proposed to increase the size not only of the army but also of the corps of officers, a well-known stronghold of reaction" (p. 316).

186. See Wolfe, *Marxism*, pp. 90–91.

187. See ibid., pp. 75–76.

188. Ibid., pp. 410–12.

189. See all articles on the subject of war in *Sozialistische Monatshefte* 2 (1914), and *Die Neue Zeit* 2 (1914).

190. See Haupt, p. 110.

191. See Engels, "Vorwort zur Broschure *Internationales* aus dem 'Volksstaat'" (1871–75), in Marx and Engels, *Werke*, vol. 22, pp. 417–18, quoted in Moore, p. 2. In *The State and Revolution* Lenin summarizes the first half of this passage and quotes the last two sentences (beginning from the words: "For Marx . . ."). He also adds the following sentence: "The names of *real* political parties, however, are ever wholly appropriate; the party develops while the name stays" (L, *SW*, 2:296).

192. Quoted in Kolakowski, *Main Currents*, vol. 2, p. 108.

193. See Haupt, pp. 104–10.

194. This took place only in 1959, at the Bad Godesberg conference of the German Social Democratic party. The process of abandoning the ideal of communism, while retaining the program of transition to socialism, was completed much earlier, in the first years after World War II. See chapter 3, section 1.

Chapter 3

1. Kolakowski, *Main Currents*, vol. 2, p. 43.

2. See Haupt, pp. 11–13.

3. See, for instance, the testimony of a Yugoslav social democratic leader, Z. Topalovitsch, in his "Mein geistiger Vater."

4. Nikolaevskii [Nikolajewsky], "Karl Kautsky in Russland," p. 92.

5. In *The State and Revolution* Lenin wrote: "Undoubtedly, an immeasurably larger number of Kautsky's works have been translated into Russian than into any other language. It is not without reason that some German Social Democrats say in jest that Kautsky is read more in Russia than in Germany" (L, *SW*, 2:314). It should be remembered that in 1905 Lenin indignantly rejected allegations about differences dividing Bolsheviks from the Kautskian orthodoxy. He emphatically stressed that he had never accused Kautsky of "opportunism" and never claimed "to have created any sort of special trend in international Social Democracy *not* identical with the trend of Bebel and Kautsky" (ibid., 1:465–66).

6. Anderson, *Considerations on Western Marxism*, p. 7.

7. See Waldenberg, vol. 1, p. 68. (Waldenberg's two-volume work is the most comprehensive monograph on Kautsky in any language.)

8. See B. Kautsky, p. 4. See also Waldenberg, vol. 1, p. 74, and Steenson, pp. 35, 45.

9. See Steenson, pp. 47–49.

10. Ibid., p. 80.

11. Kolakowski, *Main Currents*, vol. 2, p. 35.

12. See Waldenberg, vol. 1, p. 611.   13. See Fetscher, p. 89.

14. See Lukes, pp. 1–26.   15. Ibid., pp. 14–18.

16. K. Kautsky, *Ethics*, quoted in Kautsky, *Selected Political Writings*, pp. 42–43.

17. Ibid., pp. 43, 43.

18. Ibid., pp. 38, 38.

19. See Lukes, p. 16. The expression "ethical skepticism" was used by Otto Bauer.

20. Quoted in Lukes, p. 17.

21. K. Kautsky, "Allerhand Revolutionäres," *Die Neue Zeit* 22, no. 1 (1903–4): 655–56. Quoted in Steenson, p. 8.

22. K. Kautsky, *The Class Struggle (Erfurt Program)*, p. 118 (see also p. 87).

23. Kolakowski, *Main Currents*, vol. 2, p. 57.

24. See Waldenberg, vol. 1, pp. 444–45.

25. K. Kautsky, *Die Neue Zeit* 20, no. 3 (1901–2): 79. Quoted in Lenin, *What Is to be Done?* (L, *SW*, 1:121).

26. See Harding, vol. 1, pp. 161–96. (The author gave this chapter a provocative title: "The Reaffirmation of Orthodoxy.")

27. Kolakowski, *Main Currents*, vol. 2, p. 53.

28. Kolakowski, *Main Currents*, vol. 2, pp. 48, 52. Kolakowski's treatment of Kautsky reveals a certain ambiguity in his attitude toward Marxism. In the epilogue to *Main Currents* (vol. 3, p. 523), he states that "Marxism has been the greatest fantasy of our century." At the same time he criticizes Kautsky for his lack of understanding of Marx's greatest fantasy—"the paradigm of human nature returning into itself." If the Marxian esoteric conception of "self-enriching alienation of man's species essence" is a fantasy, then Kautsky's "positivism" and simple com-

mon sense, which prevented him from embracing this fantasy, should be seen in a more positive light.

29. See Waldenberg, vol. 1, pp. 88–89.

30. Steenson, p. 99.

31. K. Kautsky, *The Class Struggle*, p. 17. However, Kautsky argued at the same time that "the transition to the socialist society does not at all require the expropriation of the small artisan and the small farmer. This transition not only will deprive them of nothing, but it will bring them many advantages" (ibid., p. 132). This meant that small producers were doomed to be expropriated only under capitalism and might be saved from this lot by a quick transition to socialism.

32. Ibid., pp. 210, 164. In another context Kautsky wrote about a visible deterioration of the condition of the "educated workers" and concluded that "the educated people are being forced into the proletariat" (ibid., pp. 40–41).

33. Ibid., pp. 143, 22.

34. Ibid., pp. 22–23.

35. Ibid., pp. 214, 215.

36. Ibid., pp. 63, 99, 100–101, 138. For a critical analysis of this conception of socialist society as "a single gigantic industrial concern," see L. Szamuely, pp. 24–28, and Selucký, pp. 96–98.

37. K. Kautsky, *The Class Struggle*, pp. 149, 150, 150–51, 150.

38. Ibid., pp. 152, 152, 153, 154, 154, 157. As an example of this culture-destructive influence of capitalism, Kautsky mentioned "the movement to abolish Greek and Latin from the secondary schools" (Ibid., p. 154).

39. Ibid., p. 158.

40. K. Kautsky, *Die soziale Revolution*, p. 45.

41. K. Kautsky, *Selected Political Writings*, p. 40.

42. See Lukács's essay "The Old Culture and the New Culture," in Lukács, *Marxism and Human Liberation*, pp. 3–19.

43. K. Kautsky, *The Class Struggle*, p. 88 (article 5 of the *Erfurt Program*).

44. See L. Szamuely, p. 25.

45. K. Kautsky, *The Class Struggle*, pp. 148, 149.

46. See L. Szamuely, ch. 2: "The Ideology of War Communism."

47. For a polemic against the widespread view that War Communism was just a matter of emergency and had no ideological premises, see Boettke, "The Soviet Experiment with Pure Communism," pp. 149–82. For a more comprehensive treatment of the problem, see Boettke, *The Political Economy of Soviet Socialism*.

48. K. Kautsky, *The Class Struggle*, p. 98 (cf. L. Szamuely, *First Models*, p. 25).

49. Ibid., p. 132 (cf. L. Szamuely, *First Models*, p. 27).

50. Ibid., pp. 101–2 (cf. L. Szamuely, *First Models*, p. 27).

51. L. Szamuely, *First Models*, p. 27.

52. See Selucký's comment: "Because the market as a criterion of comparative advantage has been abolished, there would be no way to measure the latter which, once unmeasurable, loses its meaning. Therefore, Kautsky's emphasis on a maximum possible degree of self-sufficiency of individual nations appears to be the most logical, though the least economic, solution of the dilemma facing the non-market national economies" (Selucký, p. 97).

53. K. Kautsky, *The Class Struggle*, pp. 102–3.

54. Quoted in L. Szamuely, *First Models*, pp. 27–28.

55. Ibid., p. 28.

56. See Selucký, p. 97.

57. See Waldenberg, vol. 2, p. 426.

58. K. Kautsky, *The Labour Revolution*, pp. 262, 260.

59. Ibid., pp. 280–81.   60. Ibid., p. 281.

61. Ibid., p. 282.   62. Ibid.

63. For a similar critique of Marx's communism by young Mehring (not yet a Marxist), see chapter 1, section 7).

64. See K. Kautsky, *Selected Political Writings*, p. 114 (cf. K. Kautsky, *The Dictatorship of the Proletariat*, p. 43).

65. Ibid., p. 99 (cf. *The Dictatorship*, pp. 4–5).

66. Ibid., p. 100 (cf. *The Dictatorship*, p. 6).

67. Ibid., pp. 103–4 (cf. *The Dictatorship*, p. 13).

68. Kolakowski, *Main Currents*, vol. 2, pp. 53, 53.

69. K. Kautsky, *The Dictatorship*, pp. 99, 19, 20–21.

70. K. Kautsky, *Selected Political Writings*, p. 106 (cf. *The Dictatorship*, p. 17).

71. Ibid., p. 115 (cf. *The Dictatorship*, p. 45).

72. Ibid., pp. 114–15 (cf. *The Dictatorship*, pp. 44–45).

73. Ibid., p. 111 (cf. *The Dictatorship*, p. 32).

74. Ibid., p. 102 (cf. *The Dictatorship*, p. 58).

75. Ibid., p. 110 (cf. *The Dictatorship*, p. 30).

76. K. Kautsky, *The Dictatorship*, pp. 89–90.

77. Ibid., pp. 38–39 (cf. *Selected Political Writings*, p. 112).

78. Ibid., pp. 39–40 (cf. *Selected Political Writings*, pp. 112–13).

79. Ibid., pp. 121–22.

80. Ibid., pp. 148–49.

81. See K. Kautsky's July 1919 letter to his son, Benedikt, as quoted in Steenson, pp. 226–27.

82. K. Kautsky, *Terrorism and Communism*, pp. 231–32, 207.

83. Ibid., pp. 200, 200–201, 202.

84. Ibid., p. 200.

85. See Martov.

86. K. Kautsky, *Terrorism and Communism*, pp. 156, 162.

87. Ibid., pp. 176–77.   88. Ibid., pp. 123–30.

89. Ibid., pp. 140–49.   90. Ibid., p. 146.

91. See Waldenberg, vol. 1, pp. 578–85.

92. In 1920–21, Kautsky visited Georgia on the invitation of its government. "The Mensheviks who headed this short-lived government considered him a mentor, and he was treated to a long visit once he did arrive. He was in Georgia from late September until early in January" (Steenson, p. 227).

93. See Kolakowski, *Main Currents*, vol. 2, p. 34.

94. See Walicki, *A History of Russian Thought*, ch. 7.

95. See Bakunin, *Nauka i nasushchnoe revolutsyonnoe delo*, p. 32.

96. See Walicki, *A History of Russian Thought*, ch. 12.

97. See Baron, chs. 1–5. (Baron's book is the best and most comprehensive monograph on Plekhanov in English.) For an analysis of Plekhanov's intellectual

evolution from populism to Marxism, see also Walicki, *Controversy over Capitalism*, pt. 3, pp. 1–2.

98. According to Plekhanov's wife, Rosaliia Markovna, he was completely engrossed in reading Orlov's book. "It seemed that the question of whether the commune were to be or not—if it were to disintegrate or not—was for him a question of life and death" (Baron, p. 55).

99. See Vaganyan, pp. 94–95.

100. To support these views Plekhanov used to quote the *Manifesto of the Communist Party*. He was especially fond of quoting from it the sarcastic remarks about the German "true socialists" who (like the Russian populists) exhibited a nihilistic attitude toward liberalism and "bourgeois freedom" in general.

101. Plekhanov, *Sochineniia*, vol. 2, p. 166.

102. Plekhanov, *Socialism and the Political Struggle* in *Selected Philosophical Works*, vol. 1, p. 99.

103. Plekhanov, *Our Differences*, in ibid., pp. 279–80.

104. Ibid., p. 104.

105. Plekhanov, *Izbrannye filosofskie proizvedeniia*, vol. 4, p. 140.

106. Plekhanov, *Sochineniia*, vol. 19, p. 283.

107. *Vestnik Narodnoi Voli* [*What Should We Expect from Revolution?*] (Geneva, 1884), no. 2.

108. Marx's letter to Zasulich was short, but three drafts of it, found in his archive, give an elaborate argument for his general conclusion. Marx drafted them not only in connection with Zasulich's letter but also as the first sketch of the brochure that he intended to write at the request of the executive committee of the People's Will. For a detailed analysis of these important documents, see Walicki, *Controversy over Capitalism*, pp. 188–91, and Hinada. The text of the first draft is to be found in M&E, *SW*, 3:152–61.

109. Yur'evskii. Nikolaevskii questioned Yur'evskii's testimony but did not provide convincing arguments. Nikolaevskii did not even try to conceal that his motivation was to defend Plekhanov's group and, by the same token, the tradition of Menshevism against defamation. See Nikolaevskii, "Legenda ob 'utajennom pis'me' K. Marksa."

110. Plekhanov, *Izbrannye*, vol. 2, p. 621.

111. Ibid., vol. 4, pp. 113–14; vol. 1, p. 392; vol. 4, p. 86.

112. For that reason *Capital* was used by the populists as an argument against capitalist development of Russia.

113. See Plekhanov, *Izbrannye*, vol. 2, p. 360.

114. *Literaturnoe nasledye G. V. Plekhanova*, vol. 7, p. 178.

115. See Plekhanov, *On the Question of the Individual's Role in History* in *Selected Philosophical Works*, vol. 2, pp. 285–86.

116. Ibid., pp. 285, 285n, 285.

117. Ibid., p. 289.

118. Ibid., pp. 290–91.

119. Struve concluded: "We must concede that we lack culture and go to the school of capitalism." For Mikhailovskii's reply to this, see Mikhailovskii.

120. In his article Mikhailovskii quoted the following passage from Belinskii's

letter of March 1841 to Botkin (as quoted in Walicki, *The Controversy over Capitalism*):

I thank you humbly, Egor Fëdorich [Hegel], and I bow down to your philosophical nightcap; but with all due respect to your philosophical philistinism, I have the honor to inform you that even if I were to reach the highest possible level of development I should ask you for an account of all the victims of life and history, of chance, superstition, Inquisitions, Philip II and so forth. Otherwise, I shall throw myself down from the highest level. I don't want happiness, even when it is offered free, if I am not certain about the fate of all my brothers, my own flesh and blood. To say that disharmony is essential to achieve harmony may sound practical and pleasant to music lovers but certainly not to people whose part in life happens to be to express by their own fate the idea of disharmony. (p. 161)

121. Plekhanov, *Izbrannye*, vol. 4, pp. 542, 271; vol. 1, p. 458.

122. See Plekhanov, *Sochineniia*, vol. 20, p. xxviii.

123. The "abstract ideal" in question was, in this context, Russia's direct transition to socialism. Plekhanov defined abstract ideal as "a utopian ideal, born in the vague sphere of abstraction and divorced from concrete conditions of *hic et nunc*." He further commented: "An abstract ideal has too long hindered the development of humankind. And it was not without reason that Belinsky deplored the period in which he found himself under its detrimental influence" (Plekhanov, *God na rodine*, vol. 2, p. 260).

124. Plekhanov, *Selected Philosophical Works*, vol. 1, pp. 571, 572, 574.

125. Ibid., pp. 666–67.

126. Kolakowski, *Main Currents*, vol. 2, pp. 343, 342.

127. Plekhanov, *Selected Philosophical Works*, vol. 1, pp. 665, 665.

128. See Plekhanov, *Sochineniia*, vol. 18, p. 334.

129. Plekhanov, *Selected Philosophical Works*, vol. 1, p. 665.

130. Ibid., p. 432.

131. Ibid.

132. Quoted in Rubel, "Gespräche über Russland mit Friedrich Engels," pp. 22–23.

133. See Baron, pp. 230–41.

134. Plekhanov, *Sochineniia*, vol. 12, pp. 418–19. See also the English translation, "Plekhanov on Terror" (L, *CW*, 42:47–48).

135. Plekhanov, *Sochineniia*, vol. 4, p. 266.

136. Ibid., vol. 11, p. 319. "In politics," Plekhanov asserted, "he who holds state power is the dictator" (in *Leninskii sbornik*, vol. 2, pp. 60, 95).

137. See Baron, p. 265.

138. Ibid., p. 277 (see also Miliukov, p. 222).

139. This view of small producers, formulated already in the *Manifesto of the Communist Party*, was made "orthodox" by the Erfurt Program of the SPD, which saw the ruination of small, independent producers as a "natural necessity" of economic development. For a thoughtful discussion of this issue, see Mitrany.

140. According to Plekhanov's explanation, the Tartar origin of his family was indicated by the name "Ple-khan-ov." See Deutsch, p. 125 (quoted in Baron, p. 17).

141. Plekhanov, *Sochineniia*, vol. 10, p. 154 (quoted in Baron, pp. 302–3).

142. Plekhanov, *Sochineniia*, vol. 20, pp. 82–83. Plekhanov's philosophy of Russian history is best presented in the first part of his unfinished *History of Russian Social Thought*, entitled "An Outline of the Development of Social Relations in Russia."

143. Ibid., pp. 112–15.

144. Ibid., vol. 15, p. 31 (quoted in Baron, p. 305).

145. Because of this the Kadets refused to support Stolypin's agrarian reform and sided in the Duma with the left-wing defenders of the peasant commune. Leonard Schapiro was certainly right in stating that the Kadets were in fact radicals rather than liberals. See Schapiro, *Russian Studies*, pp. 89–90.

146. Plekhanov, *God na rodine*, vol. 1, p. 233.

147. Ibid., vol. 2, pp. 198, 193; vol. 1, p. 21.

148. Quoted in Baron, p. 359. "According to R. M. Plekhanova, General Krasnov asked Plekhanov to become Premier. A few months earlier, before the Bolshevik revolution, General Kornilov had wanted to appoint Plekhanov to a ministerial post in the Cabinet with which he proposed to replace the Kerensky government" (Baron, pp. 351, 382n).

149. Kuskova, p. 139 (cf. Baron, p. 358).

150. Plekhanov, *Sochineniia*, vol. 16, p. 294.

151. See above, note 130.

152. Plekhanov's argument runs as follows: "One of the creators of scientific socialism, F. Engels, once expressed a brilliant thought: without ancient slavery modern socialism would have been impossible. Let us reflect on this thought: it amounts to a relative justification of slavery, a justification within a certain historical epoch. Is this not a shameful betrayal of an ideal? Please ease your mind— there is no betrayal at all. It is only the rejection of a utopian idea born in the vague sphere of abstraction and divorced from the concrete conditions of *hic et nunc*. Engels was right to reject such an ideal, not wrong" (Plekhanov, *God na rodine*, vol. 2, p. 260). Plekhanov went on to refer to Belinskii's rejection of the "abstract ideal" (see above, note 123).

153. Nettl, vol. 1, pp. 32–33.

154. Luxemburg, *Selected Political Writings*, p. 326.

155. Nettl, vol. 1, p. 51. It is incomprehensible why S. E. Bronner, the editor of *The Letters of Rosa Luxemburg*, described her as "a Jew in Poland who spoke German at home" (p. 4) when the letters edited by him contain the information that the German language was foreign to her (p. 59; see also letter to the editors, *Die Neue Zeit*, Mar. 5, 1896).

156. It should be noted in this context that the working class of the Congress Kingdom was multiethnic, being Polish, German, and Jewish.

157. Kolakowski, *Main Currents*, vol. 2, p. 75.

158. Luxemburg, *Letters*, pp. 168–69.

159. Luxemburg, *Selected Political Writings*, pp. 122–23, 334–35.

160. Luxemburg, *Letters*, p. 153.

161. Luxemburg, *Selected Political Writings*, pp. 363, 412, 413–14.

162. See Nettl, vol. 1, pp. 53–54. Telling evidence of Luxemburg's attitude toward Polish culture is contained in her article on Adam Mickiewicz on the

occasion of the centenary of his birth. Writing for German readers, she presented Mickiewicz as one of the greatest poets of the world while at the same time contemptuously rejecting any attempt to include his ideas in the history of Polish socialism. He was the last and greatest bard of Polish gentry nationalism, and Polish workers accepted him as such, just as German workers had accepted the great heritage of German idealist philosophy (see Luxemburg, *Wybór pism*, vol. 1, pp. 107–14; the German original was published in *Leipziger Volkszeitung*, 1898).

163. For an analysis of Mickiewicz's and Slowacki's messianic historiosophy, see A. Walicki, *Philosophy and Romantic Nationalism*, pp. 239–91.

164. Kolakowski, *Main Currents*, vol. 2, pp. 75, 95, 48.

165. See Walicki, *Stanislaw Brzozowski*, ch. 2: "On Some Specific Features of Early Polish Marxism."

166. Luxemburg, *Gesammelte Werke*, p. 616.

167. Ibid., pp. 616, 612.

168. Ibid., pp. 325–26.

169. The theory that capitalism cannot develop without foreign markets was set forth by the Russian populist economist V. Vorontsov in his *Sud'by kapitalizma v Rossii* (*The Fate of Capitalism in Russia*), SPb, 1882. Vorontsov drew from this the conclusion that Russia could not develop capitalistically because all external markets had been already divided up by more advanced countries. Similar arguments were used by another populist economist, N. Danielson. Rosa Luxemburg seems to have been indebted to both of them. She referred to Vorontsov in *The Accumulation of Capital* as a "brilliant Russian theorist with whom one can spend moments of sheer delight" (p. 278). Two separate chapters of this work are devoted to analyzing Vorontsov's and Danielson's view (pp. 276–91). In her letter to K. Zetkin of December 22, 1911, she stated that Russian populists were closer to truth than Russian Marxists and even understood Marxism better than "our triumphant Church" (i.e., German Social Democracy). See Luxemburg, *Listy do Leona Jogichesa-Tyszki*, vol. 3, p. 252.

170. Luxemburg, *Selected Political Writings*, pp. 43, 48, 53, 60.

171. Ibid., pp. 54, 107, 106–7, 46, 74, 106.

172. Ibid., pp. 123, 122.   173. Ibid., p. 302.

174. Ibid., p. 304.   175. Ibid., p. 302.

176. Ibid., pp. 290, 301.   177. Ibid., pp. 305–6.

178. Ibid., p. 304.

179. See Szlezinger, p. 119. Nevertheless, *from Stalin's point of view* Luxemburg was undoubtedly a "spontaneist." In the quoted article she stressed "the limited role of the conscious initiative of the party direction in the formation of tactics," showing that "the unconscious comes before the conscious, the logic of objective historical process before the subjective logic of its bearers" (*Selected Political Writings*, p. 293). This amounted to a "cult of spontaneity" in Lenin's view. Thus, Luxemburg fought against spontaneism in her polemics with Bernstein (and Bernstein-inspired Russian "economism") but defended it against the Leninist conception of the party.

180. Ettinger, introduction to Luxemburg, *Comrade and Lover*, p. xxxii.

181. Nettl, vol. 1, p. 363.

182. Ibid., p. 319.

183. Luxemburg, *Selected Political Writings*, pp. 245, 238.

184. Ibid., pp. 240, 253.

185. Ibid., p. 252.

186. See Waldenberg, vol. 2, ch. 7. See also Dunayevskaya, *Rosa Luxemburg*, pp. 17–24.

187. Luxemburg, *Wybór pism*, vol. 2, pp. 191–93.

188. See ibid., vol. 1, pp. 598–99.

189. See Geras, pp. 71–101.

190. Luxemburg, *Wybór pism*, vol. 1, pp. 601.

191. This was later acknowledged by Trotsky himself. See Knei-Paz, pp. 171–72n.

192. Luxemburg, *Wybór pism*, vol. 2, pp. 97–98. See also Luxemburg, "Nauki Trzech Dum."

193. Luxemburg, *Selected Political Writings*, p. 324.

194. Ibid., p. 350.

195. Luxemburg, *Leninism or Marxism?*, pp. 40, 48. (The title *Leninism or Marxism?* was given to this volume by its editor.)

196. Ibid., pp. 62, 71–72, 78, 69.

197. Kolakowski, *Main Currents*, vol. 2, pp. 87–88.

198. See Dunayevskaya, *Rosa Luxemburg*, p. 72.

199. Luxemburg, *Selected Political Writings*, p. 387.

200. Ibid., pp. 368, 370–71, 367, 368, 369, 373.

201. Ibid., p. 372.

202. Ibid., pp. 374, 405, 375.

203. Ibid., pp. 406–7, 376.

204. Ibid., pp. 380–84.

205. Ibid., pp. 385–87.

206. Ibid., pp. 367, 370.

207. Ibid., p. 333.

208. Ibid., p. 415.

209. Luxemburg, *The Industrial Development of Poland*, p. 165.

210. Luxemburg, *Wybór pism*, vol. 1, p. 60.

211. This interpretation has been developed in detail by Tych.

212. See Luxemburg, *The Industrial Development*, pp. 161–65.

213. Luxemburg, *Wybór pism*, vol. 1, pp. 69–70.

214. Ibid., vol. 2, p. 14.

215. Ibid., vol. 1, p. 399n. See also Luxemburg, *Listy do Leona*, vol. 2, p. 379.

216. See Walicki, *Philosophy and Romantic Nationalism*, pp. 358–61. For another interpretation of Marx and Engels's concept of national class that is closer to Luxemburg's views, see Davis, *Nationalism and Socialism*, pp. 76–82. See also Lichtheim, pt. 3, ch. 2. (Lichtheim's interpretation fully agrees with mine.)

217. Ettinger, introduction to Luxemburg, *Comrade and Lover*, p. xxviii.

218. Nettl, vol. 2, p. 860. For a study of Luxemburg's Jewish background and of her attitude toward the Jewish question, see Wistrich.

219. Luxemburg, *Listy do Leona*, vol. 1, pp. 123, 180, 190, 196–97.

220. Quoted in Nettl, vol. 1, p. 133; vol. 2, p. 852.

221. It is important, however, to stress that Luxemburg was not fully conscious of this. Her pamphlet *W obronie narodowości* (1900) strongly condemned the "system of Germanization." But at the same time she urged the Polish workers in Posnania to break with the Polish priests and patriotic landowners (who were

the natural leaders of the resistance to Germanization) and to join forces with the German Social Democrats (who wanted to Germanize them "for their own good").

222. Luxemburg, *The National Question*, p. 96. It was necessary to modify the translation by substituting "spiritual culture" (as in the Polish original) for "intellectual heritage" and "spiritual life" for "intellectual life."

223. Luxemburg, *The National Question*, p. 135.

224. Ibid., pp. 142–43. Luxemburg tried to make this blunt statement more palatable by adding that revolutionaries in fact represented the interests of the majority and were a minority only from the point of view of the *conscious* will of the people. Nonetheless, she made it plain that "the historical mission of Social Democracy" expressed not the will of the majority but the will of the "working-class majority" (p. 143).

225. See Kolakowski, *Main Currents*, vol. 2, pp. 285–90.

226. See Nettl, vol. 2, p. 847.

227. Luxemburg, *The National Question*, pp. 215, 259.

228. Ibid., p. 265.

229. Luxemburg, *Leninism or Marxism?* p. 54. See also Luxemburg, *The National Question*, p. 298.

230. Luxemburg, *Selected Political Writings*, pp. 348, 354.

231. Luxemburg, *Leninism or Marxism?* pp. 47–53.

232. See Nettl, *Rosa Luxemburg*, vol. 2, p. 564.

233. Ibid., pp. 855–56. See Lenin's answer to Feliks Dzierżyński: "People don't want to understand that to strengthen internationalism you do not have to repeat the same words. What you have to do is to stress, in Russia, the freedom of secession for oppressed nations and, in Poland, their freedom to unite. Freedom to unite implies freedom to secede. We Russians must emphasize freedom to secede, while the Poles must emphasize freedom to unite" (L, CW, 24:298).

234. See Lichtheim's review of Nettl's *Rosa Luxemburg* in *Encounter*, June 1966. Quoted in Dunayevskaya, *Rosa Luxemburg*, p. 57.

235. Nettl, vol. 2, p. 861.

236. Ibid., p. 862.

237. See Kelles-Krauz, vol. 2, pp. 392–95.

238. Brzozowski, *Idee*, p. 225.

239. See Bergmann, pp. 64, 90, 102.

240. See above, note 222.

241. This aspect of Marxism has been thoroughly analyzed by Szporluk.

242. Nettl, vol. 2, p. 860.

243. See Luxemburg, *Comrade and Lover*, p. 16: "My Leon should speak Polish with me, but then you 'won't feel at home.' What shall we do? Your suggestion to speak both Polish and Russian at home is horrifying." (Jogiches's native language was Russian.) Despite such testimonies, it seems clear that with the passage of time Luxemburg's attachment to the Polish language and culture became weaker and weaker.

Chapter 4

1. See especially the works of such scholars as Daniels, S. Cohen, Lewin, and Fitzpatrick.

2. See Fitzpatrick, "New Perspectives on Stalinism," p. 357.

3. MacIntyre, *Against the Self-Images of the Age*, p. 43.

4. Ibid.

5. Ibid., pp. 47, 44.

6. Trotsky, *Lenin*.

7. Lenin's lack of vanity was stressed by Schapiro, who saw it as a redeeming feature and quoted approvingly the Russian nineteenth-century historian, Timothy Granovsky: "The great actors in history bear responsibility only for the purity of their intentions, and for their zeal in carrying them into effect, and not for the remote consequences of the labour which they perform" (Schapiro and Reddaway, p. 20). Of course, many people (Lenin included) would not agree with this view or would at least see it as very controversial.

8. Gorky, p. 52.   9. Turgenev, pp. 26, 26.

10. Trotsky, *Lenin*, p. 174.   11. Ibid., pp. 174–76.

12. Nove (who quoted these words out of context) saw this statement as a "rather surprising" reversal of the standard Marxist view on the priority of economics. See A. Nove, "Lenin as an Economist," in Schapiro and Reddaway, p. 188.

13. Marxist theory, Lenin argued, "subordinates the 'ethical standpoint' to the 'principle of causality'; in practice it reduces it to the class struggle" (L, CW, 1:421).

14. This involved a distinction between objectivism and materialism, which Lenin set forth as follows: "When demonstrating the necessity for a given series of facts, the objectivist always runs the risk of becoming an apologist of these facts; . . . a materialist discloses the class contradiction and in so doing defines his standpoint" (ibid., p. 401).

15. Schapiro and Reddaway, p. 13.

16. Trotsky, *My Life*, p. ix.

17. For a comprehensive analysis of this theory see Knei-Paz, chs. 3, 4.

18. See Marx's preface to the first German edition of *Capital*. For an analysis of the importance of this view for Plekhanov's interpretation of Marxism, see chapter 3, section 2.

19. For Engels's view, see chapter 2, section 3. A variation on this theme was developed, as a criticism of Lenin's views, by P. B. Akselrod in his two articles on "The Unification of Russian Social Democracy and Its Tasks," *Iskra* (Dec. 15, 1903, Jan. 15, 1904). According to a witness, it made Lenin "so furious that he looked like a tiger" (quoted in Valentinov, *Encounters with Lenin*, p. 115).

20. See Brzezinski, *The Grand Failure*.

21. Quoted in Medvedev, *Let History Judge*, p. 80. Despite Lenin's clearly expressed wish, his "Testament" was not presented to the plenum of the Central Committee. In later years, when Stalin had firmly entrenched himself in power, it was proclaimed a forgery (ibid., pp. 84–87). See also Lewin, *Lenin's Last Struggle*.

22. In fact, Bentham, a sharp critic of the theory of human rights, did not belong to those who "wrote beautifully" about freedom. Lenin seems to confuse here

two different theories: that of inalienable human rights and that of the democratic majority.

23. This has been stressed by Heller in *The Theory of Needs in Marx*.

24. For a discussion of the different meanings of the term *populism* (*narodnichestvo*) in Russian nineteenth-century thought, see Walicki, *The Controversy over Capitalism*, ch. 1, "The Concept of Populism."

25. In the broadest sense, Russian populism was, in Lenin's view, "a whole vision of the world whose history begins with Herzen" (see ibid., p. 8). This comprehensive usage of the term could be applied, of course, to Chernyshevskii. In a more narrow sense, the term *populism* was applied by Lenin to those of Chernyshevskii's disciples who combined bourgeois democratic ideas with a petty bourgeois conservative reaction against bourgeois progress.

26. Valentinov, *Encounters with Lenin*, p. 64.

27. According to Valentinov, "There was a special and hidden, yet strongly revolutionary ideological, political and psychological line running from Chernyshevskii's *What Is to Be Done?* to Lenin's *What Is to Be Done?*" (ibid., p. 68).

28. He made this distinction in his "Notes on the Founding of Political Economy by J. S. Mill" (1860), a work highly praised by Marx.

29. Valentinov, *Encounters with Lenin*, p. 67.

30. Chernyshevskii, *Polnoe sobranie sochinenii*, vol. 5, pp. 106, 217. Quoted in Lampert, p. 199.

31. Chernyshevskii, *Polnoe sobranie sochinenii*, vol. 1, pp. 110, 110.

32. Thus, expressions like *demokraticheskoe proizhozhdenie* or *demokraticheskaia sreda* in Russian mean simply "plebeian origin" and "plebeian milieu."

33. According to this usage of the term, Russian autocracy fighting the Polish uprising of 1863 represented the principle of "democracy" simply because the Polish insurgents, as Catholics and members of the gentry, were perceived as a socially conservative force. Thus, Bakunin perceived tsarism as crushing the Polish uprising in the name of democracy (Bakunin, *Filosofia, sotsyologia, politika*, p. 15). Konstantin Leontiev, an ultraconservative thinker, developed the same view in his essay *National Policy as an Instrument of World Revolution*: he sympathized with the Poles and regretted that the victory of Russian autocracy speeded up the process of social democratization.

34. Chernyshevskii, "The Party Struggle in France in the Reigns of Louis XVIII and Charles X." Quoted in T. Szamuely, p. 176.

35. See Walicki, *Controversy over Capitalism*, p. 84, as well as *A History of Russian Thought*, pp. 200–202, and *Legal Philosophies of Russian Liberalism*, pp. 60–61.

36. For a more comprehensive account, see Walicki, *Controversy over Capitalism*, pp. 80–107.

37. These words are those of Y. U. Stefanovich, one of the populist followers of Bakunin. Quoted in Levin, p. 334.

38. Walicki, *The Controversy over Capitalism*, pp. 26, 132–53.

39. A perfect example of this reasoning can be found in Eliseev's article "Plutocracy and Its Social Base" (*Otechestvennye Zapiski* [Nov. 2, 1872]) in which quotations from Marx's *Capital* were used to support the view that the Russian

autocracy, not as yet fully committed to capitalism, was in fact better than Western parliamentary systems, which were merely obedient tools of the propertied classes.

40. See Maximoff, p. 187.

41. Conquest, *Lenin*, pp. 21–22; see also Harding, vol. 1, p. 19.

42. See *Perepiska G. V. Plekhanova i P. B. Akselroda*, vol. 1, pp. 270–71. See also Haimson, pp. 106–8.

43. See Mitrany.

44. See Baron, pp. 265–66.

45. See Hobsbawm.

46. Thus, for instance, he exaggerated the importance of Lenin's casual acquaintance with M. P. Yasneva, a political associate of the "old Jacobin" P. G. Zaichhevsky. See Valentinov, *Encounters with Lenin*, pp. 73–74.

47. A useful summary of these observations is to be found in Weeks.

48. See Valentinov, *Encounters with Lenin*, p. 203. See also the paragraph on Tkachev in *What Is to Be Done?* (L, *LA*, 107).

49. See Vaganyan, p. 54, and Polevoi, p. 134.

50. See Krupskaya, pp. 517–18.

51. "To understand the roots of Communist totalitarianism," wrote Löwenthal, "it is essential that we recognize that the Communists first took power in the name of a utopian goal of perfect equality having its origin in the radical wing of the Western Enlightenment of the 18th century, and more particularly of the French Revolution" (Löwenthal, "Beyond the 'Institutionalized Revolution' in Russia and China," p. 14.) For a presentation of Babeuf's contribution to revolutionary totalitarianism see J. Talmon, pp. 179–247.

52. See Ulam, *The Bolsheviks*, pp. 156–57.

53. Harding, vol. 1, pp. 161–66/169, 169, 187–88.

54. Ibid., pp. 187, 195.

55. Ibid., pp. 194–95.

56. In "Letter to a Comrade on Organizational Tasks" (1902), Lenin wrote: "The decisions of the district groups should be determined by the committee, i.e., the committee *appoints* one or two of its members (or even comrades who are not on the committee) as delegates to this or that district and instructs them to *establish a district group*, all the members of which are likewise installed in office, so to speak, by the committee. The district group is a branch of the committee, deriving its powers only from the latter" (L, *CW*, 6:241).

57. *Oblomovism* (after the name of the chief character in Goncharov's novel *Oblomov*) was a term coined by the literary critic Nikolai Dobrolyubov to denote laziness and lack of will, characteristics of those brought up in the demoralizing hothouse conditions of privilege and lack of responsibility. Dobrolyubov's essay on oblomovism made "a shattering impression" on Lenin (see Valentinov, *Encounters with Lenin*, p. 68).

58. See Marot, pp. 241–64. Marot's views have been heavily influenced by Harding's book on Lenin.

59. See Williams, pp. 21, 38, 80.

60. See Sochor, p. 37.

61. See Brown, p. 9.

62. See Walicki, "Alexander Bogdanov and the Problem of the Socialist Intelligentsia," pp. 297–99.

63. *Vtoroi Syezd RSDRP: protokoly*, p. 29. Quoted in Knei-Paz, p. 184.

64. Quoted in Wolfe, *Three Who Made a Revolution*, p. 253.

65. Trotsky, *Nashi politicheskie zadachi*, p. 50. Quoted in Knei-Paz, p. 195.

66. See Plekhanov, "Rabochii klass i sotsyal-demokraticheskaia intelligentsia" (1904), in *Sochineniia*, vol. 13, p. 131. Lenin's views on the role of correct consciousness reminded Plekhanov of Bruno Bauer's theory of the role of "critical thought" (ibid., pp. 132–33).

67. Ibid., pp. 129–30.

68. Ibid., p. 124. Plekhanov realized that his readers might question the reasons for his delayed reaction. He explained, rather awkwardly, that he saw Lenin's errors from the very beginning but attributed them to the awkwardness of his expressions and thus minimized their importance (ibid., p. 135).

69. For the text of this amazing document, see Daniels, ed., *A Documentary History of Communism*, vol. 2, pp. 44–47.

70. See Harding, vol. 1, pp. 232–33.

71. Wolfe has rightly noticed that in this way Lenin passed from his theory of the party to a "new dream": that of "total organization *by the party*." (*Lenin and the Twentieth Century*, p. 27).

72. Ulam, *The Bolsheviks*, p. 181.

73. Hayek, following Michael Oakeshott, defined this distinction as follows: "A teleocratic order, in which the same hierarchy of ends is binding on all members, is necessarily a made order or organization, while a nomocratic society will form a spontaneous order." See Hayek, *Law, Legislation, and Liberty*, vol. 2, p. 15.

74. See above, note 6.

75. See Stuart and Williams.

76. See Walicki, *Legal Philosophies of Russian Liberalism*, ch. 1: "The Tradition of the Censure of Law."

77. Quoted in Venturi, p. 366. Sergei Nechaev (1847–82), the founder of the utterly centralized clandestine organization the People's Vengeance, frequently resorted in his revolutionary activities to mystifications, such as presenting himself as a representative of the International and a member of an all-Russian revolutionary committee. His *Catechism* recommended extremely ruthless and immoral methods. When a member of this organization protested against these methods, he was "sentenced to death" and killed. Nechaev's trial (in St. Petersburg in 1871) aroused great interest and was used to discredit the Russian revolutionary movement as a whole (for instance, in Dostoevsky's novel *The Possessed*). Marx and Engels disapproved of Nechaev's methods and used this occasion to cut themselves off from the illegal activities of revolutionary secret societies. The relationship between Nechaevism and Leninism has been discussed by many authors, most recently in Besançon, ch. 8, and also Weeks, pp. 44–50.

78. Venturi, pp. 366–67.

79. Lewin, *Lenin's Last Struggle*, p. 134.

80. Balabanoff, *Impressions of Lenin*, p. 7.

81. "What We Are Fighting For?" *News* of the Kronstadt Temporary Revolu-

tionary Committee (Mar. 8, 1921). Quoted in Daniels, ed., *A Documentary History*, vol. 1, p. 137.

82. Axelrod, "The Unification of Russian Social Democracy and Its Tasks," *Iskra* (Dec. 15, 1903, Jan. 15, 1904). Quoted in Valentinov, *Encounters with Lenin*, p. 117.

83. To translate *riadovoi Marksist* as "ordinary Marxist" (see L, CW, 13:450) would minimize Lenin's awareness of his lack of philosophical distinction.

84. See also Valentinov, *Encounters with Lenin*, pp. 235–36, and Katkov, pp. 75–76.

85. Valentinov, *Encounters with Lenin*, p. 236.

86. Lenin's "Notes" have not been published, and their fate remains unknown.

87. See Valentinov, *Encounters with Lenin*, pp. 248–49.

88. Ibid., p. 247.

89. Williams has aptly observed that Lenin "understood best that relativist myth is most effective when disguised as orthodox truth" (p. 189).

90. See Bogdanov, "Vera i nauka," in Bogdanov, *Padenie velikogo fetishizma*, pp. 145–223.

91. In Marx and Engels's view, the aggressively antireligious standpoint characterized some "prescientific" currents of revolutionary socialism, especially Blanquism. In his analysis of the "Programm der blanquistischen Kommune-flüchtinge" (1874), Engels stated: "This much is certain: the only service that can be rendered to God nowadays is to declare atheism a compulsory article of faith and to outdo Bismarck's *Kulturkampf* laws by prohibiting religion generally" (quoted in Hunt, *The Political Ideas of Marx and Engels*, vol. 2, pp. 178–79). Religion was not formally prohibited in the Soviet Union, but it was savagely repressed and persecuted, which included the killing of priests and the deliberately blasphemous vandalization of churches. By comparison, the situation of German Catholics under Bismarck's *Kulturkampf* laws can be described as almost idyllic.

92. See Maximoff, p. 118.

93. See Bakunin, *Filosofia, sotsyologia, politika*, pp. 100–101.

94. The existence of striking similarities between medieval chiliasm and the modern totalitarian movements has been noticed by Cohn: "The more carefully one compares the outbreaks of militant social chiliasm during the later Middle Ages with modern totalitarian movements, the more remarkable the similarities appear. The old symbols and the old slogans have indeed disappeared, to be replaced by new ones; but the structure of the basic phantasies seems to have changed scarcely at all" (p. xiv). For an analysis of bolshevism as a "political secular religion" of a distinctively chiliastic type, see Gurian.

95. See Schapiro, *The Origin of the Communist Autocracy*, p. 360.

96. Medvedev, *Let History Judge*, p. 645.

97. See Khoruzhii.

98. Ibid., no. 12, p. 7.

99. The first sentence in this letter indicates its purpose: "On the question of deporting the writers and professors helping the counter-revolution" (L, CW, 45:555).

100. In Lenin's view, the slogan of "national culture" should not be tolerated even in the case of oppressed and persecuted nationalities. In this connection he wrote about the Jews: "Whoever, directly or indirectly, puts forward the slogan of Jewish 'national culture' is (whatever his good intentions may be) an enemy of the

proletariat, a supporter of all that is *outmoded* and connected with *caste* among the Jewish people; he is an accomplice of the rabbis and the bourgeoisie" (L, *LA*, 655).

101. Timasheff, p. 165.

102. See, for instance, the entry devoted to this article in the Soviet *Filosofskaya Entsiklopedia*, vol. 4 (Moscow, 1967), pp. 108–9.

103. Lenin's *Philosophical Notebooks* of 1914–16 are yet another proof of his notorious lack of philosophical culture. Nine-tenths of the text consists of remarks like these: "The idealist is caught!" "Ha-ha! he's afraid!" (on Hegel), "He pities God!! the idealistic scoundrel!!" (on Epicurus), and so on (L, *CW*, 38:287, 289, 295). The main conclusion is exactly the same as in *Materialism and Empiriocriticism*: "Kant disparages knowledge in order to make way for faith: Hegel exalts knowledge, asserting that knowledge is knowledge of God. The materialist exalts the knowledge of matter, of nature, consigning God, and the philosophical rabble that defends God to the rubbish heap" (ibid., p. 171).

104. Ulam, *The Bolsheviks*, p. 353.

105. Wolfe, *An Ideology in Power*, pp. 29, 30, 29.

106. See R. Tucker, "Lenin's Bolshevism as a Culture in the Making," in Gleason et al., pp. 26–27.

107. Ulam, *The Bolsheviks*, pp. 348–49.

108. Quoted in Bronner, *Socialism Unbound*, p. 126.

109. Bahro, p. 96.

110. Friedrich and Brzezinski, pp. 9–10.

111. Thus, Tucker is perfectly right when he stresses that Lenin's conduct after the Revolution "is not to be explained by an urge to power for power's sake" ("Lenin's Bolshevism," p. 32). He is wrong, however, in assuming that this conclusion characterizes a new, "cultural" approach to bolshevism, as opposed to the totalitarian model (ibid., pp. 36–37).

112. According to Löwenthal, commitment to utopian goals is a distinctive feature of communist totalitarianism. A communist dictatorship that has abandoned the search for utopia ceases to be totalitarian. See Löwenthal, "Beyond the 'Institutionalized Revolution' in Russia and China," p. 14.

113. This critical remark fully applies to Ehrenberg's *The Dictatorship of the Proletariat*. (This book appeared when this chapter had already been written.)

114. Hunt, *The Political Ideas of Marx and Engels*, vol. 2, pp. 198, 198.

115. Ibid., p. 243.

116. Ibid., p. 244.

117. Ibid., pp. 328, 144.

118. For an analysis of Marx's notion of the "parasite state," see Hunt, *The Political Ideas*, vol. 2, pp. 4–7. According to Hunt, we can find in Marxism two theories of the state: "The one fathered by Marx, the other by Engels." "Engels' state was a mere instrument; Marx's state was autonomous, its own master. Engels' theory gave prime importance to coercion, class coercion, as the essence of state power; Marx's theory stressed its caste egoism and estrangement from civil society" (p. 4).

119. Bakunin, *Gosudarstvennost' i anarkhya*, in Bakunin, *Filosofia, sotsyologia, politika*, p. 482.

120. Unlike Lenin, Marx flatly refused to treat the "bourgeois state" as essen-

tially the same everywhere. The "present-day state," he explained, "is different in the Prusso-German Empire from what it is in Switzerland, and different in England from what it is in the United States. 'The present-day state' is, therefore, a fiction" (M&E, SW, 3:26).

121. According to Hunt, Marx and Engels saw the tendency toward a radical deprofessionalization of state functions as the most precious legacy of the Paris Commune. See Hunt, *The Political Ideas*, vol. 2, pp. 134, 367.

122. It is important to remember that the idea of "workers' councils" was first formulated by the members of the anarchist wing of the First International. See Rocker, pp. 64–67.

123. Engels claimed that legality had become a mortal danger to the bourgeoisie, while the socialists "are thriving far better on legal methods than on illegal methods and overthrow" (M&E, SW, 1:202).

124. Haupt, p. 41.

125. See also Haupt, pp. 31–32.

126. Kelsen is right to point out the significance of the anarchistic tendency prevailing in the writings of Marx and especially of Engels (see Kelsen, p. 38).

127. Polan, p. 129. In Polan's view, "the 'crime' of Lenin's text is not that it did not work: it is that it did. The 'libertarian' Lenin bears equal responsibility for the Gulag with the 'authoritarian' Lenin" (p. 130).

128. Kelsen, p. 48.

129. See Selucký, pp. 12–14, 52–53.

130. See, for instance, the Kuroń-Modzelewski "Open Letter to the Party" (1965). Reprinted in Stokes.

131. Kelsen, p. 51.

132. Deutscher, *The Prophet Armed*, p. 493.

133. Trotsky, *Terrorism and Communism*, pp. 169–70 (italics added).

134. See Hunt, *The Political Ideas*, vol. 1, pp. 37–38.

135. Liebman, pp. 261–62.

136. See Walicki, *Legal Philosophies of Russian Liberalism*, p. 95. In his review of this book, John N. Hazard has rightly noticed that this amounted to introducing "an original feature into Marxism." However, he pointed out that after the Revolution, Lenin "seems to have concluded that *zakony*, if not the more general *pravo*, had utility in controlling his bureaucrats and his people." See *Cambridge Law Journal*, (Nov. 1987): 515. In fact I have never intended to question this view. Lenin's attitude toward administrative regulations (*zakony*) and his attitude toward law in the general sense (*Recht, droit, pravo*) are two separate questions.

137. See Lapenna, p. 248.

138. Ibid.

139. Piers Beirne and Alan Hunt quote these words from Lenin's article of 1920 without mentioning that it was Lenin's quotation from his own article of 1906. This creates the false impression that Lenin's conception of "direct popular justice" was formulated only *after* the Revolution as a reaction to the civil war and other forms of class struggle in the postrevolutionary period. See P. Beirne and A. Hunt, "Lenin, Crime, and Penal Politics, 1917–1924," in Beirne, pp. 105–6.

140. Thus, for instance, in May 1918, Petrograd workers "rejected the idea of food supply detachments on the grounds that it would cause a 'deep chasm' between

workers and peasants. Some speakers demanded that workers who joined such detachments be 'expelled' from the ranks of the proletariat" (Pipes, *The Russian Revolution*, p. 561).

141. See Liebman, p. 326.   142. Ibid.

143. See J. Talmon, p. 182.   144. See also Lapenna, p. 253.

145. As indicated above, this expression was later used (in the pejorative sense) in the "Draft Revolution on the Syndicalist and Anarchist Deviation in Our Party."

146. See Kritsman.   147. Ibid., pp. 81–82.

148. Ibid., pp. 154–63, 190–93.   149. See Lapenna, p. 250.

150. Pipes, *The Russian Revolution*, pp. 69–70. This view of law was summarized thus by the police chief of Nicholas I: "Laws are written for subjects, not for the government!" (p. 70).

151. See, for instance, the following words: "We are not bureaucrats and do not want to insist on the letter of law everywhere" (quoted in Beirne, p. 78). A special advantage of the Soviet system, as distinct from parliamentarism, was, in Lenin's view, its ability to realize the people's will "without any bureaucratic [read: legal] formalities." See L, A, 399 ("Can the Bolsheviks Retain State Power?").

152. Beirne and Hunt, p. 124.

153. Ibid., p. 100.

154. Carr, *Socialism in One Country*, vol. 2, p. 421.

155. *Trinadtsatyi Syezd RKP (b)*, p. 167.

156. See P. Beirne and A. Hunt, "Law and the Constitution of Soviet Society: The Case of Comrade Lenin," in Beirne, p. 79.

157. See P. Beirne and R. Sharlet, introduction to Pashukanis, *Selected Writings on Marxism and Law*, p. 32.

158. Ibid., p. 143.

159. C. J. Arthur, introduction to Pashukanis, *Law and Marxism*, p. 13.

160. See Pashukanis, *Selected Writings*, p. 89.

161. Pashukanis, *Selected Writings*, pp. 104, 102. Pashukanis substantiated his view on ethics by pointing out that the Kantian categorical imperative was a rule of conduct based on a rational calculation of interests. Hence, he argued, "Kantian ethics are the typical ethics of a commodity-producing society" (p. 103).

162. Ibid., pp. 103–4, 104.

163. The vision of communism as a social formation in which people would be able to settle their disputes "with simplicity, without elaborately organized tribunals, without legal representation, without complicated laws, and without a labyrinth of rules of procedure and evidence" was by then very widespread among the Bolsheviks. See Hazard, p. vi.

164. Pashukanis, *Selected Writings*, pp. 60, 60.

165. In this way Pashukanis provided a Marxist justification for the view that only private law (i.e., a contractual commercial-individualistic type of legal relationship) is law par excellence, and that public law is not law at all, but administration. Because of this Kamenka and Tay refer to Pashukanis's theory as an example of what they call "the *Gesellschaft* paradigm of law" (as opposed to the "*Gemeinschaft* paradigm," on the one hand, and the bureaucratic-administrative paradigm, on the other). See E. Kamenka and A. Tay, "Social Traditions, Legal Traditions," in Kamenka and Tay, *Law and Social Control*, pp. 3–26.

166. See Marx's words: "Legislation, whether political or civil, never does more than proclaim, express in words, the will of economic relations" (Marx, *The Poverty of Philosophy*, in M&E, CW, 6:147).

167. P. Beirne and R. Sharlet, introduction to Pashukanis, *Selected Writings*, p. 6.

168. Pashukanis translated the quoted words as "the narrow horizon of bourgeois law" (*Selected Writings*, p. 46).

169. Only a part was published after Lenin's death in *Pyatyi Vserossiisky syezd deyatelei sovetskoi yustitsii*. The full text of the letter was published only in the fifth edition of Lenin's *Polnoe sobranie sochinenii*, vol. 44, pp. 396–400.

170. See R. Sharlet, "Pashukanis and the Withering Away of Law in the USSR," in Fitzpatrick, ed., *Cultural Revolution in Russia*, p. 170.

171. See Pashukanis, "The Marxist Theory of Law and the Construction of Socialism," in Pashukanis, *Selected Writings*, pp. 188–99. It is interesting to note that the view of the incompatibility of private law with socialist planning found sympathetic understanding among Western specialists in Soviet legal theory. Schlesinger summarized thus: "Under socialism, the rule of law is granted by the public interest embodied in Public Law, and by nothing else. The advantages of planning and social security cannot be combined with those of extreme decentralization" (p. 271). A similar opinion was expressed by P. Beirne and A. Hunt in Beirne, p. 91.

172. Pashukanis, *Selected Writings*, p. 194.

173. Ibid., p. 192.

174. Ibid., p. 250 ("Economics and Legal Regulation").

175. Ibid., p. 249.

176. Unfortunately, Gorbachev himself chose to look for the legitimation of his reforms in "Lenin's last writings." See his *Slovo o Lenine*.

177. In "The Chief Task of Our Day" (Mar. 12, 1918) Lenin wrote: "In the space of a few months we passed through a number of stages of collaboration with the bourgeoisie and of shaking off petty bourgeois illusions, for which other countries have required decades" (L, CW, 27:159).

178. See Lenin's vivid description of how "to forcibly move a very poor family into a rich man's flat" in "Can the Bolsheviks Retain State Power?" (L, CW, 27:403–4).

179. See Pipes, *The Russian Revolution*, pp. 686–87.

180. The word *products* has been italicized by Lenin to stress that it must not be exchange of *commodities*.

181. Boettke, *The Political Economy of Soviet Socialism*, p. 69. Malle is more cautious. In her view, during War Communism ideology "acted as a filter for acceptable alternatives, but not as blind prescription of necessary measures" (p. 24). However, her own book shows that the militantly ideological character of War Communism made it immune to pragmatic corrections and led the country to a veritable economic catastrophe.

182. For a good summary of these interpretations, see Boettke, *The Political Economy*, pp. 14–22.

183. Carr, *The Bolshevik Revolution*, vol. 2, p. 270.

184. Lewin, *Lenin's Last Struggle*, p. 17.

185. Stites, p. 4.

186. Pipes, *The Russian Revolution*, p. 673. Nevertheless, Pipes's final analysis subscribes to the thesis that War Communism was "the most ambitious attempt ever made until then to rationalize completely production and distribution through the elimination of market forces" (pp. 711–12).

187. Pipes's position on this matter is somewhat ambiguous. On the one hand, he stresses that War Communism was not a "temporary measure" but "an ambitious attempt to introduce full-blown communism" (pp. 671–72). On the other hand, however, he denies the significance of the ideological inspiration of Bolshevism, representing the Bolsheviks as merely a "cohort gathered around a chosen leader" (p. 814). I see these two interpretations as mutually exclusive.

188. See Gerschenkron, and Nove, *An Economic History of the USSR*, p. 47. See also Boettke, *The Political Economy of Soviet Socialism*, pp. 11–12.

189. The merit of stating this clearly belongs to Boettke. See his *Political Economy of Soviet Socialism*, p. 7.

190. Boettke, *The Political Economy of Soviet Socialism*, p. 3.

191. See Kritsman, p. 61.

192. Quoted in Nove, "Some Observations on Bukharin and His Ideas," p. 86.

193. *Protokoly xi syezda RKP (b)*, p. 285. Quoted in L. Szamuely, p. 94.

194. According to Pipes, "The earliest official use of 'War Communism' dates to the Spring of 1921—that is, to the time when the policies so labeled were being abandoned in favor of the more liberal New Economic Policy. It was then that the Communist authorities, in order to justify their sudden turnabout, sought to blame the disasters of the immediate past on circumstances beyond their control." See Pipes, *The Russian Revolution*, p. 671.

195. Stalin, "The Program of the Comintern." Speech delivered on July 5, 1928, in *Works*, vol. 11, pp. 152–53. Quoted in L. Szamuely, p. 8.

196. L. Szamuely, p. 8.

197. The relevant passage of *The Immediate Tasks of the Soviet Government* has been omitted in Tucker's *Lenin Anthology*.

198. Kollontai described "one-man management" as "a product of the individualist conception of the bourgeois class." From this point of view, Lenin's espousal of this principle was a clear case of "opportunism." See Kollontai, "The Workers' Opposition," in Kollontai, *Selected Writings*, p. 160.

199. See Boettke, *The Political Economy of Soviet Socialism*, p. 127.

200. See Pipes, *The Russian Revolution*, p. 674.

201. Medvedev, *La Révolution d'Octobre, était-elle inéluctable?* p. 134. (Quoted in Malle, p. 16.)

202. The systematic nationalization of Russian industry was only decreed on June 28, 1918.

203. L. Szamuely, p. 24.

204. Ibid., pp. 24–25.

205. Ibid., p. 27.

206. Ibid., p. 24. We must remember that Szamuely published his excellent, provocative book in 1974, in Kádár's Hungary. For political reasons it was more convenient for him to put the blame for antimarket dogmas on the Second International than to say plainly that these dogmas had always been the very essence of Marxist communism.

207. See Boettke, *The Political Economy of Soviet Socialism*, p. 196.

208. Bukharin, *The Politics and Economics of the Transition Period*, p. 125. Bukharin spoke glowingly about the collapse of the Russian economy, interpreting it as the collapse of capitalism. (See Pipes, *The Russian Revolution*, p. 712.)

209. Kritsman, p. 60.

210. *Ekonomicheskaia zhizn'*, no. 261 (Nov. 9, 1920): 1 (italics added). Quoted in Pipes, *The Russian Revolution*, p. 689.

211. See Fehér, Heller, and Márkus.

212. Of all the foodstuffs consumed in Russian cities in the winter of 1919–20, as measured by their calorific value, the illegal free market furnished from 66 to 80 percent. See Pipes, *The Russian Revolution*, p. 701.

213. Bellamy, *Looking Backward from the Year 2000*, pp. 126–27.

214. E. Bellamy, "Why I Wrote 'Looking Backward,' " in Bellamy, *Edward Bellamy Speaks Again!* pp. 201–2. Quoted in Kumar, p. 150.

215. Bellamy, *Looking Backward*, p. 304. For an analysis of Bellamy's "militarism," see Kumar, pp. 158–67.

216. Quoted in Kumar, p. 135. For Bellamy's influence in Russia, see Bowman, pp. 67–85.

217. Quoted in Kumar, p. 135.

218. Kovalevsky, "9 let ekonomicheskoi politiki proletariata," *Planovoe Khozyaistvo*, no. 10 (1926): 20–21. Quoted in L. Szamuely, p. 7.

219. "We must *mobilize* all who are able capable of working and *compel* them to work with us" (L, *CW*, 30:414; italics added).

220. See S. Heitman, introduction to Bukharin and Preobrazhensky.

221. Bukharin and Preobrazhensky, pp. 75, 69, 70, 70, 72.

222. Ibid., p. 95.   223. Ibid., pp. 100, 136, 137.

224. Ibid., p. 80.   225. Ibid., pp. 317, 317.

226. Ibid., pp. 233, 301, 396.   227. Ibid., pp. 143–46.

228. Ibid., p. 387.   229. Ibid., pp. 386–87, 286, 389.

230. Ibid., p. 32.   231. Ibid., p. 77.

232. Bukharin and Preobrazhensky, p. 74. In theory Lenin continued to endorse this ideal but made its realization dependent on the level of proletarian class consciousness. In *The Immediate Tasks of Soviet Government*, he wrote: "Given ideal class-consciousness and discipline on the part of those participating in the common work, this subordination would be something like the mild leadership of a conductor of an orchestra. It may assume the sharp forms of a dictatorship if ideal discipline and class-consciousness are lacking" (L, *A*, 455).

233. Bukharin and Preobrazhensky, p. 191.

234. Bukharin, *Selected Writings*, pp. 38–39. Luxemburg developed the same view in her introduction to "Political Economy" (see chapter 3, section 3).

235. Ibid., pp. 51, 67, 51.   236. Ibid., p. 55.

237. Ibid., p. 69.   238. Selucký, p. 53.

239. Bukharin, *Selected Writings*, p. 71.

240. Ibid., p. 76.

241. Ibid., pp. 78, 78/80, 78, 79.

242. Ibid., pp. 80, 80, 81, 80–81.

243. *Leninskii sbornik*, vol. 40, p. 424. Quoted in Bukharin, *Problemy teorii*, p. 451 (n. 1).

244. Ibid., pp. 454 (nn. 34, 35), 453 (n. 27), 454 (n. 32). See also Bukharin, *Selected Writings*, pp. 78, 80.

245. See especially S. Cohen, *Bukharin and the Bolshevik Revolution* (first published 1973).

246. Bukharin, "Uchenye Marksa i ego istoricheskoe znachenye." First published in *Sotsyalisticheskaya rekonstruktsya i nauka*, March–June 1933; reprinted in Bukharin, *Problemy teorii*, pp. 331–421.

247. Bukharin, *Problemy teorii*, p. 414.

248. Ibid., p. 415.

249. Quoted in ibid., 415.

250. Ibid., pp. 416, 416. The second tendency was represented, of course, by the "orthodox" Marxism of the Second International. It should be stressed that Bukharin was wrong to accuse its representatives of forgetting about the ultimate tasks of communism. In fact, the communist utopia of a marketless economy was a part of the official program of the German Social Democracy (see chapter 3, section 1).

251. Ibid., p. 416.

252. It seems proper to note that the Marxist opposition between "teleological" (or "teleocratic") order and a market order was developed by Hayek, who, of course, drew completely different conclusions. He presented convincing arguments for the thesis that "teleocratic" order is incompatible with individual freedom and that the lack of "an agreed ranking of ends" is in fact a great merit of the market order—a merit "which makes individual freedom and all its values possible" (*Law, Legislation, and Liberty*, vol. 2, p. 109).

253. Trotsky, *Terrorism and Communism*, p. 59.

254. Ibid., pp. 63, 93, 92.   255. Ibid., p. 96.

256. Ibid., pp. 142–43, 133, 138–40, 137, 149.

257. Ibid., p. 141.   258. Ibid., p. 147.

259. Ibid., p. 153.   260. Ibid., pp. 169–70.

261. See Knei-Paz, pp. 433–34.

262. Trotsky, *Terrorism and Communism*, pp. 171, 171.

263. Trotsky, *Their Morals and Ours*, pp. 51–52.

264. Ibid., p. 48.

265. Trotsky, *Literature and Revolution*, p. 189.

266. Ibid., p. 190.

267. Ibid., pp. 229, 229.

268. Ibid., p. 190.

269. Ibid., pp. 254–56.

270. The main representative of this trend within Russian Marxism is Lunacharskii. See Kline, and Tait.

271. See Knei-Paz, p. 467. The title of Trotsky's essay was "Koe-chto o filosofii 'sverkhcheloveka'" (published in 1900).

272. The title of this lecture is "The Changing Function of Historical Materialism." It is a part of Lukács's *History and Class Consciousness*.

273. Lukács, *History and Class Consciousness*, pp. 645–46.

274. Ibid., pp. 247, 251–52.

275. See the resolution about agriculture passed by the Eighth Congress of Soviets on December 28, 1920, in L. Szamuely, p. 78. This resolution contained such points as the following:

> The national plan of obligatory sowing shall be worked out by the Commissariat for Agriculture in agreement with the Commissariat for Food and the Supreme Council for National Economy. . . . The sowing plans of the regions, districts and communes shall be worked out under the national plan by the sowing committees, regions and districts; previously the plans shall be discussed by special congresses. . . .
>
> In order to support, by state means, the efforts of the best farmers aimed at improving land cultivation, the sowing committees of the provinces may prescribe—under the guidance and control of the Commissariat for Agriculture—obligatory rules for the main methods of cultivation of arable land, for soil amelioration, for sowing, as well as for maintaining the fertility of the soil.

276. Lewin, *Stalinism and the Seeds of Soviet Reform*, pp. 84, 84.

277. Tucker, ed., *The Lenin Anthology*, p. 515.

278. Lewin, *Stalinism and the Seeds of Soviet Reform*, p. 87.

279. Despite widespread opinion to the contrary, Trotsky's understanding of the inherent flaws of central planning was superior to Bukharin's because Trotsky approached this problem from the point of view of economic calculation, not merely from the point of view of the interests of the peasantry. He pointed out that only a universal mind as conceived by Laplace, "a mind that would register simultaneously all the processes of nature and society," could "a priori draw up a faultless and exhaustive economic plan, beginning with the number of hectares of wheat and down to the last button for a vest" (Trotsky, *Soviet Economy in Danger*, p. 29). Nevertheless, Trotsky did not conclude that central planning was economically impossible. Indeed, he consistently supported rigorous all-encompassing planning and demanded the elimination, albeit not immediate, of the NEP (see Knei-Paz, pp. 271–73, 304). There can be no doubt that his motivation on this point was heavily ideological, being directly connected to his understanding of communist freedom.

280. Tucker has interpreted these articles differently. In his view, "very likely Lenin would have shared much of the position that Bukharin and others of his group elaborated in the mid-twenties." See R. Tucker, ed., *The Lenin Anthology*, p. 707, editorial note to Lenin's article "On Cooperation." I see this judgment as containing an element of wishful thinking characteristic of those American Sovietologists who want to emphasize the alleged discontinuity between Leninism and Stalinism.

281. Harding, vol. 2, p. 302. Harding thinks that Lenin became a Jacobin only in his last pamphlets (ibid., p. 307). In my view, there is a remarkable continuity and consistency in Lenin's thought from *What Is to Be Done?* to "Better Fewer, But Better."

282. Boettke points out that this was Lenin's "fundamental error in political economy," stemming from his misunderstanding of the nature of economic calculation (*The Political Economy of Soviet Socialism*, p. 131). In fact, however, Lenin developed his views on the Central Control Commission in another context. In

"Better Fewer, But Better" he was concerned not so much with the uncontrollability of the market but rather with the problem of the uncontrollability of the Soviet bureaucracy. In other words, his problem was how to control those whose task was to consciously control "the blind forces of the market"—how to control the controllers!

Chapter 5

1. Twenty million dead is the estimate of Conquest (*The Great Terror*, p. 486). According to Medvedev, the total number of Stalin's victims was forty million. A compilation of his data has been given in "Tragicheskaia statistika," *Sobytiia i Vremia*, no. 6 (Mar. 1989).

2. Medvedev, *Let History Judge*, p. 455.

3. See Orwell, vol. 2, p. 135.

4. In Solzhenitsyn's view, the essence of Marxist communism "has not changed at all during 125 years of its existence" (i.e., since the *Manifesto of the Communist Party*). See Solzhenitsyn, *Publitsistika*, p. 232.

5. Trotsky, *Stalinism and Bolshevism*, p. 17.

6. See Meyer, pp. 401–8.

7. These views were subject to devastating criticism from those Polish intellectuals who defined themselves as Hayekian liberals. See Walicki, "Liberalism in Poland," pp. 8–38; see also "Totalitarianism and Liberalism," pp. 355–68.

8. Emmons, p. 33.

9. Ibid.

10. Walicki, "The Prospects for Change," p. 17. I did not predict in 1986 that *perestroika* would lead to the wholesale collapse of the Soviet Union. Nevertheless, I saw Gorbachev's reforms as entailing a thorough liberalization which "must inevitably lead to the elimination of Leninism and to other profound changes in the legitimating ideology of the system" (ibid., p. 16).

11. A notable exception to this view is Brzezinski's theory of the "retreat from communism," which conceives the disintegration of communism as a movement from "communist totalitarianism" to "communist authoritarianism," then "postcommunist authoritarianism," and, finally, "postcommunist pluralism" (Brzezinski, *The Grand Failure*, pp. 252–58). Unfortunately, this book has had no influence on current thinking on totalitarianism in postcommunist countries.

12. R. Tucker, "A Choice of Lenins?" in Urban, pp. 177–78.

13. Kolakowski, "The Devil in History," in Urban, p. 251.

14. S. Cohen, "Bolshevism and Stalinism," in R. Tucker, ed., *Stalinism*, p. 4.

15. Ibid., p. 24.

16. J. F. Hough, "The Cultural Revolution and Western Understanding of the Soviet System," in Fitzpatrick, ed., *Cultural Revolution in Russia*, pp. 244–47.

17. Ibid., p. 248. See also Hough and Fainsod, pp. 147–66, 520–21.

18. Hough, "The Cultural Revolution," p. 241–48.

19. R. Tucker, "Stalinism as Revolution from Above," in R. Tucker, ed., *Stalinism*, pp. 81, 82, 95, 99, 100.

20. R. Tucker, *Stalin in Power*.

21. Ibid., p. 65.

22. R. Tucker, "A Choice of Lenins?" pp. 163–64.

23. Ibid., p. 163.

24. Stalin, *Works*, vol. 1, p. 111.

25. S. Fitzpatrick, "Cultural Revolution as Class War," in Fitzpatrick, ed., *Cultural Revolution in Russia*, p. 37.

26. See R. Tucker, *Stalin in Power*, p. 65, and S. Cohen, "Bolshevism and Leninism," pp. 23–24.

27. Stalin, *Selected Writings*, pp. 102, 80, 61, 134, 167, 191, 147–48, 147.

28. We owe to Lewin a clearer understanding of the role of the "grain crisis" in the shaping of Stalin's policy of collectivization. Lewin's findings, however, do not justify the conclusion that collectivization was basically a nonideological response to circumstances. See Lewin, *The Making of the Soviet System*, p. 97.

29. See Mitrany.

30. Thus, for instance, Daniels proposed to regard the evolution of Soviet communism as independent of Marxism: "It was an independent development, assuming unforeseeable and uncontrollable forms in response to situational and personal factors of which Marxist theory took little or no account." See Daniels, *Trotsky, Stalin, and Socialism*, p. 25.

31. Bukharin and Preobrazhensky, p. 317.

32. Stalin was quite right to point this out. See *Selected Writings*, p. 62.

33. Erlich, pp. 170, 177.

34. McNeal, "Trotskyist Interpretations of Stalinism," in R. Tucker, ed., *Stalinism*, p. 32.

35. Trotsky, *The Revolution Betrayed*, pp. 8, 29.

36. Ibid., pp. 26–27. 37. Ibid., p. 74.

38. Erlich, p. 176. 39. See Molyneux, p. 111.

40. Deutscher, *The Prophet Unarmed*, p. 315.

41. Ibid., pp. 232, 239–40.

42. Trotsky, *The Revolution Betrayed*, pp. 30, 30.

43. See S. Cohen, "Introduction to the Oxford Edition. Bukharin and the Idea of an Alternative to Stalinism," in S. Cohen, *Bukharin and the Bolshevik Revolution*, pp. xv–xxiv.

44. Timasheff, p. 19. 45. Ibid., pp. 20–21, 343, 343.

46. Ibid., p. 412. 47. Ibid.

48. Ibid., pp. 408/411, 413. 49. Ibid., p. 131.

50. Ibid., p. 140. 51. Ibid.

52. Ibid., p. 146. 53. Timasheff, p. 137.

54. Stalin, *Selected Writings*, pp. 344–45.

55. Timasheff, p. 194. These policies were continued under the NEP; the only concession was the restoration of inheritance (ibid., p. 195).

56. Ibid., p. 205. 57. Ibid., p. 210.

58. Ibid., pp. 197, 201. 59. Ibid., pp. 228–31.

60. Ibid., pp. 240, 167, 359, 361–62.

61. Stalin, *Selected Writings*, p. 200.

62. Szporluk has rightly pointed out that planning for national modernization was the idea of Friedrich List, not of Karl Marx. See Szporluk, p. 220.

63. One of these was Sergius Hessen, theorist of "rule-of-law socialism." See Walicki, *Legal Philosophies of Russian Liberalism*, pp. 447–48.

64. Moshe Lewin, *The Making of the Soviet System*, pp. 283–84.

65. See Timasheff, p. 241.

66. Hough, "The Cultural Revolution," pp. 246–48.

67. See editor's introduction to Fitzpatrick, ed., *Cultural Revolution in Russia*. According to this view, the radicalization of Soviet Marxism that accompanied Stalin's "turn to the left" in the years 1928–31 was "both unacceptable to the Party leadership and inappropriate to its purposes" (ibid., p. 7). In reality, however, this transient phenomenon was part of the early phase of Stalin's "revolution from above." Cf. R. Tucker's comment on this issue: "Militant leftism of 1928–31 in various fields of culture was given a green light by Stalin" (Tucker, *Stalin in Power*, p. 103).

68. Kolakowski, "The Devil in History," in Urban, p. 251. This shows that "the perfect embodiment of *communism*" should be distinguished from "the perfect embodiment of communist *totalitarianism*."

69. Trotsky, *The Revolution Betrayed*, pp. 93–94.

70. Ibid., pp. 279–80.   71. Ibid., p. 138.

72. Ibid., p. 252.   73. Ibid., p. 279.

74. Ibid., p. 255.   75. Ibid., p. 115.

76. Ibid., p. 255.   77. Ibid., p. 301.

78. Ibid., pp. 176, 151.   79. Ibid., p. 154.

80. Ibid., pp. 144–45.   81. Ibid., p. 126.

82. Ibid., p. 156.   83. Ibid., pp. 116, 102, 164.

84. Timasheff, p. 103.

85. Trotsky, *The Revolution Betrayed*, p. 51.

86. Ibid., p. 161.   87. Ibid., pp. 248, 54.

88. Ibid., p. 270.   89. Ibid., p. 278.

90. Ibid., p. 260.   91. Ibid., p. 261.

92. Ibid., pp. 272, 272.   93. Ibid., p. 278.

94. Ibid., pp. 180, 181.   95. Ibid., pp. 181–85.

96. Hough, "The Cultural Revolution," p. 246.

97. See S. Cohen, "Bolshevism and Stalinism," p. 6.

98. In fact R. Tucker made a major concession to this view when he stated that "one of the forces conducive to a Stalinist revolutionary response among Bolshevik politicians was the other Lenin—the still very influential revolutionary Lenin of the War Communism and the heritage of Bolshevik revolutionism that the other Lenin symbolized" (Tucker, "Stalinism as Revolution from Above," p. 89). It remains only to add that this "other Lenin," the revolutionary Lenin, represented the essentials of Leninism and of Bolshevism as a distinct revolutionary movement. See also Tucker's statement that "Stalin followed the strategy of cult building via assertion of Lenin's infallibility" (Tucker, *Stalin in Power*, p. 154).

99. Laqueur, p. 13.

100. To show Stalinism as a continuation of Russian state building is the major achievement of R. Tucker's *Stalin in Power*. This book also contains a convincing summary of the similarities between Stalinism and Nazism. Unfortunately, Tucker drew a totally unconvincing conclusion about the "anti-Communist character" of the Stalinist regime (see ibid., pp. 591–92).

101. See Bukharin's opinion of Stalin's theoretical ambitions: "He's eaten up by

the yearnings to become a recognized theorist. He thinks that's the only thing he lacks." Quoted in R. Tucker, *Stalin in Power*, p. 80.

102. Ibid., p. 608.

103. *Pod znamenem marksizma*, no. 2 (1939). Quoted in Timasheff, p. 85.

104. See Medvedev, *Let History Judge*, p. 616.

105. Kolakowski, *Main Currents of Marxism*, vol. 3, p. 244.

106. Ibid., p. 250.

107. Ibid., p. 252.

108. In his "Lenin's Bolshevism as a Culture in the Making," R. Tucker tries to support his thesis about the absence of direct continuity between Leninism and Stalinism by arguing that Soviet communism as designed by Lenin was in essence "a new culture containing *within* itself a system of party-state power," while Stalin's totalitarianism was merely a "system of total power" (see Tucker, "Lenin's Bolshevism," in Gleason, Kenez, and Stites, pp. 36–37). This is a strange misinterpretation of both the basic facts and the basic concept. The concept of totalitarianism, as constructed by the main theorists of this subject, cannot be reduced to a "system of total power"; it contains by definition a commitment to a total transformation of culture. Stalin did not abandon this commitment; he wanted to be a supreme "engineer of human souls" rather than just a supreme political ruler.

109. See G. Sartori, foreword to Pellicani, p. xii. Pellicani was described by Sartori as "an engaged intellectual within the ranks of the Italian Socialist Party" (ibid., p. xi).

110. Gramsci, *Selected Writings*, p. 243.

111. Pellicani, pp. 58, 60.

112. Pellicani, p. 87.

113. Ibid., p. 72.

114. Sochor concluded from this that Stalinism was a combination of Leninism (emphasis on political power) and Bogdanovism (emphasis on the cultural revolution). See Sochor, p. 215. It is interesting to compare this thesis with the views of two other scholars. According to Hough, Stalinism instituted "an ever-tightening, all-encompassing network of controls" but abandoned the idea of a revolutionary transformation of culture. Therefore it was *not* totalitarian (see above, note 16). In the view of R. Tucker, Stalinism instituted "a system of total power" but, unlike Leninism, abandoned the idea of a revolutionary transformation of society. Therefore, unlike Leninism, it *was* totalitarian (see above, note 108). In fact the basic premise of these two judgments is wrong, since Stalinism did *not* abandon the idea of a revolutionary transformation of culture.

115. Pellicani, p. 90.

116. Beck and Godin, pp. 229–30. The officer of the NKVD mentioned in this quotation is described by the authors as "a former Vice-Commissar of the Kiev NKVD and chief of the administrative section" (p. 228).

117. Gramsci, *Selected Writings*, p. 339.

118. Ibid.

119. Ibid., pp. 339–40, 340, 343, 340, 340.

120. Ibid., pp. 341, 341, 341–42.

121. Kolakowski, *Main Currents*, vol. 3, p. 95.

122. *History of the Communist Party*, pp. 106–9.

123. Ibid., pp. 111, 112, 113, 105.

124. Ibid., p. 114.   125. Ibid., pp. 111, 121.

126. Ibid., p. 115.   127. Ibid., p. 110.

128. See S. Rainko, "Marksizm Stalina," in Rainko *Świadomość i determinizm*, pp. 177–78. Rainko's essay on "Stalin's Marxism" is one of the best works on this subject in any language.

129. Arendt, pp. 461–62.

130. Conquest, *The Great Terror*, pp. 393–95.

131. See Rainko, "Marksizm Stalina," p. 180.

132. *History of the Communist Party*, pp. 121–22.

133. See Stites, p. 236.

134. *History of the Communist Party*, p. 128.

135. The use of the expression "utopia in power" should not be seen as implying agreement with the interpretation of Stalinism in Heller and Nekrich.

136. Stites, p. 226. Unfortunately, in the next sentence the author states that "Stalinism did not aspire to transform human values." I regard this statement as totally untenable.

137. Stalin, *Leninism*, vol. 1, p. 20.

138. Ibid., pp. 14, 261, 73.

139. See above, note 24.

140. Stalin, *Works*, vol. 1, pp. 12, 49–50.

141. See Ree.   142. Stalin, *Works*, vol. 1, p. 97.

143. Ibid., p. 100.   144. Ibid., p. 101.

145. Stalin, *Sochineniia*, vol. 5, p. 71. Quoted in R. Tucker, *Stalin in Power*, p. 7.

146. Stalin, *Leninism*, vol. 1, pp. 278, 88–91, 283, 283, 283.

147. Ibid., pp. 275–77.

148. Ibid., p. 277.

149. Ibid., pp. 276, 277.

150. Ibid., pp. 270, 271 (italics added), 271.

151. One of the earliest instances of this policy was his attack on Bukharin for his critical views on the national character of the Russians, whom he called "the nation of Oblomovs." (See R. Tucker, *Stalin in Power*, p. 358.) Oblomov, the hero of Ivan Goncharov's novel, typifies laziness and lack of will.

152. Stalin, *Sochineniia*, vol. 15 (2), p. 204. Quoted from Daniels, ed., *A Documentary History of Communism*, vol. 1, p. 294.

153. For a sample of its style, see Daniels, ed., *A Documentary History*, vol. 1, pp. 303–6.

154. This applied also to the works of the great prerevolutionary scholar Alexander Veselovskii (1838–1906), the chief representative of the historical-comparative school of folklore in Russia.

155. Innumerable books and articles on Chernyshevskii as the greatest pre-Marxian philosopher (pre-Marxian in the dialectical sense, because chronologically he was Marx's contemporary) were an important part of the struggle against cosmopolitanism on the philosophical front. The authors of these works always referred to the high opinion of Chernyshevskii Lenin expressed in the supplement

to his *Materialism and Empiriocriticism* but carefully avoided his description of Chernyshevskii as "the great Russian Hegelian and materialist" who "was also a disciple of Feuerbach" (L, *CW*, 14:359).

156. Unfortunately, existing Western works on "Zhdanovism" (for instance, in Swayze, or chapter 13 of Armstrong) are less than satisfactory. None of them adequately conveys the horror of an outright obscurantist ideology made universally binding and supported by the repressive apparatus of a totalitarian state.

157. Shtromas, "Making Sense of Stalin," p. 437.

158. See Baczko, pp. 26–52.

159. Stalin, *Selected Writings*, pp. 339–40.

160. Ibid., p. 336.

161. Ibid., p. 337.

162. Ibid., p. 336.

163. Trotsky, *The Revolution Betrayed*, p. 249.

164. See Trotsky, *In Defense of Marxism*, pp. 15–16.

165. Ibid., pp. 13–14.

166. See, for instance, Ulam's *Stalin: The Man and His Era* in which *Economic Problems* is described as a work that "seldom rises above the level of the commonplace and then does so only to sink into confusion" (p. 729). There is no doubt about this confusion, but it was not a commonplace in 1952 to remind Communists that the existence of monetary exchange in the Soviet Union required doctrinal explanation and justification.

167. Stalin, *Economic Problems of Socialism in the USSR*, p. 9. For the quotation from Engels (in a different translation) see E, *AD*, 343.

168. Stalin, *Economic Problems*, p. 9.

169. Ibid., p. 12.

170. Ibid. (see also E, *AD*, 343).

171. Stalin, *Economic Problems*, p. 12.

172. Ibid., p. 13.

173. Ibid., p. 16.

174. Ibid., p. 17.

175. Ibid., p. 19.

176. Ibid., pp. 20, 16–17.

177. Ibid., pp. 19–20.

178. Ibid., p. 23 (see also E, *AD*, 361).

179. Stalin, *Economic Problems*, p. 69.

180. Ibid., p. 70.

181. R. Miliband, "Reflections on the Crisis of Communist Regimes," in Blackburn, pp. 9, 9.

182. Jameson, "Conversations on the New World Order," in Blackburn, p. 261.

183. Smolar, p. 104.

184. See Arendt, p. 379. To properly understand Arendt's conception of totalitarianism, it is necessary to remember that she applied this term only to the Stalinist Soviet Union and Nazi Germany. In her view Mussolini, and still more Franco, did not even attempt to establish a fully totalitarian regime (pp. 308–10).

185. Beck and Godin, p. 206. For the notions of dual consciousness and ideocratic fear, see Meerson-Aksenov and Shragin, pp. 22, 116–48, 256–90.

186. See Orwell, *Collected Essays*, vol. 2, p. 135.

187. *Trinadtsatyi Syezd RKP (f). Stenographicheskii otchet*, p. 372. Quoted in Medvedev, *Let History Judge*, p. 127.

188. Stalin, *Works*, vol. 6, pp. 238–39.

189. See Arendt, p. 307 (n. 7).

190. See Tucker and Cohen, pp. 656–57.

191. See Koestler, *The Invisible Writing*, p. 394.

192. Conquest, *The Great Terror*, p. 118.

193. Koestler, *Darkness at Noon*, pp. 82–83.

194. Ibid., p. 188.

195. Ibid., p. 190.

196. Ibid., p. 191.

197. Ibid.

198. Conquest, *The Great Terror*, p. 120.

199. Beck and Godin, pp. 211–12.

200. Admittedly, concern for his family played a role in Bukharin's case as well.

201. Solzhenitsyn himself sees the tragedy of the old Bolsheviks as infinitely less important than the tragedy of the countless victims of Bolshevism and has therefore not paid much attention to the mysteries of the Moscow Trials. Nevertheless, Koestler's explanation of Rubashov's (Bukharin's) surrender to his interrogator is consistent with Solzhenitsyn's view of the hypnotizing function of communist ideology. See Solzhenitsyn, *Publitsistika*, pp. 87, 266–67.

202. Of course, there are exceptions to every rule: one of them is Steven Lukes, whose book *Marxism and Morality* contains an excellent discussion of Koestler's relevance for the understanding of the Marxist ethic (pp. 130–38).

203. S. Cohen, "Bolshevism and Stalinism," in Tucker, ed., *Stalinism*, pp. 8–9.

204. R. Tucker, "Stalin, Bukharin, and History as Conspiracy," in Tucker and Cohen, p. xlvi.

205. Valentinov described his encounter with Piatakov and reconstructed the content of the latter's passionate speech in the article "Sut' bolshevizma v izobrazhenii Iu. Piatakova," pp. 140–61. Valentinov's testimony is accepted as entirely credible by such authorities as Schapiro (see his *The Communist Party of the Soviet Union*, pp. 380–81) and Conquest (see his *The Great Terror*, pp. 112–13).

206. The problem of double-dealers (*dvurushniki*) within the party is discussed in R. Tucker's *Stalin in Power*, pp. 307–10.

207. Valentinov, "Sut' bolshevizma," pp. 150–53. For most of Piatakov's tirade, I have used the English translation in Shafarevich, pp. 217–18.

208. Ibid., pp. 148, 160.

209. Ibid., p. 160 (published in *Pravda*, August 21, 1936).

210. Ibid.

211. Tucker and Cohen, pp. 659–60.

212. Ibid., pp. 658/660, 664.

213. Ibid., p. 665.

214. Ibid.

215. Ibid.

216. Ibid. (italics added).

217. Ibid., p. 666.

218. Ibid.

219. See R. Tucker, "Stalin, Bukharin, and History as Conspiracy."

220. See Bukharin's conversation with Theodore Dan, quoted in Abramovitch, p. 416.

221. Ibid.

222. Nikolaevskii, *Power and the Soviet Elite*, pp. 25, 25.

223. Tucker and Cohen, pp. 667, 667.

224. Ibid., p. xlvi.
226. Ibid.
228. Quoted in ibid., p. xliii.

225. Ibid., p. 667.
227. Ibid., pp. 667–68.

229. Thus, for instance, Emelyanov's book on Bukharin contains a very critical assessment of Bukharin's conduct at the trial and a firm rejection of Cohen's attempt to present "Bukharinism" as a positive alternative to Stalinism (see pp. 20–35, 268–302).

230. See Larina, "Nezabyvaemoe."

231. See Laqueur, p. 24.

232. Bukharin's widow, Anna Larina, commented that this statement recalled the fact that in November 1929 all the leaders of Bukharin's group decided to repudiate their views for the sake of party unity. She admitted, however, that in general it was impossible to be enthusiastic about her husband's declarations of loyalty. (See Larina, "Vsegda verila, chto pravda vostorzhestvuet," p. 398). Her statement was published on the occasion of Bukharin's posthumous reinstatement in the party (which took place on July 21, 1988).

233. See Conquest, *The Great Terror*, p. 111.

234. Arendt, p. 308.

235. It is tempting to see this as an archaic feature of the totalitarian mentality. Striving for unanimity characterized different forms of primitive communal democracy (including the Russian peasant commune) and was reflected in Rousseau's conception of the general will.

236. Quoted in *Mayakovsky*, pp. 283–84.

237. See Krasnov, p. 172. The debate on Koestler's book took place in March 1989 in the pages of *Literaturnaya gazeta*. The critic referred to is Vadim Kozhinov, a spokesman for the nationalist Russian writers.

238. E. Hobsbawm, "Goodbye to All That," in Blackburn, p. 117.

239. See Stalin and Wells, pp. 4–6.

240. Webb and Webb, vol. 1, pp. viii, viii. (A question mark existed after the subtitle of the first edition, published Nov. 1935.)

241. Ibid., pp. ix, ix.
243. Ibid., pp. xii–xiii.
245. Ibid., p. xxxv.
247. Ibid., pp. xxxiii, xxxiii, 415.
249. Ibid., p. 430.
251. Ibid., p. xl.
253. Ibid., p. xl.
255. Ibid., p. xxx.

242. Ibid., p. xiv.
244. Ibid., p. xxv.
246. Ibid., p. xxix.
248. Ibid., p. xxxiv.
250. Ibid., p. xxxix.
252. Ibid., p. xli.
254. Ibid., p. xxxvii, xxxviii.
256. Ibid., p. 450.

257. See R. Tucker, "Lenin's Bolshevism as Culture in the Making," p. 36.

258. Merleau-Ponty, pp. 129, 153. (This book first appeared in 1947.)

259. Ibid., p. 153.
261. Ibid., p. 110.
263. Ibid., p. 98.
265. Ibid., pp. 29, 29.
267. See ibid., pp. 30–33.
269. Ibid.

260. Ibid., p. xxi.
262. Ibid.
264. Ibid., pp. 43, 34.
266. Ibid., p. 52.
268. As quoted in ibid., p. 70.

270. Koestler, *The Invisible Writing*, p. 404.

271. Lukes, pp. 132–38.   272. Crossman, pp. 20, 23.

273. Ibid., p. 34.   274. Ibid., pp. 44–45.

275. Ibid., p. 50.   276. Ibid., pp. 65, 65.

277. Ibid., p. 98.   278. Ibid., pp. 99, 112, 113.

279. Ibid., pp. 156, 156, 156.   280. Ibid., pp. 156–57.

281. Ibid., p. 157.   282. Ibid., pp. 113, 162.

283. The other contributors to this part of the book were André Gide and Louis Fischer.

284. Crossman, p. 272.   285. Ibid., p. 167.

286. Ibid., p. 272.   287. Ibid., p. 235.

288. Ibid., p. 254.   289. Ibid., pp. 240–41, 241.

290. Ibid., pp. 271, 271.

291. I. Deutscher, "The Ex-Communist's Conscience," in Deutscher, *Marxism, Wars, and Revolutions*, pp. 52, 52, 55. Deutscher developed this view in his book on Stalin. According to him, "Stalin cannot be classed with Hitler, among the tyrants whose record is one of absolute worthlessness and futility. Hitler was the leader of a sterile counter-revolution, while Stalin has been both the leader and the exploiter of a tragic, self-contradictory but creative revolution. Like Cromwell, Robespierre, and Napoleon he started as the servant of an insurgent people and made himself its master. Like Cromwell he embodies the continuity of the revolution through all its phases and metamorphoses. . . . Like Robespierre he has bled white his own party; and like Napoleon he has built his half-conservative and half-revolutionary empire and carried out revolution beyond the frontiers of his country" (Deutscher, *Stalin*, pp. 569–70).

292. Merleau-Ponty, p. 141.

293. See Conquest's obituary of Soviet communism in "Lenin Nyet!" *The New Leader* (Sept. 9–23, 1991): 3.

294. Turchin, p. 20.

295. Ibid., p. 36.

296. Ibid., p. 21.

297. For Stalin's attitude toward the *dvurushniki*, see R. Tucker, *Stalin in Power*, pp. 307–10.

298. Beck and Godin, p. 181.

299. Ibid., p. 193.

300. Mandelstam, p. 203.

301. Ibid. Mandelstam's "Ode to Stalin" has recently been subject to a thorough literary analysis from the point of view of its place in the poet's oeuvre as a whole. The conclusion of this analysis is unambiguous: the "Ode" is not an alien body in Mandelstam's poetry but an organic and inseparable part of it. See Gasparov, p. 70.

302. Both these articles are available in English in Meerson-Aksenov and Shragin, pp. 116–47, 256–90.

303. Ibid., p. 131.   304. Ibid.

305. Ibid., p. 132.   306. Ibid., pp. 134, 135, 136.

307. Ibid., pp. 146, 117.   308. Ibid., pp. 262, 288–89.

309. Ibid., pp. 266, 259, 259, 261, 264.

310. See Orwell, *1984*, p. 220.

311. Meerson and Shragin, pp. 277, 275–76.

312. Ibid., p. 290.

313. Altaev's and Nelidov's articles were published in the journal *Vestnik RSKHD* (Vestnik Russkogo Khristianskogo Studencheskogo Dvizhenia), nos. 97, 106 (1973, 1974). Solzhenitsyn was a careful student of this journal; he read Altaev's essay and referred to it in two of his articles of 1973–74 (see Solzhenitsyn et al., pp. 95–96, 242–44). His *Letter to the Soviet Leaders* seems to have been influenced by Altaev's diagnosis, and of course the same is true of Nelidov's article. Hence, these three writings are interrelated, and Solzhenitsyn's *Letter* (written on the eve of his forced exile) may be regarded as a product of the Russian dissident movement of that time.

314. Solzhenitsyn, *Letter to the Soviet Leaders*, p. 48.

315. Ibid., p. 47.

316. A. Solzhenitsyn, "As Breathing and Consciousness Return," in Solzhenitsyn et al., p. 24.

317. Ibid., p. 274 ("The Smatterers").

318. Orwell, *Collected Essays*, vol. 2, p. 135.

319. Solzhenitsyn et al., p. 248 ("The Smatterers").

320. For an enlarged version of the following section, containing also an auto-biographical section and a theoretical discussion of the problem of totalitarianism, see Walicki, "*The Captive Mind* Revisited," pp. 51–95.

321. Hirszowicz, p. 22.

322. See the interview with Berman in Toranska, pp. 257, 334, 353, 354.

323. See Trznadel (an anthology of interviews concerning the Stalinist period in Poland).

324. Milosz, *The Captive Mind*, p. 6.

325. This article was originally published in the emigré monthly *Kultura*, no. 5 (Paris, 1951).

326. See Milosz, "Nie," pp. 208–9.

327. Ibid., pp. 206, 216.

328. In the same year, 1951, the same parallel was developed by an economic historian, Witold Kula (who was to become one of the greatest Polish historians of this century), in an interesting piece entitled "Wizardry"—an autobiographical document written for the author's small daughter to enable her to at some point in the future understand her father. It shows the tragic conflict of values represented by the ancient world, on the one hand, and by the new world of the Christians and northern barbarians, on the other. Writing about the Christian church as a mass organization in *The Apostolic History* (a very crude book, but one that helped millions of former slaves create a new and better world), Kula had in mind the Communist party and the Stalinist *History of the Communist Party of the Soviet Union*. See Kula, pp. 225–93.

329. See Kolakowski's essay "Responsibility and History," in Kolakowski, *Towards a Marxist Humanism*. My own early experience in rationalizing totalitarian oppression in terms of the Hegelian philosophy of history has been presented and analyzed in Walicki, *Spotkania z Miloszem*. For a short autobiographical

account, dealing with the years 1950–55, see A. Walicki, "An Autobiographical Digression," in Walicki, *The Captive Mind* Revisited."

330. In *The Native Realm* Milosz asked: "What is this monster, historical necessity, that paralysed my contemporaries with fear?" (p. 277).

331. C. Milosz, "Child of Europe," in Milosz, *Selected Poems*.

332. Milosz, *The Native Realm*, pp. 289, 281.

333. Ibid., pp. 57, 55.   334. Ibid., pp. 9, 4, 23.

335. Ibid., p. 5.   336. See Ibid., ch. 3, pp. 54–81.

337. Ibid., pp. 72–73.

338. Tadeusz Kroński (1907–58), a Hegelian philosopher, exercised a formative influence on Milosz's mind. See also a chapter on him in Walicki, *Spotkania z Miloszem*, pp. 47–71.

339. Milosz, *The Native Realm*, pp. 269–70.

340. Milosz, *The Captive Mind*, p. 80.

341. Milosz, *The Native Realm*, p. 270.

342. Ibid., p. 269.

343. Ibid., p. 278.

344. Ibid.

345. These words were used by Roman Zimand, himself an ex-Communist, at an academic conference in Warsaw (December 1980) organized to celebrate Milosz's Nobel Prize.

346. Such as love of comfortable life, fear, and seeking honors and privileges bestowed by the new rulers. See Z. Rafalski (a pseudonym), "Jeszcze jeden ukąszony choć poranek świta" (One more bitten before the dawn), in the underground monthly *Kultura niezależna*, no. 33 (Sept. 1987): 38–39. Rafalski's long article was a review of my *Spotkania z Miloszem*.

347. For a similar phenomenon in the USSR, see Shtromas, *Political Change and Social Development*, pp. 75–82. Shtromas describes this behavior as "positive intrastructural dissent," as opposition to the system under the cover of loyalty by pursuing different constructive (but in official terms, controversial) goals (p. 75).

348. See Walicki, "The Paradoxes of Jaruzelski's Poland," pp. 167–92. Reprinted in Fehér and Arato.

349. Nikolai Ustrialov, the leader of the *Smenovekhovist* current in Russian emigré thought, even developed a sort of gnostic justification of the Bolshevik revolution. As a result, he returned to Russia to help the new rulers to shape Russia's national destiny. By Milosz's categories this was a sort of "historiosophical," "metaphysical," and "national" Ketman. The danger of playing such games under Stalin was proved by Ustrialov's arrest and execution in 1938. See Agursky, pp. 240–51.

350. The inevitable conflicts between the covert and overt opposition, as well as the atmosphere of a self-righteous moral crusade, organized by the latter, are described in the afterword to my *Spotkania z Miloszem*. A similar situation began to develop in Russia after Solzhenitsyn's attacks on the cowardice of all those who cared about preserving their position within the system. (See especially his article "The Smatterers" of January 1974 in Solzhenitsyn et al.) But it is well to remember that Solzhenitsyn himself adopted this fundamentalist position only after his

expulsion from the Writers' Union (1969) and his debarment from any means of publication in the USSR. Before that he had wanted to continue his dissident activities from an "intrastructural" position. He would have liked to receive the Lenin Prize and did not avoid some moral compromises. Thus, for instance, he refrained from publicly condemning the Soviet invasion of Czechoslovakia. See Shtromas, *Political Change*, pp. 84, 92 (n 56).

Chapter 6

1. Brzezinski, *Ideology and Power*, p. 47.
2. Arendt, p. 325.
3. W. Gurian, "Totalitarianism as Political Religion," in Friedrich, p. 123.
4. C. Friedrich, "The Unique Character of Totalitarian Society," in Friedrich, p. 52.
5. Schapiro, *Totalitarianism*, pp. 34–35, 93.
6. E. Gellner's concluding remarks in Merridale and Ward, pp. 235–36.
7. Boffa, p. 70.
8. D. Lane, "The Roots of Political Reform," in Merridale and Ward, p. 95.
9. Schapiro, *Totalitarianism*, pp. 20, 38–43.
10. It must be remembered that this view is not the product of cold war anticommunism but was formulated by Arendt, who stressed that Mussolini's fascism, like Franco's authoritarianism, was not really totalitarian and that only Nazism and Bolshevism had succeeded in establishing a genuinely totalitarian regime. In addition, she distinguished totalitarian movements from totalitarian rule, arguing that before the war a truly totalitarian rule existed only in the Soviet Union. In Germany it was established "only during the war, after the conquests in the East furnished large masses of people and made the extermination camps possible" (Arendt, pp. 310–11).
11. E. Gellner, in Merridale and Ward, pp. 232, 233.
12. See Tsipko, "Istoki Stalinizma," and *Is Stalinism Really Dead?* pp. 82–90. (Tsipko is a philosopher who supported Gorbachev and even served on the Central Committee of the party.) See also J. Cooper, "Construction . . . Reconstruction . . . Deconstruction," in Merridale and Ward, p. 164.
13. See Lewin's concluding remarks in Merridale and Ward, p. 241.
14. Lewin, *Stalinism and the Seeds of Soviet Reform*, p. xxiv.
15. Ibid.
16. Ibid., p. 82 (italics added).
17. W. Brus, *Ogólne problemy funkcjonowania gospodarki socjalistycznej* (Warsaw, 1964). Translated into English under the title *The Market in a Socialist Economy*.
18. Brus, pp. 13, 15.
19. Ibid., pp. 25–27, 24.
20. Lewin's expression in the foreword to *Stalinism and the Seeds of Soviet Reform*, p. xxv.
21. Brus, p. 27.
22. See Rigby, *The Changing Soviet System*, p. 6. Rigby is right to point out that this "mono-organizational" vision of socialism was substantially achieved by Lenin's successors: "That single office was the Central Committee Office in Old

Square, Moscow, and its board of directors was the Politburo." See Rigby, *Changes in the Soviet Union*, p. 6.

23. Gorbachev, *Speeches and Writings*, p. 44.

24. This is Löwenthal's term. In his view, "institutionalized revolution," (synonymous with the Stalinist "revolution from above") was an unforeseen consequence of Lenin's utopianism and its failure. See Löwenthal, "Beyond the 'Institutionalized Revolution' in Russia and China," in Shtromas and Kaplan, p. 16.

25. The words in quotes are a paraphrase of Brzezinski's definition of totalitarianism in his *Ideology and Power in Soviet Politics*, p. 47.

26. C. Johnson, "Comparing Communist Nations," in Johnson, p. 2.

27. T. McNeill, "Images of the Soviet Future: The Western Scholarly Debate," in Shtromas and Kaplan, p. 318.

28. Arendt, preface to part 3 (June 1966), pp. xxv, xxxvi–xxxvii. Arendt's term *detotalitarization* means the same as *detotalitarianization*, a term used elsewhere in this book.

29. Ibid., p. xxvii.

30. Schapiro, *Totalitarianism*, pp. 124, 118–19.

31. Brzezinski, *The Grand Failure*, p. 255.

32. This is a quotation from Walzer, whose views, however, are the opposite of mine. According to him, "totalitarianism is not a regime" (which, in a sense, is true, since it is much *more* than a regime) and therefore should *not* be given "a permanent place in the typologies of political science." See M. Walzer, "On Failed Totalitarianism," in Howe, p. 119.

33. It is quite obvious that from an economic and social point of view, the differences between the Soviet Union and Nazi Germany are more important than the similarities. Hence it is necessary to distinguish carefully between communist and noncommunist totalitarianism.

34. A. Brown, "Pluralism, Power and the Soviet Political System," in Solomon, pp. 65–66. The continuing relevance of the totalitarian model as an ideal type enabling us to "see how far the Soviets have been moving from it" was first pointed out by Inkeles, who saw it as a commendable alternative to constant revision of the model. See Inkeles, p. 13.

35. Löwenthal, "Development vs. Utopia in Communist Policy."

36. Heller and Nekrich, p. 592.

37. L. Kolakowski, "Zmierzch bogów," in Kolakowski, *Pochwala niekonsekwencji*, pp. 102–10.

38. See Löwenthal, "Beyond the 'Institutionalized Revolution' in Russia and China," p. 19.

39. Gilison, p. 61.

40. Ibid., pp. 80–82.

41. Löwenthal, "Beyond the 'Institutionalized Revolution' in Russia and China," p. 18.

42. See Gilison, p. 85.

43. Breslauer, pp. 51–52, and Gilison, p. 63.

44. Gilison, p. 66.

45. See Breslauer, p. 55.

46. See Gilison, p. 63.

47. Evdokimov, p. 27. Quoted in Gilison, p. 89.

48. D. I. Chesnokov, *Ot gosudarstvennosti k obshchestvennomu samoupravleniiu* (Moscow, 1960), p. 26. Quoted in Gilison, p. 123.

49. Smirnov, p. 83.

50. Gilison, p. 110.

51. For theoretical justification of this practice, see, for instance, Lesnoi.

52. See Armstrong, pp. 324–25, and Heller and Nekrich, pp. 560–61.

53. Armstrong, p. 324.

54. Arendt, p. xxxvii.

55. See Gilison, p. 9.

56. Strumilin, *Robochii den' i kommunizm*, p. 32.

57. Gilison, p. 130.

58. Ibid., pp. 131 (quotation from Khalfina, p. 32), 148.

59. Ibid., pp. 150, 167, 179.

60. For instance, my own works on Russian intellectual history written at that time were classified in the Soviet Union as belonging to Western scholarship (or, more crudely, to the category of "Western falsifications of Russian thought") and access to them was strictly limited. One of these is my *Slavophile Controversy*, first published in Warsaw in 1964. In Poland it was hailed as representative of the works of the so-called Warsaw school of history of ideas, headed by the leading revisionist Marxists Kolakowski and Baczko, and therefore at the center of Polish intellectual life in the Gomulka period. See Walicki, "Leszek Kolakowski and the Warsaw School of the History of Ideas," pp. 5–23.

61. Świda-Ziemba, pp. 15–95.

62. See, for instance, Armstrong, pp. 343–44, and Arendt, p. xxxiv.

63. Świda-Ziemba, pp. 86–87.

64. Gilison, pp. 182–83.

65. According to Brunner, "Communist justification of party authority may be qualified as *heteronomous-teleological legitimacy doctrine*," heteronomous because it is derived from the "laws of history" and thus "independent of any human decision," teleological because it is "imparted by the eschatological goal of the classless communist society." See G. Brunner, "Legitimacy Doctrines and Legitimation Procedures in East European Systems," in Rigby and Fehér, pp. 31–32. Using Brunner's terminology, we can say that under Brezhnev the legitimacy doctrine remained heteronomous but de-emphasized the teleological (i.e., specifically communist) element.

66. Gilison, p. 181.

67. Shlapentokh, pp. 40–41.

68. Löwenthal, "Beyond the 'Institutionalized Revolution,'" p. 27.

69. Ibid., p. 32.

70. Pipes, *Survival Is not Enough*, p. 150. Pipes pointed out the similarity of this process to the eighteenth-century emancipation of the Russian gentry. In his *Russia Under the Old Regime* he had defined the latter as greatly contributing to the dismantling of patrimonial autocracy. It is strange, therefore, that he failed to notice how important the emancipation of the *nomenklatura* was for the dismantling of communist autocracy.

71. Löwenthal, "Beyond the 'Institutionalized Revolution,'" p. 23.

72. Thus, for instance, M. Voslensky treats the *nomenklatura* as the most important feature of totalitarianism. See "The Soviet System," in Shtromas and Kaplan, p. 8.

73. For this reason, Brzezinski saw the permanent purge as an essential constitutive feature of totalitarianism. See Brzezinski, *The Permanent Purge*.

74. Arendt, p. xxxiv.

75. Löwenthal, "Development vs. Utopia in Communist Policy," p. 48.

76. See Yanov.

77. The idea that a new class of dynamic, open-minded technocrats, as opposed to inept, doctrinaire bureaucrats, might decisively contribute to the dismantling of the Soviet system was put forward simultaneously by many observers of the Soviet scene, including Shtromas who, unlike Yanov, was inclined to pin his hopes to a military coup. See A. Shtromas, "How the End of the Soviet System May Come About," in Shtromas and Kaplan, pp. 201–300.

78. The pioneer of the pluralist approach to the Soviet system was H. Gordon Skilling, and its best-known, and most controversial, American representative is Jerry F. Hough. The need to take into account the pluralist structure of interests in Soviet-type societies was also emphasized by the Polish sociologist, Jerzy Wiatr. See Wiatr; see also Wiatr and Przeworski.

79. See J. F. Hough, "Pluralism, Corporatism and the Soviet Union," in Solomon.

80. Schapiro, *Russian Studies*, pp. 39, 39.

81. Shlapentokh, p. 1.

82. See Shtromas, *Political Change and Social Development*.

83. Ibid., p. 71.

84. Gray, pp. 129–30.

85. See Shtromas, *Political Change and Social Development,* pp. 74–79.

86. Heller and Nekrich, p. 609.

87. See Gilison, p. 99.

88. See Tsipko, *Is Stalinism Really Dead?* p. vii.

89. See Brzezinski, *Ideology and Power in Soviet Politics*, pp. 170–74.

90. Shtromas, "A Commentary on Sections 1 and 2," in Shtromas and Kaplan, p. 51.

91. Ibid., p. 53.

92. Siniavskii, p. 163.

93. See Leonhard, p. 21 (first published in 1984).

94. Ibid., p. 160.

95. Ibid., p. 161.

96. Ibid., p. 11.

97. Brzezinski, *The Grand Failure*, p. 255.

98. Kuroń testifies that in the 1960s Polish dissidents, the future founders of the KOR, were greatly impressed by the Russian and Ukrainian dissidents and envied them their *samizdat*. See Kuroń, p. 7.

99. See Michnik, "Does Socialism Have Any Future in Europe?" p. 183.

100. Ibid.

101. For a presentation and critique of this antitotalitarian crusade, see Walicki, "From Stalinism to Post-Communist Pluralism."

102. Waldemar Kuczyński, an economic advisor to Solidarity and a minister in

614 Notes to Pages 534–39

T. Mazowiecki's government, confesses in his recently published memoirs that he saw Jaruzelski's martial law as the only solution for Poland. In 1981 Solidarity was a revolutionary avalanche that could not be expected to stop and arrive at a compromise solution. It was a situation of war, dual power, paralysis, and economic catastrophe. Solidarity, however, could not overthrow communism, so communism, whether Polish or Soviet, had to overthrow Solidarity. Poland's best chance was an unfinished revolution—a revolution dismantled in time (i.e., before Soviet intervention). This was the fate of the Solidarity revolution: it was dismantled, but not strangled, and because of this Jaruzelski's martial law did not eliminate the opportunity for evolutionary reforms. See Kuczyński, pp. 14–15.

103. See Wlodek, ed., *Tajne Dokumenty Biura Politycznego*, pp. 570–71.

104. Kolakowski, *Main Currents of Marxism*, vol. 2, p. 514.

105. For a detailed analysis, see Walicki, "The Paradoxes of Jaruzelski's Poland." An especially visible form of protest against martial law and the suppression of Solidarity was the five-year-long boycott of television by the elite of Polish actors, who (with very few exceptions) strongly resisted both material temptations and political pressure. The participants in this protest stress that it was a spontaneous reaction, immediately understood and applauded by the theater-going public. See Roman. (This is a collection of interviews with Polish actors that was first published underground; it received Solidarity's cultural award for 1988.)

106. Friedrich and Brzezinski, pp. 9–10.

107. Gorbachev, *Perestroika*, p. 151.

108. Gorbachev, *Izbrannye rechi i stat'i*, vol. 6, pp. 347–48 (Doklad na xix Vsesoyuznoi konferentsii KPSS 28 iunia 1988 goda).

109. See Malia, "Yeltsin and U.S.," p. 24.

110. See Thom, p. 136, and Malia, "Yeltsin and U.S.," p. 21.

111. S. Cohen, "Gorbachev vedet bor'bu za reformy," p. 4.

112. Malia, "Leninist Endgame," p. 60.

113. Ibid., pp. 57, 59–60.

114. Malia, "A New Russian Revolution?" p. 31.

115. Malia, "The August Revolution," p. 22.

116. Malia, "Leninist Endgame," p. 57.

117. An illustration of this is the case of Valeria Novodvorskaya, the leader of the Democratic Union Party, who repeatedly called Gorbachev a "fascist criminal." When accused of having insulted the president, she declared that she would be happy to die in a Soviet prison in order to soil Gorbachev's *perestroika* with her blood. (See "Budu shchastliva umeret' v sovetskoi tyurme," *Kommersant*, Feb. 18–25, 1991, p. 3.) Fortunately, the court came to the conclusion that the president had not been insulted.

118. For an analysis of the situation in Russia in the last year of Gorbachev's presidency, see Walicki, "Russia, Before the Coup and After," pp. 1–35.

119. Gorbachev, "Speech at a Meeting with Cultural Leaders on Nov. 28, 1990," p. 2.

120. Quoted in Kirkpatrick, p. 280.

121. Gorbachev, *The August Coup* (Appendix C: The Crimea Article), pp. 104, 67.

122. At his 1990 meeting with the cultural leaders, Gorbachev said: "Why did I

have to start all this up? I could have hung on like that for five or 10 years, anyway. But it was impossible to live that way, Comrades." See Gorbachev, "Speech given at a Meeting with Cultural Leaders," p. 5.

123. Thom, ch. 1.

124. For a brief summary of the quite impressive achievements of the Soviet Union under Brezhnev, see White, pp. 1–3.

125. Ulam, *The Communists*, pp. 388, 389, 389.

126. Ibid., pp. 289, 289.

127. The president of Russia, Boris Yeltsin (whom the putschists could have easily arrested on the first day of the coup), courageously stood up to the challenge, boosting the morale of democratic forces and giving direction to the unexpectedly widespread popular resistance. This was undoubtedly his great merit. But equally important was the fact that the armed forces fraternized with the population, making it clear that they would not fire at civilians, and even the elite KGB Alpha unit refused to storm Yeltsin's "White House" in Moscow. Mikhail Golovatov, the leader of the Alpha group, said: "Frankly speaking, we could have fulfilled our task in 20 to 30 minutes." See "KGB, Long a Feared and Pervasive Force, Is Now Quickly Brought to Heel," *New York Times*, Aug. 28, 1991, p. 7.

128. See C. Friedrich, "The Unique Character of Totalitarian Society," in Friedrich.

129. For Malia's views on this subject, see his "To the Stalin Mausoleum," in Graubard, especially pp. 286–89. In the postscript to this article, Malia says that his analyses aimed only to express the point of view that was "long axiomatic in Warsaw and Budapest" (p. 332). If so, he did not take into account that the anti-communist opposition in Poland and Hungary was deeply biased in its view of totalitarianism, for the obvious reason that the demonization of the enemy greatly helped them in the ideological mobilization of their own ranks and in the destruction of all remnants of the legitimacy of the system. When the system collapsed, to treat it as totalitarian to the last was a self-serving, self-congratulatory move: defeating a totalitarian dragon obviously had much greater merit than defeating the regime as it really was, a weak *post*totalitarian regime unable to stand on its own feet and relying only on support from outside. It was especially true of Poland, where the regime, greatly weakened by the Solidarity movement, had lost all semblance of ideological self-confidence and willingly called itself "the lesser evil." See Walicki, "From Stalinism to Post-Communist Pluralism." For a more detailed theoretical analysis, see Walicki, "Totalitaryzm i post-totalitaryzm."

To clarify, I should add that my disagreement with Malia concerns mostly his analysis and appraisal of the descending phase of Soviet totalitarianism (which I call the "detotalitarization phase"), especially the Gorbachev period. Malia's general interpretation of the history of Soviet socialism—as presented in his book *The Soviet Tragedy: A History of Socialism in Russia, 1917–1991* (New York: Free Press, 1994), which appeared when this book was already in production—is remarkably close to my own in stressing the primacy of ideology and the ideocratic character of the Soviet system. This aspect of Malia's views is, by the way, different from the standard anticommunist opinions in Poland. Polish militant anti-communists (including the democratic opposition of the 1970's and the leaders of Solidarity) have not been inclined to take communist ideology seriously or to interpret the history of communism as tragedy. Most of them took it for granted that communism was only about power, not about ideas. See the Introduction, p. 4.

130. Gorbachev, *Izbrannye rechi i stat'i*, vol. 2, p. 81. See also Åslund, pp. 26–27, and Rigby, *The Changing Soviet System*, p. 211.

131. See White, p. 186.

132. Gorbachev, *Izbrannye rechi i stat'i*, vol. 7, p. 573.

133. See White, p. 194 (reported in *Pravda*, June 23, 1989, p. 2). See also Yakovlev, pp. 11, 76, 99–100.

134. Malia, "To the Stalin Mausoleum," p. 317.

135. Gorbachev, *The August Coup*, p. 112.

136. Malia, "To the Stalin Mausoleum," p. 317.

137. See Yakovlev's interview with Gail Sheehy (Sheehy, p. 343).

138. See Rigby, *The Changing Soviet System*, p. 225.

139. Brzezinski, *Ideology and Power*, p. 142. A good example of the initial underestimation of Gorbachev's new understanding of internationalism is the case of Adam Michnik, a Polish thinker otherwise very sympathetic to Gorbachev. In a recent article he tells us that Gorbachev's book on *perestroika* seemed to him "a rubbishy collection of phrases from the Party *nomenklatura*." See Michnik, "On the Edge of a Black Hole," p. 8.

140. Ulam, *The Communists*, pp. 383, 486.

141. See especially Gorbachev's address to the Nineteenth Party Conference of June 28, 1988 (*Izbrannye rechi i stat'i*, vol. 6, pp. 323–97).

142. See Ibid., p. 575.

143. See *Sovetskaya kultura*, Dec. 5, 1989, p. 3.

144. Globachev, p. 11.

145. "S kazhdym godom vse huzhe," *Nezavisimaya Gazeta*, March 12, 1991.

146. See Herzen, pp. 11–17.

147. See Gorbachev, *The August Coup*, p. 66.

148. See Gorbachev, "Speech given at a Meeting with Cultural Leaders," pp. 1–2.

149. Rigby, *The Changing Soviet System*, p. 234.

150. Gorbachev, "Sotsyalisticheskaia ideia i revolutsyonnaia perestroika," p. 11 (first published in *Pravda*, Nov. 26, 1989).

151. Ibid.   152. Ibid., p. 12.

153. Ibid., p. 16.   154. Ibid., pp. 16–18.

155. Heller, "The End of Communism," p. 12.

156. Gorbachev, "Sotsyalisticheskaia ideia," p. 4.

157. Ibid., pp. 5–6.   158. Ibid., p. 7.

159. Ibid., pp. 5, 7.   160. Ibid., p. 5.

161. Ibid., p. 8.   162. Ibid., pp. 8–9, 12.

163. Ibid., p. 10. It seems proper to recall in this connection that Berdyaev, a philosopher who knew very well both Kantianism and Marxism, accused Marxism of an instrumental attitude toward individual human beings. In Marxism, he wrote, "the person is never a goal and always a means" (p. 112).

164. Good examples of such humanist and "open" Marxism may be found in the pages of *Dialectics and Humanism*, an English-language philosophical journal

published in Poland under Gierek and Jaruzelski. After 1989 it became an organ of "universalism" and changed its title to *Dialogue and Humanism*.

165. See M. Dobbs and R. G. Kaiser, "He Hasn't Gone Gentle Into That Good Night," *Washington Post National Weekly Edition*, Mar. 30–Apr. 5, 1992, p. 20. For my own view on this matter, see Walicki, "Russia, Before the Coup and After," pp. 12–15.

166. See Shostakovskii.

167. Ibid.

168. Gorbachev, "Sotsyalisticheskaia ideia," p. 7.

169. Gorbachev, "Speech Given at a Meeting with Cultural Leaders," p. 3.

170. Ibid., p. 1.   171. Ibid., pp. 1–2.

172. Ibid., p. 2.   173. Ibid., p. 3.

174. Sheehy, pp. 144–45.   175. Ibid., p. 144.

176. Ibid., p. 76.

177. A good illustration of Gorbachev's way of playing with the term *communism* (paying lip service to it while in fact depriving it of its doctrinal and historical content) is his answer to the question of an American journalist "What does it mean to be a communist today, and what will it mean in years to come?" The essential part of Gorbachev's answer reads: "To be a communist, as I see it, means not to be afraid of what is new, to reject obedience to any dogma, to think independently, to submit one's thoughts and plans of action to the test of morality and, through political action, to help working people realize their hopes and aspirations and live up to their abilities. I believe that to be a communist today means first of all to be consistently democratic and put universal human values above everything else" (*Time*, June 4, 1990, p. 23).

178. Heller, p. 27.   179. See above, note 114.

180. Soros, p. 114.   181. Fehér, p. 12.

Works Cited

Abramovitch, Raphael. *The Soviet Revolution, 1917–1939*. New York, 1962.
Agursky, Mikhail. *The Third Rome: National Bolshevism in the USSR*. Boulder, Colo., 1987.
Anderson, Perry. *Considerations on Western Marxism*. London, 1976.
———. *In the Tracks of Historical Materialism*. London, 1983.
Arendt, Hannah. *The Origins of Totalitarianism*. New ed. with added prefaces. New York, 1973.
Armstrong, J. A. *The Politics of Totalitarianism: The Communist Party of the Soviet Union from 1934 to the Present*. New York, 1961.
Åslund, A. *Gorbachev's Struggle for Economic Reform*. London, 1989.
Avineri, Shlomo. *Moses Hess: Prophet of Communism and Zionism*. New York, 1985.
Baczko, Bronislaw. "Stalin-spreparowany charyzmat," *Aneks* 34 (London, 1984).
Bahro, Rudolf. *The Alternative in Eastern Europe*. London, 1978.
Bakunin, Mikhail. *Filosofia, sotsyologia, politika*. Moscow, 1989.
———. *Nauka i nasushchnoe revolutsyonnoe delo*. Geneva, 1870.
Balabanoff, Angelica. *Impressions of Lenin*. Ann Arbor, Mich., 1964.
Balibar, Etienne. "Europe After Communism." *Rethinking Marxism* 5, no. 3 (Fall 1992).
Baron, Samuel. *Plekhanov: The Father of Russian Marxism*. London, 1963.
Bazard, Armand, and Barthémely Enfantin. *La Doctrine Saint-Simonienne*. In C. H. Saint Simon and B. Enfantin, *Oeuvres*, vol. 42. Paris, 1877.
Beck, F., and W. Godin. *The Russian Purge and the Extraction of Confession*. New York, 1951.
Beirne, Piers, ed. *Revolution in Law. Contributions to the Development of Soviet Legal Theory, 1917–1938*. Armonk, N.Y., 1990.

Beirne, Piers, and Alan Hunt. "Lenin, Crime, and Penal Politics, 1917–1924." In Piers Beirne, ed., *Revolution in Law*, pp. 99–135.

Bekerman, G. *Marx and Engels: A Conceptual Accordance*. Oxford, 1986.

Bellamy, Edward. *Edward Bellamy Speaks Again!* Kansas City, Mo., 1937.

———. *Looking Backward from the Year 2000*. New York, 1973.

Berdyaev, Nikolai. "Socialism as Religion." In Bernice Glatzer Rosenthal and Martha Bohachevsky-Chomiak, eds., *A Revolution of the Spirit: Crisis of Value in Russia, 1890–1924*, pp. 107–33. New York, 1990.

Berger, Peter. *The Capitalist Revolution: Fifty Propositions About Prosperity, Equality, and Liberty*. New York, 1986.

Bergmann, Frithjof. *On Being Free*. Notre Dame, Ind., 1977.

Berlin, Isaiah. *Four Essays on Liberty*. Oxford, 1969.

———. *Karl Marx: His Life and Environment*. New York, 1959.

Besançon, Alain. *The Rise of the Gulag: Intellectual Origins of Leninism*. New York, 1981.

Blackburn, Robin, ed. *After the Fall: The Failure of Communism and the Future of Socialism*. London, 1991.

Blackwell, A. L. *Schleiermacher's Early Philosophy of Life: Determinism, Freedom, and Phantasy*. Chico, Calif., 1982.

Bloom, S. F. *The World of Nations: A Study of the National Implications in the Work of Karl Marx*. New York, 1941.

Boettke, Peter. *The Political Economy of Soviet Socialism: The Formative Years, 1918–1928*. Boston, 1990.

———. "The Soviet Experiment with Pure Communism." *Critical Review* 2, no. 2 (1988).

Boffa, Giuseppe. *The Stalin Phenomenon*. Trans. N. Fersen. Ithaca, N.Y., 1992.

Bogdanov, Aleksandr. *Empiriomonizm*. 3 vols. St. Petersburg, 1904–7.

———. *Padenie velikogo fetishizma*. Moscow, 1910.

Bottomore, Tom, ed. *A Dictionary of Marxist Thought*. Oxford, 1983.

Bowman, Sylvia, ed. *Edward Bellamy Abroad: An American Prophet's Influence*. New York, 1962.

Brenkert, George. *Marx's Ethics of Freedom*. London, 1983.

Breslauer, George. "Khrushchev Reconsidered." In Stephen F. Cohen, Alexander Rabinovich, and Robert Sharlet, eds., *The Soviet Union Since Stalin*, pp. 50–70. Bloomington, Ind., 1980.

Bronner, Stephen Eric. *Socialism Unbound*. New York, 1990.

———, ed. *The Letters of Rosa Luxemburg*. See Luxemburg. *Letters*.

Brown, E. J. *The Proletarian Episode in Russian Literature 1928–1932*. New York, 1953.

Brus, Wlodzimierz. *The Market in a Socialist Economy*. London, 1972.

Brzezinski, Zbigniew. *The Grand Failure: The Birth and Death of Communism in the Twentieth Century*. New York, 1989.

———. *Ideology and Power in Soviet Politics*. New York, 1967.

———. *The Permanent Purge*. Cambridge, Mass., 1956.

Brzozowski, Stanislaw. *Idee*. Lwów, 1910.

———. *Kultura i życie*. Warsaw, 1973.

———. *Legenda Mlodej Polski*. Lwów, 1910.

Buchanan, Allen. *Ethics, Efficiency, and the Market*. Totowa, N.J., 1985.

——. *Marx and Justice: The Radical Critique of Liberalism*. London, 1982.

Bukharin, Nikolai. *The Politics and Economics of the Transition Period*. Ed. K. J. Tarbuck. London, 1979.

——. *Problemy teorii i praktiki sotsyalizma*. Moscow, 1989.

——. *Selected Writings on the State and the Transition to Socialism*. Ed. R. B. Day. Armonk, N.Y., 1982.

Bukharin, Nikolai, and Evgeny Preobrazhensky. *The ABC of Communism*. Ann Arbor, Mich., 1966.

Bulgakov, Sergei N. *Filosofia khozyaistva*. Moscow, 1990 [1912].

Butler, E. M. *The Saint-Simonian Religion in Germany*. Cambridge, Eng., 1926.

Calvez, Jean Yves. *La pensée de Karl Marx*. Paris, 1961.

Carr, Edward. *The Bolshevik Revolution*. 3 vols. Harmondsworth, 1952.

——. *Socialism in One Country*. 3 vols. New York, 1960.

Carrère d'Encausse, Hélène. *Lenin: Revolution and Power*. Trans. Valence Ionescu. London, 1982.

——. *Stalin: Order Through Terror*. Trans. Valence Ionescu. London, 1981.

Carver, Terrell. *Marx and Engels: The Intellectual Relationship*. Bloomington, Ind., 1983.

Chernyshevskii, Nikolai G. *Polnoe sobranie sochinenii*. 16 vols. Moscow, 1939–55.

Chesnokov, D. I. *Ot gosudarstvennosti k obshchestvennomu samoupravleniu*. Moscow, 1960.

Cohen, Gerald. *Karl Marx's Theory of History: A Defence*. Oxford, 1978.

Cohen, Marshal, Thomas Nagel, and Thomas Scanlon, eds. *Marx, Justice, and History*. Princeton, N.J., 1980.

Cohen, Stephen. *Bukharin and the Bolshevik Revolution: A Political Biography, 1888–1938*. Oxford-New York, 1980 [1973].

——. "Gorbachev vedet bor'bu za reformy." *Izvestia*, Mar. 12, 1991.

Cohn, Norman. *The Pursuit of the Millennium*. London, 1957.

Conquest, Robert. *The Great Terror. A Reassessment*. New York, 1990.

——. *Lenin*. New York, 1972.

Constant, Benjamin. *Political Writings*. Cambridge, Eng., 1988.

Cornu, Auguste. *Karl Marx et Friedrich Engels: leur vie et leur oeuvre*. 3 vols. Paris, 1955–62.

Crossman, R., ed. *The God That Failed*. Salem, N.H., 1949.

Daniels, Robert. *Trotsky, Stalin, and Socialism*. Boulder, Colo., 1991.

——, ed. *A Documentary History of Communism*. 2 vols. Hanover, N.H., 1984.

Davis, Horace B. *Nationalism and Socialism: Marxist and Labour Theories of Nationalism to 1917*. New York, 1967.

——, ed. *The National Question*. See Luxemburg, *The National Question*.

Deutsch, L. "Molodost' G. V. Plekhanova." *Byloe*, no. 13 (1918).

Deutscher, Isaac. *Marxism, Wars, and Revolutions: Essays from Four Decades*. London, 1984.

——. *The Prophet Armed. Trotsky: 1879–1921*. Oxford, 1954.

——. *The Prophet Outcast. Trotsky: 1929–1940*. Oxford, 1963.

——. *The Prophet Unarmed. Trotsky: 1921–1929*. Oxford, 1959.

——. *Stalin: A Political Biography*. 2d ed. New York, 1967.

Dewey, John. "Liberty and Social Control." *The Social Frontier* 2, no. 2 (Nov. 1935): 41–42.

Dostoevsky, Fedor. *The Possessed.* Trans. A. R. MacAndrew. New York, 1962.

Dunayevskaya, Raya. *Marxism and Freedom.* London, 1975.

———. *Rosa Luxemburg, Women's Liberation, and Marx's Philosophy of Revolution.* Atlantic Highlands, N.J., 1982.

Durkheim, Emile. *The Division of Labor in Society.* Glencoe, Ill., 1960.

Dworkin, Ronald. "Why Liberals Should Believe in Equality." *New York Review of Books,* Feb. 3, 1983.

Ehrenberg, John. *The Dictatorship of the Proletariat: Marxism's Theory of Socialist Democracy.* New York, 1992.

Emelyanov, Iu. V. *Zametki o Bukharine: revolutsya, istoriia, lichnost'.* Moscow, 1989.

Emmons, Terence. "The Abusable Past." *New Republic,* Mar. 9, 1992.

Engels, Frederick. *Anti-Dühring: Herr Eugen Dühring's Revolution in Science.* Moscow, 1978 [1947].

Engels, Frederick, and Karl Kautsky. "Juridical Socialism." Trans. and int. Piers Beirne, *Politics and Society* 7, no. 2 (1977).

Erlich, Alexander. *The Soviet Industrialization Debate, 1924–1928.* Cambridge, Mass., 1960.

Evdokimov, V. I. *Vozrastaiushchaia rol' partii v stroitelstve kommunizma.* Moscow, 1960.

Fehér, Ferenc. "The Left After Communism." *Thesis Eleven,* no. 27 (1990).

Fehér, Ferenc, and Andrew Arato, eds. *Crisis and Reform in Eastern Europe.* New Brunswick, N.J., 1991.

Fehér, Ferenc, Agnes Heller, and Gyorgy Márkus. *Dictatorship over Needs.* Oxford, 1983.

Fetscher, Irvin. *Das Verhältnis des Marxismus zu Hegel.* Tübingen, 1960.

Feuerbach, Ludwig. *The Essence of Christianity.* Trans. G. Eliot. New York, 1957.

Fitzpatrick, Sheila. "New Perspectives on Stalinism." *Russian Review* 45, no. 4 (1986).

———, ed. *Cultural Revolution in Russia, 1928–1931.* Bloomington, Ind., 1984.

Friedrich, Carl, ed. *Totalitarianism.* Cambridge, Mass., 1954.

Friedrich, Carl, and Zbigniew Brzezinski. *Totalitarian Dictatorship and Autocracy.* Cambridge, Mass., 1956.

Gasparov, M. "Metricheskoe sosedstvo Ody Stalinu." *Zdes' i teper',* no. 2 (Moscow, 1992).

Gaus, Gerald. *The Modern Liberal Theory of Man.* London-Canberra, 1983.

Gellner, Ernest. *Nations and Nationalism.* Ithaca, N.Y., 1983.

———. *State and Society in Soviet Thought.* Oxford, 1988.

Geras, Norman. *The Legacy of Rosa Luxemburg.* London, 1976.

Gerschenkron, Alexander. "History of Economic Doctrines and Economic History." *American Economic Review* 59, no. 2 (May 1969).

Gilison, Jerome. *The Soviet Image of Utopia.* Baltimore, Md., 1975.

Gleason, Abbott, Peter Kenez, and Richard Stites, eds. *Bolshevik Culture.* Bloomington, Ind., 1985.

Globachev, M. "Perestroika-provokatsya apparata?" *Stolitsa,* no. 28 (1991).

Gorbachev, Mikhail. *The August Coup*. New York, 1991.

———. *Izbrannye rechi i stat'i*. 6 vols. Moscow, 1987–89.

———. *Perestroika: New Thinking for Our Country and the World*. New York, 1987.

———. *Slovo o Lenine*. Moscow, 1990.

———. "Sotsyalisticheskaia ideia i revolutsyonnaia perestroika." *Kommunist*. Dec. 18, 1989.

———. "Speech given at a meeting with cultural leaders on Nov. 28, 1990." *Current Digest of the Soviet Press* 42, no. 48 (Jan. 2, 1991).

———. *Speeches and Writings*. Oxford, 1986.

Gorky, Maxim. *Days with Lenin*. London, 1932.

Gottlieb, Roger. *Marxism, 1844–1990: Origin, Betrayal, Rebirth*. New York, 1992.

Gouldner, Alvin. *The Two Marxisms*. New York, 1988.

Graham, Keith. *Karl Marx, Our Contemporary: Social Theory for a Post-Leninist World*. Toronto, 1992.

Gramsci, Antonio. *Selected Writings, 1916–1926*. Ed. David Forgacs. New York, 1988.

———. *Selections from Political Writings (1910–1920)*. New York, 1977.

———. *Selections from the Prison Notebooks*. New York, 1971.

Graubard, Stephen R., ed., *Eastern Europe . . . Central Europe . . . Europe*. Boulder, Colo., 1991.

Gray, John. "Totalitarianism, Reform, and Civil Society." In Ellen Frankel Paul, ed., *Totalitarianism at the Crossroads*, pp. 97–142. New Brunswick, N.J., 1990.

Green, Thomas Hill. *Works*, 3 vols. London, 1889.

Gurian, Waldemar. *Bolshevism. An Introduction to Soviet Communism*. Notre Dame, Ind., 1952.

Haarscher, Guy. *L'ontologie de Marx*. Brussels, 1980.

Habermas, Jürgen. *The Theory of Communicative Action*, vol. 1. Trans. T. McCarthy. Boston, 1984.

Haimson, Leopold. *The Russian Marxists: The Origins of Bolshevism*. Cambridge, Mass., 1955.

Hamilton, Alexander, James Madison, and John Jay. *The Federalist Papers*. Ed. Clinton Rossiter. New York, 1961.

Hamowy, Ronald. "Adam Smith, Adam Ferguson, and the Division of Labour." *Economica* 35 (Aug. 1968).

Harding, Neil. *Lenin's Political Thought*. Atlantic Highlands, N.J., 1983.

Haupt, Georges. *Aspects of International Socialism 1871–1914*. Trans. Peter Fawcett, int. Eric Hobsbawm. Cambridge, Eng., 1986.

Hayek, Friedrich. *The Constitution of Liberty*. Chicago, 1960.

———. *The Counter-Revolution in Science: Studies on the Abuse of Reason*. Indianapolis, Ind., 1979 [1952].

———. *Law, Legislation, and Liberty*. 2 vols. London, 1982.

———. *New Studies in Philosophy, Politics, Economics, and the History of Ideas*. London, 1978.

Hayes, Carlton. *The Historical Evolution of Modern Nationalism*. New York, 1931.

Hayner, P. C. *Reason and Existence: Schelling's Philosophy of History*. Leiden, 1967.

Hazard, John. *Settling Disputes in Soviet Society: The Formative Years of Legal Institutions.* New York, 1960.

Heller, Agnes. "The End of Communism." *Thesis Eleven,* no. 27 (1990).

———. *The Theory of Needs in Marx.* London, 1974.

———. "Toward a Marxist Theory of Value." Trans. A. Arato. *Kinesis* (Southern Illinois University at Carbondale, 1972).

Heller, Mikhail, and Aleksandr Nekrich. *Utopia in Power. The History of the Soviet Union from 1917 to the Present.* Trans. Ph. B. Carlos. New York, 1986.

Herling-Grudzinski, Gustaw. *A World Apart.* London, 1951.

Herzen, Alexandr. *From the Other Shore and the Russian People and Socialism.* London, 1956.

Hess, Moses. *Philosophische und sozialistische Schriften 1837–1850.* Ed. A. Cornu. Berlin, 1961.

Himka, John-Paul. *Socialism in Galicia: The Emergence of Polish Social Democracy and Ukrainian Nationalism, 1860–1890.* Cambridge, Mass., 1983.

Hinada, Shizuma. "On the Meaning in Our Times of the Drafts of Marx's Letter to Vera Zasulich." *Suravu Kenkyu,* no. 20 (1975).

Hirszowicz, Maria. *Coercion and Control in Communist Society: The Visible Hand in a Command Economy.* New York, 1986.

History of the Communist Party of the Soviet Union (Bolsheviks). New York, 1939.

Hobsbawm, Eric. *Primitive Rebels.* Manchester, 1963.

Hough, Jerry F., and Merle Fainsod. *How the Soviet Union Is Governed.* Cambridge, Mass., 1979.

Howard, M. C., and J. E. King. *A History of Marxian Economics.* Vol. 1, *1883–1929.* Princeton, N.J., 1989.

Howe, Irving. *1984 Revisited.* New York, 1983.

Hunt, Richard. *The Political Ideas of Marx and Engels.* Vol. 1, *Marxism and Totalitarian Democracy, 1881–1850.* Pittsburgh, Pa., 1974.

———. *The Political Ideas of Marx and Engels.* Vol. 2, *Classical Marxism, 1850–1895.* Pittsburgh, Pa., 1984.

Inkeles, Alec. "Models and Issues in the Analysis of Soviet Society." *Survey* 60 (July 1966).

Ionin, Leonid. *Georg Simmel—Sotsyolog.* Moscow, 1981.

Jacoby, Russel. *Dialectic of Defeat: Contours of Western Marxism.* Cambridge, Eng., 1981.

Jay, Martin. *Marxism and Totality: The Adventures of a Concept from Lukács to Habermas.* Berkeley, Calif., 1984.

Johnson, Chalmers, ed. *Change in Communist Systems.* Stanford, Calif., 1970.

Kamenka, Eugene. *The Ethical Foundations of Marxism.* London, 1962.

Kamenka, Eugene, Robert Brown, and Alice Ehr-Soon Tay, eds. *Law and Society: The Crisis in Legal Ideas.* London, 1978.

Kamenka, Eugene, and Alice Ehr-Soon Tay. "The Sociology of Justice." In *Legal Change: Essays in Honour of Julius Stone,* pp. 107–22. Sydney, 1983.

Kamenka, Eugene, and Alice Ehr-Soon Tay, eds. *Law and Social Control.* London, 1980.

Katkov, George. "Lenin as Philosopher." In Leonard Schapiro and Peter Reddaway, eds., *Lenin,* pp. 71–86.

Kautsky, Benedikt, ed. *Friedrich Engels' Briefwechsel mit Karl Kautsky*. Vienna, 1955.

Kautsky, Karl. *The Class Struggle (Erfurt Program)*. Trans. W. E. Bohn. Chicago, 1910.

——. *The Dictatorship of the Proletariat*. Trans. H. J. Stenning. Manchester, 1919.

——. *The Labour Revolution*. Trans. H. J. Stenning. London, 1925.

——. *Selected Political Writings*. Trans. and ed. P. Goode. London, 1983.

——. *Die soziale Revolution*. Vol. 25, *Am Tage der sozialen Revolution*. Berlin, 1907 [1902].

——. *Terrorism and Communism*. Trans. W. H. Keridge. London, 1920.

Kelles-Krauz, Kazimierz. *Pisma wybrane*. 2 vols. Warsaw, 1963.

Kelsen, Hans. *The Communist Theory of Law*. New York, 1955.

Khalfina, R. O. "O prave lichnoi sobstvennosti v period razvernutogo stroitelstva kommunizma." *Sovetskoe gosudarstvo i pravo*, no. 12 (1960).

Khoruzhii, Sergei. "Philosopher Ship." *Literary Gazette International* (Moscow-Washington) 1, no. 11–12 (Aug. 1990).

Kirkpatrick, J. J. *The Withering Away of the Totalitarian State*. Washington, D.C., 1990.

Kline, George. *Religious and Anti-Religious Thought in Russia*. Chicago, 1968.

Knei-Paz, Baruch. *The Social and Political Thought of Leon Trotsky*. Oxford, 1978.

Koestler, Arthur. *Darkness at Noon*. Harmondsworth, Eng., 1983 [1947].

——. *The Invisible Writing: Autobiography 1931–53*. London, 1954.

Kohn, Hans. *Prelude to Nation-States: The French and German Experience*. Princeton, N.J., 1967.

Kolakowski, Leszek. "The Devil in History." In G. R. Urban, ed., *Stalinism*, pp. 246–78.

——. *Jednostka i nieskończoność: wolnosc i antynomie wolności w filozofii Spinozy*. Warsaw, 1958.

——. *Main Currents of Marxism*. 3 vols. Oxford, 1981.

——. "Le marxisme de Marx, le marxisme de Engels: signification contemporaine de la controverse." In R. Klibansky, ed., *Contemporary Philosophy: A Survey*. Florence, 1971.

——. "The Myth of Human Self-Identity." In L. Kolakowski and Stuart Hampshire, eds., *The Socialist Idea: A Reappraisal*. London, 1974.

——. *Pochwala niekonsekwencji. Pisma rozproszone z lat 1955–1968*. London, 1989.

——. *Światopogląd i życie codzienne*. Warsaw, 1957.

——. *Towards a Marxist Humanism: Essays on the Left Today*. New York, 1968.

Kollontai, Alexandra. *Selected Writings*. London, 1977.

Krasnov, Vladislav. *Russia Beyond Communism: A Chronicle of National Rebirth*. Boulder, Colo., 1991.

Kritsman, Lev. *Geroicheskii period Velikoi Russkoi Revolutsii*. Moscow, 1926.

Krupskaya, Nadezhda. *Memories of Lenin*. London, 1930.

Kuczyński, Waldemar. *Zwierzenia zausznika*. Warsaw, 1992.

Kuhn, Thomas. *The Structure of Scientific Revolutions*. Chicago, 1962.

Kula, Witold. *Rozważania o historii*. Warsaw, 1958.

Kumar, Krishan. *Utopia and Anti-Utopia in Modern Times.* Oxford, 1987.

Kurczewski, Jacek, ed. *Stalinizm.* Warsaw, 1989.

Kuroń, Jacek. *Gwiezdny czas.* London, 1991.

Kuskova, E. D. "Davno minuvshee." *Novyi zhurnal* 46 (1958).

Lampert, Eugene. *Sons Against Fathers.* Oxford, 1965.

Lapenna, Ivo. "Lenin, Law, and Legality." In Leonard Schapiro and Peter Reddaway, eds., *Lenin,* pp. 235–63.

Laqueur, Walter. *Stalin: The Glasnost' Revelations.* New York, 1990.

Larina, A. M. "Nezabyvaemoe." *Znamia,* no. 10–12 (1988).

———. "Vsegda verila, chto pravda vostorzhestvuet." In *Bukharin: chelovek, politik, uchenyi.* Moscow, 1990.

Lavoie, Don. *National Economic Planning: What Is Left?* Cambridge, Mass., 1985.

Lenin, V. I. *Collected Works.* 45 vols. Moscow, 1960–70.

———. *Polnoe sobranie sochinenii.* 5th ed. 55 vols. Moscow, 1958–65.

———. *Selected Works.* 3 vols. Moscow, 1977 [1963].

The Lenin Anthology. Ed. R. Tucker. See under Tucker.

Leninskii sbornik, vol. 2. Moscow, 1924.

Leninskii sbornik, vol. 40. Moscow, 1985.

Leonhard, Wolfgang. *The Kremlin and the West: A Realistic Approach.* New York, 1986 [1984].

Leroux, Pierre. *De l'Humanité, de son principe et de son avenir.* Paris, 1840.

Lesnoi, V. M. *Gosudarstvo, pravo i kommunizm.* Moscow, 1964.

Levin, Sh. M. *Obshchestvennoe dvizhenie v Rossii v 60-70-e gody XIX veka.* Moscow, 1958.

Levine, Norman. *The Tragic Deception: Marx contra Engels.* Santa Barbara, Calif., 1975.

Lewin, Moshe. *Lenin's Last Struggle.* New York, 1968.

———. *The Making of the Soviet System.* New York, 1985.

———. *Stalinism and the Seeds of Soviet Reform.* Armonk, N.Y., 1991.

Lichtheim, George. *Marxism: An Historical and Critical Study.* New York, 1962.

Liebman, Marcel. *Leninism Under Lenin.* London, 1975.

Lobkowicz, Nicholas. *Theory and Practice: History of a Concept from Aristotle to Marx.* Notre Dame, Ind., 1967.

Locke, John. *An Essay Concerning Human Understanding.* Ed. P. H. Nidditch. Oxford, 1975.

Lomasky, Loren. "Socialism as Classical Political Philosophy." *Social Philosophy and Policy* 6, no. 2 (1989).

Löwenthal, Richard. "Beyond the 'Institutionalized Revolution' in Russia and China." In Alexander Shtromas and Morton Kaplan, eds., *The Soviet Union and the Challenge of the Future,* vol. 1, pp. 13–34.

———. "Development vs. Utopia in Communist Policy." In Chalmers Johnson, ed., *Change in Communist Systems,* pp. 33–116.

Löwith, Karl. *From Hegel to Nietzsche.* Garden City, N.Y., 1967.

———. *Max Weber and Karl Marx.* Ed. and int. T. Bottomore and W. Outhwaite. London, 1982.

Lukács, Georg. *History and Class Consciousness.* Trans. R. Livingstone. Cambridge, Mass., 1971.

———. *Marxism and Human Liberation.* New York, 1973.

———. *Political Writings, 1919–1929.* London, 1972.

———. *The Young Hegel.* London, 1975.

Lukes, Steven. *Marxism and Morality.* Oxford, 1985.

Lunacharskii, Anatolii. *Religia i sotsyalizm.* 2 vols. St. Petersburg, 1906.

Luxemburg, Rosa. *The Accumulation of Capital.* New Haven, Conn., 1951.

———. *Comrade and Lover: Rosa Luxemburg's Letters to Leo Jogiches.* Ed. E. Ettinger. Cambridge, Mass., 1979.

———. *Gesammelte Werke,* vol. 5. Berlin, 1975.

———. *The Industrial Development of Poland.* Trans. Tessa de Carlo. New York, 1977.

———. *Leninism or Marxism? The Russian Revolution.* Ed. B. P. Wolfe. Ann Arbor, Mich., 1961.

———. *Letters.* Ed. S. E. Bronner. Boulder, Colo., 1978.

———. *Listy do Leona Jogichesa-Tyszki,* 3 vols. Ed. Feliks Tych. Warsaw, 1968–71.

———. *The National Question. Selected Writings.* Ed. H. B. Davis. New York, 1972.

———. "Nauki Trzech Dum." *Przeglad Socjaldemokratyczny,* no. 3 (May 1908).

———. *Selected Political Writings.* Ed. Dick Howard. New York, 1971.

———. *W obronie narodowości.* Poznań, 1900.

———. *Wstęp do ekonomii politycznej.* Warsaw, 1959.

———. *Wybór pism.* 2 vols. Warsaw, 1959.

MacIntyre, Alasdair. *Against the Self-Images of the Age.* Notre Dame, Ind., 1984.

———. *Marxism and Christianity.* Notre Dame, Ind., 1984 [1968].

McLellan, David. *Friedrich Engels.* Harmondsworth, Eng., 1977.

———, ed. *Marx: The First Hundred Years.* Oxford, 1983.

Malia, Martin. "The August Revolution." *New York Review of Books,* Sept. 26, 1991.

———. "Leninist Endgame." *Daedalus* (Spring 1992), pp. 57–76.

———. "A New Russian Revolution?" *New York Review of Books,* July 18, 1991.

———. "To the Stalin Mausoleum." In Stephen R. Graubard, ed., *Eastern Europe . . . Central Europe . . . Europe,* pp. 283–338.

———. "Yeltsin and U.S." *Commentary* 93, no. 4 (Apr. 1992).

Malle, Silvana. *The Economic Organization of War Communism.* Cambridge, Eng., 1985.

Mandelstam, Nadezhda. *Hope Against Hope.* Trans. Max Hayward. New York, 1970.

Mannheim, Karl. *Ideology and Utopia.* London, 1952.

Marcuse, Herbert. *Reason and Revolution: Hegel and the Rise of Social Theory.* Atlantic Highlands, N.J., 1983 [1941].

Marot, J. E. "Alexander Bogdanov, *Vpered,* and the Role of the Intellectual in the Workers' Movement." *Russian Review* 49, no. 3 (1990).

Martov, Yulii. *Mirovoi bolshevism.* Int. F. Dan. Berlin, 1923.

Marx, Karl. *Capital.* 3 vols. New York, 1967.

———. *Grundrisse: Foundations of the Critique of Political Economy.* Harmondsworth, Eng., 1973.

———. *Pre-Capitalist Economic Formations*. Int. Eric Hobsbawm. New York, 1964.

———. *Selected Writings*. Ed. David McLellan. New York, 1985.

———. *Texts on Method*. Trans. and ed. Terrell Carver. Oxford, 1975.

———. *Theories of Surplus Value*. Moscow, 1969.

Marx, Karl, and Frederick Engels. *Basic Writings on Politics and Philosophy*. Int. L. S. Feuer. London, 1984 [1959].

———. *Collected Works*. New York, 1975–.

———. *Correspondence 1846–1895*. Sel., ed., and trans. Dona Torr. London, 1936.

———. *The Russian Menace to Europe*. Glencoe, Ill., 1952.

———. *Selected Correspondence*. Moscow, 1956.

———. *Selected Works*. 3 vols. Moscow, 1969.

———. *Werke*. Berlin, 1956–.

Marx, Karl, Frederick Engels, and Vladimir Lenin. *On Communist Society*. Moscow, 1981.

Maximoff, G. P., ed. *The Political Philosophy of Bakunin: Scientific Anarchism*. Glencoe, Ill., 1953.

Mayakovsky. Trans. and ed. H. Marshall. New York, 1965.

Mayer, G. *Engels: A Biography*. New York, 1936.

Medvedev, Roy. *Let History Judge: The Origins and Consequences of Stalinism*. Rev. ed. New York, 1989.

———. *La Revolution d'Octobre, était-elle inéluctable?* Paris, 1976.

Meerson-Aksenov, Michael, and Boris Shragin, eds. *The Political, Social and Religious Thought of Russian Samizdat*. Belmont, Mass., 1977.

Mehring, Franz. *Die deutsche Sozialdemocratie: ihre Geschichte und ihre Lehre*. Brema, 1879.

Meikle, Scott. *Essentialism in the Thought of Karl Marx*. LaSalle, Ill., 1985.

Merquior, J. G. *Western Marxism*. London, 1986.

Merleau-Ponty, Maurice. *Humanism and Terror*. Trans. John O'Neill. Boston, 1969 [1947].

Merridale, Catherine, and Chris Ward, eds. *Perestroika: The Historical Perspective*. London, 1991.

Meyer, Alfred. "Coming to Terms with the Past." *Russian Review* 45, no. 4 (Oct. 1986).

Michnik, Adam. "Does Socialism Have Any Future in Europe?" *Studium Papers* 13, no. 4 (Oct. 1989).

———. "On the Edge of a Black Hole." *Quadrant* (May 1992).

Mikhailovskii, N. K. "Karl Marks peved sudom g. Zhukovskogo." In N. K. Mikhailevskii, *Polnoe sobranie sochinenii*, vol. 4, pp. 167–73. St. Petersburg, 1909.

———. "O g. Struve i ego kriticheskikh zametkakh." In N. K. Mikhailovskii, *Polnoe sobranie sochinenii*, vol. 7, pp. 889–924. St. Petersburg, 1909.

Miliukov, Pavel. *God bor'by*. St. Petersburg, 1907.

Mill, John Stuart. *On Liberty in Focus*. Ed. J. Gray and G. W. Smith. London, 1991.

Milosz, Czeslaw. *The Captive Mind*. Harmondsworth, Eng., 1980 [1953].

———. *The Native Realm*. London-Manchester, 1981.

———. "Nie." *Krytyka* (Aneks ed.), 13–14 (London, 1984).

————. *Selected Poems.* New York, 1981.

Misrahi, Robert. *Marx et la question juive.* Paris, 1972.

Mitrany, David. *Marx Against the Peasant.* Chapel Hill, N.C., 1951.

Molnár, Miklós. *Marx, Engels et la politique internationale.* Paris, 1975.

Molyneux, J. *Leon Trotsky's Theory of Revolution.* New York, 1981.

Moore, Stanley. *Marx on the Choice Between Socialism and Communism.* Cambridge, Mass., 1980.

Morgan, Louis Henry. *Ancient Society or Researches in the Lines of Human Progress from Savagery Through Barbarism to Civilisation.* London, 1877.

Nettl, Peter. *Rosa Luxemburg.* 2 vols. London, 1966.

Neurath, Otto. *Wesen und Weg zur Sozialiesierung.* Munich, 1919.

Nicolaevskii, Boris, and O. Maenchen-Helfen. *Karl Marx: Man and Fighter.* Philadelphia, 1936.

Nikolaevskii, Boris. "Karl Kautsky in Russland." In *Ein Leben für den Sozialismus.* Hannover, 1954.

————. "Legenda ob 'utajennom pis'me' K. Marksa." *Sotsyalisticheskii vestnik,* no. 5 (New York-Paris, 1957).

————. *Power and the Soviet Elite.* Ed. J. D. Zagoria. New York, 1965.

Niebuhr, Richard. "Schleiermacher." In *Encyclopedia of Philosophy,* vol. 7, pp. 317–19. New York-London, 1972.

Nove, Alec. *An Economic History of the USSR.* New York, 1984.

————. "Some Observations on Bukharin and His Ideas." In Nove, *Political Economy and Soviet Socialism.* London-Boston, 1979.

Novgorodtsev, Pavel. *Ob obshchestvennom ideale.* 3rd ed. Berlin, 1921.

Ocherki po filosofii marksizma. St. Petersburg, 1908.

O'Rourke, James. *The Problem of Freedom in Marxist Thought.* Dordrecht, 1974.

Orwell, George. *Collected Essays.* 3 vols. New York, 1968.

————. *1984.* London, 1949.

Osborn, Robert. *Freedom in Modern Theology.* Philadelphia, 1967.

Panasiuk, Ryszard. *Dziedictwo heglowskie i marksizm.* Warsaw, 1979.

Pashukanis, Evgeny. *Law and Marxism.* Ed. C. J. Arthur. Worcester, Eng., 1989.

————. *Selected Writings on Marxism and Law.* Ed. Piers Beirne and Robert Sharlet. London, 1980.

Pelczynski, Zbigniew, ed. *The State and Civil Society: Studies in Hegel's Political Philosophy.* Cambridge, Eng., 1984.

Pelczynski, Zbigniew, and John Gray, eds. *Conceptions of Liberty in Political Philosophy.* London, 1984.

Pellicani, Luciano. *Gramsci: An Alternative Communism?* Stanford, Calif., 1976.

Perepiska G. V. Plekhanova i P. B. Akselroda. 2 vols. Moscow, 1925.

Pipes, Richard. *Russia Under the Old Regime.* London, 1974.

————. *The Russian Revolution.* New York, 1990.

————. *Survival Is Not Enough: Soviet Realities and America's Future.* New York, 1984.

Plekhanov, G. V. *God na rodine.* 2 vols. Paris, 1921.

————. *Izbrannye filosofskie proizvedeniia.* 5 vols. Moscow, 1956–58.

————. *Selected Philosophical Works.* Moscow, 1977.

————. *Sochineniia.* 2d ed. 24 vols. Moscow, 1923–27.

Polan, A. J. *Lenin and the End of Politics*. Berkeley, Calif., 1984.

Polevoi, Iu. Z. *Zarozhdenie marksizma v Rossii*. Moscow, 1959.

Popper, Karl. *The Open Society and Its Enemies*. 2 vols. London, 1980 [1945].

Pyatyi Vserossiiskii Syezd deyatelei sovetskoi yustitsii, stenograficheskii otchet. Moscow, 1924.

Rainko, Stanislaw. *Świadomość i determinizm*. Warsaw, 1981.

———. *Świadomość i historia*. Warsaw, 1978.

Ree, van, Eric. "Stalin's Organic Theory of the Party." *Russian Review* 52, no. 1 (Jan. 1993).

Reuel, A. L. *Russkaia ekonomicheskaia mysl' 60–70 kh 99. XIX veka i marksizm*. Moscow, 1956.

Rigby, T. H. *Changes in the Soviet Union*. Annual lecture delivered at the Australian National University, Nov. 6, 1990. Canberra, 1990.

———. *The Changing Soviet System. Mono-organisational Socialism from Its Origins to Gorbachev's Restructuring*. Aldershot, Eng., 1990.

———. "Stalinism and the Mono-organizational Society." In Robert Tucker, ed., *Stalinism*, pp. 53–76.

Rigby, T. H., and Ferenc Fehér, eds. *Political Legitimation in Communist States*. London, 1982.

Rocker, R. "Anarchism and Sovietism." In *The Poverty of Statism: Bukharin, Fabri, Rocker*, pp. 10–25. Minneapolis, Minn., 1981.

Rodrigues, Eugene. *Nouveau Christianisme: lettres sur la religion et la politique*. Paris, 1832.

Roman, A., ed. *Komedianci: Rzecz o bojkocie*. Warsaw, 1990.

Rosdolsky, Roman. *Engels and the Non-Historic Peoples: The National Question in the Revolution of 1848*. Trans. and ed. J. P. Himka. Critique Books, 1987.

Rubel, Maximilien. *Marx critique du Marxisme*. Paris, 1974.

———, ed. "Gespräche über Russland mit Friedrich Engels. Nach Aufzeichnungen von A. M. Woden." In *Internationale wissenschaftliche Korrespondenz*. Berlin, April 1971.

Rudnytsky, Ivan. *Essays in Modern Ukrainian History*. Cambridge, Mass., 1987.

Rupnik, Jacques. *The Other Europe*. New York, 1989.

Schacht, R. *Hegel and After: Studies in Continental Philosophy Between Kant and Sartre*. Pittsburgh, Pa., 1975.

Schaff, Adam. *Alienation as a Social Phenomenon*. Oxford, 1980.

Schapiro, Leonard. *The Communist Party of the Soviet Union*. New York, 1960.

———. *The Origin of the Communist Autocracy, Political Opposition in the Soviet State*. 2d. ed. Cambridge, Mass., 1977.

———. *Russian Studies*. Ed. Ellen Dahrendorf. London, 1986.

———. *Totalitarianism*. London, 1972.

Schapiro, Leonard, and Peter Reddaway, eds. *Lenin: The Man, the Theorist, the Leader*. New York, 1967.

Schlesinger, Rudolf. *Soviet Legal Theory. Its Social Background and Development*. New York, 1945.

Selucký, Radoslav. *Marxism, Socialism, Freedom: Towards a General Theory of Labour-Managed Systems*. New York, 1979.

Shafarevich, Igor. *The Socialist Phenomenon*. Trans. W. Tjalsma. New York, 1980.

Shanin, Teodore, ed. *Late Marx and the Russian Road: Marx and "the Peripheries of Capitalism."* London, 1984.

Sheehy, Gail. *The Man Who Changed the World. The Lives of Mikhail Gorbachev.* New York, 1990.

Shlapentokh, Vladimir. *Soviet Ideologies in the Period of Glasnost': Responses to Brezhnev.* New York, 1988.

Shostakovskii, V. "Diktatura Kommunistov vozhmozhna, no slabaia i ne na dolgo." *Stolitsa*, no. 8 (1991).

Shtromas, Alexander. "Making Sense of Stalin." *The World and I* 1, no. 8 (Aug. 1986).

——. *Political Change and Social Development: The Case of the Soviet Union.* Frankfurt am Main, 1981.

Shtromas, Alexander, and Morton Kaplan, eds. *The Soviet Union and the Challenge of the Future*, vols. 1–4. New York, 1988–89.

Simmel, Georg. *On Individuality and Social Forms.* Chicago, 1971.

——. *The Philosophy of Money.* Trans. T. Bottomore and D. Frisby. Boston, 1978.

Siniavskii, Andrei (A. Tertz). *On Socialist Realism.* New York, 1965.

Smirnov, Iu. P. *Gosudarstvo i kommunizm.* Minsk, 1962.

Smolar, Aleksander. "L'utopie et science: l'économie politique dans la vision marxienne du communisme et pendant l'industrialisation soviétique." *Revue de l'Est* 5, no. 4 (Oct. 1974).

Sochor, Zenovia. *Revolution and Culture: The Bogdanov-Lenin Controversy.* Ithaca, N. Y., 1988.

Solomon, S. G., ed. *Pluralism in the Soviet Union: Essays in Honour of H. Gordon Skilling.* London, 1983.

Solzhenitsyn, Aleksandr. *Letter to the Soviet Leaders.* New York, 1974.

——. *Publitsistika: stat'i i rechi.* Paris, 1981.

Solzhenitsyn, Aleksandr, Mikhail Agursky, A. B., Eugeny Barabanov, Vadim Borisov, F. Korsakov, and Igor Shafarevich. *From Under the Rubble.* Boston, 1975.

Soros, Georg. *Opening the Soviet System.* London, 1990.

Stalin, Joseph. *Economic Problems of Socialism in the USSR.* New York, 1952.

——. *Leninism.* 2 vols. New York, n.d. (193-).

——. *Selected Writings.* New York, 1942.

——. *Sochineniia.* 13 vols. Moscow, 1946–52.

——. *Sochineniia*, vols. 14 (1)–16 (3). Ed. Robert H. McNeal. Stanford, Calif., 1967.

——. *Works.* 13 vols. London, 1952–55.

Stalin, Joseph, and H. G. Wells. *Marxism vs. Liberalism: An Interview.* New York, 1947.

Steenson, Gary. *Karl Kautsky, 1854–1938: Marxism in the Classical Years.* Pittsburgh, Pa., 1978.

Steklov, Yu. M. *N. G. Chernyshevskii, ego zhizń i deiatelnost'.* 2 vols. Moscow-Leningrad, 1928.

Stepelevich, Lawrence. "Max Stirner and Ludwig Feuerbach." *Journal of the History of Ideas* 39, no. 3 (1978).

────, ed. *The Young Hegelians. An Anthology.* Cambridge, Eng., 1983.

Stites, Richard. *Revolutionary Dreams: Utopian Vision and Experimental Life in the Russian Revolution.* New York, 1989.

Stokes, Gale, ed. *From Stalinism to Pluralism. A Documentary History of Eastern Europe Since 1945.* New York, 1991.

Strumilin, Stanislav. "Kommunizm i razdelenie truda." *Voprosy filosofii,* no. 3 (1963).

────. "Rabochii byt i kommunizm." *Novyi Mir,* no. 7 (1960).

────. *Rabochii den' i kommunizm.* Moscow, 1959.

────. "Zakon stoimosti i planirovanie." *Voprosy ekonomiki,* no. 7 (1959).

Struve, Petr. *Kriticheskie zametki k voprosu ob ekonomicheskom razvitii Rossii.* St. Petersburg, 1894.

Stuart, J. J. C., and B. Williams. *Utilitarianism: For and Against.* Cambridge, Mass., 1973.

Studies in the Philosophy of Marxism. See *Ocherki po filosofii marksizma.*

Swayze, Harold. *Political Control of Literature in the USSR, 1946–1959.* Cambridge, Mass., 1962.

Świda-Ziemba, Hanna. "Stalinizm i polskie spoleczenstwo." In Jacek Kurczewski, ed., *Stalinizm,* pp. 15–95. Warsaw, 1989.

Szamuely, László. *First Models of the Socialist Economic Systems. Principles and Theories.* Budapest, 1974.

Szamuely, Tibor. *The Russian Tradition.* Ed. R. Conquest. London, 1974.

Szlezinger, Maria. "Podstawy filozoficzne doktryny spolecznej Rózy Luksemburg." *Studia socjologiczno-polityczne,* no. 15 (1963).

Szporluk, Roman. *Communism and Nationalism. Karl Marx versus Friedrich List.* New York, 1988.

Tait, A. L. "Lunacharsky: A Nietzschean Marxist?" In Bernice Glatzer Rosenthal, ed., *Nietzsche in Russia,* pp. 275–92. Princeton, N.J., 1986.

Talmon, Jacob. *The Origins of Totalitarian Democracy.* London, 1961.

Talmon, Yonina. "Millenarism." In D. L. Sills, ed., *International Encyclopedia of Social Sciences,* vol. 10. New York-London, 1968.

Temkin, Gabriel. *Karola Marksa obraz gospodarki komunistycznej.* Warsaw, 1962.

Timasheff, Nicholas. *The Great Retreat: The Growth and Decline of Communism in Russia.* New York, 1946.

Thom, Françoise. *The Gorbachev Phenomenon: A History of Perestroika.* Trans. J. Marshall. London, 1989.

Thompson, Edward. "An Open Letter to Leszek Kolakowski." *The Socialist Register,* 1973.

Tillich, Paul. *Perspectives on 19th and 20th Century Protestant Theology.* London, 1967.

Toews, John Edward. *Hegelianism: The Path Toward Dialectical Humanism 1805–1841.* Cambridge, Eng., 1980.

Tönnies, Ferdinand. *Community and Society.* Trans. Ch. P. Loomis. East Lansing, Mich., 1957.

Topalovitsch, Živko. "Mein geistiger Vater." In *Ein Leben für den Sozialismus.* Hannover, 1954.

Torańska, Teresa. *Them: Stalin's Polish Puppets*. Trans. A. Kolakowska. New York, 1987.

Trinadtsatyi Syezd RKP (b). Moscow, 1924.

Trotsky, Leon. *In Defense of Marxism*. New York, 1965.

——. *Lenin*. London, 1925.

——. *Literature and Revolution*. Ann Arbor, Mich., 1966.

——. *My Life*. Harmondsworth, Eng., 1984.

——. *Nashi politicheskie zadachi*. Geneva, 1904.

——. *On Engels and Kautsky*. New York, 1969.

——. *The Revolution Betrayed*. New York, 1989 [1937].

——. *Sochineniia*. Moscow, 1925–27.

——. *Soviet Economy in Danger*. New York, 1931.

——. *Stalinism and Bolshevism*. New York, 1970.

——. *Terrorism and Communism. A Reply to Karl Kautsky*. Westport, Conn., 1986.

——. *Their Morals and Ours*. New York, 1975.

Trznadel, Jacek. *Hańiba domowa: rozmowy z pisarzami*. Paris, 1986.

Tsipko, Aleksandr. *Is Stalinism Really Dead?* San Francisco, 1990.

——. "Istoki Stalinizma." *Nauka i zhizń*, no. 11–12 (1988).

Tucker, D. F. B. *Marxism and Individualism*. Oxford, 1980.

Tucker, Robert. "Lenin's Bolshevism as Culture in the Making." In Abbott Gleason, Peter Kenez, and Richard Stites, *Bolshevik Culture*, pp. 25–38.

——. *Philosophy and Myth in Karl Marx*. Cambridge, Eng., 1964.

——. "Stalin, Bukharin, and History as Conspiracy." In Robert Tucker and Stephen Cohen, eds., *The Great Purge Trial*, pp. ix–xlviii.

——. "A Choice of Lenins?" In Urban, ed., *Stalinism*.

——. *Stalin in Power: The Revolution from Above, 1928–1941*. New York, 1990.

——, ed. *The Lenin Anthology*. New York, 1975.

——, ed. *Stalinism: Essays in Historical Interpretation*. New York, 1977.

Tucker, Robert, and Stephen Cohen, eds. *The Great Purge Trial*. New York, 1965.

Turchin, Valentin. *Inertsya strakha*. New York, 1978.

Turgenev, Ivan. *Hamlet and Don Quixote*. Trans. R. Nichols. London, 1930.

Tych, Feliks. "Róża Luksemburg." In B. Skarga, ed., *Polska mysl filozoficzna i spoleczna*, vol. 3, pp. 432–98. Warsaw, 1977.

Ulam, Adam. *The Bolsheviks*. New York, 1968.

——. *The Communists: The Story of Power and Lost Illusions*. New York, 1992.

——. *Stalin: The Man and His Era*. Boston, 1973.

Urban, G. R., ed. *Stalinism: Its Impact on Russia and the World*. Cambridge, Mass., 1986.

Vaganyan, V. G. *V. Plekhanov: opyt kharakteristiki sotsyalno-politicheskikh vozzrenii*. Moscow, 1924.

Valentinov, Nikolai. *Encounters with Lenin*. London, 1968.

——. "Sut' bolshevizma v izobrazhenii Iu. Piatakova." *Novyi Zhurnal* 52 (New York, 1958).

Venturi, Franco. *Roots of Revolution: A History of the Populist and Socialist Movements in Nineteenth Century Russia*. London, 1960.

Vincent, Andrew. *Modern Political Ideologies*. Oxford, 1992.

Vogel, Steven. "Nature and Natural Science in 'Traditional' and 'Critical' Marxism: Engels and Lukács." Ph.D. diss., Boston University, 1984. (Reproduced by University Microfilms International, Ann Arbor, Mich.)

Vorontsov, Vasilii. *Sud'by kapitalizma v Rossii*. SPb, 1882.

Voslensky, Michael. *Nomenklatura: The Soviet Ruling Class*. Trans. E. Mosbacher, pref. M. Djilas. Garden City, N.Y., 1984.

Vtoroi Syezd RSDRP: protokoly. Moscow, 1932.

Waldenberg, Marek. *Wzlot i upadek Karola Kautsky'ego*. 2 vols. Cracow, 1972.

Walicki, Andrzej. "Alexander Bogdanov and the Problem of the Socialist Intelligentsia." *Russian Review* 49, no. 3 (July 1990): 293–305.

――――. "*The Captive Mind* Revisited: Intellectuals and Communist Totalitarianism in Poland." In E. F. Paul, ed. *Totalitarianism at the Crossroads*, pp. 51–96. New Brunswick, N.J., 1990.

――――. *The Controversy over Capitalism: Studies in the Social Philosophy of the Russian Populists*. Oxford, 1969.

――――. *The Enlightenment and the Birth of Modern Nationhood: Polish Political Thought from the Noble Republicanism to Tadeusz Kosciuszko*. Notre Dame, Ind., 1989.

――――. "From Stalinism to Post-Communist Pluralism: The Case of Poland." *New Left Review*, no. 185 (Jan.-Feb., 1991): 92–121.

――――. *A History of Russian Thought from the Enlightenment to Marxism*. Trans. Hilda Andrews-Rusiecka. Stanford, Calif., 1979.

――――. "The Intellectual Tradition of Pre-Revolutionary Russia: A Reexamination." In Alexander Shtromas and Morton Kaplan, eds., *The Soviet Union and the Challenge of the Future*, vol. 3, pp. 3–22.

――――. "Karl Marx as Philosopher of Freedom." *Critical Review* 2, no. 4 (1988): 10–58.

――――. "Karol Marks: emancypacja ludzkości a wolność indywidualna." *Zdanie*, no. 2 (1984): 27–34.

――――. *Legal Philosophies of Russian Liberalism*. Oxford, 1987.

――――. "Leszek Kolakowski and the Warsaw School of the History of Ideas." *Critical Philosophy* 1, no. 2 (Sydney, 1984): 5–23.

――――. "Liberalism in Poland." *Critical Review* 2, no. 1 (1988): 8–38.

――――. "Marx and Freedom." *New York Review of Books*, Nov. 24, 1983.

――――. "The Marxian Conception of Freedom." In Zbigniew Pelczynski and John Gray, eds., *Conceptions of Liberty in Political Philosophy*, pp. 217–42.

――――. "Meaning of History and Meaning in History." *Dialectics and Humanism* 9, no. 1 (1982): 61–71.

――――. "The Paradoxes of Jaruzelski's Poland." *Archives Européennes de Sociologie* 26, no. 2 (1985).

――――. *Philosophy and Romantic Nationalism: The Case of Poland*. Oxford, 1982.

――――. *Polska, Rosja, Marksizm: studia z dziejów marksizmu i jego recepcji*. Warsaw, 1983.

――――. "The Prospects for Change: The Soviet Union Under Gorbachev." *Age Monthly Review*. Melbourne, Nov. 1986.

————. "Rosa Luxemburg and the Question of Nationalism in Polish Marxism." *Slavonic and East European Review* 61, no. 4 (Oct. 1983): 565–82.

————. "Russia, Before the Coup and After." *Critical Review* 15, no. 1 (1991): 1–35.

————. *The Slavophile Controversy, History of a Conservative Utopia in Nineteenth-Century Russian Thought.* Trans. Hilda Andrews-Rusiecka. Oxford, 1975.

————. *Spotkania z Miloszem.* London, 1985.

————. *Stanislaw Brzozowski and the Polish Beginnings of "Western Marxism."* Oxford, 1989.

————. "Totalitarianism and Liberalism." *Critical Review* 3, no. 2 (1989): 355–68.

————. "Totalitaryzm i post-totalitaryzm." In Z. Sadowski, ed., *Spoleczeństwa posttotalitarne: kierunki przemian,* pp. 13–26. Warsaw, 1991.

Watson, George. "Hitler's Marxism." In George Watson, *The Idea of Liberalism,* pp. 110–31. London, 1985.

Webb, Sidney, and Beatrice Webb. *Soviet Communism: A New Civilization.* 2d ed. 2 vols. London, 1941.

Weeks, A. L. *The First Russian Bolshevik: A Political Biography of Peter Tkachev.* New York, 1968.

Weyl, Nathaniel. *Karl Marx: Racist.* New Rochelle, N.Y., n.d.

White, Stephen. *Gorbachev in Power.* Cambridge, Eng., 1990.

Wiatr, Jerzy. "Elements of Pluralism in the Polish Political System." *Polish Sociological Bulletin,* no. 1 (1966).

Wiatr, Jerzy, and Adam Przeworski. "Control Without Opposition." *Government and Opposition* 1, no. 2 (1966).

Williams, Robert. *The Other Bolsheviks: Lenin and His Critics, 1904–1914.* Bloomington, Ind., 1986.

Wistrich, Robert. *Revolutionary Jews from Marx to Trotsky.* London, 1976.

Wlodek, Zofia, ed. *Tajne dokumenty Biura Politycznego: PZPR a Solidarność 1980–1981.* London, 1992.

Wolfe, Bertram. *An Ideology in Power: Reflections on the Russian Revolution.* New York, 1970.

————. *Lenin and the Twentieth Century.* Ed. L. D. Gerson. Stanford, Calif., 1984.

————. *Marxism: One Hundred Years in the Life of a Doctrine.* Boulder, Colo., 1985 [1965].

————. *Three Who Made a Revolution.* Boston, 1955.

Wood, Allen. *Karl Marx.* London, 1981.

————. "Marx on Right and Justice." In M. Cohen et al., eds., *Marx, Justice and History,* pp. 106–34.

Yakovlev, Alexandr. *Muki prochtenia bytiia.* Moscow, 1991.

Yanov, Alexandr. *Détente After Brezhnev.* Berkeley, Calif., 1977.

Yur'evskii, E. "Mysli o G. V. Plekhanove." *Sotsyalisticheskii vestnik,* no. 4 (New York-Paris, 1957).

Zlocisti, Theodor. *Moses Hess—Vorkämpfer des Sozialismus und Zionismus,* 2nd ed. Berlin, 1921.

Index of Names

In this index an "f" after a number indicates a separate reference on the next page, and an "ff" indicates separate references on the next two pages. A continuous discussion over two or more pages is indicated by a span of page numbers, e.g., "pp. 57–58." *Passim* is used for a cluster of references in close but not continuous sequence.

Akhmatova, A., 480
Altaev, O., 481f, 527, 608
Althusser, L., 113
Anderson, P., 113, 209, 559
Arendt, H., 435, 454, 465, 509f, 516, 522, 604, 610
Aristotle, 123, 171, 388
Armand, I., 200
Auer, I., 264
Axelrod, P., 310

Babeuf, G., 292, 349, 425, 498
Baczko, B., 612
Bahro, R., 325
Bakunin, M., 154, 158, 225–29 *passim*, 285f, 318, 321f, 575, 587
Balabanoff, A., 306
Ballanche, P. S., 554
Bauer, B., 130, 589
Bauer, O., 84, 211, 265
Bebel, A., 199f
Beck, F., 458
Beirne, P., 352, 592, 594

Belinskii, V. G., 228f, 234–38 *passim*, 580ff
Bellamy, E., 373f
Bentham, J., 281, 586
Berdyaev, N., 320, 560, 616
Berger, P. L., 103
Bergmann, F., 561f
Bergson, H., 473
Berlin, I., 25, 35, 44, 127
Berman, J., 485
Bernstein, E., 202, 209, 212, 220, 252f, 293, 296, 498
Besançon, A., 589
Bismarck, O., 198
Blanqui, A., 224, 226
Boehme, J., 128
Boettke, P., 594f, 598
Bogdanov, A., 297f, 301, 311–17, 428
Börne, L., 125
Bosanquet, B., 37
Brenkert, G., 560
Brezhnev, L., 465, 478, 497, 508, 510, 521–28, 531f, 539

Library of Congress Cataloging-in-Publication Data

Walicki, Andrzej.
   Marxism and the leap to the kingdom of freedom : the rise and fall of the
Communist utopia / Andrzej Walicki.
      p.   cm.
   Includes bibliographical references and index.
   ISBN 0-8047-2384-2 (cl.) : ISBN 0-8047-2863-1 (pbk.)
   1. Socialism—History.   2. Communism—History.   3. Freedom—History.
   I. Title.
HX39.W17   1995
320.5'31'09—dc20   94-32893
                                                                CIP

⊗ This book is printed on acid-free paper.